OCÉANO ATLÁNTICO

ho de Florida

Las Bahamas

zas

fuegos

CUBA

• Camagüey

Guantánamo

Santiago
de Cuba

HAITÍ

Port-au-Prince

**REPÚBLICA
DOMINICANA**

Santo
Domingo

**PUERTO
RICO**

Mayagüez

Ponce

San
Juan

Islas Vírgenes

Antigua

Kingston ★

JAMAICA

Guadalupe

Dominica

Martinique
Santa Lucía

San
Vicente

Barbados

Granada

Antillas Menores

MAR DEL CARIBE

Aruba

Bonaire

Curaçao

Isla de
Margarita

Trinidad

Tobago

★ Port-of-Spain

★ Caracas

*Canal de
Panamá*

• Colón

★ Panamá

ANAMÁ

*Golfo
de
Panamá*

R. Orinoco

VENEZUELA

GUYANA

**GUAYAN
FRANCE**

SURINAM

R. Magdalena

AMÉRICA DEL SUR

★ Bogotá

COLOMBIA

BRASIL

¡ARRIBA!
a first course

Eduardo Zayas-Bazán
EAST TENNESSEE STATE UNIVERSITY

Susan M. Bacon
UNIVERSITY OF CINCINNATI

PRENTICE HALL ENGLEWOOD CLIFFS, NEW JERSEY 07632

Library of Congress Cataloging-in-Publication Data

Zayas-Bazán, Eduardo.
    ¡Arriba! A First Course/Eduardo Zayas-Bazán, Susan M. Bacon.
        p.   cm.
    Includes index
    ISBN 0-13-319583-X. --ISBN (invalid) 0-13-329485-8 (annotated instructor's ed.)
    1. Spanish language--Textbooks for foreign speakers--English.
I. Bacon, Susan M.   II. Title.
PC4112.Z379   1995   94-44600
468.2'421--dc20   CIP

Editor-in-Chief: *Steve Debow*
Director of Development: *Marian Wassner*
Project Editor: *Isabel Picado*
Assistant Editor: *María F. García*
Editorial Assistant: *Brian Wheel*
Managing Editor: *Deborah Brennan*
Graphic Project Manager: *Ximena de la Piedra*
Interior Design and Graphics: *Kenny Beck*
Cover Design: *Christine Gehring Wolf*
Illustrations: *Andrew Lange*
Realia Design: *Paul Uhl, DesignAssociates*
Page Layout: *Paul Uhl, DesignAssociates, Ximena de la Piedra*
Cover Illustration: *Matt Walton*
Manufacturing Buyer: *Tricia Kenny*

© 1995 by Prentice Hall, Inc.
A Simon & Shuster Company
Englewood Cliffs, New Jersey 07632

Text ISBN 0-13-319583-X
Annotated Instructor's Edition ISBN 0-13-329485-8

Prentice Hall Internationnal (UK) Limited, *London*
Prentice Hall of Australia Pty. Limited, *Sydney*
Prentice Hall Canada, Inc., *Toronto*
Prentice Hall Hispanoamericana, *Mexico*
Prentice Hall of India Private Limited, *New Delhi*
Prentice Hall of Japan, Inc., *Tokyo*
Simon & Schuster Asia Pte. Ltd., *Singapore*
Prentice Hall do Brasil, Ltda., *Rio de Janeiro*

Contents

Contents

Preface

¡Arriba! **A First Course** is a streamlined introductory Spanish program for college courses that meet three or four hours per week. Rich in pedagogy and supported by carefully integrated supplementary materials, *A First Course* responds to requests for a more compact *¡Arriba!* with a greater number of exercises, activities, and opportunities for partner and group work. Its highly flexible format and ancillary package offer instructors and students a range of choices to suit individual goals, curricula, interests, and methodological preferences.

We have been grateful to the hundreds of instructors and thousands of students who have worked successfully with *¡Arriba!* **Comunicacion y cultura,** published in 1993. There is now an Alternate Testing Program available. Vocabulary lists have been recorded, and we have expanded our video program to include CD-ROM. We appreciate your support and ongoing communication, and look forward to your reactions to this adapted, activities-oriented course, which many of you may find better suits the goals of your program.

HIGHLIGHTS OF *A FIRST COURSE*

CD-ROM

Short video clips that feature international, national, and local programs, documentaries, sports programming, and other specials are one of the most exciting components of *A First Course*.

Clear and Concise Grammar Presentation

The grammar explanations in *A First Course* are clear and concise, and contrast English and Spanish with clear examples wherever possible. The *Práctica* and *Actividades* sections contain a mix of contextualized drills and activities that provide for guided, meaningful practice. *Study Tips* assist students with structures that non-native speakers of Spanish often find particularly difficult.

Instructors meeting three hours per week may wish to experiment with their grammatical syllabus, depending on the preparation and progress of their students. The *Ampliación gramatical* has been designed to offer maximum flexibility to those instructors that prefer a traditional grammar syallabus.

Information Gap Activities

Classroom-tested information gap activities in which students simulate realistic situations appear in the new recycling and review section in every chapter, entitled *Colaboración*. Students work in pairs to solve problems, supply one another with information each needs to complete charts, letters, recipes, and so on. We will be expanding these activities from time to time so that your program remains fresh.

Engaging Reading Material

The development of systematic reading skills is accomplished through serial readings and the *Mundo hispánico* magazine collages. ***Tirofijo va a Málaga y otras selecciones***, which features an illustrated detective story and an introduction to Hispanic literature with accompanying reading strategies, exercises, and discussion activities, is available with ***A First Course*** at an economical price. In addition, all readings are recorded.

This motivating introduction to literary selections has been carefully screened and selected to appeal to students' interests. The prereading and postreading activities that accompany each selection help develop skills, and take an easy-to-follow, step-by-step approach.

Design

Students and instructors using ***¡Arriba!* Comunicación y cultura** have commented favorably on its less cluttered, light, and breezy format. We have attempted to retain this feel in ***A First Course:*** accessible and less intimidating than other Spanish programs available.

Photographs and Illustrations

High quality photographs by specialists in Hispanic culture have been used again in ***A First Course,*** especially in the *¡Así es la vida!* language models and the *Mundo hispánico* informational collages. Designed to follow the format of magazines, the photographs and content in the *Mundo hispánico* stimulate the curiosity and interest of the student.

CHAPTER ORGANIZATION AND PEDAGOGY

A First Course contains ten *lecciones,* each divided intor three sections: *Primera parte, Segunda parte,* and *Colaboración.* The *Ampliación gramatical* appears after *Lección 10* for instructors wishing to experiment with the traditional grammar syllabus. Each *lección* maintains the following consistent structure:

¡Así es la vida! *(That's life!)* Each *parte* begins with a combination of lively conversations, drawings, photos, realia, or readings that sets the stage for the communicative functions, grammatical structures and culture in the *lección.*

Vocabulario y expresiones *(Vocabulary and expressions)* The vocabulary lists are grouped functionally wherever possible. Active vocabulary is listed within each section. Translations are aligned so that students may cover English during self-tests. Where a decision was needed regarding length of a list, we chose to err on the side of providing more than less. We encourage instructors to test only the words and expressions they feel are most universal and important.

¡Así lo decimos! *(That's how we say it!)* Language variation and common colloquial expressions and differences are highlighted in each *parte* of ***A First Course.***

¡A escuchar! (*Let's listen!*) *A First Course* features both in-text and laboratory audio components. The in-text *¡A escuchar!* sections contain recordings of each *¡Así es la vida!* Students are encouraged to complete accompanying listening comprehension activities at home. Some instructors using *¡Arriba!* suggest reading the *Tapescript* aloud to students and completing the listening activities in class, since bering cassette recorders to class can prove and additional challenge.

Estructuras (*Structures*) The grammar explanations in *A First Course* are clear and concise, and contrast English and Spanish with clear examples wherever possible. The *Práctica* and *Actividades* sections range from contextualized drills to guided, more communicative practice. *Study Tips* are included to assist students with structures that non-native speakers of Spanish often find particularly difficult.

A propósito... (*By the way...*) The authors have carefully designed each chapter within a culturally authentic framework. Key contrasts are highlighted in the *A propósito...* sections, which also provide insightful questions as points of departure for classroom discussion.

Colaboración (*Collaboration*) Classroom-tested information gap activities in which students simulate realistic situations appear in this popular recycling and review section in every *lección*.

Mundo hispánico (*The Hispanic World*) Six *Mundo hispánico* collages provide brief introductions to Spanish-speaking countries and regions, including the United States. Lavish collages are intended to motivate discussion and interaction. Instructors can use the information contained in each collage as a springboard for creative individualized and group activities, and class discussion.

COMPONENTS OF *A FIRST COURSE*

CD-ROM

Developed for both the IBM and MacIntosh platforms, *Multimedia ¡Arriba!* contains over forty authentic television clips, originally appearing on television in Spain. *Multimedia ¡Arriba!* develops students' ability to follow Spanish spoken at a natural pace by a variety of native speakers. Students control the pace at which they watch the video. With their mouse, students can slow speech, repeat phrases with the help of a native speaking voice tutor, look up unknown words and phrases, record and listen to their own voices, and view translations of recorded material. At present, comprehension activities are in development, but are not scheduled for release for at least one year. *Multimedia ¡Arriba!* is thematically compatible with *A First Course*, however, is not text-specific.

Multimedia ¡Arriba! is available for purchase with or without *A First Course*. Institutions adopting *A First Course* are eligible to receive a substantial discount on the CD-ROM.

Student Text or Student Text/Cassette Package

The student text is available for purchase with or without a cassette that contains recordings of the in-text *¡A escuchar!* sections. Because the text and text/cassette package have separate ISBNs, please be careful to request the correct number when ordering *A First Course*.

Student Text 0-13 319583-X
Student Text/Cassette Package 0-13-353138-4

Annotated Instructor's Edition

Marginal annotations in the *Annotated Instructor's Edition* include warm-up and expansion exercises and activities, and an array of tips and ideas specifically designed for novice teaching assistants or adjunct faculty who may be teaching Spanish for the first time in many years. The *Annotated Instructor's Edition* also contains the *Tapescript* for all in-text *¡A escuchar!* activities. We gratefully acknowledge the assistance of Joseph and Karin Collentine of East Carolina University

Customized Components

Each of the print components can be custom published to your individual specifications. The **Prentice Hall Customized Components Program** permits departments to add syllabi, extra readings, activities and exercises, and other print materials to any of its supplements at a nominal charge.

Student Activities Manual, Cassettes, and Tapescript

The organization of the *Student Activities Manual* parallels that of the main text. The listening portion of this comprehensive manual contains scripted and semi-authentic recordings that are designed to challenge the student to move beyond the in-text *¡A escuchar!* activities to guided, more realistic listening texts and contexts. Cassettes are available for unlimited duplication upon adoption of *A First Course*.

IBM Tutorial Software

The IBM tutorial software has been designed for students with little or no computer experience. Practice material is supported by detailed hints, reference files, a Spanish-English, English-Spanish dictionary, and scoring machine.

Instructor's Resource Manual

The Instructor's Resource Manual is especially useful for schools offering multiple sections of first-year Spanish. It includes a bibliography of Hispanic organizations, embassies and cultural centers for countries, video tips and activities, the Tapescript, and general guidelines and hints for novice teaching assistants.

Testing Program

The *Testing Program* for **A First Course** consists of quizzes and tests for each chapter, and alternative midterm and final examinations. Prepared by Aaron Taylor and Alison McConnell *(University of Cincinnati)*, the program utilizes a variety of techniques to address the skill areas of listening, reading, writing, and culture.

Transparencies

Beautiful transparencies with illustrations, charts, and realia provide visual support materials for the student text.

Acknowledgments

A First Course is an adaptation of **¡Arriba!,** the result of discussion, planning, and ongoing collaboration between students, instructors, and us. We sincerely hope that you will continue to tell us what you and your students need and want in a foreign language program.

We wish to express our gratitude and deep appreciation to our editors Steve Debow, José Blanco, Marian Wassner, María García, and Isabel Picado. When they approached us to adapt *¡Arriba!* to a more streamlined format, we were not contemplating another venture, but they persuaded us to do so. Their energy, enthusiasm, and ideas provided support and guidance. We extend our thanks to Isabel who contributed countless hours to the writing and adapting of materials for **A First Course.** Isabel's teaching and writing experience proved invaluable to the project.

The Prentice Hall production team deserves special thanks for seeing the project through its final phase.

We would especially like to thank Debbie Brennan, our Managing Editor for her levelheadedness and unparalleled professionalism; Ximena de la Piedra for her help with the page layout and graphic design; Paul Uhl for his page layout and realia design; Andrew Lange whose pens lend flair and whimsy to the many pages of the book; and Kenny Beck for his vivid interior design.

Our collaboration with Patrick Nee has made it possible to include authentic, lively, high quality video materials in *Multimedia ¡Arriba!*. We gratefully acknowledge Patrick's contribution for his work and for his understanding of the needs of today's foreign language student.

We recognize that aspects of the program may not perfectly fit every individual's teaching situation, but we hope that it contains new or improved ideas and materials for everyone. Many colleagues contributed comments and reactions to us. We gratefully acknowledge their participation and candid commentary:

Rita Ricaurte, *University of Nebraska*
Miguel Federico Cano Montenegro, *Fort Lewis College*
Ingrid Watson-Miller, *Hampton University*
Otto Tetzlaff, *Angelo State University*
Clara Mojica-Diaz, *Wayne State College*
Susan Bacon, *University of Cincinnati*
Renee Andrade, *Mt. San Antonio College*
Ken Fleak, *University of South Carolina*
April Koch, *University of Texas, El Paso*
Francisco Lopez, *Texas A & M University, Kingsville*
Terri Gebel, *University of Northern Iowa*
John Kellogg, *Golden West College*
SheriAnn Simpson-Sanford, *Northwestern University*
Rosalie Postma-Carttar, *University of Kansas*
Jon Bauer, *University of Missouri, Kansas City*
John Chaston, *University of New Hampshire*
Peggy Hartley, *Appalachian State University*
Barbara Ward, *Bridgewater State College*
Mara-Lee Bierman, *Rockland Community College*
Hilde Cramsie, *Mt. San Antonio Community College*
Barbara Esquival-Heinemann, *Winthrop University*
Roger Gilmore, *Colorado State University*
Peter Alfieri, *Salve Regina University*
Robert Brown, *University of the District of Columbia*
Andrea Varrichio, *West Chester University*
Fidel de Leon, *El Paso Community College*

About the Authors

Eduardo Zayas-Bazán

Eduardo Zayas-Bazán is a native of Camagüey, Cuba. He has a M.S. in foreign languages from Kansas State Teachers College, Emporia, Kansas, and a Doctor en Derecho degree from Universidad Nacional José Martí, Havana, Cuba. He participated in the Bay of Pigs Invasion as a frogman, was wounded, captured, and spent one year in prison. In April 1962 he was liberated after being ransomed by the U.S. government for $100,000.

Professor Zayas-Bazán was elected President of the American Association of Teachers of Spanish and Portuguese. In August of 1990 he was elected president of the National Association of Cuban American Educators.

Susan M. Bacon

Susan M. Bacon earned her Ph.D. in Foreign-Language Education and Spanish Linguistics form The Ohio State University. She is currently Associate Professor of Spanish at the University of Cincinnati. She has published extensively in the area of foreign-language acquisition and methodology, particularly in the use of authentic listening and reading text. In 1994, she was honored by the American Coucnil on the Teaching of Foreign languages with the Paul Pimsleur Award for Research in Foreign Language Education.

A First Course is an adaptation of *¡Arriba! Comunicación y cultura*, published in 1993 and used in hundreds of colleges and universities throughout the world. *¡Arriba!* was the result of years of research, experience, and class-testing at pilot sites with a variety of student audiences. Over the years many people contributed ideas and suggestions to us; we are most grateful.

We would especially like to acknowledge and thank José B. Fernández, of the University of Central Florida, whose participation in and contributions to **Comunicación y cultura** made **A First Course** possible. We are hopeful that his workload as Department Chair will soon lighten and that he may fully participate in future editions of *¡Arriba!*

¡ARRIBA!
a first course

¡Bienvenidos!

¡Hola! ¿qué tal?

Comunicación

- Greetings and Farewells
- Expressing Nationality and Place of Origin
- Counting and Spelling
- The Spanish Alphabet
- Classroom Expressions and Objects

Cultura

- Why study Spanish?
- Introduction to Spanish-speaking Countries

Estructuras

- Definite and Indefinite Articles
- Gender of Nouns
- Plurals of Nouns

¡Así es la vida!

Saludos y despedidas

—¡Hola! ¿Cómo te llamas?
—¡Hola! Me llamo José Delgado.
—Mucho gusto. Soy Elena Sánchez.
—El gusto es mío.

—¡Hola! ¿Cómo se llama usted?
—Me llamo Miranda Pérez.
—Mucho gusto. Soy la profesora Hoyos.
—Encantada.

—Buenos días, Luisa, ¿Qué tal? ¿Cómo estás?
—Muy bien, Carlos, ¿y tú?
—Más o menos.

—Buenas noches, señora González, ¿cómo le va?
—Bastante bien, José Manuel. ¿Cómo estás tú?
—No muy bien.
—¿De veras? Lo siento, José Manuel.

—Hasta mañana, Pepe.
—Adiós, Pedro.

Vocabulario y expresiones

Saludos

Buenos días.	*Good morning.*
Buenas tardes.	*Good afternoon.*
Buenas noches.	*Good evening.*
Hola.	*Hello, hi.*
¿Qué tal?	*What's up? How goes it?*
¿Qué hay?	*What's new?*
¿Cómo estás? (familiar)	*How are you?*
¿Cómo está usted? (formal)	*How are you?*
¿Cómo le va? (formal)	*How are you doing?*
¿Cómo te va? (familiar)	*How are you doing?*

Respuestas

Bien.	*Fine, well.*
Muy bien.	*Very well, fine.*
Muy bien, gracias. ¿Y tú/usted? (familiar/formal)	*Fine, thank you. And you?*
Bastante bien.	*Pretty well.*
Regular.	*So, so.*
Mal.	*Not well, badly.*
Más o menos.	*More or less, so-so.*
No muy bien.	*Not very well.*

Despedidas

Adiós.	*Good-bye.*
Hasta mañana.	*See you tomorrow.*
Hasta luego.	*See you later.*
Hasta pronto.	*See you soon.*

Presentaciones

¿Cómo se llama usted? (formal)	*What's your name?*
¿Cómo te llamas? (familiar)	*What's your name?*
Me llamo. . .	*My name is. . .*
Soy. . .	*I am. . .*
Encantado(a).	*Delighted.*
Mucho gusto.	*It's a pleasure (to meet you).*
El gusto es mío.	*The pleasure is mine.*
Igualmente.	*Likewise.*

Títulos

profesor (masculine)	*professor*
profesora (feminine)	*professor*
señor (Sr.)	*Mr.*
señora (Sra.)	*Mrs.*
señorita (Srta.)	*Miss*

Otras expresiones

gracias	*thank you*
muchas gracias	*thank you very much*
de nada	*you're welcome*
lo siento	*I'm sorry*
¿de veras?	*really?*
¿verdad?	*true?*

◆◆◆◆◆◆◆◆◆◆◆◆◆◆◆◆◆◆◆◆◆◆◆◆◆◆◆◆

¡Así lo decimos!

More than 362 million Spanish speakers world-wide share many cultural and linguistic features. What is less noticeable to the casual observer are the cultural and linguistic differences. Each **¡Así lo decimos!** box following the vocabulary sections presents some of the lexical and idiomatic differences among the countries and regions of the Spanish-speaking world. While it is clearly out of the scope of this text to provide an exhaustive accounting of language variation, **¡Así lo decimos!** will give you a glimpse of the breadth, richness, and flavor of the diversity that exists in the Spanish language.

In some cases, the differences you see may be perceived to be minor, and in others, there seems to be no common ground. The countries selected for inclusion reflect no a priori judgments or considerations. They were included simply because they illustrate the diversity of expression within the scope of the chapter vocabulary.

As with all languages, there are "standard" words and expressions, but as we know from English, there are often more common and sometimes colloquial ways of expressing the same idea. For example, *handbag* is the "standard" way to refer to the item of women's apparel. Yet this is rarely the word used to refer to this item in daily speech. Depending on where you are from in North America, you will use a different word, for example *bag*, *pocketbook*, *purse*, *shoulder bag*, *clutch*, and so on.

Similar regional and dialectal differences also occur in Spanish. These are the topic of **¡Así lo decimos!**

¡A escuchar!

A. Saludos y despedidas. You will hear the conversations that appear in **¡Así es la vida!** on page 1 of your text. Copy the names of the speakers on a piece of paper. Then, listen to each conversation, and identify the speaker by writing the number of the conversation next to the speaker's name. You will hear the correct responses on the tape.

____ Luisa   ____ Elena Sánchez
____ José Delgado   ____ Pedro
____ la profesora Hoyos   ____ Miranda Pérez
____ José Manuel   ____ la señora González
____ Pepe   ____ Carlos

B. You will now hear the conversations a second time. Repeat each phrase or sentence at the pause.

◆ Práctica

H-1 En la clase. Match the statements or questions in the left-hand column with the most appropriate rejoinders on the right.

1. Adiós
2. ¿Qué tal?
3. Gracias.
4. ¿Cómo se llama Ud.?
5. Mucho gusto.
6. No muy bien.

a. Me llamo Pedro Arce.
b. De nada.
c. Igualmente
d. Regular.
e. Hasta luego.
f. Lo siento.

H-2 ¡Hola! The following people are meeting for the first time. What would they say to each other? After you have finished, repeat the activity assuming they are meeting again one month later.

el profesor Solar
Ester Moniz

la Sra. Aldo
la Sra. García

Patricia
Marco

Eduardo
Samuel

H-3 En una reunión. Complete the following phrases you overhear with words from **Vocabulario y expresiones**.

1. —¿Cómo…llama usted?
2. —Soy el…Oreamuno. ¿Y usted?
3. —Me…Doris Solera.
4. —….
5. —El…es mío.
6. —¿Cómo está…?
7. —Más o…¿Y usted?
8. —…bien gracias.

H-4 Saludos. You work as an assistant in the Spanish Department. How would you greet the following people in Spanish? Practice by yourself and then, in pairs, one student role-plays the **asistente**, and the other the person named in the exercises.

1. Prof. María Garcia, 8:00 A.M.
2. Miss Perry, 3:15 P.M.
3. Mrs. Soto, 9:00 P.M.
4. José Luis, 10:00 A.M.
5. Mrs. Murphy, 5:00 P.M.
6. Prof. Ramón Suárez, 8:00 P.M.
7. Amanda, 9:00 A.M.
8. Mrs. Gómez, 12:30 P.M.

H-5 Saludos. In groups of three or four, practice saying hello to one another, telling each other your names, and saying good-bye.

H-6 Dramatizar. Choose a partner and role-play one or more of the situations presented below. Be prepared to act out your roles before the whole class. Student A must initiate the conversation.

A

1. You meet your Spanish instructor for the first time and introduce yourself to him or her.
2. You meet an elderly neighbor in the apartment building you just moved into. Greet the neighbor and introduce yourself. Assume it is 9 A.M.
3. Introduce yourself to an attractive student of the opposite sex that you just spotted in the cafeteria. Assume it is 8 P.M.
4. Introduce yourself to a student you meet in the library. Assume that the time is 3 P.M.

B

1. One of your Spanish students introduces himself/herself to you. Respond appropriately.
2. You meet the young student who just moved into the apartment above you. Greet the student and introduce yourself.
3. Respond to your fellow student's greeting but act reserved, since you are not really interested in striking up a friendship.
4. Respond to your fellow student's introduction enthusiastically, since you would like to get to know him/her better.

Pronunciación

Spanish Vowels

- The Spanish **a** is pronounced like the <u>a</u> of the English word *father*.
  casa **mañana** **papá** **Marta**

- The Spanish **e** is pronounced like the *e* of the English word *cafe*.
  Pepe **mesa** **reloj** **estudiante**

- The Spanish **i** is pronounced like the *e* in the English word *me*.
  libro **silla** **sí** **chico**

- The Spanish **o** is pronounced like the *o* in the English word *tone*.
  profesor **mucho** **poco** **Lola**

- The Spanish **u** is pronounced like the *oo* in the English word *tuna*.
  pupitre **usted** **uno** **luna**

The Spanish Alphabet

In English, some vowels consist of **two** sounds as in the words *note, mine,* and *made.* This contrasts sharply with the **one,** crisp, short sound of Spanish vowels that never vary in pronunciation.

LETTER	NAME	EXAMPLES
a	a	Anita
b	be (grande)	bebé
c	ce	casa, cero
d	de	Dios
e	e	elegante
f	efe	feo
g	ge	gente, gordo
h	hache	hacer
i	i	indio
j	jota	José
k	ka	kiosco
l	ele	Lola
m	eme	mamá
n	ene	nada
ñ	eñe	año
o	o	oso
p	pe	Pepe
q	cu	química
r	ere	pero
rr	erre	perro, radio
s	ese	sí
t	te	Tomás
u	u	mucho
v	ve (chica) *or* uve	vamos
w	doble ve	Washington
x	equis	excelente, México
y	i griega *or* ye	soy, Yolanda
z	zeta	zapato

- The Spanish alphabet contains twenty-eight letters, including two letters that do not appear in the English alphabet. The letters **rr** and **ñ** are considered individual letters. The **rr** never begins a word in Spanish, and the **ñ** has its own section in Spanish dictionaries.

- Spanish only uses the **k** and **w** in words that have been borrowed from other languages, such as **sándwich, karate, whisky,** and **kilómetro.**

- All names of letters are feminine. Thus, you would say: **la be, la jota, la eme,** etc.

- At the beginning of a word, the **r** is always pronounced as the trilled **rr.** For example: **Ramón, ramblas,** and **redondo.**

- The letter **y** can be pronounced like the semivowel **i,** as in **voy, hay, Paraguay.** It can also be pronounced as **ll,** as in **yo, Maya,** and **Yadira.**

- Note that the letter **c** followed by the vowel **e** or **i** is pronounced with the [s] sound: **cero, cinco, cerca, cima.** When followed by the vowel **a, o,** or **u,** it is pronounced with the [k] sound as in: **casa, Colombia,** and **Cuba.**

- Also note that the **g** followed by the vowel **e** or **i** is pronounced like the Spanish **j** as in: **Germán, gitano,** and **gemido.** When followed by the vowel **a, o,** or **u,** it is pronounced with the [g] sound as in: **ganar, Gómez, Gutiérrez.**

Jj

Un jaguar toma jugo en la jungla.

◆ Práctica

H-7 Mundo hispánico. Look at the proper names below. Pronounce them and identify the first letter of each word by its name. Can you locate them?

MODELO: Washington   **doble ve**

Jalisco	Valparaíso	Copán	Chichicastenango
Puntarenas	Honduras	Quito	Rosario
Guyana	Sucre	Zaragoza	Taxco

H-8 Ortografía. Prepare a list of the names of five classmates in your Spanish course or five friends on campus to spell to your partner. Do not say the name prior to spelling it. Then listen as your classmate spells five names for you to record. Exchange lists to verify your work.

MODELO: Harry Chapman   hache-a-erre-i griega   ce-hache-a-pe-eme-a-ene

A propósito...Why study Spanish?

There are over 362 million Spanish speakers in the world today. The majority of them are concentrated in Spain, and North, Central, and South America, but they can also be found in Asian countries such as the Philippines and in North Africa. An estimated 25 million Spanish speakers live in the United States, making this country the fifth largest Spanish-speaking country in the world.

The enormous diversity among Spanish speakers results in differences in pronunciation and vocabulary, similar to differences in expressions and accents in English (North America, Great Britain, Australia, for example).

The following chart contains some examples of regional vocabulary variations in Spanish.

ENGLISH WORD	SPANISH WORDS			
EE.UU.	ESPAÑA	COLOMBIA	MÉXICO	ARGENTINA
car	coche	carro	coche	auto
apartment	piso	apartamento	apartamento	departamento
bus	autobús	bus	camión	ómnibus
sandwich	bocadillo	sándwich	sándwich	sándwich

¡Vamos a comparar!

H-9 Mundo hispánico. Working in small groups, name the places in the Spanish-speaking world that match the following descriptions. Use your intuition to guess the meaning of words you do not know. Some items may have more than one correct answer.

MODELO: Nación suramericana (cuatro letras)   **Perú**

1. La capital del Perú
2. Un canal importante
3. Una isla del Caribe
4. La capital de España
5. Nación suramericana (ocho letras)
6. Nación centroamericana; sus habitantes hablan inglés
7. País suramericano; sus habitantes hablan portugués
8. Nombres de países que terminan en "y"
9. Nombres de países que comienzan con "c"
10. En Gran Bretaña, son las Islas Falkland; en la Argentina son…
11. Estrecho entre Tierra del Fuego y Argentina
12. Países centroamericanos en la costa del Océano Pacífico

H-10 Mundo hispánico. Working in small groups, prepare a list of ten place names from the Spanish-speaking world. Then challenge another team to a spelling match. *Rules:* Teams alternate naming a place for their opponents to spell. The correct spelling earns 2 points; an incorrect spelling loses 2 points. No team member may respond more than once until all team members have volunteered to spell a word. The first team to earn 20 points wins.

Así es la vida

En la clase

1	el borrador	9	el papel	17	la luz
2	el estudiante	10	la pizarra	18	el reloj
3	la estudiante	11	la tiza	19	el escritorio
4	el mapa	12	la profesora	20	la ventana
5	la silla	13	el bolígrafo	21	la pared
6	el cuaderno	14	el lápiz	22	la mesa
7	los libros	15	la puerta		
8	el pupitre	16	la mochila		

Vocabulario y expresiones

Expresiones para la clase

Abra(n)[1] **el libro.**   *Open the book.*
Cierre(n) el libro.   *Close the book.*
Conteste(n) en español.   *Answer in Spanish.*
Escriba(n) los ejercicios.   *Write the exercises.*
Escuche(n).   *Listen.*
Estudie(n) la lección.   *Study the lesson.*
Haga(n) la tarea.   *Do the homework.*
Lea(n) la lección.   *Read the lesson.*
Repita(n) las frases.   *Repeat the sentences.*
Vaya(n) a la pizarra.   *Go to the board.*
aquí   *here*
allí   *there*

Preguntas

¿Cuánto(s)…?   *How much? How many?*
¿Cuánto cuesta(n)…?   *How much is…? How much are…?*
¿Qué hay en…?   *What's in…?*
¿Qué es esto?   *What's this?*
¿Cómo es…?   *What is … like?*

Respuestas

Hay[2]   *There is, There are*
Esto es   *This is*
Cuesta(n)   *It costs, They cost*
Necesito un/una…   *I need a…*

Otras palabras

barato(a)   *cheap, inexpensive*
caro(a)   *expensive*
hombre   *man*
mujer   *woman*

---

[1]In general, verb forms that end in **n** indicate that you are talking to or about more than one person or thing.

[2]Note that **hay** has the same form for both singular and plural.

¡Así lo decimos!

Saludos

The are many ways to greet people in Spanish. In addition to the expressions **¡Hola! ¿qué tal?** and **¿Cómo te va?**, most countries share the following informal expressions with different degrees of use. These expressions are often linked together as part of one greeting, e.g., **¡Hola! ¿cómo estás? Qué hay de nuevo?**

¿Cómo andas?
¿Qué hay de nuevo?
¿Qué novedades?
¿Qué onda?
¿Qué tal amaneciste?
¿Qué (te) cuentas?, ¿Qué me cuentas?, ¿Qué se cuenta?
¿Qué es de tu vida?

In Colombia, México and Venezuela, you will hear the greeting: **¿Qué hubo?**, which, when pronounced quickly, is run together and routinely results in: **¿Quiubo?**

The tendency of Mexican Spanish to add **-le** to many words creates another variation of this expression: **¿Quiúbole?**

Spanish from Cuba, Puerto Rico, and the Dominican Republic frequently uses subject pronouns and often does not invert word order in questions. These grammatical variations produce this typical greeting: **¿Cómo tú estás?**

Ampliación

Los números 0–30

0	cero				
1	uno	11	once	21	veintiuno
2	dos	12	doce	22	veintidós
3	tres	13	trece	23	veintitrés
4	cuatro	14	catorce	24	veinticuatro
5	cinco	15	quince	25	veinticinco
6	seis	16	dieciséis	26	veintiséis
7	siete	17	diecisiete	27	veintisiete
8	ocho	18	dieciocho	28	veintiocho
9	nueve	19	diecinueve	29	veintinueve
10	diez	20	veinte	30	treinta

- Before masculine nouns **uno** becomes **un.**
  un libro   **un** profesor

- Before feminine nouns **una** is used.
  una lección   **una** profesora

- In compound numbers **–uno** becomes **–ún** before a masculine noun and **–una** before a feminine noun.
  veinti**una** profesoras   veinti**ún** libros

- The numbers **dieciséis**, **diecisiete**, **dieciocho**, **diecinueve**, and **veintiuno** to **veintinueve** can be written as one word (shown here) or as three words: **diez y seis**, **diez y siete**, **diez y ocho**, **diez y nueve**, **veinte y uno**, etc. Throughout this text they appear as one word.

¿Cuál es el número del billete?

📼 ¡A escuchar!

¿Qué es esto? You will hear the question **¿Qué es esto?** followed by an answer. Indicate whether the answer matches the object in the drawing by deciding whether each answer is **Cierto** (*True*) or **Falso** (*False*). You will hear the correct responses on the tape.

MODELO: ¿Qué es esto?   Es una tiza.

Cierto   (Falso)

1. **Cierto   Falso**

4. **Cierto   Falso**

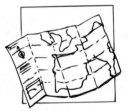

7. **Cierto   Falso**

2. **Cierto   Falso**

5. **Cierto   Falso**

8. **Cierto   Falso**

4. **Cierto   Falso**

6. **Cierto   Falso**

◆ Práctica

H-11 En la clase. How does your instructor...

1. tell a student to respond in Spanish?
2. tell students to open the book?
3. tell them to read the lesson?
4. tell them to do the homework?
5. tell them to close the book?
6. tell a student to answer a question?
7. tell a student to go to the blackboard?
8. tell a student to repeat the sentences?

H-12 Problemas de matemáticas. Your fourth-grade nephew needs help with his math homework. As you help him solve the following problems, read them aloud in Spanish. The following terms are used in mathematical operations.

más (+)   menos (−)   por (x)   entre (÷)   son/es (=)

MODELO: $2 + 3 = 5$ Dos más tres son cinco.
$\ 4 − 3 = 1$ Cuatro menos tres es uno.
$\ 3 \times 5 = 15$ Tres por cinco son quince.
$\ 10 ÷ 2 = 5$ Diez entre dos son cinco.

1. $5 \times 5 =$
2. $16 ÷ 4 =$
3. $14 − 2 =$
4. $10 \times 2 =$
5. $8 + 9 =$
6. $11 ÷ 11 =$
7. $9 \times 3 =$
8. $15 + 15 =$
9. $19 − 1 =$
10. $20 ÷ 2 =$
11. $6 \times 2 =$
12. $23 ÷ 23 =$
13. $12 + 7 =$
14. $29 − 17 =$
15. $30 ÷ 5 =$

H-13 Objetos en la clase. Write at least seven sentences naming in Spanish as many items in your classroom as you can.

MODELO: Hay una pizarra.

H-14 Completar. Complete the statements by identifying the objects or persons shown in the illustrations.

1. Hay una _____ en la de clase.

3. Esto es un _____.

5. Es una_____ matemáticas.

2. Es una _____ grande.

4. Es un _____.

6. Hay un _____ en el escritorio.

H-15 Objetos en un círculo. The first student names an item visible in the classroom. The student to his or her left repeats that item and names a new one. Each person in turn repeats all previously named items and adds a new one, until someone breaks the circle by failing to name all items or to come up with a new item.

MODELO: ESTUDIANTE A: En la clase hay una profesora.
              ESTUDIANTE B: En la clase hay una profesora y una mesa.
              ESTUDIANTE C: En la clase hay una profesora, una mesa y un reloj. Etc.

H-16 ¡Pumba! Form a circle. Take turns counting from 1 to 30, substituting the word **¡pumba!** for each Spanish number that falls into the categories described below.

MODELO: All numbers divisible by 2.
              ESTUDIANTE A: Uno
              ESTUDIANTE B: **¡Pumba!**
              ESTUDIANTE C: Tres
              ESTUDIANTE D: **¡Pumba!**

1. Numbers divisible by 3
2. Numbers divisible by 4
3. Numbers divisible by 5
4. Numbers divisible by 7

H-17 ¿Cuánto cuesta...? Take turns with a classmate asking questions about the price of each item. Decide if the item is expensive or cheap. Use the model as a guide.

MODELO: ESTUDIANTE A: ¿Cuánto cuesta el libro?
          ESTUDIANTE B: Cuesta veinte dólares.
          ESTUDIANTE A: ¿Es caro o barato?
          ESTUDIANTE B: Es caro.
          ESTUDIANTE A: Sí, es verdad. Es caro. **or**
                      No es verdad. No es caro.

1.

2.

3.

4.

5.

6.

7.

8.

H-18 Más matemáticas. Working in small groups, devise ten math problems in Spanish and determine their solutions. Make sure no problem element or solution is grteater than 30. Then, using the problems you prepared, challenge another group to solve them. Each team alternates presenting and solving problems. No team member may present or solve more than one problem until all team members have had a turn. Score 2 team points for each correct answer. Subtract two points for incorrect answers.

Pronunciación

Syllabification

Spanish words are divided into syllables according to the following rules.

- Single consonants (including **rr** and **ñ**) are attached to the vowel that follows: **na-da, ma-ña-na, bo-rra-dor.**

- Two consonants are generally separated: **tar-des, i-gual-men-te.** If a consonant is followed by **l** or **r**, both consonants are attached to the following vowel: **li-bro, Pe-dro, Ga-brie-la;** except in the groups **nl, rl, sl, tl, nr** and **sr,** where they are divided: **Car-los.**

- In groups of three or more consonants, only the last consonant, or the one followed by **l** or **r** (with the exceptions listed in the rule above) begin a syllable: **in-glés, es-cri-to-rio, cons-tar.**

- Adjacent strong vowels **(a, e, o)** form separate syllables: **le-an, ma-es-tro,** whereas in a diphthong—the combination of a strong **(a, e, o)** and a weak **(i, u)** vowel—both vowels appear in the same syllable: **E-duar-do, puer-ta, es-tu-dian-te.** However, in some instances the diphthong may be broken when the stress falls on either of the weak vowels **i** or **u.** In such cases, the weak vowel carries an accent mark: **bio-lo-gí-a, Ma-rí-a.**

Word Stress

- Words that end with a vowel, **n,** or **s** are stressed on the next-to-last syllable: **ma-***ña***-na,** *to*-**man,** *to*-**dos.**

- Words that end with consonants other than **n** or **s** are stressed on the last syllable: **us-***ted*, **to-***tal***,** **pro-fe-***sor***.**

- Words that do not follow the previous rules require a written accent mark on the stressed syllable: *ú*-**til,** *Víc*-**tor,** **lec-***ción***.**

- A written accent is also used to differentiate between words that are spelled the same but have different meanings: **tú** *(you),* **tu** *(your),* **él** *(he),* **el** *(the),* **sí** *(yes),* **si** *(if).* A written accent is also used on the stressed syllable of *all* interrogative and exclamatory words: **¿cuántos?** *(how many?),* **¿qué?** *(what?),* **¡Qué lindo!** *(How nice!),* **¡Cómo no!** *(Of course!).*

H-19 Sílabas. Divide the following words in syllables.

MODELO: cuadrado   cua-dra-do

buenos	gusto	lápiz	estudie
gracias	usted	hagan	señor
pupitre	puerta	profesor	reloj
lápices	luego	días	lecciones
bolígrafo	encantado	pizarra	lea

H-20 Categorías. With a partner, match each word in the previous exercise with one of the categories given under *Word Stress* on the preceding page. Explain the rule that governs the stress of each word.

 Estructuras

1. Definite and Indefinite Articles

In Spanish, the forms of the definite and indefinite articles vary according to the gender and number of the noun to which they refer.

Definite Articles

	MASCULINE		FEMININE	
SINGULAR	**el** bolígrafo	*the pen*	**la** silla	*the chair*
PLURAL	**los** bolígrafos	*the pens*	**las** sillas	*the chairs*

- The definite article is required with titles when talking about someone (indirect address) and omitted when addressing someone directly.

  Es **el** profesor Bonilla.   *It's Professor Bonilla.*
  ¡Buenos días, profesor Bonilla!   *Good morning, Professor Bonilla!*

Indefinite Articles

	MASCULINE		FEMININE	
SINGULAR	**un** libro	*a book*	**una** mesa	*a table*
PLURAL	**unos** libros	*some books*	**unas** mesas	*some tables*

- **Unos** and **unas** are equivalent to *some.*

  Hay **unos** cuadernos en la mesa.   *There are some notebooks on the table.*
  Unas clases son largas, otras cortas. *Some classes are long, others short.*

- **Un** and **una** are usually omitted with the verb **ser** when stating nationality, profession, membership in an organization, or occupation.

Marcos es **dentista**.	*Marcos is a dentist.*
Paulina es **demócrata cristiana**.	*Paulina is a Christian Democrat.*
Betina es **argentina**.	*Betina is Argentinian.*

- As in English, the indefinite article can be omitted after the verb **hay** to express the availability of something.

Hay **café** en la cafetería.	*There's coffee in the cafeteria.*
Hay **bananos** en el mercado.	*There are bananas in the market.*

◆ Práctica

H-21 La forma correcta. Provide the correct form of the definite article.

1. sillas	6. borrador	11. libro
2. pupitre	7. papel	12. microscopio
3. puerta	8. mochila	13. luz
4. relojes	9. cuaderno	14. mapa
5. pared	10. bolígrafo	15. tiza

H-22 Identificar. Using the definite article, identify the objects that you see in the picture.

H-23 Otra vez (*again*). Now identify the same objects in the illustration using the indefinite article.

H-24 Presentaciones. Complete the paragraph below using the definite and indefinite articles. In some cases, the article must be omitted.

— ¡Buenos días! ¿Cómo está? Yo soy _____ profesora Isolina Sequeira.
— Encantada, profesora. Yo soy _____ estudiante. Me llamo Flory Solano.
— _____ gusto es mío. ¿Es estudiante en _____ clase de español?
— Sí señora, en _____ clases de español y de italiano.
— Excelente. Lea _____ lección y haga _____ tarea para *(for)* mañana.
  Escriba _____ ejercicios tres y cuatro.
— Sí, profesora. Necesito _____ libro, _____ cuaderno, _____
  lápices, _____ bolígrafos y _____ mochila.
— Muy bien. En la clase hay _____ pizarra, _____ tiza, _____
  bolígrafos y _____ papel. Hay _____ mapa, _____ sillas,
  _____ pupitres, _____ escritorio para _____ profesora,
  _____ reloj y _____ mesa para _____ diccionarios.

2. Gender of Nouns

• Words that identify persons, places, or objects are called nouns. Spanish nouns—even those denoting nonliving things—are either masculine or feminine in gender.

MASCULINE		FEMININE	
el muchacho	the boy	**la muchacha**	the girl
el hombre	the man	**la mujer**	the woman
el profesor	the professor	**la profesora**	the professor
el lápiz	the pencil	**la pluma**	the pen
el libro	the book	**la mesa**	the table
el mapa	the map	**la clase**	the class

- Most nouns ending in **-o** or those denoting male persons are masculine: **el libro, el hombre.** Most nouns ending in **-a** or those denoting female persons are feminine: **la mujer, la mesa.**

- Some common exceptions are: **el día** *(day)* and **el mapa** *(map)*, which end in **-a** but are masculine. Another exception is: **la mano** *(hand)*, which ends in **-o** but is feminine.

▼▼▼▼▼▼▼▼▼▼▼▼▼▼▼▼▼▼▼▼▼▼▼▼▼▼▼▼▼

STUDY TIPS

Some nouns do not follow patterns. The following basic rules may help you determine the gender of many Spanish nouns.

1. Many masculine nouns ending in **-o** have a corresponding feminine form ending in **-a**: **el muchacho/la muchacha** *(boy/girl)*.
2. Some masculine nouns ending in a consonant simply add an **-a** to form the corresponding feminine form: **el profesor/la profesora** *(male professor/female professor)*.
3. Certain nouns, which often end in **-e**, have the same form for both genders: **el estudiante/la estudiante** *(male student/female student)*.
4. The article that accompanies each noun will help you identify its gender: **un pupitre, una clase**.
5. Most nouns ending in **-ad** and **-ión**, such as **la verdad** *(the truth)*, **la mitad** *(half)*, and **la nación** *(the nation)*, are feminine. Nouns ending in **-ez, -ud**, and **-umbre** are also feminine: **la pesadez** *(heaviness)*, **la juventud** *(youth)*, **la legumbre** *(vegetable)*.

H-25 Femenino y masculino. Give the feminine equivalents of the following words.

1. el profesor
2. el estudiante
3. el hombre
4. el muchacho
5. el señor
6. el doctor
7. el conductor del carro
8. el técnico
9. el estudiante
10. el artista

H-26 ¿Qué tienes? Copy the list below on a separate piece of paper. Circulate around the class looking for people who meet the criteria in the list. Write the name of each person who responds affirmatively to one of your questions next to the question. You may ask each person only one question, and you must allow each person to ask you a question. You have five minutes to find at least one person for each item.

MODELO: —¿Tienes (do you have) un bolígrafo rojo?
                      —¿Cómo te llamas?
          —Me llamo ... *(name)*

1. ¿Tienes una clase interesante?
2. ¿Tienes una mochila grande?
3. ¿Tienes un lápiz?
4. ¿Tienes papel?
5. ¿Tienes un amigo inteligente?
6. ¿Tienes un diccionario de español?
7. ¿Tienes un reloj bueno?
8. ¿Tienes un cuaderno?
9. ¿Tienes un mapa?
10. ¿Tienes un bolígrafo?

3. Plurals of Nouns

SINGULAR	PLURAL
el muchacho	**los** muchacho**s**
el hombre	**los** hombre**s**
la mujer	**las** mujer**es**
el profesor	**los** profesor**es**
el lápiz	**los** lápi**ces**
la mochila	**las** mochila**s**

- Singular nouns ending in a vowel add an **-s** to form the plural:
  hombre → hombres, mesa → mesas.

- Singular nouns ending in a consonant add **-es:**
  mujer → mujeres, profesor → profesores.

- Singular nouns ending in -**z** change the **z** to **c**, and add **-es: lápiz → lápices.**

When the last syllable of a word has an accent mark, the accent is omitted in the plural form: **lección → lecciones.**

H-26 Cambiar. Give the plural of the following nouns:

1. el borrador
2. la lección
3. el lápiz
4. la mochila
5. la ventana
6. el papel
7. el reloj
8. el día
9. la pluma
10. la mano
11. el mapa
12. la pared

H-27 En la clase de español. Complete the following paragraph about a Spanish class using the correct form of the definite or indefinite article.

En _____ clase de español, hay _____ mapa, _____ pizarra, _____ escritorio, _____

sillas y _____ pupitres. _____ estudiantes son *(are)* muy inteligentes. _____

profesor/profesora es _____ señor/señorita/señora…

H-28 En el apartamento. Work in groups of four or five. Assume that your group is sharing an apartment for the school year and that you are about to go shopping for the things you need to settle in. Make a list of who needs each item below and record the totals so that you will know what to buy.

MODELO: —Yo necesito un escritorio.
        —Yo también *(also)*. ¿Y tú, Juan?
        —Yo no. Tengo un escritorio. etc.

1. sillas
2. papel
3. mochilas
4. lápices
5. mapas

6. escritorios
7. cuadernos
8. relojes
9. bolígrafos
10. libros

Colaboración

Estudiante A

H-29A ¿Qué hay? ¿Qué no hay? Working with a classmate, find at least five differences between the drawing below and the one in 29B on page 24. You should not look at the drawing on that page, and your partner should not look at the one on this page.

MODELO: —Hay un borrador de pizarra.
          —Sí, hay. (No, no hay.)

H-30A Personajes y lugares. Spell the names of the five Spanish-speaking countries and cities in the left-hand column to your partner. Then, working together, match the place names with the descriptions in the column to the right.

MODELO: Chile   ce-hache-i-ele-e

1. Argentina
2. Lima
3. Panamá
4. Cuba
5. Madrid

a. capital del Perú
b. capital de España
c. canal
d. nación suramericana
e. isla

Now listen as your partner spells the names of five famous people from the Spanish-speaking world, and write what you hear on a piece of paper. Then, working together, match the names of the people in the list with these professions.

MODELO: Fidel Castro   efe-i-de-e-ele ce-a-ese-te-ere-o

a. cantante popular (m)
b. jugador de golf
c. cantante popular (f)
d. cómico
e. jugador de béisbol

H–31A El mundo latinoamericano. Working with your partner, complete the information missing from the chart below and help your partner complete the chart on page 25. Note that the charts do not necessarily contain the same information, nor is the information arranged in the same order. Some information may be missing from *both* charts.

MODELO: —Un país pequeño, en Centroamérica; la capital es San Salvador.
          —Es El Salvador.

EXTENSIÓN: Un país (grande/pequeño)
CAPITAL: La capital es …
LUGAR: En (Suramérica, Centroamérica, Norteamérica, el Caribe)

PAÍS	EXTENSIÓN	CAPITAL	LUGAR
El Salvador	pequeño	San Salvador	Centroamérica
Colombia	1.	Bogotá	2.
México	grande	3.	Norteamérica
Paraguay	4.	5.	Suramérica
6.	pequeño	Santo Domingo	el Caribe
7.	grande	Lima	Suramérica
8.	9.	Guatemala	Centroamérica
Argentina	grande	10.	Suramérica
11.	pequeño	Panamá	12.
Cuba	pequeño	La Habana	13.
14.	15.	San Juan	el Caribe
Honduras	16.	Tegucigalpa	Centroamérica
Brasil	17.	18.	Suramérica

¿Qué países son?

Estudiante B

H-29B ¿Qué hay? ¿Qué no hay? Working with a classmate, find at least five differences between the drawing below and the one in 29A on page 22. You should not look at the drawing on that page, and your partner should not look at the one on this page.

MODELO: —Hay un borrador de pizarra.
              —Sí, hay. (No, no hay.)

H-30B Personajes y lugares. Listen as your partner spells the names of five Spanish-speaking countries, and write what you hear on a piece of paper. Then, working together, match the place names with these descriptions.

MODELO: Chile   ce-hache-i-ele-e

a. capital del Perú
b. capital de España
c. canal
d. nación suramericana
e. isla *(island)*

Now spell the names of the five famous people from the Spanish-speaking world in the left-hand column to your partner. Then, working together, match the names of the people with the professions in the column to the right.

MODELO: Fidel Castro   efe-i-de-e-ele ce-a-ese-te-ere-o

1. Fernando Valenzuela   a. cantante popular (m)
2. Julio Iglesias   b. jugador de golf
3. Gloria Estefan   c. cómico
4. Severino Ballesteros   d. jugador de béisbol
5. Cheech   e. cantante popular (f)

H–31B El mundo latinoamericano. Working with your partner, complete the information missing from the chart below and help your partner complete the chart on page 23. Note that the charts do not necessarily contain the same information, nor is the information arranged in the same order. Some information may be missing from *both* charts.

MODELO: —Un país pequeño, en Centroamérica; la capital es San Salvador.
              —Es El Salvador.

EXTENSIÓN: Un país (grande/pequeño)
   CAPITAL: La capital es….
     LUGAR: En (Suramérica, Centroamérica, Norteamérica, el Caribe)

PAÍS	EXTENSIÓN	CAPITAL	LUGAR
El Salvador	pequeño	San Salvador	Centroamérica
1.	grande	2.	Norteamérica
Argentina	grande	3.	Suramérica
Paraguay	pequeño	4.	Suramérica
Perú	5.	6.	Suramérica
Guatemala	pequeño	7.	Centroamérica
Puerto Rico	8.	San Juan	9.
La República Dominicana	10.	11.	el Caribe
12.	grande	Brasilia	13.
Colombia	grande	14.	15.
Cuba	pequeño	16.	17.
Honduras	18.	Tegucigalpa	19.
20.	21.	Panamá	22.

¿Qué países son?

Lección 1

¿De dónde eres?

Comunicación

- Expressing Nationality and Place of Origin
- Asking and Responding to Simple Questions
- Describing Yourself and Others
- Talking about Daily Activities
- Expressing Your Age
- Expressing *to be* in Spanish

Cultura

- Spanish Names and Nicknames

Mundo hispánico: ¡362 millones hablan español!

Estructuras

Primera parte

- Form, Position, and Agreement of Adjectives
- Subject Pronouns
- The Present Tense of **ser** *(to be)*
- Questions and Negation

Segunda parte

- The Present Tense of **-ar** Verbs in the Indicative
- The Present Tense of **tener** *(to have)*

PRIMERA PARTE
¡Así es la vida!

¿Quién es?

—¡Hola! Me llamo Antonio Pacheco. Éstos son mis amigos:

José Morales de Nueva York.

Se llama Isabel Madrid Davis. Es argentina. Es inteligente y muy trabajadora. También es muy simpática. ¿De dónde eres tú?

Se llama Leví Gómez Mansur. Es de Madrid, la capital de España. Es alto y delgado. ¿Cómo eres tú?

¿De dónde eres?

PACO: ¿De dónde eres tú, María?
MARÍA: Yo soy de Miami, pero mis padres son de Cuba. Y tú, ¿de dónde eres?
PACO: Yo soy de Puerto Rico.

CARLOS: ¿Ustedes son colombianas?
LUPE: No, somos venezolanas.
CARLOS: ¿De veras? Yo también soy de Venezuela.
LUPE: ¿Sí? ¿De qué ciudad eres?
CARLOS: De Maracaibo.
SARA: ¡Ay! ¡Nosotras también!
LUPE: ¡Qué pequeño es el mundo!

Vocabulario y expresiones

Palabras y expresiones interrogativas

¿Cómo ...?	How ...?, What ...?
¿Cuál / cuáles ...?	Which (one / ones) ...?
¿Cuándo ...?	When ...?
¿Cuánto / cuántos ...?	How much ./ many...?
¿Dónde ...?	Where ...?
¿De dónde ...?	From where ...?
¿Adónde ...?	To where ...?
¿Qué ...?	How ...? What ...?
¿De qué ...?	From which...?, Of what...?
¿Por qué ...?	Why ...?
¿Quién / quiénes ...?	Who ...?
¿Cómo eres?	What are you like?
¿Con quién(es) ...?	With whom ...?
¿De quién(es) ...?	Whose ...?

Adjetivos descriptivos

alto(a)	tall
antipático(a)	unfriendly
bajo(a)	short
bello(a)	beautiful
bonito(a)=lindo(a)	pretty
bueno(a)	good
delgado(a)	thin, slender
feo(a)	ugly
gordo(a)	fat
grande	big
guapo(a)	handsome
inteligente	intelligent
joven	young
malo(a)	bad
pequeño(a)	small
perezoso(a)	lazy
simpático(a)	nice, friendly
tonto(a)	dumb
trabajador(a)	hardworking
viejo(a)	old

Adjetivos de nacionalidad

argentino(a)	Argentinian
boliviano(a)	Bolivian
canadiense	Canadian
colombiano(a)	Colombian
costarricense(a)	Costa Rican
cubano(a)	Cuban
chileno(a)	Chilean
dominicano(a)	Dominican
ecuatoriano(a)	Ecuadorian
español(a)	Spanish
estadounidense	American (U.S.)
guatemalteco(a)	Guatemalan
japonés(a)	Japanese
mexicano(a)	Mexican
norteamericano(a)	North American (U.S., Canada)
panameño(a)	Panamanian
paraguayo(a)	Paraguayan
peruano(a)	Peruvian
puertorriqueño(a)	Puerto Rican
uruguayo(a)	Uruguayan
venezolano(a)	Venezuelan

Otras palabras

el amigo	friend
el año	year
el apellido	surname
la capital	capital
la ciudad	city
con	with
de	of, from
la edad	age
entonces	then, therefore
la isla	island
el mundo	world
muy	very
el país	country
pero	but
porque	because
el pueblo	town
ser	to be
sí / ¿Sí?	yes / Really?
si	if
también	also

¡Así lo decimos!

Los amigos

When we talk about friends, we often choose words that indicate that we have a closer bond with some friends: *best friend*, *buddy*, *pal*, *girlfriend* (used by women to denote a special friendship), *confidant(e)*, etc. In Spanish, **amigo** is the generic word for *friend*. However, throughout the Spanish-speaking world, there is a wide variety of words used in informal conversation to express close friend.

Colombia	**llave, pana**
Cuba	**socio/a**
Ecuador	**pana**
España	**compañero/a, colega, coleguilla**
Guatemala, México	**cuate**
Perú	**pata**
Venezuela	**pana, panadería**

Rocío y yo somos cuates desde la escuela primaria.

Rocío and I have been pals since elementary school.

When native speakers of Spanish address their friends (or even strangers of the same age group), they frequently use a word in place of the person's name. The colloquial use of *man* or *dude* is the closest American English equivalent.

Argentina	**che, flaco/a**
Colombia	**hermano/a**
Cuba	**chico/a, viejo/a**
España	**tío/a**
Guatemala, Puerto Rico	**'mano/a**
México	**'manito/a**
Venezuela	**chamo/a, chico/a**

Oye, chamo, ¿hay clase hoy?

Hey, man, is there class today?

Somos cuates desde la escuela primaria.

📼 ¡A escuchar!

¿Quién es? You will hear Antonio describe his friends as they appear in **¡Así es la vida!** (p. 27). After each description, indicate whether the statements that follow are **Cierto** or **Falso**.

	Cierto	Falso			Cierto	Falso
1.	_____	_____		3.	_____	_____
2.	_____	_____		4.	_____	_____

¿De dónde eres? You will now hear the other conversations on page 27. First listen to the conversation, then mark **Cierto** or **Falso** after each statement.

	Cierto	Falso			Cierto	Falso
1.	_____	_____		4.	_____	_____
2.	_____	_____		5.	_____	_____
3.	_____	_____		6.	_____	_____

Ampliación

Los colores

blanco(a)	*white*
rojo(a)	*red*
negro(a)	*black*
amarillo(a)	*yellow*
anaranjado(a)	*orange*
morado(a)	*purple*
rosado(a)	*pink*
gris	*gray*
verde	*green*
marrón	*brown*
azul	*blue*

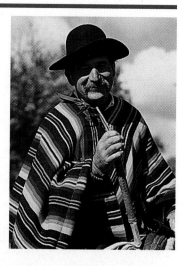

¿Qué colores hay?

◆ Práctica

1–1 ¿De qué color es? Look for the objects listed below in your classroom, then give the colors for each object.

1. una pizarra
2. un lápiz
3. los pupitres
4. unos cuadernos
5. un mapa (si hay)
6. una mochila
7. la tiza
8. unos libros
9. las sillas
10. un borrador
11. la pared
12. unos bolígrafos

1–2 En la clase. Use words and expressions from **¡Así es la vida!** and **Vocabulario y expresiones** to complete the following exchanges.

MARIO: ¿De _____ eres tú, María?

MARÍA: Yo _____ de Santiago.

TERE: ¿_____ son norteamericanos?

GLORIA: No, no _____ norteamericanos. Somos _____.

CARLOS: El profesor no es chileno; es _____.

JORGE: Y también es _____.

1–3 ¿Cómo son? Choose the correct word from the corresponding list to complete each sentence.

MODELO: Lucila es de Bogotá. Es ___**c.**___

       a. venezolana   b. española   c. colombiana   d. puertorriqueña

1. Barcelona es una _____ de España.

   a. capital   b. joven   c. país   d. ciudad

2. Chepe es de Acapulco. Es _____.

   a. mexicano   b. norteamericano   c. panameño   d. bueno

3. ¡Qué _____ es el mundo!

   a. antipático   b. perezoso   c. pequeño   d. delgado

4.   OLGA: Tú eres dominicana, ¿no?

   CARMEN: No, yo _____ hondureña.

   a. soy   b. son   c. es   d. somos

5.   PEPE: ¿_____ es la capital de Ecuador?

   TOÑO: Es Quito.

   a. Quién   b. Por qué   c. Cuál   d. Dónde

6.   CHELA: ¿_____ es María Teresa?

   MARCOS: Es baja, pequeña y bonita.

   a. Cómo   b. Dónde   c. Por qué   d. Qué

7.   JUAN: ¿_____ es el estudiante alto y gordo?

   GLORIANA: Es de Santiago, Chile.

   a. Cómo   b. Quién   c. De dónde   d. De qué

1–4 Emparejar. Match the words in the left-hand column with the word that has the opposite meaning at the right.

_____ 1. alto   a. trabajador

_____ 2. gordo   b. bueno

_____ 3. simpático   c. inteligente

_____ 4. perezoso   d. bajo

_____ 5. malo   e. feo

_____ 6. bonito   f. delgado

_____ 7. pequeño   g. antipático

_____ 8. tonto   h. grande

1–5 ¿Cómo son? With a partner, describe the people in the following illustration.

1. Eugenio
2. María Eugenia
3. Antonio
4. María Antonia
5. Gonzalo
6. Virginia
7. Alicia
8. Juan Manuel

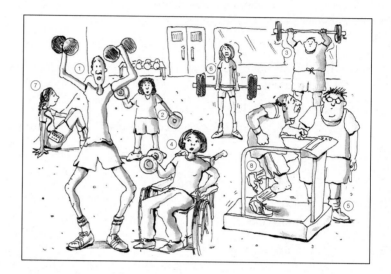

Pronunciación

Linking

In Spanish as well as in English, speakers group words into units that are separated by pauses. Each unit or breath group is pronounced as if it were one long word. Spanish speakers link words within a unit if the second word to be linked begins with a vowel. The following will serve as a guide.

- If a word ends in a vowel and the following word begins with a vowel, pronounce them as one syllable.

    Tú eres de la capital. (**Tué**-res-de-la-capital.)

- If the two vowels that are adjacent to each other are the same, pronounce them as if they were one.

    Luis**a a**ctúa bien. (Lui-**sac**-tú-a-bien.)

- If the two vowels that are adjacent are strong vowels but not the same, pronounce them as one syllable.

    ¿Cóm**o e**stás tú? (¿Có-**moes**-tás-tú?)

- When a word ends in a consonant and the following word begins with a vowel, they also form a single syllable.

    ¿Él **e**s de Puerto Rico? (¿É-**les**-de-Puer-to-Ri-co?)

 Estructuras

1. Form, Position, and Agreement of Adjectives

La profesora Monge es
trabajadora.

El profesor Figueres es
viejo.

- Adjectives agree in gender and number with the noun they modify and are
generally placed after the noun.

el profesor **colombiano**	the **Colombian** professor
las señoras **mexicanas**	the **Mexican** ladies
los libros **interesantes**	the **interesting** books

- Adjectives whose masculine form ends in **-o** have a feminine form ending in **-a.**

el profesor **mexicano**	the **Mexican** professor
la profesora **mexicana**	the **Mexican** professor

- Adjectives that end in a consonant or in **-e** have the same masculine and feminine
forms.

un libro **interesante**	an **interesting** book
una clase **interesante**	an **interesting** class
un coche **azul**	a **blue** car
una silla **azul**	a **blue** chair

- Adjectives of nationality that end in a consonant, and adjectives that end in
-dor, add **-a** to form the feminine. If the adjective ends in a consonant and has
an accent on the last syllable, both the feminine and the plural forms will drop
the accent. Adjectives of nationality are not capitalized in Spanish.

el profesor **español**	the **Spanish** professor
la estudiante **española**	the **Spanish** student
el señor **trabajador**	the **hardworking** man
la profesora **trabajadora**	the **hardworking** professor
un libro **francés**	a **French** book
una mochila **francesa**	a **French** backpack

• Generally, adjectives follow the same rules as nouns to form the plural.

SINGULAR		PLURAL
mexicano	→	mexicanos
española	→	españolas
inteligente	→	inteligentes
trabajador	→	trabajadores

◆ Práctica

1–6 ¿Cómo son? Complete the following descriptions of people and objects you know. Use colors, adjectives of nationality, descriptive adjectives, and so on.

1. El libro de español es....
2. El cuaderno es....
3. El profesor/la profesora es....
4. Las sillas son....
5. Los estudiantes son....
6. La pizarra es....
7. La clase es....
8. La cafetería de la universidad es....

1–7 Él y ella. Change the male characters in the sentences to female characters.

MODELO: El profesor de francés es muy inteligente y feo.
              La profesora de francés es muy inteligente y fea.

1. El profesor de historia es mexicano y muy interesante.
2. El estudiante español es alto y gordo.
3. El boliviano es un hombre inteligente.
4. El muchacho grande es muy perezoso y antipático.
5. El señor gordo es muy simpático y honesto.
6. El doctor trabajador es dominicano.
7. El panameño en la clase es muy alto.
8. El venezolano es pequeño y joven.

1–8 La clase. Choose the most logical words from the list to complete the paragraph below. There may be more than one possibility for a few of the choices.

blancas	escritorio	francesa	guatemalteca
hay	interesante	mapa	norteamericanos
pared	patrióticos	pequeños	pizarra
puertas	mesa	simpática	ventana

La clase de español es muy _____. La profesora es _____ y es muy
_____. Todos (all) los estudiantes son _____, menos (except)
Michelle Poirot que es _____. En la clase _____ una _____
verde con tiza y borrador, y un _____ de España y otro (another) de América
Latina. Los pupitres de los estudiantes son _____, pero el _____ de
la profesora es grande. También hay un reloj gris en la _____ y una
_____ blanca con sillas _____. Las _____ son rojas y la
_____ es azul. ¡Los colores de las clases son muy _____!

2. Subject Pronouns

- Subject pronouns in Spanish are used to refer to people. Spanish does not generally use subject pronouns to refer to inanimate objects or animals.

- Spanish speakers frequently omit subject pronouns because the verb form indicates who the speaker is.

  ¿Eres de Cuba?   *Are you from Cuba?*
  Sí, soy de Cuba.   *Yes, I'm from Cuba.*

- In many instances, subject pronouns can be used for clarification or emphasis:

  Yo estudio derecho y **ella** medicina.   *I study law and she studies medicine.*

- Spanish has two equivalents for the English singular *you:* **tú** and **usted. Tú** is used informally with friends, family, and children. **Usted** is used to denote formality with people with whom you are not well acquainted, with those in a position of authority (supervisor, boss, instructor), and with older people. **Usted** and **ustedes** are commonly abbreviated as **Ud.** and **Uds.** or as **Vd.** and **Vds.**

- In Latin America, the plural of **tú** and **usted** is **ustedes.** In Spain, the **vosotros/vosotras** forms are used to address more than one person in a familiar context. In this book, **ustedes** is used as the plural of **tú.**

3. The Present Tense of *ser (to be)*

Nosotras somos bailarinas!

- **Ser** is used to express origin, occupation, and to describe inherent qualities of people and things.

  Soy un profesor de ciencias   *I'm a science professor from Madrid.*
  de Madrid.
  El libro **es** interesante.   *The book is interesting.*

ser *(to be)*			
SINGULAR FORMS		PLURAL FORMS	
yo soy *I am*		**nosotros/nosotras somos** *we are*	
tú eres *you are* (fam.)		**vosotros/vosotras sois** *you are* (fam. pl.)	
usted es *you are* (formal)		**ustedes son** *you are* (pl.)	
él es *he is*		**ellos son** *they are*	
ella es *she is*		**ellas son** *they are*	

▼▼▼▼▼▼▼▼▼▼▼▼▼▼▼▼▼▼▼▼▼▼▼▼▼▼▼▼▼▼▼▼▼▼▼▼▼

STUDY TIP

To *conjugate* verbs in Spanish, you have to memorize six sets of endings (per verb), including the form for **vosotros/as**. **Usted**, **él**, and **ella** (third person singular) and **Ustedes**, **ellos** and **ellas** (third person plural) require one set of endings each.

We suggest repeating the forms out loud many times until you are able to produce them automatically, without thinking. Or, write each subject pronoun on a separate index card and test yourself by shuffling them and trying to produce the verb form that corresponds to the subject pronoun on each card. Practicing a few minutes every day produces better results than practicing several hours only once a week.

◆ Práctica

1–9 ¿De dónde son?
Indicate where the following people are from based on the information provided in the map.

MODELO: Yo soy de
Colombia.

1–10 ¿De dónde son? Complete the following paragraphs, using appropriate forms of **ser.**

— ¡Hola! Nosotros _____ Fernando Mendoza Vareta, Marta Pérez Caicedo y Adela Guzmán Soler. Nosotros _____ chilenos. Fernando _____ de Viña del Mar, Marta _____ de Valparaíso y yo _____ de Santiago, que _____ la capital del país. Santiago _____ una ciudad muy bonita. ¿De dónde _____ tú?

— ¡Ah, Uds. _____ chilenos! Chile _____ un país lindo y la capital _____ muy interesante. Yo _____ de Jalapa, México. México _____ un país muy grande, pero Jalapa _____ una ciudad relativamente pequeña. _____ muy bonita también. ¿Uds. _____ estudiantes? Yo _____ estudiante en la Universidad Autónoma de México.

1–11 Preguntas indiscretas. Write the following interview questions using the verb **ser**.

1. Ask your professor what his/her surnames *(sus apellidos)* are.
2. Ask two classmates where they're from.
3. Ask your professor where he/she is from.
4. Ask a classmate what his girlfriend *(tu novia)*/boyfriend *(tu novio)* is like.
5. Ask two classmates what they are like. Where are they from?

◆ Actividades

1–12 Una descripción. Briefly describe yourself to a classmate. Follow the model. Then describe your Spanish professor and at least one of the students in the class.

MODELO: Me llamo…. Soy norteamericano(a). Soy inteligente.

1–13 Descripciones. Working in small groups, make up five descriptions of famous people. Include information such as physical characteristics, the person's profession, and place of residence. Then challenge another team to alternate with yours in describing and identifying the people you chose. Award two points for each correct answer. A list of cognates (words derived from the same root in Spanish and English) appears in the chart below.

MODELO: —Es muy alto, joven,
deportista y vive *(lives)* en Orlando.
            —¿Es Shaquille O'Neal?
            —Sí, sí es.

PROFESIÓN	CÓMO ES	
actor (m)/actriz (f)	tradicional	cómico
agente secreto	andrógino	conservador
boxeador	artístico	demócrata
dictador	autoritario	idealista
doctor	cínico	intelectual
poeta	dramático	liberal
político	nervioso	realista

1–14 ¿Cómo es? While the rest of the class takes notes, each person stands up and says his or her name, the city and state or country he or she is from, and gives a brief description of himself/herself. Then, in groups of three, describe three other students in your class, in as much detail as possible. Add your own details. Following is a list of words you may want to use.

MODELO: (you)   Me llamo Katie Deller. Soy de Atlantic City, New Jersey.
                       Soy de pelo negro, no muy alta, y muy trabajadora.

    (in groups)   —¿De dónde es Katie Deller?
                       —Es de New Jersey. Es de Atlantic City.
                       —¿Cómo es ella?
                       —Es de pelo negro. No es muy alta. Es trabajadora.

rubio(a)	*blond*
pelirrojo(a)	*redhead*
de pelo (negro, café oscuro, claro)	*black, dark brown, light brown hair*
de pelo corto/largo	*short, long hair*
de ojos azules/negros/ café/verdes	*blue, black, brown, green eyes*

1–15 ¿Cuál es tu opinión? Work in small groups. Find out what your classmates think about these people/things. Record at least five opinions on a separate sheet of paper. (*Note:* Be sure to conjugate the verb **ser** and make certain that all adjectives agree with the nouns they describe.)

MODELO: —En tu opinión, ¿cómo es la vida del estudiante?
               —Es difícil.

    Según *(According to)* … (nombre), la vida del estudiante es difícil.

la vida del (de la) profesor(a)	las mujeres inteligentes
los estudiantes de la universidad	los hombres simpáticos
los profesores	la ciudad
los futbolistas	la universidad
los políticos	

ser

bueno/malo	tonto/inteligente
terrible	antipático/simpático
estupendo	viejo/joven
rico/pobre	magnífico
trabajador	…(original)
feo/guapo/bonito	

4. Questions and Negation

Using Interrogative Words

- Interrogative words are commonly used at the beginning of a sentence to form questions in Spanish. The most commonly used interrogative words are:

¿Cómo…?	*How …?*
¿Cuál…?	*Which (one)…?*
¿Cuáles…?	*Which ones…?*
¿Cuándo…?	*When…?*
¿Dónde…?	*Where…?*
¿De dónde…?	*From where…?*
¿Por qué…?	*Why…?*
¿Qué…?	*What…?*
¿De qué…?	*From which…?, From what…?*
¿Quién…?	*Who…?* (singular)
¿Quiénes…?	*Who…?* (plural)
¿De quién…?	*Whose…?*

- Note that questions in Spanish are punctuated with two question marks: an inverted, backward question mark at the beginning of the question (¿) and a question mark (?) at the end.

¿Qué? vs. ¿Cuál?

In general, the interrogatives **¿qué?** and **¿cuál?** are similar in English and Spanish, although both may be translated as *what* or *which* in different circumstances.

When **¿qué?** is used alone, it is a request for a definition and is translated as *what?* in English. When followed by a singular or plural noun, **¿qué?** means *which?* and requests information about one or some among many.

¿Qué tienes?	**What** *do you have?*
¿Qué es la vida?	**What** *is life?*
¿Qué área(s) de estudio prefieres?	**Which** *field(s) of study do you prefer?*

¿Cuál?, meaning *which?,* is generally used alone and implies selection from a group. It may also be translated as *what?* in English.

¿Cuál(es) prefieres?	**Which** *(one[s]) do you prefer?*
¿Cuál es la fecha de hoy?	**What** *is today's date?*
¿Cuál es la capital de Colombia?	**What** *is the capital of Colombia?*

Yes/No Questions

- A yes/no question is formed by inverting the position of the subject and the verb in a declarative statement, by modifying the intonation pattern, or by adding a "tag" phrase at the end of a declarative statement.

INVERSION:	**Tú eres** de México. → ¿**Eres tú** de México?
MODIFIED INTONATION:	¿**Ellos son** de los Estados Unidos?
TAG PHRASE:	Adela es de Madrid, **¿verdad?**

- Other frequently used tag questions are:

¿Cierto? *Right?*   **¿Sí?** *Yes?*   **¿De veras?** *Truly? Really?*

Negation

- To make a sentence negative in Spanish simply place the word **no** immediately in front of the verb.

Elena **no** es de la capital.	*Elena's **not** from the capital.*
Nosotros **no** somos de España.	*We're **not** from Spain.*

- When answering a question in the negative, the word **no** also precedes the verb.

¿Son ellos de Caracas?	*Are they from Caracas?*
No, ellos **no** son de Caracas.	*No, they're **not** from Caracas.*

◆ Práctica

1–16 ¿De veras? Look at the list in exercise **1–15** (**¿Cuál es tu opinión?**) page 38. Use it to make at least three intonation questions and three tag questions.

1–17 ¡Cuántas preguntas! Look at the conversations in **¡Así es la vida!** on page 27. Pick out the questions and say which ones are inversion questions and which ones are intonation questions. Are there any tag questions?

1–18 Una compañera de clase. Complete the following exchange using the correct interrogative expression.

— ¿_____ te llamas?   — Soy María.
— ¿De _____ eres, María   — De Puerto Rico.
— ¿De _____ ciudad?   — De San Juan.
— ¿_____ son tus padres?   — Son los señores Ramírez.
— ¿_____ es tu clase de inglés?   — Es por la tarde.
— De _____ es tu profesor?   — Es de aquí.
— ¿_____ es?   — Es trabajador.

1–19 ¿Es verdad? You didn't quite hear what a classmate said. Ask questions by inverting the subject and verb in the following statements.

MODELO: El profesor es de Costa Rica. ➜ ¿Es el profesor de Costa Rica?

1. Los estudiantes son norteamericanos.
2. La profesora es inteligente.
3. Nosotros somos trabajadores.
4. La señora Martínez es de la Ciudad de México.
5. Las muchachas españolas son simpáticas.
6. Nosotros somos inteligentes.
7. Isabel es de Valparaíso.
8. El profesor es activo.

1–20 ¿Quiénes son? In pairs, answer the following questions affirmatively or negatively based on the information provided on the ID cards below. First read "Spanish Names and Nicknames" in **A propósito** on page 43 and answer this question: What would Luisa's name be if she married Rodolfo?

1. Luisa es de Colombia, ¿verdad?
2. Rodolfo es muy delgado, ¿no?
3. Los apellidos de Luisa son Cardona Gómez, ¿cierto?
4. ¿Rodolfo es de la República Dominicana?
5 Luisa es muy alta, ¿verdad?
6. El apellido de la mamá de Rodolfo es Gómez, ¿verdad?
7. ¿Dónde estudia Luisa?
8. ¿En qué universidad está Rodolfo?

1–21 Entrevista. Aracely Fernández is a candidate for admission in the freshman class at Florida State. Complete her conversation with an alumnus in the screening interview. Compare your paragraph with that of a partner.

—¿…?
—Yo soy de la Florida.

—¿…?
—De Orlando.

—Pero Ud. no es cubana, ¿verdad?
—….

—¿De veras? ¡Yo también! Soy de Buenos Aires. ¿También Ud. es de Buenos Aires?
—….

—¡Tucumán! ¡Bella ciudad! Mercedes Sosa, la cantante más famosa de Argentina también es de Tucumán.
—Sí,… .

—Así es. ¡Qué pequeño es el mundo!

1–22 No y no. Look at Exercise **1–19 (¿Es verdad?)** on the preceding page. Turn the affirmative sentences into negative sentences.

◆ Actividades

1–23 El carnet de identidad. A new student at *La Universidad Complutense* is being interviewed in order to obtain a university ID card. First, on a separate piece of paper, complete the sentences at the top of the following page with the appropriate interrogative word. Then, take turns acting out the roles of student and interviewer. As interviewer, you must write down the information and create an ID with the following items: (1) *Nombre*, (2) *Apellidos*, (3) *Edad*, (4) *País de origen*, and (5) *Descripción física*.

1. ¿_____ te llamas?
2. ¿_____ son tus apellidos?
3. ¿_____ años tienes?
4. ¿_____ país eres?
5. ¿_____ eres (físicamente)?

1–24 ¿Quién eres? Work in groups of three or four. Follow these steps:

1. Create your own identity card. Include name, two last names, place of birth, a short physical description, and the name of the institution that issues the card.
2. Give your identity card to the person to your right.
3. Prepare a list of questions to ask about the identity card you just received from the person to your left. Use interrogative words and yes-and-no questions.
4. When done, pass your classmate's identity card to the person to your right.
5. Take turns asking the questions you wrote about the person to your left, to the person to your right who is now holding your classmate's identity card.

A propósito... Spanish Names and Nicknames

People with Hispanic backgrounds have both paternal and maternal surnames. A person named **María Fernández Ulloa** takes her first surname, **Fernández,** from her father, and the second, **Ulloa,** from her mother. In some Hispanic countries, women still keep their father's surname when they marry (giving up their mother's surname) and may attach their husband's paternal surname using the preposition **de.** Thus, if **María Fernández Ulloa** married **Carlos Alvarado Gómez,** her new name would be **María Fernández de Alvarado.** It would also be common for people to refer to her as **la señora de Alvarado** *(Mrs. Alvarado)* and to the couple as **los Alvarado.** The use of nicknames in place of first names is as common as it is in the United States.

MALE		FEMALE	
Alejandro	Alex, Alejo	Ana	Anita
Antonio	Tony, Toño	Carmen	Menchu
Enrique	Quique	Concepción	Concha
Francisco	Paco, Pancho	Dolores	Lola
Guillermo	Memo, Guille	Graciela	Chela
José	Pepe, Chepe	Guadalupe	Lupe
Ignacio	Nacho	Isabel	Chabela
Luis	Lucho	María Isabel	Maribel
Manuel	Manolo	María Luisa	Marilú
Rafael	Rafa	Mercedes	Mencha, Meche
Ramón	Moncho	Rosario	Charo, Chayo
Roberto	Beto	Teresa	Tere

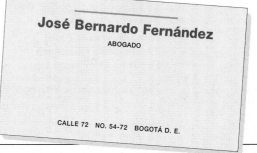

¡Así es la vida!

¿Qué haces?

Andrea Alvarado Salinas,
28 años, Santiago de Chile

Hablo español e italiano,
y estudio medicina en la
Universidad de Chile. Hoy
tengo que estudiar mucho
porque mañana tengo un
examen de biología.

Marco Aurelio Mora Arce,
22 años, San José, Costa Rica

Hablo español y un poco de inglés. Estudio
historia en la Universidad Nacional y por las
tardes trabajo en una librería. Hoy tengo
que practicar el fútbol con mis amigos.

Rosalía Bermúdez Fiallo,
19 años, Santo Domingo,
República Dominicana.

Estudio ingeniería. Esta noche
mis amigos y yo vamos a bailar
a una discoteca. No tenemos
clases mañana.

Vocabulario y expresiones

Actividades

bailar	to dance
caminar	to walk
conversar	to converse, to chat
escuchar	to listen
enseñar	to teach
estudiar	to study
hablar	to talk
hacer	to make, to do
mirar	to look, to watch
nadar	to swim
practicar	to practice
preparar	to prepare
regresar	to return
trabajar	to work

Áreas de estudio

administración de empresas	business administration
arte	art
biología	biology
derecho	law
filosofía y letras	humanities/liberal arts
geografía	geography
historia	history
ingeniería	engineering
medicina	medicine

Idiomas

el alemán	German
el español	Spanish
el francés	French
el inglés	English
el italiano	Italian
el portugués	Portuguese

Algunos deportes

el béisbol	baseball
el fútbol	soccer
la natación	swimming
el tenis	tennis

Otras palabras y expresiones

compañera de cuarto	roommate
discoteca	discotheque
esta noche	tonight
el examen	exam
la galería	gallery
la librería	bookstore
mañana	tomorrow
mucho	a lot, plenty, much
por las tardes	in the afternoon
sobre	about
sólo	only
vamos a + inf.	we are going to

Expressions with tener (to have)

tener calor	to be hot
tener cuidado	to be careful
tener frío	to be cold
tener hambre	to be hungry
tener miedo	to be afraid
tener prisa	to be in a hurry
tener razón	to be right (correct)
tener sed	to be thirsty
tener sueño	to be sleepy
tener _____ años	to be _____ years old
tener que + inf.	to have to (do something)

◆◆◆◆◆◆◆◆◆◆◆◆◆◆◆◆◆◆◆◆◆◆◆◆◆◆◆◆◆◆

¡Así lo decimos!

mucho

To express *a lot of*, most Spanish-speaking countries use **mucho, un montón de, una pila de**, or **cualquier cantidad de**. Regional variations of these expressions are very common; some are listed below.

Argentina	**un toco de**
Colombia	**un resto de, un tarrado de**
Cuba	**una barbaridad de**
España	**un mogollón de, la tira de, la (re)leche de**
México	**un resto de**
Perú	**horrores (de), harto(a) (ej. hubo harta gente)**
Venezuela	**una burda de, un bojote de**

Hoy hice **un mogollón de** trabajo.   *I did **a lot of** work today.*

conversar

In most countries **conversar, charlar**, or **hablar** is used to refer to the act of conversing. There is one very notable variant.

México   **platicar**

Me gusta **platicar** por teléfono con mis cuates.
*I like to **talk** on the telephone with my best friends.*

🔊 ¡A escuchar!

¿Qué haces? You will hear the descriptions that appear in **¡Así es la vida!** (p. 44). Indicate whether the statements that follow each description are **Cierto** or **Falso**.

	Cierto	Falso			Cierto	Falso			Cierto	Falso
1.	_____	_____		4.	_____	_____		7.	_____	_____
2.	_____	_____		5.	_____	_____		8.	_____	_____
3.	_____	_____		6.	_____	_____		9.	_____	_____

◆ Práctica

1–25 ¡Fuera de lugar! Circle the letter corresponding to the word that is out of place.

1. a. biología   b. francés   c. italiano   d. alemán
2. a. tenis   b. sociología   c. natación   d. fútbol
3. a. ingeniería   b. derecho   c. mañana   d. historia
4. a. trabajar   b. practicar   c. estudiar   d. mucho
5. a. portugués   b. examen   c. español   d. italiano
6. a. arte   b. derecho   c. geografía   d. béisbol

1–26 ¿Qué hacen? Match the activities depicted in the illustrations with the following statements.

1. Ellos estudian para el examen.
2. Yo hablo francés.
3. Pablo trabaja en una librería.
4. Nosotros practicamos el fútbol.
5. Jorge y Teresa conversan.
6. Ana mira la televisión.

a.   b.   c.

d.   e.   f.

1–27 Confesiones. Complete the following description using words and expressions from **¡Así es la vida!** and **Vocabulario y expresiones.**

¡Hola! Me _____ María Cecilia Facio. _____ de San Pedro de Sula, Honduras. Tengo (I have) 18 _____ .

_____ francés y un poco de italiano. _____ en la universidad por la mañana, por la tarde _____ en una oficina y por la noche generalmente _____ música. También tengo clases de _____ y _____ . Hoy tengo _____ estudiar porque mañana tengo un _____ de biología. Por la noche mis amigas y yo _____ a practicar la _____ . Después de (after) bailar, vamos a _____ a la residencia. No vamos en carro.

Vamos a _____ .

◆ Actividades

1–28 Entrevistas. Walk around and greet as many classmates as you can. Ask them for their name, what they are studying, what languages they speak, whether they practice a sport and if so, which. Write the answers on a piece of paper. Following is a list of additional subjects you and your classmates may be studying. Then, in groups of three or four, share what you learned about your fellow classmates.

—¿Cómo te llamas?   —Me llamo Pompilio Robles.

—¿Qué estudias?   —Estudio higiene dental.

—¿Qué idiomas hablas?   —Sólo hablo español, pero estudio inglés.

—¿Practicas deportes?   —Sí, practico el fútbol.

agronomía	matemáticas
ciencias políticas	servicios sociales
informática *(computer science)*	*(social service)*
química *(chemistry)*	ciencias atmosféricas
arquitectura	enfermería *(nursing)*
ecología	música

Pronunciación

Spanish Intonation in Questions

Intonation refers to the rise and fall of the voice pitch in normal speech in accordance with the type of message that is being conveyed. In questions with interrogative words, the pitch level at the beginning is high and gradually falls toward the end of the question.

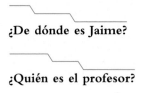

¿De dónde es Jaime?

¿Quién es el profesor?

With yes/no questions, the tone of voice rises to an above-normal pitch at the end of the questions.

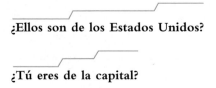

¿Ellos son de los Estados Unidos?

¿Tú eres de la capital?

Estructuras

5. The Present Tense of *-ar* Verbs in the Indicative

hablar *(to speak, to talk)*							
SINGULAR FORMS				PLURAL FORMS			
	STEM	ENDING	VERB FORM		STEM	ENDING	VERB FORM
yo	habl	+ **o**	→**hablo**	nosotros(as)	habl	+ **amos**	→**hablamos**
tú	habl	+ **as**	→**hablas**	vosotros(as)	habl	+ **áis**	→**habláis**
Ud. ⎫ él ⎬ ella ⎭	habl	+ **a**	→**habla**	Uds. ⎫ ellos ⎬ ellas ⎭	habl	+ **an**	→**hablan**

- In Spanish there are three verb groups: **-ar, -er,** and **-ir,** depending on the ending of the infinitive (which is the verb form listed in the dictionary). The chart above shows how to form the present tense of verbs ending in **-ar.**

- The Spanish present tense has several equivalents in English.

Yo estudio ingeniería. $\begin{cases} \textit{I study engineering.} \\ \textit{I am studying engineering.} \\ \textit{I do study engineering.} \end{cases}$

▼▼▼▼▼▼▼▼▼▼▼▼▼▼▼▼▼▼▼▼▼▼▼▼▼▼▼▼▼▼▼▼▼▼▼

STUDY TIP

Practice conjugating each **-ar** verb in the vocabulary list in writing first. Next, create two sets of index cards, one for subject pronouns, another for verbs in the infinitive form. Select one card from each set and conjugate the verb with the selected pronoun. Then, practice saying the complete conjugation for each verb in the list out loud. Try to internalize the forms so they become "second nature" and you don't have to think as much.

◆ Práctica

1–29 ¿Quién es? Who is the person carrying out the actions listed below? Give the appropriate subject pronoun.

1. trabajamos
2. miro
3. preparas
4. escuchan
5. practica
6. hablas
7. conversamos
8. nado
9. regresan
10. baila
11. camino
12. estudiamos

1–30 ¿Quienes son? Complete the following descriptions with the correct forms of the verbs below. Some may be used more than once.

bailar   estudiar   mirar
practicar   ser   trabajar

1. Montserrat Pons

Montserrat Pons _____ de Barcelona. _____ española. Montserrat _____ derecho en la Universidad de Nebraska. De noche _____ en una librería. Después de trabajar, ella y sus amigas _____ en una discoteca.

2. Pedro López, Raúl Andrade y yo

Pedro, Raúl y yo _____ colombianos y _____ filosofía y letras en la Universidad de Clemson. Hoy, vamos a _____ para el examen de español. Después de estudiar, Pedro _____ la televisión, Raúl _____ por teléfono con María, y yo _____ en la cafetería.

1–31 Son muy activos. Write at least ten complete, logical sentences by combining one word or expression from each column.

Yo	bailar	por teléfono
Alicia y María	caminar	música rap
Tú	conversar	el tenis
Rosamaría	escuchar	a la casa
Juliano y yo	estudiar	en la discoteca
Ellos	hablar	en la librería
Nosotros	mirar	por *(by)* la universidad
Ustedes	nadar	la lección
Mariano	practicar	en la biblioteca *(library)*
	preparar	con Roberto y su mamá
	regresar	en el océano
	trabajar	la televisión
		con el/la profesor(a)

1–32 ¿Qué hacen ahora? Match the names of the person or persons in each drawing with the activities listed below. Follow the model.

MODELO: Eugenia practica el tenis.

1. escuchar la música
2. mirar la televisión
3. conversar en el café
4. trabajar en el laboratorio
5. caminar por las tardes

6. hablar por teléfono
7. estudiar en la biblioteca
8. nadar en la piscina
9. bailar en la fiesta
10. preparar una pizza

a.

b.

c.

d.

e.

f.

g.

h.

i.

j.

◆ Actividades

1–33 Más preguntas. Copy the list below on a separate piece of paper. Walk around and ask as many members of your group as possible questions based on the items on the list. Write the names of those who answer affirmatively next to the corresponding item.

MODELO: —¿Practicas el piano?   —Sí, practico el piano. (No, no practico el piano)
           —¿Cómo te llamas?   —Me llamo….

(a la clase) —_____ practica el piano.

1. practicar el fútbol
2. caminar por la noche
3. regresar a casa *(home)* tarde *(late)*
4. nadar en la piscina
5. preparar la comida *(food)*

6. hablar otro idioma (¿cuál?)
7. trabajar mucho
8. estudiar biología
9. escuchar música "country"

1–34 Las actividades. Combine elements from each column below to form meaningful sentences to say to your partner. Your partner will react to your statements by saying **Te creo** *(I believe you)* or **No te creo** *(I don't believe you)*.

MODELO: —Trabajo en un bar.
           —(No) te creo.

(yo)	trabajar	en un bar	esta noche
(tú)	bailar	en la clase	todos los días
Los profesores	nadar	francés	20 horas a la semana
Los amigos	hablar	japonés	
(Tú y yo)	preparar	comida mexicana	por la mañana
Mi mamá	escuchar	comida española	mañana por la tarde
Mi papá	conversar	en la universidad	
Mi compañero/a	estudiar	en casa	
de cuarto	la tarea	con los amigos	
		música clásica	
		la lambada	
		por teléfono	

6. The Present Tense of *tener* (to have)

tener *(to have)*	
SINGULAR FORMS	PLURAL FORMS
yo **tengo**	nosotros(as) **tenemos**
tú **tienes**	vosotros(as) **tenéis**
usted ⎫ él ⎬ **tiene** ella ⎭	ustedes ⎫ ellos ⎬ **tienen** ellas ⎭

- The verb **tener** is irregular in Spanish. In addition to expressing possession, it is used in many day-to-day expressions. In English these are frequently expressed with the verb *to be*.

Ellos **tienen** muchos amigos.	*They **have** many friends.*
Yo **tengo** hambre.	*I **am** hungry.*
Adela **tiene** frío.	*Adela **is** cold.*
Los niños **tienen** sueño.	*The children **are** sleepy.*

- **Tener** is also used in Spanish to express age.

¿Cuántos años **tiene**?	*How old are you?*
Yo **tengo** veintidós años.	*I'm twenty-two years old.*

- The verb **tener** may be used with **que** and an infinitive to express the idea of obligation. In English, **tener que** + *infinitive* is the equivalent of *to have to*.

Yo **tengo que** estudiar para el examen.	*I **have to** study for the exam.*
Tenemos que practicar hoy.	*We **have to** practice today.*

◆ Práctica

1–35 ¿Qué tienen? Describe how the following people feel.

1. Yo… .

2. Alicia y Juanita… .

3. José Luis… .

4. Tú… .

5. Rosa y yo… .

6. Los chicos… .

1–36 ¿Qué tienen? Complete the exchange between two friends using the correct form of **tener.**

—Roberto, hoy es tu cumpleaños, ¿verdad? ¿Cuántos años _____?

—_____ veintidós.

—¿_____ que trabajar esta noche?

—No, pero _____ que estudiar un poco. Mañana _____ examen de física.

—Bueno, Marta y yo _____ hambre. Vamos al café.

—¿No _____ (tú) que practicar el béisbol?

—No. Hoy _____ (nosotros) partido a las seis. Los jugadores (*players*)

_____ que ir más tarde al estadio.

1–37 ¿Qué tienes que hacer? Now write sentences saying what you *have to do* tomorrow, following the model. Some possible answers are depicted below.

MODELO: —¿Qué tienes que hacer mañana?
           —Mañana tengo que practicar el fútbol y tengo que hablar con
             el profesor. ¿Y tú?
           —Yo tengo que hablar por teléfono con mi novio(a) *(boy/girlfriend).*

1. 2. 3.

4. 5.

◆ Actividades

1–38 ¿Qué tiene la universidad? With your partner, decide whether or not your university has…

- un bar estudiantil
- un salón de baile *(ballroom)*
- un estadio o un gimnasio
- muchas residencias
- edificios *(buildings)* grandes
- buenas clases
- confrontaciones políticas

- una buena cafetería
- el sistema de semestres
- el sistema de cuatrimestres *(quarters)*
- un excelente equipo *(team)* de fútbol americano
- una persona famosa

1–39 ¿Quién tiene qué? Copy the list below on a separate piece of paper. Then, use the expressions with **tener** to ask as many classmates as you can questions based on the list. Write the name of each person that says yes to your questions next to the corresponding item.

MODELO: 21 años   —¿Tienes veintiún años?   —Sí, tengo veintiún años.
           (you write)   _____ tiene veintiún años.

1. 21 años
2. calor en la clase
3. hambre en la clase
4. frío en casa *(at home)*
5. sed en la fiesta
6. menos de *(less than)* 20 años
7. siempre *(always)* razón
8. sueño por la mañana
9. miedo en una película *(movie)* de horror
10. más de 25 años
11. prisa en un examen
12. que practicar un instrumento musical

Colaboración

Estudiante A

1-40A ¿De dónde es? Tell your partner in which city the famous people in the first column live. (2) Ask your partner what country they are from. (3) Using the place names in the second column, tell your partner what country the people on his/her list are from. (4) Match your names and your partner's with the professions in the third column. You have some of the professions, your partner the remaining ones.

MODELO: Diana (Londres)
          —La princesa Diana vive in Londres. ¿De dónde es?
          —Es de Inglaterra. Es princesa.

Fidel Castro (La Habana)	los Estados Unidos	una autora chicana
Alberto Fujimori (Lima)	Rusia	el presidente de México
Gabriel García Márquez (Bogotá)	Paraguay	el presidente de Argentina
	Argentina	el presidente de Rusia
Gloria Estefan (Miami)	México	la presidenta de Argentina

1-41A ¿Quién es? ¿Qué es? Read the following descriptions to your partner, who will try to match them with a person, place, or thing. The last description should be original and precise enough for your partner to guess.

1. Es muy larga.
2. Es difícil.
3. Es conservador.
4. Es muy buena.
5. Es muy bonito.
6. Son muy inteligentes.
7. Son muy guapos.
8. (original)

Now listen to your partner's descriptions and match them logically to the following names.

Robin Williams	Michael Jordan
Michelle Pfeiffer	Nueva York
San Nicolás	los profesores
Bill Clinton	....(*original*)

1-42A ¡Se perdió mi...! *(I lost my...)* Your companion has wandered away from you at the mall. Describe him or her to the security guard.

Se perdió mi... [compañero(a)]	gordo(a) / delgado(a)
Se llama (nombre, apellido paterno, apellido materno)	malo(a) / bueno(a)
	joven / viejo(a)
Tiene... años.	bonito(a) / feo(a)
Es...	...
alto(a) / bajo(a)	

Estudiante B

1-40B ¿De dónde es? Your partner will tell you in which city some famous people live. When asked, tell him or her what country they are from using the place names in the second column. Then, tell your partner in which city the famous people in the first column live. Ask what country they are from. Finally, match your names and your partner's with the professions in the third column. You have some of the professions, your partner the remaining ones.

MODELO: El Rey Juan Carlos (Madrid)
                      —El Rey Juan Carlos vive in Madrid. ¿De dónde es?
                      —Es de España. Es rey.

Carlos Menem (Buenos Aires)	Puerto Rico	el presidente de Perú
	Perú	el presidente de Japón
Sandra Cisneros (Chicago)	los Estados Unidos	el presidente de Cuba
Boris Yeltsin (Moscú)	Cuba	un autor (Premio Nobel)
Ernesto Zedillo (Ciudad de México)	Colombia	una cantante famosa

1-41B ¿Quién es? ¿Qué es? Listen to your partner's descriptions and match them logically to the following names.

Cancún	una novela de Jame Michener
La Madre Teresa	Ronald Reagan
Los estudiantes de esta clase	Tom Cruise y Kevin Costner
La clase de español	…(original)

Now read the following descriptions to your partner, who will try to match them with a list of persons, places, and things. The last person and description should be original and precise enough for your partner to guess.

1. Es liberal.
2. Es muy bonita.
3. Es atleta.
4. Es muy gordo y generoso.

5. Son excelentes.
6. Es muy activa.
7. Es muy cómico.
8. …(Original)

1-42B Se perdió mi… ! *(I lost my…)* You are a security guard at a mall. A shopper has lost his/her companion. Listen to the description and fill in the missing person report.

PERSONA PERDIDA

Nombre…   Apellidos…
Relación…   Edad…
Rasgos físicos…

 # Mundo hispánico

¡362 milliones hablan español!

El mundo hispánico es enorme: 20 países independientes, situados en 4 continentes. Además de España y México, hay 6 países hispanos en la América Central y 9 países en la América del Sur. En el Mar Caribe hay 2 países hispanos y Puerto Rico, un Estado Libre Asociado. En los Estados Unidos más de 25 millones de personas hablan español. El español es una de las lenguas más habladas en el mundo.

El español, una lengua universal

1. chino	1.300.000.000
2. panjabi	600.000.000
3. inglés	456.000.000
4. indostani	383.000.000
5. español	362.000.000
6. ruso	293.000.000
7. árabe	208.000.000
8. bengalí	189.000.000

Source: The World Almanac, 1993

Ciudades principales (habitantes)

1. México, D.F. (México)—27.000.000
2. Buenos Aires (Argentina)—11.625.000
3. Bogotá (Colombia)—5.788.849
4. Santiago (Chile)—4.364.497
5. Lima (Perú)—4.164.597
6. Madrid (España)—3.188.297
7. Caracas (Venezuela)—2.386.367
8. La Habana (Cuba)—1.952.373
9. Ciudad de Guatemala (Guatemala)—
   1.629.189
10. Santo Domingo (República Dominicana)—
    1.313.172

Países de mayor población

1. México—85.950.000
2. España—43.522.000
3. Argentina—36.321.000
4. Colombia—33.800.000
5. Perú—23.450.000
6. Venezuela—19.800.000
7. Chile—12.820.000
8. Cuba—11.950.000
9. Ecuador—10.230.000
10. Guatemala—9.073.000

◆ Actividades

1-43 ¿La América Central o la América del Sur?

1. El Salvador
2. Bolivia
3. Honduras
4. Uruguay
5. Panamá
6. Paraguay
7. Argentina
8. Venezuela
9. Chile
10. Perú

1-44 ¿Capital de qué país?

1. Buenos Aires
2. Santo Domingo
3. San José
4. Bogotá
5. Quito
6. Caracas
7. Montevideo
8. San Salvador
9. La Habana
10. Lima

Países de mayor extensión (km2)

1. Argentina—2.779.221
2. México—1.958.201
3. Perú—1.285.215
4. Colombia—1.141.748
5. Bolivia—1.098.581
6. Venezuela—916.445
7. Chile—736.902
8. España—504.750
9. Paraguay—406.752
10. Ecuador—275.800

1-45 ¿Qué lengua(s) asocia Ud. con...?

1. Pekín
2. Nueva York
3. Moscú
4. Toronto
5. Bombay

Lección 2

¿Qué estudias?

Comunicación

- Exchanging Information about Classes
- Asking for and Telling Time
- Expressing Possession and Location
- Expressing Feelings, Likes, and Dislikes
- Extending Simple Invitations
- Asking for and Giving Simple Directions

Cultura

- Universities in Spanish-speaking Countries

Mundo hispánico: Los Estados Unidos hispánicos.

Estructuras

Primera parte

- Telling Time
- Possessive Adjectives
- Possession with **de**

Segunda parte

- The Verbs **estar** (*to be*) and **ir** (*to go*)
- Expressing Future Actions: **ir a** + infinitive
- The Present Tense of **-er** and **-ir** Verbs
- Expressing *to like*: **gustar**

PRIMERA PARTE
¡Así es la vida!

¿Qué materias vas a tomar?

ALBERTO: ¡Oye, Luis! ¿Tienes tu horario de clases?

LUIS: Sí, ¿y tú? ¿Qué materias vas a tomar?

ALBERTO: Mi horario es bastante complicado. Voy a tomar cinco materias: álgebra, química, historia, inglés e informática.

LUIS: ¡Estás loco! Yo solamente voy a tomar cuatro materias este semestre…

ALBERTO: ¿Vas a tomar la clase de inglés con el profesor Smith?

LUIS: ¡No, chico! Es un profesor muy exigente.

En la Universidad de Barcelona.

¿Dónde se encuentra esta universidad?

¿Qué hora es?

MELISA: Carmen, ¿qué hora es?

CARMEN: Son las nueve en punto.

MELISA: ¿De veras? ¿Ya son las nueve?

CARMEN: Sí, mira el reloj.

MELISA: Me voy ahora mismo. ¡Mi clase de biología es en cinco minutos! Tú no tienes clase ahora?

CARMEN: Los martes no tengo clases por la mañana.

¿Adónde vas?

ANA: ¡Hola, Roberto! ¿Qué tal?

ROBERTO: ¡Muy bien, Ana! ¿Y tú? ¿Adónde vas?

ANA: Voy al departamento de idiomas. Tengo clase de francés a las diez y cuarto.

ROBERTO: Pero, ¿vas a tomar idiomas?

ANA: Pues sí, Roberto. Ahora es muy necesario aprender idiomas.

61

Vocabulario y expresiones

Algunas materias

el álgebra	*algebra*
la arquitectura	*architecture*
la biología	*biology*
las ciencias políticas	*political science*
las ciencias sociales	*social sciences*
la economía	*economics*
la historia	*history*
las humanidades	*humanities*
el idioma	*language*
la informática	*computer science*
la literatura	*literature*
las matemáticas	*math*
la música	*music*
la psicología	*psychology*
la química	*chemistry*
la sociología	*sociology*

Adjetivos

aburrido(a)	*boring*
complicado(a)	*complicated*
difícil	*difficult*
exigente	*challenging, demanding*
fácil	*easy*
interesante	*interesting*

Adverbios

bastante	*rather*
solamente	*only*
tarde	*late*
ya	*already*

Expresiones de tiempo

el día	*day*
la estación	*season*
el mes	*month*
la semana	*week*
por la mañana	*in the morning*
por la noche	*in the evening*
por la tarde	*in the afternoon*
de la mañana	*in the morning (**a.m.**)*
de la noche	*at night (**p.m.**)*
de la tarde	*in the afternoon (**p.m.**)*

La universidad

la biblioteca	*library*
la cafetería	*cafeteria*
la calculadora	*calculator*
el centro estudiantil	*student center*
el curso	*course, class*
el diccionario	*dictionary*
la especialización	*major*
el gimnasio	*gynmasium*
el horario de clases	*class schedule*
la librería	*bookstore*
la materia	*academic subject*
el microscopio	*microscope*
la residencia estudiantil	*dorm*
el semestre	*semester*

Otras palabras y expresiones

¿Adónde vas?	*Where are you going?*
ahora mismo	*right now*
chico(a)	*boy, girl, young person (colloquial)*
deportes	*sports*
llegar	*to arrive*
Me voy	*I am leaving…*
tomar	*to take; to drink*
Vas a…	*You're going…*
Voy a…	*I'm going…*

◆◆◆◆◆◆◆◆◆◆◆◆◆◆◆◆◆◆◆◆◆◆◆◆

¡Así lo decimos!

Do you *study hard* or *cram?*

The most common expression for *to study hard* is **matarse estudiando** (literally, to kill oneself studying). Spanish-speaking students express this in many different ways.

Argentina	**tragar libros**
Chile	**calentar el examen**
Cuba	**embotellarse**
España	**empollar**
México	**echar el rollo**
	machetear
	hacerle al buey
Perú	**chancar (una lección)**
Puerto Rico	**estofarse**
Venezuela	**meterse un puñal**
	apuñalearse

Anoche me metí un puñal.   *I studied really hard last night.*

¡A escuchar!

El horario de clases. You will hear the three conversations that appear in **¡Así es la vida!** Listen to the questions that follow and choose the correct answer.

1. ____ Todas mis clases son por la mañana.
   ____ Sí, es complicado, pero las clases son muy buenas.
2. ____ Exigente sí es, pero también es muy inteligente.
   ____ No, no es simpático.
3. ____ No, tengo clase de matemáticas.
   ____ Sí, tengo clase de biología.
4. ____ A los 9:05.
   ____ A las 3:30.
5. ____ Voy a tomar un idioma, francés.
   ____ Sí, tengo clases por la mañana.

Ampliación

A. Las estaciones del año

el verano	*summer*
el otoño	*fall*
el invierno	*winter*
la primavera	*spring*

The definite article is used with the seasons, and they also are not capitalized unless they begin a sentence.

¿Cómo es **la primavera** aquí?   *What is the **spring** like here?*

B. Los días de la semana

- The days of the week in Spanish are not capitalized and are all masculine.

- Calendars begin the week with Monday, not Sunday.

- The definite article is not used after **ser.**

    Hoy es jueves.   *Today is Thursday.*

- The definite article **los** is used with the plural: **los lunes, los martes,** etc. **Sábado** and **domingo** add **s** to form the plural: **los sábados.** In their plural forms, the days of the week express the idea of doing something regularly.

- *On Monday . . . on Tuesday...* etc., is expressed by using the definite article + the singular:

    El lunes tengo álgebra.   ***On Monday** I have algebra.*
    Los lunes estudio español.   *I study Spanish **on Mondays.***
    La clase de biología es **los martes** y **los jueves.**   *Biology is on **Tuesdays** and **Thursdays.***

C. Los meses del año

enero	*January*
febrero	*February*
marzo	*March*
abril	*April*
mayo	*May*
junio	*June*
julio	*July*
agosto	*August*
septiembre	*September*
octubre	*October*
noviembre	*November*
diciembre	*December*

- Months are also not capitalized in Spanish unless they begin a sentence.

D. La fecha

¿Cuál es la fecha de hoy?	*What's today's date?*
Hoy es el veintiuno de marzo.	*Today is March twenty-first.*
Es el ocho de septiembre.	*It's September eighth.*
El primero de abril es mi cumpleaños.	*My birthday is April first.*

- When asking for the date, some Spanish speakers also say:

¿A qué fecha estamos hoy?	*What's today's date?*
Hoy estamos a 15 de octubre.	*Today's the 15th of October.*

E. Los números 30–1.000.000

30	treinta
31	treinta y uno *(and so on)*
40	cuarenta
41	cuarenta y uno *(and so on)*
50	cincuenta
60	sesenta
70	setenta
80	ochenta
90	noventa
100	cien(to)
101	ciento uno
200	doscientos, –as
300	trescientos, –as
400	cuatrocientos, –as
500	quinientos, –as
600	seiscientos, –as
700	setecientos, –as
800	ochocientos, –as
900	novecientos, –as
1.000	mil
4.000	cuatro mil
100.000	cien mil
1.000.000	un millón (de)
3.000.000	tres millones (de)

- **Cien** is used when it precedes a noun or when counting.

   Aquí hay **cien** estudiantes.
   noventa y nueve, **cien,** ciento uno, etc.

- **Ciento** is used in compound numbers between 100 and 200.

   ciento diez, ciento treinta y cuatro, etc.

- When 200-900 modify a noun, they agree in gender with it.

   cuatrocient**os** libros   quinient**as** tizas   doscient**as** pesetas

- **Mil** is never used with **un** and is never used in the plural for counting.

   mil, dos mil, tres mil, etc.

- The plural of **mil** is **miles** and of **millón** is **millones.** When followed by a noun, they take the preposition **de.**

   Hay **miles de** personas interesantes.
   Son dos **millones de** dólares.

- In Spain and most of Latin America, thousands are marked by a period, and decimals by a comma.

U.S./Canada	Spain/Latin America
$1,000	$1.000
$2.50	$2,50
$10,450.35	$10.450,35

◆ Práctica

2-1 Las fechas. Give the date of the following celebrations.

1. Independence Day
2. Christmas
3. New Year's Eve
4. Valentine's Day
5. New Year's Day

6. Flag Day
7. St. Patrick's Day
8. Halloween
9. Martin Luther King Day
10. April Fool's Day

2-2 Admisiones. Answer the questions based on the advertisement below.

PONTIFICIA UNIVERSIDAD CATÓLICA MADRE Y MAESTRA

DEPARTAMENTO DE ADMISIONES

El Departamento de Admisiones de la Pontificia Universidad Católica Madre y Maestra, Recinto Santo Tomás de Aquino, les informa las fechas de Examen de Admisión y las fechas límites para depositar los documentos o requisitos de admisión (previos al examen).

FECHA EXAMEN DE ADMISION	FECHA LÍMITE PARA DEPOSITAR DOCUMENTOS
Sábado 17 de marzo, 1995	9 de marzo, 1995
Sábado 21 de abril, 1995	17 de abril, 1995
Sábado 23 de junio, 1995	15 de junio, 1995

Para mayor información debe dirigirse al Departamento de Admisiones de la Pontificia Universidad Católica Madre y Maestra y/o llamar al teléfono 555-7786, Ext. 70.

1. ¿Cómo se llama la universidad?
2. ¿Cuál es el teléfono del Departamento de Admisiones?
3. ¿Cuántos exámenes de admisión hay?
4. ¿Cuáles son las fechas del examen de admisión?
5. ¿Cuál es la fecha límite para depositar documentos para el examen de admisión del 17 de marzo?

2-3 Un calendario. Answer the following questions.

1. What's today's date?
2. When is your birthday?
3. When are your next exams scheduled?
4. When is the next holiday?
5. When is your spring vacation?

2–4 Las materias. Match the words in the left-hand column with the school subjects to the right.

1. Romeo y Julieta
2. Freud
3. George Washington
4. diccionario
5. microscopio
6. computadora
7. piano
8. más, menos, por y entre
9. gimnasio
10. mapa

a. matemáticas
b. geografía
c. biología
d. informática
e. música
f. literatura
g. deportes
h. historia
i. psicología
j. español

2–5 ¡A practicar! Say the numbers in Spanish.

1. 35 profesoras
2. 50 diccionarios
3. 200 mesas
4. 90 relojes
5. 500 estudiantes
6. 640 casas
7. 925 personas
8. 150 materias

9. 365 días
10. 3.004 pupitres
11. 575 borradores
12. 1000 mapas
13. 101 calculadoras
14. 3.296.000 chicos
15. 441 mochilas
16. 3234 computadoras

2–6 Completar. Complete the statements with the subject depicted in the illustrations.

1. Yo estudio…

2. Tú practicas…

3. Ana tiene clase de…

4. Clemencia
   estudia…

5. Teresita y Manolo
   estudian….

2-7 Los días de la semana. Look at the calendar and indicate on which day of the week the following dates fall.

MODELO: El 3 de abril es lunes.

17
21
30
4
27
8

L	M	M	J	V	S	D

ABRIL

					1	2
3	4	5	6	7	8	9
10	11	12	13	14	15	16
17	18	19	20	21	22	23
24	25	26	27	28	29	30

2-8 Los meses y las estaciones. Match the months with the corresponding season of the year in the Northern Hemisphere. Then do it with the seasons in the Southern Hemisphere.

otoño   invierno
verano   primavera

NORTHERN   SOUTHERN
HEMISPHERE   HEMISPHERE

_____	febrero	_____
_____	agosto	_____
_____	julio	_____
_____	diciembre	_____
_____	marzo	_____
_____	octubre	_____
_____	mayo	_____
_____	septiembre	_____
_____	enero	_____
_____	abril	_____
_____	noviembre	_____
_____	junio	_____

2-9 Horario de clases. Make your own *horario de clases* indicating your present class schedule. Then compare schedules with another student.

MODELO: —Tengo español los lunes. ¿Y tú?
             —Tengo francés y álgebra los lunes.
              ¿Qué clase tomas los martes?

2-10 Más horarios. Now describe the class schedules the following students are likely to have.

1. un estudiante inteligente y trabajador
2. un estudiante no muy trabajador
3. una estudiante de arte
4. una estudiante de matemáticas
5. un estudiante que va a estudiar (*going to study*) medicina

	LUNES	MARTES	MIÉRCOLES	JUEVES	VIERNES

◆ Actividades

2–11 ¡Firma aquí! Copy the following list on a separate piece of paper. Walk around and ask your classmates questions based on it (only one question per person). Write down the names of those who answer affirmatively next to the corresponding item. Be prepared to share your findings with the class.

MODELO: —¿Tu *(your)* estación favorita es el invierno?
—Sí, es el invierno.
—¿Cómo te llamas?
—Me llamo…

(You write) El invierno es la estación favorita de _____.

1. va a la biblioteca por las noches
2. su día favorito es el viernes
3. tiene un horario de clases fácil
4. toma un curso de química
5. tiene computadora
6. tiene clases los lunes, miércoles y viernes
7. toma 5 materias
8. va a ir al gimnasio el sábado
9. va a un laboratorio de ciencias
10. Su *(his/her)* estación favorita es el verano

2–12 ¿Cuánto cuesta…? Ask a classmate, who will play the role of the clerk at Budget, the following questions about prices for different vehicles.

MODELO: —¿Cuánto cuesta un Minibus por día?
—Cuesta diecisiete mil doscientas cincuenta pesetas por día.

1. ¿…un Renault 5 por siete días?
2. ¿…un Fiat Uno por día adicional?
3. ¿…un Minibus por siete días?
4. ¿…un Renault 21 por un día y por siete días?
5. ¿…en dólares americanos un Seat Ibiza por un día? (What was the exchange rate today?)

Budget rent a car

Tarifa econoplan

Madrid
Tarifas locales
Estébanez Calderón, 5 — Tel. (91) 571 66 60
Gran Vía, 49 — Tel. (91) 248 90 40
Aeropuerto (para reservas) — Tel. (91) 747 99 03

Tarifas locales
Todo incluido
Precios en pesetas

Grupo	Codigo CR	Modelos de coche	Por día 1-6 días	Por día 7 días	Día adicional
A	ECMN	Fiat Uno Renault 5	5.200	33.650	4.800
B	EXMN	Ford Fiesta 1.1	6.200	40.350	5.750
C	CCMN	Ford Escort 1.3 Seat Ibiza	6.900	44.850	6.400
D	ICMN	Ford Orion 1.4 Fiat Tipo	8.600	56.100	8.050
I	LXMR	Ford Sierra 2.0 Renault 21	13.800	89.700	12.800
M	MVMN	Minibus	17.250	112.125	16.050

Estos precios incluyen: Kilometraje ilimitado, eguro a todo riesgo, Seguro de ocupantes e IVA.
No incluyen: Gasolina.
Alquile un coche a **PRECIO FIJO,** sin sorpresas de última hora.

Pronunciación

Sounds of Spanish *b*, *v*, and *p*

In Spanish the letters **b** and **v** are pronounced in exactly the same manner. They have two possible pronunciations.

- At the beginning of a breath group or after the letters **m** or **n,** the **b** and **v** are pronounced like the *b* in the English word *boy*.

  buen   **vaso**   **bastante**   **vino**

- In any other position, the **b** and **v** are pronounced with the lips slightly open.

  una biblioteca   **ellos van**   **nosotros vivimos**

The **p** is pronounced like the English *p*, but without the strong puff of air.

  papá   **papel**   **poco**

 # Estructuras

1. Telling time

- The verb **ser** is used to express the time of day in Spanish. Use **es + la** with **una** *(one o'clock)*. With all other times, use **son + las.**

Es la una.	*It's one o'clock.*
Son las tres.	*It's three o'clock.*

- In Spanish use **y** to signify *past* or *after*; **menos** for *to* or *till*; **el mediodía** for *noontime* and **la medianoche** for *midnight*; use **cuarto** for *quarter* and **media** for *half*. You can also use numbers in place of the expressions **cuarto (quince)** y **media (treinta).**

Son las cuatro **y** cinco.	*It's five past four.*
Son las cinco **menos** diez.	*It's ten minutes to five.*
Es **el mediodía.**	*It's noon.*
Es la una y **cuarto.**	*It's a quarter after one.*

- To ask what time it is, **¿Qué hora es?** is used. To ask *at* what time an event takes place, **¿A qué hora es...?** is used. To answer, use **a + la** or **las** + *time*.

¿A qué hora es la clase de química?	*At what time is the chemistry class?*
Es **a las** cuatro y media.	*It's at four thirty.*

- The expressions **de la mañana, de la tarde,** or **de la noche** are used when telling specific time. **En punto** is used as the equivalent of *on the dot* and *sharp*.

La clase es a las nueve **en punto.**	*Class is at nine sharp.*
La reunion es a las ocho menos cuarto **de la noche.**	*The meeting is at a quarter to eight in the evening.*

◆ **Práctica**

2-13 ¿Qué hora es... ?

1. _____ 2. _____ 3. _____ 4. _____

5. _____ 6. _____ 7. _____ 8. _____

2-14 El horario de Gloria. Answer the questions by looking at Gloria's class schedule.

1. ¿Qué clases tiene Gloria por la mañana?
2. ¿A qué hora es la clase de informática?
3. ¿A qué hora es la clase de español?
4. ¿Qué clase tiene Gloria a las cinco menos cuarto?
5. ¿Qué clase tiene Gloria por la noche?
6. ¿A qué hora es la clase?
7. ¿Cómo es el horario de Gloria?
8. ¿A qué hora va a la cafetería?

inglés	9:00 a.m.
química	11:00 a.m.
informática	1:10 p.m.
español	3:30 p.m.
historia	4:45 p.m.
biología	7:15 p.m.

2-15 ¿A qué hora es? Write complete sentences saying at what time each of the events will be.

MODELO: la clase / 2:00 p.m.   La clase es a las dos.

1. el concierto de rock / 8:45 p.m.
2. el fútbol / 10:20 a.m.
3. la clase de literatura / 9:50 a.m.
4. la clase de matemáticas / 1:15 p.m.
5. la fiesta / 7:30 p.m.
6. el béisbol / 3:40 p.m.
7. el examen / 12 p.m.
8. la clase de ingeniería / 4:05 p.m.
9. la lección / 7:00 a.m.
10. la cena (dinner) / 7:35 p.m.

2–16 ¿A qué hora? Use the expressions **de la mañana, de la tarde, del mediodía,** and **de la noche** to describe when the following activities take place.

MODELO: Marina va a la escuela a las ocho
y media de la mañana.

1.

4.

2.

5.

3.

6.

◆ Actividades

2–17 ¿Qué hora es en...? In small groups, discuss what time it is in the cities that appear in the chart below. Follow the model.

MODELO: —Cuando son las cinco de la tarde en San Diego, ¿qué hora es en
Asunción?
—Son las nueve de la noche.

San Francisco	San Diego	17:00
Santa Fé	Boise	18:00
Houston	Tegucigalpa	19:00
Miami	San Juan	20:00
Buenos Aires	Asunción	21:00
Madrid	Bilbao	22:00

2–18 En el aeropuerto. You work at Arrivals Information at the Las Américas Airport in Santo Domingo. With another student assuming the role of a tourist, answer questions about flight arrival times. Use the information provided in the chart.

MODELO: —¿A qué hora llega el vuelo de Iberia de San José?
          —Llega a las siete y cinco de la mañana.

LLEGADA DE VUELOS				
AEROLÍNEA	VUELO NO.	PROCEDENCIA	HORA DE LLEGADA	PUERTA
Iberia	551	San José	7:05	15
Avianca	972	Bogotá	8:45	10
Lacsa	333	Madrid	9:15	4
American	76	Nueva York	13:30	16
Iberia	951	Londres	14:25	12
Dominicana	23	Miami	15:55	11
Air France	643	París	18:34	9
Varig	223	Río de Janeiro	21:38	10

2–19 ¿A qué hora? Working in small groups, find out the following information from your classmates and record it on a piece of paper. Then regroup with a different set of classmates and report some of your findings to the new group.

MODELO: *(you report)* La clase favorita de Mirta es a las ocho de la mañana.

¿A qué hora...

1. llegas a la universidad los lunes? ¿los martes?
2. es tu clase favorita?
3. es tu clase más exigente?
4. preparas tu clase de español?
5. estudias para las otras *(other)* clases?
6. regresas a tu casa?
7. hablas con tu mejor *(best)* amigo(a)?

2. Possessive Adjectives

Possessive Adjectives			
	SINGULAR	PLURAL	PRONOUN
yo	**mi**	**mis**	*my*
tú	**tu**	**tus**	*your* (familiar)
usted			*your* (formal)
él	**su**		*his*
ella			*her*
nosotros	**nuestro(a)**	**nuestros(as)**	*our*
vosotros	**vuestro(a)**	**vuestros(as)**	*your* (familiar)
ustedes			*your* (formal)
ellos		**sus**	*their*
ellas			

- Possessive adjectives agree in number with the nouns they modify, not with the possessor. **Nuestro(a)** and **vuestro(a)** are the only possessive adjectives that show both gender and number agreement.

- Spanish possessive adjectives are placed before the noun they modify and, unlike English, they never receive intonational stress.

Mis libros son azules.	*My books are blue.*
Tu profesora es muy simpática.	*Your professor is very nice.*
Nuestras amigas son chilenas.	*Our friends are Chilean.*

- Because the possessive adjectives **su** and **sus** can have different referents *(your, their, his, her)*, the context in which they are used can often help clarify who the possessor is.

María estudia **su** lección.	*María studies **her** lesson.*
Ramón y José hablan con **sus** amigos.	*Ramón and José speak with **their** friends.*

- When the context does not clearly indicate the identity of the possessor, the construction **de** + *noun* or **de** + *subject pronoun* is used for clarification.

Es **su** libro. Es el libro **de Paco**.	*It is **his** book. It is **Paco's** book.*
¿Son **sus** amigas?	*Are they **her** friends?*
Sí, son las amigas **de ella**.	*Yes, they are **her** friends.*

3. Possession with *de*

- In Spanish, the construction **de** + *noun* can also be used to indicate possession. It is equivalent to the English apostrophe.

El libro **de Raúl** es interesante.	***Raul's** book is interesting.*
La hermana **de Laura** estudia derecho.	***Laura's** sister studies law.*

- When the preposition **de** is followed by the definite article **el,** it contracts to **del: de + el → del**

Los libros **del** profesor son interesantes.	*The professor's books are interesting.*

◆ Práctica

2–20 En la cafetería. Fill in the blanks with the correct form of the possessive adjective.

A las 7:30 de la mañana yo tomo _____ primer café del día porque _____ clase de historia es a las 8:00. Chalo y Beto llegan a _____ clases a las 9:00 y 10:00 de la mañana, pero después *(after),* nosotros vamos a la cafetería de _____ universidad al mediodía. En la cafetería, hablamos con _____ amigos y con _____ amigas. Estudiamos _____ lecciones. Yo practico inglés con _____ amigos norteamericanos y _____ amigas Carol y Kim practican el español con _____ amigos mexicanos. Los mexicanos escuchan _____ música y nosotros escuchamos _____ música y la música de los mexicanos. Es muy bonito. ¿Vas tú a la cafetería de _____ universidad con _____ amigos?

2–21 ¿De quién es? Using the correct possessive adjective, answer each question affirmatively. Follow the model.

MODELO: —¿Es el libro de Marlene?   —Sí, es su libro.
        —¿Es mi amiga al teléfono?   —Sí, es tu amiga.

1. ¿Es el diccionario de Luis?
2. ¿Es la mochila de Alicia?
3. ¿Son mis bolígrafos?
4. ¿Es tu cuaderno?
5. ¿Son los mapas de Ángel?
6. ¿Son los lápices de nuestro profesor?
7. ¿Es tu calculadora?
8. ¿Son los bolígrafos de Uds.?
9. ¿Es tu ciudad en la foto?
10. Marta, ¿son nuestras tareas?
11. ¿Es la respuesta del Sr. Morales?
12. ¿Es la mesa de Anita y Chabela?

2–22 En la universidad. Describe or show possession of the following items. Follow the model.

MODELO: la clase/el señor Pineda   →   Es la clase del señor Pineda.

1. el examen/clase/ingeniería
2. la profesora/matemáticas
3. profesor/alemán
4. la pizarra/la clase/sociología
5. amiga/señora mexicana/Acapulco
6. cafetería/centro estudiantil
7. clase/geografía/el profesor Martínez
8. mapas/universidad

2–23 No, no es. Answer in the negative according to the cues. If the cue is in English, translate it. Follow the model.

MODELO: —¿Angelina es francesa? (italiana)   —No, es italiana.
        —¿Son los cuadernos de Jean? (de mí)   —No, son mis cuadernos.

1. El hijo *(son)* del Dr. Mena es alto y gordo, ¿no es cierto? (bajo y delgado)
2. Los pupitres de los estudiantes son pequeños, ¿no? (grandes)
3. ¿La calculadora de Ana y Patricia es buena? (mala)
4. ¿Tu estéreo es barato? (caro)
5. La nacionalidad de Roberto es chilena, ¿no? (uruguaya)
6. ¿Es grande mi laboratorio? (pequeño)
7. ¿Son los lápices de Moncho y Frank? (de nosotros)
8. ¿Son los exámenes de la profesora de álgebra? *(your exams, Mrs. Pérez)*
9. ¿Es el horario de clases de Daniel? *(my class schedule)*
10. ¿Es el mapa de África de María del Carmen? (mapa de China de Diana y Cristina)

2–24 ¿De qué color es? Take turns asking a classmate questions about the color of items in the classroom. Follow the model.

MODELO: tu libro

—¿De qué color es tu libro? —Mi libro es rojo.

1. tu cuaderno
2. nuestras sillas
3. tus lápices
4. la pizarra del (de la) profesor(a)
5. el escritorio del (de la) profesor(a
6. el reloj de _____

7. mi pupitre
8. el libro del (de la) profesora
9. nuestra mesa
10. mis bolígrafos
11. tu diccionario
12. nuestros borradores

2–25 Nuestra clase. In small groups, discuss your classes and professors at the university.

MODELO: ESTUDIANTE 1: ¿Cómo es tu clase de español?
ESTUDIANTE 2: Mi clase de español es muy buena.
ESTUDIANTE 1: ¿Y tu profesor?
ESTUDIANTE 3: Es profesora, ¡y es muy exigente!

A propósito...Universities in Spanish-speaking countries

The curriculum at universities in Spanish-speaking countries is structured differently than in the United States or Canada, where students generally choose a major during their first or second year of college. Students in Spain and Latin America must choose their field of study prior to enrolling in a university. Each specialization has a set of carefully prescribed courses to be taken each semester. Few, if any, elective courses are available outside the designated field of concentration.

Generally speaking, classes are conducted in a very formal and structured environment. Classes tend to be larger than in North America, ranging from 50 to 500 students per class. They almost always take the form of a lecture, with little time allowed for discussion. Final grades quite often depend on the results of one all-encompassing final exam. Classes generally tend to meet once or twice per week.

Most universities in Spanish-speaking countries do not have dormitories like those in North American colleges and universities. Students either live at home with their families or, if studying away from home, rent rooms in a boarding house known as a **residencia estudiantil,** a **casa de huéspedes,** or **a pensión.** These boarding homes are usually run by a family and students often must share a room without such amenities as a telephone, television, or private bathroom. Most **residencias** include meals served at set times.

In Spain and Latin America, sports are important, but never on a scale comparable with the United States and Canada. Fraternities and sororities are nonexistent. However, around the university there are usually numerous inexpensive cafes and restaurants that foster social gatherings. Also, festivities and cultural life bring students together, not to mention national and international politics. In general, students tend to be highly politicized.

¡Vamos a comparar!

Compare university systems, their advantages and disadvantages.

SEGUNDA PARTE
¡Así es la vida!

¿Dónde está la librería?

Son las once y media de la mañana. Eda y Dora conversan en un café cerca de la universidad mientras comen un sándwich y beben un refresco.

EDA: ¿Qué vas a hacer después del almuerzo?

DORA: Tengo que ir a la librería para comprar un diccionario inglés-español. Necesito escribir una composición para mañana.

EDA: ¿Y dónde está la librería? Yo también tengo que ir mañana.

DORA: Está detrás de la biblioteca. ¿Por qué no vamos juntas ahora?

EDA: No, gracias Dora. Ahora tengo que ir a la Clínica Universitaria.

DORA: Yo voy para la Facultad de Medicina que está al lado. Vamos juntas.

EDA: ¡Ah, qué bien! Vamos.

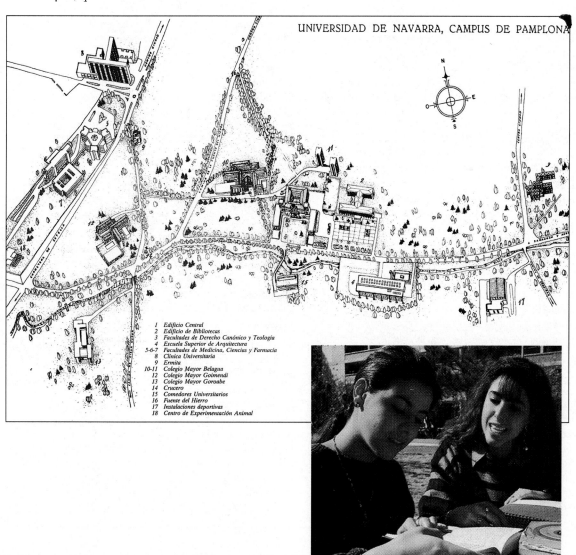

UNIVERSIDAD DE NAVARRA, CAMPUS DE PAMPLONA

1 Edificio Central
2 Edificio de Bibliotecas
3 Facultades de Derecho Canónico y Teología
4 Escuela Superior de Arquitectura
5-6-7 Facultades de Medicina, Ciencias y Farmacia
8 Clínica Universitaria
9 Ermita
10-11 Colegio Mayor Belagua
12 Colegio Mayor Goimendi
13 Colegio Mayor Goroabe
14 Crucero
15 Comedores Universitarios
16 Fuente del Hierro
17 Instalaciones deportivas
18 Centro de Experimentación Animal

Vocabulario y expresiones

Actividades

abrir	to open
añadir	to add
aprender	to learn
asistir a	to attend
beber	to drink
caer bien / mal	to like / dislike a person
comer	to eat
comprar	to buy
creer	to believe
deber	to ought to; to owe
decidir	to decide
doblar	to turn
encantar	to love (colloquial)
escribir	to write
estar	to be
faltar	lack, miss; to skip (a class)
gustar	to like, to be pleasing to
hacer	to do; to make
hay que	one has to
insistir en	to insist
interesar	to interest/to be interested in
leer	to read
molestar	to bother/to be bothered
quedar	to have left
recibir	to receive
vender	to sell
vivir	to live

Edificios universitarios

la facultad de...	the school of...
arte	art
ciencias	science
derecho	law
ingeniería	engineering
medicina	medicine
el laboratorio	laboratory
la rectoría	administration building

Comidas y bebidas

el café	coffee
la ensalada	salad
la hamburguesa	hamburger
el jugo	juice
la leche	milk
el refresco	refreshment, soda

Dar direcciones

a la derecha	to the right
a la izquierda	to the left
al lado (de)	next to
antes (de)	before
cerca (de)	near
debajo (de)	under
delante (de)	in front of
derecho	straight ahead
después (de)	after
detrás (de)	behind
encima (de)	on top of
enfrente (de)	in front, facing
en la esquina	on the corner
entre	between
lejos (de)	far
al este	to the east
al norte	to the north
al oeste	to the west
al sur	to the south
en el centro	downtown

Adjetivos

apurado(a)	in a hurry
cansado(a)	tired
casado(a)	married
contento(a)	happy
divorciado(a)	divorced
enfadado(a)	angry
enfermo(a)	sick
libre	free
ocupado(a)	busy
perdido(a)	lost
soltero(a)	single
triste	sad

Otras palabras

el almuerzo	lunch
la cena	dinner
la comida	meal; food
junto (a, os, as)	together
la lengua	language
mientras	while
el (la) novio(a)	boyfriend/girlfriend
la taquilla	ticket booth

¡Así lo decimos!

Dropping a class?

Many countries share the same terms for dropping a class from your schedule. These expressions tend to be used interchangeably, generally with one expression predominating. On the other hand, there are many variations in colloquial student speech to express to skip class.

to drop a class	**darse de baja**
	abandonar el curso/la clase
	dejar la clase

Voy a darme de baja de esta clase. Está muy difícil.
I'm going to drop this class. It's very hard.

Skipping a class?

Below are some alternatives to **faltar a clase.**

Chile	**capear**
Colombia	**echarse la leva**
España	**fumarse una clase, hacer novillos, hacer pira**
Guatemala	**capearse**
México	**irse de pinta**
Perú	**tirarse la pera, hacerse la vaca, borrarse**
Puerto Rico	**irse a comer jobo**
Uruguay	**hacer la rabona, hacer la rata**
Venezuela	**jubilarse**

(Nos) Capeamos la clase de matémáticas ayer.
We skipped math yesterday.

Vamos a tirarnos la pera hoy.
We'e going to skip class today.

📼 ¡A escuchar!

A. Eda y Dora. You will hear the conversation that appears in **¡Así es la vida!**. Indicate whether the statements that follow the conversation are **Cierto** or **Falso**.

	Cierto	Falso
1.	_____	_____
2.	_____	_____
3.	_____	_____
4.	_____	_____
5.	_____	_____
6.	_____	_____

B. ¿Dónde está? Look at the campus map on page 79. Listen to the statements and indicate whether they are **Cierto** or **Falso** based on the map.

	Cierto	Falso			Cierto	Falso
1.	_____	_____		4.	_____	_____
2.	_____	_____		5.	_____	_____
3.	_____	_____				

◆ Práctica

2–26 En la cola. It's the first basketball game of the season and students are waiting in line to buy tickets. Indicate where each student is in line by choosing the correct word in parentheses.

1. Pepe está _____ Marcela y Paula. (entre / al lado de)
2. Mercedes y Adrián están _____ la taquilla. (cerca de / lejos de)
3. Marcela está _____ la taquilla. (delante de / detrás de)
4. Adrián está _____ de Mercedes. (al lado de / delante de)
5. Marcela, Pepe y Paula están _____ Mercedes y Adrián. (delante de / detrás de)
6. Paula está _____ Pepe. (delante de / detrás de)

2–27 ¿Dónde están? Complete the sentences below with the appropriate school from the list. Use the illustrations as a cue.

Facultad de Arte   Facultad de Filosofía y Letras
Facultad de Ciencias   Facultad de Ingeniería
Facultad de Derecho   Facultad de Medicina

1. El profesor Robles hace un experimento en el laboratorio de la….
2. Andrina está en una clase en la….
3. Vicente está en el laboratirio de lenguas de la….
4. Juana y Germán están en la….
5. Alfredo y Jacobo son compañeros en la….
6. La licenciada Estrada trabaja en la corte y es profesora en la….

1.

4.

2.

5.

3.

6.

2–28 Emparejar. Use the phrases at the top of each group of four sentences to form logical thoughts.

---
si vas a la playa o no / en la biblioteca / jugo / en la residencia estudiantil
---

1. Marta lee…
2. Yo bebo…
3. Tú decides…
4. Los estudiantes viven…

---
en el cuaderno / a la izquierda del centro estudiantil /
la puerta del club / una lengua
---

5. La cafetería está…
6. Ana aprende…
7. Nosotros escribimos…
8. Hugo abre…

el diccionario viejo / en los extraterrestres /
al laboratorio de química / leche al café

9. Mario asiste…   11. Uds. creen…
10. Yo añado…   12. Ellas venden…

la lección 3 / ir a la Facultad de Medicina /
Lolita / en estudiar a las tres

13. Tú debes…   15. Ud. insiste…
14. Él hace…   16. Me cae bien…

◆ Actividades

2–29 En la Universidad de Navarra. With a classmate, look at the map of
the University of Navarra campus in **¡Así es la vida!,** and using the vocabulary in
Vocabulario y expresiones, take turns asking and answering questions about the
location of the different buildings. Locate as many buildings as you can.

MODELO: ESTUDIANTE A: ¿Dónde está la ermita?
          ESTUDIANTE B: Está enfrente de la Facultad de Medicina.

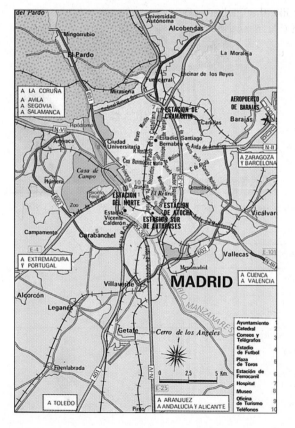

2–30 ¿Dónde está? In pairs, look at the map of Madrid and
find the following places.

MODELO: —¿Dónde está el Parque
            de El Retiro?
            —Está… (al sur/al norte/al
            este/al oeste/en el centro)
            de la ciudad.

1. La estación de Chamartín
2. La carretera a Segovia
3. El hipódromo
4. La estación de Atocha
5. Villaverde
6. La ciudad Universitaria
7. El aeropuerto de Barajas

2–31 ¿Dónde está...? Working in small groups, prepare a skit in which one of you plays a new student on campus and the remainder of you describe the location of the following places. Make your skit as natural as possible—for example, you may disagree with a fellow student and interrupt to correct information. Be prepared to present the skit before the rest of the class.

1. la librería
2. la cafetería
3. la Facultad de Ciencias
4. una pizzería buena
5. la Facultad de Letras
6. el cine (en la ciudad donde está la universidad)
7. el laboratorio de lenguas
8. otro *(another)*

Pronunciación

Sounds of Spanish *k*, *c,* and *z*

1. The **k,** and the combinations **qu, ca, co** and **cu,** are pronounced like the English *c* in the word *cut,* but without the puff of air.

   kilómetro   Quito   casa   color   cuna

2. The letter **c** before **e** or **i,** and the letter **z** are pronounced like the English *s* of the word *sense* in Latin America, and in Spain, like the English *th* in *think.*

   cine   cena   ciudad   zapato   zona   manzana

 # Estructuras

4. The verbs *estar* *(to be)* **and** *ir* *(to go)*

Both **ser** and **estar** mean *to be,* and both are irregular verbs. You already learned **ser** in **Lección 1**. Another important Spanish irregular verb is **ir** (*to go*). The following charts show the present tense forms of **estar** and **ir**.

estar (*to be*)			
yo	**estoy**	nosotros(as)	**estamos**
tú	**estás**	vosotros(as)	**estáis**
usted		ustedes	
él	**está**	ellos	**están**
ella		ellas	

- **Estar** is used to indicate the location of objects and people.

Los chicos **están** en la taquilla.	*The kids are at the ticket booth.*
La cafetería **está** al lado del centro estudiantil.	*The cafeteria is next to the Student Center.*

- **Estar** is used to express a condition or state, such as how someone is feeling, or marital status.

Estoy casada con Jorge.	*I'm married to Jorge.*
Carlos **está** apurado.	*Carlos is in a hurry.*
Mamá **está** bien, gracias.	*Mother is doing well, thank you.*

estar **vs.** *hay*

- Use **estar** to indicate the location of a specific, definite subject.

- Use **hay** (*there is/there are*) when the subject is indefinite.

La librería **está** en la Avenida Bolívar.	*The bookstore is on Bolívar Avenue.*
Hay una librería detrás de la biblioteca.	*There is a bookstore behind the library.*

ir (*to go*)			
yo	**voy**	nosotros(as)	**vamos**
tú	**vas**	vosotros(as)	**vais**
usted		ustedes	
él	**va**	ellos	**van**
ella		ellas	

Expressing Future Actions: *ir a* **+ infinitive**

- Use the construction **ir** + **a** + *infinitive* to express future action. It is equivalent to the English construction *to be going to* + *infinitive.*

¿Qué **vas a hacer** mañana?	*What are you going to do tomorrow?*
Voy a comprar un CD ROM.	*I'm going to buy a CD ROM.*

- When the definite article **el** follows the preposition **a,** they contract to **al.** The preposition **a** does not contract with **la, las, los** or with the subject pronoun **él.**

> Vamos **al** gimnasio.   *We are going to the gym.*
> Ernesto va **a la** rectoría.   *Ernesto goes to the Administration building.*

◆ Práctica

2–32 Una conversación telefónica. Paco and Manolo are talking on the telephone. Complete their conversation with the correct form of **estar.**

PACO: Hola, Manolo.

MANOLO: Hola, Paco ¿cómo _____ tú?

PACO: Yo _____ bastante bien, gracias. ¿Y tú?

MANOLO: Muy bien. Oye, *(Listen)* ¿dónde _____ tú ahora?

PACO: _____ en la cafetería.

MANOLO: ¿_____ Raúl y Roberto allí?

PACO: No, ellos _____ en la residencia estudiantil.

MANOLO: ¿Por qué? ¿_____ enfermos?

PACO: No, solamente _____ cansados. Y, oye, ¿dónde _____ María Aurora?

MANOLO: _____ muy ocupada en la biblioteca, porque tiene un examen.

PACO: Nosotros también _____ muy ocupados con los exámenes, pero vamos al fútbol esta noche. ¿_____ libres Uds.?

MANOLO: No, tenemos que estudiar. Bueno, hasta luego.

PACO: Adiós.

2–33 Los amigos. Complete the paragraph using the correct form of **ir.**

Felipe, Paloma, Silvia y yo somos buenos amigos. Nosotros _____ juntos a la universidad todos los días. Felipe _____ a la clase de español a las nueve y luego _____ a la clase de inglés. Paloma y Silvia _____ a la clase de geografía a las once y a las doce _____ a la clase de biología. Yo también _____ con ellas a la clase de geografía pero después _____ a la cafetería. Nosotros _____ a la biblioteca a las tres y por la tarde regresamos a casa. ¿A qué hora _____ tú a la universidad?

◆ Actividades

2–34 Los planes. In pairs, make plans to do something together. Use the following questions to guide your discussion.

1. ¿Qué vamos a hacer?
2. ¿Con quiénes vamos?
3. ¿Qué día vamos?
4. ¿Adónde?
5. ¿A qué hora?
6. ¿Cómo vamos? ¿En carro, en autobús, en tren o a pie *(walking)?*
7. ¿Cuándo vamos a regresar?

2-35 En la tele. With a partner, say which sports events you are going to watch and at what time. Write down your partner's selections and time. Then, change partners and tell the new person your previous partner's selections.

MODELO: *(to the first partner)*   Voy a ver el fútbol a las once y media de
                                                    la noche (23.30).
                (to the second partner)   _____ va a ver golf a las tres de la tarde.

Retransmisiones Deportivas

SÁBADO

Fútbol

❖ Final del campeonato de la Liga Brasileña Flamengo-Botafogo (Canal +, 23.27)

❖ Resumen de los partidos de fútbol correspondientes a la liga 1991–92. Real Madrid-FC Barcelona y FC Barcelona-Real Madrid (Canal 33, 22.00)

Ciclismo

❖ Tour, final de la etapa Saint Gervais-Sestrières en directo (La 2, 14.00)

Golf

❖ Open Británico desde Muirfield (Escocia), tercera jornada, retransmitida en directo (Canal +, 16:00)

Atletismo

❖ V Juegos Iberoamericanos desde Sevilla (Canal Sur, 20.30)

Tenis

❖ Semifinales de la Copa Federación femenina desde Stuttgart (Canal 33, 16.00)

DOMINGO

Tenis

❖ Final de la Copa Federación femenina desde Stuttgart (Canal 33, 13.00)

Atletismo

❖ V Juegos Iberoamericanos desde Sevilla (Canal 33, 18.00 / Canal Sur, 21.00)

Fútbol

❖ Final del campeonato de la Liga Brasileña Flamengo-Botafogo (Canal +, 0.54) ● Barcelona-Atlético de Madrid, partido correspondiente a la Liga 1991–92 (Canal Sur, 0.10)

Golf

❖ Open Británico desde Muirfield (Escocia) ● Última jornada, en directo (Canal +, 15.52)

Ciclismo

❖ Tour, final de la etapa Sestrières-L'Alpe-d'Huez en directo (La 2, 11.30)

Motociclismo

❖ Campeonato del Mundo de Velocidad Gran Premio de Francia (125cc, 50cc y 250cc) desde el circuito de Magny-Cours (La 2, *Domingo* deporte)

2–36 ¿Qué van a hacer? With a partner, write at least eight complete sentences combining elements from each column. You will have to conjugate the verbs, add articles or the contraction **al** as necessary, and make adjectives agree in gender and number with the subject. Sentences can be positive or negative.

MODELO: Las chicas no van al laboratorio porque están cansadas.

Los jóvenes	ir a	cafetería	los estudiantes dar una fiesta
Tú		restaurante porque	dar un bufet barato
Elvira y Luisa		club	estar (apurado, cansado, enfermo, contento)
Las chicas		clínica	estar aburrido de (estudiar, trabajar)
Yo		oficina	estar ahí los amigos y amigas
Tú y yo		librería	tener que estudiar
Pilar y yo		laboratorio	tener (hambre, sed)

5. The Present Tense of *-er* and *-ir* Verbs

You have already learned the present tense forms of regular **-ar** verbs in **Lección 1**. The following chart includes the forms for regular **-er** and **-ir** verbs.

	trabajar (*to work*)	**comer** (*to eat*)	**vivir** (*to live*)
yo	trabaj**o**	com**o**	viv**o**
tú	trabaj**as**	com**es**	viv**es**
usted } él } ella }	trabaj**a**	com**e**	viv**e**
nosotros(as)	trabaj**amos**	com**emos**	viv**imos**
vosotros(as)	trabaj**áis**	com**éis**	viv**ís**
ustedes } ellos } ellas }	trabaj**an**	com**en**	viv**en**

- The present tense endings of **-er** and **-ir** verbs are identical except for the **nosotros** and **vosotros** forms which show a vowel change.

- Some commmom **-er** and **-ir** verbs are listed below:

aprender	~~to open~~ to learn	**abrir**	*to open*
beber	*to drink*	**añadir**	*to add*
creer	*to believe*	**asistir a**	*to attend*
deber	*to owe, to ought to*	**decidir**	*to decide*
leer	*to read*	**escribir**	*to write*
		insistir en	*to insist*
		recibir	*to receive*
		vender	*to sell*

◆ Práctica

2–37 Enrique y Laura. Enrique and Laura are good friends. Complete the following statements with the correct form of the verbs in parentheses to describe a typical day for them at the university.

1. Enrique y yo (asistir) _____ a la universidad.
2. Él (vivir) _____ en una residencia estudiantil pero yo (vivir) _____ en un apartamento.
3. Nosotros (comer) _____ en la cafetería por la noche porque la comida que ellos (vender) _____ en la cafetería es buena.
4. Enrique siempre (beber) _____ refrescos y yo (beber) _____ leche.
5. Nosotros siempre (insistir) _____ en estudiar en la biblioteca por la noche.
6. Nosotros (aprender) _____ español.
7. Enrique (leer) _____ la lección de español y yo (escribir) _____ en el cuaderno.
8. Nosotros (creer) _____ que el español es necesario para nuestro futuro.

2–38 ¡Por la causa! A group of friends is sponsoring a dance-a-thon at Margarita's house to raise money to fight AIDS. Each person does something different before or at the party. Form logical sentences by using phrases from the list below and conjugating the verb.

porque tiene mucho calor
de su novio antes (*before*) de la fiesta
las bebidas y la comida de la fiesta
en la taquilla en el garaje de la casa

la puerta a las seis de la tarde en punto
hamburguesas, ensalada, café con leche
bailar con Rosalinda
a bailar la lambada con Raquel

1. Usted/vender/entradas para la fiesta…
2. Moncha y Dolores/comprar…
3. Cheo y yo/abrir…
4. Luis Tomás/beber/muchos refrescos…
5. Yo/aprender…
6. María Marta/recibir flores…
7. Tú/insistir en…
8. Priscila y Raimundo/comen…

2–39 ¡Hola Lupe! Help Rodrigo complete the following letter to his sister Lupe, using words from the list below. Each word is used only one time.

añadimos	escribo	hacen	aprenden
comemos	beber	aprendo	compro
hay que	asiste	deben	asisto
asistimos	escriben	leen	leer

Querida Lupe:

¿Qué tal? ¿Cómo estás? Yo estoy muy bien. _____ para contarte (tell you) sobre mi semestre. Los lunes, miércoles y viernes _____ a tres clases: química, biología y anatomía. _____ mucho, especialmente en química.

Después de las clases, Francisca y yo vamos a la cafetería a _____ jugo, leche o refrescos y _____ hamburguesas que son muy buenas. A veces _____ café al menú, si _____ que estudiar mucho por la tarde. Después vamos a la biblioteca a _____ y escribir. Todos los estudiantes _____ ir a la biblioteca donde _____ la tarea (homework), _____, _____ y _____ mucho. Los martes y jueves por la mañana _____ un sándwich y un refresco y voy al ginmasio a hacer deportes con Marilú y Gonzalo. Después, por la tarde, Marilú _____ a una clase de arte y Gonzalo y yo _____ a una clase de psicología. Es un horario muy fácil.

◆ Actividades

2–40 Mi compañero(a). Chat briefly with another student using the following questions as a guide. Then, report your findings to another classmate.

1. ¿Dónde vives?
2. ¿Con quién vives?
3. ¿Dónde comes el almuerzo?
4. ¿Qué comes en el almuerzo?
5. ¿Qué bebes con el almuerzo?
6. ¿Por qué aprendes español?
7. ¿A qué hora asistes a la clase de español?
8. ¿A qué hora lees el libro de español?
9. ¿A qué otras (other) clases asistes?
10. ¿Vendes tus libros al final del semestre?

2–41 Ordenar. To tell a story about a reception at the Engineering School, order the sentences in a logical way and conjugate each verb. Begin with the first sentence. If the subject is not obvious, let the context help you figure it out. There are several possible ways of telling the story. Work in groups of three or four.

_____ El sábado 5 de abril **ser** el Día de los Ingenieros.

_____ Por la noche **dar** una recepción en la Facultad de Ingeniería.

_____ Los estudiantes **leer** el anuncio *(announcement)* en la pared de la cafetería.

_____ Muchos chicos **escribir** la información en sus cuadernos.

_____ Todos los estudiantes de informática **estar** invitados.

_____ Los ingenieros **preparar** comida y muchas bebidas.

_____ Si tú **asistir** a la recepción, yo también **ir**.

_____ Hay muchos ingenieros simpáticos, ¿no **creer**?

_____ **Deber** ir juntas, porque **ser** más divertido *(fun)*.

_____ En la fiesta **comer, beber** y después bailamos con los ingenieros.

_____ ¿Qué **decidir** tú?

6. Expressing to like: *gustar*

Me gusta el cereal nuevo.

- The verb **gustar** is used to express preferences, likes, and dislikes. This verb is always accompanied by a word such as **me** and **te**.

  Me gusta la ensalada.   *I like the salad.*
  *(Literally, the salad is pleasing **to me**.)*

  ¿Te gusta el café?   *Do you (informal) like the coffee?*
  *(Is the coffee pleasing **to you?**)*

- The subject of the verb **gustar** is whatever is doing the pleasing, usually one or several things. For this reason, **gustar** is most often conjugated in the third person singular, **gusta**, with one item, or the third person plural, **gustan**, for several items. The words **me** and **te** indicate who is being pleased.

  Me gusta el arte.   *I like art. (Art is pleasing to me.)*
  ¿Te gustan las ciencias?   *Do you like the sciences?*
  (Are the sciences pleasing to you?)

- To express the idea that one likes *to do something,* **gustar** is followed by an infinitive. In such cases the singular form is used.

> Me **gusta escribir** en mi diario.   *I like to write in my diary.*
> ¿Te **gusta comer** hamburguesas?   *Do you like eating hamburgers?*

- Some speakers of Spanish use **gustar** to express the idea that they are *attracted* to a person.

> Me **gusta** María.   *I like María. (I'm attracted to María).*
> ¿Te **gustan** los hombres rubios?   *Do you like blond men?*
> *(Are you physically attracted to blond men?)*

- Use **caer bien** or **caer mal** to express the idea that you like or dislike a person because of their personality or taste.

> Me **caen mal** los hombres chovinistas.   *I don't like chauvinistic men.*
> ¿Te **cae bien** tu profesora?   *Do you like your professor?*

- Verbs that are grammatically similar to **gustar** are:

encantar	Me **encantan** los bananos.	*I love bananas.*
molestar	¿Te **molesta** el cigarrillo?	*Does the cigarrette bother you?*
interesar	¿Te **interesa** la química?	*Are you interested in chemistry?*
faltar	Me **falta** una página.	*I'm missing a page.*
quedar	Te **quedan** treinta dólares.	*You have thirty dollars left.*
caer bien	Maritza me **cae** muy bien.	*I like Maritza.*
caer mal	Ana me **cae** mal.	*I don't like Ana.*

◆ Práctica

2–42 Opiniones. Complete elements from each column to form logical questions in Spanish. Then interview a classmate.

¿Te	gusta(n)	nadar en el verano?
	cae(n) bien	encantar las películas?
	cae(n) mal	las ciencias atmosféricas?
	interesa(n)	los estudiantes en clase?
	falta(n)	much práctica para hablar bien el español?
	queda(n)	los estudiantes de la clase?
	molesta(n)	horas para estudiar?
	encanta(n)	los exámenes?
		los mosquitos?
		el café?
		el profesor de…?
		las noticias internacionales?
		…?

2–43 ¡A escribir! Write a little paragraph using the verbs in the previous exercise. Talk about what you like, dislike, what interests you, or bothers you, etc. Share it with another classmate.

Colaboración

2-44A Inventarios. ¿Qué tienes? ¿Qué tiene tu compañero(a)? Compare your inventory list on this page with your partner's list to find out what you have in common. Make a list of the items that your partner has that you do not.

MODELO: —Tengo dieciséis bolígrafos.
          —Yo también *(Me too.)*/Yo no.

22 relojes	1 computadora	1.000.000 de hojas de papel
101 amigas	55 mochilas	1 silla
44 diccionarios	33 mapas	666 mesas
1.000 lápices	99 tizas	11 escritorios
510 pianos	6 profesores	

2-45A Las materias y la hora. With a partner, ask each other questions to complete the chart with the information needed. Write on a separate piece of paper.

MODELO: —¿A qué hora es la clase de… ?
          —¿Qué clase es a… ?
          —¿Dónde es la clase de… ?
          —¿Qué enseña el (la) profesor(a)… ?

HORA	CLASE	LUGAR	PROFESOR(A)
8.30	cálculo	1	2
3	lingüística	Facultad de Arte	4
9.00	5	Facultad de Arte	Ramón Sánchez Guillón
10.35	6	Facultad de Medicina	7
1.55	biología	Facultad de Ciencias	8

2-46A ¿Qué tienen en común? Ask your partner what these people have in common and write down the answers on a separate piece of paper. Then, tell your partner what the people on his/her list have in common.

MODELO: —¿Qué tienen en común Mickey Mouse y Donald Duck?
            —Viven en Disney World.

LOS PERSONAJES	ALGUNAS RELACIONES
Rita Moreno y Whitney Houston	*comer* en McDonald's
Donald Trump y Lee Iacoca	*escribir* poesía
Gabriel García Márquez y Hemingway	*cantar* bien (mal)
	bailar bien (mal)
Bill, Hillary, Chelsea y Socks	*beber* cerveza (café, Coca-cola)
el Rey de España y la Reina de Inglaterra	*ir* a los bares los viernes
	trabajar mucho (poco)
… y… (*original*)	*Tener* mucha tarea
	¿…? (*original*)

2-47A ¿Cómo estás…? Ask your partner how he/she feels in the situations in the first column. Write the answers down on a separate piece of paper. Then, using **estar**, say how you feel in the situations your partner will mention to you. Use items from the second column for your answer.

MODELO: —¿Cómo estás en clase?
            —Estoy…

cuando vas a ver una
    película romántica
en una fiesta
con la familia
en su coche
después de un examen
en el invierno
por la mañana
…(*original*)

Estoy…

contento(a)
enfadado(a)
apurado(a)
aburrido(a)
loco(a)
triste
cansado(a)
romántico(a)
sentimental
serio(a)
perdido(a)
enferno(a)
ocupado(a)
muerto(a)
asustado(a) *(frightened)*

Estudiante B

2-44B Inventarios. ¿Qué tienes? ¿Qué tiene tu compañero(a)? Compare your inventory list on this page with your partner's list to find out what you have in common. Make a list of the items that your partner has that you do not.

MODELO: —Tengo dieciséis bolígrafos.
　　　　　—Yo también *(Me too.)* / Yo no.

23 relojes	65 mochilas	30 mapas
6 profesores	1 silla	99 tizas
1.000 lápices	100 amigas	666 mesas
500 pianos	4 diccionarios	1.000.000 de hojas
1 computadora	11 escritorios	de papel

2-45B Las materias y la hora. With a partner, ask questions to complete the chart with the information needed. Write on a separate piece of paper.

MODELO: —¿A qué hora es la clase de… ?
　　　　　—¿Qué clase es a… ?
　　　　　—¿Dónde está la clase de… ?
　　　　　—¿Qué enseña el (la) profesor(a)… ?

HORA	CLASE	LUGAR	PROFESOR(A)
12.00	1	Facultad de Arte	Juan Ramón Jiménez
2	diseño *(Design)*	3	Ramón Sánchez Guillón
4	física	5	Carlos Santos Pérez
6	cálculo	Facultad de Informática	María Gómez García
10.35	7	8	Ligia Gómez Salazar

2-46B ¿Qué tienen en común? Ask your partner what these people have in common and write down the answers on a separate piece of paper. Then, tell your partner what the people on his/her list have in common.

MODELO: —¿Qué tienen en común Mickey Mouse y Donald Duck?
                    —Viven en Disney World.

LOS PERSONAJES	ALGUNAS RELACIONES
Gloria Estefan y Gregory Hines	*vivir* en la Casa Blanca
Mi familia y tu familia	*tener* mucho dinero
Los estudiantes norteamericanos y los españoles	*vivir* en Europa (en...)
	cantar bien (mal)
Pablo Neruda y Walt Whitman	*escribir* novelas
Willie Nelson y Julio Iglesias	*tener* problemas
...y...(*original*)	¿...? (*original*)

2-47B ¿Cómo estás...? Using **estar**, say how you feel in the situations your partner will mention to you. Then ask him/her how he/she feels in the situations below. Write the answers on a separate piece of paper.

MODELO: —¿Cómo estás en clase?
                    —Estoy...

Estoy...

contento(a)   en la biblioteca
enfadado(a)   en una película de
apurado(a)   horror
aburrido(a)   con los amigos
loco(a)   en un bar
triste   en un examen
cansado(a)   en el verano
romántico(a)sentime   a medianoche
    ntal   ...(*original*)
serio(a)
perdido(a)
enfermo(a)
ocupado(a)
muerto(a)
asustado(a) *(frightened)*

Mundo hispánico

Los Estados Unidos hispánicos

Hoy día viven más de 24 millones de hispanos en los Estados Unidos. Casi un 35% de la población de California es de ascendencia hispánica. Los hispanos constituyen el grupo minoritario de mayor crecimiento en el país. Se calcula que para el año 2.000 habrá más de 33 millones de hispanos en los Estados Unidos.

Los hispanos en los EE.UU. se pueden dividir en tres grupos principales: los mexicanoamericanos, los puertorriqueños y los cubanoamericanos.

Los mexicanoamericanos forman casi el 60% de la población hispana de los Estados Unidos. La mayoría de ellos vive en los estados de California, Texas, Nuevo México, Colorado, Nevada y Arizona. Hay aproximadamente 1.800.000 puertorriqueños en los Estados Unidos hoy día. La mayoría vive en Nueva York, Nueva Jersey y Chicago. Hay más de un millón de cubanoamericanos en los EE.UU. y más de medio millón vive en Miami.

CIUDADES CON EL MAYOR NÚMERO DE HISPANOHABLANTES	
1. Los Angeles	4.780.000
2. Nueva York	2.780.000
3. Miami	1.100.000
4. San Francisco	970.000
5. Chicago	890.000
6. Houston	770.000
7. Dallas	520.000
8. Phoenix	345.000
9. Denver	226.000
10. Washington	225.000

CONCENTRACIÓN DE HISPANOHABLANTES EN LOS ESTADOS UNIDOS

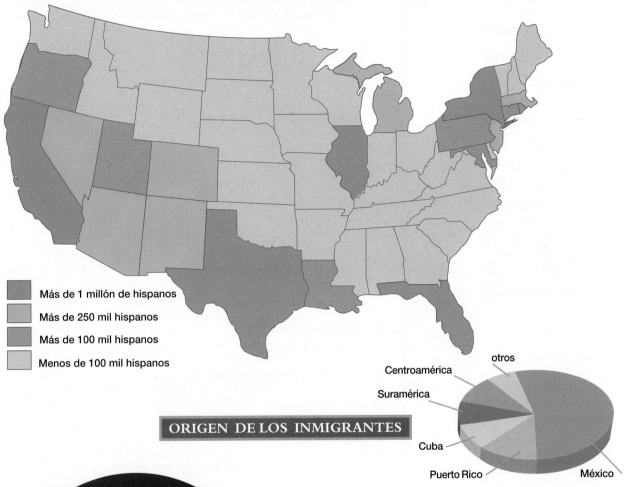

Más de 1 millón de hispanos

Más de 250 mil hispanos

Más de 100 mil hispanos

Menos de 100 mil hispanos

otros

Centroamérica

Suramérica

Cuba

Puerto Rico

México

ORIGEN DE LOS INMIGRANTES

◆ Actividad

2-48 ¿Quién es? ¿De dónde es?

1. Gloria Estefan
2. Antonio Banderas
3. Isabel Allende
4. César Chávez
5. Henry Cisneros
6. Antonia Novelo
7. Chi Chi Rodríguez

Lección 3

Las relaciones personales

Comunicación

- Talking about Family and Friends
- Extending and Responding to Invitations
- Planning Activities
- Making Comparisons and Contrasts
- Expressing Ongoing Actions

Cultura

- Hispanic Families
- Social Gatherings

Mundo hispánico: México

Estructuras

Primera parte

- Comparisons of Equality and Inequality
- Superlatives
- The Present Progressive

Segunda parte

- Stem-changing Verbs (**e→ ie**); **querer, venir**
- Summary of uses of **ser** and **estar**

PRIMERA PARTE

¡Así es la vida!

Una carta

José Joaquín Jiménez recibe una carta de su nueva amiga mexicana Marilú Fuentes. Ella estudia en la universidad con él y está contándole de su familia con la que está pasando unos días.

Querido José Joaquín:

Aquí estoy con mi familia en Guadalajara. Es fabuloso estar con ellos y descansar. Mi familia y yo somos muy unidos. Mi papá es dentista y mamá trabaja como profesora en una escuela secundaria. Mi hermana mayor se llama Carmen y es abogada. Ernesto es menor que yo y va al colegio. Finalmente está la menor, mi hermanita Lucía, que es muy alegre y tan bonita como mi mamá.

Mis abuelos, los padres de papá, viven con nosotros, y mis tíos Julia y Evelio viven bastante cerca. Ellos tienen un hijo único, mi primo Pedrito, que es tan majadero como mi hermano Ernesto. Los dos son muy traviesos. Ahora mismo están jugando y haciendo mucho ruido. Gracias a Dios que ya estoy acabando esta carta.

Regreso a la universidad el domingo próximo. ¿Cuándo regresas tú? Espero verte pronto.

Cariñosamente,

Marilú

Vocabulario y expresiones

La familia

el (la) abuelo(a)	*grandfather/mother*
el (la) cuñado(a)	*brother-/sister-in-law*
el (la) esposo(a)	*husband/wife*
el (la) hermano(a)	*brother/sister*
el (la) hermanastro(a)	*stepbrother/sister*
el (la) hijo(a)	*son/daughter*
el (la) hijastro(a)	*stepson/daughter*
el (la) hijo(a) único(a)	*only son/daughter*
el (la) nieto(a)	*grandson/daughter*
la nuera	*daughter-in-law*
la madrastra	*stepmother*
la madrina	*godmother*
la mamá, madre	*mother*
el padrastro	*stepfather*
el papá, padre	*father*
el padrino	*godfather*
los padres	*parents*
el (la) primo(a)	*cousin*
el (la) sobrino(a)	*nephew/niece*
el (la) suegro(a)	*father-/mother-in-law*
el (la) tío(a)	*uncle/aunt*
el yerno	*son-in-law*

Otras palabras y expresiones

el (la) abogado(a)	*lawyer*
la boda	*wedding*
cariñosamente	*with love*
la carta	*letter*
el casamiento	*wedding*
como	*since, as*
descansar	*to rest*
enseñar	*to teach; to show*
jugar	*to play*
más	*more*
menos	*less*
pasar	*to spend*
Querido(a)...	*Dear...*
ruido	*noise*
tan...como	*as...as*
tanto...como	*as much as*

Adjetivos

activo	*active*
agresivo	*aggressive*
alegre	*happy*
amable	*kind*
atractivo(a)	*attractive*
casado(a)	*married*
débil	*weak*
disciplinado	*disciplined*
divertido(a)	*fun, amusing*
elegante	*elegant*
famoso(a)	*famous*
fascinante	*fascinating*
fuerte	*strong*
guapo(a)	*handsome, beautiful*
lento	*slow*
majadero(a)	*annoying*
mayor	*older*
menor	*younger*
paciente	*patient*
responsable	*responsible*
rico(a)	*rich*
tímido(a)	*shy*
travieso(a)	*mischievous*
unido(a)	*close, close-knit*

Queridos abuelos...

¡Así lo decimos!

Los padres

The generic word in Spanish for parents is **padres**. However, in Mexico, the general word for parents is **papás**. In more colloquial speech, **mis viejos** is a very common way to refer to one's parents. Children of all ages address their parents in diverse ways throughout the Spanish-speaking world. These forms of address range from **mami/papi** (general) and **pipo/mima** (Cuba), to the more formal **Ud.** that is used by some people from Colombia, Mexico, the Andean countries, and parts of Central America.

fascinante

In English we can show our excitement or interest in something by saying *That's great!, Neat!, How interesting!* or even *awesome!* The choice of expression often relates to a specific generation or age group. The following expressions in Spanish are now generally cross-generational and are used to show one's approval, interest and liking.

Argentina	**bárbaro**, **macanudo**
Cuba	**un fenómeno**, **de película**
España	**alucinante**
México	**padre**
Puerto Rico	**nítido**
Venezuela	**chévere**

El concierto anoche estuvo chévere.
Last night's concert was great.

¡A escuchar!

Una carta. You will hear the letter that appears in **¡Así el la vida!** Listen to the questions that follow and choose the correct answer.

1. a. Guanajuato b. Guadalajara c. Mérida
2. a. dentista b. abogado c. profesor
3. a. en una escuela secundaria b. en una escuela primaria c. en una escuela de karate
4. a. uno b. dos c. tres
5. a. sus abuelos b. sus tíos c. sus primos
6. a. amable b. alegre c. majadero

◆ Práctica

3-1 ¿Quién es quién? Describe the members of the García family.

Pedro García   María García

Pedro García Jr.   Lola García

Ana Juárez   Juan Gómez

3-2 Los abuelos. Like all grandparents, Blanca and Javier love to brag about their family. What are they saying? Be sure to change nouns, verbs and adjectives, as necessary.

MODELO: nieto/Tito/paciente
          Nuestro nieto Tito es muy paciente.

1. nieto/Marilú/inteligente
2. hijo/Julia/bueno
3 hijo/Luis Javier/alegre
4. nieto/Ernesto y Pedrito/guapo
5. sobrino/Ramona y Meche/simpático
6 nieto/Carmen/trabajador
7. nieta/Marilú y Lucía/bonito
8. sobrino/José Miguel/responsable
9. yerno/Evelio/famoso
10. nuera/Berta/divertida
11. sobrina/Mabel/rico
12. cuñado/Sonia/elegante

3-3 El casamiento. Answer the following questions based on the wedding announcement.

1. ¿Cómo se llama el padre de la novia?
2. ¿Cómo se llama la madre?
3. ¿Cuál es el nombre completo de Marcela?
4. ¿Quién es el novio?
5. ¿Dónde es el casamiento?
6. ¿Cuándo es el casamiento y a qué hora?
7. ¿Qué apellidos va a usar Marcela después del casamiento?
8. ¿En qué ciudad es el casamiento?
9. ¿Cuál es el apellido del padre de Fernando?
10. ¿Cuál va a ser el apellido de Marcela después de la boda?
11. Si Marcela y Fernando tienen hijos, ¿cuáles van a ser sus apellidos?

> **ADRIAN J. SPERANZA**
> Y
> **MERCEDES MAGNASCO DE SPERANZA**
> PARTICIPAN A USTED EL CASAMIENTO DE SU HIJA
> **MARCELA**
> CON EL SEÑOR
> **FERNANDO, ALBERTO VAUDAGNA**
> Y LE INVITAN A ACOMPAÑARLOS EN LA CEREMONIA RELIGIOSA
> QUE SE EFECTUARA EN LA
> **IGLESIA STELLA MARIS**
> EL SÁBADO 15 DE JULIO A LAS 19.
>
> LOS NOVIOS SALUDARAN EN EL ATRIO   BUENOS AIRES, 1995.
> COMODORO PY Y CORBETA URUGUAY

3-4 Una familia. Answer the questions based on the family tree.

MODELO: —¿Es Carmen la abuela de Pablo?
          —Sí, Carmen es la abuela.
          —¿Es Armando el hermano de Pablo?
          —No, Armando no es el hermano, es el primo.

1. ¿Qué relación hay entre María y Pablo?
2. ¿Son Paco y Teresa los tíos de Carmen?
3. ¿Es Amalia la prima de Carlos?
4. ¿Se llama Ramón el hermano de Gustavo?
5. ¿Qué es Carmen de Pablo?
6. ¿Es Elena la esposa de Gustavo?
7. ¿Es Elena la cuñada de Teresa?
8. ¿Qué relación hay entre Rosendo y María?

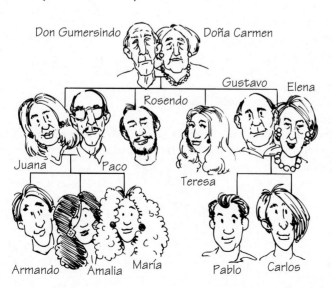

3-5 ¿Cómo es tu familia? Copy the list below on a separate piece of paper. Then, walk around the class and ask your classmates questions based on items on the list (one question per person). Write down the names of those who answer affirmatively to your questions next to the corresponding item.

MODELO: su esposo(a) es rico(a)
—¿Tu esposo(a) es rico(a)?
—Sí, mi esposo(a) es rico(a).
—No, mi esposo(a) no es rico(a).

1. sus abuelos viven en esta ciudad
2. tiene amigos casados
3. sus tíos son ricos
4. asiste a muchas fiestas familiares
5. tiene más de 15 primos
6. su familia es grande
7. su familia viaja mucho
8. es hijo/hija único/única
9. tiene madrastra o padrastro
10. tiene hermanos menores

◆ Actividades

3-6 Un árbol genealógico. Draw a family tree and describe it to other members of the class.

3-7 Preguntas personales. Interview another student about his/her family using the following questions.

1. ¿Dónde vive tu familia?
2. ¿Es grande o pequeña tu familia?
3. ¿De dónde son tus padres?
4. ¿Dónde trabajan?
5. ¿Cómo son tus padres?
6. ¿Cuántos hermanos tienes?
7. ¿Cómo se llaman?
8. ¿Cuántos años tienen?
9. ¿Viven en casa tus hermanos?
10. ¿Trabajan o estudian tus hermanos?

3-8 El informe. Now write a brief description about your classmate's family based on the conversation you have just had. Be prepared to share it with the class or another classmate.

Pronunciación ━━━━━━━━━━━━

Sounds of Spanish *d* and *t*

1. The Spanish **d** has two distinct sounds. At the beginning of a breath group or after the letters **l** or **n,** the **d** is pronounced with the tip of the tongue pressed against the back of the upper front teeth. In all other cases, the **d** is pronounced by allowing some air to escape between the tongue and the teeth, like the weak English *th* in *that.*

HARD SOUND		SOFT SOUND (*th*)
dar	**senda**	**modo**
Daniel	**Aldo**	**cada**
andar	**caldera**	**verdad**

2. The Spanish **t** is pronounced in the same position as the **d,** against the back of the upper front teeth. In contrast with English, no puff of air is produced with the **t.**

torre	**meta**	**tú**
Tomás	**puerta**	**otoño**
tanto	**octubre**	**taco**

 # Estructuras ━━━━━━━━━━━━

1. Comparisons of Equality

•   In Spanish, comparisons of equality are formed with the construction **tanto como** *(as much as).*

> Yo leo **tanto como** tú.   *I read as much as you do.*

•   Comparisons of equality with nouns are formed with the construction **tanto(-a, -os, -as)** + noun + **como.** The English translation is *as much as* (with a singular noun) or *as many as* (with a plural noun). The adjective **tanto** agrees in gender and number with the noun it modifies.

> Ana lee **tantas** novelas **como** Marina.   *Ana reads as many novels as Marina.*
>
> Vilma tiene **tantos** hermanos **como** Rodolfo.   *Vilma has as many brothers as Rodolfo.*
>
> Tú tienes **tanta** hambre como yo.   *You are as hungry as I am.*

•   Comparisons of equality with adjectives or adverbs are formed using the following construction: **tan...como** *as...as.*

> Pedro es **tan** amable **como** Rafael.   *Pedro is as kind as Rafael.*
>
> Eida habla **tan** rápido **como** su tía.   *Eida speaks as fast as her aunt.*

▼▼▼▼▼▼▼▼▼▼▼▼▼▼▼▼▼▼▼▼▼▼▼▼▼▼▼▼▼▼▼▼▼▼▼

STUDY TIP

Tanto functions as a quantifier and is used to compare amounts and qualitities.
Tan functions as a qualifier and is used to compare the manner or aspect in which the actions are carried out.

Hoy tengo **tanto** dinero **como** ayer.   *Today I have as much money as*
                                                                   yesterday.

Roberto es **tan** atractivo **como** Toño.   *Roberto is as attractive as Toño.*

◆ Práctica

3-9 ¡Arreglar! Form comparisons using **tanto(a) como** or **tanto(a, os, as)...como.**

MODELO: Yo/trabajar/mi hermano
                  Yo trabajo tanto como mi hermano.

                  Luis/tener/prisa/Fernando
                  Luis tiene tanta prisa como Fernando.

1. Mi hermanastra/beber/jugo/mi prima Olga
2. Yo/comer/hamburguesas/mi padrino
3. Mi abuelo/tener/dólares/nuestros padres
4. Nuestras tías/comprar/cosas/tu abuela
5. Tu madre/hablar/mi cuñado Pedro
6. Su cuñada/escribir/cartas/su novio
7. Mi padre/comer/yo
8. Anselmo/asistir/clases/Flory
9. Sus nietos/descansar/él
10 Nuestro sobrino/tener/sueño/nosotros

3-10 En una fiesta familiar. Tía Rigoberta and tía Tatiana are gossiping about family members. Form comparison using **tanto(a) como** or **tanto(a, os, as)...como.**

MODELO: Chema/trabajar/su hermano
                  Chema trabaja tanto como su hermano.

                  Luis/tener/dinero/su esposa
                  Luis tiene tanto dinero como su esposa.

1. Mi hermanastra/bailar/yo
2. Mi padrino/comer/mi padre
3. Mi abuelo/tener/libros/sus amigos
4. Tu cuñada/hablar/idiomas/tú
5. Tus sobrinos/escribir/cartas/sus amigos
6. Tus nietos/gritar/mis nietos
7. Nuestro primo/tener/sueño/los otros jóvenes
8. Mi yerno/tener/excusas/tu yerno

2. Comparisons of Inequality

- The following construction is used to express comparisons of inequality.

$$\left.\begin{array}{c} \textbf{más} \\ \text{or} \\ \textbf{menos} \end{array}\right\} + \text{adjective/adverb} + \textbf{que}$$

Mercedes es **más atractiva que** Carmen.	*Mercedes **is more attractive than** Carmen.*
Pedro es **menos paciente que** Julio.	*Pedro **is less patient than** Julio.*
Tu casa está **más lejos que** mi casa.	*Your house is **farther than** my house.*

- In numerical expressions, **de** is used instead of **que**.

Tengo **más de** cinco buenos amigos.	*I have **more than** five good friends.*

3. Regular and Irregular Comparatives

ADJECTIVE	REGULAR FORM	IRREGULAR FORM	
bueno(a)	más bueno	mejor	*better, best*
malo(a)	más malo	peor	*worse, worst*
viejo(a)	más viejo	mayor	*older, oldest*
joven	más joven	menor	*younger, youngest*

- The irregular forms **mejor** and **peor** are more commonly used than the regular forms **más bueno** and **más malo. Mejor** and **peor** are used to describe quality and performance related to both people and objects, while **más bueno** and **más malo** usually refer to moral, ethical and behavioral qualities.

El coche de Lucinda es **mejor que** el de Carlos.	*Lucinda's car is **better than** Carlos's.*
Pedro es **más bueno que** Luis.	*Pedro is **nicer** (he's a kinder person) **than** Luis.*

- **Más grande** and **más pequeño** are almost always used to refer to size, while **mayor** and **menor** refer primarily to age.

Mi casa es **más grande que** la casa de Domingo.	*My house is **bigger than** Domingo's house.*
Lucía **es menor** que Beba y yo soy **mayor** que Lucía.	*Lucía is **younger** than Beba and I am **older** than Lucía.*

◆ Práctica

3-11 Opiniones. Express your opinions by forming comparisons similar to the model.

MODELO: El español y el inglés (fácil)
                 El español es tan fácil como el inglés.
                 El inglés es más fácil que el español.

1. Robin Williams y Eddie Murphy (guapo, famoso, cómico, simpático)
2. España y los Estados Unidos (interesante, fascinante, rico, fuerte)
3. Jodie Foster y Meg Ryan (atractivo, amable, elegante, famoso)
4. Donald Trump y Lee Iacocca (inteligente, rico, trabajador, majadero)
5. Nelson Mandela y Martin Luther King (famoso, responsable, bueno, fuerte)
6. Oprah Winfrey y Geraldo Rivera (rico, majadero, fascinante, escandaloso)

3-12 La familia de Rodrigo. Look at the illustration and compare one family member to another using the cues provided. Follow the model.

MODELO: tía Ligia/elegante/tía Norma
                 Tía Ligia es más elegante que tía Norma.
                 Rodrigo es menos elegante que tía Ligia.

1. Jorge/alto/Rodrigo
2. Pili y Mili/menor/Rodrigo
3. el abuelo/contento/tía Norma
4. Elena/mayor/Pili y Mili
5. Elena/gordo/Rodrigo
6. el abuelo/viejo/tía Norma y tía Ligia

7. tía Norma/alegre/tía Ligia
8. tío Rafa/perezoso/Rolando
9. Rolando/ocupado/Rodrigo
10. tía Ligia/delgada/Elena
11. Rodrigo/travieso/Pili y Mili
12. tía Norma/triste/Rodrigo

4. Superlatives

- To express the superlative in Spanish, the definite article is used with **más** *(more)* or **menos** *(less)*.

   Mercedes es **la más responsable** de la clase y **la menos agresiva**.
   *Mercedes is **the most responsible** one in the class and **the least aggressive**.*

- When a noun is used, the definite article precedes the noun in Spanish.

   Cuautéhmoc es **el muchacho más fuerte** de la clase.
   *Cuautéhmoc is **the strongest boy** in the class.*

- The equivalent of *in* or *of* after a superlative is **de**.

   Nieves es la chica más fascinante **de** la clase.
   *Nieves is the most fascinating girl **in** the class.*

◆ Práctica

3-13 Exageraciones. Change the following statements to the superlative. Follow the model.

MODELO: Mi primo Nacho es un chico simpático. (la familia)
               Mi primo Nacho es el chico más simpático de la familia.

1. Mi abuela Chabela es una mujer elegante. (la ciudad)
2. El padrastro de Juan es un hombre fuerte. (la isla)
3. Nuestros abuelos son unas personas pacientes. (la familia)
4. Tu cuñada Rosa es una mujer fascinante. (el grupo)
5. La prima de Mayela es una chica majadera. (la clase)
6. Mis hermanas Paula y Ana son unas estudiantes responsables. (la universidad)
7. Nuestra familia es una familia unida. (Sevilla)
8. Fernando es un doctor amable. (el hospital)
9. El casamiento de Elizabeth y Luis es una fiesta famosa. (el año)
10. La vieja profesora es una mujer buena. (el pueblo)

3-14 Una encuesta. Read the following chart and make at least six comparisons based on the ratings each person has received for each category.

	INTELIGENTE	ATRACTIVO(A)	AMABLE	POPULAR
Rosa	5	4	1	2
Antonia	2	5	3	3
Manuela	3	3	4	5
Guadalupe	4	2	5	4

MODELO: Rosa es más inteligente que Antonia.
               Rosa es la más inteligente del grupo.

◆ Actividades

3-15 Preguntas personales. Find a partner and take turns asking each other questions comparing different members of your families. Make sure the adjectives agree in gender and number with the subject. You may use an adjective more than once. Give as much information as you can.

MODELO: ¿Quién es más liberal, tu papá o tú?

Yo soy más liberal que mi papá, pero mamá es más conservadora que él.

alto/bajo	feo/guapo
delgado/gordo	menor/mayor
fuerte/débil	simpático/antipático
inteligente/tonto	trabajador/perezoso
paciente/impaciente	liberal/conservador
alegre/triste	responsable/irresponsable
interesante/aburrido	ocupado/desocupado

3-16 Una encuesta. Conduct a survey of restaurants, clubs, and stores in the area. Select at least three of each and rate them in each of the categories below. In small groups, compare your opinions to those of other members of the class.

BUENO(A)	MALO(A)	EL (LA) MEJOR	EL (LA) PEOR
restaurante			
discoteca			
tienda			

3-17 Contrastes. In small groups, find out the following information about the members in your group. Write it down. Be prepared to report it to the class.
En su grupo, ¿quién...

1. ...tiene más hermanos?
2. ...tiene el (la) hermano(a) menor más joven?
3. ...vive más lejos ahora de su casa familiar?
4. ...trabaja más horas cada semana?
5. ...es el (la) mayor del grupo?
6. ...es el (la) menor del grupo?
7. ...es el (la) más extrovertido(a) del grupo? ¿y el (la) más introvertido(a)?
8. ...tiene el (la) pariente *(relative)* más famoso(a)?
9. ...tiene el (la) pariente más divertido(a)?
10. ...pasa más tiempo hablando por teléfono todos los días?

5. The Present Progressive

- The present progressive tense describes an action that is in progress at the time the statement is made. The progressive is formed using the present indicative of **estar** and the present participle of the main verb.

Present Progressive of *hablar*		
yo	estoy	hablando
tú	estás	hablando
usted ⎫ él ⎬ ella ⎭	está	hablando
nosotros(as)	estamos	hablando
vosotros(as)	estáis	hablando
ustedes ⎫ ellos ⎬ ellas ⎭	están	hablando

- To form the present participle of regular **–ar** verbs, add **–ando** to the verb stem.

    hablar: **habl– + ando → hablando**

- To form the present participle of **–er** and **–ir** verbs, add **–iendo** to the verb stem.

    comer: **com– + iendo → comiendo**
    escribir: **escrib– + iendo → escribiendo**

- The present participle is invariable. Its ending never changes regardless of the subject. Only the verb **estar** is conjugated when using the present progressive forms.

- Unlike English, the Spanish present progressive is not used to express future time. Instead, Spanish uses the present indicative.

Vamos al cine el domingo próximo.	*We are going to the movies next Sunday.*
Salgo mañana para Buenos Aires.	*I am leaving for Buenos Aires tomorrow.*

Common Irregular Present Participles			
caer	to fall	**cayendo**	falling
decir	to say	**diciendo**	saying
dormir	to sleep	**durmiendo**	sleeping
leer	to read	**leyendo**	reading
oír	to hear	**oyendo**	hearing
pedir	to ask for	**pidiendo**	asking for
repetir	to repeat	**repitiendo**	repeating
reír	to laugh	**riendo**	laughing
servir	to serve	**sirviendo**	serving
seguir	to follow	**siguiendo**	following
traer	to bring	**trayendo**	bringing

◆ Práctica

3-18 ¿Qué están haciendo?

MODELO: Mi hermana/una carta
          Mi hermana está escribiendo una carta.

1. Mi hermano/ la televisión   2. Mis padres/un libro   3. Yo/un refresco

4. Mis tías/sándwiches   5. Mi abuela/por teléfono   6. Mi hermana/ la siesta

3-19 ¿Dónde están? Match the phrases below with the situations to describe what each person is doing.

MODELO: Julio Antonio está en la biblioteca.
           Está leyendo un libro.

leer un libro	jugar al tenis	charlar con Bill Clinton
bailar mucho	comprar un libro	hacer una película
comer sándwiches	jugar al béisbol	tocar el piano
escuchar al profesor	preparar una comida	

1. Mario y Alicia están en una fiesta.
2. Nosotros estamos en la cafetería.
3. Tú estás en la librería.
4. Juan Carlos y Ana están en la clase de español.
5. José Canseco está en el estadio.
6. El rey Juan Carlos está en Washington.
7. Julia Child está en la cocina.
8. Mi hermano está en la cancha (*field*).
9. Meryl Streep está en Hollywood.
10. Billy Joel está en el concierto.

◆ Actividad

3-20 Lo siento. Carmen and Paula are in charge of organizing a birthday party at the office for their boss. Carmen e-mails her colleagues asking them to meet for five minutes to finalize plans, but they all have an excuse. In pairs, first take turns role-playing the colleague answering Carmen. Then, take turns role-playing Carmen reporting back to Paula. Follow the model.

MODELO: *(the colleague to Carmen)*   Cecilia/escribir una carta
                                          Ahora estoy escribiendo una carta. Lo siento.
           (Carmen to Paula)   Ahora Cecilia está escribiendo una carta.

1. Ligia/hablar por teléfono
2. María Fernanda y yo/preparar un informe
3. Marcos y Nidia/aprender un programa de computadora
4. Julio/añadir un párrafo al informe
5. Eduardo/conversar con el Sr. Márquez
6. Adolfo/leer el nuevo plan de acción
7. Felicia y Hortencia/abrir la correspondencia *(the mail)*
8. Consuelo/pedir una nueva extensión de teléfono
9. Esteban/beber un chocolate muy caliente *(hot)*
10. Los clientes/decidir ahora mismo si venden o no
11. El Sr. Gómez/dormir una siesta
12. La Sra. Facio/escribir una carta
13. Don Pepe/pedirle un informe al Departamento de Estadísticas
14. Ana María/seguir un programa de vídeo
15. Lorenzo y Pepita/estudiar para la clase de informática

A propósito...Hispanic Families

Hispanic families tend to be fairly large and stay together for longer periods than families in the United States. Unmarried sons and daughters usually live at home, even while holding full-time jobs or attending school. It is not uncommon for family members such as grandparents, aunts, uncles, and even cousins to live under the same roof. This "extended family" is very loyal and affords stability and security to each of its members. Most relatives outside the nucler family live in the same city and often in the same neighborhood.

The importance of family relationships is reflected in the following words for which there is no equivalent in English. If Paco and Ileana are married, Paco's parents are the **consuegros** of Ileana's parents. Paco's brother Miguel is a **cuñado** to Ileana and a **concuñado** to Ileana's brother José or Ileana's sister Ivette. In other words, the two sets of parents of the couple are **consuegros,** and the two sets of brothers and sisters of the couple are **concuñados (con** = *with*; *joint in-laws*).

Finally, if Paco and Ileana have a child, Evita, and they ask Paco's brother Miguel to be Evita's godfather **(padrino)** and Ileana's sister Ivette to be the godmother **(madrina)**, then Miguel and Ivette are **compadres,** because they jointly share the joy and responsibility of the child.

How does the Hispanic notion of extended family compare with yours?

¿Cuántas personas hay en la familia?

¿Tienen nietos?

¡Así es la vida!

Entre jóvenes

LAURA: Aló.

RAÚL: Sí, con Laura, por favor.

LAURA: Habla Laura.

RAÚL: Laura, es Raúl. ¿Cómo estás?

LAURA: Muy bien. ¡Qué sorpresa!

RAÚL: Pues, voy a pasear por el centro. ¿Quieres ir?

LAURA: Prefiero conversar en un café.

RAÚL: Está bien. Y después, en el Cine Rialto dan una de tus películas favoritas, *Lágrimas de amor*....

LAURA: ¡Sí! Pues vamos. ¿A qué hora es la función?

RAÚL: Es a las siete.

LAURA: De acuerdo. Vamos al cine.

En una fiesta

117

Vocabulario y expresiones

Actividades y pasatiempos

bailar en la fiesta	to dance at the party
bailar en la discoteca	to dance at the discotheque
conversar en un café	to chat at a cafe
correr por el parque	to run/jog in the park
dar un paseo	to take a stroll
ir al cine	to go to the movies
ir a la playa	to go to the beach
pasear por el centro	to stroll downtown
visitar	to visit
tomar el sol	to sunbathe

Verbos (e → ie)

comenzar	to begin
entender	to understand
pensar	to think
preferir	to prefer
querer	to want; to love
venir	to come

Cómo hacer una invitación

¿Vamos a...?	Should we go to...?
¿Quieres ir a...?	Do you want to go to...?
¿Puedes ir a...?	Can you go to...?

Cómo rechazar una invitación

Gracias, pero no puedo:...	Thanks, but I can't...
Lo siento, tengo que...	I'm sorry, I have to...

Cómo aceptar una invitación

Está bien, vamos.	O.K., let's go.
Me encantaría.	I would love to.
Sí, claro.	Yes, of course.

Otras palabras y expresiones

aló	hello (telephone)
contigo	with you
de acuerdo	fine with me; O.K.
la función	the show
la lágrima	tear
la orquesta	orchestra
pasar	to go by
solo(a)	alone
la sorpresa	surprise
vamos	let's go
la verdad	truth

Invitación a Una Boda

Lo siento, tengo que...

◆◆◆◆◆◆◆◆◆◆◆◆◆◆◆◆◆◆◆◆◆◆◆◆◆◆◆◆◆

¡Así lo decimos!

El teléfono

In Canada and the U.S., we generally say *Hello?* when our home phone rings. Throughout the Spanish-speaking world, there are a handful of expressions that are generally understood, but some countries have a typical way of answering the phone at home.

Argentina, Uruguay	**hola**
Cuba	**dígame, oigo**
Guatemala, Perú, Puerto Rico, Venezuela	**¿Aló?**
España	**dígame, diga**
México	**bueno**

El sol

In general, the majority of these expressions mening *to sunbathe* will be understood anywhere. However, most countries tend to show a preference for certain expressions.

to sunbathe

Argentina	**tomar sol**
Cuba	**coger sol**
España	**tomar el sol, broncearse**
Guatemala	**asolearse, broncearse**
México	**tostarse, asolearse, hacerse a la lagartija**
Puerto Rico	**quemarse**

¡A escuchar!

Una invitación. Listen to the phone conversation in **¡Así es la vida!** Then, listen to the questions that follow and match them with the correct answer. Read the rejoinders before starting.

____ a. ¿Adónde?

____ b. No, me gusta más el plan original.

____ c. Pues por la noche me encantaría ir al cine a ver "Contigo en Acapulco".

____ d. ¡Ay, sí! Me encantaría. Está un poco triste en el hospital.

____ e. Es a las 9:30 de la noche.

____ f. Estoy un poco aburrida de estar en casa.

◆ Práctica

3-21 Los pasatiempos. Form complete sentences with elements from the columns below.

1. Nosotros corremos…	a. en una discoteca
2. Alicia toma el sol…	b. en la boda
3. Voy a ver una película…	c. en el cine
4. ¿Hoy visitas…?	d. en un café
5. La fiesta está cerca…	e. del parque
6. Nosotras vamos…	f. por el parque
7. Me gusta conversar…	g. a la playa
8. Qué divertido es bailar…	h. por la playa
9. Vamos a tomar champán…	i. en la playa
10. Yo camino todos los días…	j. a tu abuela

3-22 ¿Aló? Complete the following telephone conversation between Aurelio and Noemí with words from the list. Do not use any word more than once.

aburrida	que	dar	paso
madrina	contigo	pasear	sorpresa
puedes	orquesta	sol	encantaría
acuerdo	siento	divertida	presentando
más			visitar

AURELIO: ¡Hola! ¿Cómo estás?

NOEMÍ: Más o menos, un poco _____.

AURELIO: ¿Quieres ir a la playa a tomar el _____ esta tarde?

NOEMÍ: Lo _____. Me _____, pero tengo _____ visitar a una tía que está en el hospital. Es tía Eulalia, mi _____. De todos mis tíos y tías, ella es la _____ alegre.

AURELIO: Sí, es cierto, es muy simpática tu tía. Bueno, ¿por qué no voy _____ y después vamos a _____ un paseo por la ciudad.

NOEMÍ: ¡Ay, sí, qué bueno! Vamos a _____ a tía Eulalia y a _____ por el centro.

AURELIO: De _____. _____ por ti a las 2:15. Ah, y están _____ una película de misterio en el Cine San Miguel. ¿_____ ir el sábado?

NOEMÍ: No. Tengo una _____ para ti. Hay una fiesta con _____ en el club. Es muy elegante y va a ser muy _____. Quieres ir, ¿verdad?

AURELIO: Sí claro, pero me gusta más estar solo contigo.

◆ Actividades

3-23 Conversación. Invite two members of your class to a party. One declines
the invitation and gives you a reason; the other accepts your invitation. Use the
expressions in **Vocabulario y expresiones.**

3-24 El fin de semana. In groups of four, make plans for this coming weekend.
Use the following questions to guide your decision.

1. Where are you going to go?
2. Who is going?
3. What are you going to do there?
4. On what day are you going?
5. At what time will everybody arrive?

Pronunciación ────────────────────

Sounds of Spanish *j* and *g*

- The Spanish **j** is pronounced like a forceful English *h* in the word *hat*. The letter
  x, in words such as **Xavier** and **México,** is pronounced like the **j** sound.

jamón	**Texas**	**caja**
jugar	**Jaime**	**jarra**

- The letter **g** has three distinct sounds.

  a. Before **e** or **i** it is pronounced like the **j.**

gitano	**agitar**	**gemir**
Germán		

  a. At the start of a breath group or after **n,** the combinations **ga, go, gu, gue**
  and **gui** are pronounced like the English *g* as in *gate*.

guerra	**gol**	**mango**
ganar	**guitarra**	**manga**

  c. Everywhere else (except with **ge** and **gi**) the sound is weaker.

suegra	**agricultura**	**agua**
albergue	**ogro**	**negro**

 Estructuras

3. Stem-changing Verbs (e→ie)

Some verbs require a change in the stem vowel of the present indicative form in the first, second, and third person singular, and in the third person plural, when the stress falls on the stem. Note the conjugation of **querer.**

querer *(to want, to love)*			
yo	qu**ie**ro	nosotros(as)	queremos
tú	qu**ie**res	vosotros(as)	queréis
usted él ella	qu**ie**re	ustedes ellos ellas	qu**ie**ren

- Some common regular **e → ie** verbs are:

    pensar, preferir, entender, comenzar

- Some irregular, stem-changing **e → ie** verbs such as **tener,** which you studied in **Lección 1**, are also irregular in the first person singular. Notice the insertion of the **g** between the stem and the ending in the first person singular in the verb **venir.**

venir *(to come)*			
yo	ven**g**o	nosotros(as)	venimos
tú	v**ie**nes	vosotros(as)	venís
usted él ella	v**ie**ne	ustedes ellos ellas	v**ie**nen

◆ Práctica

3-25 María y Pedro. María and Pedro Janzow have plans for the weekend but there is a slight problem. Find out what it is by completing the paragraph with the correct form of a logical verb.

comenzar	pensar	querer
entender	preferir	tener

Mi esposo y yo _____ planes para este fin de semana. Nosotros _____ ir al cine el sábado por la noche. Pedro _____ ver una película cómica porque no _____ las películas de misterio. Yo _____ las películas de misterio y _____ ir a ver una. ¡Qué problemas! Las dos películas _____ a las nueve. ¿Qué _____ tú de esta situación? _____ Uds. venir con nosotros? ¿Qué _____ Uds.?

3-26 En la universidad. Complete the paragraph by choosing the right word from the list.

comienza	gustan	tiene
comienzan	hay	tienen
conversar	piensa	viene
entiende	prefiero	vienen
entiendo	quiero	venir

Las clases de la universidad _____ hoy. Todos los estudiantes _____ que tomar las humanidades: historia, filosofía y castellano. También _____ que tomar una ciencia. Yo no _____ por qué. No me _____ las ciencias. _____ las letras y las artes. Mamá sí *(does)* _____ y ella _____ que debo tener una actitud más positiva. Ella _____ razón, pero yo _____ tomar muchas clases de sicología, antropología, etc. Mamá y papá _____ de Santiago el sábado y vamos a _____ de mis estudios. Mi hermanita Lucía también _____ a visitarme. Ella _____ la secundaria la semana próxima *(next)*. Está muy contenta de _____ a visitar mi universidad.

3-27 En la cafetería. Match each item in the left-hand column with a logical completion or rejoinder to the right.

1. Pienso ir a la playa esta tarde.
2. No entienden que tengo que estudiar.
3. ¿Mañana vienes a la cafetería?
4. ¿Qué tienes que hacer por la noche?
5. Mañana vengo tarde a casa.
6. ¿Qué prefieres, el cine o un paseo?
7. ¿A qué hora comienzan las clases?
8. No entiendo la lección de álgebra.
9. ¿Viene tu hermano el lunes?
10. ¿Comenzamos a correr?

a. Nada. ¿Quieres ir a la discoteca a bailar?
b. No, quiere venir el jueves.
c. Creo que al mediodía.
d. Me gusta pasear por el parque.
e. Quiero consultar con el profesor.
f. Aquí no. Prefiero en el parque sin carros.
g. Prefiero el restaurante chino.
h. ¿Quieres venir?
i. Si quieres, estudiamos juntos.
j. Quiero ver *Schindler's List* en cablecolor.

◆ Actividades

3-28 La fiesta de graduación. You are organizing a graduation party for a friend. Discuss your plans with a classmate.

1. ¿Cuándo piensas dar la fiesta?
2. ¿A qué hora comienza la fiesta?
3. ¿Vienen todos sus amigos?
4. ¿Piensas invitar a los padres de tu amigo(a)?
5. ¿Quiénes más *(else)* vienen a la fiesta?
6. ¿Tienes un estéreo?
7. ¿Qué música prefieres para la fiesta?
8. ¿Qué quieres darle de regalo *(gift)* de graduación?

3-29 Una entrevista. Interview a fellow student and find out the information below. Then write a brief summary of his/her responses.

1. si entiende las películas en español
2. el tipo de película que prefiere ver
3. la película que piensa ver el viernes, sábado o domingo
4. la hora que comienza la película
5. quiénes van a ver la película

3-30 Las películas. In groups of 3 or 4, read the movie listings. Decide which movie each of you wants to see and explain your reasons. Select one member in your group to report to the class which movie is the most popular.

MODELO: Quiero ver *La casa de los espíritus* porque prefiero las películas cómicas.

★★**Delicias turcas**, de *Paul Verhoeven*. En su momento causó cierto escándalo en Europa, y hoy se une ese aliciente al de la posterior carrera de su realizador, autor de **Robocop**. Comedia.

★★**Hombres, hombres...**, de *Doris Dörrie*. Oportunidad de repescar algo tan insólito como una comedia alemana. Dörrie ha seguido después una trayectoria irregular, pero este vodevil sobre lo peculiares que son los hombres cara a los celos tiene mucha miga. Comedia.

★★★**Adiós, muchachos**, de *Louis Malle*. El director francés, curtido en el cine americano, vuelve a sus raíces con una historia autobiográfica sobre la ocupación alemana, relatada con emoción. Drama.

★**Las aventuras del barón Munchausen**, de *Terry Gillian*. El creador de **Brazil** vuelve con una comedia disparatada, ideada especialmente para los críos: la historia del oficial de caballería que dijo haber estado en la Luna. Comedia.

★★★**Salaam Bombay**, de *Mira Nair*. Una imagen real de la India, rodada con gente de la calle y sin concesiones a lo que en Occidente se entiende por melodrama. Drama.

4. Summary of uses of *ser* and *estar*

Ser

- **Ser** is used with the preposition **de** to indicate origin, possession, and to describe physical characteristics.

Evelio **es de** Guatemala.	*Evelio **is from** Guatemala.*
Es una camisa **de** seda.	*It's a silk shirt.*
Los libros **son de** Luisa.	*The books **are** Luisa's.*

- When combined with an adjective, **ser** expresses characteristics that define the subject such as size, color, shape, religion, nationality and occupation.

Tomás **es** alto y delgado.	*Tomás **is** tall and thin.*
Los jóvenes **son** católicos.	*The young men **are** Catholic.*
Somos españolas.	*We **are** Spaniards.*
Mi hermana **es** abogada.	*My sister **is** a lawyer.*

- **Ser** indicates where and/or when events take place.

La fiesta **es** en mi casa el viernes.	*The party **is** at my house on Friday.*

- **Ser** is also used to express dates, days of the week, months, seasons of the year, and time.

Es el 28 de octubre.	*It's October 28.*
Son las cinco de la tarde.	*It's five o'clock in the afternoon.*

Estar

- **Estar** indicates location of persons and objects.

La librería **está** detrás de la cafetería.	*The bookstore **is** behind the cafeteria.*
Rosa **está** en el hotel.	*Rosa **is** at the hotel.*

- **Estar** is used with the **-ndo** form of the main verb to form the progressive construction.

Carlos y Ana **están comiendo.**	*Carlos and Ana **are eating**.*

- **Estar** is used with adjectives to describe the state or condition of the subject.

Las chicas **están** contentas.	*The girls **are** happy.*
Pedro **está** enfermo.	*Pedro **is** sick.*

Some adjectives have different meanings when used with **ser** or **estar**.

WITH *ser*	ADJECTIVE	WITH *estar*
to be good, kind	**bueno(a)**	*to be well, fit, recovered*
to be funny	**divertido(a)**	*to be amused*
to be clever	**listo(a)**	*to be ready*
to be bad, evil	**malo(a)**	*to be sick, ill*
to be handsome	**guapo(a)**	*to look handsome*
to be pretty	**bonito(a)**	*to look pretty*
to be ugly	**feo(a)**	*to look ugly*
to be alert, smart	**vivo(a)**	*to be alive*

◆ Práctica

3-31 ¿Dónde está Juancho? Complete the sentences with the correct form of **ser** or **estar**. Then arrange them in a logical order to find out what Juancho is doing.

___ La comida _____ a las ocho.

___ En casa viven los abuelos, los padres, y cinco hijos.

___ Hoy _____ sábado y (yo) _____ en la casa de mi amigo Roberto.

___ La hija menor tiene cuatro años y todavía _____ con su mamá.

___ Los abuelos _____ mexicanos, pero los padres _____ de aquí.

___ En este momento la mamá _____ preparando comida para todos: chiles rellenos, que _____ su especialidad.

___ Roberto vive en un pueblo que _____ cerca de aquí.

___ Cuando todos (nosotros) _____ ella sirve la comida. ¡_____ deliciosa!

___ La casa _____ grande porque su familia _____ grande.

3-32 La familia Andrade. Use the correct form of **ser** or **estar** to complete the descripton of the Andrade family.

La familia Andrade _____ una familia hispana que ahora _____ en Pasadena. Raúl, el papá, _____ mexicano y muy trabajador. Graciela, la mamá, _____ uruguaya y _____ muy amable. Ellos tienen tres hijos. Francisco _____ muy responsable y _____ en el Pasadena Community College. María _____ muy inteligente y _____ en la Universidad de California, Los Angeles. Marc _____ todavía muy joven. Esta noche la familia _____ muy contenta porque ellos van a un concierto. El concierto _____ a las nueve de la noche. _____ en el un estadio que _____ cerca de su casa. Ya _____ hora de salir y todos _____ listos.

3–33 Una boda. Complete the description of Aureliano and Rebeca's wedding with the appropriate form (which may sometimes be the infinitive), of verbs **ser** or **estar**.

La boda de Aureliano y Rebeca _____ el 25 de abril. Los padrinos _____ don Armando y doña Soledad, y el mejor amigo _____ Ramón, el primo de Aureliano. Ramón _____ de Guatemala pero ahora _____ trabajando aquí. Viene toda la familia y muchos amigos.

La novia _____ muy bonita y amable. _____ estudiando pedagogía en la Universidad Nacional. El novio no _____ guapo, pero _____ el hombre más trabajador del mundo. Ahora _____ trabajando para la compañía Tricorisa. Los padres de Rebeca _____ muy contentos con él. Los novios _____ nerviosos porque hay mucho que hacer. Ahora _____ pensando en la música. Quieren música para bailar, y la Orquesta Salomón _____ la mejor orquesta de salsa de la ciudad.

La boda _____ en la Iglesia de los Ángeles que _____ al lado del Salón Señorial. _____ muy conveniente porque la boda _____ a las cinco de la tarde, la fiesta comienza a las 6:30 y el Salón Señorial _____ al lado de la iglesia. Va a _____ una fiesta muy bonita.

◆ Actividades

3-34 Describir. Get together with several classmates and describe what you see in the photos using **ser** and **estar.**

3-35 Un(a) compañero(a) de clase. Write a description of one of your friends to present the rest to the class. You might mention their

- age
- physical features
- place of origin
- where he/she is now
- what he/she is like as a person

3-36 Conversación. With a partner, ask each other the following questions.

1. ¿De dónde eres?
2. ¿Qué estás estudiando?
3. ¿Qué clases estás tomando?
4. ¿Estás contento(a) con tus clases?
5. ¿Dónde son tus clases?
6. ¿Qué estás pensando hacer el año próximo *(next)?*
7. ¿Qué estás pensando hacer para tu graduación?
8. ¿Cómo es tu compañero(a) de cuarto?
9. ¿Cómo es tu cuarto?
10. ¿Dónde está tu cuarto, en una residencia estudiantil, apartamento o casa?

3-37 En grupo. One student gives a clue and another turns it into a complete sentence anyway he or she wants. Walk around the class and take turns providing clues and creating complete sentences. If given the same clue twice, try to come up with a different sentence each time.

MODELO: estoy estudiando
          Estoy estudiando lenguas y música.

1. estoy viviendo…
2. el (la) profesor(a) es…
3. La clase de…es…
4. Los estudiantes están…
5. Tú y yo estamos…
6. Estoy pensando en…
7. Soy…
8. Nosotros…

Colaboración

Estudiante A

3-38A La familia. With a partner, take turns asking and answering questions about this family. If there are any differences, write them down.

MODELO: — ¿Cómo se llama el abuelo?
— Se llama…

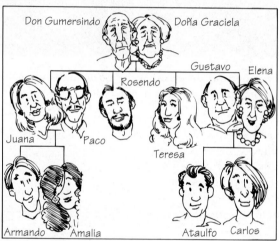

3-39A La familia real española. With a partner, complete the family tree of the Spanish Royal family.

MODELO: —¿Cómo se llama el abuelo de Juan Carlos?
— Se llama…

La familia real española

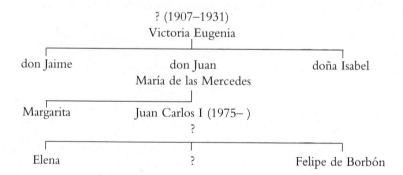

Now answer these questions:

1. ¿Quién es Juan Carlos I?

2. ¿Quién es María de las Mercedes?

128

3-40A ¿Qué prefieres? Interview a classmate. Write down his/her answers.

MODELO: —¿Prefieres Coca Cola o cerveza?
                — Prefiero…

preferir	té frío o caliente	café con leche o solo
querer	vivir en una ciudad grande o en un pueblo pequeño	pasar las vacaciones en la playa o en las montañas
tener que	preparar la tarea o leer	escribir una carta o llamar a un amigo.

3-41A ¿Con qué frecuencia…? Interview a classmate. Then work together and write a summary of your findings.

MODELO: —¿Con qué frecuencia escribes cartas?
                —Nunca *(never)* escribo cartas.

ACTIVIDAD	TODOS LOS DÍAS	MUCHO	POCO	UNA VEZ AL MES	CASI NUNCA	NUNCA
hablar por teléfono						
comer comida española						
leer novelas de detectives						
escribir poesía						
asistir a clase						
escribir cartas						

Estudiante B

3-38B La familia. With a partner, take turns asking and answering questions about this family. If there are any differences, write them down.

MODELO: — ¿Cómo se llama el abuelo?
           — Se llama…

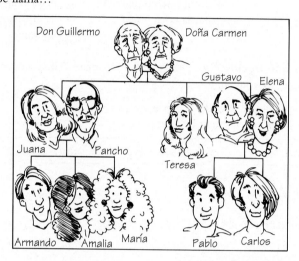

3-39B La familia real española. With a partner, complete the family tree of the Spanish Royal family.

MODELO: —¿Cómo se llama el abuelo de Juan Carlos?
           — Se llama…

La familia real española

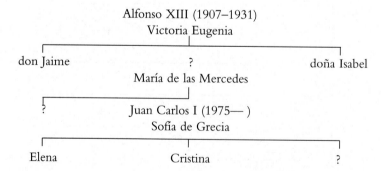

Now answer these questions:

1. ¿Quién es don Jaime?   2. ¿Quién es Elena?

3-40B ¿Qué prefieres? Interview a classmate. Write down his/her answers.

MODELO: — ¿Prefieres Coca Cola o cerveza?
          — Prefiero…

preferir	vino o agua mineral	ver una película romántica o una película de horror
querer	vivir en los Estados Unidos o en otro país	escuchar música o las noticias
tener ganas de	comer comida mexicana o italiana	tomar cerveza o coca cola

3-41B ¿Con qué frecuencia…? Interview a classmate. Then work together and write a summary of your findings.

MODELO: —¿Con qué frecuencia escribes cartas?
          —Nunca *(never)* escribo cartas.

ACTIVIDAD	TODOS LOS DÍAS	MUCHO	POCO	UNA VEZ AL MES	CASI NUNCA	NUNCA
beber cerveza						
leer el periódico						
insistir en hablar inglés						
recibir cartas						
comer pizza						
ir al cine						

 # Mundo hispánico

México

México es una de las naciones que ofrece más contrastes, variedad y creatividad. Además de ciudades coloniales del siglo XVI, catedrales barrocas y elegantes haciendas, tiene edificios ultra modernos como el Centro Bursátil y la Torre Latinoamericana en el Distrito Federal. México tiene artistas y artesanos en abundancia, música y danza de muchos tipos y comidas exóticas.

Datos básicos de México

Nombre oficial: Estados Unidos Mexicanos
Población: 91.000.000
Ciudades principales: Ciudad de México, Guadalajara, Monterrey, Netzahualcóyotl , Tijuana, Puebla.
Grupos étnicos y raciales: Mestizos 60%, indígenas 30%, europeos 9%

Arqueología

- Más de 14.000 ruinas arquelógicas
- las ruinas toltecas de Teotihuacán, con su magnífica Pirámide del Sol
- las ruinas olmecas en la costa del Golfo de México
- las ruinas mayas de Chichén Itzá y Palenque en la jungla de Chiapas y la Península de Yucatán
- las ruinas de Montealbán y de Mitla en Oaxaca
- El Museo de Antropología, uno de los más importantes del mundo en historia precolombina

Ciudades pintorescas

- Guanajuato
- Mérida
- Morelia
- Cuernavaca
- San Miguel de Allende
- Puebla
- Oaxaca
- Taxco

Artesanía famosa

- sarapes[1]—Saltillo
- alfarería[2]—Oaxaca y Puebla
- platería[3]—Taxco
- cestos y hamacas—Mérida

[1]shawls   [2]pottery   [3]silver crafts

Playas

- Cancún, Cozumel e Isla Mujeres en la Península de Yucatán
- Acapulco, Puerto Vallarta y Mazatlán en la costa del Pacífico

Comidas

- tacos, burritos, enchiladas, chalupas
- mole, frijoles, tortillas, cochinita pibil

Arte y literatura

- Música de mariachis y otros ritmos tradicionales
- Ballet Folklórico de México
- *Murales y pintura:* José Clemente Orozco (1883–1949), Diego Rivera (1886-1957), *Mercado de Tenochtitlán;* David Alfaro Siqueiros (1896–1974), *Historia de la humanidad*; Rufino Tamayo (1900–1991), *El cantante;* y Frida Kahlo (1910–1954), *Autorretrato.*
- *Escritores famosos:* Sor Juana Inés de la Cruz (1651–1695), poetisa y monja, *Inundación castálida;* Octavio Paz (1914–), escritor y diplomático, *El laberinto de la soledad, Piedra del sol* (ensayo), Premio Nóbel 1990; Juan Rulfo (1918–1986), escritor, *Pedro Páramo* (novela); Carlos Fuentes (1928–), esctitor, *La muerte de Artemio Cruz* (novela); Elena Poniatowska (1933–), escritora y periodista, *La noche de Tlatelolco* (ensayo); José Emilio Pacheco (1939 -), escritor, *Ayer es nunca jamás* (poesía); Laura Esquivel (1950–), escritora, *Como agua para chocolate* (novela).

◆ Actividades

3-42 ¿Cierto o falso? Correct any false statements.

1. México tiene menos de 90.000.000 de habitantes.
2. México es nuestro vecino del norte.
3. La tierra de los mayas está en la costa del Pacífico.
4. Chichén Itzá es una ruina maya.
5. La vida en estas ciudades es muy tranquila.
6. Cada región de México tiene una artesanía diferente.
7. Mazatlán es el mejor lugar para observar el mundo submarino.
8. La cochinita pibil es una comida exótica.
9. Octavio Paz es diplomático.
10. Laura Esquivel escribe novelas.

3-43 ¿Qué es?

1. Cozumel
2. Guanajuato
3. Pirámide del Mago en Uxmal, Yucatán
4. sarapes de Saltillo
5. chalupas
6. Centro Bursátil
7. Chichén Itzá
8. Isla mujeres
9. cerámica de Puebla
10. La Torre Latinoamericana

a. ruina arqueológica
b. arquitectura moderna
c. playa turística
d. ciudad pintoresca
e. artesanía
f. comida

Lección 4

¡A divertirnos!

Comunicación

- Making Suggestions
- Reacting to Suggestions
- More on Extending and Responding to Invitations
- Expressing Interest, Emotion, and Indifference

Cultura

- **Las diversiones**
- **Los deportes**

Mundo hispánico: América del Sur

Estructuras

Primera parte

- The Present Tense of **salir**, **ver**, **traer**, **decir, poner**, and **hacer**
- **saber** and **conocer**
- Direct Object Pronouns and the Personal **a**

Segunda parte

- The Present Tense of Stem-changing Verbs: **o → ue** and **e → i**
- Indirect Object Pronouns and Prepositional Pronouns
- The Verb **dar**

PRIMERA PARTE
¡Así es la vida!

El fin de semana

Escena 1

Karen Banks, Ricardo Rubio, Linnette Ortiz y Scott Breslow estudian en la Universidad de Puerto Rico. Es sábado por la mañana.

RICARDO: Oye, Karen, ¿por qué no vamos al partido de básquetbol?

KAREN: No sé. Hoy hace buen tiempo y no quiero estar dentro de un gimnasio.

RICARDO: Tienes razón. ¿Qué tal si vamos a la feria internacional?

KAREN: ¡Buena idea! Pero, mira, allí están Scott y Linnette. Vamos a ver qué piensan hacer ellos.

Escena 2

KAREN: Hola, ¿qué piensan hacer hoy?

LINNETTE: Pues, hoy es un día perfecto para ir a la playa.
Hace sol y mucho calor. ¿Por qué no vamos a Luquillo a nadar en el mar y después hacemos un picnic?

RICARDO: ¡Estupendo!

SCOTT: Yo hago los sándwiches.

LINNETTE: No, mejor los hago yo.

SCOTT: Entonces, yo voy a comprar los refrescos.

KAREN: ¿Y quién trae la sombrilla?

RICARDO: Yo la traigo.

Hoy es un día perfecto.

Escena 3

Al llegar a la playa.

KAREN: ¿Qué te parece si nadamos?

SCOTT: ¡Fabuloso! Está ideal para nadar.

LINNETTE: Oye, Scott, ¿dónde está la bolsa con los trajes de baño? No la veo en el baúl.

SCOTT: ¡Qué desgracia! Están en la residencia de estudiantes.

LINETTE: ¡Qué suerte la nuestra! No vamos a poder nadar en el mar.

RICARDO: Pero podemos cantar con la guitarra.

¿Dónde está la bolsa…?

135

Vocabulario y expresiones

Actividades

dar	*to give*
dar un paseo	*to take a walk*
hacer la cama	*to make the bed*
las compras	*to do the shopping*
los ejercicios	*to exercise*
los mandados	*to run errands*
un pícnic	*to have a picnic*
una merienda	
ir a un concierto	*to go to a concert*
un partido	*to go to a game*
llevar	*to wear*
nadar en el mar	*to swim in the ocean*
poner atención	*to pay attention*
la mesa	*to set the table*
la música	*to play music*
la radio	*to turn on the radio*
tocar música	*to play music*
ver la televisión	*to watch television*

Cómo pedir opiniones y sugerencias

¿Por qué no vamos...?	*Why don't we go...?*
¿Qué piensas...?	*What do you think?*
¿Qué crees...?	*What do you think?*
¿Qué tal si...?	*What if . . .?*
¿Qué te parece?	*What do you think?*

Cómo reaccionar ante opiniones y sugerencias

Es una buena/mala idea.	*It's a good/bad idea.*
Estoy de acuerdo.	*I agree.*
¡Estupendo!	*Terrific!*
¡Ideal!	*Ideal!*
¡Magnífico!	*Great! Wonderful!*
¡Qué desgracia!	*How unfortunate!*
Tienes razón.	*You're right.*
No tienes razón.	*You're wrong.*
No sé.	*I don't know.*
Me da igual.	*It's all the same to me.*

Palabras para conectar

además	*besides*
a menudo	*often*
a veces	*sometimes*
casi	*almost*
durante	*during, for*
luego	*then*
ni...ni	*either/neither...or/nor*
por eso	*for that reason, that's why*
siempre	*always*

Otras palabras y expresiones

adentro	*inside*
afuera	*outside*
los apuntes	*notes*
el baúl	*trunk*
la bolsa	*bag*
el cesto	*basket*
el disco compacto	*compact disk*
el estéreo	*stereo*
la heladera	*cooler*
el hielo	*ice*
listo(a)	*ready*
nada	*nothing*
otro(a, os, as)	*other, another*
saludar	*to say hello*
la sombrilla	*beach umbrella*
la televisión (la tele)	*television*
temprano	*early*
el tiempo	*weather, time*
la toalla	*towel*
el tocacassettes	*cassette player*
todo(a)	*everything*
todos(as)	*all, everyone*
el traje de baño	*bathing suit*

¡Así lo decimos!

me da igual

There are various ways to say that something is not important to you.
In addition to **me da igual**, most countries also use **me da lo mismo**,
¿Qué me importa?, or **me importa un bledo**. Other interesting
variations are listed below.

Cuba	**Me importa un pito...**
España	**Me tiene sin cuidado...**
México	**Me vale...**

Me tiene sin cuidado lo que pienses.
It doesn't matter to me what you may think.

hacer mandados

In many countries **hacer mandados** is the typical expression for *to run
errands* (especially *to buy things*), and while it would generally be understood
in the countries listed below, other expressions are normally used.

Argentina ⎫	
Colombia ⎪	
Cuba ⎬	**hacer diligencias**
Venezuela ⎭	
España	**hacer un encargo**, **hacer un recado**
México	**ir al mandado**

If the purpose of the errand is to process paperwork (e.g., paying bills), the
general expression is **hacer trámites** or **hacer una gestión**.

Ampliación

Para hablar del clima

The verb **hacer** *(to do* or *to make)* is used in the third person singular with weather
expressions in Spanish.

¿Qué tiempo hace?	*What's the weather like?*
Hace buen tiempo.	*It's nice out.*
Hace (mucho) calor.	*It's (very) hot.*
Hace (mucho) frío.	*It's (very) cold.*
Hace (mucho) sol.	*It's (very) sunny.*
Hace (mucho) viento.	*It's (very) windy.*
Hace fresco.	*It's cool.*
Hace mal tiempo.	*The weather is bad.*

- **Hace** is not used when talking about rain or snow, but rather **llueve**
  (it's raining) and **nieva** *(it's snowing)*.

📼 ¡A escuchar!

El fin de semana. You will hear the conversations that appear in **¡Así es la vida!**. Complete the sentences that follow each conversation by choosing the appropriate answer.

Escena 1

1. a. estar adentro   b. estar afuera   c. estudiar
2. a. un partido de béisbol b. una fiesta   c. una feria

Escena 2

3. a. hace muy buen tiempo   b. llueve   c. hace fresco
4. a. las hamburguesas   b. la sombrilla   c. jugo y leche

Escena 3

5. a. muy malo   b. difícil   c. fabuloso
6. a. la residencia de estudiantes   b. el baúl   c. la casa de Linnette

◆ Práctica

4–1 ¿Qué hacer? Some friends are talking about their plans for the weekend. Complete their statements below with an appropriate word from **Vocabulario y expresiones.**

1. Yo quiero ir a escuchar música. Voy a un _____.
2. Hace buen tiempo. ¿Por qué no vamos al parque, llevamos sándwiches y hacemos un _____?
3. Hoy hace sol. Voy a dar un _____ por el parque.
4. Los refrescos están en la _____.
5. El sábado va a hacer mucho calor. ¿Por qué no vamos a nadar en el _____?
6. El domingo hay un _____ de básquetbol en el gimnasio.
7. El sábado dan una película muy buena. ¿Qué te _____ si vamos?
8. Va a ser un fin de semana magnífico, ni mucho calor ni mucho _____.
9. Hace frío. No es un buen día para ir a la _____.
10. Los trajes de baño están en la bolsa, las frutas en el _____.

4–2 El tiempo. Describe the weather in each drawing using expressions from **Vocabulario y expresiones.**

1.   2.   3.   4.   5.

4–3 Las entradas. Your professor has two tickets to give away and she has just offered you one. Answer the following questions to help you decide which of the tickets below you will accept.

1. ¿Qué hay en el Centro Cultural Conde Duque?
2. ¿En qué ciudad es el Festival Internacional?
3. ¿En qué ciudad es el ballet?
4. ¿Cuándo es el ballet?
5. ¿Cómo se llama la orquesta que va a tocar en el festival?
6. ¿A qué hora es la actividad en el Conde Duque?
7. ¿Cuándo toca la orquesta? ¿A qué hora?
8. ¿Cuánto cuesta el ballet? ¿la orquesta?
9. ¿A cuál de estas actividades quieres ir?

4–4 ¡Emparejar! Match the words and expressions in the lefthand column with those in the righthand column.

_____ 1. hace frío	a. en el mar
_____ 2. ¡Ganamos!	b. en la playa
_____ 3. un partido	c. diciembre, enero, febrero
_____ 4. el otoño	d. en una discoteca
_____ 5. el tenis	e. hay refrescos en la heladera
_____ 6. hacer un picnic	f. llueve
_____ 7. bailar	g. nieva
_____ 8. Me da	h. septiembre, octubre, noviembre
_____ 9. hace mal tiempo	i. igual
_____ 10. hace calor	j. una raqueta
_____ 11. nadar	k. de básquetbol
_____ 12. el invierno	l. ¡Estupendo!

◆ Actividades

4–5 Situaciones. In pairs, develop each situation by writing the questions your friends would ask and the answers you would give.

1. Your friends invite you to a concert, but you are not sure whether you want to go or not.
2. You have forgotten to bring your bathing suit to a beach party.
3. You want to go to the beach today but would like to find out if your roommate knows what the weather will be like.
4. It's a nice day and your professor suggests holding class outside.
5. A friend is in charge of organizing an outing and he/she wants to know who is bringing what. You and other friends volunteer.

4–6 No es verdad. With a classmate, make five statements about the weather. Your partner will contradict you every time. Follow the model.

MODELO:　—Nieva.
　　　　　—No es verdad, llueve.

4–7 Entrevista. Use the following questions to guide your conversation with several students in the class.

1. ¿Qué haces cuando hace calor?
2. ¿Qué haces cuando llueve?
3. ¿Qué haces cuando hace mucho frío?
4. ¿Qué haces cuando hace fresco?
5. ¿Qué haces cuando nieva?
6. ¿Qué haces cuando hace buen tiempo?

Pronunciación

The Sounds of Spanish *r* and *rr*

The Spanish **r** has two distinct sounds. The **rr** represents a strongly trilled sound produced by having the tip of the tongue strike behind the upper front teeth in a series of rapid vibrations. A single **r** at the beginning of a word or after the consonants **l, n** or **s,** is pronounced like the **rr.**

Roberto	**repetir**	**correr**	**cerro**
cerrar	**ratón**	**enredo**	**Israel**

The single **r** in all other positions is pronounced with one "flap" of the tongue against the gums directly behind the upper front teeth. The sound is similar to the English *dd* and *tt* in the words *ladder* and *putter*.

cero	**oro**	**arena**	**abrir**
ladra	**mira**	**pero**	**cara**

Estructuras

1. **The Present Indicative of** *decir,* *hacer,* *poner,* *salir,*
   traer, **and** *ver.*

- Some Spanish verbs are irregular in the present tense *only* in the first person
  singular form (the **yo**-form). All other forms follow the regular conjugation
  patterns. **Decir** is also an **e → i** stem-changing verb..

		YO	TÚ	ÉL, ELLA, UD.	NOSOTROS	VOSOTROS	ELLOS, ELLAS, UDS.
decir	*(to say, to tell)*	digo	dices	dice	decimos	decís	dicen
hacer	*(to do, to make)*	hago	haces	hace	hacemos	hacéis	hacen
poner	*(to put)*	pongo	pones	pone	ponemos	ponéis	ponen
salir	*(to leave, to go out)*	salgo	sales	sale	salimos	salís	salen
traer	*(to bring)*	traigo	traes	trae	traemos	traéis	traen
ver	*(to see)*	veo	ves	ve	vemos	véis	ven

Expressions with *salir*

Salir means *to leave* and is often combined with a variety of prepositions.

- **Salir de** means *to leave a place* or *to leave on a trip.*

    Salimos de viaje el lunes.   *We **leave on** a trip on Monday.*

*(Expressions with **salir** continue on the next page.)*

- **Salir para** means *to leave for* (*a place*), *to depart*

  Mañana **salen para** Perú.   *They're **leaving** tomorrow for Perú.*

- **Salir con** means *to go out with, to date*

  Anita **sale con** Adolfo.   *Anita **is going out with** Adolfo.*

- **Salir a** means *to go out* (*to do something*)

  ¿**Sales a** caminar por la tarde?   ***Do you go out** walking in the afternoon?*

◆ Práctica

4–8 Mis planes para hoy. Complete the following paragraph using the correct first person singular form of the verbs in parentheses.

Hoy (salir) _____ para la playa con Karen muy temprano. Antes de salir, (hacer) _____ la cama y unos sándwiches para el grupo. Como hoy hace mucho calor, (traer) _____ muchos refrescos. (Poner) _____ los refrescos en la heladera. Después, (poner) _____ todo en el baúl y (ver) _____ si Karen está lista. Como queremos nadar, (poner) _____ los trajes de baño y dos toallas en la bolsa de Karen. También (traer) _____ cassettes para el carro porque siempre (poner) _____ música. Yo (decir) _____ que es mejor estar preparado para todo.

4–9 Los planes. Describe what Linnette does during the week by completing each sentence with an appropriate form of the verb **salir** and the correct preposition.

Linnette _____ Scott son novios. Los fines de semana ellos _____ sus amigos Ricardo y Karen. A menudo van a una película y después _____ comer. Ellos _____ el restaurante a las diez de la noche y después _____ bailar. Si es viernes, Marcos y yo también _____ ellos, pero después de comer no vamos a bailar. Nosotros preferimos _____ caminar. Los sábados yo _____ hacer mandados y por la noche Marcos y yo _____ cenar, si el domingo no tenemos que _____ viaje.

2. *saber* and *conocer*

Both **saber** and **conocer** translate to the English verb *to know,* but they are not interchangeable.

saber			
yo	**sé**	nosotros	**sabemos**
tú	**sabes**	vosotros	**sabéis**
usted		ustedes	
él	**sabe**	ellos	**saben**
ella		ellas	

conocer			
yo	**conozco**	nosotros	**conocemos**
tú	**conoces**	vosotros	**conocéis**
usted		ustedes	
él	**conoce**	ellos	**conocen**
ella		ellas	

- **Saber** means *to know a fact* or *to have knowledge or information* about someone or something.

  No **sé** la dirección de Lily.   *I don't **know** Lily's address.*
  No **sé** el número de teléfono.   *I don't **know** the phone number.*

- When used with the infinitive, **saber** means to *know how to do something.*

  Sabemos nadar muy bien.   *We know how to swim very well.*
  ¿Sabes bailar?   *Do you know how to dance?*

- **Conocer** means *to be acquainted* or *to be familiar with a person, place, or thing.*

  ¿Conoces la Ciudad de México? *Do you know Mexico City?*
  Miriam **conoce** a Paco, pero no *Miriam knows Paco, but she doesn't*
    sabe dónde vive él.   *know where he lives.*

- **Conocer** cannot be followed by an infinitive. When it expresses *to know a specific person,* it is always followed by the preposition **a.**

  La profesora **conoce a** mi hermano. *The teacher knows my brother.*

◆ Práctica

4–10 Preguntas. Answer the following questions.

1. ¿Conoces a Gloria Estefan?
2. ¿Conoces uno o más países hispanos? ¿Cuáles?
3. ¿Sabes el número de oficina del (de la) profesor(a)?
4. ¿Sabes hablar francés?
5. ¿Qué deportes sabes jugar?
6. ¿Conoces a tu profesor bien?
7. ¿Sabes dónde está la biblioteca?
8. ¿Conoces al presidente de la universidad?

4–11 Una conversación. Lizette and Emilia are gossiping. To find out what they're saying, complete their conversation with the correct form of **saber** or **conocer.**

LIZETTE: ¿_____ a Marcela Rodríguez?

EMILIA: Bueno, _____ quién es, pero no la _____ bien.

LIZETTE: ¿_____ quien es la chica mexicana que está en una de tus clases?

EMILIA: Sí, yo _____. _____ a Marcela porque está en mi clase de biología.

LIZETTE: ¿Ah, sí? Pues, a Marcela le gusta Roberto, ¡tu hermano!

EMILIA: ¿De veras? Y, ¿a Roberto le gusta Marcela?

LIZETTE: Sí. Van al cine esta noche. Marcela y yo somos amigas, pero ella no _____ que tú eres hermana de Roberto o que eres mi amiga.

EMILIA: ¿_____ tú a los padres de Marcela? ¿_____ cuántos años tiene ella?

LIZETTE: Mis padres y yo _____ a sus padres porque viven cerca de mi abuela. Nosotros no _____ mucho de ellos, pero es una familia muy unida.

4–12 Nuestro fin de semana. Complete the paragraph about Lola and Guillermo's weekend activities by selecting words from the list below. Do not use any word more than once. Who is telling the story?

conocemos	hago	sé	traigo
decimos	pone	sale	ve
dice	ponemos	salgo	vemos
hacer	pongo	salimos	veo
hacemos	sabe	trae	

Yo _____ mucha televisión. Lola _____ que yo no _____ nada, pero no es cierto. Hay mucha información en la tele. Yo _____ las noticias *(news)* y veo programas científicos. También me gusta leer y a menudo _____ muchos libros de la biblioteca. Los sábados por la mañana Lola _____ a _____ compras y yo leo. Por la tarde yo _____ a hacer mandados y ella _____ música. Por la noche Lola y yo _____ a caminar. Luego regresamos a casa y _____ la tele, pero Lola no _____ la televisión ni me pone atención si yo hablo. Tú _____ que ella prefiere leer. Lola _____ palomitas *(popcorn)* y refrescos. Durante horas nosotros no _____ nada. Los domingos vamos al cine y _____ una película. Nosotros no _____ a otra persona con una rutina tan regular.

◆ Actividades

4–13 Preguntas. Exchange answers to the following questions with another student.

1. ¿A qué hora sales para la playa?
2. ¿Con quiénes vas a la playa?
3. ¿Quién hace los sándwiches cuando van a la playa?
4. ¿Dónde pones los refrescos?
5. ¿Quién trae la sombrilla?
6. ¿Qué ves en la playa?
7. ¿A qué hora salen de la playa?

2. Direct Object Pronouns and the Personal *a*

- The direct object is the noun directly affected by the verb. It can either be an object or a person.

Pablo va a comprar **un helado.**	*Pablo is going to buy **an ice cream.***
Anita está llamando a **su amiga Julia.**	*Anita is calling **her friend Julia.***
Veo a **Jorge** y a **Elisa** allá.	*I see **Jorge** and **Elisa** there.*

- Direct object nouns are often replaced by direct object pronouns. The chart shows the forms of the direct object pronouns.

SINGULAR		PLURAL	
me	*me*	**nos**	*us*
te	*you* (informal)	**os**	*you* (informal) (Spain)
lo	*you* (masculine), *him,* *it* (masculine)	**los**	*you* (masculine), *them*
la	*you* (feminine), *her, it* (feminine)	**las**	*you* (feminine), *them*

- Direct pronouns agree in gender and number with the noun to which they refer.

Quiero el libro.	**Lo** quiero.
Quiero los discos.	**Los** quiero.
Llamo a Teresa.	**La** llamo.
Llaman a las chicas.	**Las** llaman.

- Direct object pronouns are usually placed immediately *before* the conjugated verb.

¿Dónde ves a **Jorge** y a **Adela?**	*Where do you see **Jorge** and **Adela?***
Los veo en clase.	*I see **them** in class.*
¿Quieres **la blusa,** Mili?	*Do you want **the blouse,** Mili?*
Sí, **la** quiero.	*Yes, I want **it.***

- In constructions with the infinitive or the present progressive forms, they may either precede the conjugated verb, or be attached to the infinitive or the present participle (**-ndo**).

Adolfo va a comprar **un cesto.**	*Adolfo is going to buy **a basket.***
Adolfo va a comprar**lo.** ⎫ Adolfo **lo** va a comprar. ⎭	*Adolfo is going to buy **it.***
Ana está llamando a **Pepa.**	*Ana is calling **Pepa.***
Ana está llamándo**la.** ⎫ Ana **la** está llamando. ⎭	*Ana is calling **her.***

- In negative sentences, the direct object pronoun is placed between **no** and the conjugated verb. It may also be attached to the infinitive or to the present participle.

Adolfo no **lo** va a comprar. ⎫ Adolfo no va a comprar**lo.** ⎭	*Adolfo is not going to buy **it.***

- The direct object pronouns **lo, la, los, las** can refer to inanimate *and* animate objects.

Adolfo **lo** va a comprar.	*Adolfo is going to buy **it**.*
Adolfo **la** va a llamar.	*Adolfo is going to call **her**.*

The Personal *a*

- When the direct object is a specific person or persons (or a personified animal), Spanish requires that an **a** precede the noun. This is known as ther personal **a.**

Veo **a** Juan todos los días.	*I see Juan every day.*
Quiero mucho **a** mi papá.	*I love my father a lot.*
Quiero mucho **a** mi gato.	*I love my cat.*
Llaman **al** hombre.	*They are calling the man.*
Alicia visita **al** abuelo.	*Alice visits her grandfather.*

- If the direct object is an indefinite or unspecific person, the personal **a** is *not* used.

Ana quiere un novio inteligente.	*Ana wants an intelligent boyfriend.*

- When interrogative **quién(es)** requests information about the direct object, the personal **a** precedes it.

¿A quién está llamando Juanita?	***Whom** is Juanita calling?*

- The personal **a** is required before every specific, human, direct object in a series.

Visito **a** Jorge y **a** Elisa.	*I'm visiting Jorge and Elisa.*

- The personal **a** is not normally used with the verb **tener.**

Marta y Tomás tienen un hijo.	*Marta and Tomás have a son.*

◆ Práctica

4–14 Los amigos. Complete the conversation two people are having about their friends with the personal **a** whenever necessary.

— ¿Ves _____ Karen todos los días?

— Siempre veo _____ Karen y _____ Paulina en la cafetería de la universidad. Los viernes por la tarde Karen y yo visitamos _____ Lisette y _____ Rodolfo. Nosotras conversamos o vemos _____ libros de arte, y Rodolfo trabaja o ve _____ el fútbol en la tele.

— Rodolfo tiene _____ un primo muy simpático, ¿no es cierto?

— Sí, Rigoberto. Cuando no va a ver _____ Rita, su novia, él viene con nosotros a ver _____ una película. Rita va a menudo a ver _____ su mamá que está enferma. Entonces Rigoberto ahora ve más _____ sus amigos.

4–15 ¿Quién hace qué? You and your roommate have forgotten who is doing what.

MODELO: ¿Quién va a comprar los sándwiches? (tú)
          Tú vas a comprarlos.

1. ¿Quién va a llamar a las chicas? (Pancho)
2. ¿Quién va a buscar el hielo? (Hilda)
3. ¿Quién va a preparar el cesto con la comida? (yo)
4. ¿Quién va a llevar un radio? (nosotros)
5. ¿Quién va a comprar los refrescos? (ellos)
6. ¿Quién va a traer a las chicas a la residencia de estudiantes? (tú y yo)
7. ¿Quién va a llevar la heladera? (Ana Laura y Silvia)
8. ¿Quién va a poner la mesa? (Milton)
9. ¿Quién va a traer los discos compactos y el estéreo? (tú)
10. ¿Quién va a hacer la cama? (Uds.)

◆ Actividades

4–16 Vamos a la playa. With some friends, organize a day at the beach.

MODELO: ¿Quién lleva la bolsa? (tú)
          Yo la llevo.

1. ¿Quién hace los sándwiches? (tú)
2. ¿Quién compra los refrescos? (la profesora)
3. ¿Quién busca la heladera? (Glauco)
4. ¿Quién lleva la sombrilla? (nosotros)
5. ¿Quién lleva el cesto? (Uds.)
6. ¿Quién pone el hielo en la heladera? (los amigos)
7. ¿Quién prepara la bolsa con las toallas? (las chicas)
8. ¿Quién trae los trajes de baño? (Aida)
9. ¿Quién pone las cosas en el baúl? (Jorge)
10. ¿Quién lleva las hamburguesas? (Odilia)

4–17 Responder. In pairs, make plans to attend an outdoor concert. Match the questions in the left-hand column with the rejoinders at the right.

1. ¿Traen el cesto del profesor?
2. ¿Abres el baúl, por favor?
3. ¿A qué hora es el concierto?
4. ¿Estás haciendo la tarea ahora?
5. Está María haciendo los sándwiches?
6. ¿Qué están haciendo con la heladera?
7. ¿Abren el parque temprano?
8. ¿Vas a llamar a Berta y a Alejandro?

a. Estamos poniéndola en el baúl.
b. Estoy llamándolos ahora mismo.
c. No, la voy a hacer esta noche.
d. Sí, con mucho gusto lo abro.
e. El concierto comienza a las tres.
f. Sí, aquí está. ¿Dónde lo ponemos?
g. Sí, está preparándolos.
h. Sí, lo abren a las siete de la mañana.

4–18 El fin de semana. With two or three students, make plans to attend a patio party this weekend. Write a dialogue based on a series of questions and answers. Be prepared to present it as a skit to the class.

MODELO: ¿Quién va a llevar la sombrilla? ¿Quiénes preparan los sándwiches?

A propósito...Las diversiones y los deportes

Como a los norteamericanos, a los hispanos les gusta celebrar la vida y dedicar mucho tiempo a las actividades recreativas. En general estas actividades son de tipo social y son por la noche: visitar a la familia y a los amigos íntimos; salir en grupo al cine, al teatro, a un concierto, a dar un paseo por el parque; ir a un partido de fútbol, béisbol o básquetbol; o simplemente ver la televisión en casa o jugar juegos *(play games)* con la familia como canasta y ajedrez *(chess)*.

Un deporte muy popular en el mundo hispano es el fútbol. En los países hispanos vemos a niños pequeños con una pelota de fútbol en los parques. Los jugadores profesionales de fútbol son extremadamente populares y las estrellas *(stars)* como Hugo Sánchez de México y Emilio Buitagueño de España son héroes nacionales. En el Caribe, el béisbol es un deporte muy popular. Peloteros *(baseball players)* de Cuba, la República Dominicana y Puerto Rico son estrellas de las Grandes Ligas norteamericanas. En Colombia hay muchos aficionados al ciclismo, y en la Argentina, Chile y España el esquí es muy popular. En España y algunos *(some)* países hispanoamericanos como México, Venezuela, Perú, Ecuador y Colombia, las corridas de toros *(bullfighting)* tienen muchos aficionados.

¡Vamos a comparar!

1. En tu opinión, ¿cuáles son los dos deportes más populares en los Estados Unidos? ¿en el Canadá?
2. ¿Cuál es la diferencia entre el fútbol y el fútbol americano?

¡Así es la vid!

Los deportes

Marina Silva Wierna (*argentina*)

Me encantan los deportes. En verano, cuando hace calor, juego al tenis y practico ciclismo y natación. En invierno, cuando hace frío, me gusta esquiar en Bariloche. Mi deportista favorita es la tenista argentina, Gabriela Sabatini.

Julio Prenat Anzola (*uruguayo*)

Soy entrenador de un equipo de fútbol. Yo les enseño a mis jugadores a ser agresivos y disciplinados. Por eso casi siempre juegan bien.

Norberto Vásquez Guerra (*dominicano*)

Yo practico vólibol, básquetbol y béisbol, pero el deporte que más me gusta es el béisbol. Soy jardinero izquierdo del equipo de la universidad. No soy una estrella pero generalmente bateo bastante bien. La temporada de la liga de béisbol dominicana es de noviembre a enero.

Albertina Morales Rulfo (*mexicana*)

Hay deportes que me gustan mucho y hay otros que no. El tenis me fascina, porque es un deporte muy rápido; pero el golf no me gusta, porque lo encuentro lento y muy aburrido. El boxeo no me gusta porque es violento y, aunque no entiendo el fútbol americano, lo encuentro emocionante.

Vocabulario y expresiones

Algunos deportes

el atletismo	*track and field*
el básquetbol	*basketball*
el ciclismo	*cycling*
el esquí	*skiing*
el esquí acuático	*water skiing*
el fútbol	*soccer*
el fútbol americano	*football*
la gimnasia	*gymnastics*
el golf	*golf*
el hockey	*hockey*
el tenis	*tennis*
el vólibol	*volleyball*

Algunos términos deportivos

el(la) aficionado(a)	*fan*
el balón	*ball (soccer, basketball, volleyball)*
el bate	*bat*
la bicicleta	*bicycle*
el(la) campeón(a)	*champion*
el campeonato	*championship*
la cancha	*court, playing field*
el(la) deportista(a)	*one who participates in a sport; a sports fan*
el(la) entrenador(a)	*coach*
el equipo	*team*
los esquís	*skiis*
el estadio	*stadium*
la estrella	*star*
el guante	*glove*
el jardinero	*outfielder*
el juego	*game*
el(la) jugador(a)	*player*
la pelota	*ball*
la piscina	*swimming pool*
la raqueta	*racquet*
la temporada	*season*

Actividades deportivas

batear	*to bat*
esquiar	*to ski*
ganar	*to win*
nadar	*to swim*
patear	*to kick*
patinar	*to skate*
perder (ie)	*to lose*
trotar	*to jog*

Verbos o→ue y e→i

almorzar (ue)	*to have lunch*
contar (ue)	*to tell; to count*
conseguir (i)	*to get, to obtain*
costar (ue)	*to cost*
decir (i)	*to say, to tell*
dormir (ue)	*to sleep*
encontrar (ue)	*to find*
jugar (ue) (a)	*to play*
llover (ue)	*to rain*
mostrar (ue)	*to show*
pedir (i)	*to ask for*
poder (ue)	*to be able, can*
seguir (i)	*to follow*
servir (i)	*to serve*
soñar (ue) (con)	*to dream*
reñir (i)	*to quarrel*
repetir (i)	*to repeat*
volar (ue)	*to fly*
volver (ue)	*to return, come back*

📼 ¡A escuchar!

Los deportes. Listen to the people featured in **¡Así es la vida!** as they talk about their favorite sport. Then indicate below whether the statements that follow are **Cierto, Falso,** or **No se sabe**. You will hear the correct answers on the tape.

	CIERTO	FALSO	NO SE SABE		CIERTO	FALSO	NO SE SABE
1.	_____	_____	_____	6.	_____	_____	_____
2.	_____	_____	_____	7.	_____	_____	_____
3.	_____	_____	_____	8.	_____	_____	_____
4.	_____	_____	_____	9.	_____	_____	_____
5.	_____	_____	_____				

◆ Práctica

4–19 ¿Qué necesito para jugar? Complete the sentences with an appropriate word from **Vocabulario y expresiones.** Use the drawings as a clue.

1. Voy a comenzar a practicar el
   _____.

2. Es un deporte violento pero emocionante. Soy aficionado al
   _____.

3. Me gusta correr mucho y patear el balón. Mi deporte es el _____.

4. Es el mejor jardinero del equipo, pero necesita un
   _____
   nuevo.

5. Practico con una amiga en una cancha. Necesitamos muchas pelotas y dos raquetas. Nuestro deporte es el _____.

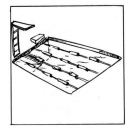

6. Voy a la piscina todos los días. Me gusta _____.

4–20 En las Olimpiadas. Identify the Olympic sports depicted in the drawings.

1.

2.

3.

4.

5.

6.

7.

8.

4–21 Un partido. Look at the advertisement. Answer the following questions to see if you are interested in going to the game.

1. ¿Qué hay el 3 de mayo?
2. ¿A qué hora es?
3. ¿De dónde son los equipos?
4. ¿Cómo se llaman los equipos?
5. ¿Cuánto cuestan las entradas?
6. ¿Dónde van a jugar los equipos?
7. ¿Dónde puedes comprar las entradas?
8. ¿Quieres ir?

4–22 Excusas. Juan José hates to exercise, but likes to pretend that he's a sports fan with his friend Ana. Choose the correct word from the list to complete the paragraph.

atletismo	esquí	patear
balón	esquí acuático	patinar
batear	fútbol americano	perder
bicicleta	gimnasia	vólibol
boxeo	guantes	

ANA: Juan José, ¿por qué no practicas deportes?

JUAN JOSÉ: Bueno…, el _____ es emocionante, pero hay que correr mucho. El béisbol me encanta, pero no puedo _____. El _____ es violento y hay que ser muy fuerte. El hockey me gusta mucho, pero no sé _____ bien. Soy aficionado al _____ pero no me gusta la nieve. ¡Hace mucho frío!

ANA: ¿Y el _____?

JUAN JOSÉ: Pues es estupendo, pero no puedo nadar bien y siempre tengo miedo. El fútbol es interesante pero no puedo _____ el _____. No tengo _____ para practicar el ciclismo. La _____ es más bonita para las mujeres. Soy muy bajo para el básquetbol o el _____. El _____ también es violento y los _____ son muy caros.

ANA: ¿Por qué no practicas golf?

JUAN JOSÉ: Es muy aburrido y no me gusta _____.

◆ Actividades

4–23 Mis opiniones. Discuss sports with another student. Follow the model and use the adjectives below in your conversation.

emocionante	fácil
interesante	violento
aburrido	difícil
divertido	fascinante

MODELO: —Creo que el golf es muy interesante.
　　　　　—Pues yo lo encuentro (*find*) muy aburrido.

4–24 ¿Qué deporte practicas? Copy the list on a separate piece of paper. Walk around and ask your classmates questions based on the list. Ask one question only of each person. Write the name of each person that answers affirmatively next to the corresponding item. Be prepared to report your findings to the class.

1. practicar el ciclismo
2. batear muy bien
3. tener guantes de boxeo
4. patinar
5. estar en un equipo de fútbol o de fútbol americano
6. practicar el básquetbol
7. hacer gimnasia
8. practicar el atletismo
9. estar en un equipo de vólibol
10. tener esquís (¿de nieve o acuáticos?)

Pronunciación

Sounds of Spanish *n* and *l*

1. The Spanish **n** is pronounced like the English *n* in the word *never*.

   nunca   **andar**   **nada**

   However, before the letters **b, v, m** and **p,** it is pronounced like the letter *m*.

   un beso   **en vano**   **inmediato**
   un padre   **sin mamá**   **con prisa**

2. To pronounce the Spanish **l,** place the tip of your tongue slightly higher above the front teeth of your mouth than for the English *l*.

   Luis   **vela**   **sal**

 Estructuras

3. The Present Tense of Stem-changing Verbs
o → *ue* and *e* → *i*

o → ue volver *(to return, to come back)*			
yo	**vue**lvo	nosotros(as)	volvemos
tú	**vue**lves	vosotros(as)	volvéis
usted ⎱ él ⎰ ella	**vue**lve	ustedes ⎱ ellos ⎰ ellas	**vue**lven

e → i pedir *(to ask, request)*			
yo	**pi**do	nosotros(as)	pedimos
tú	**pi**des	vosotros(as)	pedís
usted ⎱ él ⎰ ella	**pi**de	ustedes ⎱ ellos ⎰ ellas	**pi**den

- You have already learned about stem-changing verbs in **Lección 3**. Verbs like **volver** (*to return*), **poder** (*to be able*), **dormir** (*to sleep*) and **encontrar** (*to find*) belong to a different category of stem-changing verbs in which the stressed **o** of the stem changes to **ue.**

- As with **e → ie** verbs, there is no stem change in the **nosotros** and **vosotros** forms of **o → ue** or **e → i** verbs.

- All **e → i** stem-changing verbs have the **–ir** ending.

  The verb **jugar** (*to play*) follows the same conjugation pattern as **o → ue** verbs, even though its stem vowel is **u.**

> Nuestro equipo j**ue**ga bien.   *Our team plays well.*
> Ellos j**ue**gan al tenis.   *They play tennis.*

◆ Práctica

4–25 Planes para una excursión. The coach and others are talking about a game they'll play in another city. Conjugate and complete each sentence with a logical verb.

almorzar	dormir	mostrar	volar
costar	jugar	poder	volver
encontrar	soñar		

1. Antes del viaje, los jugadores _____ en la cafetería.
2. El equipo _____ en avión.
3. Los boletos para el partido _____ veinte dólares.
4. Juan y yo _____ con ser jugadores de fútbol.
5. Los jugadores no tienen sueño; _____ poco antes del viaje.
6. Carlos busca su balón pero no lo _____.
7. El entrenador les _____ una técnica nueva.
8. El equipo _____ bien y gana el partido.
9. El entrenador no lo _____ creer.
10. Todos _____ muy contentos.

4–26 En la playa. Complete each sentence by conjugating a logical verb from the list below.

conseguir	pedir	repetir	servir
decir	reñir	seguir	

1. Antes de salir para la playa, nosotros _____ hielo para la heladera.
2. Mamá _____ que hay refrescos en el refrigerador.
3. Abuela siempre _____ una sombrilla grande.
4. Conchita nos _____ en su convertible.
5. Los niños _____ mucho. Son muy majaderos.
6. En la playa, papá _____ los refrescos.
7. Mamá _____ las reglas (*rules*) para nadar.
8. Los abuelos nos _____, "hasta luego", y nosotros vamos a nadar.

4–27 Completar. Complete the sentences with the correct verb form of the verb in parentheses.

1. ¿_____ (tú) los tomates en el supermercado? (conseguir)
2. Mamá _____ que no hay refrescos en la heladera? (decir)
3. Abuela siempre _____ una sombrilla grande en la playa. (pedir)
4. Conchita, ¿_____ saliendo con Jorge Manuel? (seguir)
5. ¿Por qué _____ tanto Uds.? (reñir)
6. En la cafetería _____ el almuerzo a las doce en punto. (servir)
7. La profesora siempre _____ cosas importantes. (decir)
8. Yo siempre _____ que el dinero no es tan importante. (decir)
9. No me gusta cuando mis padres _____. (reñir)
10. ¿A qué hora _____ tú el almuerzo? (servir)

4–28 Las vacaciones de Luciana. Luciana talks about her family's vacation planning. To find out more, complete her story by choosing the correct word from the list.

almorzamos	consiguen	cuentan	cuesta	dice	duermen
compran	juegan	pueden	puedo	siguen	sirve
sueño					

Tres días antes de salir, todos _____ juntos para hacer planes. Tío Federico _____ cuánto _____ más o menos el viaje. Mamá y Papá _____ el dinero. Tía Sofía _____ el almuerzo. Yo soy grande y _____ ayudar *(help)*. Mis hermanos y primos _____ afuera. Después, Papá y tío _____ haciendo planes. Mamá y tía _____ la comida para el viaje en el supermercado. Yo _____ con la playa y los pequeños _____ que la vacación es tan fabulosa, que no _____ pensar en otra cosa. La noche antes no _____ de la emoción.

4–29 Luciana en la playa. Organize the events in a logical way and conjugate the verbs in parentheses.

1. Tía Sofía (contar) cuentos (stories) fascinantes, y los niños los (repetir) muchas veces.
2. Luego por la noche los papás *(dormir)* en sus cuartos, y nosotros *(dormir)* en hamacas *(hammocks)* en la terraza *(porch)*.
3. Poco después Papá le *(mostrar)* las fotos a toda la familia.
4. Al final de las vacaciónes todos *(volver)* a la ciudad.
5. Cuando estamos de vacaciones, los padres descansan y nosotros *(jugar)* en la playa todo el día.

◆ Actividades

4–30 Una persona curiosa. Take turns interviewing and being interviewed by a classmate to find out more about each other. Use the following questions to get started. Then report to your class what you found out.

1. ¿Me muestras una foto de tu familia?
2. ¿Dónde almuerzas todos los días?
3. ¿Duermes una siesta *(take a nap)* después de almorzar?
4. ¿Qué haces después de la clase si llueve?
5. ¿Puedes ver la televisión o escuchar música por la tarde? ¿Que ves? ¿Qué escuchas?
6. ¿Sueñas mucho o poco? ¿Con qué sueñas por lo general?
7. ¿Riñes mucho con tus padres o con tus hermanos?
8. ¿Dónde compras tu ropa *(clothes)*?
9. ¿Dónde encuentras gente interesante?
10. ¿Cuánto cuesta tu estéreo? ¿tu computadora? ¿tu carro?
11. ¿Qué dices cuando quieres salir con un(a) muchacho(a) y él(ella) no quiere?
12. ¿A qué hora sirven la comida en la cafetería?
13. ¿Repites la conjugación de los verbos irregulares todas las noches?
14. ¿Vuelas en avión a menudo?
15. ¿Cuentas tu dinero todos los días?
16. ¿Qué deportes juegas?
17. ¿Cuándo vuelves a hablar conmigo?

4–31 ¡A escribir! In small groups, write a short story using as many of the verbs on the list as you can. It can be prose, a skit, or a poem or a rap song. Be prepared to share it with the class.

almorzar	mostrar	poder
jugar	repetir	volver
soñar	costar	dormir
contar	pedir	seguir
llover	volar	encontrar
reñir	decir	servir
conseguir		

4. Indirect Object Pronouns and Prepositional Pronouns

¿Le traigo un café, señor?

No, gracias. Mejor me trae un té con leche.

An indirect object indicates *to* or *for whom* an action is carried out, and in Spanish, it is also used to indicate *from whom* something is bought, borrowed or taken away. You have already been using indirect object pronouns when constructing sentences with the verb **gustar**. The following chart shows the forms of the indirect object pronouns.

SINGULAR		PLURAL	
me	*(to) me*	**nos**	*(to) us*
te	*(to) you* (familiar)	**os**	*(to) you* (familiar) (Spain)
le	*(to) you* (formal)	**les**	*(to) you* (formal)
	(to) him		*(to) them* (masculine and feminine)
	(to) her		

- The indirect object pronouns are identical to the direct object pronouns, except for the third person singular and plural.

- Indirect object pronouns agree only in number with the noun to which they refer. There is no gender agreement.

Le acaban de traer una bicicleta.	*They have just brought **her** a bike.*
(a María)	*(Mary)*

- Like direct object pronouns, the indirect object pronoun usually precedes the conjugated verb; in negative sentences it is placed between **no** and the conjugated verb; and in constructions with an infinitive or progressive verb forms, the indirect object pronoun may either precede or follow the verb.

Le doy una oportunidad.	*I'm giving **you** an opportunity.*
Te presto mi estéreo.	*I'm lending **you** my stereo.*
No les escribo nunca.	*I never write **to them**.*
Le estoy diciendo la verdad. ⎫	
Estoy diciéndo**le** la verdad. ⎭	*I'm telling **you** the truth.*

- When the indirect object of a verb is a person, the corresponding indirect object pronoun also precedes the verb. This redundant structure has no equivalent in English.

Le doy el dinero **a Julia.**	*I'm giving **Julia** the money.*
¿**Les** muestro las fotos **a mis primos?**	*Shall I show **my cousins** the photos?*

PREPOSITIONAL PRONOUNS			
mí	*me*	**nosotros(as)**	*us*
ti	*you* (familiar)	**vosotros(as)**	*you* (Spain)
usted	*you* (formal)	**ustedes**	*you*
él	*him*	**ellos**	*them* (masculine)
ella	*her*	**ellas**	*them* (feminine)

- In the examples above, **Julia** and **mis primos** can be replaced by the prepositional pronouns **ella** and **ellos.** These pronouns always follow a preposition. They have the same form as subject pronouns, except for the first and second person singular, **mí** and **ti,** which with the preposition **con** become **conmigo** and **contigo.**

  Para **mí** es importante estudiar.   *For **me** it is important to study.*
  Le hablo a **ella,** no a **Ud.**   *I'm speaking to **her**, not to **you**.*
  ¿Vas **conmigo?**   *Are you coming **with me**?*

- The prepositional phrase **a + prepositional pronoun** is used for clarification and emphasis with direct and indirect object pronouns.

  Le doy la carta **a él.**   *I give **him** the letter.*
    (*vs.* a Ud., a ella)
  A mí me gustan los tacos.   ***I** like tacos.*

◆ Práctica

4–32 Xinia y Tito. Two friends are discussing which sports they like. Complete the dialog with the correct prepositional pronouns.

XINIA: Mis padres no quieren ir esta noche al partido de fútbol americano con Mario y conmigo. Para _____ *(us)* el fútbol americano es muy interesante, pero para _____ *(them)* es demasiado violento y difícil de entender.

TITO: ¿De veras? Y, ¿el vólibol les gusta? Para _____ *(them)* es un deporte elegante. El sábado hay un partido muy bueno. ¿A _____ *(you)* te gusta?

XINIA: Me encanta. Para _____ *(me)* todos los deportes son fabulosos, menos el boxeo.

TITO: Y a Mario, ¿le gusta el boxeo? A _____ *(me)* me gusta, pero no mucho.

XINIA: No, a _____ *(him)* no le gusta mucho, pero a mi cuñado Franco le encanta. Por eso Mario a veces va con _____ *(him)*.

TITO: Y, ¿tú vas también?

XINIA: No, ellos van sin _____ *(me)*. A _____ *(me)* no me gusta.

4–33 Eduardo y Celina. Two friends are making plans to go to a baseball game. Complete each sentence by selecting the appropriate item from the box below.

conmigo	contigo	él	ella
ellos	mí	nosotros	ti
Uds.			

EDUARDO: Hola, Celina, ¿quieres ir al estadio _____?

CELINA: ¿Al estadio? ¿Quién juega y con quién más vas?

EDUARDO: Juegan Los Tigres contra Los Leones. Y quiero ir _____, si aceptas y también vienen Mayela y Andrés.

CELINA: Y, ¿a _____ les gusta el béisbol?

EDUARDO: A Mayela le encanta, pero a _____ no le gusta tanto como a todos _____.

CELINA: Pues, como soy aficionada al béisbol, acepto. Es una mujer entrenadora, ¿no? Quiero ver a los jugadores hablándole a _____ para ver cómo la tratan. Ay, ¿y los boletos?

EDUARDO: Mayela y Andrés van a comprar sus boletos, y yo voy a comprar dos, uno para _____ y para _____. Yo voy a pasar por todos _____ a las dos. ¿OK?

4–34 ¡A ti te lo digo! A classmate will ask you the following questions. Be emphatic in your response. Follow the model.

MODELO: —¿Me quieres, mamá?
—Sí, Paulina, **a ti te** quiero mucho.

1. ¿Me ves cuando juego al béisbol?
2. ¿Te cae bien el entrenador?
3. ¿Les gusta cómo juegan los jugadores?
4. ¿Te interesa ir al partido?
5. ¿Te molesta ir a un concierto de música clásica?
6. ¿Me escuchas?
7. ¿Les gusta tener que practicar el tenis todos los días?
8. ¿Le interesa (a tu amigo) jugar al vólibol hoy?
9. ¿Les gusta (a tus amigas) el atletismo?
10. ¿No te fascinan las películas de amor?
11. ¿Me escribes de Bolivia?
12. ¿Nos cuentan Uds. un cuento (a story)?

4–35 ¡A jugar! A group of friends are at a sports camp. To find out who's doing what, complete the following sentences with the correct form of the indirect object pronoun.

1. _____ doy las raquetas. (a ustedes)
2. _____ traigo el balón. (a ti)
3. ¿_____ llevas una toalla? (a mí)
4. _____ enseño a jugar al tenis. (a ellos)
5. _____ dices dónde están los esquís. (a él)
6. _____ pides la pelota. (a ellas)
7. ¿_____ gusta el esquí acuático? (a usted)
8. _____ da igual. (a mí)
9. _____ pido, por favor, tus esquís. (a ti)
10. ¿_____ sirvo el almuerzo? (a Ud.)
11. _____ dan las raquetas mañana. (a nosotros)
12. _____ dice que no puede venir. (a mí)
13. ¿_____ conseguiste el cuaderno? (a Luisito)
14. Julia _____ muestra la carta. (a sus padres)

4–36 Planes. The same group of friends is discussing their afternoon plans at the sports camp. Change the following sentences by placing the indirect object pronouns before the verb.

MODELO: Voy a escribirle una carta. → Le voy a escribir una carta.
           Estoy diciéndole la verdad. → Le estoy diciendo la verdad.

1. Vamos a enseñarle a jugar al básquetbol.
2. Quieren darles nuestros guantes.
3. Paco piensa pedirles los patines.
4. Están mostrándole el bate.
5. ¿Estás explicándoles cómo patinar?
6. Estamos enseñándole cómo batear.
7. ¿Vas a escribirle a Luisa?
8. Van a pedirnos los guantes de boxear.
9. Está contándole un cuento a Rosita.
10. Necesitamos pedirle la cancha de tenis.

4–37 Una carta. Complete the following letter with the correct forms of the indirect object pronouns.

Querida Ana María,

Hoy _____ voy a hablar de los deportes. A mí _____ gustan mucho todos los deportes pero a mi hermano Carlos no _____ gustan. Por ejemplo, a Carlos no _____ gusta el boxeo porque dice que es muy violento. A mis padres _____ gusta el fútbol pero no el fútbol americano porque dicen que es demasiado violento. ¿Qué deportes _____ gustan? ¿_____ gusta la natación? A Roberto y a mí _____ fascina. Si a ti _____ gusta nadar, este verano vamos a ir a la playa todos los días.

Hasta pronto,
Eduardo

◆ Actividades

4–38 ¿Adónde vamos? With a new friend from a summer exchange program, look at the schedule of events below and discuss those events that interest you the most, your likes and dislikes, etc. Arrange to go to at least two events together.

4–39 ¡A contestar! In pairs take turns answering the following questions in the affirmative or in the negative.

MODELO: —¿Les pides dinero a tus padres?
          —Sí, les pido dinero.
            o No, no les pido dinero.

1. ¿Les escribes a tus padres?
2. ¿Le cuentas tus problemas a tu mejor amigo(a)?
3. ¿Le dices siempre la verdad a tu novio(a)?
4. ¿Les das dinero a las personas que no conoces?
5. ¿Le enseñas a jugar al tenis a tu amigo(a)?
6. ¿Les das regalos *(gifts)* a tus amigos especiales?

4–40 Mis opiniones. In small groups, take turns expressing opinions about the following using **gustar** and other similar verbs.

MODELO: ¿Te gusta el hockey?
          A mí me encanta.

1. swimming
2. your Spanish professor
3. boxing
4. springtime
5. American football
6. winter
7. summertime
8. mystery movies
9. television
10. homework

4–41 ¿Quiénes te caen bien/mal? Discuss with another student several people whom you like and other whom you dislike and explain why. You may use some of the descriptive adjectives listed below.

MODELO: Me cae bien María porque es muy buena persona.

simpático   agradable *(pleasant)*
agresivo   egoísta *(selfish)*
interesante   chismoso *(loves to gossip)*
travieso   hablador *(talks too much)*
majadero   aficionado de…

 Colaboración

Estudiante A

4-42A Vamos a hacer un viaje. With a classmate, make plans for a trip. Decide where, when, with whom you are going, what you are taking, what the weather will be like, how long you are going to stay there, etc. Ask your classmate questions based on the items on the list. Follow the model.

MODELO: ¿Adónde/ir (nosotros) a hacer un viaje?
—¿Adónde vamos a hacer un viaje?

¿Adónde/ir (nosotros) a hacer un viaje?
¿En qué fecha y a qué hora/salir (nosotros)?
¿Qué tiempo/hacer?
¿Quiénes/ir con nosotros?
¿Qué/ir (nosotros) a llevar?
¿Cuánto tiempo/ir (nosotros) a pasar allí?
¿Qué/poder (nosotros) ver?
¿Qué/poder (nosotros) visitar?
¿Cuándo/volver (nosotros)?

4-43A Consejos: Los pasatiempos. You're moody and don't know quite what to do. Ask your classmate for advice and react to his/her suggestions. Write down the piece of advice given.

MODELO: —Estoy impaciente.
—¿Por qué no escuchas música?
—Buena idea.

EMOCIÓN	REACCIÓN
aburrido(a)	Tienes razón.
triste	Me da igual….
emocionado(a)	¡Fabuloso!
impaciente	¡Ideal!
cansado(a)	No sé….
nervioso(a)	¡Buena idea!
distraído(a)	¡Vamos!
¿…? (original)	¡Magnífica idea!
¿…? (original)	¡Es una mala idea!

4-44A Entrevista para *El Norte*. You are a reporter from the Mexican newspaper *El Norte*. Interview a famous person. Follow the first model. Then, answer your classmate's questions. Follow the second model.

MODELO 1: —¿Conoce usted a la autora de *Como agua para chocolate*?
—Sí, la conozco. (No, no la conozco.)

MODELO 2: —¿Escribe usted sus artículos en inglés también?
—Sí, los escribo en inglés también. (No, no los escribo en inglés.)

PREGUNTA

practicar el tenis	querer mucho a su familia
conocer al presidente de México	pensar visitar México este año
llamar a su esposo(a) todas las noches	conocer el periódico *El Norte*
decir siempre la verdad	…(*original*)
leer el periódico todos los días	

4-45A ¿Qué tal? Tell your classmate your impression of different people, activities, or places. Follow the model. Then, ask your classmate his/her impressions of the people, activities, and places on the list below.

MODELO: —¿Te gusta la clase de español?
—Me gusta.

(No) Me…	PERSONAS, ACTIVIDADES, LUGARES
gustar	la clase
caer bien	Fidel Castro
caer mal	la comida mexicana
fascinar	los coches rápidos
importar	los profesores de esta unversidad
interesar	la película
impresionar bien	la música clásica
molestar	jugar al ráquetbol

Estudiante B

4-42B Vamos a hacer un viaje. With a classmate, plan a trip. Decide where, when, with whom you are going, what you are taking, what the weather will be like, how long you are staying, etc. Answer your classmate's questions according to the model.

MODELO: ¿Adónde/ir (nosotros) a hacer un viaje?
                —¿Adónde vamos a hacer un viaje?
                —Vamos a hacer un viaje a…

Algunas sugerencias:

LUGARES	CLIMAS	COMPAÑEROS
Buenos Aires	hace calor, frío, etc.	todos los amigos
La Habana	nevar	el profesor
San José, Costa Rica	llover	(la profesora)
Caracas	viento	nuestros padres
Cozumel	sol	nuestros(as) novios(as)
		alguien tan rico como
		Ross Perot

SE NECESITA	PASATIEMPOS	LUGARES DE INTERÉS
toallas	jugar al ajedrez	las playas
traje de baño	ir a la playa	los estadios de fútbol
esquís	ir a las discotecas	las fábricas de cigarros
la tarjeta de crédito	ver los museos	el salto Ángel
la bicicleta	conocer los restaurantes	el teatro

4-43B Consejos: Los pasatiempos. Your classmate is moody and doesn't know quite what to do. Give him/her advice fromt he list below.

MODELO: —Estoy impaciente.
                —¿Por qué no escuchas música?
                —Buena idea.

ACTIVIDAD

dar un paseo	jugar al tenis
ir a la playa	trabajar en la biblioteca
visitar un museo	hacer la tarea
ir a un concierto	comprar un helado
ir de picnic	escuchar música

4-44B Entrevista para *El Norte*. You are a famous person (decide who). A reporter from the Mexican newspaper *El Norte* is going to interview you. Introduce yourself to the reporter and then answer his/her questions using the direct object pronoun. Follow the first model. Then, ask the reporter questions about his/her experience as a journalist.

MODELO 1: —¿Conoce usted a la autora de *Como agua para chocolate*?
—Sí, la conozco. (No, no la conozco.)

MODELO 2: —¿Escribe usted sus artículos en inglés también?
—Sí, los escribo en inglés también. (No, no los escribo en inglés.)

ACTIVIDAD

escribir bien el inglés
hablar inglés en su trabajo
visitar su país con frecuencia
…(*original*)

preferir los periódicos mexicanos
siempre escribir la verdad
conocer a (otra persona famosa)

4-45B ¿Qué tal? Ask your classmate his/her impression of the different people, activities, or places on the list below. Follow the model. Then, tell your classmate your impression of the different persons, activities, or places he/she mentions.

MODELO: —¿Te gusta la clase de español?
—Me gusta.

(No) Me…

caer bien
caer mal
fascinar
gustar
importar
impresionar mucho
interesar
molestar

PERSONAS, ACTIVIDADES, LUGARES

la clase
Gloria Estefan
el rey Juan Carlos de España
la cerveza mexicana
las películas de horror
la música "country"
el boxeo
los árbitros de béisbol

Mundo hispánico

América del Sur

América del Sur tiene nueve países de habla hispana, todo tipo de clima y varias lenguas indígenas como el guaraní, aimará y quechua.

¿Cuántos países y capitales puedes nombrar?

POBLACIÓN AFROHISPANA

México
Honduras
Cuba
Santo Domingo
El Salvador
Panamá
Nicaragua
Costa Rica
Venezuela
Colombia
Ecuador
Brasil
Perú
Bolivia
Paraguay
Uruguay
Chile
Argentina

La población afrohispana ha dasaparecido o se ha mezclado en su mayoría (1% o menos)

La población afrohispana existe, pero es una pequeña minoría (2 -5%)

Una significante minoría de población afrohispana (6-30%)

Probablemente en estos países el grupo más grande de la población, es afrohispano.

Source: Leslie B. Rout, Jr.
The African Experience in Spanish America: 1502 to the Present Day. New York: Cambridge Unviversity Press, 1976

169

◆ Argentina

Capital: Buenos Aires (10.500.000);
Ciudades principales: Córdoba, Rosario, Mendoza, San Miguel de Tucumán
Población: 32.860.000
Etnicidad y raza: europeos (españoles, italianos, otros) 98%, mestizos y otros 2%

Dato: el país de habla hispana más grande del mundo; es uno de tres países del sistema fluvial del Río de la Plata (formado por los ríos Paraná y Uruguay), un sistema muy importante de comercio

Personas famosas: General José de San Martín, liberador; Domingo Fausto Sarmiento, escritor; Bernardo Houssay, Premio Nóbel de Medicina; Jorge Luis Borges, escritor; Julio Cortázar, novelista

Productos: ganado[1], agropecuarios e industriales

Atracciones turísticas: Buenos Aires, centro intelectual de gran importancia, con muchas casas editoriales, monumentos majestuosos, arte y museos. Parece una gran ciudad europea; la Patagonia (ecoturismo)

Buenos Aires

Arte

Literatura: Ricardo Güiraldes (1886–1927), *Don Segundo Sombra* (novela sobre los gauchos); Leopoldo Lugones (1874–1938), escritor modernista, *Lunario sentimental* (poesía); Alfonsina Storni (1892– 1938), poetisa feminista, *El dulce daño* (poesía); Jorge Luis Borges (1900–1986), escritor, poeta y filósofo, *Ficciones* (cuento y ensayo); Julio Cortázar (1914–1984), *Rayuela* (novela); Ernesto Sábato (1911–), *El túnel* (novela existencialista); Silvina Ocampo (1905–), *Viaje olvidado* (cuentos fantásticos); Manuel Puig (1932–1990), *El beso de la mujer araña* (novela)

Música: tango, música folclórica gaucha, chacarera, milonga

Platos típicos: churrasco, salsa chimichurre

◆ Bolivia

Capital administrativa: La Paz (1.669.000);
Ciudades principales: Santa Cruz, Cochabamba, Potosí, Sucre
Población: 7.243.000
Etnicidad y raza: indígenas 55%, (quechua 30%, aimará 25%), mestizos 25-30%, europeos 5-15%

Nombre: se llama así en homenaje a Simón Bolívar

Tres zonas: el frío altiplano andino; los cálidos valles y yungas[1]; y los llanos tropicales. No tiene salida al mar.

Productos: gas natural, estaño, plata, cinc, cobre

La Paz: la capital más alta del mundo (3.636 metros); mucha gente necesita oxígeno al llegar

Arte

Literatura: Renato Prada Oropeza (1927–), *Argal*

Música y danza: la tradicional de los quechuas y aimarás; huayna, cueca y lambada

[1]Warm Valleys

◆ Colombia

Datos básicos de Colombia

Capital: Sante Fe de Bogotá (4.819.000);
Ciudades principales: Medellín, Cali, Barranquilla,
Cartagena de Indias
Población: 33.170.000
Etnicidad y raza: mestizos 58%, europeos 20%, mulatos
14%, africanos 4%

Dos océanos: es el único país en Suramérica con costas en el
Pacífico y el Atlántico.

Leyenda de El Dorado: los españoles oyeron de un cacique[3]
de los Chibchas que era tan rico que en los ritos religiosos se
cubría[4] con polvo de oro[5] y después se bañaba[6] en un lago en
los Andes.

Productos: café, petróleo, carbón, bananas.

Atracción turística: El Museo del Oro (Bogotá); la antigua
ciudad de Cartagena de Indias; la catedral de sal de Zipaquirá

Arte

Literatura: José Eustaquio Rivera (1888–1928), *La vorágine*
(novela sobre los llanos del Orinoco y la selva amazónica);
José Asunción Silva (siglo XIX), poeta lírico
(poesía modernista); Gabriel García Márquez 1928–), *Cien
años de soledad* (novela de realismo mágico), Premio Nóbel
(1982)

Pintura: Fernando Botero

Música y danza: pasillo, bambuco, danzón, cumbia

[3]chief [4]covered himself; [5]gold dust; [6]bathed

Museo del Oro Bogotá, Colombia

◆ Chile

Datos básicos de Chile

Capital: Santiago (5.236.000)
Ciudades principales: Concepción, Viña del
Mar, Valparaíso
Población: 13.395.000
Etnicadad y raza: europeos y mestizos 95%,
indígenas 3%

Dato: un país largo y angosto con 10.000 km de
costas y buen clima todo el año, excepto en el
extremo sur y en los Andes donde hace frío; la
corriente Humboldt afecta el clima.

Productos: cobre, frutas y vegetales, harina de
pescado, nitrato de sodio

Persona famosa: Bernardo O'Higgins, Libertador
y Director Supremo (1817–1823)

Arte

Literatura: Gabriela Mistral (1889–1957),
educatora, poetisa y diplomática, Premio Nóbel
(1945), *Desolación* (poesía); Pablo Neruda
(1904–1973), poeta y diplomático, Premio Nóbel
(1971), *Veinte poemas de amor y una canción
desesperada* (poesía); José Donoso (1924–),
escritor, *El obsceno pájaro de la noche* (novela);
María Luisa Bombal (1910–1981), novelista, *La
última niebla* (novela); Isabel Allende (1942–),
novelista, *La casa de los espíritus* (novela de realismo
mágico)

Música: zamacueca

Platos típicos: torta mil hojas

Quito

◆ Ecuador

Datos básicos del Ecuador

Capital: Quito (1.500.000)
Ciudades principales: Guyaquil, Cuenca, Machala, Portoviejo
Población: 10.880.000
Etnicidad y raza: mestizos 62%, indígenas 22%, africanos 10%, europeos 6%

Cuatro regiones: la selva amazónica; la costa del Pacífico; la región andina; y las islas Galápagos.

Productos: petróleo, pescado y mariscos, café, bananas

Atracción turística: Quito, ciudad colonial al pie de la montaña Pichincha en los Andes; Islas Galápagos; las ruinas de Ingapirca

Arte

Literatura: Demetrio Aguilera Malta (1909–1982), escritor de carácter social y defensa de los indios *El secuestro del general* (novela): Jorge Icaza (1906–1978), *Huasipungo* (novela sobre explotación de los indios)

Pintura: Osvaldo Guayasamín

Música y danza: folclórica

◆ Paraguay

Datos básicos de Paraguay

Capital: Asunción (607.000)
Ciudades principales: Ciudad del Este, Concepción
Población: 4.871.000
Etnicidad y raza: mestizos 95%, europeos e indígenas 5%

Lenguas oficiales: el español y el guaraní

Detalle geográfico: no tiene costa al mar, pero tiene los ríos el Paraguay y el Paraná que le dan acceso al Atlántico a través del Río de la Plata

Productos: madera[1], ganado, agrícolas

Atracción turística: Asunción, una capital colonial

Arte

Literatura: Augusto Roa Bastos (1917–), *Hijo de hombre* (novela); Gabriel Casaccia (1907–1980), *La babosa* (novela)

Música: de arpa paraguaya

Platos típicos: costillas de cerdo en vinagre, tallarines con salsa de hongos, Chepa—pan de queso, torta de pasa.

[1] wood

◆ Perú

Capital: Lima (5.826.000)
Ciudades principales: Arequipa, Callao, Trujillo,
Chiclayo, Piura
Población: 22.585.000
Etnicidad y raza: indígenas 45%, mestizos 37%,
europeos 15%

Tiempos precolombinos: centro del imperio inca

Tres zonas: la costa; la sierra o cordillera de los Andes; y
la selva amazónica (62% del país)

Productos: cobre, harina de pescado, petróleo, café

Atracciones turísticas: el Cuzco, antigua capital de los
incas; las ruinas de Machu Picchu, centro ceremonial
inca; Museo Nacional de Antropología y Arqueología
(Lima)

Arte

Literatura: César Vallejo (1892–1938), *Los heraldos negros*
(poesía); José María Arguedas (1911–1969), *Los ríos
profundos* (novela); Mario Vargas Llosa (1936–), escritor
y político, *La ciudad y los perros* (novela)

Música: las típicas de los quechuas; marinera, huayno.

Cuzco

◆ Uruguay

Capital: Montevideo (1.310.000)
Ciudades principales: Salto, Paysandú
Población: 3.130.000
Etnicidad y raza: europeos 88%, mestizos 8%,
africanos 4%

Tamaño: el país más pequeño del continente

Nivel de educación: su población es muy instruida y
disfruta de excelentes servicios públicos y medios de
transporte.

Productos: ganado, agrícolas

Atracción turística: Montevideo es una activa metrópolis
con playas estupendas

Arte

Literatura: José Enrique Rodó (1872-1917), escritor
modernista, pensador y humanista, *Ariel* (ensayo);
Delmira Agustini (1886–1914), poetisa modernista, *El
libro blanco* (poesía); Horacio Quiroga (1878– 1937),
Cuentos de amor, de locura y de muerte (cuentos); Juana de
Ibarbourou (1895–1979), escritora, *El cántaro fresco*
(poesía); Juan Carlos Onetti (1909–), *La vida breve*
(novela); Mario Benedetti (1920–) *El cumpleaños de Juan
Ángel* (novela)

Música: candombe, milonga

Platos típicos: chivito, cacerola de pavo, calamares a la
plancha, cazuela de mariscos, pan de maíz

Postre: chaja

◆ **Venezuela**

Nombre: los españoles la llamaron "pequeña Venecia" por las casas de los aborígenes en el lago de Maracaibo.

Tres zonas: al norte Los Andes; en el centro los llanos[1] alrededor del río[2] Orinoco que tiene 2.200 km. navegables; al sur la selva virgen.

Productos: petróleo, aluminio, acero, hierro.

Persona famosa: Simón Bolívar, Libertador (1783–1830)

Atracción turística: el Salto Ángel *(Angel Falls)*; la Isla Margarita

Arte

Literatura: Rómulo Gallegos (1884–1969), escritor y político (presidente), *Doña Bárbara* (novela sobre los llanos); Arturo Uslar Pietri (1906–), escritor y político, *El camino de El Dorado* (novela)

Música, y danza: joropo, tono, gaitas navideñas

[1]plains, [2]river

Datos básicos de Venezuela

Capital: Caracas (1.290.000)
Ciudades principales: Maracaibo, Valencia, Barquisimeto
Población: 20.430.000
Etnicidad y raza: mestizos y mulatos 67%, europeos 21%, africanos 10%, indígenas 2%

◆ Actividades

4-46 ¿Qué es? Although you may not understand all the information given, if you scan the charts, you will be able to provide answers to the following.

1. Sólo tiene cerca de siete millones de habitantes. Su nombre se deriva de una persona muy famosa. Tiene la capital más alta del mundo y el 55% de sus habitantes son indígenas.
2. Es un río muy grande, en el que los barcos *(ships)* pueden andar por más de dos mil kilómetros. Se llama…
3. Dos países especialmente importantes en la antropología y la arqueología precolombinas son…
4. El héroe de este país andino tiene un nombre irlandés *(Irish)*. Es un país muy largo, con muchos kilómetros de costas que llegan hasta el Polo Sur.
5. Es un país que tiene una parte en Los Andes, otra en los llanos del Orinoco y otra en la selva. Tiene una población de unos veinte millones de habitantes. Los indios vivían en casas sobre el lago Maracaibo.
6. La mayoría de los habitantes son de origen europeo. Está al lado de un río muy grande. Su capital es famosa por su belleza, su cultura y sus casas editoriales. Es el país donde nació el libertador José de San Martín.
7. Entre sus productos principales están el cobre, el petróleo y el café. Antes de llegar los españoles existía la civilización indígena más conocida de Suramérica.
8. Una de las lenguas oficiales es el guaraní. Tiene salida al mar por medio del Río de la Plata. La capital tiene mucha arquitectura colonial.
9. Es el único país en Suramérica en que uno puede ir a la playa en el Océano Pacífico o en el Atlántico. En la capital está el museo más importante de artefactos de oro.
10. Es una atracción turística para las personas a las que les interesa la naturaleza. Son islas y es una de las cuatro regiones del Ecuador. Se llama…
11. Las ruinas precolombinas más conocidas en Sur América son de…
12. Es una capital grande donde uno puede ir a la playa. Está en el país más pequeño del continente que tiene un buen sistema de transporte y donde la gente recibe muy buena educación.

4-47 La bibliotecaria. You are a reference librarian at a big university. In small groups, respond to the questions and requests put to the librarian by students.

1. Quiero hacer un trabajo sobre la participación de los intelecuales en la vida política de América Latina. ¿Me puede recomendar unos cinco autores or autoras?
2. Me interesa la música folclórica de América del Sur, en especial, la música de arpa. ¿Por cuál país debo comenzar? ¿Qué otros tipos de música hay?
3. Tengo que hacer un trabajo comparando el ensayo de dos autores latinoamericanos, uno de fines del siglo XIX y otro del siglo XX, ¿Qué autores me recomienda?
4. Trabajo medio tiempo como chef en un restaurante. Un cliente quiere una salsa chimichurre. ¿Sabe Ud. en qué país se origina esta salsa?
5. Tengo que hacer una presentación para mi clase de español, sobre los distintos temas de la novela latinoamericana, pero no sé nada. ¿Me puede ayudar a hacer una lista de algunos de los temas que aparecen en la literatura de América del Sur? Voy a hablar por lo menos de cuatro temas.
6. Voy a escribir sobre la poesía femenina latinoamericana. ¿Me da los nombres de algunas poetisas? Voy a incluir unas cuatro mujeres.
7. Necesito los nombres de cuatro escritores modernistas para una clase de cultura y civilización latinoamericana.
8. Tengo que preparar una lista de autores y autoras latinoamericanos que han ganado el Premio Nóbel. Ya tengo a Octavio Paz de México, pero necesito por lo menos tres más.
9. Quiero hacer una comparación entre un cuentista hombre y una cuentista mujer. ¿Puede darme los nombres de algunos cuentistas suramericanos?
10. Quiero conocer unos dos pintores suramericanos de dos países distintos.

Lección 5

La comida

Comunicación

- Discussing Foods
- Obtaining Service in a Restaurant
- Requesting Information at a Restaurant
- Talking about Past Activities

Cultura

- **Las comidas**
- **La preparación de comida**

Estructuras

Primera parte

- Demonstrative Adjectives and Pronouns
- Double Object Pronouns

Segunda parte

- The Preterite
- Affirmative and Negative Expressions

¡Así es la vida!

¡Buen provecho!

Escena 1

MARTA: Tengo mucha hambre, Arturo. ¿Por qué no vamos a almorzar?

ARTURO: Está bien. Vamos a este restaurante. Sirven unas hamburguesas deliciosas con papas fritas.

MARTA: Pero no me gustan las hamburguesas. Mejor vamos al restaurante Don Pepe. Allí sirven platos típicos latinos.

Escena 2

ARTURO: Camarero, nos trae el menú, por favor.

CAMARERO: Enseguida se lo traigo. Mientras tanto, ¿desean algo de beber?

MARTA: Sí. Me trae una copa de vino, por favor.

ARTURO: Y yo quisiera una Coca-Cola, por favor.

Escena 3

MARTA: ¿Podría Ud. decirme cuál es la especialidad de la casa?

CAMARERO: Con mucho gusto. La especialidad del chef son los camarones a la parrilla.

MARTA: ¿A la parrilla?

CAMARERO: Sí, señorita. Son realmente exquisitos. ¿Los quiere probar?

MARTA: No, prefiero el bistec de solomillo y una ensalada.

ARTURO: Yo sí voy a pedir los camarones.

¿Cuál es la especialidad de la casa?

Escena 4

MARTA: ¿Qué vas a pedir de postre?

ARTURO: No me gusta comer postre con el almuerzo, pero quiero un café con leche.

MARTA: ¡A mí me encantan los postres! Yo quiero un flan de coco y un café negro.

Vocabulario y expresiones

Las comidas

Quisiera + inf.	*I would like + inf.*
¿Podría + inf?	*Could you + inf?*
desayunar	*to have breakfast*
almorzar	*to have lunch*
cenar	*to have dinner*
el desayuno	*breakfast*
el almuerzo	*lunch*
la comida o cena	*dinner*
la merienda	*afternoon snack*

Las carnes

el bistec de solomillo	*sirloin steak*
las chuletas de cerdo	*pork chops*
el filete de res	*beef steak*
el pollo asado	*broiled chicken*
el jamón	*ham*
la ternera	*veal*

Los pescados y mariscos

el atún	*tuna*
los camarones	*shrimp*
el filete de pescado	*fish fillet*
la langosta	*lobster*
la merluza	*hake*

Los granos y derivados

el arroz	*rice*
el cereal	*cereal*
los frijoles	*beans*
el pan	*bread*
las tostadas	*toast*

Las bebidas

el agua (f) mineral	*mineral water*
el café con leche	*coffee with milk*
el café negro o solo	*black coffee*
la cerveza	*beer*
la copa de vino	*glass of wine*
la gaseosa, el refresco	*soft drink*
el jugo de naranja	*orange juice*
el té	*tea*

Los vegetales

la cebolla	*onion*
los espárragos	*asparagus*
las habichuelas, las judías	*green beans*
la lechuga	*lettuce*
la papa	*potato*
el tomate	*tomato*
la zanahoria	*carrot*

Las frutas

el(la) banano(a)	*banana*
la fresa	*strawberry*
la manzana	*apple*
la naranja	*orange*
la pera	*pear*
el plátano	*plantain, banana*
la uva	*grape*

Los postres

el flan	*caramel custard*
el helado	*ice cream*
la torta	*cake*

Otras comidas

el azúcar	*sugar*
los huevos fritos	*fried eggs*
los huevos revueltos	*scrambled eggs*
la mantequilla	*butter*
la mayonesa	*mayonnaise*
la mermelada	*jam, marmalade*
la miel	*honey*
la mostaza	*mustard*
las papas fritas	*french fries*
la pimienta	*pepper*
el queso	*cheese*
la sal	*salt*
el sándwich	*sandwich*
la salsa de tomate	*ketchup*
la sopa	*soup*

La mesa

la cuchara	*tablespoon*
la cucharita	*teaspoon*
el cuchillo	*knife*
el mantel	*tablecloth*
el plato	*dish*
la servilleta	*napkin*
la taza	*cup*
el tenedor	*fork*
el vaso	*glass*

En el restaurante

el(la) camarero(a)	*waiter/waitress*
el(la) cliente(a)	*client*
la cuenta	*bill*
desear	*to want*
la especialidad de la casa	*the specialty of the house*
el menú	*menu*
probar(ue)	*to try (taste)*
la propina	*tip*
reservar una mesa	*to reserve a table*

Adjetivos

bien cocido(a)	*well done, well-cooked*
caliente	*hot (temperature)*
crudo(a)	*rare, raw*
delicioso(a)	*delicious*
exquisito(a)	*exquisite*
fresco(a)	*fresh*
frío(a)	*cold*
horrible	*horrible*
largo(a)	*long*
medio crudo(a)	*medium rare*
nuevo(a)	*new*
picante	*hot (spicy)*
término medio	*medium*
sabroso(a)	*savory, tasty*
sucio(a)	*dirty*

Otras expresiones

a eso de	*at around* (time)
ahí	*there*
a la parilla	*on the grill*
allí	*there*
allá	*over there*
aunque	*even though*
Buen provecho.	*Enjoy your meal.*
enseguida	*right away*
mientras tanto	*in the meantime*
por favor	*please*
todavía	*still*
¡Salud!	*to your health (a toast)*

◆◆◆◆◆◆◆◆◆◆◆◆◆◆◆◆◆◆

¡Así lo decimos!

las comidas

The names of foods often reflect the geographic and cultural diversity of the Spanish-speaking world. In some cases, the names are completely different, whereas in others, the difference is one of gender.

	BANANA	PEACH
Argentina	**la banana**	**damasco**
Colombia	**guineo, el banano**	**durazno**
Cuba	**plátano**	**melocotón**
España	**plátano**	**melocotón**
México	**chabacano**	**durazno**
Puerto Rico	**guineo**	
Venezuela	**cambur**	

la tortilla

While people in the U.S. tend to think immediately of a flat cornmeal *pancake*, this is not the case throughout the Spanish-speaking world. In many parts of Central America and México, the cornmeal tortilla is the norm (although it varies in shape, size and taste from country to country). However, in many other parts of the world, particularly Spain and the Caribbean, a **tortilla** refers to an egg and potato omelette. In addition to the Mexican **tortilla**, other typical cornmeal dishes are: Cuba: **tamal en hoja**; Puerto Rico: **zorullos**; and Venezuela: **arepas**.

el camarero

While most of these terms will be understood anywhere in the Spanish-speaking world, each country generally shows a preference for certain words.

Argentina	**mozo**, **garzón** (in an expensive restaurant)
España	**camarero**
Guatemala	**mesero**
México	**joven**, **mese**ro
Perú	**mozo**
Venezuela	**mesonero**

📼 ¡A escuchar!

A. Contesta. Listen to the conversations that appear in **¡Así es la vida!** Indicate whether the following statements are **Cierto** or **Falso**.

Cierto	Falso		Cierto	Falso
1. _____	_____	3. _____	_____
2. _____	_____	4. _____	_____

B. ¡Buen provecho! Look at the illustration. Then listen to the questions and answer them.

1. _____   5. _____
2. _____   6. _____
3. _____   7. _____
4. _____   8. _____

◆ Práctica

5–1 ¡Fuera de lugar! Circle the word or expression that does not belong in each group below.

1. a. lechuga   b. zanahoria   c. leche   d. frijoles
2. a. cereal   b. tostadas   c. huevos   d. postre
3. a. agua mineral   b. refrescos   c. vino   d. espárragos
4. a. habichuelas   b. uvas   c. fresas   d. banana
5. a. jamón   b. filete   c. arroz   d. chuletas
6. a. café   b. cuchara   c. tenedor   d. cuchillo
7. a. camarones   b. langosta   c. pollo   d. servilleta
8. a. papas   b. fresas   c. peras   d. uvas

5–2 Tengo hambre. Choose the most logical word to complete the sentences.

1. ¿Quieres _____ para el desayuno?
   a. espárragos   b. huevos revueltos   c. helado

2. El _____ es mi postre favorito.
   a. café   b. flan   c. jamón

3. Camarero, necesito _____ para el café.
   a. sal   b. pimienta   c. azúcar

4. El _____ es un pescado.
   a. atún   b. filete de res   c. camarón

5. Siempre bebo _____ en el desayuno.
   a. té   b. naranjas   c. cerveza

6. Voy a hacer una ensalada de _____.
   a. flan   b. filete   c. frutas

7. Quiero comer arroz con _____ negros.
   a. frijoles   b. quesos   c. helados

8. ¿Me trae _____ para la langosta, por favor?
   a. mermelada   b. miel   c. mantequilla

9. ¿Te gustan los _____? Hoy hay camarones en casa.
   a. postres   b. mariscos   c. granos

10. Vamos a poner la mesa. ¿Dónde está el _____?
    a. propina   b. mantel   c. carnes

11. Sí, sí, el bistec de solomillo está muy _____. Gracias.
    a. sabroso   b. sucio   c. frío

12. Quisiera una copa de _____, por favor.
    a. leche   b. jugo de naranja   c. vino

5–3 ¿Qué comen? State what the following people are eating or drinking.

MODELO: Antonio está comiendo una hamburguesa. Él bebe un vaso de agua.

 1.

 2.

 3.

 4.

 5.

 6.

5–4 ¿Qué restaurante? Answer the following questions based on these advertisements that you found in your hotel in Madrid.

1. ¿Qué tipo de restaurante es Parrilla el Gaucho?
2. ¿Cuáles son las especialidades de Las Cuevas del Duque?
3. ¿Qué tipo de comida sirven en La Galette?
4. Si no tengo mucho tiempo, ¿a qué lugar voy? ¿Por qué?
5. Si quieres escuchar música clásica, ¿adónde vas a comer?
6. ¿Cuál es la especialidad del restaurante norteamericano?
7. A mi esposo y a mí nos gusta mucho el pescado. ¿Qué restaurante nos recomiendas?
8. Si quiero reservar una mesa en La Galette, ¿a qué número debo llamar?

¿Cuál es tu comida preferida?

¿Dónde prefieres comer hoy?

◆ Actividades

5–5 Entrevista. Ask someone about his/her eating habits.

MODELO: —¿Qué comes en el desayuno?
—Como pan con mantequilla.

	DESAYUNO	ALMUERZO	CENA
HORA			
COMIDA			
BEBIDA			

5–6 ¿Qué dices? In pairs, role-play the following situations.

1. Your waiter suggests that you order the *especialidad de la casa,* but you would rather have the lobster.
2. Your soup is cold. The waitress asks if the food is O.K.
3. You need a table for four in a restaurant. A waiter greets you.
4. Your customers are in a hurry for their food and drinks.
5. You want to know about the specialty of the house.

5–7 Casa Botín. In groups of three or four, enact a complete restaurant scene using the menu below. Several tourists have just arrived at *Casa Botín* for dinner. The waiter is very gracious and answers the tourists' questions about the menu.

ENTREMESES Y JUGOS DE FRUTA

Pomelo 1/2	355
Jugos de Tomate, Naranja	300
Entremeses variados	750
Lomo de cerdo Ibérica	1.550
Jamón de Bellota	2.100
Melón con Jamón	1.825
Jamón con Piña	1.825
Ensalada Riojana	750
Ensalada de luchuga y tomate	380
Ensalada BOTIN (con pollo y jamón)	895
Ensalada de endivias	650
Ensalada de endivia con Queso	880
Morcilla de Burgos	415
Croquetas de Pollo y Jamón	625
SALMON AHUMADO	1.685
URTIDO DE AHUMADOS	1.850

SOPAS

Sopa al cuarto de hora (de pecados y mariscos)	1.295
Sopa de Ajo con huevo	450
Caldo de Ave	375
Gazpacho campero	550

HUEVOS

Huevos revueltos con patatas y morcilla	490
Huevos revueltos con salmon ahumado	850
Huevos revueltos con champiñon	510
Huevos a la flamenca	550
Tortilla con gambas	885
Tortilla con jamón	520
Tortilla con chorizo	520
Tortilla con esparragos	625
Tortilla con escabeche	510

LEGUMBRES

Espárragos dos salsas	1.110
Guisantes con jamón	700
Alcachofas salteadas con jamón	700
Judias verdes con tomate y jamón	700
Setas a la Segoviana	800
Champiñon salteado	700
Patatas fritas	290
Patatas asadas	290

RESTAVRANTE
ANTIGVA CASA
SOBRINO DE
BOTIN
(1725)
TELEFONO 2664217
28005 MADRID
CVCHILLEROS, 17

ASADOS Y PARRILLAS

COCHINILLO ASADO	1.875
CORDERO ASADO	1.990
Pollo asado 1/2	690
Pollo en cacerola 1/2	990
Pechuga "Villeroy"	900
Perdiz estofada (o escabeche) 1/2	1.100
Chuletas de cerdo adobadas	975
Filete de ternera con patatas	1.500
Escalope de ternera con patatas	1.500
Ternera asada con guisantes	1.500
Solomillo con patatas	2.190
Solomillo con champiñon	2.190
Entrecot a la plancha, con guarnición	1.990
Ternera a la Riojana	1.600

POSTRES

Cuajada	500
Tarta helada	500
Tarta de crema	500
Tarta de manzana	475
Tarta de limón	550
Tarta de frambuesa	690
Flan	300
Flan con nata	500
Helado de vainilla, chocolate o caramelo	400
Espuma de chocolate	500
Fruta del tiempo	450
Queso	700
Piña natural al Dry-Sack	480
Fresón al gusto	575
Sorbete de limón	450
Sorbete de frambuesa	450
Natillas	490
Melón	490

Pronunciación

Sounds of y, ll and ñ

- The Spanish **y** has two distinct sounds. At the beginning of a word or within a word, it is pronounced like the *y* in the English word *yes,* but with slightly more force.

yo	o**y**e	**Y**olanda
le**y**es	**y**a	arro**y**o

- When **y** is used to mean *and,* or appears at the end of a word, it is pronounced like the Spanish vowel **i.**

Jorge **y** María	hay	cantar **y** bailar	voy

- The letter group **ll** is pronounced like the **y** in **yo.**

llamar	bri**ll**a	**ll**orar	se**ll**o

- The **ñ** is pronounced by pressing the middle part of the tongue against the roof of the mouth or palate. Its sound is similar to the *ny* sound in the English word *onion.*

ma**ñ**ana	pu**ñ**o	ni**ñ**o	se**ñ**al

Estructuras

1. Demonstrative Adjectives and Pronouns

Demonstrative Adjectives

Demonstrative adjectives are used to point out people and objects and to indicate the relative position and distance between the speaker and the object or person that is being modified.

	SINGULAR	PLURAL	
MASCULINE	**este**	**estos**	*this/these*
FEMININE	**esta**	**estas**	
MASCULINE	**ese**	**esos**	*that/those*
FEMININE	**esa**	**esas**	
MASCULINE	**aquel**	**aquellos**	*that/those*
FEMININE	**aquella**	**aquellas**	*(over there)*

- Demonstrative adjectives are usually placed before the modified noun and agree in number and gender with that noun.

¿De quién es **ese** carro?	*To whom does **that** car belong?*
Ese carro es de Daniel.	***That** car belongs to Daniel.*

- The **ese/esos** and **aquel/aquellos** forms and their feminine counterparts are equivalent to the English *that/those*. These forms are interchangeable with the **aquel** forms, but the latter are preferred to point out objects and people that are relatively farther away than others.

Yo voy a comprar **esas** peras y **aquellas** naranjas.	*I am going to buy **those** pears and **those** oranges (over there).*

- Demonstrative adjectives are usually repeated before each noun in a series.

Este jugo, **esa** manzana y **aquel** sándwich son míos.	***This** juice, **that** apple, and **that** sandwich are mine.*

Demonstrative Pronouns

No, quiero ésa.

Demonstrative adjectives function as pronouns when the noun they modify is omitted. To differentiate them from demonstrative adjectives, an accent mark is written on the stressed vowel of the demonstrative pronoun.

MASCULINE		FEMININE		NEUTER
SINGULAR	PLURAL	SINGULAR	PLURAL	
éste	éstos	ésta	éstas	esto
ése	ésos	ésa	ésas	eso
aquél	aquéllos	aquélla	aquéllas	aquello

Esta cafetería y **aquélla** son
muy buenas.

*This cafeteria and **that one** are
very good.*

No me gustan aquellos postres,
pero me encantan **éstos.**

*I don't like those desserts, but I
love **these.***

- **Esto, eso** and **aquello** have no written accent or plural forms. They are used to point out ideas, actions concepts, or to refer to unspecified objects, and to inquire generally about the nature of objects or things.

Aquello no me gusta.   *I don't like **that.***
No digo **eso.**   *I'm not saying **that.***
¿Qué es **eso?**   *What's **that?***
Es un caracol.   *It's a snail.*

◆ Práctica

5–8 En el supermercado. Alejandro and Sandra are in a supermarket. Complete their conversation with the correct form of the demonstrative adjectives. Use the illustration to determine the location of all food items.

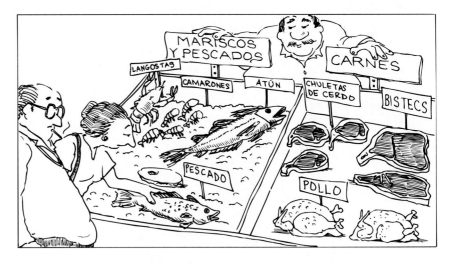

SANDRA: Mira, Alejandro, ¡qué fresco está _____ pescado!
ALEJANDRO: Sí, pero yo prefiero _____ chuletas de cerdo que están allí y
_____ bistec.
SANDRA: Voy a comprar el atún y también voy a comprar _____ camarones
y _____ langostas porque quiero hacer una sopa de mariscos.
ALEJANDRO: Yo solamente voy a comprar _____ pollo que está aquí porque
todas _____ carnes están muy caras.

5–9 En un restaurante. Using demonstrative adjectives, make five comparisons about dinner at a restaurant.

MODELO: —Esas uvas son muy sabrosas.
—Sí, pero estas manzanas son más sabrosas que esas uvas.

5–10 En una cena familiar. Tía Lucía dominates the conversation with statements about *this* and *that*. Complete the sentences with the correct demonstrative adjective.

MODELO: Estoy comiendo _____ manzana.
                    Estoy comiendo esta manzana.

1. _____ cesto que está aquí en la mesa es para las frutas.
2. _____ sopa que sirven en el restaurante Botín es exquísita.
3. _____ frijoles en mi plato están fríos.
4. _____ cucharitas que están allá son para el postre.
5. _____ es muy importante. Tienen que poner atención.
6. ¡Qué huevos fritos tan sabrosos! _____ desayuno está muy bueno.
7. Ahí están _____ sándwiches de jamón, pero necesitan queso.
8. Sólo pienso en _____ postre exquisito del restaurante de anoche.
9. ¿Deseas miel o mermelada con las tostadas? _____ mermelada es muy buena.
10. La especialidad de _____ restaurante en Sevilla es mejor que ésta aquí en Madrid.

5–11 Cambiar. If Tía Lucía repeated herself, she would probably use demonstrative pronouns instead of adjectives. Change the sentences in the previous exercise according to the model.

MODELO: Estoy comiendo esta manzana.
                    Estoy comiendo ésta.

5–12 De compras. Your friends have stopped at a local vegetable stand. Complete their thoughts using appropriate demonstrative pronouns.

1. No quiero estas legumbres; quiero _____. (allá lejos, en otro mercado)
2. Aquellas manzanas no me gustan; prefiero comprar _____. (ahí)
3. No me gustan esos espárragos, pero _____ me encantan. (en mi plato)
4. No voy a comprar esta naranja; quiero _____ en la ventana. (allá)
5. No quiero aquel arroz; quiero _____ en esta caserola. (aquí)
6. Estos frijoles no parecen buenos. Mejor compro _____. (allá muy lejos)
7. No me gusta esa pera; prefiero _____. (aquí)
8. No quiero aquellos tomates; quiero _____. (allá)
9. Este camarero es antipático. Me cae mejor _____. (allá por la puerta)
10. Estas habichuelas están frías. ¿Puedo comer _____? (ahí)

◆ **Actividades**

5–13 En la clase. Look for different objects in your class and describe them to a classmate using appropriate demonstrative adjectives and/or pronouns.

MODELO: Esta mochila es mi mochila. (*it's next to you, in your desk or hand*)
                    Esa ventana es muy pequeña. (*It's somewhat close to you*)
                    Aquel libro es de María Eugenia. (*It's far from you*)

5–14 En un restaurante vegetariano. In pairs, take turns asking the questions and answering them negatively.

MODELO: ¿Vas a comer en este restaurante? (que está cerca de la universidad)
           No, voy a comer en ése que está cerca de la universidad.

1. ¿Vas a pedir esas frutas? (que están cerca de ti)
2. ¿Va a hablar Mario con aquel camarero? (que está ahí)
3. ¿Lucila y Elsa van a ver esos menús? (que están aquí)
4. ¿Vas a hablar con esa camarera? (que está allá lejos)
5. ¿Nosotros vamos a beber de aquellos vasos? (que están allá)
6. ¿Tú vas a pedir esta ensalada de papas? (que está allá lejos)

2. Double Object Pronouns

INDIRECT OBJECT PRONOUNS	DIRECT OBJECT PRONOUNS
me	
te	
le → se	lo/la
nos	
os	
les → se	los/las

- When both a direct and an indirect object pronoun are used together in a sentence, they are usually placed before the verb, and the indirect object pronoun precedes the direct object pronoun.

  Te traigo el menú ahora.   *I'll bring **you** the menu now.*
  Te lo traigo ahora.   *I'll bring **it to you** now.*

- The indirect object pronouns **le** *(to you, to her, to him)* and **les** *(to you, to them)* change to **se** when they appear with the direct object pronouns **lo, los, la, las.**

  El camarero **les** trae el menú.   *The waiter is bringing **them** the menu.*
  El camarero **se lo** trae.   *The waiter is bringing **it to them.***

- As with single object pronouns, the double object pronouns may be attached to the infinitive or the present participle. In this case, the order of the pronouns is maintained and an accent mark is added to the stressed vowel of the verb.

  Camarero, ¿puede traerme un   *Waiter, can you bring me a glass of water?*
  vaso de agua?
  Enseguida voy a **traérselo.**   *I'll **bring it to you** right away.*
  ¿El chef nos está preparando una   *Is the chef preparing us a French salad?*
  ensalada francesa?
  Sí, está **preparándonosla.**   *Yes, he's **preparing it for us**.*

◆ Práctica

5–15 Sí quiero. You are having breakfast at a friend's house. Your friend is very obsequious and you are very hungry, so you accept most of his/her offers of food. Write down both your friend's question and your answer.

MODELO: el filete de pescado (servir)   ¿Te sirvo el filete de pescado?
                   Sí, me lo sirves, por favor.

1. el pan   5. el café con leche
2. el arroz y los frijoles   6. la ensalada de frutas
3. los huevos fritos   7. las tostadas
4. el jugo de naranja   8. el cereal

5–16 Don Francisco. Don Francisco is a very conscientious restaurant owner who worries about his customers' satisfaction. His son, Pancho, agrees with everything don Francisco says. Complete Pancho's responses with the appropriate object pronouns.

MODELO: ¿Les vas a dar el menú a los señores de la mesa seis?
                   PANCHO: ¡Claro, se lo voy a dar!

1. ¿Les preparas una ensalada a los señores de la mesa tres?
   ¡En seguida _____ preparo!
2. ¿Le das esta propina de la mesa dos a Carmen?
   ¡Ahora _____ doy!
3. ¿Me traes esos menús?
   ¡Sí, papi, _____ traigo!
4. ¿Les sirves más vino a la señora de la mesa uno?
   ¡Cómo no! _____ sirvo.
5. ¿Les puedes mostrar el bar a los clientes? ¡En seguida _____ muestro!
6. ¿Les llevas esta cuenta a las señoras de la mesa cinco?
   ¡Claro, _____ llevo!
7. ¿Me compras los camarones frescos hoy en el mercado?
   ¡Con mucho gusto _____ compro!
8. ¿Le traes un tenedor a este señor?
   ¡En seguida _____ traigo!

5–17 Una escena cinemática. A young film director intends to turn her family's reunion into a model for a scene in her next film. Change the nouns in the sentences to object pronouns.

MODELO: Le están enseñando el restaurante a Irma.
                   Se lo están enseñando.   *OR*   Están enseñándoselo.

1. Las camareras les están poniendo los manteles a las mesas.
2. El camarero les está dando los menús a tío Juan Manuel y a tía Rosita.
3. Tío Vinicio le está pidiendo más agua a la camarera.
4. Felipe les está consiguiendo unos refrescos a los más pequeños.
5. Nos van a traer un plato de chuletas de cerdo y otro de jamón. ¡Qué delicia!
6. Leonardo se está comiendo un cóctel de camarones.
7. Mamá le está sirviendo la sopa a mi hermanita Teresa.
8. Patricia me está sirviendo las habichuelas.
9. Le estoy sirviendo agua mineral a abuelita Celina.
10. Me están haciendo un bistec de solomillo por ser la invitada de honor.

5-18 La gallina roja. Esmeralda has a very well-known restaurant. Now her godchild Manuel Enrique is about to open a restaurant near a university in another part of the city. He seeks her advice in an informal note. Answer his questions affirmatively using double object pronouns.

MODELO: ¿Le compra la lechuga al *(from)* Sr. González de la verdurería del sur?
                 Sí se la compro al Sr. González.

1. ¿Me puede vender sus tazas de cerámica de Puebla, México, si no las usa?
2. ¿Me vende también los tenedores especiales para postre?
3. ¿Le consigue buena carne su chef a Ud. en el mercado de las Cruces?
4. ¿Les vende Ud. la comida más barata a los estudiantes?
5. ¿Les vende vino a los estudiantes?
6. ¿Para ocasiones especiales, me puede Ud. preparar unos platos de mariscos?
7. ¿Le añade crema al capuccino?
8. A veces le añade su salsa picante al arroz, ¿verdad?
9. ¿Siempre le pone la cebolla cruda a la ensalada de papas?
10. ¿Les pone manteles buenos a todas las mesas?
11. ¿Me puede dar su receta de filete de pescado con espárragos?
12. ¿Debo servirles desayuno a los clientes?
13. ¿Les debo servir verduras crudas a los clientes?
14. ¿Les doy la cuenta a los clientes después de comer?
15. ¿Les preparo tres postres diferentes a los clientes todos los días?

Querida Madrina:

Le escribo esta notita porque como Ud. sabe, voy a abrir un restaurante nuevo. Se va a llamar "La gallina roja". Como Ud. cocina tan bien y sabe mucho de restaurantes, quiero hacerle unas preguntas. Sus respuestas me pueden ayudar mucho. Mil gracias por todo. Muy pronto la llamo. Ahí van las preguntas.

Un abrazo respetuoso,
Manuel Enrique

◆ Actividades

5-19 El camarero. You are at a restaurant with a group of friends and everyone wants something from the waiter. In groups, take turns role-playing the waiter and the customers. Use the list as a guide; add at least five original items.

MODELO: traer el cóctel de camarones
                 —Camarero, ¿me trae un cóctel de camarones?
                 —Sí, se lo traigo enseguida. **or** No hay. ¿Le traigo otra cosa?

1. conseguir una mesa para ocho
2. preparar un bistec
3. servir una ensalada mixta
4. traer el pan y la mantequilla
5. conseguir una botella de vino
6. dar un vaso de agua
7. traer la salsa de tomate y la mostaza
8. servir más vino
9. mostrar los postres
10. traer la cuenta

5–20 Un jefe exigente. The manager of *El Pollo Dorado* is very demanding and is always asking the waiters what they are doing. With another classmate, write a restaurant scenario using the expresions from the box below. Use the model as a guide only. Be prepared to present it to the class.

MODELO: —¿A quién le llevas el vino tinto?
—Se lo llevo a aquellos jóvenes.

aquellas señoritas	la joven rubia
esa señora	aquellas muchachas
este señor	estos chicos
esa pareja	aquel hombre

1. ¿A quiénes les reservas esa mesa?
2. ¿A quién le vas a dar el menú?
3. ¿A quiénes les sirves la sopa de pollo?
4. ¿A quiénes les traes el pan y la mantequilla?
5. ¿A quién le preparas la ensalada?
6. ¿A quiénes les llevas el flan y la torta?
7. ¿A quién le das la especialidad de la casa?
8. ¿A quién le das la cuenta?

5–21 ¿Me haces el favor de...? There are two scrambled conversations below. Student A covers column B and student B covers column A. Student A starts by choosing the best opening statement or questions in the first conversation, and student B responds by choosing an appropriate item. Student A continues by choosing the next logical statement, and so on. Switch roles for conversation 2.

CONVERSACIÓN 1

A	B
_____ ¿Me lees las tiras cómicas (*comics*)?	_____ Te lo hago ahora mismo.
_____ Sí, ¿me lo sirve con leche, por favor?	_____ ¿Te sirvo cereal?
_____ ¿Me las haces con mermelada, por favor?	_____ Está bien, te las hago con mermelada de fresa.
_____ Papá, ¿me haces el desayuno?	_____ Te las leo después de desayunar.
	_____ Bien, te la pongo en la mesa y tú te sirves. ¿Te hago tostadas también?

CONVERSACIÓN 2

A	B
_____ Te las compro donde don Armando. Y también unos camarones, si quieres.	_____ Ahora mismo te la hago.
_____ Si me la haces ahora, voy esta mañana.	_____ Mejor me los compras en el mercado de pescados y mariscos.
_____ Tengo que ir al mercado. Te puedo hacer las compras si quieres.	_____ ¿Me las puedes hacer hoy? Te hago una lista.
_____ ¿Tienes un cesto para las verduras?	_____ Te lo pongo en la mesa. ¿Me compras habichuelas y zanahorias?

A propósito...Las comidas

Los hábitos de comer de los hispanos son diferentes a los hábitos de los norteamericanos. Dependiendo del país, el desayuno es entre las cuatro y media y las seis de la mañana—en las áreas rurales—y entre las seis y las ocho en las áreas urbanas. En el primer caso es un desayuno grande. Puede ser arroz y frijoles con tortilla y café. En la ciudad casi siempre es más pequeño y consiste en café con leche, té o chocolate caliente, con pan y mantequilla o pasteles. El almuerzo es, por lo general, la comida más importante del día, y según el país, ocurre entre las doce y las cuatro de la tarde. Un almuerzo típico puede consistir en una sopa, pescado o carne y verdura, arroz (y frijoles), postre y café. A eso de las tres, en unos países, y las seis, en otros, es común la merienda que puede ser pasteles, pan, sándwiches de jamón y queso, refrescos o café con leche. La cena puede ser entre las seis y las once de la noche, dependiendo del país, y a menudo es menos abundante que el almuerzo.

Otra diferencia importante es que, aunque los supermercados ya son muy populares, todavía es común ir al mercado típico dos o tres veces por semana. Éste puede estar en un edificio enorme con pequeñas tiendas donde venden todo tipo de comida. Hay carnicerías, pescaderías, fruterías, panaderías *(bakeries)*, pastelerías y heladerías *(ice cream shops)*. En general, la comida es muy importante para los hispanos, quienes viven para comer, en lugar de comer para vivir.

¡Vamos a comparar!

Compara las horas de comida del mundo hispano con las horas de comida de tu familia. También, compara los lugares donde tú y tu familia compran la comida con el mercado típico hispano.

SEGUNDA PARTE
¡Así es la vida!

El arroz con pollo de tía Julia

Mi tía Julia tiene un programa de cocina en la televisión. Cocina delicioso. Ayer hizo un plato exquisito, el arroz con pollo. No hay plato más popular en la región del Caribe. Le pregunté: —Tía Julia, ¿cómo preparaste el arroz con pollo? —y esto me contestó.

— Primero corté el pollo en pedazos pequeños y luego los metí en un recipiente. Le añadí jugo de limón y un poco de ajo picado.

— Después, calenté un poco de aceite de oliva en una cazuela, añadí los pedazos de pollo y lo freí a fuego mediano. Añadí una cebolla y un ají verde bien picados. Lo cociné todo unos cinco minutos.

— Luego añadí una taza de salsa de tomate, una cucharada de sal, una pizca de pimienta y azafrán, media taza de vino blanco y dos tazas de caldo de pollo. Lo cociné unos cinco minutos más.

— Enseguida añadí dos tazas de arroz blanco a la cazuela. Mezclé todo bien y cuando volvió a hervir, tapé la cazuela y cociné todo a fuego lento unos veinticinco minutos.

— El arroz con pollo quedó delicioso.

Vocabulario y expresiones

Las medidas

la cucharada	*tablespoon*
la cucharadita	*teaspoon*
el kilo	*kilogram (=2.2 lb.)*
el litro	*liter (= 1.05 quarts)*
una pizca	*a pinch*
la taza	*cup*

Aparatos de cocina

el congelador	*freezer*
la estufa	*stove*
el fregadero	*sink*
el horno	*oven*
el lavaplatos	*dishwasher*
el microondas	*microwave*
el refrigerador	*refrigerator*
la tostadora	*toaster*

Utensilios de cocina

la cafetera	*coffeepot*
la cazuela	*stewpot, casserole dish, saucepan*
el recipiente	*container, bowl*
la(el) sartén	*frying pan, skillet*

Actividades de cocina

añadir	*to add*
batir	*to beat*
calentar(ie)	*to heat up*
cocinar	*to cook*
cortar	*to cut*
echar	*to add*
freír (i)	*to fry*
hervir (ie)	*to boil*
hornear	*to bake*
meter	*to put in*
mezclar	*to mix*
pelar	*to peel*
picar	*to chop*
prender	*to light*
tapar	*to cover*
tostar (ue)	*to toast*
voltear	*to turn over*

Ingredientes y expresiones de la cocina

el aceite de oliva	*olive oil*
el ají o chile verde	*green pepper*
el ajo	*garlic*
el azafrán	*saffron*
el caldo	*broth*
los cubiertos	*silverware, place setting*
el fuego (alto, mediano, lento)	*heat (high, medium, low)*
el limón	*lemon*
la receta	*recipe*
la tortilla española	*Spanish egg omelette*

Expresiones indefinidas

algo	*something*
alguien	*someone, anyone*
algún, alguno	*any, some*
cada	*each*
nada	*nothing*
nadie	*nobody, no one, not anybody*
ni...ni	*neither ...nor*
ninguno(a)	*no, none, not any*
nunca, jamás	*never*
o...o	*either...or*
para nada	*at all*
también	*also*
tampoco	*neither, not either*

Expresiones de tiempo

anoche	*last night*
anteayer	*the day before yesterday*
el año pasado	*last year*
ayer	*yesterday*
el mes pasado	*last month*
la semana pasada	*last week*

◆◆◆◆◆◆◆◆◆◆◆◆◆◆◆◆◆◆◆◆◆◆◆◆◆◆◆

¡Así lo decimos!

los aparatos de cocina

There is a wide variety of words in Spanish-speaking countries to refer to *stove*, *refrigerator*, and the *burners* on the stove. In some cases, the words are completely different; in others, it is the difference between masculine and feminine. As often happens, for example, with Kleenex or Band-Aid in English, sometimes brand names are used to refer to the item (★ from the brand name Frigidaire).

stove

Argentina, Cuba, Perú	**cocina, fogón**
España	**hornillo, infiernillo, cocina, encimera**
México	**fogón, estufa**
Puerto Rico	**estufa**

refrigerator

Argentina	**heladera**
España	**frigorífico, refrigerador, nevera**
Colombia, Cuba, Puerto Rico, Venezuela	**nevera, refrigerador**
Chile	**refrigerador, "fishider"★**
México	**refrigerador**
Perú	**refrigeradora, "frijider"★**

burners on stove

Argentina	**hornallas**
España	**fogones, quemadores**
Cuba, Perú	**hornillas**
México	**quemadores**

📼 ¡A escuchar!

¡Un arroz con pollo exquisito! You will hear the conversation that appears in **¡Así es la vida!** Complete tía Julia's statements by choosing the correct answer.

1. a. añadí sal y pimienta   b. corté el pollo   c. añadí jugo de limón

2. a. la sartén   b. un recipiente   c. una cazuela

3. a. pescado   b. carne   c. pollo

4. a. limón   b. mantequilla   c. pimienta y azafrán

5. a. cociné todo a fuego lento   b. lo serví caliente   c. le añadí arroz

◆ Práctica

5–22 Consejo de tía Julia. Complete each sentence with a logical expression from the list below.

la cafetera	el fregadero	el recipiente
la cazuela	el horno	el sartén
el congelador	el refrigerador	la tostadora

1. Voy a freír el pescado en …
2. Mezclo los huevos en …
3. Lavas los platos en …
4. Tienes que tostar el pan en …
5. Hay una botella de agua en …
6. Preparamos el café en …
7. Cocinas el arroz en …
8. Meto el pastel en …
9. Para conservar la carne nosotros la metemos en …

los cubiertos	fuego mediano	la receta
la estufa	hervir	tapar bien
freír	el microondas	voltearla

10. Si tienes prisa puedes calentar tu comida en …
11. Siempre horneo la torta a …
12. Cuando todo está listo para cocinar, prendes …
13. Si preparas café puedes usar …
14. Pones la mesa con el mantel, la sal, pimienta y …
15. No cocino sin …
16. Por último la tortilla española tienes que …
17. Para preparar un arroz sabroso, lo debes …
18. El sartén sirve para…

5–23 Describir. Tell what the people in the illustrations are doing. Use words and expressions from **Vocabulario y expresiones.**

MODELO: Mario pone el pollo en el horno.

1.

2.

3.

4.

5.

6.

5–24 Ordenar. How do you make a Spanish tortilla? Find out by conjugating each verb in italics and sequencing the items below in a logical way. Compare your version with that of a classmate.

Hoy voy a hacer una tortilla española.

_____ *batir* los huevos con un poco de agua.
_____ *añadir* sal y pimienta.
_____ *mezclar* los ingredientes en un recipiente.
_____ *picar* la cebolla y el chile verde.
_____ *poner* la sartén a fuego lento.
_____ *pelar* las papas y las corto en rodajas *(slices)*.
_____ *voltear* la tortilla y la cocino otros diez minutos.
_____ La *servir* con pan francés, cerveza o una copa de vino.
_____ Primero *mirar* la receta.
_____ *pasar* todo a una sartén.
_____ Las *freír* en la sartén y las seco *(dry)* en una servilleta de papel.
_____ La *cocinar* durante diez minutos.

◆ Actividades

5–25 Comparación. What kitchen appliances do you have? Compare your kitchen with that of a classmate.

MODELO: Tengo un congelador grande, ¿y tú?
                     Tengo un congelador pequeño dentro del refrigerador.

5–26 Tu comida favorita. Explain to your partner how to prepare your favorite dish.

MODELO: Primero hay que añadir…
                     Después debes…
                     Luego tienes que…

5–27 Una dieta balanceada. In small groups, write a recipe for a simple main dish. Choose several side dishes from the food pyramid to make a balanced menu. Then, switch recipes with another group and write a shopping list for the recipe given to your group.

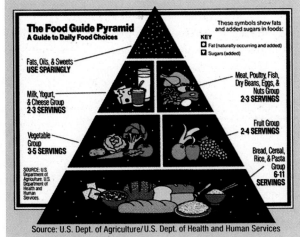

Pronunciación

Sounds of *ch* and *h*

- The Spanish letter group **ch** is pronounced much like the initial sound in the English word *chop*.

chica	**ch**ocolate	no**ch**e	cu**ch**arada
e**ch**ar	**ch**ile	mu**ch**o	le**ch**e

- The Spanish **h** is silent.

habla	**h**ora	**H**ernán	**H**éctor
Hola	**h**acer	alco**h**ol	**h**ielo

Estructuras

3. The Preterite of Regular Verbs

¿Comieron suficiente?

Spanish has two simple past tenses that refer to events in the past: the preterite and the imperfect. In this chapter, you will learn about the preterite.

The Preterite Forms			
	–AR	–ER	–IR
	tomar	**comer**	**vivir**
yo	tomé	comí	viví
tú	tomaste	comiste	viviste
Ud./él/ella	tomó	comió	vivió
nosotros(as)	tomamos	comimos	vivimos
vosotros(as)	tomastéis	comistéis	vivistéis
Uds./ellos/ellas	tomaron	comieron	vivieron

- The preterite tense is used to report completed actions and to narrate past events.

> Anoche **los padres cenaron** en   *Last night **the parents had dinner** at*
> el restaurante Don Pepe.   *Don Pepe's.*
> Los chicos **comieron** en la   ***The children ate** at the store's cafeteria.*
> cafetería de la tienda.

- The preterite forms for **nosotros** are identical to the present tense forms for **–ar** and **–ir** verbs. The situation or context of the sentence will clarify the meaning.

> Siempre **compramos** mucha ropa.   ***We** always **buy** a lot of clothes.*
> El mes pasado **compramos**   *Last month **we bought** two shirts.*
> dos camisas.
> **Vivimos** aquí ahora.   ***We live** here now.*
> **Vivimos** allí el año pasado.   ***We lived** there last year.*

- Always use an accent mark for the first and third person singular forms.

> **Compré** un cuaderno para la   ***I bought** a notebook for Spanish class.*
> clase de español.
> Ana **vendió** el anillo ayer.   *Ana **sold** the ring yesterday.*

◆ Práctica

5–28 Una conversación. Alina and Mario are talking about how hectic their final exam period was. Complete their exchange with the preterite form of the verb in parentheses.

— La semana pasada no me (gustar) _____ para nada.
— A mí tampoco. Yo (estudiar) _____ muchísimo y no (dormir) _____ más de cinco horas cada noche.
— Yo también. Además (trabajar) _____ en la tienda *(store)* veinte horas. No (salir) _____ de la biblioteca y sólo (comer) _____ en la cafetería. (Perder) _____ más de dos kilos.
— Yo no, porque la tensión me (abrir) _____ el apetito. (Ganar) _____ más de un kilo de peso. Pero después, los _____ (perder) en el gimnasio.

5–29 ¡Un terrible error! You and your friends forgot to follow the recipe when you were cooking. Complete each sentence to contrast what you usally do (present), with what you did (preterite) this time.

MODELO: Normalmente (tú: *picar*) las cebollas, pero esta vez …
          Normalmente picas las cebollas, pero esta vez no las picaste.

1. Normalmente (yo: *echo*) la sal después de probar la sopa, pero esta vez …·
2. Normalmente (tú: *preparar*) la comida usando una receta, pero esta vez …
3. Normalmente mis amigos (*comprar*) vegetales frescos en el mercado, pero esta vez …
4. Normalmente (nosotros: *beber*) vino con la comida, pero esta vez …
5. Normalmente mi amigo Julio (*añadir*) una pizca de pimienta a la sopa, pero esta vez …
6. Normalmente Julio (*batir*) los huevos, pero esta vez …
7 Normalmente (yo: *hornear*) la torta por 45 minutos, pero esta vez…
8. Normalmente (tú: *pelar*) las papas, pero esta vez …
9. Normalmente tía Julia (*cocinar*), pero esta vez tú y yo…
10. Normalmente mi mamá (*llegar*) a las 11 de la noche, pero esta vez…

5–30 ¿Por qué? Several members of a family are explaining to each other the reason behind the events of last week.

1. Me (molestar) _____ el ruido del refrigerador y entonces (llamar) _____ al técnico.
2. A ti te (gustar) _____ la salsa de los camarones porque yo la (preparar) _____ con vino.
3. Arnaldo no (recibir) _____ una carta de Amalia porque la semana pasada (conversar) _____ con ella.
4. El vino que Uds. (tomar) _____ es especial porque (llegar) _____ de España ayer.
5. Los padres nos (vender) _____ su carro viejo, porque (comprar) _____ uno nuevo.
6. Nosotros (vivir) _____ en Maracaibo y por eso nuestros amigos venezolanos nos (visitar) _____ anoche.
7. Las clases (comenzar) _____ la semana pasada, por eso los chicos ya (aprender) _____ a patinar.
8. Grisel (regresar) _____ de la tienda ya porque (correr) _____ mucho.
9. Tú no (practicar) _____ los verbos de español con nosotros, porque (descansar) _____ toda la tarde en aquella silla.
10. Luis Alberto (enseñar) _____ español en la universidad pero no le (gustar) _____. Por eso (cambiar) _____ de trabajo.
11. Yo (entender) _____ la lección de geometría. Por eso no (preguntar) _____ nada.
12. Nosotros no (llegar) _____ temprano a la clase de las nueve, porque (bailar) _____ toda la noche en la discoteca.
13. Uds. (regresar) _____ a las playas todos los años, pero nunca (visitar) _____ el museo. Por eso no lo conocen.
14. Mis primos (almorzar) _____ tarde hoy, por eso no (comer) _____ nada.
15. Sara (patinar) _____ todo ayer y (esquiar) _____ anteayer. Por eso hoy está muy cansada.

5–31 La comida en casa de mi abuela. Mirta's grandchildren are reporting on the tasks they have done to help her with dinner. First, select a logical word or phrase to complete each sentence and then put the verbs into the past tense.

en el fregadero.	el aceite de oliva.	con mantequilla y a fuego lento.
el pan.	en el recipiente.	durante más de una hora.
en la sartén.	para hacer café.	para ponerlas en la mesa.
la cebolla y el ají verde.	para freírlas.	la ensalada de lechuga y tomate.
la tortilla.	en el horno.	los huevos.

1. Ana *cocinar* las habichuelas…
2. Su mamá *cortar* las papas…
3. Mario *lavar* las uvas y las manzanas…
4. Tú *freír* las papas…
5. Nosotros *hornear* el pollo…
6. Yo *prender* la estufa para calentar…
7. Ligia *voltear*…
8. Uds. *mezclar* los ingredientes…
9. Eugenio *picar*…
10. Las chicas *tostar*…
11. Tú *batir*…
12. Uds. *calentar* la cazuela…
13. Rodrigo y José *poner* los platos…
14. Sonia le *echar* sal y pimienta a …
15. Yo *hervir* el agua…

◆ Actividades

5–32 Entrevista. With a classmate, take turns interviewing each other about your recent activities. Use the preterite tense.

1. ¿Estudiaste mucho ayer?
2. ¿Con quién hablaste por teléfono anoche?
3. ¿Qué comiste en el almuerzo ayer?
4. ¿Visitaste a tus padres la semana pasada?
5. ¿Leíste el periódico hoy?
6. ¿Compraste comida anoche?
7. ¿Fuiste al cine anoche?
8. ¿A qué hora saliste esta mañana para la universidad?
9. ¿Caminaste o tomaste un autobús?
10. ¿Compraste muchas cosas el mes pasado? ¿Qué compraste?
11. ¿Qué artículo te costó más?
12. ¿Miraste bien las ventas y liquidaciones *(sales)*?
13. ¿Gastaste mucho dinero? ¿Cuánto?
14. ¿A qué hora regresaste ayer a tu casa?

5–33 Ayer. What did you do yesterday afternoon? Write down the list on a separate piece of paper. Walk around and find out who among your classmates did the same things yesterday. Write down the name of each person who answers affirmatively next to the corresponding activity. Report your findings to the class.

MODELO: correr   ¿Corriste ayer?

1. *estudiar* en la biblioteca
2. *abrir* el libro de español
3. *beber* una gaseosa
4. *comer* en la cafetería
5. *escribir* una carta
6. *leer* una revista *(magazine)*
7. *llegar* tarde a clase
8. *visitar* a un amigo o a una amiga
9. *caminar* a la universidad
10. …*(orginal)*

4. Indefinite and Negative Expressions

AFFIRMATIVE	NEGATIVE
algo	nada
alguien	nadie
algún, alguno (-a, -os, -as)	ningún, ninguno(a)
siempre	nunca, jamás
también	tampoco
o...o	ni...ni

- Spanish negative sentences may have other negative expressions in addition to the adverb **no**, forming double and triple negatives. In such cases **no** precedes the verb and negatives either immediately follow the verb or are placed at the end of the sentence. When a sentence is negative, all the indefinite words in it are also negative.

  Lucía **no** conoce a **nadie** tampoco.   *Lucía doesn't know **anybody** either.*
  No como **nunca** con Samuel.   *I **never** eat with Samuel.*
  No como, **ni** bebo **ni** leo antes   *I do**n't** eat, or drink or read before*
    de dormir.   *sleeping.*

- When the negative expression precedes the verb, **no** is omitted.

  Nunca como con Samuel.   *I **never** eat with Samuel.*
  Ni como, **ni** bebo, **ni** leo antes   *I **neither** eat, **nor** drink, **nor** read before*
    de dormir.   *sleeping.*

- The expressions **nadie** and **alguien** refer only to persons and require the personal **a** when they appear as direct objects of the verb.

  No veo **a nadie**.   *I don't see **anyone**.*
  ¿Visitas **a alguien** especial?   *Are you visiting **someone** special?*

- The adjectives **alguno** and **ninguno** drop the **-o** before a masculine singular noun just as the number **uno** shortens to **un**.

  Ningún estudiante viene a   ***No** student is coming to dinner.*
    la comida.
  Preparé **algún** pollo sabroso.   *I prepared **some** tasty chicken.*

◆ Práctica

5–34 Una cena desastrosa. Answer the following questions in the negative.

MODELO: ¿Va alguien a la fiesta?
          No va nadie a la fiesta.

1. ¿Alguien va a planear la cena?
2. ¿Tienes algo que preparar?
3. ¿Alguno de nosotros sabe cocinar?
4. ¿Siempre comemos el postre al final?
5. ¿También te gusta el atún?
6. ¿O repites la carne o el pescado?
7. ¿Hay algo en el recipiente?
8. Alguien pone la cafetera en la estufa?
9. ¿Siempre pones los platos sucios o en el fregadero o en el lavaplatos?
10. ¿También bates los huevos?
11. ¿O calientas el pan o picas la cebolla?
12. ¿Algunos de los platos están fríos?

5–35 Las recetas de Enrique. Choose the correct indefinite and/or negative expression to complete one viewer's opinion about Enrique's cooking show.

No me gusta _____ (nadie, alguno, ninguno) de los programas de recetas de Enrique. El _____ (siempre, jamás, nada) da suficientes explicaciones. Si _____ (algún, alguno, ningún, ninguno) día yo tengo un programa de televisión como el de Enrique, yo _____ (algún, alguno, ningún, ninguno, nunca, siempre) voy a explicar muy bien las recetas. _____ (también, nunca, siempre, nada) voy a hablar rápido porque _____ (también, nunca, siempre, nadie, alguien) me van a entender. _____ (nunca, ni…ni, o…o) planeo el programa bien, _____ (nunca, ni…ni, o…o) no lo tengo. Si no, a la gente _____ (nunca, ni…ni, o…o) le gusta _____ (nunca, ni…ni, o…o) lo vuelve a poner. A _____ (tampoco, alguno, nadie) le interesa un programa difícil de entender. A mí _____. (tampoco, también, siempre)

5–36 ¡De ninguna manera! Your friend wants to go to a new restaurant that has just opened but you don't think it's a good one. Answer the following questions in the negative using the correct form of **ningún.**

MODELO: —¿Sirven platos típicos?
                    —No, no sirven ningún plato típico.

1. ¿Preparan platos de dieta?
2. ¿Tienen buenas ensaladas?
3. ¿Sirven pescado fresco?
4. ¿Tienen vinos españoles?
5. ¿Sirven platos muy picantes?
6. ¿Hay alguna especialidad de la casa?
7. ¿Tienen postres exquisitos?
8. ¿Preparan sándwiches vegetarianos?
9. ¿Hacen algún plato con azafrán?
10. ¿Hay mesas para fumadores *(smokers)?*

◆ Actividades

5–37 Contestar. Interview a classmate using the following questions, then report your findings to another classmate.

1. ¿Invitaste a alguien a salir este fin de semana?
2. ¿Conociste a alguien interesante?
3. ¿Estudiaste con algún amigo la semana pasada?
4. ¿Comiste algo antes de venir a la clase?
5. ¿Cocinaste algo especial este fin de semana?
6. ¿Miraste mucha televisión anoche?
7. ¿Bebiste vino o cerveza durante el fin de semana?
8. ¿Les escribiste a tus padres, abuelos, o a algún amigo o amiga?
9. ¿Descansaste mucho durante el fin de semana?
10. ¿Leíste algo interesante ayer?

Colaboración

Estudiante A

5-38A Los utensilios de la mesa. What differences are there between your drawing and that of your classmate? Ask each other questions and make a list of the differences.

MODELO: ¿Tienes sal?
—Sí, la tengo.
—No, no la tengo.

5-39A ¡Camarero, por favor...! Enact the roles of waiter/waitress and client. Using the lists from the previous exercise, order the items you don't have. Follow the model.

MODELO: —¡Camarero! Por favor, necesito un vaso.
—Se lo traigo enseguida, señor/señorita.

5-40A Soluciones. You complain about your problems and your classmate makes suggestions. Write down the suggestions your classmate gives you. Then, listen to his/her complaints, and give an appropriate suggestion.

MODELO: —No tengo mucha hambre.
—Puedes comer una ensalada verde.

QUEJAS

1. *tener* mucha hambre
2. *estar* a dieta
3. *querer* el solomillo pero tener poco dinero
4. no *querer* comida picante
5. *querer* algo de desayuno

SUGERENCIAS

- *tomar* la sopa de pollo de su mamá
- *tomar* una cerveza
- *tomar* algo como leche, agua mineral o una gaseosa
- *pedir* un flan
- *beber* una taza de café

5-41A El gazpacho. You and your classmate want to prepare a gazpacho, a cold, tomato-based soup, but you are not sure if you have all of the ingredients. Make a list of the things you need to buy. One of you has the recipe, the other knows what you have in the kitchen.

MODELO: —Necesitamos un kilo de tomates.
—Tenemos medio kilo. Hay que comprar otro medio kilo.

1 kilo de tomates
3 pepinos (cucumbers)
1 ají grande
1 cebolla grande
3 dientes de ajo machacados (crushed)
2 rebanadas (slices) de pan francés
media taza de aceite de oliva
media taza de vinagre de vino tinto (red)
1 taza de agua
1 cucharadita de sal

Menú

Fecha: _____

Número de personas: _____

Primer plato: _____

Segundo plato: _____

Vegetales: _____

Postre: _____

Bebida: _____

¿Café? _____

5-42A Una cena especial. You and your classmate have to decide what you will serve the dean of students when he/she comes to dinner tomorrow night. Work together on your menu. Then check the sales ad to make your shopping list. You must stay within your $75.00 budget.

Mercado
Gómez

Pescados y mariscos
Atún atlántico **$15/k**
Camarones del
   Golfo de México **$15/k**
Langosta de Main **$30/k**
Filete de bacalao **$10/k**

Carnes
bistec de solomillo **$8/k**
chuletas de cerdo **$8.50/k**
pollo **$3/k**
ternera **$20/k**

Bebidas
vino tinto de Calif **$5**
v. blanco de Portugal **$10**
vindo rosado de NY **$7.50**
cerveza mexicana **6@$7**
cerveza de Wisc. **6@$4**
agua mineral **$2.50/litro**
café colombiano **$6/500gr**

Vegetales
zanahorias **$1/k**
espárragos **$3/k**
papas **50¢/k**
lechuga **$2.50/k**
tomates **$2/k**

Frutas
bananas **$1/k**
fresas **$5/cesta**
uvas **$3/k**
peras **6@$2**
naranjas **6@$3**

Flores
violetas **$5**
rosas **$25**
margaritas **$4.99**

Postres
helado **$4**
torta de queso **$15**

Estudiante B

5-38B Los utensilios de la mesa. What differences are there between your drawing and that of your classmate? Ask each other questions and make a list of the differences.

MODELO: ¿Tienes sal?
           —Sí, la tengo.
           —No, no la tengo.

5-39B ¡Camarero, por favor…! Enact the roles of waiter/waitress and client. Using the lists from the previous exercise, order the items you don't have. Follow the model.

MODELO: —¡Camarero! Por favor, necesito un vaso.
           —Se lo traigo enseguida, señor/señorita.

5-40B Soluciones. You complain about your problems and your classmate makes suggestions. Write down the suggestions your classmate gives you. Then, listen to his/her complaints, and give an appropriate suggestion.

MODELO: —No tengo mucha hambre.
           —Puedes comer una ensalada verde.

QUEJAS

1. *tener* mucha sed, pero no *querer* una bebida alcóholica
2. *estar* enfermo(a)
3. *tener* que estudiar, pero *querer* dormir
4. no me *gustar* el vino
5. *querer* comer un dulce liviano *(light)*

SUGERENCIAS

- *comer* una ensalada de vegetales o un filete de pescado asado
- *pedir* un sándwich de jamón y queso
- *pedir* una hamburguesa con queso y papas fritas con salsa de tomate
- *comer* huevos fritos con tostadas
- *pedir* el pollo asado que es más barato

5-41B El gazpacho. You and your classmate want to prepare a
gazpacho, a cold, tomato-based soup, but you are not sure if you
have all of the ingredients. Make a list of the things you need to
buy. One of you has the recipe, the other knows what you have
in the kitchen.

MODELO: —Necesitamos un kilo de tomatoes.
          —Tenemos medio kilo. Hay que comprar otro
            medio kilo.

En la cocina:

✓ medio kilo de tomates
✓ 1 pepino (cucumber) viejo
✓ 1 ají pequeño
✓ 2 cebolla grandes
✓ pan integral (whole wheat)
✓ una cabeza grande de ajo
   (garlic head)
✓ una botella de aceite de maíz
✓ una botella de vinagre blanco
✓ una botella de agua
✓ sal y pimienta

5-42B Una cena especial. You and your classmates have to decide what you will serve the dean of students when
he/she comes to dinner tomorrow night. Work together on the menu. Then check the sales ad to make your
shopping list. You must stay within your $75.00 budget.

COMIDA	CANTIDAD	COSTO TOTAL
Gran total		

¡De compras!

Comunicación

- Shopping
- Reading and Responding to Advertisements
- Reporting Events in the Past
- Describing Situations and Conditions in the Past

Cultura

- **De compras**
- **Las tiendas especializadas**

Estructuras

Primera parte

- More on the Preterite
  - Irregular Verbs
  - Stem-changing Verbs
  - Verbs with Spelling Changes
- The Imperfect Tense

Segunda parte

- Preterite or Imperfect?
- Adverbs ending in **-mente**

¡Así es la vida!

De compras

VILMA: Ayer Victoria, Manuel y yo fuimos de compras.

PITI: ¿Ah sí? ¿Dónde fueron?

VILMA: Bueno, antes de salir Victoria puso el televisor y vio todas las ofertas del día en los almacenes y tiendas de Lima. Decidimos ir al centro comercial.

PITI: ¿Y estuvieron mucho tiempo ahí?

VILMA: Anduvimos de allá para acá más de cuatro horas. Manuel hizo muchas compras de camisas, pantalones, medias y un par de zapatos.

PITI: Y tú, ¿qué compraste?

VILMA: Para mí no pude encontrar nada, pero le compré a tía Zoila varios artículos de cuero interesantes, una billetera y un cinturón, para su cumpleaños.

PITI: Y por la noche, ¿no salieron?

VILMA: ¡Imposible! Llegamos súper cansados a la casa. Victoria durmió tres horas antes de la cena. Mamá no dijo nada pero a todos nos pidió silencio. Yo no dormí pero tuve que descansar.

En el Almacén Wong

En verano mi familia siempre iba al Almacén Wong porque ofrecía muchas gangas y podíamos pagar con tarjeta de crédito o con cheque. Si uno lo pedía, daban buenas rebajas. Tenían camisas de algodón, corbatas de seda, chaquetas y bolsos de cuero a un descuento del 30% o más. Mamá nos compraba mucha ropa para la escuela. Eran compras baratas pero de buena calidad. Y cuando había una venta-liquidación, salíamos de la casa temprano, hacíamos las compras y luego íbamos a comer. Siempre ahorrábamos mucho en el Almacén Wong.

Vocabulario y expresiones

La ropa

el abrigo	overcoat
la billetera	wallet
la blusa	blouse
el bolso	purse, handbag
las botas	boots
la camisa	shirt
la cartera	purse, wallet
el cinturón	belt
la chaqueta	jacket
la corbata	necktie
la falda	skirt
los guantes	gloves
el impermeable	raincoat
los jeans	jeans
las medias	socks/stockings
los pantalones	pants, slacks
las pantimedias	pantyhose
el pañuelo	handkerchief
las sandalias	sandals
el sombrero	hat
el suéter	sweater
el traje	suit
el vestido	dress
los zapatos	shoes
los (zapatos de) tenis	tennis shoes

Las tiendas

el almacén	department store
la caja	cash register
el centro comercial	shopping center, mall
el mostrador	counter
el piso	floor
el probador	fitting room
la sección de ropa	clothing section
la tienda	store
la vitrina	display case

Materiales

el algodón	cotton
el cuero	leather
la lana	wool
la seda	silk

Descripciones

bello(a)	beautiful
corto(a)	short
de buena/mala calidad	good/bad quality
de cuadros	plaid
de manga corta	short sleeve
de manga larga	long sleeve
de rayas	striped
hermoso(a)	beautiful
largo(a)	long
lindo(a)	pretty

Sobre el dinero

al contado	cash
el cheque	(bank) check
el descuento	discount
el dinero	money
en efectivo	cash
la ganga	bargain
la oferta	offer, sale
el precio	price
la rebaja	sale, discount
el recibo	receipt
la venta-liquidación	clearance sale

Palabras claves

al poco rato	a little bit later
el(la) dependiente(a)	clerk
la etiqueta	price tag
hasta	until
luego	then, afterwards, later
el par	pair
según	according to
la talla	size (with clothes)
la tarjeta de crédito	credit card
abrazar	to hug
ahorrar	to save
andar	to walk, to go
aprovechar	to take advantage
atender(ie)	to wait on someone
ayudar	to help
buscar	to look for
cerrar(ie)	to close
cumplir (años)	to be someone's birthday
empezar(ie)	to begin
entrar	to enter
explicar	to explain
llevar	to wear
necesitar	to need
obligar	to force
oír	to hear
pagar	to pay (for)
rebajar	to lower (in price)
recordar(ue)	to remember

¡Así lo decimos!

la ropa

The Spanish words for many items of clothing are often different from country to country. Sometimes several countries share one word to refer to the same item (**vaquero**s—Argentina and México); but other times the same word is used to refer to different items (**saco**—Perú and Cuba). The regional differences of some words from this lesson are listed here.

jeans

Argentina	**jeans, vaqueros**
Cuba	**pitusas**
España	**vaqueros**
México	**pantalones de mezclilla, jeans**
Puerto Rico	**mahones**
Uruguay	**vaqueros**
Venezuela	**bluyín**

sports coat

Argentina, Cuba	**saco**
Colombia, España	**americana de sport, americana**
México	**saco esport**
Venezuela	**palto**

jacket

Argentina, Uruguay	**campera**
España	**jersey** (if it is closed), **chaqueta** (if it is open), **cazadora**
México	**chamarra**
Perú	**saco**
Puerto Rico, Venezuela	**chaqueta**

t-shirt

Argentina, Uruguay	**remera**
Cuba	**pulóver**
España	**camiseta**
México	**playera, camiseta**
Perú	**polo**
Venezuela	**franela**

Ampliación

Ordinal numbers

primero(a)	*first*		**sexto(a)**	*sixth*
segundo(a)	*second*		**séptimo(a)**	*seventh*
tercero(a)	*third*		**octavo(a)**	*eighth*
cuarto(a)	*fourth*		**noveno(a)**	*ninth*
quinto(a)	*fifth*		**décimo(a)**	*tenth*

• Ordinal numbers in Spanish agree in gender and number with the noun they modify. **Primero** and **tercero** are shortened to **primer** and **tercer** before masculine singular nouns. In Spanish, ordinal numbers are rarely used beyond **décimo** (tenth). The cardinal numbers are used instead.

Es la **primera** rebaja del año.	*It's the **first** sale of the year.*
El almacén está en el **tercer** piso.	*The store is on the **third** floor.*
La oficina del presidente está en el piso **doce**.	*The president's office is on the **twelfth** floor.*

 ¡A escuchar!

A. De compras. You will hear a recording of Vilma and Piti's conversation in **¡Así es la vida!** Answer the questions that follow by choosing the correct answer.

1. a. una   b. dos   c. tres
2. a. en Quito   b. en Lima   c. en La Paz
3. a. Manuel   b. Victoria   c. Vilma
4. a. para Manuel   b. para Victoria   c. para tía Zoila
5. a. una hora   b. dos horas   c. tres horas

B. En el Almacén Wong. You will hear the paragraph about *el Almacén Wong*. Complete the statements that follow by choosing the appropriate item.

1. a. invierno   b. verano   c. el centro comercial
2. a. camisas de lana   b. gangas   c. recibos
3. a. a grandes descuentos b. a precios muy altos c. de mala calidad
4. a. a grandes descuentos b. a precios muy bajos c. de buena calidad

◆ Práctica

6–1 En un almacén. Answer the questions based on the information in the illustration.

1. ¿Qué está comprando la señora?
2. ¿De qué forma paga ella?
3. ¿Quién está detrás del mostrador?
4. ¿Cuáles son los artículos que están en rebaja?
5. ¿Cómo son las camisas que miran las jóvenes?
6. ¿Quién las atiende?

6–2 Las rebajas. Answer the questions based on the advertisement from a department store in Peru.

1. ¿Cuáles son los artículos que están en rebaja?
2. ¿Cuántos modelos de suéter hay?
3. ¿De qué material es la playera (polo shirt)?
4. ¿Cuáles son las tallas de la playera? ¿del suéter?
5. ¿Cuántos modelos de jeans hay?
6. ¿Cuál es el precio normal de suéter?
7. ¿Cuánto cuesta el suéter que está en rebaja?
8. ¿Cuántos colores de pantalón hay? ¿Cuáles son?

SUETER PARA DAMA
en acrilán 100%, 7 modelos, gran variedad e colore, tallas: 7 a 11.
de 49,999.00 a
29,990⁰⁰

JEAN PARA DAMA
"MAGIC CLUB"
en mezclilla de algodón 100% acid wash, corte vaquero, 4 modelos, tallas: 7 a 15.
de 54,990.00 a
34,990⁰⁰

PLAYERA TIPO POLO PARA CABALLERO,
en algodón 100%, colores: rojo, mamey, amarillo, blanco, azul cielo tallas: 36-42
de 22,990.00 a
11,990⁰⁰

DE IMPORTACIÓN:
PANTALÓN SPORT
PARA CABALLERO, en algodón 100%, con cinturon, colores: negro, beige, azul, blanco y gris, tassas: 28 a 36
de 69,990.00 a
34,990⁰⁰

6–3 En la tienda. Ask a store clerk for these items. Use the expressions in the model.

MODELO: Quisiera… Busco…
          Me gustaría… Me puede mostrar…

1. a pair of leather boots
2. a cotton shirt for women
3. a woolen sweater
4. a silk dress
5. a blouse on sale
6. a black leather jacket

7. a long-sleeved shirt
8. a pair of tennis shoes
9. a size 37 skirt
10. a good quality handkerchief
11. a wallet with a section for credit cards
12. a short-sleeved jacket

6–4 Sobre la ropa. Complete the statements with words and expressions from **Vocabulario y expresiones.**

1. María lleva un _____ y un par de _____ porque hace mucho frío.
2. Yo llevo un _____ porque está lloviendo mucho.
3. A Tito le quedan muy bien las _____ de playa, pero a Luis los _____ le quedan muy grandes. No va a poder caminar.
4. Aquí no aceptan _____ personales. Hay que pagar con _____.
5. Eduardo pone su dinero en su _____ y Anita pone las entradas dentro de su _____.
6. La _____ de rayas no va bien con la camisa de _____.
7. ¿Estás lista para pagar? Ahí está la _____.
8. ¿Dónde está la _____ de señoras?
9. Quisiera ver cómo me quedan los _____. ¿Dónde está el _____?
10. No uso _____ porque prefiero los kleenex.
11. Me gustan las camisas de _____. No tienen nada artificial.
12. Esos sombreros están en la _____ de hombres. Tienen un _____ del 25%.

6–5 De compras. José Miguel is in the habit of talking to himself as he goes about his business. Complete the paragraph with the appropriate word from the box below.

almacén	artículos	caja	cuadros	dependiente
descuento	dinero	etiqueta	mostrador	oferta
piso	probador	queda	recibo	sección
talla	tarjetas	vitrina		

Tengo el _____ y mis _____ de crédito en la billetera. Ahora estoy en un _____ muy grande porque hay una excelente _____. Estoy en el segundo _____ porque allí está la _____ de ropa de hombres. Todos los _____ están en rebaja. Quiero comprar la camisa de _____ que vi (I saw) en la _____. Según la _____ cuesta dos mil pesetas, pero con el _____ sale en menos. El _____ me la muestra y yo voy al _____ a probármela (try it on). Me _____ muy bien. Es mi _____. Me la llevo y pago la cuenta en la _____ que está detrás del _____. El dependiente me da el _____ y me voy.

6-6 En busca de rebajas. Organize the conversation below in a in a logical way.
Start with number 1.

___ No, sólo los abrigos, pero mañana hay una venta-liquidación en la Miraflores.
___ Sí, es un centro nuevo con muchos pisos y vitrinas. Si quieres, vamos.
___ ¿Va a pagar las cuentas? Debe *(owes)* mucho dinero en ese almacén, ¿no?
___ ¿Y las corbatas no están en rebaja? Necesito una de seda.
___ Si quieres lo ayudo. Aquí tengo mi tarjeta de crédito.
___ Anda en la tienda El Caballero Elegante.

___ Busca un abrigo y en El Caballero Elegante están en rebaja. Es una ganga.
___ ¿Dónde está Lucho?
___ Sí, debe bastante, pero no tiene dinero.
___ Esa tienda está en el centro comercial de San Luis, ¿no es cierto?
___ ¿Me puedes explicar entonces por qué anda en El Caballero Elegante?
___ Gracias, pero mejor no. Lucho necesita aprender a ser responsable.

◆ Actividades

6–7 Describir. Describe how students in class are dressed today.

MODELO: Tom lleva una camisa azul de manga larga y de algodón.
         Lleva pantalones negros, etc.

6–8 El anuncio. In pairs, and using the ads below as a model, create your own
newspaper advertisement for at least four items.

FALDAS PARA NIÑAS DE ESCUELA

En mezclilla (denim).
De cuadros, de rayas, en colores
sólidos. lar gas y cortas.
Tallas 4 a 10.
Originalmente $ 1.200.
Ahora a $ 850.

ZAPATOS PARA HOMBRE

Cuero italiano, muy fino
Colores negro, marrón, azul.
Tallas 38 a 42
De $4.300 a 3.800

Gran oferta

Descuentos del 40% en artículos
de mujer.
Blusas para damas. 100% seda
4 modelos. En tonos pasteles:
celeste, rosa, verde claro y blanco.
Tallas 6 a 12.
De 1.500 a 2.500

6–9 En el centro comercial. In pairs, role-play a clerk and a customer in a
department store. Use words and expressions from **Vocabulario y expresiones.**
Use the expressions below as a guide.

DEPENDIENTE
¿En qué puedo servirle?
¿Necesita ayuda?
¿Ya lo atienden?
¿Cuál es su talla?
Ya se lo muestro.
Le queda (bien/mal).
Es una ganga.
¿Cómo va a pagar?

CLIENTE
Quisiera….
Busco….
¿Me puede mostrar…?
¿Qué tal me queda?
Esta talla no me queda bien.
¿Aceptan…?

 Estructuras

1. More on the Preterite: Irregular Verbs

- The verbs **ser** and **ir** have the same form in the preterite. The context of the
  sentence or the situation will clarify the meaning

  Fui de compras.   *I **went** shopping.*
  Fui su alumno.   *I **was** her student.*

VERB	YO	TÚ	UD./ÉL/ELLA	NOSOTROS(AS)	VOSOTROS(AS)	UDS./ELLOS/ELLAS
andar	anduve	anduviste	anduvo	anduvimos	anduvisteis	anduvieron
estar	estuve	estuviste	estuvo	estuvimos	estuvisteis	estuvieron
tener	tuve	tuviste	tuvo	tuvimos	tuvisteis	tuvieron
dar	di	diste	dio	dimos	disteis	dieron
decir	dije	dijiste	dijo	dijimos	dijisteis	dijeron
traer	traje	trajiste	trajo	trajimos	trajisteis	trajeron
ir	fui	fuiste	fue	fuimos	fuisteis	fueron
hacer	hice	hiciste	hizo	hicimos	hicisteis	hicieron
ser	fui	fuiste	fue	fuimos	fuisteis	fueron
oír	oí	oíste	oyó	oímos	oísteis	oyeron
poder	pude	pudiste	pudo	pudimos	pudisteis	pudieron
poner	puse	pusiste	puso	pusimos	pusisteis	pusieron
querer	quise	quisiste	quiso	quisimos	quisisteis	quisieron
saber	supe	supiste	supo	supimos	supisteis	supieron
venir	vine	viniste	vino	vinimos	vinisteis	vinieron

- **Andar, estar, poder, poner, saber,** and **tener** have a similar pattern with a **u** in the stem.

Estuve en Madrid.	*I was in Madrid*
Pudo ir a la tienda.	*He was able to go to the store.*
¿**Pusiste** la mesa?	*Did you set the table?*
No **supimos** quién era.	*We didn't find out who it was.*

- **Decir, hacer, querer,** and **venir** have a similar pattern with an **i** in the stem.

Dijo la verdad.	*She told the truth.*
¿**Hiciste** la tarea?	*Did you do the homework?*
Quisimos ver la película.	*We wanted to see the movie.*
Vine temprano.	*I came early.*

- **Decir** and **traer** have a **j** in the stem. The third person plural form ends in **-eron** not **-ieron.**

Dijeron que no.	*They said no.*
Trajeron los zapatos.	*They brought the shoes.*

- The forms for **dar** are the same as for regular **-er** and **-ir** verbs, but without the accent in the first and third person, because these forms only have one syllable.

Me **dio** su número de teléfono	*He gave me his phone number*
y yo le **di** el mío.	*and I gave him mine.*

◆ Práctica

6–10 La semana pasada. Describe what the following people did last week.

MODELO: La semana pasada Jorge tuvo que trabajar en la tienda. (Nosotros)
La semana pasada, nosotros tuvimos que trabajar en la tienda.

1. Yo estuve en el Almacén El Globo. (Lucho y Lucía)
2. Yo quise hablar con la dependienta pero no pude. (Tú)
3. Yo traje las sillas de la tienda. (Ellos)
4. El dependiente te hizo un gran descuento. (Nosotros)
5. Lorenzo pudo pagarlo al contado. (Yo)
6. Tania le dijo a Claudio de la oferta en el almacén. (Rufino y Clara)
7. Vine a verlo a la residencia. (Anita)
8. La dependienta puso el vestido en el mostrador. (Yo)
9. No quise el cinturón de cuero. (Tú)
10. No vimos las faldas en la vitrina. (Uds.)
11. No supo sobre la venta-liquidación. (Yo)
12. Nos trajeron una camisa de manga corta. (Él)
13. No vinieron a la tienda. (Nosotros)
14. No tuve que usar la tarjeta de crédito. (Tú)
15. ¿A qué hora anduvieron tus amigos en las tiendas? (Benita)

6-11 ¿Qué hicieron todos en el Corte Inglés? Combine subjects and complements to create novel sentences in Spanish to say what you and others did (preterite) the last time you were in the Spanish department store.

Yo	**poder** conseguir su talla
Nosotros	**decir** que no aceptanm tarjetas de crédito
La dependienta	**andar** por todo el almacén
Mis amigos	**venir** conmigo
Mi compañera española	**hacernos** un buen descuento
Miguel de Cervantes (no)	**saber** una gran oferta
Tú	**darme** un suéter de lana
Mis padres	**estar** en el probador por una hora
Algunos estudiantes extranjeros	**ir a buscar** ropa en la sección de hombres
Los reyes de España	**querer** ver los aparatos domésticos
La infanta *(princess)* Christina	**querer** aceptar un cheque de viajero
	poder encontrar unas gangas
	traer zapatos de rayas verdes y amarillos
	poner todo el dinero en el mostrador

6–12 Ayer. Describe what made yesterday an unusual day. Use the direct or indirect object pronouns, when appropriate to avoid repeating the noun objects mentioned.

MODELO: Siempre hago la tarea por la noche, pero ayer….
Siempre hago la tarea por la noche, pero ayer no la hice.

1. Mi mamá siempre puede hablar con el director de ventas, pero ayer no….
2. El novio de Sonia siempre dice la verdad, pero ayer no….
3. Todas las noches Roberto y Julia ven televisión, pero ayer no….
4. Todas las tardes hacemos nuestra tarea, pero ayer no….
5. Siempre ponen las cazuelas en el lavaplatos, pero ayer no….
6. Todos los días les traemos café con leche, pero ayer no….

6–13 El día de los enamorados *(Valentine's Day)*. Complete Celestino's letter to
Julián by using the correct preterite forms of the verbs in parentheses.

Querido Julián:

   Ayer Paco y yo (andar) _____ por el centro. (Ir)
_____ de compras al centro comercial de Guadalupe.
(Estar) _____ en tres tiendas. (Poder) _____ ver
muchos pañuelos. Yo (tener) _____ mucho cuidado cuando
(hacer) _____ la selección del pañuelo, porque no (poder)
_____ conseguir mucho dinero para la ocasión. En la Tienda
París la dependienta me (traer) _____ un pañuelo de seda
muy bonito y a buen precio. Lo (ver) _____ y ahí mismo
decidí comprarlo. Le pedí un descuento y me lo (dar) _____.
Después yo (ir) _____ a la casa de Maribel y le (dar)
_____ el pañuelo para el Día de los enamorados. (Ser)
_____ un momento muy romántico. Ella me (dar)
_____ muchos besos y abrazos y me (decir)
_____: —Gracias Celestino, te quiero.
   Después Maribel y yo (ir) _____ a comer a un
restaurante italiano. Invitamos a sus padres, pero ellos no (querer)
_____ venir. Nosotros no (saber) _____ por qué
ellos no (venir) _____ con nosotros, pero (ser) _____
_____ mejor. Me caen súper bien, pero cuando (estar)
_____ solos en el restaurante (hacer) _____
planes para nuestra boda. Te vamos a invitar, por supuesto (of
course).
   Te dejo porque tengo que estudiar.

   Un fuerte abrazo,
   Celestino

6–14 La aventura de Beatriz. Beatriz went to the beach last week with a friend. Find out what they did by completing her letter with the correct word from the list.

anduvimos	conocí	conoció	di
dijo	dio	estuve	estuvo
fue	pude	pudimos	puse
supe	trajo	tuvimos	vino

Querida María Antonia:

La semana pasada Marisa y yo _____ ir a la playa. El jueves _____ por la arena y el viernes _____ la oportunidad de conversar con muchos chicos guapos. ¡Ja, ja, ja! Yo _____ a Marcos y _____ que el año pasado él _____ en Tennessee Tech, pero ahora estudia ingeniería en nuestra universidad. No _____ saber cuánto tiempo pasó en los Estados Unidos. Marcos me _____ que me _____ en una fiesta, pero no _____ posible recordar en cuál. Anoche Marcos _____ a verme. Me _____ unas flores muy bellas y me _____ un poema que él escribió. Yo _____ las flores en la mesa y le _____ las gracias y un besito. Pero yo _____ nerviosa todo el tiempo. Creo que me gusta mucho este hombre. ¿Qué piensas de todo esto? Debes escribirme pronto.

Tu amiga,

Beatriz

2. Stem-changing Verbs in the Preterite

- Stem-changing **-ir** verbs also have a stem change in the preterite in the third person singular and plural only. The changes are either **e→i** or **o→u**.

	PEDIR	DORMIR
yo	pedí	dormí
tú	pediste	dormiste
Ud./él/ella	p**i**dió	d**u**rmió
nosotros(as)	pedimos	dormimos
vosotros(as)	pedisteis	dormisteis
Uds./ellos/ellas	p**i**dieron	d**u**rmieron

6–15 ¿Qué hicieron? A group of friends from Almacén Victoria are having dinner on a Friday night. They're all talking at once, discussing bits and pieces about their life. Fill in both blank spaces in each sentence with the appropriate preterite forms of the verbs in parentheses.

1. Yo _____ muy bien, pero Toño y Ángel _____ muy mal por el problema que tuvieron ayer en el almacén. (dormir)
2. Después de que tú les _____ el dinero a los clientes, ¿no te _____ ellos un recibo? (pedir)
3. Le dije a doña Hilda cuando llegó: —Un momento, ya estoy con Ud. — y _____ atendiendo a la cliente; pero doña Hilda _____ interrumpiéndome. (seguir)
4. ¿Te _____ tus compañeros de trabajo?—No, fue la jefa quien me _____.(reñir)
5. Vilma me _____ las instrucciones y después yo te las _____ a ti. ¿No es cierto? (repetir)
6. Ellos llegaron temprano porque _____ bailando hasta la una, pero yo llegué tarde porque, ¡_____ bailando hasta las tres! (seguir)
7. Ayer después del accidente Antonio y Lulú _____ en su casa, pero como era tarde, nosotros también _____ en su casa. Por eso llevamos la misma ropa hoy. (dormir)
8. ¿Dónde _____ tú ese sombrero? —Roberto me lo _____ en la sombrería. Es muy bonito, ¿no? (conseguir)
9. Uds. _____ pañuelos de seda en la tienda de al lado del almacén, ¿verdad? Es una buena tienda. Nosotros _____ chaquetas de lana ahí. (conseguir)
10. Nosotros _____ el bistec de solomillo, pero ellos _____ el pescado porque ya comieron carne en el almuerzo. (preferir)
11. Esta mañana yo _____ cuatro huevos con queso y Cecillia _____ cinco huevos con jamón; por eso no queremos nada con huevo ahora. (freír)
12. —¿Tú me _____ el jugo?
    —No, te lo _____ Ana Isabel. (servir)

6–16 El Globo. Complete Lidia's narration about a day of shopping with her friend Abelardo. Conjugate the verbs in parentheses.

Ayer yo (ir) _____ de compras al centro comercial de Escazú con mi amigo Abelardo. Yo (llegar) _____ allí a las diez de la mañana y Abelardo (llegar) _____ poco después. Entramos al Almacén El Globo y (ir) _____ al tercer piso. Un dependiente muy simpático nos (atender) _____ y nos (decir) _____: —¿En qué puedo servirles—? Yo le (dar) _____ los buenos días y le contesté: —Necesito una chaqueta de cuero—. Él me (conseguir) _____ muchas chaquetas hermosas. Finalmente me (traer) _____ una en rebaja, ¡la más linda de todas! Yo (ir) _____ al probador. (Querer) _____ comprarla porque me quedó muy bien. La (poner) _____ en el mostrador, pero no la (pagar) _____ con mi tarjeta. (Tener) _____ que pagarla al contado porque allí no aceptan tarjetas de crédito.

Abelardo también (hacer) _____ algunas compras. Le (poder) _____ comprar una blusa y una falda a su novia. Nosotros (hacer) _____ otras compras en otras tiendas y (estar) _____ en el centro hasta las dos de la tarde. Nosotros (poder) _____ aprovechar el día muy bien. (Andar) _____ por todas partes y ahorramos mucho dinero porque (poder) _____ aprovechar las grandes rebajas. (Ser) _____ fabuloso.

3. Verbs with Other Spelling Changes in the Preterite

- Verbs that end in **-car, -gar,-** and **-zar** have a spelling change in the first person singular of the preterite. In all other forms, they are conjugated regularly.

c→qu	**buscar**	yo **busqué**	Te **busqué** esta mañana.
g→gu	**llegar**	yo **llegué**	**Llegué** tarde a clase.
z→c	**almorzar**	yo **almorcé**	**Almorcé** al mediodía.

- When an **i** is found between two vowels as in **oír, creer,** and **leer,** in the third-person singular or plural forms it changes to **y.**

Atahualpa no le **creyó** nada.	*Atahualpa did not **believe** him at all.*
Roxana y Rafael **leyeron** la noticia en el periódico.	*Roxana and Rafael **read** the news in the newspaper.*
Ella **oyó** el concierto ayer.	*She **heard** the concert yesterday.*

◆ Práctica

6-17 La verdad es, mamá... Your mother wants to know everything you've been doing since leaving home. Answer her questions in a letter.

1. ¿A qué hora llegaste después de tu visita en casa?
2. Practicaste tus lecciones ayer?
3. ¿La explicaste la lección a tu compañero?
4. ¿Comenzaste a comer mejor?
5. ¿Le buscaste un regalo a tu papá?
6. ¿Tocaste la puerta antes de entrar en tu departamento?
7. ¿Empezaste a estudiar para tus exámenes finales?
8. Pagaste la cuenta de tu tarjeta de crédito?
9. Jugaste al ajedrez con tu amiga?
10. Almorzaste con tu profesora?

6–18 ¿Me puedes contar? In pairs, ask your partner what he/she did last week. Then have him/her ask you the same questions.

MODELO: —¿Jugaste al béisbol?
          —Sí, jugué al béisbol. o —No, no jugué al béisbol.

1. almorzar en un restaurante
2. pagar con cheque en un almacén
3. practicar el fútbol
4. explicarle el juego a un amigo(a)
5. comenzar a hablar español
6. buscar ayuda de alguien
7. abrazar a tu mamá
8. perder la billetera
9. pedirle el recibo al(a la) dependiente(a)
10. freír huevos en la sartén
11. hervir agua para hacer una sopa
12. volar en avión
13. entender la película
14. conseguir algo interesante en las tiendas
15. jugar algún juego violento

◆ Actividades

6–19 La última vez... When was the last time that your partners did the following things? Interview at least two partners.

MODELO: ir a la playa
          —¿Cuándo fue la última vez que fuiste a la playa?
          —En septiembre, antes de las clases.

1. ver a tus padres
2. dar una fiesta
3 pedirles dinero a tus padres
4. andar por tu ciudad o pueblo
5. explicarle la tarea a un compañero(a)
6. tener un examen (y en qué materia)
7. traerle un regalo (gift) a alguien
8. estar enfermo(a)
9. dormir hasta las 10:30 de la mañana
10. salir a bailar (y con quién)
11. jugar a algún deporte (y cuál)
12. ir a algún sitio que no te gustó (y adónde)

6–20 El pretérito. Interview your partners about their recent activities. Write the names of those who answer affirmatively to your questions.

MODELO: llevar corbata la semana pasada
          —¿Llevaste corbata la semana pasada?
          —Sí, llevé corbata una vez. (No, no llevé corbata la semana pasada.)

ir al cine esta semana
salir con tu novio(a) ayer
hacer la tarea para hoy
ir a un centro comercial el sábado
ver un buen programa en la televisión esta semana
jugar al básquetbol esta semana
practicar un instrumento musical ayer
almorzar en McDonald's esta semana
tener buenas noticias la semana pasada

6–21 ¿Qué hiciste? Meet with two or three partners and find out what they did last weekend. Use irregular verbs in the preterite tense to ask each other questions.

MODELO: ¿Qué hiciste…?   ¿Estuviste en…?   ¿Le trajiste…?
           ¿Tuviste que…?   ¿Anduviste por…?   ¿Fuiste a…?

6–22 Y anoche, ¿qué hiciste? In small groups, talk about what each of you did last night. Try to use some of the irregular verbs you have learned in this lesson like **poder, poner, venir, traer, decir, querer, saber, dar, andar,** etc. Be prepared to report your findings to the class.

Estructuras

4. The Imperfect

- As we discussed in **Lección 5** there is a second past tense in Spanish: the imperfect. To form the imperfect, use the endings in the chart below.

CAMINABAMOS,   SUBIAMOS CERROS

Y NOS SENTIAMOS LOS DUEÑOS DEL MUNDO.
NISSAN TERRANO, DE CIDEF.

	HABLAR	COMER	ESCRIBIR
yo	hablaba	comía	escribía
tú	hablabas	comías	escribías
Ud./él/ella	hablaba	comía	escribía
nosotros(as)	hablábamos	comíamos	escribíamos
vosotros(as)	hablabais	comíais	escribíais
Uds./ellos/ellas	hablaban	comían	escribían

- The first person plural of **-ar** verbs has a written accent mark. **-Er** and **-ir** verbs take the same imperfect endings, and all forms have a written accent mark.

- The imperfect is used to describe repeated or continuous actions in the past, with no reference to the beginning or end of the action.

Cuando yo **estaba** en la secundaria **tenía** muchos amigos.	*When **I was** in high school **I had** many friends.*
El joven **tenía** una camisa amarilla.	*The young man **had** a yellow shirt.*
Yo **almorzaba** allí con mucha frecuencia.	*I **used to have lunch** there quite frequently.*

- The Spanish imperfect has three common English equivalents: the simple past, the past progressive, and the *used to* + infinitive construction.

Yo vivía en la capital.	**I lived** in the capital.
	I was living in the capital.
	I used to live in the capital.

- The imperfect is also used to describe an event or action occurring at the same time as another event or action. The other event or action may be expressed by the imperfect or the preterite.

Mientras Eloísa **leía,** Joaquín **escribía** cartas.	*While Eloísa **was reading,** Joaquín **was writing** letters.*
Leonor y Juan **hablaban** cuando **entró** Dulce.	*Leonor and Juan **were talking** when Dulce **came in.***

Irregular verbs in the imperfect

There are three irregular verbs in the imperfect.

¡Cuando era joven yo tenía mejor gusto para la música!

	IR	SER	VER
yo	**iba**	**era**	**veía**
tú	**ibas**	**eras**	**veías**
Ud./él/ella	**iba**	**era**	**veía**
nosotros(as)	**íbamos**	**éramos**	**veíamos**
vosotros(as)	**ibais**	**erais**	**veíais**
Uds./ellos/ellas	**iban**	**eran**	**veían**

Only the first person plural forms of **ir** and **ser** have a written accent mark; all forms of **ver** require a written accent.

◆ Práctica

6–23 Las vacaciones. During the summers Carlos used to work part time at a beach paraphernalia store on the boardwalk. Based on the illustrations, describe what Carlos used to do. Use the given times and expresions as a guide.

MODELO: Cuando Carlos estaba de vacaciones,
          comenzaba el día a las 8 de la mañana.

1. Al poco rato…

2. Luego….

3. A las diez….

4. Siempre….

5. Con frecuencia….

6. A menudo….

7. Todas las tardes….

8. A veces por la noche….

9. Muy a menudo….

10. Por fin….

6–24 Cuando vivíamos en casa. Carlos is reminiscing with his twin sister about what they and their numerous family members used to do when they were living at home. Use the correct form of the imperfect tense.

MODELO: ir a la biblioteca (nosotros)
          íbamos a la biblioteca

1. poner la mesa / yo
2. hacer la cama / tú
3. cocinar la comida / Lucrecia
4. hacer las compras en el supermercado / papá
5. preparar la cena / Lucía y Alfonso
6. atender al abuelo / mamá y yo
7. conseguir flores para la mesa / tú y Lucrecia
8. pasear al perro (the dog) / yo
9. escuchar música después de cenar / todos
10. leer muchas novelas románticas / tú

6–25 En Arequipa. Beatriz Loret de Mola used to live in a city in Peru. Complete her autobiographic description with the imperfect tense of the verbs in parentheses.

Cuando yo (ser) _____ joven, mi familia (vivir) _____en Arequipa, una ciudad de los Andes. Nuestra casa (estar) _____ cerca de la escuela, y mis hermanos y yo (ir) _____ caminando a las clases todas las mañanas. En la escuela yo (tener) _____ muchas amigas y siempre (estar) _____ contenta. Nuestra casa (ser) _____ grande y vieja. (Tener) _____ un sólo piso y (haber) _____muchos cuartos (rooms). Mi hermana Berta y yo (dormir) _____ en uno y mis hermanos Hugo y Juancho en otro. (Ser) _____ mejor así porque ellos (ser) _____ mayores y (necesitar) _____ espacio y silencio. Hugo (trabajar) _____ en un almacén y Juancho (estudiar) _____ en la universidad. Berta y yo (jugar) _____ mucho y (hacer) _____ ruido. Por eso (preferir) _____ estar afuera cuando no (llover) _____. Todas las noches nosotros (ver) _____ televisión, (leer) _____ o (cantar) _____ con la guitarra. (Ser) _____ una familia muy unida.

6–26 En Los Yoses. Complete the paragraphs about Isabel and Norma's shopping trips by selecting the correct verb from the list and conjugating it in the imperfect. Do not use any word more than once.

atender	buscar	hacer	llevar	ver
ayudar	encantar	ir	trabajar	

A mi hermana Norma y a mí nos _____ ir al Almacén Los Yoses. Siempre _____ de compras y _____ las vitrinas. Conchita, una amiga, _____ ahí, y nos _____ muy bien. Para empezar nos _____ a encontrar la mejor ropa. _____ nuestra talla y nos _____ los artículos al probador. También nos _____ muy buenos descuentos.

aprovechar	costar	gustar	ser	poder
comprar	dar	saber	tener	querer

Norma _____ para comprar zapatos. Yo _____ que a ella le _____ los pañuelos y a veces le _____ uno de seda. Como Norma _____ mayor que yo, _____ más dinero y _____ comprar más. A veces yo _____ algo especial pero _____ muy caro y ella me lo _____.

deber	estar	hacer	obligar	regresar	tener
decir	gustar	molestar	querer	ser	traer

Otras veces nosotros _____ a nuestro hermanito menor, Rolando. _____ pequeño y nos _____ mucho. Le _____ andar de allá para acá y nos _____ a caminar mucho. _____ y _____ cosas que no _____, y en general _____ muy travieso. Pero nosotros lo _____ y además, a menudo _____ que ayudar a mamá con el niño. Al final todos _____ muy cansados y con mucha hambre y sed.

◆ Actividades

6–27 Los cambios en mi vida. In small groups, discuss what you do differently now than what you used to do four or five years ago.

MODELO: Ahora compro ropa cara, pero cuando estaba en la escuela secundaria, compraba ropa barata.

6–28 Entrevista. Interview a partner about his/her high school experiences, using the following questions.

1. ¿Eras tímido(a) o sociable?
2. ¿Ibas mucho al cine, al centro comercial, a las tiendas?
3. ¿Tenías novio(a)? ¿Cómo era? ¿Lo/La veías a menudo?
4. ¿Te gustaba estudiar? ¿Sacabas buenas notas?
5. ¿Leías libros o revistas? ¿Cuándo?
6. ¿Cómo era tu escuela? ¿Cómo eran tus clases? ¿Cómo eran tus compañeros?
7. ¿Cuáles eran tus clases favoritas? ¿Por qué?
8. ¿Practicabas deportes? ¿Cuáles?

A propósito...De compras

Ir de compras en un país hispano es una experiencia diferente que en Norteamérica. En España, por ejemplo, las tiendas generalmente abren a las nueve o diez de la mañana y cierran a las dos de la tarde durante tres horas para el almuerzo y la siesta. Vuelven a abrir a las cinco de la tarde y cierran a las ocho o nueve de la noche. Las tiendas están abiertas de lunes a viernes y el sábado por la mañana. Pero esto está cambiando. Los centros comerciales más grandes y modernos con frecuencia abren durante todo el fin de semana, igual que en los Estados Unidos y Canadá. En México y en otros países hispanoamericanos, es posible regatear *(to bargain)* el precio de un artículo en el mercado público o a vendedores ambulantes *(street vendors).* En España y muchos otros países hispanos tanto los empleados (employees) como muchos de los dueños *(owners)* toman un mes de vacaciones al año, casi siempre durante el verano. Muchos comercios cierran por un mes. El turista que va a España en los meses de julio y agosto va a encontrar muchas tiendas y restaurantes cerrados.

En el mundo hispano hay grandes almacenes y supermercados, y también hay una gran cantidad de tiendas especializadas. Es fácil identificar estas tiendas porque por lo general llevan el nombre del producto en el que se especializan y éste casi siempre termina en **-ería.** Así en muchas ciudades hay joyerías, perfumerías, zapaterías, sastrerías, sombrererías, peleterías (fur shops), pastelerías, panaderías, tabaquerías, etc. Los mismos dueños hacen sus propios (own) productos y a menudo son de excelente calidad.

¡Vamos a comparar!

Si vas de compras en un país hispano, ¿en qué cosas tienes que pensar? Con tus compañeros de clase, conversen sobre qué tipo de artículo se vende en las diferentes tiendas en los países hispanos.

¡Así es la vida!

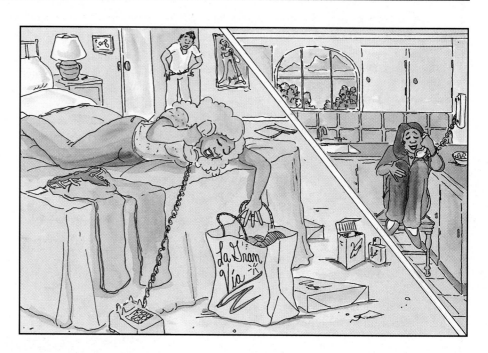

¿Qué compraste?

Andrina ya estaba de vuelta en casa y estaba conversando sobre sus compras con su hermano Armando, cuando sonó el teléfono.

ANDRINA: ¿Oigo?

VIVIANA: Hola, Andrina. Te habla Viviana. ¿Cómo estás?

ANDRINA: Muy bien. ¿Qué tal, Viviana?

VIVIANA: Oye, te llamé tres veces a tu casa y no estabas. Nadie contestó. ¿Dónde andabas?

ANDRINA: Fui de compras a la Gran Vía. Generalmente voy ahí cuando tengo algo especial que comprar.

VIVIANA: ¿Ah sí? ¿Y tenías algo especial que comprar?

ANDRINA: Sí, Gustavo cumple años. Pero, primero compré uno de esos jeans que estaban de moda el verano pasado. ¿Recuerdas? Me quedan perfectamente. Luego fui a la joyería y le compré un llavero de plata a Gustavo. Finalmente fui a la farmacia y le compré una colonia a papá y un perfume a mamá.

VIVIANA: Gastaste muchísimo, ¿no?

ANDRINA: Pues no salió barato, pero lo bueno es que no tuve que pagar al contado. Usé la tarjeta de crédito de papá.

VIVIANA: ¡Pero Andrina!

ANDRINA: Bueno, no es para tanto. El mes que viene se lo pago.

ARMANDO: Siempre dices lo mismo pero nunca lo haces. ¡Pobre papá!

Vocabulario y expresiones

Tipos de tienda

la carnicería	*butcher shop*
la farmacia	*drugstore*
la frutería	*fruit store*
la heladería	*ice cream shop*
la joyería	*jewelry store*
la panadería	*bread shop*
la pastelería	*pastry shop*
la perfumería	*perfume shop*
la pescadería	*fish shop*
la sastrería	*tailor shop*
la sombrerería	*hat shop*
la tabaquería	*tobacco shop*
la verdurería	*vegetable store*
la zapatería	*shoe store*

Las joyas y los metales preciosos

el anillo	*ring*
los aretes	*earrings*
la cadena	*chain*
el collar	*necklace*
el llavero	*key chain*
la medalla	*medal*
el oro	*gold*
los pendientes	*earrings*
la plata	*silver*
la pulsera	*bracelet*
el reloj pulsera	*wristwatch*

Artículos de tocador

la colonia	*cologne*
el champú	*shampoo*
el desodorante	*deodorant*
el jabón	*soap*
la pasta de dientes	*toothpaste*
el perfume	*perfume*
el talco	*powder*

Verbos

aceptar	*to accept*
arreglar	*to fix*
bajar	*go down, get off, to descend*
cumplir años	*to complete (birthday)*
devolver(ue)	*to return (something)*
gastar	*to spend*
pescar	*to fish*
sonar	*to ring*
subir	*to climb, go up, get on*

Adjetivos

amable	*friendly, nice*
cómodo(a)	*comfortable*
enorme	*huge*
frecuente	*frequent*
lento(a)	*slow*
rápido(a)	*fast*
magnífico(a)	*magnificent*
maravilloso(a)	*marvelous*
tranquilo(a)	*calm*
único(a)	*only*

Otras palabras y expresiones

aunque	*even though*
estar de moda	*to be in style*
estar de vuelta	*to be back*
finalmente	*finally*
hacer(le) juego	*to match, go well with*
el lago	*lake*
la montaña	*mountain*
el traje a la medida	*custom-made suit*

¡Así lo decimos!

Earrings

Note the variety of words that are used throughout the Spanish-speaking world to refer to *earrings*.

Argentina	**aros**
Cuba, México	**aretes**
España	**pendientes**
Puerto Rico	**pantallas**
Uruguay	**caravanas, aros (only if they are round)**
Venezuela	**zarcillos**

estar de moda

In most Spanish-speaking countries, you say that **algo está de moda** to mean that something is *in* or *in style*. When you want to say that a person is stylish, you say **Fulana está a la moda.** In addition to the expression **está de moda,** some countries use other variants in everyday speech to convey the same thing.

Argentina, Uruguay	**está de onda**
Chile, México	**está "in"**
Ecuador	**está chic**
España	**es lo que mola, está a la última**

Usar las gorritas al revés **está de onda** en los EE.UU.
Wearing caps backwards is "in" in the U.S.

¡A escuchar!

¿Qué compraste? You will hear the conversation that appears in **¡Así es la vida!** Complete the statements that follow by choosing the correct answer.

1. a. nadie contestó
   b. estaban ocupados
   c. nadie sabía donde estaba
2. a. comprar jeans de moda
   b. llevar a la mamá
   c. comprar algo especial
3. a. la joyería
   b. la farmacia
   c. la panadería
4. a. baratas
   b. caras
   c. ni muy baratas ni muy caras
5. a. y siempre lo hace
   b. pero nunca lo hace
   c. e insiste en que es cierto

◆ Práctica

6–29 De compras. Choose the word or phrase that best completes each statement.

1. En una joyería no venden . . .
   a. pulseras   b. anillos   c. desodorante

2. El vestido le hace juego con el . . .
   a. collar   b. oro   c. talco

3. Voy a la papelería a comprar . . .
   a. un cuaderno   b. champú   c. una pulsera

4. Mi mamá compra el champú en la . . .
   a. joyería   b. sastrería   c. farmacia

5. Los pendientes, el collar y la pulsera hacen . . .
   a. moda   b. a la medida   c. juego

6. Necesito arreglar mi…Voy para la joyería.
   a. traje nuevo   b. reloj pulsera   c. teléfono

7. María Cecilia va a…a eso de las tres de la tarde.
   a. estar de moda   b. pagar con cheque   c. estar de vuelta

8. Elida fue a comprar el pan a la . . .
   a. pastelería   b. panadería   c. tabaquería

9. El nuevo centro comercial es . . .
   a. lento   b. rápido   c. enorme

10. No me gusta comprar en una tienda grande. Prefiero una tienda
    pequeña porque es más…
    a. lenta   b. tranquila   c. frecuente

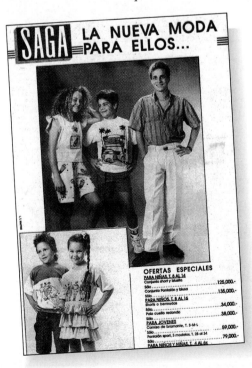

Vamos a Saga. Hay unas
gangas increíbles esta semana.

6-30 ¿Dónde se compra? Match the articles with the illustrations of the store or shop in which they would be found.

1. un anillo de oro
2. unos bolígrafos
3. un vestido
4. un par de botas
5. una colonia
6. una pulsera de plata
7. unos jeans de moda
8. pasta de dientes

9. un pan francés
10. un pastel de manzana
11. un traje a la medida
12. un helado de chocolate
13. un talco
14. una cadena de plata
15. ropa exótica o diferente

a. la heladería

b. la sastrería

c. la zapatería

d. la panadería

e. la joyería

f. la farmacia

g. la pastelería

h. la perfumería

i. la papelería

j. la boutique

6–31 El Corte Inglés. Answer the following questions based on the brochure from *El Corte Inglés,* a famous department store in Spain.

1. ¿Cómo se llama el departamento donde están la perfumería y la joyería?
2. ¿En qué planta está ese departamento?
3. ¿En qué planta está el departamento de ropa para niños?
4. ¿Dónde está la cafetería?
5. Si una señora necesita una talla especial, ¿adónde tiene que ir?
6. ¿En qué planta puede uno llamar por teléfono?
7. ¿En qué departamento puedes conseguir una tarjeta de crédito de El Corte Inglés?
8. ¿En qué planta hay un servicio de intérpretes?
9. ¿En qué planta hay zapatos de tenis para jóvenes?
10. ¿Cuántos departamentos están en el sótano?

MADRID - PRECIADOS

EL CORTE INGLES GUIA DE DEPARTAMENTOS Y SERVICIOS

P / 3-2 / P-1

Servicios: Aparcamiento.

Servicios: Aparcamiento. Carta de Compra. Taller de Montaje de accesorios de automóvil.

1.er SOTANO

Departamentos: Tejidos. Boutique. Mercería. Sedas. Lanas. **Supermercado.** Alimentación. Limpieza. **Imagen y Sonido.** Hi-Fi. Ordenadores. Radio. TV. Vídeos. Librería. Papelería.

Servicios: Patrones de moda. Reparación de Calzado. Plastificado de Carnet. Duplicado de llaves. Grabación de objetos. Consultorio Esotérico.

PLANTA BAJA

Departamentos: Complementos de Moda. Perfumería y Cosmética. Joyería. Bisutería. Bolsos. Fumador. Marroquinería. Medias. Pañuelos. Relojería. Sombreros. Turismo. Fotografía.

Servicios: Reparación relojes y joyas. Estanco. Quiosco de Prensa. Información. Servicio de Intérpretes. Objetos perdidos. Optica 2000. Revelado rápido de Fotografías. Empaquetado de Regalos.

1.a PLANTA

Departamentos: Hogar Menaje. Artesanía. Cerámica. Cristalería. Cubertería. Accesorios Automóvil. Bricolaje. Loza. Orfebrería. Porcelanas (Lladró, Capodimonte). Platería. Regalos. Vajillas. Saneamiento. Electrodomésticos. Muebles de Cocina.

Servicios: Listas de Boda.

2.a PLANTA

Departamentos: Niños/as. (4 a 10 años) Confección. Boutiques. Complementos. Juguetería. **Chicos/as.** (11 a 14 años) Confección. Boutiques. **Bebés.** Confección. Carrocería. Canastillas. Regalos bebé. Zapatería bebé. **Zapatería.** Señoras, Caballeros y Niños.

Servicios: Estudio Fotográfico y realización de retratos.

3.a PLANTA

Departamentos: Confección Caballeros. Confección. Ante y Piel. Boutiques. Ropa Interior. Sastrería a Medida. Artículos de Viajes. Complementos de Moda. Zapatería. Tallas Especiales.

4.a PLANTA

Departamentos: Señoras. Confección. Punto. Peletería. Boutiques Internacionales. Lencería y Corsetería. Futura Mamá. Tallas Especiales. Complementos de Moda. Zapatería. Pronovias.

Servicios: Peluquería Señoras. Conservación de pieles.

5.a PLANTA

Departamentos: Juventud. Confección. Tienda Vaquera. Lencería y Corsetería. Punto. Boutiques. Complementos de Moda. **Deportes.** Prendas deportivas. Zapatería deportiva. Armería. Complementos. Marcas internacionales.

6.a PLANTA

Departamentos: Muebles y Decoración. Dormitorios. Salones. Lámparas. Cuadros. **Hogar Textil.** Mantelerías. Toallas. Visillos. Alfombras y Moquetas. Cortinas. Edredones. Ropa de cama y mesa.

Servicios: "Creamos Hogar". Post-Venta. Enmarque de cuadros. Realización de Retratos. Centro de Comunicaciones (Llamadas telefónicas nacionales e internacionales). Cambio de Moneda Extranjera.

7.a PLANTA

Departamentos: Oportunidades. Promociones.

Servicios: Cafetería. Buffet. Restaurante.

ANEXOS

Preciados, 1. Vídeo-Tienda (Discos, Cassettes, Películas Vídeo, Vídeo-Club).

Preciados, 2. Lainez (Tienda especializada en confección de caballeros).

◆ Actividades

6–32 Muchas compras, poco dinero. In pairs role-play a transaction between a store clerk and a customer. The customer needs four presents for family and friends. He/She has $600 and must make all these purchases within that budget. The clerk gives the price of each article and reasons for buying it. Use the model and the lists below as a guide.

MODELO: —Necesito (me gustaría quisiera, etc.)…¿Cuánto cuesta?
—Cuesta…y está en rebaja.
—¡Ay, qué caro! (Es demasiado./¿Me puede hacer un descuento?, etc.)

ARTÍCULOS	PRECIOS	COMENTARIOS
reloj pulsera	$200	Es/Son una ganga.
aretes de plata	$39,50	Le queda/n muy bien.
un perfume francés	$15,99	No puedo rebajar el precio.
un collar de perlas	$500	Está/n de moda.
un llavero de oro	$350	Usted va a ahorrar mucho.
unos zapatos de cuero	$10,95	Le hago un descuento.

6–33 De compras. You and your friends are giving a dinner party for 15 people. In groups of three or four, look at the menu, make a list of what you have to buy, and agree on labor division. Who is going to buy what at what shop?

MODELO: Pepe va a comprar el pescado en la pescadería.

Menú

Plato principal:

Shis-ke-bab de carne, pollo, mariscos, pescado y vegetales

■

Platos secundarios:

ensalada de papas; pan francés

■

Bebidas:

vino, cerveza, té y café

■

Postres:

ensalada de frutas con helados, pastel de fresa con chantilly, torta de chocolate

Estructuras

3. Preterite or Imperfect?

- In Spanish, the use of the preterite or the imperfect reflects the way the speaker views the action or event being expressed. Compare the two tenses in the following chart.

PRETERITE	IMPERFECT
1. Narrates past actions or events that the speaker views as completed or finished. It tells what happened. **Fui** a Londres. I *went* to London. Paco **estudió** tres años en la universidad. *Paco studied for three years at the university.*	1. Describes what was happening in the past, usually in relation to another event or to a given time, but with no reference to the beginning or end of the action. It tells the way things were. Paco **estudiaba** en la universidad. y **trabajaba** en una tienda. *Paco was studying at the university and working at a store.* **Era** una noche fría. *It was a cold night.*
2. Expresses the beginning or end of past events or actions. Las clases ya **comenzaron**. *Classes have begun already.* La fiesta **terminó** a la una de la mañana. *The party ended at 1:00 a.m.*	2. Expresses habitual actions or events in the past. Las clases siempre **comenzaban** por la mañana. *Classes always started in the morning.* Las fiestas nunca **terminaban** antes del amanecer. *The parties never ended before dawn.*
3. Narrates events that occur in a series. Carlos **entró** en la clase, **vio** a María y **se sentó** con ella. *Carlos came into class, saw María, and sat with her.*	3. Expresses time in the past. **Eran** las cuatro de la tarde. *It was 4 o'clock in the afternoon.*
	4. Expresses mental, physical, and emotional conditions or states in the past. No **sabía** que estabas triste. *I didn't know that you were sad.* Eduardo **se sentía** mal. *Eduardo was feeling badly.*

• The preterite and the imperfect are often used together. The imperfect describes what was happening and sets the scene for other actions and events that take place. The preterite expresses the action being completed while the first action was in progress.

Comía cuando Eloísa **entró.**	*He **was eating** when Eloísa **came in.***
Las chicas **estaban** caminando cuando **vieron** a la profesora.	*The girls **were walking** when **they saw** the professor.*
Llovía cuando aterrizaron en Madrid.	***It was raining** when they landed in Madrid.*
Él y yo **hablábamos** cuando su esposa llamó.	*He and I **were talking** when his wife called.*

STUDY TIPS: Distinguishing between the preterite and the imperfect

Here are a few hints for using the preterite or the imperfect in Spanish.

1. Analyze the context and ask yourself, Does the verb describe the way things *were* or does it tell *what happened?* Use the imperfect to describe and the preterite to tell what happened.

> **Era** de noche cuando **aterrizaron** en Barcelona.
> **Era**—This describes → *It was nighttime.*
> **aterrizaron**—It tells what happened → *They landed.*

2. In many instances the use of the preterite or the imperfect will produce a grammatically correct sentence. However, your choice will communicate how you view the action or event.

> Así **fue.**   *That's **how it happened.***
> Así **era.**   *That's **how it used to be.***

3. Here are some temporal expressions that are frequently used with the tense under which they are listed.

IMPERFECT	PRETERITE
a menudo	anoche
con frecuencia	anteayer
de vez en cuando	ayer
muchas veces	esta mañana
nunca	el fin de semana pasado
siempre	el mes pasado
todas las semanas	el lunes/martes, etc. pasado
todos los días/meses	el lunes/martes, etc. por la mañana
todos los lunes/martes, etc.	

◆ Práctica

6–34 ¿Descripción o acción? What did Sócrates and his buddy used to do during the summer? Change the focus of the sentences from description to action. Use the cues provided.

MODELO: Siempre íbamos al centro comercial. /Ayer
          Ayer fuimos al centro comercial.

1. Durante el verano Sócrates y yo trabajábamos por la mañana en una tienda de artículos deportivos. / El verano pasado

2. Sócrates trabajaba en la caja y yo en el mostrador de artículos especiales. /Anteayer

3. A veces yo trabajaba decorando las vitrinas. / Este lunes que pasó

4. Siempre les vendíamos mucho a nuestros clientes. / El mes pasado

5. Con frecuencia comprábamos artículos deportivos a grandes descuentos. / Ayer

6. Podíamos pagar con cheque o tarjeta de crédito. / Hoy

7. Hacíamos mucho ejercicio todo el tiempo. / El mes pasado

8. A menudo jugábamos al básquetbol o al vólibol con otros compañeros de la tienda. / El jueves por la noche

9. Los domingos andábamos en bicicleta. / El domingo pasado

10. Tú a veces venías con nosotros. / El fin de semana pasado

11. Como Sócrates y yo ya éramos compañeros de cuarto, pasábamos mucho tiempo juntos. / El año pasado

12. Yo usaba las corbatas y los cinturones de Sócrates./ La semana pasada

13. Muchas veces comíamos exageradamente. / Anoche

14. Todas las mañanas Sócrates preparaba un desayuno enorme. / Esta mañana

15. Por la tarde Sócrates y yo asistíamos a clases. / Ayer

16. Los lunes y miércoles íbamos a la biblioteca por tres horas. / Anteayer

17. Todos los martes Sócrates se encontraba contigo para almorzar. / Anoche

18. Yo prefería almorzar en casa de mis padres. / El verano pasado

19. Los viernes todos comíamos en un restaurante chino. / Este viernes

20. Los sábados tú y Ligia venían a la casa. / El sábado pasado

6–35 En esta ocasión. Lucinda and her family are discussing changes or obstacles in their routines. Complete the sentences with the correct form of the preterite or imperfect of the verbs in parentheses.

1. Yo (ver) _____ a tío Luis todos los días en la joyería, pero esa vez no lo (ver) _____ porque (estar) _____ en el dentista.

2. Antes (vender) _____ unos anillos de oro muy bonitos. Ahora no los venden porque tío Luis (traer) _____ muchos aretes y pulseras de plata de Taxco, México.

3. Antes (hacer) _____ buenas rebajas, pero después (subir) _____ mucho los precios.

4. Mi reloj de pulsera no (funcionar) _____, pero tío Luis me lo (arreglar) _____.

5. Ayer yo (gastar) _____ todo mi dinero en la perfumería. Antes no (gastar) _____ tanto.

6. Cuando yo era más joven Uds. nunca me (devolver) _____ mis aretes o collares. Anteayer me (devolver) _____ la cartera porque yo (estar) _____ furiosa.

7. Marina no le (aceptar) _____ joyas a Carlos Luis, pero ayer le (aceptar) _____ una pulsera de plata.

8. Antes Paquita (comprar) _____ los cuadernos en la papelería Luna, pero este año no los (comprar) _____ ahí porque la papelería (cerrar) _____.

9. A menudo ellos (venir) _____ a buscarme a la perfumería, pero ese viernes no (venir) _____ porque yo no (poder) _____ ir a la heladería con ellos.

10. Rigoberto con frecuencia me (comprar) _____ champú, loción o colonia, pero como el año pasado (ganar) _____ mucho dinero, ahora todo me lo compro yo.

11. El perfume de la casa Rimbaud (estar) _____ de moda antes, pero el verano pasado (ser) _____ el perfume de la casa Baudelaire el que más (gustar) _____.

12. Mauricio siempre (pescar) _____ en un lago tranquilo, pero el mes pasado (empezar) _____ a pescar en el mar.

6–36 De compras en el supermercado. Fernando is telling about the errands he had to do today. Complete his story by providing the appropriate form of the imperfect or the preterite.

Yo (tener) _____ que comprar pasta de dientes, pero cuando (llegar) _____ a la farmacia, ya (estar) _____ cerrada. Creo que la farmacia (cerrar) _____ temprano porque el esposo de doña Violeta (estar) _____ enfermo. Entonces (ir) _____ al supermercado y (comprar) _____ un poco de comida para la casa. También (aprovechar) _____ para comprar la pasta de dientes, un desodorante, dos jabones y un talco. Mis compras me (costar) _____ menos porque ayer (bajar) _____ los precios para celebrar el Día de la Independencia. En total (gastar) _____ como treinta dólares que no está mal.

Después del supermercado (pasar) _____ por la panadería. (Ofrecer) _____ un pan español maravilloso, pero sólo (tener) _____ dos bollos (loaves). Los (aceptar) _____ y los (llevar) _____ a casa. Antes (visitar) _____ la pastelería. (Querer) _____ (comprar) un postre porque (venir) _____ mis primas a cenar por la noche. No (tener) _____ los pasteles que siempre compro, pero (ver) _____ unas empanadas de frijoles y (pedir) _____ una para probarla. Me (dar) _____ una pequeña y me (encantar) _____, por eso (pedir) _____ doce más. Finalmente (ir) _____ a la heladería, donde (vender) _____ unos helados de mango deliciosos. (Llegar) _____ a casa muy contenta pero muy pobre.

◆ Actividades

6–37 Entrevista. Interview a partner about what he/she did yesterday. Use the following questions as a guide.

1. ¿A qué hora te levantaste ayer? ¿Cómo te sentías?
2. ¿Qué comiste en el desayuno?
3. ¿Cómo estaba el tiempo?
4. ¿Qué hiciste en la universidad?
5. ¿Qué hora era cuando regresaste a casa?
6. ¿Qué hiciste al regresar a casa?
7. ¿Qué hora era cuando cenaste?
8. ¿Qué tal dormiste?

6–38 Queríamos.... You and some friends wanted to do a great many things today, but were unable to do so. Explain to a partner why you couldn't do what you wanted to do. Then exchange roles. Follow the model.

MODELO: Iba a ver a mi novio(a) esta tarde…
                    Iba a ver a mi novio esta tarde pero tuve que estudiar.

1. Quería cenar en un restaurante mexicano esta noche pero…
2. Pensaba ir a clases esta mañana pero…
3. Tenía deseos de ver una buena obra de teatro pero…
4. Planeaba ir al café con mis amigos pero…
5. Esperaba asistir al concierto con Pedro pero…
6. Tenía ganas de ir a casa este fin de semana pero…
7. Le quería comprar un reloj pulsera a mi hermano(a) pero…
8. …(original)

4. Adverbs ending in *-mente*

¡Están locamente enamorados!

- In Spanish, many adverbs are formed with the addition of **-mente** (equivalent to the English *-ly*) to the feminine singular form of adjectives that end in **-o/-a.**

    lento → **lentamente**   *slow → slowly*
    rápido → **rápidamente**   *rapid → rapidly*

- If the adjective had a written accent mark, the accent remains on the adverb.

    Lucrecia escribe **rápidamente.**   *Lucrecia writes **rapidly**.*
    Esteban lee **lentamente.**   *Esteban reads **slowly**.*

- If the adjective ends in **-e** or a consonant, **-mente** is added directly to the form.

    alegre → **alegremente**
    fácil → **fácilmente**

◆ Práctica

6-39 Transformar. Change the adjectives to adverbs.

1. enorme
2. tranquilo
3. cómodo
4. difícil
5. regular

6. alto
7. único
8. elegante
9. amable
10. brutal

6–40 Mi amigo Orlando. Complete the story of Orlando and his propensity to spend money on friends, by changing the adjectives in parentheses to adverbs.

Antes mi amigo Orlando y yo íbamos juntos de tiendas (frecuente) _____ .
Caminábamos (tranquilo) _____ por las calles y veíamos muchas vitrinas
porque (general) _____ él no tenía dinero. La razón de esto es que Orlando
era (enorme) _____ generoso con sus amigos y amigas. Ahorraba dinero
muy (lento) _____ y (difícil) _____ , pero luego lo gastaba súper
(rápido) _____ en las tiendas, que le encantan, y también en fiestas y en
restaurantes. Invitaba a todos sus amigos (regular) _____ a comer pizza
y tomar cerveza a su casa. Por eso a veces cuando íbamos de tiendas, yo le daba
un poco de dinero, pero él lo aceptaba (único) _____ si veía algo que
le gustaba mucho. Siempre me pagaba (rápido) _____ porque a él le gustaba
hacer las cosas (correcto) _____ . Ahora Orlando es más serio y (alto)
_____ responsable. Siempre es muy generoso, pero cuando se trata de
gastar demasiado dinero, ya sabe decir que no (amable) _____ . Ahora
cuando vamos de compras, (normal) _____ no pensamos mucho en
asuntos de dinero. Orlando ya sabe ahorrar más y gastar menos.

◆ Actividades

6–41 Preguntas personales. In pairs, ask each other the following questions. Try to respond using adverbs formed with the adjectives in the box. Follow the model.

MODELO   —Cómo haces los exámenes?
              —Los hago cuidadosamente.

cuidadoso	difícil	rápido	maravilloso
amable	animado	elegante	excelente

1. ¿Qué tal dormiste anoche?
2. ¿Cómo estabas vestido anoche?
3. ¿Cómo te trataron en el hotel en Costa Rica?
4. ¿Qué tal bailaron tus amigos en la discoteca anoche?
5. ¿Cómo practicaste el tenis esta mañana?

6–42 Semejanzas y diferencias. How do you and your partner do the following activities? What do you have in common? How are you different?

MODELO: —Yo bailo divinamente.
                —Yo no. Yo bailo raramente y muy mal.

ACTIVIDAD		SUGERENCIAS	
cantar	dormir	lento	fácil
aprender cosas nuevas	vestirse	amable	tranquilo
pelearse con su novio(a)	escribir cartas	ansioso	rápido
limpiar la casa	jugar a . . .	difícil	animado
tratar a sus amigos	tratar a los mayores	frequente	brutal
bailar	montar a caballo	respetuoso	cuidadoso
(original)	*(original)*	elegante	raro
		cómodo	alegre

Colaboración

Estudiante A

6–43A ¿Qué llevas cuando…? Interview your partner. Ask him/her what he/she wears on the following occasions.

OCASIÓN

quiere impresionar a la familia
   de su novio(a)

va de vacaciones a Cancún

es un día de enero

es el día del examen final

sus amigos vienen a su casa a
   tomar cerveza

6-44A ¿Qué compras para tu familia? Ask your partner what he or she is going to buy these people for their birthday. Ask about the article, its size, color, and the material.

MODELO: —¿Qué vas a comprarle a tu mamá?
          —Voy a comprarle . . .
          ¿Cuál es su talla? ¿Qué color le gusta? ¿Qué material prefiere?

la mamá

el(la) hermano(a)

el(la) profesor(a)

el(la) novio(a)

el(la) mejor amigo(a)

6-45A Excusas. Your partner wants to know why you did not carry out your responsibilities. Invent excuses using the preterite of the verbs.

MODELO: —¿Por qué no asististe a clase ayer?
          —No asistí porque fui a Acapulco.

ALGUNAS EXCUSAS

ir a . . .

tener que …

comer …

estar…(enfermo, cansado,
    durmiendo, en …)

llegar (tarde)

comprar…

6-46A ¿Es cierto? You like to brag about your experiences and relate some of them to your partner. He/she decides whether to believe you or not. When finished, switch roles.

MODELO: —Una vez visité México.
          ¿Cuándo visitaste México?
          —En el año 1988.
          —Te creo. (No te creo.)

6-47A ¿Cómo era cuando…? Describe to your partner what was going on *(imperfect)* when you first started studying in college *(preterite)*. Your partner will ask you for more details.

MODELO: querer estudiar
          —Cuando empecé mis estudios en esta universidad, quería estudiar….
          —¿Sí? ¿Qué querías estudiar?

SUGERENCIAS

ser (19__)

haber muchos (pocos) estudiantes en mis clases

la universidad **ser** más (menos) grande

conocer a mucha (poca) gente

tener…años

salir con

trabajar en…

pensar estudiar

querer aprender

tener que…

creer…

me **gustar**…

Estudiante B

6-43B ¿Qué llevas cuando…? Interview your partner. Ask him/her what he/she wears on the following occasions.

OCASIÓN

el presidente lo/la invita a la Casa Blanca   limpia la casa

trabaja en su coche   asiste a una boda

la temperatura es 98 grados Fahrenheit

6-44B ¿Qué compras para tu familia? Tell your partner what you are going to buy for the birthday of the people he or she mentions.

MODELO: —¿Qué vas a comprarle a tu mamá?

—Voy a comprarle….

—¿Cuál es su talla? ¿Qué color le gusta? ¿Qué material prefiere?

ALGUNAS PRENDAS

vestido	pañuelo	blusa	suéter
cinturón	camisa	saco	bolsa
billetera	medias	corbata	…

ALGUNOS COLORES

amarillo	rosado	negro	de cuadros
morado	blanco	pardo	…
beige	rojo	de rayas	

ALGUNOS MATERIALES

algodón	nylon	poliéster
lana	seda	pieles *(fur)*
rayón	fuerte azul *(denim)*	cuero

6-45B Excusas. You want to know why your partner did not carry out his/her duties. Ask him/her questions in the preterite.

MODELO: —¿Por qué no asististe a clase ayer?

—No asistí porque fui a Acapulco.

PREGUNTA

no **asistir** a clase ayer	no **hacer** la tarea	**volver** tarde anoche
no **llamar** a su madre ayer	no **dormir** mucho anoche	**terminar** el trabajo
no **estudiar** para el examen	no **trabajar** ayer	**leer** el periódico ayer

6-46B ¿Es cierto? Your partner brags a lot about his/her experiences. You must decide whether you believe him/her or not. When done, switch roles.

MODELO: —Una vez visité México.

¿Cuándo visitaste México?

—En el año 1988.

—Te creo. (No te creo.)

POSIBLES EXPERIENCIAS

| ir a… | ver… | trabajar en… | salir con… | comprar… |
| visitar… | conocer a… | vivir en… | besar a… | |

6-47B ¿Cómo era cuando…? Your partner is going to describe to you what was going on *(imperfect)* when he or she first started studying in college *(preterite)*. Ask him or her for more details and take notes.

MODELO: querer estudiar

—Cuando empecé mis estudios en esta universidad, quería estudiar…

—¿Sí? ¿Qué querías estudiar?

Lección 7

La rutina diaria

Comunicación

- Describing your Habits and Daily Routine
- Expressing Needs Related to Personal Care
- Performing Household Chores
- Giving Instructions

Cultura

- **La tertulia y la peña literaria**
- **Las tareas domésticas**

Mundo hispánico: El Caribe y Centroamérica

Estructuras

Primera parte

- Reflexive Constructions
- The Relative Pronouns **que**, **quien** and **lo que**

Segunda parte

- Formal Commands
- **por** and **para**

PRIMERA PARTE
¡Así es la vida!

El arreglo personal

Antonio, Beatriz y Enrique Castillo son tres hermanos que viven en Barquisimeto, Venezuela. He aquí su rutina de todas las mañanas.

Antonio es madrugador. Siempre se despierta a las seis de la mañana. Después de levantarse, se cepilla los dientes, se ducha y se seca con una toalla. Luego, le prepara el desayuno a su mamá y ella se pone muy contenta.

Beatriz es madrugadora también, pero como anoche no durmió bien, hoy no se despertó temprano. Cuando se levantó esta mañana, se lavó la cara; se vistió rápidamente y salió de casa sin maquillarse. Se puso muy nerviosa cuando llegó a la universidad, porque estaba atrasada.

Enrique nunca se despierta cuando suena el despertador. Le gusta dormir por las mañanas porque, por las noches, siempre se acuesta muy tarde. Después de levantarse, se afeita, se pone loción, se peina y se mira en el espejo. Muchas veces llega tarde al trabajo y su jefe se pone furioso.

Vocabulario y expresiones

El arreglo personal

afeitarse	to shave
bañarse	to take a bath
cepillarse	to brush
ducharse	to take a shower
lavarse	to get washed
maquillarse	to put on makeup
mirarse	to look at oneself
peinarse	to comb
pintarse	to makeup (to polish one's nails)
ponerse	to put on
quitarse	to take off
secarse	to dry oneself
vestirse(i, i)	to get dressed

Otros verbos reflexivos

acordarse(ue) (de)	to remember
acostarse(ue)	to go to bed
alegrarse (de)	to become happy
despedirse(i, i)	to say good-bye
despertarse(ie)	to wake up
divertirse(ie, i)	to have fun
dormirse(ue, u)	to fall asleep
enamorarse (de)	to fall in love (with)
enfermarse	to get sick
enojarse (con)	to get angry (at)
irse	to go away, to leave
levantarse	to get up
llamarse	to be called
morirse(ue, u)	to die
olvidarse	to forget
pelearse	to fight
quedarse	to remain, stay
reírse(i, i)	to laugh
sentarse	to sit down
sentirse(ie, i)	to feel, to regret

Cambios emotivos

ponerse contento(a)	to become happy
ponerse furioso(a)	to get angry
ponerse impaciente	to become impatient
ponerse nervioso(a)	to get nervous
ponerse triste	to become sad

Artículos de uso personal

el cepillo	brush
el cepillo de dientes	toothbrush
el colorete	rouge, blush
la cuchilla (navaja) de afeitar	razor
la crema de afeitar	shaving cream
el desodorante	deodorant
el enjuague	mouthwash
el esmalte	nail polish
el espejo	mirror
el jabón	soap
el lápiz labial	lipstick
la loción	shaving lotion
el maquillaje	makeup
la máquina de afeitar	razor
el peine	comb
la secadora	hair dryer
las tijeras	scissors
la toalla	towel

Algunas partes del cuerpo

la boca	mouth
la cara	face
los dientes	teeth
los dedos	fingers
los labios	lips
las manos	hands
los ojos	eyes
el pelo, cabello	hair
las uñas	nails

Otras palabras y expresiones

atrasado(a)	late, behind schedule
el despertador	alarm clock
he aquí	here is
lo siento	I'm sorry
madrugador(a)	early riser
madrugar	to get up early
temprano	early

◆◆◆◆◆◆◆◆◆◆◆◆◆◆◆◆◆◆◆◆◆◆◆◆◆◆◆◆◆◆

¡Así lo decimos!

enojarse

The standard ways to express *to get angry* are: **enfadarse** (Spain) and **enojarse** (elsewhere). But, in many countries, the idea of getting angry often means losing control over your emotions, and there are many colorful ways of expressing anger, which may be unacceptable in polite conversation. The following colloquial expressions can be used in most informal situations in the country indicated.

Argentina, Uruguay	**calentarse, chivarse, embroncarse**
Cuba	**ponerse bravo, emberrinchinarse, encabronarse**
España	**cabrearse, enfadarse**
México	**enchilarse**
Perú	**amargarse**
Puerto Rico	**enfogonarse**
Venezuela	**arrecharse, cabrearse**

Me calenté cuando me enteré.
I got very angry when I found out.

afeitarse

In previous lessons, you saw several examples in which only one country has a different but standard way of saying something. This is the case with the verb *to shave*.

México, Guatemala   **rasurarse**

¡A escuchar!

Por las mañanas. Listen to the descriptions of daily routine that appear in **¡Así es la vida!** and indicate whether the statements that follow best describe Antonio, Beatriz or Enrique.

ANTONIO	BEATRIZ	ENRIQUE
1. _____	_____	_____
2. _____	_____	_____
3. _____	_____	_____
4. _____	_____	_____
5. _____	_____	_____
6. _____	_____	_____

◆ Práctica

7–1 Fuera de lugar. Circle the word or expression that doesn't belong.

1. a. acostarse   b. bañarse   c. dormirse   d. despertarse
2. a. la secadora   b. la máquina de afeitar   c. los labios   d. las tijeras
3. a. el peine   b. el cepillo de dientes   c. la pasta de dientes   d. las uñas
4. a. afeitarse   b. ducharse   c. ponerse contento   d. peinarse
5. a. el pelo   b. el esmalte   c. el lápiz labial   d. el colorete
6. a. despertador   b. levantarse temprano   c. madrugador   d. estar atrasado
7. a. jabón   b. loción   c. desodorante   d. toalla
8. a. enojarse   b. ponerse furioso   c. ponerse contento   d. estar molesto
9. a. secarse   b. ducharse   c. bañarse   d. lavarse
10. a. pintarse   b. las uñas   c. el esmalte   d. los dientes
11. a. loción   b. cepillo   c. pelo   d. champú
12. a. morirse   b. enamorarse   c. divertirse   d. reírse

7–2 Los artículos de tocador *(dressing table)*. Create a chart with three columns: **hombres, mujeres, los dos.** Using words from **Vocabulario y expresiones,** make three lists of the bathroom articles used by each.

7–3 ¿Qué haces con eso? What do people do with the following items?
MODELO: Juan / tijeras
      Juan usa las tijeras para cortarse el pelo.

1. yo / lápiz labial
2. tú / pasta de dientes
3. mi hermano y yo / peine
4. mi hermano / secadora de pelo
5. María / jabón
6. Pedro y Ramiro / crema de afeitar
7. nosotros / champú
8. Manuel / toalla
9. María Elena / esmalte
10. Julita / el enjuague
11. tú / el espejo
12. yo/ la navaja

7–4 Emparejar. Match the words in the two columns below.

____ 1. vestirse   a. cuchilla
____ 2. afeitarse   b. ropa linda
____ 3. cortarse el pelo   c. espejo
____ 4. bañarse   d. despertador
____ 5. secarse   e. dientes
____ 6. pintarse la boca   f. toalla
____ 7. peinarse   g. lápiz labial
____ 8. madrugar   h. jabón
____ 9. mirarse   i. perfume
____ 10. maquillarse   j. tijeras
____ 11. ponerse   k. los ojos
____ 12. cepillarse   l. peine

7–5 Mi rutina. Create a simple chart of your daily routine hour by hour.

MODELO: 7:00   Despertarme
          7:20   Levantarme y ducharme
          7:30   …

7–6 Las emociones. Complete the sentences by choosing an appropriate expression with **ponerse** from **Vocabulario y expresiones.**

1. Mi hermanita menor me despertó con un vaso de hielo. Yo me puse _____.
2. Tú tienes una clase a las nueve y quince de la mañana y el autobús no llega. Te pones _____.
3. Doris quiere salir con Alberto, pero a él no le interesa. Ella se pone _____.
4. Tenemos un examen muy difícil mañana. Nos ponemos muy _____.
5. Mañana es sábado y voy a dormir hasta el mediodía. Me pongo _____.
6. Claudio necesitaba hablar inmediatamente con la Sra. Brenes, pero el teléfono estaba ocupado. Se puso _____.
7. Roberto y Quique tenían que estar en la escuela para tomar un examen a las ocho de la mañana, pero el despertador no sonó. Se pusieron _____ porque no querían llegar tarde.
8. Yo me iba a poner desodorante pero no había. Mi hermano Camilo lo usó todo ayer y no compró más. Me puse _____.

◆ Actividades

7–7 Las necesidades del viaje. You and a classmate are going to travel together. Make a list of the things you have to buy before leaving. You might share some articles such as toothpaste. Do not spend more than $25 between the two.

MODELO: Para el viaje necesito…
          Yo también. (Yo no, ya tengo…, pero tengo que comprar…) or
          No es necesario. Yo tengo… y podemos compartirlo(la). (share)

ARTÍCULO	COSTO	ARTÍCULO	COSTO
cepillo de dientes	1,00	peine	1,00
crema de afeitar	2,00	tijeras	5,00
desodorante	2,50	jabón	0,50
enjuague	2,50	secadora	15,00
loción	2,00	despertador	10,00
navajas	1,50	espejo	4,00

Estructuras

1. Reflexive Constructions

A reflexive construction is one in which the subject both performs and receives the action expressed by the verb. The verb is always a reflexive verb, which means that it is accompanied by a reflexive pronoun.

Isabel **se peina**.
Isabel combs her hair.

Isabel **peina** a su hermana.
Isabel combs her sister's hair.

Reflexive Pronouns		
SUBJECT PRONOUNS	REFLEXIVE PRONOUNS	
yo	**me**	*(myself)*
tú	**te**	*(yourself)*
él, ella, Ud.	**se**	*(himself, herself, yourself)*
nosotros	**nos**	*(ourselves)*
vosotros	**os**	*(yourselves)*
ellos, ellas, Uds.	**se**	*(themselves, yourselves)*

• Reflexive pronouns have the same forms as direct and indirect object pronouns, except in the third person singular and plural **(se).**

• As with the object pronouns, reflexive pronouns are placed immediately before the conjugated verb, or attached to the **-ndo** form of the progressive or attached to the infinitive.

Me peino.	*I'm combing **myself**.*
Te estás bañando. (Estás bañándo**te**.)	***You** are taking a bath.*
Ema **se** va a maquillar. (Ema va a maquillar**se**.)	*Ema **is going to** put on makeup.*

Reflexive verbs

- Verbs that describe personal care and daily habits carry a reflexive pronoun if the same person performs and receives the action. The same verbs can also be used nonreflexively.

Me acuesto temprano.	*I go to bed early.*
Acuesto temprano a mi hermano.	*I put my brother to bed early.*
¿**Te afeitaste** hoy?	*Did you shave today?*
La enfermera **afeitó** al paciente.	*The nurse shaved the patient.*

- In Spanish, verbs that express feelings, moods and changes in condition or emotional state are often used with reflexive pronouns. In English, verbs like *to get* or *to become,* or nonreflexive verbs are used to describe feelings, moods, and changes in condition or emotional state.

Me alegro de verte.	*I'm happy to see you.*
Se enoja si pierde.	*He gets angry if he loses.*
Tiqui **se enamoró** de Luis.	*Tiqui fell in love with Luis.*
Nos divertimos mucho juntos.	*We have a lot of fun together.*
No **me acuerdo** de nada.	*I don't remember anything.*
Eusebio **se enfermó.**	*Eusebio got sick.*
Nos peleamos ayer.	*We had a fight yesterday.*

- Some verbs have different meanings when used with a reflexive pronoun than when used without it.

NON REFLEXIVE		REFLEXIVE	
acostar	to put to bed	**acostarse**	to go to bed
dormir	to sleep	**dormirse**	to fall asleep
ir	to go	**irse**	to go away
levantar	to lift	**levantarse**	to get up
llamar	to call	**llamarse**	to be called
poner	to put, to place	**ponerse**	to put on, to become
quitar	to remove	**quitarse**	to take off
vestir	to dress	**vestirse**	to get dressed

- The plural reflexive pronouns **nos, os,** and **se,** may be used with certain verbs to express reciprocal actions. These actions are expressed in English by *each other* or *one another.*

Nos queremos mucho.	*We love each other a lot.*
Se ven todos los días.	*They see one another everyday.*

◆ Práctica

7–8 ¿Qué hicieron? Look at the chart and write nine sentences in the preterite describing what these people did and at what time.

GERARDO Y ROXANA	NOSOTROS	EMILIA
8:00 a.m.	vestirse rápidamente	6:30 a.m.
despedirse de su mamá	1:00 p.m.	servirse el desayuno
verse en la cafetería y	irse a la biblioteca y	9:00 a.m.
sentarse juntos	quedarse hasta las 3:00	sentirse enferma y
11:00 a.m.	9:00 p.m.	olvidarse de llamar a
	divertirse en el baile	Lucía
		6:00 p.m.
		acostarse temprano
		dormirse en el sofá

7–9 En el campamento de verano. You are new at summer camp and you have a million questions about everything.

MODELO: lavarse las manos ahora (nosotros)
          ¿Nos lavamos las manos ahora?

1. levantarse a las 8:00 a.m., ¿verdad? (yo)
2. ducharse a las 8:30 a.m., ¿no? (nosotros)
3. vestirse a las 9:00 a.m., ¿sí? (José)
4. poderse sentar cerca de la televisión (Uds.)
5. lavarse los dientes después de comer (tú)
6. acostarse tarde, ¿verdad? (Ud.)
7. enamorarse el año pasado (los consejeros)
8. enojarse con Cecilia ayer (tú)
9. morirse el mes pasado (el director)
10. enfermarse seriamente (Gonzalo)

7–10 Mi mejor amigo y yo. Form complete sentences that explain some of the things you and your spouse or roommate, children, or best friend do together.

MODELO: escribirse cartas cuando…
          Nos escribimos cartas cuando estamos separados(as).

1. verse por las mañanas…
2. encontrarse después de las clases…
3. contarse todas las cosas…
4. entenderse perfectamente…
5. conocerse muy bien…
6. visitarse por la tarde…
7. llamarse por teléfono…
8. juntarse para ir…
9. acordarse de nuestros cumpleaños…
10. enojarse de vez en cuando…
11. sentarse juntos en…
12. ponerse contentos…

7–11 Marcela y yo. Complete this person's melancholy reminiscenses about last summer with the correct preterite or imperfect form of the reflexive verbs in parentheses.

El verano pasado Marcela y yo (irse) _____ a menudo a la playa con Gisela, la hermana de Marcela, y su esposo Lalo. Yo (divertirse) _____ mucho. Los sábados por la noche, después de que Gisela y Lalo (acostarse) _____, nosotros (quedarse) _____ en la playa hablando por horas. (Sentarse) _____ frente al mar y no (acostarse) _____ hasta muy tarde. La última vez que (ir) _____ fue muy especial. A la hora de dormir yo (irse) _____ a mi cuarto a las 10 p.m., pero de la emoción no (dormirse) _____ hasta la medianoche. ¡(Sentirme) _____ tan contento!

El domingo Gisela y Lalo (bañarse) _____ en el mar muy temprano y (irse) _____ para la ciudad mientras Marcela y yo (dormir) _____ . Nosotros (despertarse) _____ tarde, (bañarse) _____ en el mar, (vestirse) _____ y regresamos a la ciudad. Pero por la tarde Marcela (enojarse) _____ conmigo y nosotros (pelearse) _____ muy seriamente. Yo (ponerse) _____ furioso y no le hablé más. Ella (ponerse) _____ muy triste.

Cuando llegamos a la casa nosotros (despedirse) _____ y aunque después hablamos varias veces por teléfono, ya no (volver a verse) _____ más. Por eso ayer cuando la vi (alegrarse) _____ mucho. Fuimos a un café y (divertirnos) _____ recordando los buenos tiempos. No (enamorarse) _____ otra vez, pero ya (olvidarse) _____ del pasado y ahora podemos ser buenos amigos otra vez.

7–12 ¿Cómo se pusieron? Express how each person felt in the following situations.

MODELO: Quería salir a jugar al tenis pero llovía mucho. Me puse triste.

1. Mi compañera de cuarto me iba a llevar a la universidad. Yo tenía mucha prisa porque estaba atrasado, pero ella se peinaba, se maquillaba y se miraba muchas veces en el espejo.
2. Tú tenías una fiesta muy importante y era la primera vez que ibas a cortarte el pelo con esa persona.
3. Los niños estaban viendo una película y el perro del héroe se murió.
4. Nuestros padres nos llamaron para contarnos que ganaron $10.000 en la lotería.
5. Yanina ya estaba prácticamente dormida cuando Esteban puso una música rock a todo volumen *(very loud)*.

◆ Actividades

7–13 Contestar el teléfono. Your roommate is preparing for a difficult exam and has asked you to screen his/her calls. Prepare six excuses that you can use so that he/she doesn't have to come to the phone. In pairs, take turns playing the caller and the roommate answering the phone.

MODELO: —¿Puedo hablar con… ?
                     —No, está bañandose. (No, se está bañando.)

7–14 Entrevista. Interview another person and create a chart about his/her routine on a typical day. Use the questions below as a starting point. Be prepared to report your findings to another person or to the whole class in the third person.

MODELO: Clemente se despierta a las cinco y media de la mañana.
                A las seis en punto se desayuna. Después…

1. ¿A qué hora te despiertas (te levantas)?
2. ¿Te duchas o te bañas? ¿A qué hora?
3. ¿A qué hora te desayunas? ¿Qué desayunas?
4. etcétera

7–15 Una relación especial. In pairs, take turns asking each other questions about a special relationship, be it with a close friend, a boyfriend or girlfriend, husband or wife, or a pet.

1. ¿Cuándo se conocieron?
2. ¿Con qué frecuencia se ven?
3. ¿Dónde se encuentran generalmente?
4. ¿Cuántas veces al día se llaman por teléfono?
5. ¿Se quieren mucho?
6. ¿Se enojan a veces? ¿Por qué?
7. etcétera

7–16 La rutina diaria. First write questions about each item below on a separate piece of paper. Then, in small groups, interview your classmates about their daily routine. Write at least one answer per item.

MODELO: afeitarse los sábados
    —¿Te afeitas los sábados?
    —Sí, me afeito los sábados. (No, no me afeito los sábados.)

1. peinarse muchas veces al día
2. dormirse normalmente antes de la doce
3. alegrarse cuando lo(la) invitan a salir
4. enojarse cuando recibe una mala nota
5. divertirse en clase
6. levantarse tarde los fines de semana
7. ducharse por la mañana
8. secarse el pelo con secadora
9. vestirse antes o después de desayunar
10. olvidarse de su tarea

2. The Relative Pronouns *que, quien,* and *lo que*

¡Éste es, papá! ¡Éste es el coche que quiero!

- Relative pronouns are used to join two sentences that have something in common.

Tenemos un **apartamento** grande.	*We have a big **apartment**.*
El **apartamento** está en la playa.	*The **apartment** is on the beach.*
Tenemos un apartamento grande **que** está en la playa.	*We have a big apartment **that** is on the beach.*

- The relative pronoun **que,** meaning *that, which, who* or *whom,* may be used for both people and objects.

El folleto **que** te di está en la mesa.   *The brochure (that) I gave you is on the table.*

Esa chica **que** ves allí es mi novia.   *That girl (that) you see there is my girlfriend.*

- The relative pronoun **quien(es),** meaning *who* or *whom,* refers only to persons and is mostly commonly used as an indirect object or after a preposition.

Ésas son las chicas **con quienes** te vi.   *Those are the girls **with whom** I saw you.*

La persona **a quien** me recomendó no estaba en su oficina.   *The person **to whom** you recommended me was not in his office.*

- The relative pronoun **lo que,** meaning *what* or *that which,* is a neuter form and refers to a previous idea, event, or situation.

No me gustó **lo que** hiciste.   *I didn't like **what** you did.*

¿Entiendes **lo que** dice el profesor?   *Do you understand **what** the professor says?*

- In Spanish, the use of the relative pronoun **que** is never optional as it is in many instances in conversation in English.

Estoy buscando la guía **que** compraste.   *I'm looking for the travel book (that) you bought.*

La Coca-Cola **que** te trajo la azafata está caliente.   *The Coca Cola (that) the flight attendant brought you is warm.*

◆ Práctica

7–17 Completar. Fill in the blanks with the correct forms of the relative pronouns **que, quien, quienes** or **lo que.**

1. ¿Dónde está la señorita tan simpática con _____ hablé ayer?
2. El señor _____ está delante de mí, va primero.
3. El espejo _____ está en la silla no es el nuestro.
4. El problema _____ más me procupa es _____ no tenemos mucho dinero para las compras.
5. _____ usted necesita es ir al aeropuerto temprano.
6. Los cepillos de dientes _____ compramos ayer están en la mesa.
7. Ésa es la nueva dependiente _____ comenzó a trabajar hoy.
8. El muchacho a _____ te presenté ayer es muy madrugador.
9. _____ tenemos que hacer es comparar precios.
10. ¿Quiénes son las señoras con _____ conversabas ayer?

7–18 Lo que necesito. Restate each sentence using the relative pronoun **lo que.**

MODELO: Necesito más tiempo.
          Lo que necesito es más tiempo.

1. Digo la verdad.
2. Necesito tu ayuda.
3. Te hace falta dinero.
4. Tengo que comprarme un coche nuevo.
5. Dices tonterías *(foolishness)*.
6. Me hace falta tu presencia.
7. Necesito diez dólares.
8. El ruido de la calle despierta a la bebé.
9. Me gusta maquillarme.
10. Me enoja no encontrar las tijeras en su lugar.
11. No me acuerdo si compré el colorete.
12. Nos encanta pintarnos los ojos.

7–19 Una telenovela *(soap opera).* Complete the paragraph with the relative pronouns **que** or **quien.**

Mi amor es la telenovela _____ más público tiene. El actor principal, Álvaro Montalbán, es el actor de _____ todos hablan. Dicen que este año va a ganar el premio Talía, _____ es el equivalente al Óscar norteamericano. Las chicas dicen que Álvaro es el actor con _____ les gustaría salir. Silvina Bermúdez, la actriz principal de la telenovela, a _____ todo el mundo quiere, está enamorada de Álvaro, pero Álvaro no la quiere. Esmeralda del Norte es la chica a _____ él quiere, pero Esmeralda no es buena. Es una chica a _____ sólo le interesa el dinero de Álvaro. La telenovela _____ pasan por televisión al mediodía es muy melodramática. Siempre hay problemas _____ mantienen el interés del público.

◆ Actividades

7–20 Una conversación entre amigos. Jorge is going to a party tomorrow and still doesn't have a date. He's in the cafeteria talking with his friend Eduardo when Angélica walks in. Complete the conversation between Jorge and Eduardo using the relative pronouns **que** and **quien.** Compare your conversation with that of a classmate.

JORGE: Ésa es la chica a…
EDUARDO: ¿Conoces a Angélica?
JORGE: No, no la conozco, pero sé…
EDUARDO: ¡Por favor, Jorge! Angélica es la chica a… Es… Además…
JORGE: No importa. Mi corazón me dice…
EDUARDO: ¡Qué ridículo estás! No te voy a presentar a Angélica sino a un psiquiatra…

7–21 En el centro comercial de Santa Ana. In pairs, take turns role-playing a clerk at the information booth of a large shopping center and the customers seeking information. The different customers ask for items on the list. The clerk sends them to the appropriate places according to the layout of the shopping center.

MODELO: Lo que quiero es la sección de ropa para hombres.
                  Lo que tiene que hacer es ir al primer piso a…
                  Lo que necesita es subir al segundo piso y…
                  La tienda que tiene eso está en… y se llama…

1. querer conseguir un buen perfume
2. necesitar unos jeans para niños
3. buscar un anillo de compromiso
4. comer un pollo asado
5. desear una crema para quitarse el maquillaje
6. desear un traje a la medida
7. tener sed / querer café y algún pastel
8. andar buscando una secadora de ropa
9. querer un jabón y desodorante
10. buscar unas buenas botas de cuero

A propósito... Otras costumbres de la vida diaria

En la gran mayoría de los países hispanos el costo de la mano de obra *(manual labor)* todavía es relativamente barato. Es por eso que muchas familias todavía tienen empleados domésticos o sirvientes que ayudan con la cocina, la limpieza, el jardín y otros quehaceres del hogar. En algunos países hispanos, los electrodomésticos como las lavadoras, los lavaplatos y los hornos microondas son un lujo y, entonces, la gente hace las tareas a mano. Como no hay tanta tecnología, la vida es más lenta y un poco más tranquila que en los países altamente desarrollados. Esto significa que hay más tiempo. Por eso, y también porque los hispanos en general son muy sociables, otras dos costumbres muy populares son **la tertulia** y **la peña literaria.** La tertulia consiste de un grupo de amigos que van a la casa de uno de ellos o a un café a una hora determinada para conversar y beber algo. En la tertulia conversan de muchas cosas como la política, los deportes y las películas. La peña literaria es similar a la tertulia, pero es una reunión más formal. La gente va para conversar sobre autores u obras *(works)* literarias.

Otras dos costumbres diarias son la siesta, y el café o el té de la tarde. Muchas personas todavía se acuestan a dormir una o dos horas después del almuerzo, por lo menos los domingos y, según el país, por la tarde se toman un café o un té a las tres, las cuatro o las cinco. Este café o té con frecuencia se toma con pasteles, pan o tostadas.

¡Vamos a comparar!

¿Hay en su casa empleados domésticos? ¿Por qué? ¿Cuál es la diferencia entre una tertulia y una peña literaria? ¿Duerme siestas? ¿Cuándo?

¡Así es la vida!

La agente de bienes raíces

AGENTE: Pasé por la casa del señor Dalí. ¡Es fabulosa! Creo que le va a interesar.

CLIENTE: ¿Ah, sí? Dígame, ¿cuándo puedo verla?

AGENTE: Mañana si quiere. Vaya y véala porque es ideal para Ud. En la planta alta tiene tres dormitorios grandes y dos baños completos. La sala está debajo del cuarto principal en la planta baja. Es enorme y tiene una terraza. Mañana no deje de salir al jardín. ¡Es maravilloso!

CLIENTE: Me interesa. Cuénteme más.

AGENTE: Pues, el comedor no es muy grande, pero puede poner un aparador contra la pared grande y una mesa para ocho o diez personas. La cocina en cambio es muy grande y está al lado del garaje. Es un garaje doble, para dos carros. Ah, y me olvidaba, en la planta baja, entre la cocina y el comedor, hay un medio baño. También tiene una despensa suficientemente grande para guardar comida, la aspiradora y la escoba. Lo que no tiene es lavandería, pero como la cocina es grande, podría poner la lavadora de ropa y la secadora ahí.

CLIENTE: Bueno, no hay más que hablar. Deme una cita para la mañana. ¿Le parece bien?

Los quehaceres domésticos de María Isabel

María Isabel es una chica trabajadora. Se levanta a las seis de la mañana. Se cepilla los dientes, se ducha y se pone a hacer los quehaceres de la casa. Hace la cama y ordena el cuarto. Enseguida pasa la aspiradora y plancha la ropa que se va a poner. Cuando termina se prepara un buen desayuno. A las ocho sale de la casa, se sube a su carro y se va para la agencia de bienes raíces Castillo y Peralta. Ahí trabaja de asistente de los agentes de bienes raíces de nueve de la mañana a cinco de la tarde. Le encantan las casas bellas y sueña con tener una algún día. Por la noche, si no sale con amigos, llega a la casa, prepara la comida, pone la mesa y se sienta a comer frente a la televisión en el comedor. Después de la comida, sacude el sofá, barre el piso de la cocina y saca la basura. Finalmente se acuesta a leer novelas de misterio.

Vocabulario y expresiones

Los quehaceres domésticos

barrer el piso	*to sweep the floor*
cortar la hierba	*to mow the lawn*
lavar la ropa	*to wash clothes*
limpiar la casa	*to clean the house*
ordenar el cuarto	*to straighten up one's room*
pasar la aspiradora	*to vacuum*
planchar la ropa	*to iron*
preparar la comida	*to prepare the meal*
sacar la basura	*to take out the garbage*
sacudir los muebles	*to dust the furniture*

Las partes de una casa

la cocina	*kitchen*
el comedor	*dining room*
el cuarto/dormitorio	*bedroom*
el baño	*bathroom*
la despensa	*pantry*
la escalera	*stairs*
el garaje	*garage*
el jardín	*garden, yard*
la lavandería	*laundry room*
el pasillo	*hall*
el piso	*floor, apartment (Sp.)*
la planta alta/baja	*upstairs/downstairs*
la sala	*living room*
la terraza	*terrace, porch*

Los muebles

la alfombra	*rug*
el aparador	*china cabinet*
la cama	*bed*
la cómoda	*dresser*
el estante	*shelf*
la lámpara	*lamp*
el librero	*bookcase*
la mesa de noche	*night table*
la mecedora	*rocking chair*
el sofá	*sofa*
el sillón	*armchair*

Accesorios

la aspiradora	*vacuum cleaner*
el basurero	*garbage can*
la escoba	*broom*
la lavadora	*washer*
la plancha	*iron*
la secadora	*dryer*
el equipo de sonido	*sound system*

Preposiciones de lugar

arriba de	*above*
contra	*against*
debajo de	*under*
dentro de	*within, inside of*

Expresiones con *por*

por aquí (ahí/allí)	*around there*
por ahora	*for now*
por cierto	*by the way, for certain*
por Dios	*for God's sake*
por ejemplo	*for example*
por fin (último)	*finally*
por lo general	*in general*
por lo visto	*apparently*
por poco	*almost*
por suerte	*luckily*

Otras palabras y expresiones

la agencia	*agency*
el(la) agente	*agent*
los bienes raíces	*real estate*
cambiar	*to change*
de vez en cuando	*from time to time, once in a while*
donde	*where*
en cambio	*instead*
guardar	*to put away*
pesado(a)	*tedious, dull*
el(la) sirviente(a)	*maid*
la visita	*guest(s), visitors*

¡Así lo decimos!

pesado(a)

It is human nature to comment on what we think of people and of different experiences. In this chapter, you learned that **pesado(a)** is used to remark about a dull or tedious situation. In Spanish, the same word can be used to refer to people, e.g., **Esa persona es pesada**. The closest English equivalent is: *That person is such a drag/bore.* There are many colorful regional variations of this expression.

Argentina	**es densa, es un plomo**
Chile	**es un cargante**
Cuba	**es un bofe, es un hígado**
España	**es un(a) plasta, es un palizas**
Uruguay	**es imbancable, es un plomo/plomazo**

Esa persona es un hígado.
That person is a real drag.

el baño

When you travel, it is often necessary to ask where the restrooms are located. The word **baño** is generally used for bathrooms in a house. Other words are used to refer to public restrooms.

Argentina	**el servicio**
Cuba	**el baño público**
Ecuador	**el wáter, WC**
España	**los servicios, el wáter, WC**
México	**el sanitario, el excusado**
Uruguay	**los toilettes**

In the midwest of the United States and Canada, some people use a different word for restroom. Do you know the word?

car

Other than colloquial words, any of the three standard words for *car* will generally be understood in most Spanish-speaking countries. Note the word that is preferred in the following countries.

Argentina, Uruguay	**auto**
Cuba	**carro, máquina (colloquial)**
España	**coche, buga(ati) (colloquial)**
México	**coche**
Venezuela	**carro**

¡A escuchar!

A. La casa del Sr. Dalí. Listen to the conversation about Mr. Dalí's house in **¡Así es la vida!** Then, decide whether the statements that follow are **cierto** or **falso**.

CIERTO   FALSO

1. _____   _____
2. _____   _____
3. _____   _____
4. _____   _____

B. La rutina de María Isabel. Listen to the description of María Isabel's daily routine from **¡Así es la vida!** and label the illustrations in their proper sequence.

_____

_____

_____

_____

_____

_____

_____

_____

_____

◆ Práctica

7–22 Emparejar. Match the items in the two columns.

___ 1. escalera   a. comedor
___ 2. escoba   b. mesa de noche
___ 3. ropa   c. planta alta
___ 4. cuadro   d. escritorio
___ 5. cómoda   e. pared
___ 6. ducha   f. aspiradora
___ 7. aparador   g. planchar
___ 8. basurero   h. barrer
___ 9. cama   i. garaje
___ 10. lámpara   j. baño
___ 11. limpiar la casa   k. oficina
___ 12. estante de libros   l. dormitorio

7-23 Mi vida es muy diferente. Complete this person's reminiscence about how things used to be by choosing the appropriate word from the list.

aspiradora	limpiaba	mueren	secaba
barría	limpio	ordenaba	sucio
lavaba	mesa	ordeno	
quehaceres	muebles	planchaba	

Cuando yo era niño, mi vida era diferente. Nosotros teníamos muchos _____ domésticos. Todos los días yo pasaba la _____ en la sala, _____ y _____ los cuartos y _____ la terraza con la escoba. Mi hermana Pilar siempre _____ , _____ y _____ la ropa. Mis hermanos Tito y Gilberto casi siempre sacudían los _____ y ponían la _____. Cuando nuestros padres llegaban del trabajo todo estaba listo y perfecto. Ahora mi cuarto siempre está _____ porque ni lo _____ ni lo _____ muy a menudo. Si mis padres vienen yo creo que se _____.

7–24 Los quehaceres domésticos. Write at least ten complete, logical sentences about who did what in this family by combining elements from the columns below.

MODELO: Hoy lavé los platos en la cocina.

Yo	poner	la cocina
Mi tía	lavar	la basura
Sus abuelos	limpiar	los muebles
Nuestros padres	planchar	la cama
Tus hermanos	sacar	los platos
Pepe y yo	barrer	la mesa
Juan y tú	sacudir	la ropa
Tú	hacer	la terraza
Marla	ordenar	el cuarto
Uds.	preparar	la comida
Nosotros	cortar	la hierba
La sirvienta	pasar	la aspiradora

7–25 Mirando un plano. Looking at the floor plan below, answer the questions.

1. ¿Es el plano de un piso o una casa?
2. ¿Cuántos cuartos tiene?
3. ¿Cuántos baños hay? ¿Son baños completos?
4. ¿Dónde está la sala?
5. ¿Dónde está la cocina?
6. ¿Cuántas personas pueden pasar la noche cómodamente ahí?
7. ¿Es grande la sala?
8. ¿Hay una terraza? ¿Dónde?
9. ¿Hay alfombras?
10. ¿Qué muebles hay?

PISOS

ESTRUCTURA:	Hormigón armado con pilares y vigas planas.
FORJADOS:	Unidireccionales de vigueta pretensada y bovedilla.
ACRISTALAMIENTO:	Doble acristalamiento tipo Climalit.
CALEFACCIÓN:	Centralizada en fuel-oil con contadores individuales. Producción de ague caliente centralizada.
SOLADOS:	Pavimento de gres en cocina y aseos, mármol en portal y escaleras y ferrogres en terrazas, parquet de espiga resto del edificio.
COCINA:	Totalmente amueblada.
VARIOS:	Ascensor, Antena TV. FM. Canalización para C.T.N.E.

7–26 Mi casa. Write a paragraph about your house or apartment and the furniture it has. Give as much detail as you can.

◆ Actividades

7-27 Los quehaceres domésticos. Discuss household chores with a classmate. Use the model as a starting point.

MODELO: —¿Cuántas veces a la semana ordenas o limpias tu cuarto?
          —Lo limpio una vez a la semana. ¿Y tú?
          —¿Quién lava los platos, tu compañero(a) de cuarto o tú? etc.

7–28 División del trabajo. You and your roommate need to reach an agreement as to who does what around the house. With a classmate, divide house chores.

MODELO: Poner la mesa
           —¿Quieres poner la mesa?
           —Pongo la mesa si tú preparas la comida.
           —De acuerdo *(I agree)*. Yo preparo la comida si tú…

barrer el piso	ordenar el cuarto
cocinar la carne	pasar la aspiradora
cortar la hierba	sacar la basura
hacer la cama	sacudir los muebles
poner la mesa	secar la ropa
lavar la ropa	comprar la comida
planchar la ropa	lavar el carro
lavar los platos	

7–29 Los muebles. In pairs, look at the floor plan and tell each other how you would furnish the house.

MODELO: —Entre la cama y el sillón quiero poner la mesa de noche.
           —Pues a mí me gustaría poner la cómoda contra la ventana.

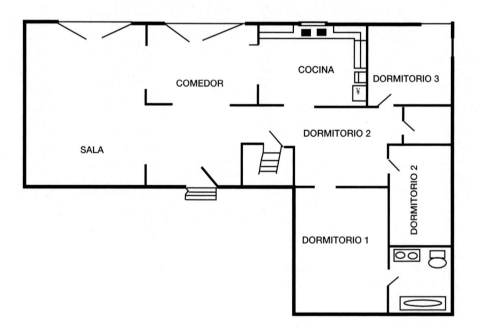

Estructuras

3. Formal commands

- Commands (imperatives) are used to give instructions or to ask people to do things.

- In Spanish, commands have different forms for formal **(usted/ustedes)** and familiar **(tú/vosotros)** address. The following chart summarizes the formation of the formal commands.

INFINITIVE	PRESENT INDICATIVE		FORMAL COMMANDS	
	1ST PERS.SING.	STEM	USTED	USTEDES
hablar	hablo	**habl-**	hab**le**	hab**len**
pensar	pienso	**piens-**	pien**se**	pien**sen**
comer	como	**com-**	co**ma**	co**man**
atender	atiendo	**atiend-**	atien**da**	atien**dan**
escribir	escribo	**escrib-**	escri**ba**	escri**ban**
pedir	pido	**pid-**	pi**da**	pi**dan**

- Formal commands of **-ar** verbs add **-e,** and formal commands of **-er** and **-ir** verbs add **-a** to the stem of the first person singular of the present indicative.

  Piense antes de hablar.   *Think before speaking.*
  Coma con el tenedor.   *Eat with your fork.*
  Pídale un refresco al camarero.   *Ask the waiter for a soda pop.*

- For plural commands, add **-n** to the **usted** command form.

  Piensen antes de hablar.   *Think before speaking.*
  Atiendan bien a la visita.   *Take good care of the guest.*

- The following verbs have irregular formal commands:

estar	dar	ir	saber	ser
esté(n)	**dé(den)**	**vaya(n)**	**sepa(n)**	**sea(n)**

  No **vayan** al cine esta noche.   *Don't go to the movies tonight.*
  Sepan la lección para mañana.   *Know the lesson for tomorrow.*
  Sea buena gente. Ayúdeme.   *Be a nice guy. Help me.*
  Estén de vuelta a las diez.   *Be back by ten.*
  Dele la leche al niño.   *Give the milk to the child.*

- The singular **dar** command **dé** has a written accent when it stands alone to distinguish it from the preposition **de.**

    No le **dé** dulces al niño.   *Don't **give** candy to the child.*

- Verbs ending in **–car, –gar,** and **–zar** change spelling in the formal command: **c** changes to **qu, ga** changes to **gu,** and **z** changes to **c.**

    Saque la basura.   ***Take** the garbage out.*
    No **lleguen** tarde.   *Don't **arrive** late.*
    Comience ahora mismo.   ***Start** right now.*

- With affirmative commands, direct and indirect object pronouns follow the command form and are attached to it. An accent mark is added to commands of two or more syllables so the stress of the original verb remains the same.

    Prepáre**les** la cena.   ***Prepare** dinner **for them.***
    Prepáre**sela** hoy.   ***Prepare** it **for him** today.*

- Negative commands are formed by placing **no** in front of the command form. With negative commands, direct and indirect object pronouns are placed between **no** and the command form.

    No **les** prepare la comida.   *Don't prepare dinner **for them.***
    No **se la** prepare hoy (la comida).   *Don't prepare it **for him** today.*

- Subject pronouns may be used with commands for emphasis or clarification. As a rule, they are placed after the verb.

    Piense **usted** en esto.   ***You** think about this.*
    No hablen **ustedes** ahora.   *Don't talk now.*

◆ Práctica

7–30 Hágalo Ud. You are coordinating a big dinner at your house. Distribute the work among the people you have hired by changing each sentence to a command.

MODELO: Cristina prepara el menú.
           Cristina, prepare el menú.

1. Marcos pasa la aspiradora.
2. Doña Consuelo limpia las ventanas.
3. Pepe y Toño traen las mesas de la planta alta.
4. Mercedes y Juliana ponen las mesas.
5. Manuel corta la hierba del jardín.
6. Carmencita sacude los muebles.
7. La señora Pérez prepara las carnes.
8. Elena pone los manteles y las servilletas en la lavadora.
9. Anita plancha el mantel y las servilletas.
10. Ud. trae el equipo de sonido.
11. Uds. sacan la basura.
12. Marcos pone el champán en el refrigerador.

7–31 El gerente del restaurante. You are a restaurant manager and you are giving instructions to a recently hired waiter/waitress about what to do and what not to do.

MODELO: atender bien a los clientes
Atienda bien a los clientes.

1. no llegar tarde al trabajo
2. no comer en el trabajo
3. poner los cubiertos correctamente en las mesas
4. ser amable con los clientes
5. estudiar el menú
6. tomar bien los pedidos
7. servir rápido
8. estar siempre listo(a)

9. limpiar las mesas
10. hablar con los clientes
11. lavarse las manos
12. ordenar la cocina
13. vestirse bien
14. sacar la basura
15. acordarse de las flores de las mesas

7-32 La hora de acostarse. Although it may seem strange to people from other Spanish-speaking countries, in Costa Rica it is not unusual for parents and their children to address each other formally. That doesn't mean that the conversation cannot be intimate. Complete the family conversation by providing the correct form of the **Ud.** command of the verbs in parentheses.

NIDIA: Niños, es tarde, (acostarse) _____ ya. A ver, Rebeca, (levantarse) _____ ya del sofá. Bernabé, (despertarse) _____… Bernabé, m'hijo, (sentarse) _____… vamos, no (dormirse) _____ en el sofá.

REBECA: Ay mami, el programa en la tele es muy interesante. ¿Puedo quedarme media hora más?

NIDIA: Está bien, (quedarse) _____, pero (acordarse) _____: mañana hay que levantarse muy temprano. Y Bernabé, ¿qué le pasa a este muchacho? Vamos, (lavarse) _____ las manos y (cepillarse) _____ los dientes. Rápido.

BERNABÉ: Y, ¿por qué Rebeca puede quedarse y yo no? ¿Me siento con ella?

NIDIA: Bernabé, Ud. se estaba durmiendo y ahora quiere quedarse. Ay, ¡por Dios! (Olvidarse) _____. No (sentarse) _____ a ver la tele o vamos a estar aquí toda la noche.

BERNABÉ: Pero, mamá…

NIDIA: Hijo, no (ponerme) _____ impaciente. Todas las noches lo mismo. Rebeca es mayor. Vamos, (despedirse) _____ de papá y (acostarse) _____.

BERNABÉ: Está bien, mami, no (enojarse) _____. Hasta mañana, papá.

PAPÁ: ¿Sin darme las buenas noches? (Venir) _____, (darme) _____ un abrazo. Eso es, así bien grande como a mí me gusta. ¿A qué hora lo levanto?

BERNABÉ: (Despertarme) _____ a las 6:30, por favor. Quiero pasear al perrito.

PAPÁ: A las 6:30 pues. (Soñar) _____ con cosas bonitas.

BERNABÉ: Sí, papá. Voy a soñar que mañana ganamos el partido de fútbol.

7–33 Una tortilla española. A friend from Madrid is showing you how to cook a Spanish tortilla. Complete the sentences with the correct **usted** command of the verbs in parentheses.

1. (comprar) _____ seis huevos, dos cebollas y cinco papas.
2. (lavar) _____ las papas.
3. (pelar) _____ las papas.
4. (cortar) _____ las papas y las cebollas en trozos pequeños.
5. (poner) _____ aceite de oliva en una sartén.
6. (calentar) _____ el aceite.
7. (freír) _____ las papas y las cebollas.
8. (batir) _____ los huevos en un plato.
9. (añadir) _____ un poco de sal y los huevos a la sartén.
10. (mover) _____ los ingredientes con la espátula.
11. Luego, (voltear) _____ la tortilla.
12. (Servir) _____ la tortilla bien caliente.

7–34 Sopa de mariscos. You are showing a friend how to make seafood chowder. Answer the questions he/she asks using commands with object pronouns.

MODELO: —¿Debo cortar las cebollas? (sí)
         —Sí, córtelas.

1. ¿Debo pelar las papas y las zanahorias? (sí)
2. ¿Debo hervir el agua en la cazuela? (sí)
3. ¿Tengo que añadir sal y pimienta? (no)
4. ¿Tengo que lavar el pescado y los camarones? (sí)
5. ¿Debo prender la estufa a fuego alto? (no)
6. ¿Tengo que añadir la salsa de tomate? (no)
7. ¿Debo dejar la sopa en la estufa dos horas? (sí)
8. ¿Tengo que servir la sopa muy caliente? (sí)

7–35 Mi receta. Using commands, write the directions (recipe) for one of your favorite dishes. Then, share it with a partner.

Mi receta

◆ Actividades

7–36 El programa de radio. You are hosting a cooking show. A number of people call in to ask questions about the recipes you demonstrate. Today you are making **Arroz con pollo.** Some of your answers will be in the affirmative and some will be in the negative. Role-play this situation with a classmate using the illustrations as a guide. (The recipe appears in **Lección 5.**)

MODELO: —Tía Julia, ¿le echo salsa de tomate al arroz con pollo?
                 —No le eche salsa de tomate al arroz con pollo; échele sal.

7–37 En casa. With another classmate, take turns using the words below to design your new apartment or house.

MODELO: —Y este aparador, ¿dónde lo pongo?
                 —Póngalo en el comedor.

el reloj
la sala
el sofá
el estante
las sillas
las camas
la cómoda
las mesas de noche
la alfombra
la mesa
las lámparas
la lavadora
el aparador
los sillones
la mecedora

el piso
el dormitorio
el comedor
el pasillo
la cocina
aquí
la pared
el baño

7–38 Los consejos. In groups of three or four, give a context for each problem and find a solution for it using a command form. Be prepared to share some of your group's problems and solutions with the class.

MODELO: (Problema) encantarle la comida frita
                  (Contexto) un enfermo del corazón y su médico
                  (Solución) Coma menos grasa.

PROBLEMAS
- no tener suficiente dinero para pagar los estudios
- querer levantarse temprano y no tener despertador
- morirse de miedo con las películas de horror
- necesitar secarse pero no tener toalla
- desear acostarse temprano pero dar una película en la televisión
- querer quitarse la ropa pero la puerta no cerrar bien
- tener hambre y sed
- *(original)*

7–39 Una multitud de soluciones. Invent a problem and tell it to as many classmates as you can in a five-minute period. Write down your classmates' names and the advice they give you.

4. *Por* and *para*

Por and **para** are both often translated as *for* in English, but they are not interchangeable. Each word has a distinctly different use in Spanish:

por

- Expresses the time during which an action takes place *(for, during)*

Vamos a visitarla **por** la tarde.	*We are going to visit her **during** the afternoon.*
Pienso estudiar en Ecuador **por** tres meses.	*I am planning to study in Ecuador **for** three months.*

- Expresses *because of, in exchange for, on behalf of*

El piloto tuvo que aterrizar inesperadamente **por** una emergencia.	*The pilot had to land unexpectedly **because of** an emergency.*
¿Quieres cinco dólares **por** esa corbata?	*Do you want five dollars **(in exchange) for** that tie?*
Lo hizo **por** su madre.	*She did it **for (on behalf of)** her mother.*

- Expresses motion *(through, by, along, around)*

Pasé **por** tu casa anoche.	*I went **by** your house last night.*
Las chicas salieron **por** la puerta central.	*The girls went out **through** the main door.*

- Expresses means or manner by which an action is accomplished *(by)*

¿Viajaron a Quito **por** avión?	*Did you travel to Quito **by** plane?*
La casa fue construida **por** el arquitecto.	*The house was built **by** the architect.*

- Expresses the object of an action *(for)*

Venimos **por** usted a las dos.	*We'll come by **for** you at two.*
Los estudiantes fueron **por** los helados.	*The students went **for** the ice cream.*

- Is used in many idiomatic expressions, such as **por favor** and **por fin.** Refer to the chart on page 279.

para

- Expresses goal, purpose, recipient or destination *(for, in order to)*

Este regalo es **para** ti.	*This present is **for** you.*
Mañana partimos **para** México.	*Tomorrow we depart **for** Mexico.*
Estudian **para** maestras.	*They are studying **to be** teachers.*
Vamos a casa **para** comer.	*We're going home **in order to** eat.*

- Expresses time limits or deadlines *(for, by)*

Necesito el pasaje **para** esta tarde.	*I need the ticket **for** this afternoon.*
Pienso estar en Acapulco **para** el mes de junio.	*I plan to be in Acapulco **by** June.*

- Expresses comparison with others (stated or implicit)

Para él los idiomas son muy fáciles.	***For** him languages are very easy.*
Para tener cinco años, ella es muy alta.	***For** being five years old, she is very tall.*

- Expresses readiness (to be about to do something) when used with **estar** + *infinitive*

Estoy **para** salir.	*I am **about to** leave.*
El avión está listo **para** despegar.	*The plane **is ready** for takeoff.*

¿por o para?

- It may be helpful to link the uses of **por** and **para** to the questions **¿para qué?** (for what purpose?) and **¿por qué?** (for what reason?).

¿Por qué vino?	*Why (**for what reason**) did you come?*
Vine **porque** necesitaba verlo.	*I came **because** I needed to see you.*
¿Para qué vino Ud.?	*For what purpose did you come?*
Vine **para** ayudar a mi familia.	*I came (**in order**) to help my family.*

- In many instances the use of either **por** or **para** will be grammatically correct, but each one will express a different meaning. Compare the following sentences.

Mario va **para** el parque. *(destination)*	*Mario is going **to (toward)** the park.*
Mario va **por** el parque. *(motion)*	*Mario is going **through (in)** the park.*
Lo hice **para** ti.	*I did it **for** you. (recipient)*
Lo hice **por** ti.	*I did it **because of** you. (because of)*

◆ Práctica

7-40 ¿Por o para? Say whether the following sentences would involve **por** or **para** in Spanish. Explain your rationale.

1. I got this shirt for my mother.
2. 'm working in order to make more money.
3. Art for art's sake.
4. The ball went through the door.
5. For being as dumb as he is, he sure has a good job.
6. We're leaving for Florida tomorrow.
7. got this for five dollars.
8. For me, you shouldn't have.
9 Let's do it in the morning.
10. Good Lord.
11. He didn't get the job on account of his lack of experience.

7–41 Completar. Complete the sentences with **por** or **para**.

1. _____ mí las orquídeas son las flores más bonitas.
2. Vamos a pescar _____ el río *(river)*.
3. ¿Es verdad que mandas la carta _____ avión *(airplane)*?
4. Pasamos _____ tu residencia _____ verte.
5. Francisca, estas rosas son _____ ti.
6. _____ Dios, no me hagas más preguntas.
7. Te doy mi fruta _____ tu ensalada.
8. Rita estudia en la biblioteca _____ la mañana.
9. Estoy preparándome _____ ser profesora de español.
10. Anduvimos _____ el parque con nuestras novias.
11. El arroz con pollo es _____ el almuerzo.
12. _____ ser un niño de siete años, es muy inteligente.

7–42 ¿Por o para? Complete the sentences with **por** or **para.**

LUCAS: Ayer _____ la tarde pasé _____ tu casa _____ ir al cine, pero no estabas. Iba _____ el parque cuando vi que ibas _____ tu clase. Te llamé pero no me oíste _____ el ruido del tráfico.

CONSUELO: Ah, ¿sí? Iba _____ mi clase de portugués con el profesor Nascimento.

LUCAS: ¿Caminas siempre a la universidad o a veces vas _____ autobús?

CONSUELO: Con frecuencia camino _____ hacer ejercicio y porque los autobuses son famosos _____ lentos. No me gusta llegar tarde a clase.

LUCAS: Y, ¿_____ qué quieres aprender portugués? ¿Es porque vas a Europa?

CONSUELO: Bueno, es un requisito _____ la carrera. _____ mí, es la clase más interesante de mi horario _____ el profesor. ¡Él es tan dinámico! Además, quiero aprender portugués _____ la música de Brasil que, ¡me encanta! ¿Oíste alguna vez Beleza Tropical, compilada ____ David Byrne? ¡Es excelente!

LUCAS: Pues, qué bien.

CONSUELO: Oye, Lucas, ¿vienes conmigo a la farmacia un momentito?

LUCAS: ¿_____ qué?

CONSUELO: Es que ayer no hice mandados _____ la lluvia y necesito un esmalte _____ las uñas, maquillaje _____ los ojos, colorete, café, pan y jugo de naranja. Ah, y no se te olvide, un lápiz labial _____ la boca.

LUCAS: ¿Todo ese maquillaje es _____ ti? Debe ser caro ser mujer.

CONSUELO: ¡No te imaginas cuánto! Pero en esta ocasión el maquillaje es _____ una clase de teatro. Voy a enseñar a un grupo de actores a pintarse la cara. _____ hacerlo necesito mucho maquillaje.

Idiomatic expressions with *por*

por ahí	*around there*	**por favor**	*please*
por ahora	*for now*	**por fin**	*finally*
por aquí	*around here*	**por lo general**	*in general*
por cierto	*by the way*	**por lo visto**	*apparently*
por Dios	*for God's sake*	**por poco**	*almost*
por eso	*that's why*	**por supuesto**	*of course*
por ejemplo	*for example*	**por último**	*finally*

Colaboración

Estudiante A

7-43A Las emociones. Ask your partner how he or she reacts in the situations below. Then, tell how you react in the situations he or she asks you about. Use expressions with **ponerse.**

MODELO: Hace buen tiempo
—¿Cómo te sientes cuando hace buen tiempo?
—Me pongo contento(a).

LAS CIRCUNSTANCIAS

- no suena el despertador
- sale bien en un examen
- conoce a un(a) muchacho(a) interesante
- el profesor llega tarde a un examen
- ve una comedia

- hace mal tiempo
- pasa una hora esperando el autobús
- recibe una mala noticia
- pierde su billetera o su cartera
- compró algo por $10 y ahora está en rebaja en otra tienda por $5

7-44A ¿Qué hiciste con eso? Tell your partner what you did with the items he or she mentions. Then ask him or her what he or she did with the items on your list.

MODELO: el peine
—¿Qué hiciste con el peine?
—Me peiné y lo dejé en el cuarto (baño, sala, etc.).

ARTÍCULOS

la secadora
la pasta de dientes
las tijeras

la máquina de afeitar
el desodorante
el enjuague

7-45A Credibanco. You are an employee at **Credibanco**. Tell the director the problem and he or she will give you instructions. Then reverse roles.

MODELO: —No tenemos café para la conferencia esta tarde.
—Pues, ¡cómprelo!

PROBLEMAS

No tenemos el informe para la reunión.
El señor García no está en la oficina.
Le llama el señor Ramírez. ¿Qué le digo?
No sé dónde están los papeles para la reunión.
No hay suficiente dinero en la caja.

INSTRUCCIONES

ayudar
terminar
llamar
empezar
comprar

7-46A Por favor, ¿dónde está... ? You are new at the university and you ask a stranger how to get to the places on the list. He or she answers. Then switch roles.

MODELO: —¿Dónde está la Facultad de Ciencias?
                —Vaya por el pasillo, doble a la izquierda, salga y camine...

1. el centro estudiantil
2. la cafetería
3. el gimnasio
4. el banco más cercano *(nearest)*

7-47A ¿Cómo es tu casa? Compare your house or apartment with that of your partner. Take notes.

MODELO: —Mi casa tiene...
                —Mi casa también, pero no tiene...

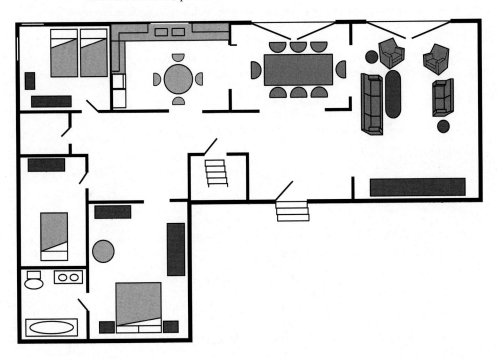

Estudiante B

7-43B Las emociones. Tell your partner how you react in the situations he or she asks you about. Then ask your partner how he or she reacts to the situations below. Use expressions with **ponerse.**

MODELO: hace buen tiempo
—¿Cómo te sientes cuando hace buen tiempo?
—Me pongo contento(a).

LAS CIRCUNSTANCIAS

- ve a una persona que no tiene casa
- quiere afeitarse pero no tiene navaja
- habla con un(a) amigo(a) muy querido(a)
- encuentra un billete de $20 en la calle
- va a salir con alguien por primera vez

- lleva una hora esperando a alguien
- ve una película de horror
- sale mal en un examen
- hace mal tiempo
- compra un reloj de oro por menos de $100

7-44B ¿Qué hiciste con eso? Ask your partner what he or she did with the items on your list. Then tell him or her what you did with the items he or she mentions.

MODELO: el peine
—¿Qué hiciste con el peine?
—Me peiné y lo dejé en el cuarto (baño, sala, etc.).

ARTÍCULOS

el jabón   el cepillo
la cuchilla   el esmalte
el espejo   la loción

7-45B Credibanco. You are the director at **Credibanco.** An employee will tell you a problem and you give him or her instructions. Then reverse roles.

MODELO: —No tenemos café para la conferencia esta tarde.
—Pues, ¡cómprelo!

PROBLEMAS	INSTRUCCIONES
Tengo que empezar un proyecto nuevo.	buscar
La Srta. Ortega está enferma en la casa.	llamar
Necesito terminar este proyecto.	escribir
No tengo basurero para mi escritorio.	ir al banco
Si no ayudo a Lolita, no va a terminar.	decirle que

7-46B Por favor, ¿dónde está... ? A new student approaches you and asks you how to get to a variety of places. Tell him or her how to get there and then switch roles.

MODELO: —¿Dónde está la Facultad de Ciencias?
—Vaya por el pasillo, doble a la izquierda, salga y camine...

1. la biblioteca
2. la librería
3. el laboratorio de lenguas
4. el cine más cercano *(nearest)*

7-47B ¿Cómo es tu casa? Compare your house or apartment with that of your partner. Take notes.

MODELO: —Mi casa tiene…
—Mi casa también, pero no tiene…

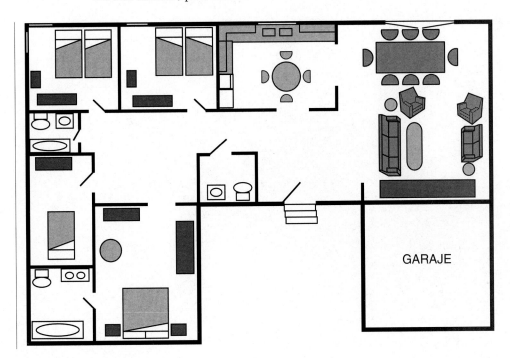

Mundo hispánico

El Caribe

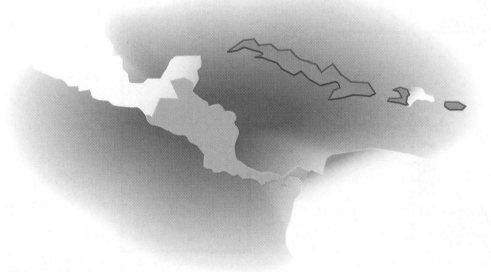

◆ **Cuba**

Cuba
Capital: La Habana (2.077.000)
Ciudades principales: Santiago de Cuba, Camagüey
Población: 10.785.000
Etnicidad y raza: mulatos 51%, europeos 37%, africanos 11%

Bahías: Las más conocidas son las de Guantámo, Santiago, Cienfuegos y La Habana.

Islas: más de 1,600 cayos, islotes e islas que forman archipiélagos

Productos: azúcar, ron, frutas cítricas, níquel

Las artes

Literatura: José Martí (1953–1895), escritor y político, *Versos sencillos* ("Guantanamera" was based on one of the poems); Alejo Carpentier (1904–1980), *El reino de este mundo* (novela de realismo mágico); Guillermo Cabrera Infante (1929–) *Tres tristes tigres* (novela)

Música y danza: conga, rumba, cha-cha-cha, mambo

Pintura: Wilfredo Lam

◆ República Dominicana

República Dominicana
Capital: Santo Domingo (2.411.900)
Ciudad principal: Santiago de los Caballeros
Población: 8.124.000
Etnicidad y raza: mulatos 73%, europeos 16%, africanos 11%

Geografía: La isla compone de la Española junto con Haití.

Santo Domingo fue fundada por Bartolomé Colón, hermano de Cristóbal Colón; es la ciudad más antigua del hemisferio occidental

Universidad Autónoma de Santo Domingo: la más antigua de las Américas

Productos: oro, azúcar, café, níquel

Las artes

Literatura: Juan Bosch (1909–) escritor y político.

Música y danza: merengue

Platos típicos: sopa hamaca (pescado, verduras), carne de cerdo guisada, sancocho prieto de siete carnes, torta de coco

◆ Puerto Rico

Puerto Rico
Capital: San Juan (1.200.000)
Población: 3.528.000
Etnicidad y raza: mulatos, europeos, africanos

Nombre: Los indios la llamaron Boriquén (Borinquen).

Productos: químicos, farmacéuticos, alimentos

Personas famosas: Rita Moreno, actriz; Roberto Clemente, beisbolista

Atracciones turísticas: El fuerte San Felipe del Morro en el Viejo San Juan; El Yunque, bosque húmedo tropical; playas

Las artes

Litertura: Rosario Ferré (1942–), *Árbol y sus sombras*

Música y danza: salsa, plena

Centro América

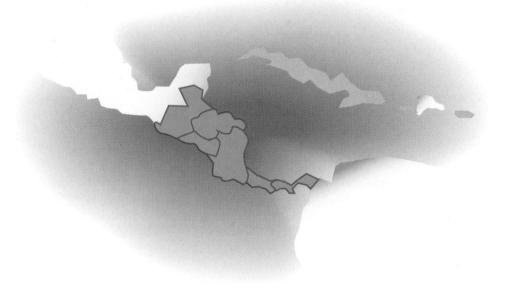

◆ **Costa Rica**

Costa Rica
Capital: San José (890.000)
Ciudades principales: Limón, Puntarenas, Alajuela, Cartago, Heredia
Población: 3.151.000
Etnicidad y raza: europeos y mestizos 96%, africanos 3%, indígenas 1%

Distinción: País que no tiene ejército.

Productos: café, banano, flores, turismo

Persona famosa: Óscar Arias, ex-presidente y Premio Nóbel de la Paz (1987)

Atracciones turísticas: Parques nacionales de Manuel Antonio, Volcán Poás, Volcán Irazú y Volcán Arenal

Las artes

Literatura: Fabián Dobles (1918–), *Ése que llaman pueblo* (novela); Carmen Naranjo (1931–), escritora y figura política, *Memorias de un hombre palabra* (novela), Quince Duncan (1940–) *Una canción en la madrugada*

Pintura: Max Jiménez; César Valverde

Platos típicos: tamal, chorreadas, pozol

◆ El Salvador

Densidad de población: el índice más alto de la región

Productos: café, algodón, azúcar, frutas

Persona famosa: El Arzobispo Romero, defensor de los derechos humanos, fue asesinado en su iglesia.

El Salvador
Capital: San Salvador (1.400.000)
Ciudades principales: Santa Ana, San Miguel Sonsonate, San Vicente
Población: 5.473.000
Etnicidad y raza: mestizos 89%, indígenas 10%, europeos 1%

Las artes

Literatura: Manlio Argueta (1936–), *Cuzcatlán*; Claribel Alegría (poesía)

Música: mariachi y música folclórica

Platos típicos: pupusas, gallo en chicha

◆ Guatemala

Guatemala
Capital: Ciudad de Guatemala (1.095.000)
Ciudades principales: Quetzaltenango, Puerto Barrios, Antigua
Población: 9.386.000
Etnicidad y raza: "ladinos" (mestizos e indígenas de habla hispana) 45%, indígenas 55%

Cultura: el elemento indígena más puro del área; se hablan muchos dialectos indígenas
Productos: café, banano, tabaco, algodón

Personas famosas: Rigoberta Menchú, Premio Nóbel de la Paz (1992); Miguel Ángel Asturias, escritor

Atracciones turísticas: Antigua; región del lago Atitlán; las ruinas de Tikal

Las artes

Literatura: Miguel Ángel Asturias (1899–1974), Premio Nóbel de Literatura (1967), *El Señor Presidente* (novela política), *Hombres de maíz* (novela de realismo mágico); Augusto Monterroso, cuentos

Arte: artesanía indígena

Música y danza: mariachi y ritmos de origen indígena

◆ Honduras

Honduras
Capital: Tegucigalpa (550.000)
Ciudades principales: San Pedro Sula, La Ceiba, Puerto Cortés, Choluteca
Población: 5.342.000
Etnicidad y raza: mestizos 90%, indígenas 7%, africanos 2%, europeos 1%

Productos: agrícolas y maderas

Atracciones turísticas: ruinas mayas de Copán

Las artes

Literatura: Roberto Sosa (1930–), *Mar interior*

Música: música folclórica y mariachi

Platos típicos: tamales, tortillas, arroz y frijoles

◆ Nicaragua

Nicaragua
Capital: Managua (1.000.000)
Ciudades principales: León, Granada, Matagalpa, Masaya, Chinandega
Población: 3.805.000
Etnicidad y raza: mestizos 69%, europeos 17%, africanos 9%, indígenas 5%

Productos: café, algodón, azúcar

Personas famosas: Rubén Darío, figura más importante del modernismo

Las artes

Literatura: Rubén Darío (1867–1916), poeta, *Azul;* Ernesto Cardenal, poeta, *Epigramas* (poesía)

Cine: *Alsino y el Cóndor* (1983) dir. Miguel Littín

Pintura: Armando Morales

◆ Panamá

Panamá
Capital: Ciudad de Panamá (440.000)
Ciudades principales: Colón, David
Población: 2.503.000
Etnicidad y raza: mestizos y mulatos 70%, africanos 14%, europeos 10%, indígenas 6%

Carnaval de Panamá

Persona famosa: Rubén Blades, abogado, actor de cine y músico

Atracción turística: Canal de Panamá

Las artes

Música: cumbia, tamborito y otros ritmos

Platos típicos: picante de almejas, sancocho (cazuela de carne y verduras)

◆ Actividades

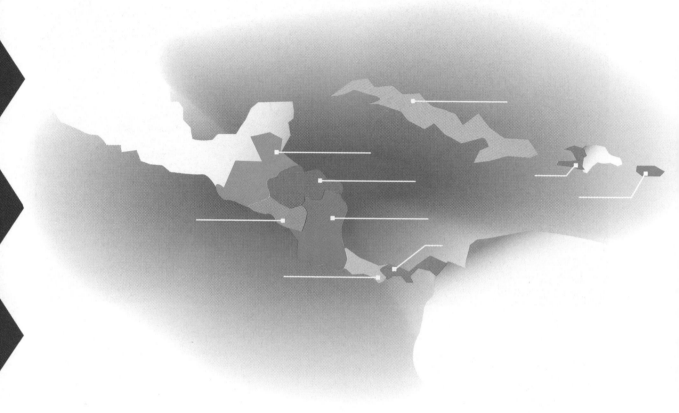

¿Puedes nombrar los países y capitales de Centro
América y el Caribe?

7-48 ¿Qué es?

1. Es una ciudad que fue fundada por Bartolomé Colón.
2. La capital es Tegucigalpa. Tiene unas ruinas mayas muy importantes.
3. Es el país donde vive Óscar Arias.
4. Es la tierra del merengue, del sancocho prieto y las tortas de coco.
5. Primero se llamó Boriquén; es la tierra de la salsa.
6. Ganó el Premio Nóbel de Literatura en 1987.
7. Autor de la novela *Tres tristes tigres*.
8. Ganó el Premio Nóbel de la Paz de 1992.
9. Tiene 10.785.000 millones de habitantes; es la tierra de José Martí y del mambo.
10. Tiene un carnaval muy famoso en Centroamérica en el que se baila el tamborito.
11. Es un arzobispo muy famoso que dio la vida por los derechos humanos.

7-49 La agencia de viajes. As a travel agent, people ask you all the time for special places to go. In pairs, take turns making recommendations to travellers based on their interests or profession.

1. una historiadora-se especializa en ciudades coloniales antiguas
2. un botánico-se especializa en plantas y flores tropicales
3. un matrimonio pacifista-no quieren que sus hijos sirvan en ningún ejército
4. un antropólogo-es experto en la civilización maya
5. una profesora de ciencias políticas-estudia la relación religión y política
6. un profesor de literatura-está escribiendo un trabajo sobre el realismo mágico.
7. un turista-quiere viajar en un bote pequeño de isla en isla
8. un músico-estudia la influencia de la música mariachi fuera de México
9. un historiador-está interesado en la población negra de Centroamérica
10. un crítico literario-le interesan los orígenes del modernismo en Centroamérica

Lección 8

¡Buen viaje!

Comunicación

- Requesting Travel Information
- Making Travel Arrangements
- Talking about Needs, Wishes, Preferences, Requests, Feelings, and Emotions
- Describing Travel Experiences

Cultura

- **Las aerolíneas de los países hispanos**
- **Las monedas**

Estructuras

Primera parte

- Informal **tú** Commands
- Introduction to the Spanish Subjunctive
- Impersonal and Passive Constructions with **se**

Segunda parte

- The Subjunctive in Noun Clauses
- The **nosotros** Command
- Indirect Commands

Un viaje de luna de miel

Armando Perera y Grisel Esteban son dos jóvenes cubanoamericanos de Miami que
van a casarse pronto. Están en la oficina de Rosario Díaz, una amiga de Grisel que
trabaja en una agencia de viajes.

ROSARIO: Hola, ¿cómo están? ¿Qué
dicen los futuros esposos?

GRISEL: Pues, aquí nos tienes,
corriendo de un lado
para otro.

ROSARIO: Bueno, ¿y ya saben
adónde van de luna de
miel?

ARMANDO: Yo quiero ir a Cancún,
porque allí fue donde
nos conocimos.

GRISEL: A Cancún no. Hay
demasiados turistas.

ARMANDO: Pero, ¡Grisel!

ROSARIO: (Mostrándoles un
folleto.) Un momento.
No vayan a pelearse
ahora. Miren, aquí
ofrecen un viaje
por dos semanas
a Costa Rica.

GRISEL: ¿Qué incluye el viaje?

ROSARIO: Incluye pasaje de ida y vuelta, hospedaje, comidas y excursiones.
¡Todo esto por sólo 800 dólares por persona!

GRISEL: ¡Maravilloso!

ARMANDO: Pues, sí, está muy bien. ¡Vamos a Costa Rica!

Un mes más tarde Armando y Grisel se casan. Después de la boda salen para Costa
Rica de luna de miel. Ahora se encuentran en la sala de espera de LACSA, en el
aeropuerto internacional de Miami. Al poco rato oyen la voz del agente...

AGENTE: Buenas tardes, señores pasajeros. LACSA
anuncia la salida del vuelo 621 con
destino a San José. Favor de pasar a la
puerta de salida número 22. ¡Buen viaje!

Vocabulario y expresiones

En la agencia de viajes

el alojamiento	*lodging*
el boleto	*(airline) ticket*
la excursión	*tour*
el folleto	*brochure*
el(la) guía	*tour guide*
la guía	*guidebook*
el hospedaje	*lodging*
el hotel	*hotel*
el pasaje	*fare, ticket*
el pasaje de ida y vuelta	*roundtrip fare*
el vuelo sin escalas	*nonstop flight*

En el aeropuerto

la aduana	*customs*
el equipaje	*luggage*
facturar el equipaje	*to check in the luggage*
la lista de espera	*waiting list*
la llegada	*arrival*
la maleta	*suitcase*
el mostrador de la aerolínea	*airline counter*
la puerta de salida	*gate*
la sala de espera	*waiting room*
la salida	*departure; exit*
el tablero	*information board*
la tarjeta de embarque	*boarding pass*

El avión

abordar	*to board*
abrocharse	*to fasten (seat belt)*
el asiento	*seat*
el aterrizaje	*landing*
el(la) azafata	*flight attendant*
la cabina	*cockpit*
el cinturón de seguridad	*seat belt*
la clase turista	*coach class*
el despegue	*takeoff*
el(la) pasajero(a)	*passenger*
el pasillo	*aisle*
el(la) piloto	*pilot*
la primera clase	*first class*
la salida de emergencia	*emergency exit*
la sección de no fumar	*no-smoking section*
la ventanilla	*window*

Algunos lugares turísticos

el bosque	*forest*
el jardín	*garden*
el monumento	*monument*
el museo	*museum*
el río	*river*
la vista	*view*
el volcán	*volcano*

Algunas actividades

asolearse	*to tan, get some sun*
escalar	*to climb (mountains)*
montar a caballo	*to ride horses*
recorrer el país	*to go around (across) the country*

Objetos de viaje

los binoculares	*binoculars*
la cámara fotográfica	*camera*
la cámara de video	*cam recorder*
las gafas de sol	*sunglasses*
el rollo de película	*roll of film*

Otros verbos

averiguar	*to find out*
caer(se)	*to fall; to fall down*
escoger	*to choose*
incluir	*to include*
sonreír	*to smile*

Otras palabras y expresiones

la cita	*appointment, date*
como	*since*
demasiado(a)	*too much*
de repente	*suddenly*
desde	*since, from*
la flor	*flower*
la luna de miel	*honeymoon*
no hay lugar	*there's no room*
las orquídeas	*orchids*
solo	*alone*
el(la) viajero(a)	*traveler*

¡Así lo decimos!

la maleta

In this lesson, you learned **maleta,** the typical word for *suitcase* throughout the Spanish-speaking world. In a few countries, however, the standard word is entirely different (although the word **maleta** will be understood).

Argentina, Uruguay	**valija**
México	**petaca, veliz**

la(el) azafata(o)

As with many professions that have traditionally been associated with one gender, the Spanish language is struggling to come up with terminology to express the concept of male flight attendants. English has resolved this issue by using the expression *flight attendant* to avoid the peculiar use of *steward*, which is generally associated with ships, not planes.

In some Spanish-speaking countries, the traditional roles still have not changed. In many countries, for example, waiters are men and flight attendants are women, and the language reflects this situation. The use of the definite article in the following examples indicates whether the word applies to males, females, or both.

Argentina	**la azafata, la camarera**
Ecuador	**la azafata, el(la) cabinero(a), el asistente de vuelo**
España	**la azafata, el sobrecargo**
México	**la azafata, el(la) sobrecargo, aeromozo(a), la angelita**
Uruguay	**la(el) azafata(o)**
Venezuela	**el(la) aeromozo(a)**

¡A escuchar!

Un viaje de luna de miel. You will hear the conversations that appear in **¡Así es la vida!** After listening to the recording, indicate whether the statements that follow are **Cierto**, **Falso** or **No se sabe**.

	Cierto	Falso	No se sabe
1.	_____	_____	_____
2.	_____	_____	_____
3.	_____	_____	_____
4.	_____	_____	_____
5.	_____	_____	_____
6.	_____	_____	_____

◆ Práctica

8–1 De viaje. Choose the word or expression that best completes each sentence.

1. Desde mi _____ se ve el motor del avión.
   a. sala de espera　　　　　b. pasillo　　　　　　　　c. ventanilla

2. Puse mi chaqueta dentro de la _____.
   a. puerta de salida　　　　b. maleta　　　　　　　　c. agente de aduana

3. Le enseñé mi _____ al agente de aduana.
   a. pasaporte　　　　　　　b. luna de miel　　　　　　c. agente de aduana

4. El piloto está dentro de la _____ del avión.
   a. cabina　　　　　　　　b. aduana　　　　　　　　c. salida

5. Ese tablero indica la _____ del avión.
   a. llegada　　　　　　　　b. ventanilla　　　　　　　c. azafata

6. Mi boleto cuesta muy caro porque es un boleto de _____.
   a. clase turista　　　　　b. la ventanilla　　　　　　c. primera clase

7. El _____ del avión fue peligroso.
   a. aterrizaje　　　　　　　b. equipaje　　　　　　　c. alojamiento

8. Le di mi tarjeta de embarque a la _____.
   a. cabina　　　　　　　　b. pasajera　　　　　　　c. azafata

9. El avión va directo a Bogotá. Es un vuelo _____.
   a. de embarque　　　　　b. de ida y vuelta　　　　　c. sin escalas

10. Me molesta el humo del cigarrillo. Voy a pedir _____.
    a. el pasaporte　　　　　b. la sección de no fumar　c. la ventanilla

8–2 De excursión. Match the items in the columns.

1. el pasaporte　　　　　　　　　a. el equipaje
2. el pasaje　　　　　　　　　　　b. de espera
3. el alojamiento　　　　　　　　c. turística
4. la cabina　　　　　　　　　　d. el rollo de película
5. las maletas　　　　　　　　　e. para recorrer el país
6. escalar　　　　　　　　　　　f. el piloto
7. el cinturón de seguridad　　　g. la aduana
8. las flores　　　　　　　　　　h. de ida y vuelta
9. la sala　　　　　　　　　　　i. el hotel
10. la cámara fotográfica　　　　j. las montañas
11. la guía　　　　　　　　　　　k. el asiento
12. la excursión　　　　　　　　l. las orquídeas

8–3 En la agencia de viajes. Complete the conversation between a travel agent and a client using the correct words from **Vocabulario y expresiones.**

—Buenos días, señorita. ¿En qué
　puedo servirle?
—Quiero hacer un _____ a Brasil.
—Bien, ¿quiere que le muestre un _____?
—Sí, por favor.
—Aquí tiene.
—¿Incluye _____ en un hotel?
—Sí, incluye el _____ de ida y vuelta
　y también una _____ por Río de Janeiro.

—¿Habla español el _____?
—Sí, por supuesto.
—¿Y hay _____ sin escalas?
—Sí, señorita.
—Entonces, deme un _____ de
　_____ turista.
—Muchas gracias y ¡_____!

8–4 Anuncios. Read the advertisements and answer the questions.

1. ¿Cómo se llama la agencia de viajes?
2. ¿Qué está anunciando la agencia?
3. ¿Cuál es el viaje más caro?
4. ¿Cuál es el más barato?
5. ¿Cómo se llama la aerolínea que viaja a Cancún?
6. ¿Cuál de los viajes no es por avión?
7. ¿Cuál de los viajes va a la República Dominicana?
8. ¿Cuál de las islas que anuncian está muy cerca de la costa de Venezuela?
9. ¿Dónde está la agencia de viajes Jackie?
10. ¿Cuál de los viajes te gusta a tí? ¿Por qué?

¿Cuál de los viajes te gusta a ti?

8–5 Javier. Javier is a fourteen-year-old computer wiz. He dreams of traveling the world, but for now, he can travel only in virtual reality. To find out what he sees in the simulation, complete the paragraph by choosing words from the list below.

abordar	clase	factura	puerta	sonríe
agencia	despegue	folletos	sala	viaje
asiento	emergencia	ida	se abrocha	
azafata	espera	lugar	seguridad	
cabina	excursión	mostrador		

Javier va a la _____ de viajes. El agente le muestra varios _____ de Centro América. Javier compra un pasaje de _____ y vuelta a Guatemala y una _____ para ir a Antigua, Chichicastenango y las ruinas de Tikal. No hace reservaciones en el avión. En el aeropuerto va al _____ de la aerolínea, pero le dicen que no hay _____. Lo ponen en la lista de _____ y se sienta en la _____ de espera al lado de la _____ de salida de su vuelo. Ahí ve llegar a una chica muy bonita. Javier se queda mirándola. Los pasajeros ya comienzan a _____ el avión. Llaman a Javier y le dicen que lo van a sentar en primera _____. Javier se alegra pero se siente solo y piensa en la chica bonita.

Javier _____ el equipaje rápidamente y aborda el avión. Le toca una ventanilla cerca de la salida de _____. _____ el cinturón de _____. En el _____ de al lado no hay nadie. El piloto ya está en la _____ preparándose para el _____. De repente se sienta alguien a su lado. Vuelve a ver y es la chica bonita. Ella le _____. Javier mira el boleto de la chica y dice: ¡Guatemala! La _____ les trae un refresco. Javier piensa que va a ser un _____ fabuloso, pero... ¡ay! la electricidad se corta y el programa de simulación termina abruptamente.

8–6 El viaje a Costa Rica. Organize the sentences in a logical manner to tell a story. Start with number 1.

___ Hoy fui a ver a mi amigo Arturo que trabaja para una agencia de viajes.

___ El viaje incluye pasaje de ida y vuelta, alojamiento, comida y excursiones por todo el país.

___ Cuando entré a la agencia tuve que esperar una hora por Arturo.

___ ¡Por fin voy a poder visitar Costa Rica!

___ La agencia está por la calle Flores.

___ Fui a la agencia a comprar dos boletos para un viaje que vamos a hacer mi hermano y yo a Costa Rica.

___ Por fin, Arturo llegó y le compré los boletos.

___ El viaje es por avión y los boletos me costaron ochocientos dólares por persona.

___ Para ser un viaje tan largo, no está caro.

___ El viaje es para este sábado y sale de Miami a la una de la tarde.

◆ Actividades

8–7 Especiales de viaje. With several classmates, decide on a travel destination based on the following advertisement. Discuss the information below.

- el país a visitar
- el número de días de la excursión
- los precios y la aerolínea en la que van a viajar
- ¿Hay algún plan que incluye traslado al aeropuerto?
- ¿Cuántos días de alojamiento incluye cada plan?
- Compare los servicios de los diferentes planes. ¿Cuáles incluyen comidas? ¿actividades deportivas? ¿casino? ¿actividades para niños?

Cuatro Destinos
Llenos de Sol y Fantasía

MIAMI

Hotel Sol Meliá Miami Beach
$ 538
en habitación triple
al cambio del día
INCLUYE:
- Boleto aéro con VIASA CCS-MIA-CCS
- Alojamiento por 5 días y 4 noches
- Impuesto y propinas a maleteros

NEW YORK

Hotel Wellington
$ 706
en habitación triple al cambio del día
INCLUYE:
- Boleto aéro con VIASA CCS-NYC-CCS
- Alojamiento por 6 días y 5 noches
- Traslados Aeropuerto / Hotel / Aeropuerto
- Impuesto y propinas a maleteros

CURACAO

Hotel Holiday Beach Resort & Casino
$ 269
en habitación triple al cambio del día
INCLUYE:
- Boleto aéro por ALM
- Alojamiento 3 días y 2 noches
- Traslado Aeropuerto / Hotel / Aeropuerto (por Taber Tour)
- Desayuno Americano diario
- 12% de servicio sobre la habitación y desayuno
- Recargo de energía diario
- Excursión de medio día por Taber Tour
- Una camiseta del Hotel
- Invitación al cocktel de la gerencia
- Uo gratuito de la cancha de tenis durante todo el día
- Traslado gratis ida vuelta al centro

ARUBA

Plan Munda Sonesta
$ 261
en habitación triple
al cambio del día
INCLUYE:
- Boleto aéreo CCS-Aruba-CCS con Air Aruba
- Alojamiento 3 días y 2 noches
- 11% de servicio 5% impuesto gubernamental
- Desayuno americano diario
- Una franela Sonesta por persona
- Entrada al festival Bon Bini (solo los martes)
- Talonario con descuento para diferentes tiendas del Seaport Village Mall
- Bono del casino Match Play por $25 por habitación
- Cocktel de recepción con el staff del Hotel (los miércoles)
- Firma con cargo a la habitación en 10 restaurantes asociados al hotel
- Servicio de lancha del lobby del hotel a la isla privada
- Servicio de silla y toallas en la piscina y en la playa
- Programa gratis de actividades para niños entre 5 y 12 años

VIAJES DEL MUNDO, S.A.
Torre Británica, P.B., Local C, Altamira Sur.
Telfs. 555.07.13-555.06.02
Fax. 555.71.64

8–8 En el mostrador de LACSA. In pairs, write a conversation between a LACSA agent and a passenger checking in for a flight. Include the following exchanges:

- Agent greets him/her
- Agent asks passenger for his/her airline ticket
- Agent asks passenger for his/her seating preference
- Agent asks passenger for his/her luggage
- Agent tells passenger where to board the plane
- The flight's departure is announced

8–9 El agente de viajes. In groups of three, role-play a couple planning their honeymoon trip with a travel agent. Cover the following topics:

- countries and cities you would like to visit
- time and dates of travel
- preferred method of travel
- type of hotel you would like to stay in
- special activities you would like to plan for

8–10 ¡Un viaje inolvidable! In small groups, discuss your most memorable trip. Briefly describe where you went, with whom, and what happened that made it unforgettable. After each person describes his/her experience, the other students may ask questions such as the following:

1. ¿Qué fue lo que más te gustó del viaje?
2. ¿Piensas volver algún día?
3. ¿Qué actividades hiciste en el viaje?
4. ¿Cuánto dinero gastaste?
5. ¿Qué regalos compraste?

8–11 Las vacaciones de primavera. You have just spotted this advertisement in the newspaper and you call your travel agent to find out additional information. With a classmate, act out the conversation.

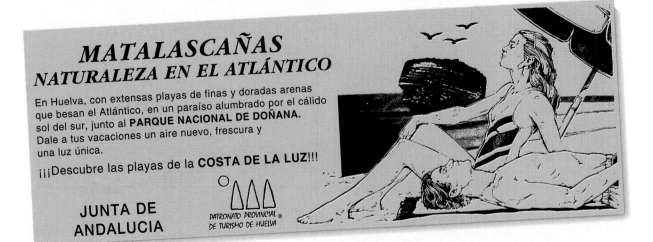

¿Qué agencia de viajes usaste la última vez que hiciste un viaje? ¿Adónde fuiste?

Estructuras

1. Informal *tú* Commands

In **Lección 7**, you learned about formal **(Ud.)** commands. The following chart presents the familiar **(tú)** command forms for regular verbs.

INFINITIVE	AFFIRMATIVE	NEGATIVE
comprar	compra	no compres
comenzar	comienza	no comiences
comer	come	no comas
atender	atiende	no atiendas
escribir	escribe	no escribas
pedir	pide	no pidas

- The affirmative **tú** commands are identical in form to the third person singular of the present indicative. Compare:

INDICATIVE	AFFIRMATIVE **tú** COMMAND	
Él **llega.**	—Oye, Miguel, ¡**llega** a tiempo!	*Listen, Miguel, **arrive** on time.*
Ella **piensa.**	—Rosa, **piensa** en mí.	*Rosa, **think** about me.*
Ud. **come.**	—Tony, **come** pescado.	*Tony, **eat** some fish.*

- The negative **tú** commands of **-ar** verbs are formed by adding **-es,** and that of **-er** and **-ir** verbs by adding **-as,** to the stem of the first person singular form of the present indicative.

<table>
<tr><td>¡No hables con Rita!</td><td>Don't speak to Rita.</td></tr>
<tr><td>No hagas la cama.</td><td>Don't make the bed.</td></tr>
<tr><td>No pidas más dinero.</td><td>Don't ask for more money.</td></tr>
</table>

Irregular Command Forms

¡Ten cuidado!

- The following verbs have irregular **affirmative** command forms.

decir	**di**	**Di** por qué.	***Tell*** *(say) why.*
hacer	**haz**	**Haz** la tarea.	***Do*** *the homework.*
ir	**ve**	**Ve** a la tienda.	***Go*** *to the store.*
poner	**pon**	**Pon** la mesa.	***Set*** *the table.*
salir	**sal**	**Sal** de aquí.	***Get*** *out of here.*
ser	**sé**	**Sé** inteligente.	***Be*** *intelligent.*
tener	**ten**	**Ten** paciencia.	***Be*** *patient.*
venir	**ven**	**Ven** conmigo.	***Come*** *with me.*

- The negative **tú** commands of these verbs are regular, with the exception of **ir.**

No **salgas** de la tienda.	***Don't leave*** *the store.*
No **seas** tan exigente.	***Don't be*** *so demanding.*
No **vayas** a la playa hoy.	***Don't go*** *to the beach today.*

- When object pronouns are used with affirmative commands, they are always placed immediately after the verb and are attached to it. If the affirmative command has two or more syllables, a written accent is added to show that the stress remains the same. With negative commands object pronouns are placed between the negative and the conjugated verb.

Cómpra**lo.**	*Buy it.*	No **lo** compres.	*Don't buy it.*
Vénde**selo.**	*Sell it to him/her.*	No **se lo** vendas.	*Don't sell it to him/her.*

◆ Práctica

8–12 Agencia Ticotour. Complete the television commercial with the familiar command form of the verbs in parentheses.

(Ser) _____ inteligente. No (perder) _____ tiempo. (Ir) _____ hoy mismo a la Agencia Ticotour Av. 7, calles 6 y 8, o (llamar) _____ al 225-5232. (Aprovechar) _____ las superofertas y (ahorrar) _____ dinero en un viaje maravilloso. (Averiguar) _____ sobre nuestras fabulosas excursiones. No (esperar) _____ más. (Visitarnos) _____ y (hablar) _____ con nuestros amables agentes. (Hacer) _____ reservaciones hoy y (pagar) _____ después. (Llamar) _____ a tus amigos y (decirles) _____ que vengan también. ¡No lo (pensar) _____ ni un minuto más! (Viajar) _____ con la Agencia Ticotour.

8–13 Consejos. Two business colleagues are planning separate trips and are exchanging advice. Change all verbs, including commands, from formal *(Usted)* to informal *(tú)* commands.

MODELO: —Llame a la Agencia Ticotour.   —Llama a la Agencia Ticotour.
          —No viaje por esa aerolínea.   —No viajes por esa aerolínea.

1. No pida un asiento en la sección de fumar porque llega enfermo.
2. Lleve poco equipaje, así puede traer más compras.
3. Pida un asiento con ventanilla y duerma un poco si el viaje es largo.
4. Facture el equipaje en el mostrador de la aerolínea.
5. Coma bien antes de viajar porque la comida en el avión no es buena.
6. Póngale su nombre a todas las maletas.
7. Tenga la tarjeta de embarque a mano *(in hand)* antes de abordar el avión.
8. Confirme en el tablero la hora de salida de su vuelo.
9. No use su computadora portátil durante el despegue.
10. Si se pone nervioso viajando, siéntese cerca de la salida de emergencia.
11. Al aterrizar, acuérdese de mirar por la ventanilla porque la vista es muy bonita.
12. Haga las reservaciones para regresar inmediatamente, así después no se olvida.
13. Si no le gusta el hotel, busque otro hotel.
14. Si va a los parques nacionales, lleve binoculares.

8–14 José Martí y Felicia. José Martí, an architecture student, is visiting Felicia, his girlfriend, in Barcelona. But she has three more days before she goes on vacation. Tell José Martí some of the things he can do until then. Use informal commands.

1. caminar por toda la cuidad para conocerla bien
2. tomar transporte público
3. llamar a Pepe, un amigo de Felicia que te va a llevar a una feria de libros
4. pasear por las Ramblas
5. ir a ver la Catedral de Santa Eulalia y la iglesia de Santa María del Mar
6. no dejar de entrar a la Catedral de la Sagrada Familia
7. dar un paseo por los parques Güell o Montjuich
8. ver una corrida de toros
9. asolearse un poco en la plaza
10. probar la paella en el restaurante de al lado de la casa
11. beber vino y comer tapas en el bar
12. mirar a la gente bailar la sardana enfrente de la catedral

8–15 Consejos para el viajero. Your friend wants to visit a foreign country. Give him/her useful traveling tips using the phrases below.

MODELO: escoger bien la agencia de viajes
                Escoge bien la agencia de viajes.

1. leer muchos folletos sobre los países que más te interesan
2. decidir si quieres ver la ciudad o la naturaleza, o si quieres hacer un poco de todo
3. escoger bien el país que vas a visitar
4. conversar con amigos que ya conocen el país
5. visitar la biblioteca para leer sobre ese país
6. comparar con cuidado los servicios de diferentes planes de viaje
7. averiguar qué planes incluyen comidas
8. preguntar si el hotel ofrece excursiones
9. comprar un pasaje de ida y vuelta en clase turista para ahorrar dinero
10. tomar un vuelo sin escalas
11. no llevar demasiado equipaje
12. llegar al aeropuerto temprano
13. traer cámara fotográfica o cámara de vídeo y también muchos rollos de película
14. no olvidarse de unas buenas gafas de sol
15. no asolearse demasiado en la playa
16. al regreso no traer flores ni comida
17. llevar todas las fotografías o cintas de vídeo *(videotape)* a revelar inmediatamente
18. poner todas las fotos en un álbum para mostrárselas a los amigos y a la familia

◆ Actividades

8–16 Problemas de viajes. In pairs, take turns stating each traveling problem, using your imagination to complete the idea when necessary. Then, use the phrases in parentheses as a guide to formulate suggestions for solving the problem.

MODELO: querer un asiento… en el avión (reservar…)
                —Quiero un asiento cómodo en el avión.
                —Reserva un asiento de primera clase.

1. querer hacer un viaje a… (llamar a…)
2. los aterrizajes me dan miedo (pedir un vuelo…)
3. el pasaje de ida y vuelta sale más… (ahorrar…)
4. no tener reservaciones en el avión (llegar temprano a…)
5. no encontrar la puerta de salida de mi vuelo (preguntar o preguntarle…)
6. qué hacer con el equipaje (facturarlo en…)
7. tener sed (pedirle a la azafata…)
8. no encontrar mi… (buscar en…)
9. la azafata querer ver mi tarjeta de embarque (mostrar…)
10. nunca acordarme de ponerme el cinturón de seguridad (no olvidarse de…)
11. cuando llegar *(preterite)* de… mi equipaje no estar *(imperfect)* (ir a… y preguntar)
12. en mi hotel no haber excursiones (venir a mi…)
13. el parque nacional estar cerrado los… (visitar…)
14. querer montar a caballo pero tener miedo (pedir un caballo manso *[gentle]*)
15. querer ver la vista del volcán pero no tener binoculares (tomar mis binoculares)
16. hacer demasiado sol (ponerse las gafas de sol)
17. querer tomar muchas fotografías (comprar…)
18. *(original)*

8–17 Consejos sobre la comida. Two friends are having a few health problems while on a trip. With a classmate, play the roles of two friends and give each other advice on the food-related problems in the left hand column. Possible solutions appear in the right hand column.

MODELO: desear un café pero no poder comer nada con azúcar
          —Deseo un café pero no puedo comer nada con azúcar.
          —Pide un café con miel (honey).

PROBLEMAS	CONSEJOS
no tener mucha hambre	tomar una sopa de pollo y descansar
tener una sed terrible, pero no	beber cerveza
querer alcohol	esperar un poco antes de comer
estar a dieta	comprar hamburguesas y papas
estar enfermo(a)	comer una ensalada
querer escribir cartas, pero necesitar dormir	sacar una gaseosa del refrigerador
querer comer algo dulce	mirar a ver si hay torta en la cocina
querer comer un bistec de solomillo,	acostarse por dos horas nada más
pero tener poco dinero	hacer una sopa de gazpacho
no querer comida caliente	
no gustar el vino	

8–18 Mi hermanita. Your six-year old sister is spending the summer with your grandparents in Puerto Rico. Help her pack her suitcase. In pairs, take turns role-playing the little sister and her older brother/sister. Answer her questions using affirmative and negative **tú** commands, and add an explanation to your answer. You may need to use different verbs than those used in the questions.

MODELO: —¿Llevo la cámara fotográfica?
          —Sí, llévala. Hay muchas cosas lindas que ver. **o**
          —No, no la lleves. Abuelo tiene una excelente.

1. ¿Pongo los libros de cuentos en la maleta grande o en la pequeña?
2. ¿Qué hago con los binoculares que le compré al abuelo?
3. ¿Tengo que llevar cosas de playa como sombrilla y la heladera?
4. ¿Llevo el guante de béisbol para jugar con los abuelos?
5. ¿Cuántas toallas de playa necesito?
6. ¿Traigo la bicicleta?
7. ¿Meto el tocacasetes en la maleta grande?
8. El vestido de baño me queda pequeño. ¿Qué hago?
9. Tengo los zapatos blancos, los rojos y las sandalias. ¿Qué otros zapatos necesito?
10. Ya puse el cepillo de pelo, la pasta y el cepillo de dientes en la maleta pequeña. ¿Incluyo también el jabón y el champú?
11. Quiero llevar el vestido blanco y azul, pero está sucio. ¿Ahora qué hago?
12. No tengo dinero. ¿Crees que lo necesito?

2. Introduction to the Spanish Subjunctive

The **indicative mood** is used to describe actions or events that are real, definite or factual. Up to this point you have been exchanging ideas and information in the **indicative mood.**

The **subjunctive mood** is used to describe a speaker's attitudes, wishes, feelings, emotions, or doubts about an action or event. Unlike the indicative, which deals with real, factual actions, the subjunctive describes reality subjectively.

Es importante que **compres** un boleto de ida y de vuelta.	*It's important that you **buy** a round trip ticket.*
La azafata **quiere** que te **sientes** en primera clase.	*The flight attendant **wants** you to **sit** in first class.*

¡Quiero que me compres ése!

Like the formal commands, the present subjunctive stem is formed by deleting the final **-o** of the first person singular of the present indicative. The endings associated with **-er** verbs are added to the **-ar** verbs and those associated with the **-ar** verbs are added to the **-er** and **-ir** verbs which have identical endings.

habl**ar**	hablo → habl	+	**e** → habl**e**
com**er**	como → com	+	**a** → com**a**
viv**ir**	vivo → viv	+	**a** → viv**a**

	HABLAR	COMER	VIVIR
yo	habl**e**	com**a**	viv**a**
tú	habl**es**	com**as**	viv**as**
Ud./él/ella	habl**e**	com**a**	viv**a**
nosotros	habl**emos**	com**amos**	viv**amos**
vosotros(as)	habl**éis**	com**éis**	viv**áis**
Uds./ellos/ellas	habl**en**	com**an**	viv**an**

◆ Práctica

8-19 ¿Es importante, o no? Respond whether the following circumstances are important or not to you and your friends. In each response, conjugate the subordinate verb in the subjunctive.

MODELO: nosotros: vivir cerca de los padres
                    Es importante que vivamos cerca de los padres. (or)
                    No es importante que vivamos cerca de los padres.

yo: comer en casa todos los días
mis compañeros y yo: estudiar más de seis horas por día
yo: leer las noticias internacionales
mi mejor amigo: trabajar más de 20 horas por semana
mis padres: comprarme un coche nuevo
nosotros: asistir a clase todos los días
yo: aprender a hablar bien el español
mis amigos: creer en su futuro
nosotros: recibir buenas notas en la universidad
yo: vivir en la casa de mis padres

8-20 El matrimonio. Grisel is telling her mother what people want her and Armando to do as they plan their wedding, honeymoon, and married life. Complete each phrase logically, changingthe infinitives to the subjunctive mood.

MODELO: Para la luna de miel, Armando quiere que (yo) ...
                    Para la luna de miel, Armando quiere que (yo) compre una guía turística.

Mi jefe quiere que (yo)

La tía Consuelo quiere que
    Armando y yo

Armando quiere que (yo)

Rosario Díaz quiere que (nosotros)

Mi amiga Ema quiere que (yo)

Los abuelos quieren que (nosotros)

Papá quiere que (nosotros)

Armando y su primo José quieren
    que (yo)

Tú quieres que (nosotros)

Mis compañeras de la oficina
    quieren que (nosotros)

Yo quiero que Armando

llevar el vestido que compré en Panamá

pasar la luna de miel en las cataratas de
    Niágara

cortarse el pelo antes de la boda

mirar un vídeo de Costa Rica

hablar con un amigo costarricense

visitar el pueblo donde ellos se conocieron

vivir en un apartamento pequeño después
    de la boda

comer poco el día de la boda

buscar mi cámara

terminar todo mi trabajo antes de salir

escribir un artículo para el periódico después
    de la luna de miel.

leer toda la información sobre el viaje a
    Costa Rica

The Present Subjunctive of Irregular Verbs

- There are six Spanish verbs that have irregular present subjunctive forms.

	DAR	ESTAR	HABER	IR	SABER	SER
yo	dé	esté	haya	vaya	sepa	sea
tú	des	estés	hayas	vayas	sepas	seas
Ud./él/ella	dé	esté	haya	vaya	sepa	sea
nosotros(as)	demos	estemos	hayamos	vayamos	sepamos	seamos
vosotros(as)	deis	estéis	hayáis	vayáis	sepáis	seáis
Uds./ellos/ellas	den	estén	hayan	vayan	sepan	sean

◆ Práctica

8-21 ¿Es necesario? Your boss is always ordering you around with demands that are sometimes necessary and other times not. Verify that each of the following really are necessary by asking the question, ¿Es necesario que ...? and using the subjunctive with the subject indicated.

MODELO: Es necesario ir por café. ¿Yo?
            ¿Es necesario que yo vaya por café?

1. Es necesario darle este trabajo a la secretaria. ¿Yo?
2. Es necesario ir a la tienda a comprar papel. ¿La secretaria?
3. Es necesario estar aquí a las ocho en punto todos los días. ¿Nosotros?
4. Es necesario saber quién es el jefe de la Agencia de Viajes. ¿Usted?
5. Es necesario ser cortés con los clientes. ¿Nosotros?
6. Es necesario ir mañana a Acapulco. ¿Usted y yo?
7. Es necesario haber flores en mi oficina.
8. Es necesario saber la temperatura hoy en Roma. ¿Nuestro cliente Rossini?
9. Es necesario estar a tiempo en la reunión. ¿Los empleados?
10. Es necesario haber café en la reunión.
11. Es necesario darles esta información a los miembros del comité. ¿Yo?
12. Es necesario saber quiénes van a asistir a la reunión. ¿Usted?

The Present Subjunctive of Regular and Stem-changing Verbs

- Verbs with an irregular **yo** form in the present indicative use the **yo** form as the base of the present subjunctive.

INFINITIVE	1ST PERS. SING. PRESENT INDICATIVE	1ST PERS. SING. PRESENT SUBJUNCTIVE
caer	caigo	**caiga**
decir	digo	**diga**
hacer	hago	**haga**
poner	pongo	**ponga**
tener	tengo	**tenga**
traer	traigo	**traiga**
venir	vengo	**venga**
ver	veo	**vea**

- In order to maintain the [k], [g], and [s] sounds corresponding to the letters **c, g,** and **z**, verbs whose infinitives end in **-car, -gar,** and **-zar** have spelling changes in all forms of the present subjunctive.

buscar	c → **qu**	bus**qu**e	→ bus**qu**es…
llegar	g → **gu**	lle**gu**e	→ lle**gu**es…
empezar	z → **c**	empie**c**e	→ empie**c**es…

- The subjunctive forms of **-ar** and **-er** stem-changing verbs have the same pattern as that of the present indicative.

PENSAR (IE)		DEVOLVER (UE)	
p**ie**nse	pensemos	dev**ue**lva	devolvamos
p**ie**nses	penséis	dev**ue**lvas	devolváis
p**ie**nse	p**ie**nsen	dev**ue**lva	dev**ue**lvan

- In **-ir** stem-changing verbs, the unstressed **e** changes to **i,** and the unstressed **o** changes to **u** in the **nosotros** and **vosotros** subjunctive forms.

SENTIR (IE,I)		DORMIR (UE, U)	
s**ie**nta	s**i**ntamos	d**ue**rma	d**u**rmamos
s**ie**ntas	s**i**ntáis	d**ue**rmas	d**u**rmáis
s**ie**nta	s**ie**ntan	d**ue**rma	d**ue**rman

◆ Práctica

8–22 Pobre Paco. Paco's mother, the owner of Agencia Ticotour, wants him to take over the business as soon as possible. She's planned his entire summer so that he can learn the ropes. Complete the statements with the correct subjunctive form of the verbs in parentheses.

1. Quiero que (venir) _____ a la agencia todas las tardes.
2. Te insisto en que (llegar) _____ temprano a la agencia.
3. Los lunes sugiero que (ayudar) _____ a Gracia con las reservaciones de avión.
4. Los martes te pido que (llamar) _____ a los hoteles para ver si tienen habitaciones vacías *(empty)*.
5. Los miércoles recomiendo que (observar) _____ a Marisa con las excursiones.
6. Los jueves te aconsejo que (estudiar) _____ los precios de los boletos de avión.
7. Los viernes necesito que (hacer) _____ las cuentas.
8. Los sábados y domingos te recomiendo que (divertirse) _____ y (descansar) _____ mucho porque entre semana *(on weekdays)* hay que trabajar mucho.
9. Te ruego que en la agencia no (hablar) _____ demasiado por teléfono con amigos.
10. Quiero que (comenzar) _____ a trabajar la semana que viene.

8–23 ¡A divertirnos! You work at Agencia Ticotour and are organizing a party to welcome Paco. Tell your co-workers what you want them to do for the party.

MODELO: Marta / traer los vasos
           Quiero que Marta traiga los vasos.

1. Alberto / prestar el carro
2. Julia y Chichi / preparar la comida
3. Norma / comprar los refrescos
4. Roberto / traer el estéreo
5. Mauricio y Berta / poner la mesa
6. Ángela / cocinar el cerdo
7. Nosotros / preparar los postres
8. Betina / escoger la música
9. Santiago / decorar la casa
10. Alonso / conseguir sillas extras
11. Tino y Norberto / leer sus poesías
12. Ema y Blanca / empezar el baile
13. Isolina y Jaime / tocar la guitarra
14. Todos / ayudar a limpiar

8–24 Una excursión. You and your friends are going on a camping trip. What does David tell all of you to do before the trip in his note?

MODELO: Preparar unos sándwiches
           David dice que preparemos unos sándwiches.

llamar a Federico
desayunar bien antes de salir
traer refrescos y comida
poner gasolina al carro
acordarse de llevar bañera
cepillar al perro antes de subirlo al carro

pasar por María
salir bien temprano
no olvidar la guitarra
cerrar todas las ventanas de la casa
guardar todo lo que no van a llevar
vestirse apropiadamente

8–25 El viaje de Yanina. Yanina is going to Quito. To find out about her trip, conjugate the verbs in parentheses with the correct subjunctive form.

En el mostrador de la aerolínea me piden que (mostrar) _____ mi pasaporte. Yo les pido que (darme) _____ un boleto de primera clase. Ellos sugieren que (cambiarlo) _____ por un pasaje de ida y vuelta que es más barato. Como no tengo reservaciones les pido que (ponerme) _____ en la lista de espera. Como el vuelo sale pronto me dicen que (ir) _____ a la puerta de salida número 18. No me permiten que (facturar) _____ el equipaje por si acaso *(in case)* no hay lugar. Pronto invitan a los pasajeros a que (abordar) _____ el avión. Todos suben y a mí me piden que (esperar) _____ y que (tener) _____ paciencia. Por fin me piden que (mostrarles) _____ la tarjeta de embarque. Me invitan a que (sentarme) _____ en primera clase. Enseguida la azafata nos pide que (abrocharnos) _____ el cinturón de seguridad. El piloto nos prohíbe que (fumar) _____ durante el despegue, pero cuando ya estamos en el aire la azafata nos dice que podemos fumar. La señora de al lado me pide que (levantarme) _____ porque tiene que ir al baño. Poco después, nos piden que (quedarnos) _____ en nuestros asientos durante el aterrizaje. Es una aerolínea excelente. Te recomiendo que (viajar) _____ en ella.

▼▼▼▼▼▼▼▼▼▼▼▼▼▼▼▼▼▼▼▼▼▼▼▼▼▼▼▼▼▼

STUDY TIP: How to listen for the subjunctive

Most of the time the subjunctive appears in a clause introduced by **que.**
To train your ear to recognize the subjunctive in conversation, practice the
conjugations with the word **que** in front: **que venga, que llegue,** and
so on. Practice them with some of the most typical verbs that often elicit
the subjunctive, such as **querer** and **decir.**

Dice que venga.   **Quiere que vaya.**

◆ Actividades

8–26 Evangelina la miedosa. Evangelina wants to go on a trip, but she's afraid
of everything. In pairs, take turns role-playing Evangelina and her friend, who has a
piece of advice for every one of Evangelina's preoccupations.

MODELO: Desear hacer un viaje a México   Deseo hacer un viaje a México.
                buscar un folleto sobre México   Te recomiendo que busques un folleto
                                                                              sobre México.

PREOCUPACIONES   SUGERENCIAS
no saber qué tipo de pasaje comprar   no facturarlo / llevarlo en…
¿viajar en primera clase o en turista?   sentarse cerca de…
¿comprar una guía?   ir a…
no gustarme aterrizar en muchos lugares   conseguir…
tener claustrofobia   pedirle a la azafata…
querer un hotel seguro pero no muy caro   tomar un vuelo…
llevar poco equipaje   comprar un pasaje…
tener miedo del aterrizaje   cambiarse a un asiento…
no tener un pasaporte válido   buscar un hotel…
molestarme el humo de los pasajeros   sentarse en…
¿y si tener que ir al baño a menudo?   viajar en…
¿y si en mi hotel no haber excursiones?   ir al consulado de…

8–27 La fiesta de mamá. Your mother, a travel agent, is having a party for some
of her most important clients. She wants you and your siblings to get the house ready.
In small groups, write and be prepared to present a skit about all the things she wants
you to do. Use the lists below as a guide.

MODELO: —¿En qué te ayudamos, mamá?
                —Necesito que limpies la cocina. Y tú, ayuda a tu hermana a sacar los platos.
                —Y yo, ¿qué hago?
                —Ah, Julita, por favor, quiero que…

necesitar   barrer el piso   preparar la comida
querer   lavar los platos   planchar la ropa
desear   pasar la aspiradora   sacar la basura
pedirte   cortar la hierba   sacudir los muebles
                           ordenar los cuartos   secar el baño
                           poner la mesa   arreglar las flores
                           escoger la música   sacar el gato al jardín

3. Impersonal and Passive Constructions with *se*

The impersonal *se* to express people, *one, we, you, they*

- The pronoun **se** may be used with the third person singular form to express an idea without attributing the idea to anyone in particular. These expressions are equivalent to English sentences that have impersonal subjects such as *people, one, we, you, they.* The third person plural of the verb may be used alone to express these impersonal subjects.

  Se dice que viajar es un placer.   ***People say*** *that traveling is a pleasure.*
  Se puede fumar aquí.   ***One can*** *smoke here.*
  Dicen que la profesora es simpática.   ***They say*** *that the professor is likable.*

The passive *se*

Detrás de estas tarjetas se encuentra algo más que su firma.

¿Qué tarjetas de crédito tienes?

- The pronoun **se** may also be used with the third person singular or plural form of a verb as a substitute for the passive voice in Spanish. The doer of the action is **not** expressed. The verb must agree with the noun that follows.

  Allí **se compran** libros usados.   *Used books **are bought** there.*
  Se habla español.   *Spanish **is spoken.***

◆ Práctica

8–28 Mi agencia de viajes favorita. Susana and Jorge use the Costamar travel agency because of the special services it offers. Find out what they like about it by completing the following paragraph with the impersonal **se** and the correct form of the verbs from the box.

hablar	atender	conseguir
decir	trabajar	poder

Nos gusta la Agencia de viajes Costamar. _____ que es la mejor agencia de viajes de Miami y allí _____ todo el día. En Costamar _____ español y _____ rápidamente al cliente. En esa agencia _____ todo muy barato y _____ pagar con tarjetas de crédito.

8–29 Se dice que... With a classmate, explain why you want to travel to a particular country. Use impersonal expressions with **se**.

MODELO: —Quiero ir a Guatemala porque se dice que la cultura indígena es muy interesante. Dicen que las ruinas de Tikal son maravillosas. Y además, se habla español y puedo practicarlo bastante.

¡Así es la vida!

En el aeropuerto

Paulino, un joven de Los Ángeles, California, va para Paraguay como voluntario del Cuerpo de Paz. Toda la familia va al aeropuerto a despedirlo.

MAMÁ: ¿Tienes todo tu equipaje mi hijo? ¿Y tu pasaporte y los cheques de viajero?

PAULINO: Sí, mamá, te ruego que no te preocupes y que estés tranquila.

MAMÁ: Al llegar quiero que me avises enseguida.

ABUELA: Mi niño, ¡qué falta nos vas a hacer! Te ruego que nos escribas.

PAULINO: Te lo prometo abuela. Ahora te sugiero que acompañes a mamá. Te pido que no la dejes sola. ¿Está bien?

ABUELA: Vete tranquilo. Todos la vamos a cuidar mucho. ¡Y te aconsejo que tengas mucho cuidado tú también!

PAPÁ: Paulino, quiero que abras una cuenta corriente en guaraníes en el Banco Central de Paraguay en Asunción. Ya sabes a cómo está el cambio, ¿no?

PAULINO: Sí, papá.

PEPITA: Paulino, yo… yo te pido que me traigas un souvenir de Paraguay.

PAULINO: Sí Pepita, y yo a ti te pido que te portes bien y ayudes a mamá en todo.

PAPÁ: Te recomiendo que no firmes los cheques de viajero antes de usarlos.

PAULINO: Sí, papá, por supuesto. Y ahora yo les prohibo a Uds. que me hagan más recomendaciones. Todo va a salir bien.

ABUELA: Tienes razón, hijo. A ver, dejémoslo en paz.

Las aerolíneas del mundo hispano

Muchas de las aerolíneas hispanas pertenecen a los gobiernos de los países en donde operan y mantienen un monopolio sobre las rutas internas del país. En los últimos años, sin embargo, la tendencia a "privatizar" las empresas estatales ha ocasionado la privatización de aerolíneas nacionales como Aerolíneas Argentinas, Aeroméxico, LAN Chile y otras. A continuación aparece una lista de las principales aerolíneas del mundo hispano:

Argentina	Aerolíneas Argentinas	Ecuador	Saeta
Chile	LAN Chile	Perú	Aeroperú
España	Iberia	Venezuela	VIASA
Colombia	AVIANCA	Panamá	Air Panamá
México	Mexicana, Aeroméxico		

Vocabulario y expresiones

En el banco

el billete	bill (dollars)
el(la) cajero(a)	teller
el cambio	exchange
la cuenta corriente	checking account
la cuenta de ahorros	savings account
el cheque de viajero	traveler's checks
el giro monetario	money order
la moneda	coin: currency
el presupuesto	budget
la ventanilla de pagos	cashier's window

En el correo

el buzón	mailbox
la carta	letter
el correo	mail; post office
el correo aéreo	air mail
el(la) destinatario(a)	addressee
la dirección	address
el(la) remitente	sender
el sello	stamp
el sobre	envelope
la tarjeta	postcard

Verbos de volición

aconsejar	to advise
avisar	to warn, to inform
esperar	to hope; to wait
lamentar	to regret
mandar	to order, lead; send
notificar	to notify
ordenar	to order
permitir	to permit, allow
recomendar(ie)	to recommend
rogar(ue)	to beg
sorprender(se)	to surprise, be surprised
sugerir(ie)	to suggest
temer	to fear

Otros verbos

acompañar	to accompany; to keep company
cobrar	to cash; to collect
cuidar	to take care of
dejar	to leave; to allow
depositar	to deposit
endosar	to countersign; endorse
enviar	to send
firmar	to sign
hacer falta	to miss; to lack
indicar	to indicate
pedir prestado	to borrow
portarse bien / mal	to behave well / poorly
preocupar(se)	to worry, be worried
prestar	to lend

Otras palabras y expresiones

al llegar	upon arrival
al mismo tiempo	at the same time
casi	almost
dejémoslo en paz	let's leave him in peace
otra vez	again
por lo menos	at least
por supuesto	of course
pronto	soon
todo va a salir bien	everything is going to turn out alright

◆◆◆◆◆◆◆◆◆◆◆◆◆◆◆◆◆◆◆◆◆◆◆◆◆◆◆◆◆◆

¡Así lo decimos!

El dinero

You already know the standard word for money: **dinero**. However, in many parts of the Spanish-speaking world, money is commonly referred to as **plata** (literally, silver) in everyday conversation. More colloquial expressions like English bread, which was popularized in the 1960s, and dough are frequently used.

Argentina, Uruguay	**guita, mosca**	España	**pelas**
Chile	**billetes**	México	**lana, feria, luz**
Colombia	**pasta, billete**	Puerto Rico	**chavos**
Cuba	**guano**	Venezuela	**real**
Ecuador	**guita**		

Ese tipo tiene **la mosca** loca.   *That guy has a lot of money.*

A propósito... Las monedas

Cada uno de los países que integran el mundo hispano emite *(issues)* su propia moneda cuyo valor en relación con el dólar fluctúa de día a día. A continuación aparece una lista de las monedas de todos los países hispanos. Puedes consultar un periódico *(newspaper)* local en la sección financiera para saber el valor actual de cada una de las monedas.

ARGENTINA	peso	MÉXICO	nuevo peso
BOLIVIA	boliviano	NICARAGUA	córdoba
CHILE	peso	PANAMÁ	balboa
COLOMBIA	peso	PARAGUAY	guaraní
COSTA RICA	colón	PERÚ	nuevo sol
CUBA	peso	PUERTO RICO	dólar (US)
ECUADOR	sucre	REPÚBLICA	
ESPAÑA	peseta	DOMINICANA	peso
EL SALVADOR	colón	URUGUAY	nuevo peso
GUATEMALA	quetzal	VENEZUELA	bolívar
HONDURAS	lempira		

¡Vamos a comparar!

¿Qué países usan el peso? ¿Por qué usa Puerto Rico el dólar? ¿A cuánto está la peseta en estos momentos comparada con el dólar? ¿el dólar de Canadá?

¿Cuánto te dan de cada moneda por US $20.00?

🔊 ¡A escuchar!

En el aeropuerto. You will hear the conversation that appears in **¡Así es la vida!** After listening, choose a letter that best completes each sentence.

1. a. las monedas   b. los guaraníes   c. los cheques de viajero

2. a. les escriba   b. que abra una cuenta   c. que los llame por teléfono

3. a. cuide a Pepita   b. acompañe a su mamá   c. le escriba

4. a. de ahorros   b. en dólares   c. corriente

5. a. un souvenir   b. una tarjeta   c. un cheque de viajero

6. a. que le escriba   b. se porte bien   c. que acompañe a mamá

8–30 Fuera de lugar. Circle the letter of the word or expression that does not belong.

1. a. buzón   b. código postal   c. sello   d. billete
2. a. el sobre   b. la cuenta corriente   c. la cuenta de ahorros   d. el cheque de viajero
3. a. aconsejar   b. portarse bien   c. recomendar   d. sugerir
4. a. el cheque   b. el correo aéreo   c. la ventanilla de pagos   d. el cambio
   de viajero
5. a. endosar   b. firmar   c. cobrar   d. indicar
6. a. ordenar   b. mandar   c. acompañar   d. permitir
7. a. avisar   b. notificar   c. sorprender   d. indicar
8. a. el presupuesto b. lamentar   c. cuidar el dinero   d. la cuenta de ahorros
9. a. el sobre   b. el cambio   c. la tarjeta   d. la carta

8–31 Completar. Choose the correct word or expression to complete each statement.

1. Eché todas las cartas en el…
   a. correo aéreo   b. buzón   c. sobre

2. ¿Cuántos… le pusiste al sobre?
   a. billetes   b. cheques de viajero   c. sellos

3. Compré los sellos en el…
   a. correo   b. banco   c. buzón

4. A la dirección le falta el…
   a. código postal   b. recibo   c. billete

5. El… en el banco me atendió muy rápidamente.
   a. destinatario   b. viajero   c. cajero

6. Yo envié la carta. Soy el…
   a. destinatario   b. remitente   c. presupuesto

7. Si quiere depositar este cheque tiene que…
   a. mandarlo   b. cobrarlo   c. endosarlo

8. Ya conté los billetes y las monedas, pero si quieres lo hago…
   a. otra vez   b. por lo menos   c. por supuesto

8–32 Anselmo. Anselmo is going to college next year. His parents want to make sure he has the right financial set up. Complete the statements with words and expressions from **Vocabulario y expresiones.**

Mañana voy para el _____. Mis padres me _____ que abra una cuenta de _____. Esa cuenta no la debo tocar, así, el próximo año, si quiero un carro mis padres no me tienen que _____ dinero. A mis papás les _____ que yo no tenga suficiente dinero en el banco. Me _____ que también abra una cuenta _____ en la que ellos puedan depositar dinero si es necesario. _____ que yo consiga algún trabajo y que yo por lo _____ ayude un poco con las cuentas de la universidad. El _____ para mis estudios es limitado. Ellos me van a _____ un cheque por correo. Yo lo tengo que _____ y depositarlo en el banco. Me sugieren que no firme los cheques hasta llegar al banco para más seguridad. Por _____, también me ruegan que me _____ bien, que les escriba, que estudie mucho, que duerma suficiente, que coma bien. ¡Tú sabes cómo son los papás!

◆ Actividad

8–33 El recibo. In pairs, role-play a monetary transaction between the person who made the payment and the person who issued the receipt below. You may find it helpful to first answer or (when the information does not appear in the receipt), to invent an answer to the following questions.

1. ¿Qué tipo de transacción monetaria es?
2. ¿Cómo se llama la persona que cambió el dinero?
3. ¿Cuál es su número de pasaporte?
4. ¿Dónde cambió el dinero?
5. ¿Cuándo cambió el dinero?
6. ¿En qué ciudad está?
7. ¿A cómo estaba el cambio ese día?
8. ¿Cuántos dólares cambió?
9. ¿Cuántas pesetas?
10. ¿Le cobraron comisión a la persona que hizo el cambio monetario?

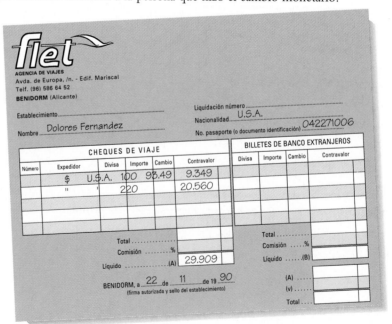

Estructuras

4. The Subjunctive in Noun Clauses

¡Espero que tengas un buen viaje!

- A clause is a group of words consisting of a subject and a predicate. A main clause can stand alone as a sentence, while a dependent clause is incomplete without the main clause. In Spanish, one type of compound sentence consists of two conjugated verbs and two subjects, one in the main clause, the other in the dependent clause. The dependent clause often begins with **que.**

MAIN CLAUSE   DEPENDENT CLAUSE

subject + verb   **que** + 2nd subject + verb in subjunctive

- A noun clause is a clause that can take the place of a noun. It can function as the direct object or subject of the verb, or as an object of a preposition. The subjunctive appears in the noun clause (dependent clause), and indicates that the act or event referred to has not yet occurred. Note some of the different English equivalents of the Spanish subjunctive in the examples that follow: the infinitive, the future, the present, or the auxiliary word might.

Dice la azafata que **abordemos** el avión.   *The flight attendants says **to board** the plane.*

Dudo que nos **den** almuerzo en el vuelo.   *I doubt they**'ll give** us lunch during the flight.*

Espero que el avión **aterrice** a salvo.   *I hope the plane **lands** safely.*

Puede que no nos **pidan** el pasaporte.   *They **might** not **ask** us for our passport.*

- If there is only one subject in a sentence, there is no noun clause, and therefore the infinitive rather than the subjunctive is used. Compare:

El piloto desea **aterrizar** en Logan.   *The pilot wants **to land** at Logan.*

Yo deseo que el piloto **aterrice** en Logan.   *I want the pilot **to land** at Logan.*

The Subjunctive to Express Volition

- When the verb in the main clause expresses volition and the subject is different from the subject in the dependent clause, the verb of the noun clause must be in the subjunctive. Verbs of volition express the needs, wishes, preferences, suggestions, requests, and implied commands of the speaker. The use of these verbs indicates that the subject in the main clause is trying to influ-

ence the behavior of the subject in the dependent noun clause. Some verbs of volition are: **aconsejar, decir, desear, insistir (en), mandar, necesitar, ordenar, pedir(i), permitir, preferir(ie,i), prohibir, querer(ie), recomendar(ie), rogar(ue), sugerir(ie, i).**

Insiste en que (ella) **vuele** en primera clase.	*He insists on her **flying** in first class.*
Prefiero que tú **hagas** las reservaciones.	*I prefer that you **make** the reservations.*
Recomiendan que no **fumemos.**	*They recommend that we don't **smoke**.*

- Verbs such as **aconsejar, decir, pedir, recomendar,** and **sugerir** require an indirect object pronoun. This indirect object refers to the subject of the dependent clause and is understood as the subject of the subjunctive.

¿**Me** aconsejas que **vuele** por LACSA?	*Do you advise **me** to fly on LACSA?*
Te sugiero que no **viajes** mañana.	*I suggest **you** don't travel tomorrow.*
Me pide que **me siente** en la ventanilla.	*She asks **me** to sit by the window.*

- Verbs such as **avisar, decir, escribir,** and **notificar** in the main clause may take either the indicative or the subjunctive in the dependent clause. If the subject in the main clause is simply reporting information, the dependent clause is in the indicative. But if the main clause verb is used in the sense of a command or a request, the dependent clause is in the subjunctive.

Avísale a Ramón que **vamos** a Perú.	*Tell Ramón **we're going** to Peru.*
Notifícale que no se **vaya** en ese vuelo.	*Tell him not **to take** that flight.*
Dice el piloto que ya **vamos** a despegar.	*The pilot says we're about **to take off**.*
Dice la azafata que nos **abrochemos** los cinturones para el despegue.	*The flight attendant says **to fasten** our seatbelts for takeoff.*

The Subjunctive to Express Feelings and Emotions

- When the verb in the main clause expresses emotions such as hope, fear, surprise, regret, pity, anger, joy, and sorrow, and the subject is different from the subject in the dependent clause, the subjunctive is used. Some of these verbs are: **alegrarse (de), enojarse, entristecerse, esperar, estar contento (triste/furioso/etc. [de], lamentar, molestar, ponerse (triste/furioso/etc. [de]), sentir (ie, i), sorprender(se), temer, tener miedo (de).**

Julia se lamenta de que Carlos no **esté** aquí.	*Julia regrets that Carlos **isn't** here.*
Nos sorprende que no **venga** a la fiesta.	*We are surprised that **he's** not **coming** to the party.*

The Subjunctive vs. Other Moods

There are four moods in Spanish:

1. **Infinitive.** The verb is not conjugated.
   Quiero **hablar** contigo.   *I want **to talk** to you.*

2. **Indicative.** Expresses simple statements and facts about reality.
   Hoy **es** martes.   *Today **is** Tuesday.*

3. **Imperative.** Expresses direct commands.
   No **hables** con Jacinto.   *Don't **talk** to Jacinto.*

4. **Subjunctive.** Expresses the attitudes of the person speaking, such as indirect
   commands and the desire to influence others. It is used to talk about things that
   either do not yet exist or may never exist, as well as events that have not yet
   happened or may not be said with certainty to happen. This is illustrated in the
   English translations of the examples below.

   Quiero que **haga** sol.   *I want it **to be** sunny.* (You don't control the sun.)
   Ojalá que el avión **salga** *I **hope** the plane **leaves** on time.* (Since it hasn't left
   a tiempo.   yet you don't know if it will leave on time or not.)
   Dudo que **llueva**.   *I doubt it **will rain**.* (But you don't say it with
                                      certainty.)

◆ Práctica

8–34 Brian y Jill. Brian and Jill, from Minneapolis, are running out of money while
on vacation in Mexico. Provide the correct form of the verbs in parentheses—it may
be the infinitive—and fill in the remaining blanks with the correct word from the
following box.

aeropuerto	correo	carta	giro monetario
billetes	cheques de viajero	de ahorros	monedas

Brian le (avisar) _____ a Jill que ya no tienen muchos _____. Sólo
les quedan unos _____ en dólares, unos en pesos y unas _____. Ellos
quieren que Sean, el hermano de Brian, les (enviar) _____ un _____ a
su hotel en la Ciudad de México. Pero a Jill le (preocupar) _____ que se pierda
en el _____. Entonces le (notificar) _____ a Sean por fax que les (mandar)
_____ el dinero a la oficina de American Express en la Ciudad de México.
Mientras tanto, Sean les (recomendar) _____ que usen las tarjetas de crédito.
Ellos aceptan, pero (lamentarse) _____ de no tener mucho dinero en su
cuenta _____ en Minneapolis. En una _____ le (rogar) _____ a
Sean que les (prestar) _____ dinero para pagar las tarjetas de crédito a su
regreso. También le (avisar) _____ que vuelven el sábado 16 a Minneapolis
y le dan el número de vuelo. Le piden que no les diga nada a los padres porque los
quieren _____ (sorprender).
   Al llegar al _____ en Minneapolis, Sean los está esperando. Les (ordenar)
_____ que se pongan sus abrigos inmediatamente porque hace mucho frío.
No les (permitir) _____ que lo (acompañar) _____ a traer el carro.
(Temer) _____ que su hermano y su cuñada se enfermen con el cambio de
clima tan fuerte. Sean es el mayor de los hermanos, por eso cree que (deber)
_____ tanto a sus hermanos.

8–35 El viaje de Katie. Katie, a Spanish major, is home recovering from a turbulent flight. Complete her letter to a friend with the correct present subjunctive form of the verbs in parentheses.

... y como te decía, el viaje de regreso fue horrible y el aterrizaje peor. Llegué sintiéndome enferma. Por suerte el doctor Facio, nuestro médico, llegó a verme. Es nicaragüense, como tú, y es un médico tradicional. Se preocupa por todos, viene a la casa y da muchos consejos. Le encanta que nosotros le (hablar) _____ en español. No nos permite que le (conversar) _____ en inglés, porque quiere que nosotros (aprender) _____ el español bien. Le aconseja a papá que (comer) _____ y (beber) _____ poco. Insiste en que la comida no (tener) _____ mucha grasa o sal y le ruega que (consumir) _____ más verduras. Le prohíbe a mamá que (fumar) _____ y le sugiere que (ir) _____ todos los años a que (hacerse) _____ un examen físico. A mi hermana Rosalía le recomienda que (llevar) _____ una dieta balanceada, que (practicar) _____ deportes y que (dormir) _____ por lo menos ocho horas al día. Finalmente, a mí, como soy un poco nerviosa, siempre me pide que (ser) _____ más tranquila y que (seguir) _____ sus consejos. Es una gran persona. Espero que (continuar) _____ siendo mi doctor para siempre. Ah, y tengo que contarte otra cosa. ¿Sabes quién venía en el avión? Te acuerdas de...

8–36 La bienvenida de Katie. Some friends are having a dinner party at Rosamaría and her roommates' house to welcome Katie. Complete the description of their early morning plans with words from the list below.

aconsejo	lamenta	maquilles	ponga
ayuden	levantemos	pide	pongamos
despertemos	limpiemos	ruego	quedemos
duche	llames	ordenemos	seas
			vaya

Mañana hay mucho que hacer. Te _____ que nos acostemos, que _____ el despertador y nos _____ temprano. Prefiero que Rosamaría se _____ primero. No quiero que ella se _____ impaciente por el baño. Y por favor, te _____ que te seques el pelo y te _____ en tu cuarto. Rosamaría no quiere que nos _____ horas y horas en el baño, lógicamente.

Me alegra que Gerardo nos _____ a ayudar. Nos _____ que lo llamemos por teléfono y lo _____ temprano. Rosamaría insiste en que _____ tú quien prepara la comida. _____ que ella no pueda ayudarte, pero sugiere que tú _____ a Clotilde y a Gloria y les digas que te _____. A Gerardo y a mí nos pide que _____ y _____ la casa. Queremos estar completamente listas para la fiesta esta tarde.

8–37 El papá estricto. Matilde and Sandra are complaining about their authoritarian, loving father. Form complete sentences by using the correct form of the verb in the indicative or the subjunctive.

MODELO: Papá *querer* que tú *ir* al partido con él.
         Papá quiere que tú vayas al partido con él.

1. papá *insistir* en que todos nosotros *levantarse* temprano
2. no *permitir* que nadie *ducharse* antes que él
3. *ponerse* furioso de que nosotras *maquillarse* tanto
4. *preferir* que mamá *peinarse* de una forma tradicional
5. no le *gustar* que nosotras *mirarse* mucho en el espejo
6. no *permitir* que ninguno de nosotros *cepillarse* con su cepillo
7. *mandar* que todos *lavarse* los dientes tres veces al día
8. no le *gustar* que nosotras *secarse* el pelo en el baño. —Vayan a sus cuartos—dice
9. *ponerse* impaciente de que mamá *pintarse* cuando él necesita el baño
10. *reírse* de que Juan José le *decir* que es demasiado exigente
11. *ordenar* que todos *quitarse* los zapatos dentro de la casa
12. *ponerse* nervioso de que Juan José *llegar* tarde los sábados por la noche
13. cuando nosotros salimos nos *aconsejar* que *vestirse* y *portarse* bien
14. *ponerse* triste de que todos *salir* de la casa al mismo tiempo
15. le *divertir* que nosotros *ir* con él y mamá al cine los fines de semana

8–38 En el hotel. Describe what happens when Guillermo Suárez arrives at a hotel in Mexico City. Form complete sentences in the subjunctive or indicative.

MODELO: Guillermo / querer / que / le *servir* / bien en el restaurante
         Guillermo quiere que le sirvan bien en el restaurante.

1. después de aterrizar / Guillermo / les *pedir* / a unos señores / que le *indicar* / la parada *(stop)* de taxis
2. *esperar* / /que / el taxista / le *aceptar* / dólares
3. le *pedir* / al taxista / que lo *llevar* / al hotel
4. en el hotel / Guillermo / *querer* / que los empleados / lo *ayudar* / con el equipaje
5. le *molestar* / que / no / lo *atender* / rápidamente
6. *alegrarse* de que / la recepcionista / le *sonreír* / y / lo *querer* ayudar
7. la recepcionista / le *pedir* / que le *dar* / el pasaporte
8. él le *pedir* / a ella / que le *guardar* / las cosas de valor
9. ella / le pregunta / si *querer* / que le *conseguir* / una excursión a Cuernavaca
10. él le responde /que *preferir* / que le *dar* / información sobre el Museo de Antropología
11. pero / él / sí *querer* / que ella / le *conseguir* / un guía
12. *desear* / que el guía / le *enseñar* / lo más interesante del museo
13. también / *querer* / que alguien / le *recomendar* / un lugar donde comer
14. le *pedir* / a la recepcionista / que le *aconsejar* / un lugar para escuchar mariachis
15. ella / le *recomendar* / que *comprar* / una guía turística
16. Guillermo *soñar* / con que la recepcionista le *aceptar* / una invitación a salir, pero no le dice nada porque no sabe si es apropiado o no

8–39 El segundo viaje de Guillermo. Despite Guillermo's traveling experience everyone has something to say or a piece of advice to give him. In pairs, take turns conjugating the verb in the main clause and completing each sentence with an appropriate dependent clause in the subjunctive.

MODELO: Yo querer que Guillermo…
            Yo quiero que Guillermo vuelva a México porque ya lo conoce.

1. La señora de la agencia le *recomendar* que…
2. Su mejor amigo *estar* contento de que…
3. Su madre *tener* miedo de que…
4. A mí me *gustar* que Guillermo…
5. Los amigos le *aconsejar* que…
6. Su novia no *querer* que…
7. Sus padres *preferir* que…
8. El abuelo *temer* que…
9. Yo le *decir* que…
10. Tú *insistir* en que…
11. Nosotros le *sugerir* que…
12. Su hermanita menor le *pedir* que…
13. La abuelita le *rogar* que…
14. Su profesor de portugués *desear* que…
15. Todos *esperar* que…

◆ Actividades

8–40 Los mensajes. In small groups, take turns role-playing receiving messages from a boss and an assistant. Combine elements from the columns below.

MODELO: Srta. Cañas, su mamá dice que por favor la llame.

su mamá	escribir(le) una carta
el profesor de…	mejor reservar el libro que necesita
su prima Ileana	guardar(le) comida porque va a llegar tarde
el doctor Facio	almorzar con… mañana
Guillermo	conversar con nadie
la entrenadora	visitar a abuelo porque está enfermo
su padrastro	hacer(le) una rebaja
sus compañeras de cuarto	llamar a la farmacia y…
la señora de la biblioteca	no salir con su novio esta noche
la abogada	conseguir unos zapatos de tenis nuevos
el jardinero	ir a patinar con…
los clientes nuevos	aprovechar la comida en el refrigerador
su novio	comprar aspirina
la dependiente del Almacén	prestarle su vestido nuevo para la fiesta
la directora	comprar(le) una botella de vino
sus amigos	no faltar al partido de vólibol
	ver su carro antes de comprar uno nuevo
	pagarle lo que le debe del mes pasado

8–41 ¡Por fin, mis pasajes! Silvia had trouble getting the flights she wanted for an upcoming trip. Complete her story with the appropriate form of the preterite or the imperfect according to the context.

1. Yo (estar) _____ en el trabajo cuando el agente de viajes *(travel agent)* me (llamar) _____.
2. El agente me (decir) _____ que (tener) _____ mis pasajes *(tickets)* en la mano.
3. Yo (pedir) _____ que no (ir) _____ a poder ir de vacaciones, pero por fin el agente me (dar) _____ las buenas noticias.
4. Yo (pedir) _____ permiso para irme temprano del trabajo y (ir) _____ directamente a la agencia de viajes.
5. Sin embargo, yo (caminar) _____ lentamente, porque (tener) _____ miedo de tener otro problema.
6. El agente (leer) _____ un folleto nuevo cuando yo (entrar) _____ en la agencia.
7. Cuando el agente me (ver) _____, inmediatamente (buscar) _____ mis pasajes.
8. Yo (pagar) _____ con tarjeta de crédito porque no (tener) _____ dinero.

8–42 Un día en el lago. Complete the following description with the correct form of the preterite or imperfect of the verbs in parentheses.

Ayer Cecilia y yo (pasar) _____ el día en un lago en las montañas. El lago (ser) _____ muy grande y bonito. (Tener) _____ una playa con arena *(sand)* y (estar) _____ rodeado *(surrounded)* de montañas muy altas. Por la mañana (ir) _____ a pescar en el bote de Carlos, un amigo de la universidad. Cecilia (pescar) _____ dos pescados muy pequeños y ella (tener) _____ que echarlos otra vez en el lago. Por la tarde, (subir) _____ una montaña y (ver) _____ muchas flores, especialmente unas orquídeas que (ser) _____ muy bonitas. Yo (cortar) _____ una y se la (poner) _____ en el pelo *(hair)* a Cecilia. Ella se (ver) _____ muy bella con la orquídea. Sí, ayer (ser) _____ un día maravilloso para nosotros y vamos a tratar de volver al lago la semana próxima.

8–43 Malila. Malila, or Malilita as her grandchildren call her, is eighty years old and needs a cane to walk, but has a fabulous spirit. She wants to take a trip abroad. With a classmate, create a conversation between her and a travel agent. Malila asks questions, makes requests, states preferences, and the agent makes suggestions, gives advice, and states what she will do herself or what she will ask her assistant to do.

5. The *nosotros* Command

- There are two ways to give a direct command to a group of persons in which you include yourself: **vamos a** + *infinitive* or the **nosotros** form of the present subjunctive.

Vamos al banco.	***Let's go*** *to the bank.*
Cambiemos el cheque hoy.	***Let's cash*** *the check today.*
Enviemos la carta el martes.	***Let's send*** *the letter on Tuesday.*

- **Vamos** is used to express *let's go* in Spanish. However, to express *let's not go,* the subjunctive **no vayamos** is required.

Vamos al teatro.	***Let's go*** *to the theater.*
No vayamos al concierto.	***Let's not go*** *to the concert.*

- As with all other direct command forms, object pronouns are attached to the affirmative commands and precede the negative commands. In affirmative commands, an accent mark is added to maintain the original stress.

Escribámosle al director del periódico.	***Let's write*** *to the publisher of the newspaper.*
No les escribamos a los reporteros.	***Let's not write*** *to the reporters.*

- When the pronoun **nos** is attached to the **affirmative** command of reflexive verbs, the final **-s** is deleted from the verb ending.

Vámonos.	***Let's leave.***
Levantémonos.	***Let's get up.***
No nos sentemos.	***Let's not sit down.***

- Stem-changing **-ir** verbs, also change in the **nosotros** command.

pedir (i, i)	**Pidamos** café.	***Let's order*** *coffee.*
dormir (ue, u)	**Durmámonos.**	***Let's go to sleep.***

◆ Práctica

8–44 Un problema. Complete the following messages sent by a bank employee using the verbs in the box below and the **nosotros** commands.

MODELO: cambiar
          Cambiemos el cheque.

abrir	enviar	indicar	prestarle
cambiar	firmar	notificar	
endosar	hacer	permitirles	

1. No _____ el dinero porque nunca paga.
2. _____ el giro monetario por correo.
3. _____ al público el nuevo cambio.
4. _____ pedir $20.000 prestados.
5. _____ una cuenta corriente.
6. _____ un presupuesto nuevo.
7. _____ los dólares por balboas.
8. _____ los cheques.
9. _____ los documentos.
10. _____ a cómo está el cambio.

8–45 Los reporteros. As two television reporters, you and a classmate are called to report on a serious accident. Discuss what you have to do by completing each sentence with the **nosotros** command of the verbs in parentheses.

1. (Levantarse) _____ rápidamente.
2. (Vestirse) _____ ahora mismo.
3. (Llevar) _____ nuestras cámaras.
4. (Buscar) _____ más información.
5. (Salir) _____ en el carro.
6. (Hacer) _____ muchas preguntas.
7. (Preparar) _____ el reportaje *(article)*.
8. (Irse) _____ a la oficina.

8–46 Acuerdos y desacuerdos. While on vacation together, two friends can never agree on anything. One always agrees with you on what to do and the other disagrees. React to the situations below.

MODELO: —Vamos a leer la cartelera.
          —Sí, leamos la cartelera.
          —No, no la leamos.

1. Vamos a ese cine.
2. Vamos a ver esa película.
3. Vamos a comprar las entradas.
4. Vamos a sentarnos allí.
5. Vamos a levantarnos del asiento.
6. Vamos a volver a casa temprano.
7. Vamos al correo.
8. Vamos a enviar la tarjeta.
9. Vamos a poner el correo en el buzón.
10. Vamos a cerrar los sobres.
11. Vamos a portarnos bien.
12. Vamos a pedir el carro prestado.

◆ Actividades

8–47 Planes para el fin de semana. With two or three classmates, propose several activities for this weekend.

MODELO: —Vamos a la discoteca "La caja de Pandora."
                —Sí, es una buena idea. Invitemos a Pedro y a Martín.
                —Pues, llamémoslos enseguida.

6. Indirect Commands

- You have already learned how to use direct commands. Commands may also be expressed indirectly, either to the person with whom you are speaking or to express what a third individual should do.

- The basic formula of the indirect command is as follows.

    Que + subjunctive verb + (subject)

Que **vaya** Raquel.	***Have (Let)** Raquel **go**.*
Que lo **haga** él.	***Have (Let)** him **do** it.*
¡Que lo **pases** bien!	***Have a good time!***
¡Que **vayas** tú a verlo!	***You go see** him!*

¡Que te diviertas!

- When **que** introduces an indirect command, it translates roughly as *have, let,* or *I wish*.

- When a subject is expressed, it generally follows the verb.

¡Que lo hagas **tú**!	***You** do it!*
¿La cocina? ¡Que la limpien **ellos**!	*The kitchen? Let **them** clean it!*

◆ Práctica

8–48 La agencia de excursiones. Your inconsiderate boss is asking you to do all
the work at the travel agency where you work. Tell your boss to have someone else
do some work. Follow the model changing noun objects to object pronouns.

MODELO: —Llama a la Srta. Núñez a la aerolínea.
                —Que la llame Ester.

1. Dale los folletos al Sr. Von Thalen.
2. Haz reservaciones en el avión para treinta y seis personas.
3. Consigue tres asientos en la sección de no fumar.
4. Pon a las hermanas Karamasoff en la lista de espera.
5. Aconseja a los turistas que lleven suficiente rollos de película.
6. Recomiéndale a la recepcionista del hotel que atienda bien a los viajeros.
7. Sugiéreles a los participantes de la excursión que lleven cheques de viajero.
8. Diles a todos que estén en el mostrador de la aerolínea a las 7:45 de la mañana.
9. Factúrales el equipaje.
10. Ve al aeropuerto y despídelos.

◆ Actividad

8–49 Planes. In groups of three or four write and be prepared to present a skit
about one of the following situations. Use at least one of each: the subjunctive,
a **tú** command, a **nosotros** command, an indirect command.

1. You are having a party and you want help from your roommates with house
   chores and food preparation.

2. Your elderly grandparents have been visiting and want to fly back home. Your
   parents want you to help them make reservations, buy return tickets, get to
   the airport, check their luggage, get to the gate, etc.

3. You are going on a trip to the rainforest. With friends discuss what to take
   and how much money to bring: currency, travelers' checks, credit cards, and
   so on.

Colaboración

Estudiante A

8-50A Planes para un viaje. You have one list of necessary steps to plan a trip. Your partner has another. Together draft a new list of the necessary steps in order of importance. You don't have to follow all the steps, but if you don't use one, you have to explain why.

MODELO: —Vamos a viajar a...
—Número 1, tenemos que (hay que) llamar al agente de viajes.
—Número 2, podemos (debemos)...

comprar ropa para el viaje
hacer cola *(line up)* para abordar el avión
facturar el equipaje
comprar una guía turística
llamar al agente de viajes

llamar un taxi
comprar una novela de detectives
ponerse los audífonos y cerrar los ojos
 antes del despegue
sacarse la foto para el pasaporte
sentarse en la sala de espera

8-51A ¿Se permite...? Ask your partner for permission to do the things on your list. Then tell him/her to go ahead and do the things on his/her list. Use **tú** commands.

MODELO: permitir fumar en esta universidad
—¿Se permite fumar en esta universidad?
—Sí, fuma.

ACTIVIDAD/OPINIÓN
guardar la bicicleta aquí
quitarse los zapatos en clase
levantarse tarde

cocinar en la cocina de la residencia estudiantil
sacar libros de referencia de la biblioteca
vestirse informalmente
hacer una fiesta en la residencia estudiantil

8-52A Los deseos. You don't feel well. Tell your partner what you want him/her to do for you. Your partner will then respond to your request.

MODELO: me *traer* un refresco
—Quiero que me traigas un refresco.
—¿Quieres que te traiga un refresco? ¡Olvídate! *(Forget it!)*

LA ACCIÓN
me *preparar* un bocadillo
me *poner* la televisión
me *leer* el periódico
me *buscar* una novela
llamar al doctor por mí

me *traer* el Kleenex
me *tomar* la temperatura
me *pedir* una cita con el médico
me *traer* una aspirina
me *comprar* unas frutas

8-53A Consejos. You ask your partner for advice. Write what he/she recommends in each situation.

MODELO: —Tengo un examen de química mañana.
—Recomiendo que estudies mucho.
—Me recomienda que estudie mucho.
—Buena idea. (No tengo tiempo, etc.)

LA SITUACIÓN
Tengo un examen de química mañana.
Quiero salir con una persona de la clase de español.
Necesito un carro nuevo.
No tengo dinero para comprarle un regalo a mi mamá.
Quiero ver… en la televisión pero no voy a estar en casa.
(original)

Mis padres quieren que los visite este fin de semana.
No tengo nada en el refrigerador.
Hay una buena película esta noche, pero el examen de español es mañana.
Estudié tanto anoche; estoy muerto(a).
Mi novio(a) quiere salir, pero tengo que estudiar.

8-54A ¿Escuchas bien? Tell your partner what's going on in your life. Write down his/her reactions. Then switch roles.

MODELO: —Tengo un examen de matemáticas hoy.
—Lamento que tengas un examen.

LO QUE USTED LE CUENTA
Tengo un examen de…
Mañana tengo que…
Este verano voy a…
Esta noche necesito…

El año que viene…
Ahora…
Siempre estoy…
Nunca hago…
Pronto voy a…

ALGUNAS EXPRESIONES DE EMOCIÓN

POSITIVAS
Me alegro de…
Me sorprende…
Espero…
Estoy contento(a) de…

NEGATIVAS
Me enoja…
Me molesta…
Lamento…
Siento…
Temo…
Tengo miedo de…

8-55A Una cuestión de dinero. With a partner, match each other's list of definitions and expressions.

MODELO: —¿Dónde se cambia el dinero en España?
—En…

LA EXPRESIÓN
el sobre
la cuenta corriente
la ventanilla de pagos
la cuenta de ahorros
el buzón
el recibo

LA DEFINICIÓN/EL USO
el lugar donde se cambia dinero
es más seguro llevar éstos que efectivo
lo doblas y lo metes en el bolsillo
en España es la peseta
esta persona te atiende en el banco
no te olvides de ponerlo en el sobre

Estudiante B

8-50B Planes para un viaje. You have one list of necessary steps to plan and make a trip. Your partner has another. Together draft a new list of all necessary steps in order of importance. You don't have to follow all the steps, but if you don't use one, you have to explain why.

MODELO: —Vamos a viajar a…
           —Número 1, tenemos que (hay que) llamar al agente de viajes.
           —Número 2, podemos (debemos)…

ir al aeropuerto	hacer las reservaciones
comprar cheques de viajeros	llamar al agente de viajes
escribir un cheque para el pasaporte	darle al agente su boleto
subir al avión	sentarse y abrocharse el cinturón
completar la solicitud del pasaporte	de seguridad
y llevarla al correo	bajar del avión

8-51B ¿Se permite… ? Tell your partner to go ahead and do the things on his/her list. Use **tú** commands. Then ask him/her to do the things on your list.

MODELO: permitir fumar en esta universidad
           —¿Se permite fumar en esta universidad?
           —Sí, fuma.

ACTIVIDAD/OPINIÓN

comer papas fritas	entrar a la biblioteca después de las 11 p.m.
acostarse tarde de domingo a viernes	terminar los estudios universitarios en
tomar cerveza en la cafetería	menos de cuatro años
llegar tarde a clase	pagar la cuenta con tarjeta de crédito

8-52 Los deseos. Your partner doesn't feel well and asks you to do a lot of things for him/her. Rephrase each request as in the model and then say whether you will do it or not.

MODELO: —Quiero que me traigas un refresco.
           —¿Quieres que te traiga un refresco? ¡Olvídate! *(Forget it!)*

ALGUNAS RESPUESTAS

POSITIVAS	NEGATIVAS
Está bien.	¡Hazlo tú!
Con mucho gusto.	No puedo ahora. Tengo que…
Ahora mismo.	¡Olvídate!
¡Claro que sí!	No tengo tiempo.
	Que lo haga…(nombre)

8-53B Consejos. Your partner asks you for advice. Tell him/her what you recommend in each situation.

MODELO: —Tengo un examen de química mañana.
            —Recomiendo que estudies mucho.
            —Buena idea. (No tengo tiempo, etc.)

ALGUNOS VERBOS DE INFLUENCIA		ALGUNAS ACCIONES	
Te aconsejo	Te prohíbo	estudiar…	llegar…
Te recomiendo	Deseo	ir a…	aprender…
Te sugiero	Te digo	trabajar…	invitar a…
Insisto en	Espero	buscar…	salir con…
Te permito	Te pido	venir…	tener…

8-54B ¿Escuchas bien? Your partner will tell you what's going on in his/her life. Write it down. Next, react to each situation. Then, switch roles.

MODELO: —Tengo un examen de matemáticas hoy.
            —Lamento que tengas un examen.

ALGUNAS EXPRESIONES DE EMOCIÓN

POSITIVAS	NEGATIVAS	LO QUE USTED LE CUENTA
Me alegro de…	Me enoja…	Tengo un examen de…
Me sorprende…	Me molesta…	Mañana tengo que…
Espero…	Lamento…	Este verano voy a…
Estoy contento(a) de…	Siento…	Esta noche necesito…
	Temo…	El año que viene…
	Tengo miedo de…	Ahora…
		Siempre estoy…
		Nunca hago…
		Pronto voy a…

8-55B Una cuestión de dinero. With a partner, match each other's list of definitions and expressions.

MODELO: —¿Dónde se cambia el dinero en España?
            —En…

LA EXPRESIÓN
el banco
el billete
el sello
la moneda
el(la) cajero(a)
los cheques de viajero

LA DEFINICIÓN/EL USO
aquí se recibe el dinero en un banco
aquí tienes dinero reservado para comprarte un coche nuevo
aquí tienes dinero para pagar las cuentas
necesitas esto cuando quieres devolver un artículo al almacén
ahí echas las cartas
en éste escribes el nombre del remitente y del destinatario

Lección 9

¡Su salud es lo primero!

Comunicación

- Talking about the Condition of Oneself and Others
- Talking about Health Care
- Giving Advice

Cultura

- **Las farmacias**
- **El ejercicio y la dieta**

Mundo hispánico: España

Estructuras

Primera parte

- The Past Participle
- The Present Perfect
- **hacer** with Expressions of Time

Segunda parte

- The Pluperfect
- Possessive Adjectives (Long Forms) and Pronouns
- **pero** vs. **sino**

PRIMERA PARTE
¡Así es la vida!

¡Qué mal me siento!

Don Evelio no se siente bien. Le duele todo el cuerpo. Su esposa
Refugio quiere que vaya al doctor.

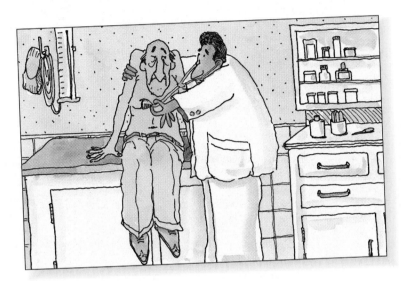

DON EVELIO: ¡Aaay, Refu! ¡Qué mal me siento!

DOÑA REFUGIO: Pero Evelio, ya te he dicho que llames al doctor. Hace tres días que estás enfermo.

DON EVELIO: De ninguna manera.

DOÑA REFUGIO: Evelio. ¡qué terco eres! No has visto al Dr. Estrada Fernández desde hace más de un año.

DON EVELIO: ¡Está bien, mujer. ¡No me molestes! Llama al Dr. Estrada Fernández. Pídele una cita, pero ya te he dicho que yo no confío en los médicos.

En el consultorio del doctor Estrada Fernández

DR. ESTRADA: Don Evelio, ¡qué gusto! ¡Hace tiempo que no lo veo!

DON EVELIO: ¿Cómo está, doctor? Sí, hace más de un año que no vengo.

DR. ESTRADA: Y, ¿cómo se siente? ¿Qué tiene?

DON EVELIO: Pues me duele mucho la garganta y también el pecho y el estómago.

DR. ESTRADA: A ver…respire…tosa… Pues mire, lo que Ud. tiene es la gripe. Le voy a recetar un antibió…¡Ah, se me olvidaba! Ud. me dijo que era alérgico a los antibióticos, ¿no es cierto?

DON EVELIO: Bueno, alérgico no. Es que no me gustan porque soy naturalista, pero si hay que tomarlos, ¡ni modo!

DR. ESTRADA: Bueno, evitemos los antibióticos. Tómese estas pastillas y le garantizo que se va a sentir mejor. Pero lo más importante es que tenga mucho reposo. Y quiero que venga la semana próxima para hacerle el examen físico anual.

DON EVELIO: ¿Venir otra vez?

DR. ESTRADA: Vamos, don Evelio, hay que ser racional.

335

Vocabulario y expresiones

Las partes del cuerpo humano

la boca	mouth
el brazo	arm
la cabeza	head
la cara	face
el corazón	heart
el cuello	neck
el dedo de la mano	finger
el dedo del pie	toe
la espalda	back
el estómago	stomach
la frente	forehead
la garganta	throat
el hombro	shoulder
el hueso	bone
la lengua	tongue
la mano	hand
la muñeca	wrist
el músculo	muscle
la nariz	nose
el oído	inner ear
la oreja	ear
el pecho	chest
el pie	foot
la pierna	leg
el pulmón	lung
la rodilla	knee
la sangre	blood
el tobillo	ankle
la uña	nail, (finger or toe)

Medicinas comunes

el antiácido	antacid
el antibiótico	antibiotic
el antihistamínico	antihistamine
la aspirina	aspirin
el jarabe	cough syrup
la pastilla	pill, lozenge
la penicilina	penicillin

Adjetivos

alérgico(a)	allergic
enfermo(a)	sick
saludable, sano(a)	healthy
terco(a)	stubborn

Otras palabras y expresiones

¡Más ánimo!	Cheer up!
ni modo	what the heck (colloquial)
según	according to

Verbos relacionados con la salud

componerse	to get well
darle la gripe	to catch the flu
darle dolor de...	to get an ache
doler(ue)	to hurt
enfermarse	to get sick
guardar cama	to stay in bed
operar	to operate
recetar	to prescribe
reposar	to rest
respirar	to breathe
romper(se) (un hueso)	to break (a bone)
torcerse	to twist
toser	to cough

Palabras asociadas a la salud

la alergia	allergy
el cirujano	surgeon
el consultorio	doctor's office
el dolor	ache, pain
la dosis	dose
la enfermedad	sickness
el(la) enfermero(a)	nurse
el examen físico	physical exam
el(la) farmacéutico(a)	pharmacist
la fiebre	fever
la gripe	flu
la infección	infection
la inyección	shot
el malestar	discomfort
las muletas	crutches
las náuseas	nausea
el(la) paciente	patient
la presión	blood pressure
la prueba/el examen	test
la radiografía	X-ray
la receta	prescription
el resfriado	cold
el síntoma	symptom
la temperatura	temperature

Otros verbos

confiar (en)	to trust
cubrir	to cover
descubrir	to discover
evitar	to avoid
garantizar	to guarantee
estar ido(a)	to be distracted
estar muerto de...	to be deadly...
tener confianza (en)	to trust

¡Así lo decimos!

cabeza

A typical, colloquial way to refer to the head in many Spanish-speaking countries is **el coco**, which literally means *coconut*. For example, if you try very hard to remember something you can say:

Me rompí el coco tratando de   *I broke my head trying to remember.*
   acordarme.

In many situations, slang words are often used to refer to the head. Do you recognize any of these words?

Argentina, Uruguay	**zabeca, el mate**
España	**azotea, chola**
México	**testa, melón**

terco(a)

In place of **terco**, there are many regional variations in Spanish that are used to mean *stubborn*. Like English, a lot of these expressions utilize some form of the word for head. What are the English expressions that use *head* to mean *stubborn*? Some Spanish variants are listed below.

Argentina, Uruguay	**testarudo, cabeza dura**
Chile	**porfiado, duro**
Cuba	**cabezón**
España	**cabezota, burro, tozudo**
México	**necio**
Puerto Rico	**cabeciduro**

📼 ¡A escuchar!

¡Qué mal me siento! You will hear the conversation in **¡Así es la vida!** First read the list below. Then, as you listen, answer the questions or complete the sentences that follow with items from the column at the right.

1. _____   a. hacía más de un año

2. _____   b. naturalista

3. _____   c. dolor de garganta, del pecho y del estómago

4. _____   d. no confía en ellos

5. _____   e. llame al doctor

6. _____   f. que se tome unas pastillas y que repose mucho

◆ Práctica

9–1 El cuerpo y la salud. Choose the word that best completes each sentence.

1. Ana no puede bailar porque le duelen los _____.
   a. oídos   b. pies   c. brazos

2. La _____ es roja.
   a. sangre   b. cabeza   c. pierna

3. Fui al _____ del doctor Duranza.
   a. resfriado   b. consultorio   c. antiácido

4. Juan se rompió un _____.
   a. corazón   b. pelo   c. brazo

5. La lengua está dentro de la _____.
   a. rodilla   b. pierna   c. boca

6. Respiramos con los _____.
   a. dientes   b. pulmones   c. músculos

7. Me corté las uñas de los _____.
   a. pies   b. tobillos   c. pulmones

8. Me duelen las _____ por el frío.
   a. orejas   b. muletas   c. alergias

9. Saque la _____.
   a. lengua   b. boca   c. cara

10. Tengo _____ de cabeza.
    a. gripe   b. fiebre   c. dolor

11. Hoy me pusieron la _____ contra la polio.
    a. infección b. inyección c. presión

12. Voy a tomarle la temperatura para ver si tiene _____.
    a. prueba   b. dolor   c. fiebre

13. Tiene apendicitis. Lo van a _____.
    a. operar   b. cubrir   c. romper

14. Dice el doctor que tiene que guardar _____.
    a. la pastilla   b. cama   c. la receta

9-2 ¿Cierto o Falso?

1. Encima de la cabeza nos ponemos el sombrero.
2. El cuello digiere la comida.
3. Caminamos con los pies y las piernas.
4. Hay sangre en las uñas.
5. Una persona que tiene la gripe debe guardar cama.
6. A veces es necesario operar cuando una persona se rompe un hueso.
7. Para tomarse la temperatura es necesario sacar la lengua.
8. Cuando una persona guarda cama es posible torcerse el tobillo.
9. Es necesario tomar un jarabe cuando hace una cita con el doctor.
10. A muchas personas les da náuseas comer pescado o mariscos.

9–3 ¿Qué les pasa? Look at the illustrations and say what's wrong with these people.

MODELO: Alicia
          A Alicia le duele el estómago.

1. Alberto

2. Ana María

3. Samuel y Ricardo

4. Luis

5. Ramiro y yo

9-4 El cuerpo. To what part of the body does each of the following expressions refer?

1. tomarse la presión.
2. tomarse la temperatura
3. fumar
4. tener fiebre
5. tener un resfriado
6. pintar
7. tener náuseas
8. respirar
9. toser
10. sacar

9–5 El cuerpo humano. Label the numbered parts of the body in the illustrations.

1. _____	8. _____
2. _____	9. _____
3. _____	10. _____
4. _____	11. _____
5. _____	12. _____
6. _____	13. _____
7. _____	14. _____

9–6 Emparejar. Match the words in left-hand column with a related word at the right.

___ 1. el anillo	a. el cuello
___ 2. el zapato	b. el jarabe
___ 3. el arete	c. el antibiótico
___ 4. el sombrero	d. el pie
___ 5. la radiografía	e. el dedo
___ 6. la bufanda *(scarf)*	f. el antihistamínico
___ 7. el esmalte	g. la aspirina
___ 8. el guante	h. la presión
___ 9. la alergia	i. la oreja
___ 10. la infección	j. la cabeza
___ 11. toser	k. las uñas
___ 12. la sangre	l. la temperatura
___ 13. la fiebre	m. el hueso
___ 14. la receta	n. la mano
___ 15. el dolor de cabeza	o. la farmacia

9-7 Un buen amigo. Eusebia is not feeling very well. Claudio comes to visit her.
Complete their conversation with words from **Vocabulario y expresiones.**

CLAUDIO: Hola, ¿qué tal? ¿Cómo te sientes?

EUSEBIA: Pues, ya lo ves, estoy un poco _____.

CLAUDIO: ¿Qué te pasa? Cuéntame.

EUSEBIA: Para empezar tengo un dolor de _____ horrible. Me duele la
_____ y además tengo _____.

CLAUDIO: ¿Cómo lo sabes? ¿Te tomaste la _____?

EUSEBIA: Sí, y tenía 40 grados. No me estoy muriendo, pero me duele todo el
_____.

CLAUDIO: ¡Pues más ánimo, mujer! ¿Llamaste al médico? Si no te _____ debes
llamar al _____ y pedir una cita. ¿O es que no te gustan los médicos?

EUSEBIA: No, no, yo _____ completamente en mi doctora. Pero como me
siento mal no quiero salir.

CLAUDIO: Pues te sugiero que te tomes una _____ para bajar la fiebre y muchos
líquidos. ¿Necesitas medicinas? Puedo ir a la _____ en un momentito.

EUSEBIA: Bueno, lo único que quiero es un _____ por si empiezo a toser.

CLAUDIO: Y, ¿un _____ no? ¿No eres alérgica?

EUSEBIA: No, felizmente, no, pero sí necesito unos jugos. ¿Puedes ir al mercado?

CLAUDIO: Claro, mujer, para eso estoy aquí, para cuidarte. Pero debes prometerme
que vas a _____ cama. Quédate ahí. Regreso enseguida.

EUSEBIA: Gracias, Claudio. ¡Qué buen amigo!

9–8 Examen médico. Complete the conversation between a doctor and her patient
by choosing the correct word from the list.

alérgico	enfermo	me duele	repose	se componga
antiácido	farmacéutico	me siento	respire	se siente
antibióticos	infección	pastillas	saque	
consultorio	inyección	pulmones	sea	

PACIENTE: Buenos días, Dra. Méndez. Me temo que estoy _____.

DOCTORA: Buenos días, Carlos Roberto. ¿Cómo _____?

PACIENTE: No me duele nada en especial, pero _____ mal.

DOCTORA: Bueno, por favor _____ la lengua y _____ profundo. Quiero
oír sus _____.

PACIENTE: Espero que no _____ nada serio.

DOCTORA: No, pero temo que Ud. tenga una _____ en la garganta.

PACIENTE: ¿En la garganta? Me sorprende que diga eso. A mí nunca _____ la
garganta.

DOCTORA: De acuerdo, pero ahora tiene una infección. Le voy a poner una
_____ de penicilina. No es _____ ¿verdad? Realmente quiero
que _____ rápido.

PACIENTE: No, por suerte no me dan alergias. Lo único, doctora, es que con los
_____ el estómago se me pone muy mal.

DOCTORA: Tómese las _____ con las comidas, así no le molestan. También le
aconsejo que _____ unos dos o tres días. Las infecciones son
delicadas. Si tiene problemas pídale al _____ que le recomiende
algún _____ . Si no se siente mejor, llámeme al _____ o al
hospital por las mañanas.

PACIENTE: Muchas gracias por todo, doctora.

9–9 Tito y Laura. Tito and his wife Laura are talking about Tito's health, but their conversation is scrambled. First read each item and decide who is speaking (Tito or Laura). Then organize the conversation in a logical way.

_____ Ya fui. Me dijo que tenía que ir al hospital.

_____ Bueno, Tito, es que comes como un caballo y no vas nunca al gimnasio. No es un estilo de vida muy saludable.

_____ ¿Te sigue doliendo el pecho?

_____ Sí, Laura, pero la vida es corta. También hay que pensar en la salud del espíritu.

_____ Sí, y no puedo respirar bien. Me tomé un té caliente.

_____ ¿Vas a ir al consultorio del Dr. Peraloca?

_____ Bueno, entonces no necesitas preocuparte. Y, ¿no pidió otros exámenes?

_____ ¡¿Al hospital?! ¡Pero entonces tienes síntomas de pulmonía!

_____ También quiere que me haga una prueba de sangre. El doctor no está contento con mi sobrepeso.

_____ No, no, mujer, tranquila. Es sólo un resfriado. Pero para estar seguros quiere que me saque una radiografía. Acuérdate que es mi examen físico anual.

9–10 Sugerencias personales. In groups of three or four, one of you plays the role of a doctor and tells the others what they should do. Medical problems are listed in the first column, verbs in the second column, and appropriate remedies in the third column.

MODELO: enfermo(a): Doctor, tengo mucha tos.
                doctor(a): Le sugiero que tome dos cucharadas de jarabe al día.

1. dolor de cabeza	aconsejarle	ponerse hielo
2. dolor de estómago	recomendarle	inmediatamente
3. tener libras de sobrepeso	sugerirle	comer cereal de avena
4. problemas cuando respiro	querer	reposar durante unos días
5. el colesterol alto	pedirle	tomar dos aspirinas
6. me torcer la muñeca	desear	ponerse una inyección
7. me sentir muy cansado(a)	esperar	de penicilina
8. tener una infección en	rogarle	tomar un antiácido
los oídos		hacerse una radiografía
		de los pulmones
		ir al gimnasio

9–11 En la farmacia. While traveling in Mexico you come down with a bad cold and you go to a pharmacist for advice about what to take. In pairs, write a short conversation about this situation. Be prepared to present it to the class.

9–12 ¿Cómo mejorar la salud? In small groups, prepare a list of at least ten specific suggestions for staying healthy.

MODELO: Les recomiendo que coman muchos vegetales.

9–13 Diálogos. In groups of three or four, create a conversation between several people in one of the following situations. Be prepared to share your skit with the class.

1. someone just broke a foot and needs an X-ray
2. someone you care for very much, a smoker, has been coughing an awful lot
3. a middle aged member of your family works under a lot of stress, eats fatty foods, is slightly overweight, and is feeling a little strange lately, but refuses to see a doctor

9-14 Mis reacciones. In pairs, take turns role-playing an employee in a health and fitness center giving a daily report to his/her boss. Express the boss' reactions by combining elements from the columns below.

MODELO: Mario/llegar/temprano.
         Me sorprende que Mario llegue temprano.

1. Pilar/llegar/tarde
2. Arturo casi nunca/practicar/la natación
3. Elena/no estar comiendo/frutas
4. las hermanas Quirós/correr/todas las tardes
5. Aurelio ya/no fumar
6. los señores/no pagar/la cuenta
7. el director/ir a comprar/más máquinas de pesas (*weights*)
8. mañana/venir/la nueva profesora de aeróbicos
9. Isolina/estar fumando/otra vez
10. Mariquita/no querer hacer/ejercicio
11. a Sonia/no le gustar/las bicicletas
12. ese chico/no bañarse/después de la clase
13. doña Marta siempre/llevarse/las toallas
14. don Manuel/ser/muy disciplinado
15. el profesor/poner/la música muy alto

alegrarse de
enojarse
esperar
estar contento(a)
gustar
lamentar
molestar
ponerse…
sorprenderse
temer
tener miedo

Estructuras

1. The Past Participle

- Form the past participle in Spanish by adding **-ado** to the stem of **-ar** verbs and **-ido** to the stem of **-er** and -**ir** verbs.

INFINITIVE	PAST PARTICIPLE
tomar	**tomado** (*taken*)
comer	**comido** (*eaten*)
vivir	**vivido** (*lived*)

- Past participles of **-er** and **-ir** verbs whose stems end in **-a, -e,** or **-o** add an accent mark.

INFINITIVE	PAST PARTICIPLE
caer	**caído**
creer	**creído**
leer	**leído**
oír	**oído**
reír	**reído**
traer	**traído**

- The following verbs have irregular past participles.[1]

INFINITIVE	PAST PARTICIPLE
abrir	**abierto**
cubrir	**cubierto**
decir	**dicho**
descubrir	**descubierto**
escribir	**escrito**
hacer	**hecho**
ir	**ido**
morir	**muerto**
poner	**puesto**
romper	**roto**
ver	**visto**
volver	**vuelto**

- In both English and Spanish, past participles may be used as adjectives to modify a noun. In Spanish, when the past participle is used as an adjective, it agrees in gender and number with the noun it modifies.

Lucinda tenía el estómago **irritado.**   *Lucinda's stomach was **irritated**.*
Tengo las piernas **dormidas.**   *My legs are **numb (asleep)**.*
Tenía la barba **afeitada.**   *His beard was **shaved**.*

---
[1] Although **limpiar** has a regular past participle, to qualify a noun, use the adjective **limpio(a)** instead of the past participle **limpiado(a).** EXAMPLE: La cocina ya está **limpia.** But, Ya **he limpiado** la cocina.

◆ Práctica

9–15 ¡Ya está hecho! You work at a hospital cafeteria where your boss is after you every minute to get things done. Respond affirmatively to all the questions using past participles.

MODELO: —¿Abrió la puerta del comedor?
—Sí, ya está abierta.

1. ¿Lavó todas las servilletas?
2. ¿Guardó los cubiertos en el aparador?
3. ¿Rompió la lista vieja de platos del día?
4. ¿Puso las mesas?
5. ¿Arregló la mesa de los postres?
6. Parece que va a llover. ¿Cerró las ventanas?
7. ¿Sacó la basura?
8. ¿Ordenó la cocina?
9. ¿Peló las papas?
10. ¿Picó las cebollas y los chiles?
11. ¿Batió los huevos?
12. ¿Tostó el pan de ajo?
13. ¿Metió los helados en el congelador?
14. ¿Cubrió la cazuela en el horno?
15. ¿Preparó la ensalada?
16. ¿Hizo la torta de chocolate?
17. ¿Le puso caramelo al flan?
18. ¿Atendió a los clientes de la mesa 14?

9-16 El viaje de Moncho. Moncho and his mother are going on a trip to Belize to visit Tato, Moncho's grandfather, who is sick and in the hospital. Provide the appropriate past participle for each verb in parentheses.

MAMÁ: El mostrador de la aerolínea ya está (abrir) _____. Vamos hijo.

(Unos minutos después)

MAMÁ: Ya todo está (decir) _____ y (hacer) _____. Estamos (poner) _____ en la lista de espera. Y según la azafata, todavía hay lugar en el avión.

MONCHO: Mami, ¿en qué hotel vamos a estar?

MAMÁ: Papá ha (descubrir) _____ uno muy bonito cerca del hospital donde está Tato. Moncho, ¿pudiste ver a qué hora salía el vuelo, en el tablero de información?

MONCHO: No, mami, no pude. El tablero estaba (cubrir) _____ con un papel. Ah, ¡mira! Ahí dice: Sale a las 2:15.

MAMÁ: Felizmente el equipaje ya está (facturar) _____.

MONCHO: ¿Te acordaste de escribirle una cartita a mi maestra explicando que iba a faltar a clase?

MAMÁ: Sí, ya está (escribir) _____ , y tu hermana se la va a llevar.

(En el avión)

MONCHO: Mami, la tarjeta de embarque no sirve. Está (romper) _____.

MAMÁ: No te preocupes. Ya no la necesitamos. Moncho…, Moncho…, hijo, ¡estás (ir) _____! ¿En qué piensas? ¡Abróchate el cinturón!

MONCHO: Esta bién. Ya está (abrochar) _____.

MAMÁ: ¿Qué te pasa? ¡Ay, mi amor, pero si estás (morir) _____ de miedo!

MONCHO: No mamá, no tengo miedo. Lo que tengo es náuseas.

MAMÁ: Tómate estas pastillas. Ya pronto te vas a sentir muy bien.

9–17 En el hospital. An administrator at a large health clinic is asking questions and reminding his very efficient staff of their various tasks. React to her questions and reminders by using the past participle of the verb in italics.

MODELO: ¿Quién va a preparar a la Sra. Blades para la prueba?
               Ya está preparada.

1. ¿Ya le *sacó* la radiografía al paciente del Dr. Molina?
2. ¿Quién le va a *hacer* la prueba de sangre a la Srta. Bonilla?
3. El Dr. Azógar nos pide que *ordenemos* más antibióticos a la farmacia central.
4. La Dra. Darío sugiere que *guardemos* la penicilina en la despensa.
5. El Dr. Discúa quiere que le *pongan* una inyección a esta niña.
6. Los doctores Sánchez y Rojas desean que *compremos* más muletas.
7. Hágame el gran favor y le *toma* la presión al Sr. Esquivel.
8. Ligia, *envía* los antihistamínicos que pidió el Dr. Machado hoy mismo.
9. Por favor, *cierren* la puerta del laboratorio.
10. ¿Cuándo *operan* al Sr. Facio de su brazo?
11. Hay que *atender* a dos pacientes nuevos.
12. Hay que *cubrir* a la paciente.
13. Hay que *romper* los documentos viejos.
14. ¿Es cierto que la Sra. Girón *se murió*?

◆ Actividades

9–18 ¿Ya lo hiciste? Your mother had knee surgery and is coming home from the hospital tomorrow. You and your siblings want to make sure that all the house chores are done and everything is taken care of. In pairs, interview each other to find out who has done what.

MODELO: —¿Ordenaste tu cuarto?
               —Ya está ordenado. *(or)*
               —No, todavía no está ordenado, pero lo voy a hacer…
                   (mi compañera de cuarto lo va a hacer) (mi cuarto nunca está ordenado)

1. ¿Compraste la comida?
2. ¿Pasaste la aspiradora?
3. ¿Sacaste la basura?
4. ¿Cortaste la hierba?
5. ¿Lavaste la ropa?
6. ¿Barriste el piso?
7. ¿Planchaste la ropa?
8. ¿Sacudiste los muebles?
9. ¿Ordenaste tu cuarto o la casa?
10. ¿Pagaste los recibos?
11. ¿Contestaste las cartas que mamá te pidió?
12. ¿Leíste las instrucciones del doctor?
13. ¿Devolviste todas las llamadas telefónicas de la gente que preguntó por mamá?
14. ¿Pusiste las maletas en el cuarto de mamá?
15. ¿Metiste los refrescos en el refrigerador?

9-19 ¿Quién lo va a hacer? Your friend María del Carmen has just graduated from nursing school. You and your friends are having a party to celebrate. With a classmate, take turns asking who is going to do a certain task, and answering that it has already been done.

MODELO: *comprar* la cerveza
—¿Quién va a comprar la cerveza?
—Ya está comprada.

1. *comprar* la cerveza
2. *decorar* el salón
3. *invitar* al (a la) profesor(a)
4. *preparar* las tapas
5. *alquilar* el salón
6. *contratar* a los músicos
7. *planear* el menú
8. *hacer* el pastel

9. *hacer* las compras
10. *escoger* el vino
11. *escribir* las invitaciones
12. *sacar* las fotos
13. *preparar* el café
14. *hablar* con la policía
15. *pagar* la comida
16. *limpiar* el salón después

9–20 ¿Qué estabas haciendo? In groups of three or four, take turns improvising a short scenario for each situation. Use past participles. Use the list of verbs as a guide for your answers.

MODELO: —¿Cómo estabas cuando sonó el teléfono?
—Estaba dormida.

(bien) atender (por el camarero)	encantar	interesar
patear, pero contento(a)	incluir (en los planes)	adelgazar
sentar (frente a la tele descansando)	necesitar (de dinero)	escoger
olvidar (de todos)	(muy bien) preparar	sorprender
perder (en la avenida 10)	descansar	enojar
vestir (y listo/a para salir)	preocupar	dormir
decidir (a ir a…)		

¿Cómo estabas…

1. cuando volviste de jugar al fútbol?
2. cuando te dijeron que te ganaste la lotería?
3. después de dormir diez horas?
4. después de consultar con la agente de viajes?
5. cuando te mostraron un carro muy bueno y barato?
6. cuando te encontraron caminando por la ciudad?
7. cuando pasaron por ti en tu casa?
8. después de trabajar muchas horas?
9. en el restaurante?
10. después de pagar todas tus cuentas?
11. después de muchos meses de no recibir cartas de nadie?
12. cuando tu novio(a) te dejó por otro(a)?
13. cuando fuiste al examen final?
14. cuando todos tus amigos te llamaron para invitarte a una fiesta?
15. cuando te dijeron que eras el(la) mejor atleta del año?
16. cuando te rompiste una pierna?
17. después de darte gripe y no comer mucho?
18. después de tomar un antihistamínico muy fuerte?

2. The Present Perfect

- The present perfect is a compound tense. To form the present perfect tense use two verbs: the present tense of an auxiliary verb + a *past participle*. In English the auxiliary verb is *to have* (in Spanish **haber**). The verb **haber** is not interchangeable with **tener**, but is translated as *to have* when used as an auxiliary verb with the past participle.

	haber	PAST PARTICIPLE
yo	he	
tú	has	
Ud./él/ella	ha	tomado
nosotros(as)	hemos	comido
vosotros(as)	habéis	vivido
Uds./ellos/ellas	han	

	to have	PAST PARTICIPLE
I	*have*	
you	*have*	
you, he, she	*has*	*taken*
we	*have*	*eaten*
you (pl)	*have*	*lived*
you (pl), *they*	*have*	

- The auxilliary verb **haber** agrees with the subject. The past participle is invariable when it forms part of a perfect tense.

  Luci **ha hecho** una cita para hoy.   *Luci **has made** an appointment for today.*
  ¿Sol y Ana **han tenido** fiebre hoy?   ***Have** Sol and Ana **had** a fever today?*

- Do not put another word between the auxiliary verb **haber** and the past participle. Always place object pronouns and negative words before **haber.**

  ¿**Me** han traído la penicilina?   *Have they brought **me** the penicillin?*
  No, **no te la** han traído todavía.   *No, they haven't brought it **for you** yet.*
  Nunca **se** ha enfermado.   *He has never been sick.*

- In general, the present perfect is used to refer to a past action or event that is perceived as having some bearing on the present. In Spain, however, the present perfect is used interchangeably with the preterit.

  | Jaime no **ha tomado** aspirina. | *Jaime **hasn't taken** an aspirin.* |
  | **¿Has visto** mis pastillas? | ***Have you seen** my pills?* |

- Use the present tense of **acabar de** + *infinitive* to describe an event that has just happened, even though in English the present perfect is used instead.

  | **Acabamos de** hablar con el doctor. | *We **have just** spoken with the doctor.* |
  | **Me acaban** de tomar la presión. | *I've just had my blood pressure taken.* |

◆ Práctica

9–21 Juana. A team of nurses is going on a humanitarian trip to a small village in Colombia where there's been a huge mudslide. They ask Juana to coordinate the details of the trip. Here's her report on what has been done.

MODELO: avisarle a la jefa qué enfermeras van a ir (María)
          Ya Marina le ha avisado a la jefa qué enfermeras van a ir.

1. preparar un presupuesto (yo)
2. hablar con la agente de viajes (Eugenia y Loló)
3. decidir qué tipo de pasajes comprar (tú)
4. pedir más dinero al Departamento de finanzas (Ana María y Loló)
5. preguntar a cómo está el cambio (Ana María)
6. comprar cheques de viajero (Manolo y Juan)
7. averiguar qué tipo de alojamiento nos van a dar en Colombia (Rodolfo)
8. conseguir más antibióticos (nosotras)
9. mandar a traer más aspirinas, antiácidos y otras medicinas (Nidia)
10. poner la penicilina en un recipiente especial para transportarla (nosotros)
11. enviar el fax pidiendo información sobre el equipo para sacar radiografías (tú)
12. hacer las maletas (Francisco y yo)

9–22 Una llamada de Madrid. You are on a short trip to Madrid with your Spanish class. In a phone call to your parents, tell them what you and your friends have done up to this point.

MODELO: yo/comer en un lugar diferente todos los días
          Yo he comido en un lugar diferente todos los días.

1. Ben y Sally/ir a la Puerta del Sol
2. Fred/caminar por el Paseo del Prado
3. Georgina/gastar todo su dinero
4. Jason and Jillian/cambiar muy pocos cheques de viajero
5. Ed y yo/todavía no comer tapas en la Plaza Mayor
6. Heidi/visitar el Palacio Real
7. Tonya/cenar en la Casa Botín
8. todos/ir a tres conciertos
9. Nancy/tomar una clase de flamenco
10. yo/ir a escuchar a Joan Manuel Serrat cantar
11. nosostros/ver una corrida de toros *(bullfight)*
12. Tom y Betty/hacer una excursión a Toledo

9–23 Paquito. Complete the telephone conversation between Paquito's mother and his doctor, by conjugating the verbs in parentheses in the present perfect.

MAMÁ: Dr. de la Torre, muchas gracias por llamar.

DOCTOR: De nada, señora. ¿Cómo sigue Paquito? ¿(guardar) _____ cama?

MAMÁ: Sí, desde hace tres días está en cama.

DOCTOR: Y ¿(tomar) _____ el jarabe y las pastillas que le recomendé?

MAMÁ: Cómo no, doctor. Ya (tomárselas) _____. Y Gracias a Dios que no (volver) _____ a toser. También ya le (bajar) _____ la fiebre.

DOCTOR: ¡Qué bueno! ¿Desde hace cuánto no le sube la temperatura?

MAMÁ: No le (subir) _____ desde el viernes.

DOCTOR: Bueno, eso significa que ya la infección pasó. Los antibióticos (trabajar) _____ bien por lo que veo.

MAMÁ: Sí, doctor, Paquito y yo (seguir) _____ todos sus consejos. Paquito ya (componerse) _____ mucho y las últimas dos noches él, su papá y yo (poder) _____ dormir mejor.

DOCTOR: ¡Magnífico! Para estar seguros quiero que continúe con la misma dosis de penicilina por dos días más. Y, las náuseas, ¿(quitársele) _____?

MAMÁ: Sí, completamente, ¿verdad, Paquito? Las náuseas no (volverte) _____.

PAQUITO: No mamá, pero tú (tener) _____ muchos dolores de cabeza.

MAMÁ: Sí, bueno, yo ya (tomar) _____ varias aspirinas.

DOCTOR: ¿Cómo dice?

MAMÁ: Ah, no nada doctor, todo está bien. Mil gracias por su llamada.

◆ Actividades

9–24 ¿Qué has hecho hasta ahora? In pairs, discuss what you have done up until this moment in the day.

MODELO: He preparado la tarea para tres clases, he ido al laboratorio de lenguas y he hecho los ejercicios. Y tú, ¿qué has hecho?

9–25 Cinco cosas. In groups of three or four, share two special things that you have done in your life, and three things that you haven't done but would like to.

MODELO: He ido al Polo Norte. No he montado a caballo, pero me gustaría.

3. *hacer* with Expressions of Time

- To talk about length of time in Spanish, use **hace que** or **desde hace.** If the event started in the past and continues in the present, use **hace** + *length of time* + **que** + the verb *in the present tense.* When **desde hace** is used, the word order in Spanish is the same as in English.

Hace una hora **que** estoy tosiendo. *I've been coughing for an hour.*
Hace tres años **que** está enferma. *She's been sick for three years.*
No se enferma **desde hace** mucho tiempo. *She hasn't been sick for a long time.*

- When the event is mentioned first, use **desde hace** to express *for* + *length of time.*

La enfermera trabaja ahí **desde hace** seis meses. *The nurse has been working there **for** the last six months.*
Está enferma **desde hace** una semana. *She's been ill **for** a week now.*

- To express *how long ago* an event occurred, use **hace** + *length of time* + **que** + *verb in the preterite.* If **hace** comes after the event, omit **que.**

     Hace media hora **que** pedí la cita. *I asked for the appointment half an hour ago.*
     El doctor llamó **hace** cinco minutos. *The doctor called five minutes ago.*

- To ask about length of time use **¿Cuánto tiempo hace que…? ¿Cuánto hace que…?** or **¿Desde hace cuánto…?**

     ¿Cuánto (tiempo) hace que   *How long have you been sick?*
     estás enfermo?
     ¿Cuánto hace que ves al   *How long have you been seeing Dr. Ruiz?*
     Dr. Ruiz?
     ¿Desde hace cuánto no fuma?   *How long has it been since you last smoked?*

- Use **hacía** + *length of time* + **que** and a verb in the imperfect or **desde hacía** + *length of time* to express how long ago something had been happening in the past.

     ¿Cuánto **hacía que** no lo veías?   *How long had it been since you'd seen him?*
     No lo veía **desde hacía** un mes.   *I hadn't seen him for a month.*

9–26 Nicolás. Read about Nicolás' visit to the doctor, and then answer the questions.

DR. APUI: Don Nicolás, hace dos años que no lo veo. A su edad es peligroso.
NICOLÁS: Lo sé, pero…
DR. APUI: Pero, no hay excusas. Tiene que hacerse un examen físico al año. Y le duele el estómago y el pecho. ¿Cuántos cigarrillos se está fumando al día?
NICOLÁS: Estaba fumándome un paquete, pero ahora tengo un mes de no fumar.
DR. APUI: ¡Felicidades! Y, dígame, ¿ha tenido mucha tos últimamente?
NICOLÁS: No, no he tenido tos desde hace quince días.
DR. APUI: La última vez que lo vi su dieta era muy grasosa y alta en colesterol. ¿Todavía come carne de cerdo, mantequilla y jamón?
NICOLÁS: La verdad es que me encanta comer. Ayer me comí un plato de paella muy grande. Me tomé dos copas de vino tinto y tres tazas de café negro. Pero no probé las chuletas de cerdo. Hace tres meses que no como carne.
DR. APUI: Excelente. Pero…, mire don Nicolás, no le puedo mentir. Eso de comer así está bien para un muchacho, pero un hombre de su edad tiene que ser más moderado. En el pecho no le oigo nada. Ud. tiene una indigestión. Tómese tres cucharadas de antiácido líquido y coma arroz blanco, sopa de pollo, o tostadas sin mantequilla por unos días. Pero de las comidas grandes, vino y café negro, ¡olvídese!
NICOLÁS: ¡Qué aburrido!
DR. APUI: Don Nicolás, Ud. ha tenido mucha suerte. No todos llegamos a los noventa años comiendo paella y tomando vino y café. Lo felicito.

1. ¿Cuánto tiempo hace que Nicolás no va al doctor?
2. ¿Hace cuánto tiempo que Nicolás no fuma?
3. ¿Desde hace cuánto no tiene tos Nicolás?
4. ¿Hace cuántos días que Nicolás se comió una deliciosa paella?
5. ¿Desde hace cuánto no prueba la carne Nicolás?

9–27 ¿Cuánto tiempo hace... ? Say how long you've done or not done these things. Give a real answer if it applies to you, or use the suggestion in parentheses.

MODELO: ¿Hace cuánto que no te enfermas? (un año)
           Hace un año que no me enfermo.

1. ¿Cuánto tiempo hace que no comes carne? (cinco años)
2. ¿Hace cuánto que no fumas? (tres meses)
3. ¿Hace cuánto que no ves al doctor? (siete meses)
4. ¿Desde hace cuánto te están doliendo los músculos de la pierna? (ocho días)
5. ¿Cuánto tiempo hace que tienes mala la muñeca? (un año y medio)
6. ¿Hace cuánto que no te haces una prueba de sangre? (seis meses)
7. ¿Hace cuánto no te sacas una radiografía de los pulmones? (un año)
8. ¿Desde hace cuánto no te da un gran dolor de cabeza? (dos días)

9–28 ¿Cuánto tiempo hacía... ? Say how long it had been since you had done these things. Give a real answer if it applies to you, or use the suggestion in parentheses.

MODELO: ...que no ponerme una inyección de ningún tipo (cinco años)
           Hacía cinco años que no me ponía una inyección de ningún tipo.

1. ...que no darme una alergia al polen (dos años)
2. ...que no sentirme tan bien (tres semanas)
3. ...que no tener confianza en un doctor (muchos años)
4. ...que no tomarme un jarabe para la tos tan horrible (cinco días)
5. ...que no necesitar la penicilina (diez años)
6. ...que no tener fiebre (tres meses)
7. ...que no darme una gripe tan fuerte (cuatro años)
8. ...que no dolerme el hombro (seis meses)

◆ Actividades

9–29 Entrevista. Interview a classmate about some current situations. Use the list as a guide but add at least three original items.

MODELO: —¿Cuánto hace que no vas al cine?
           —Hace un mes que no voy al cine.
           —Y eso, ¿por qué?
           —Porque hace un mes que empezaron mis clases por la noche.

1. no visitar a tus padres
2. estudiar español
3. salir con tu novio(a)
4. vivir donde vives ahora
5. no divertirse
6. ir a una fiesta
7. no ir a un doctor
8. no romperse un hueso
9. darle gripe

9–30 Otra entrevista. Now interview each other about some recent past events.

MODELO: —¿Cuánto hacía que no venías a clase?
—Hacía una semana que no venía a clase.
—Y eso, ¿por qué?
—Porque hacía una semana que estaba enfermo.

1. no escribirle una carta a nadie
2. no comprar zapatos de tenis
3. no salir con nadie especial
4. no guardar cama
5. no ir a la biblioteca a estudiar por la noche
6. comer algo delicioso en la cafetería
7. cocinar algo especial para alguien
8. no leer un buen libro

A propósito...Temas de salud

Las farmacias

Las farmacias en España e Hispanoamérica son tiendas especializadas en las que sólo se venden medicinas y artículos de aseo personal *(personal care products)* como jabones, jarabes, pasta de dientes, lociones y champú. Aunque existen "cadenas" de farmacias que funcionan como parte de grandes corporaciones, hoy día todavía son más numerosas las farmacias pequeñas. En estas farmacias de barrio, el mismo propietario es el farmacéutico y la gente del barrio va a consultarlo cuando están enfermos o sufren de algún malestar. Debido a que la venta de medicamentos no está tan estrictamente controlada como en los Estados Unidos, los dueños de farmacias y sus empleados con frecuencia les recetan medicinas a sus clientes. De esta forma, es posible comprar antibióticos como la penicilina y otras drogas sin necesidad de obtener una receta médica. Poco a poco, hoy día, esta costumbre va cambiando a medida que los gobiernos modernizan y reglamentan la venta de productos farmacéuticos.

El ejercicio y la dieta

La preocupación por las dietas saludables y por mantenerse en forma es un fenómeno bastante reciente en los países de habla española. Tradicionalmente, los hispanos comen platos con un alto contenido de grasa animal como la carne de cerdo y la de res. Sin embargo, es también costumbre en el mundo hispano que muchas de las comidas se preparen con ingredientes naturales y frescos. Esto contrasta con los Estados Unidos, en donde la proliferación de alimentos que se preparan en la fábrica mediante el uso de preservativos y otros químicos es mucho más frecuente. Según muchos expertos, la abundancia de ingredientes naturales en los alimentos puede resultar en menos casos de cáncer y de otras enfermedades.

Los hispanos, por lo general no hacen ejercicios o se mantienen en forma con la misma intensidad que los norteamericanos. Pero esta situación está cambiando, especialmente entre los jóvenes que viven en las grandes ciudades. Los centros de gimnasia y de danza aeróbica han aumentado en número en los últimos años, y cada día es más común ver a gente corriendo por las calles o por los parques de las grandes ciudades del mundo hispano.

¡Vamos a comparar!

1. ¿Qué diferencias existen entre las farmacias de los Estados Unidos y Canadá, y las farmacias de los países hispanos?
2. ¿Crees que los norteamericanos se preocupan excesivamente por las dietas saludables y por mantenerse en forma? ¿Qué tipo de dieta mantienes? ¿Qué actividades practicas para mantenerte en forma?

¡Así es la vida!

Mejora tu salud

Una buena dieta para un corazón saludable

Todos sabemos lo importante que es vigilar la alimentación para mantener un buen estado de salud. Mantener un control del consumo de azúcar en su dieta contribuye a su bienestar. Otras cosas que se deben tener en cuenta son los alimentos que contribuyen a las enfermedades del corazón.

Las enfermedades del corazón cobran más vidas que cualquier otra complicación que genere la diabetes. Esto no debería ocurrir. Cambios en su dieta pueden reducir el riesgo de las enfermedades cardíacas significativamente. Para disminuir estos riesgos, La

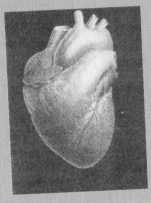

Asociación Diabetes ha hecho las siguientes recomendaciones dietéticas:

• Limite su consumo de colesterol a 300 mg. o menos por día. El colesterol está presente en todos los productos de origen animal. También trate de consumir más alimentos ricos en proteínas, tales como avena, o los frijoles.

• Aléjese de los alimentos con alto contenido de grasa. Utilice aceites vegetales y de olivas en su cocina en lugar de mantequilla y manteca.

• Obtenga del 50% al 60% de sus calorías diarias de los carbohidratos (panes, cereales), del 12% al 20% de la proteína (carne, pescado, leche) y no más del 30% de la grasa.

• No coma más de lo necesario. Comer en exceso aumenta el nivel de azúcar en la sangre.

Naturalmente, para la buena salud, el peso adecuado, el ejercicio, el control de los niveles de glucosa y el evitar el alcohol son importantes. Hable con su médico quien le ayudará a planear la dieta adecuada.

Vocabulario y expresiones

Los alimentos

la avena	oatmeal
los carbohidratos	carbohydrates
la grasa	fat
la manteca	lard
la proteína	protein
los productos lácteos	milk products

Otros sustantivos

las bebidas alcohólicas	alcoholic beverages
el cansancio	fatigue
el cigarrillo	cigarette
el colesterol	cholesterol
la complexión	body structure
la estatura	height
el peso	weight
el reposo	rest
el riesgo	risk
el sobrepeso	overweight
la tienda naturalista	health store
la vista	eye sight

Actividades para ponerse en forma

adelgazar	to lose weight
bajar de peso	
reducir de peso	
aumentar de peso	to gain weight
engordar	
subir de peso	
cuidarse	to take care of oneself
estar a dieta	to be on a diet
guardar la línea	to stay trim
hacer ejercicios aeróbicos	to do aerobics
levantar pesas	to lift weights
mantenerse en forma	to stay in shape
ponerse a dieta	to go on a diet
ponerse en forma	to get in shape
correr	to jog; to run

Otros verbos

contribuir	to contribute
controlar	to control
limitar	to limit
mantener	to keep, maintain
obtener	to obtain
pesar	to weigh
reducir	to reduce
tratar	to try

Otras palabras

grasoso(a)	greasy
nublado(a)	foggy
quizás	maybe
sin embargo	however

Otra expresión

llevarla suave	to take it easy

¡Así lo decimos!

drinks

Whether you want to accept or reject an invitation for drinks and **tapas** in Spain, the **once** in Chile, an afternoon drink in a **confitería** in Argentina, or a **piña colada** in Old San Juan, Puerto Rico where this drink was invented, you will need to know the typical colloquial words for *drink*.

Chile	**cañas, pencazos**
Colombia, Cuba	**tragos**
España	**copas, cañas**
México	**bebidas, copas, pistos**
Puerto Rico, Venezuela	**palos**

Vamos a darnos unos palos.   *Let's go for drinks.*

hangover

For some people, one of the unfortunate consequences of a night out on the town is a hangover, even though we have learned a lot about the adverse effects of alcohol from the current interest in healthy eating and living. A common, although not universal, word for *hangover* throughout the Spanish-speaking world is **resaca**. More colloquial and euphemistic terms are generally used to refer to this condition.

Argentina	**resaca, descompostura**
Chile	**la mona, la caña viva**
Cuba	**curda**
Ecuador	**chuchaqui**
España	**resaca**
México	**cruda**
Venezuela	**ratón**

¡A escuchar!

Una buena dieta... Listen to parts of the article that appears in **¡Así es la vida!** Then indicate whether the statments that follow are **Cierto** or **Falso**.

	CIERTO	FALSO		CIERTO	FALSO
1.	_____	_____	4.	_____	_____
2.	_____	_____	5.	_____	_____
3.	_____	_____	6.	_____	_____

◆ Práctica

9–31 La salud. Choose the most logical word or expression to complete each sentence.

1. _____ es un cereal que se come generalmente en el desayuno.
   a. La avena   b. El colesterol   c. La proteína

2. La manteca tiene un alto contenido de _____.
   a. grasa   b. proteína   c. carbohidratos

3. Los frijoles y la avena son _____ saludables.
   a. bebidas   b. alimentos   c. grasas

4. El _____ está presente en los productos de origen animal.
   a. alcohol   b. carbohidrato   c. colesterol

5. Mi médico dice que fumar _____ es malo para la salud.
   a. avena   b. cigarrillos   c. manteca

6. Peso mucho. Tengo que _____.
   a. subir de peso   b. bajar de peso   c. comer más mantequilla

7. Elvira practica la natación todos los días para _____.
   a. trotar   b. estar a dieta   c. mantenerse en forma

8. Cuando necesito comprar alimentos saludables siempre voy a _____.
   a. la tienda naturalista   b. la farmacia   c. la rectoría

9. Para tener buena salud hay que _____.
   a. cuidarse   b. subir de peso   c. levantar pesas

10. Algunas personas no comen helados porque son alérgicas a _____.
    a. la grasa   b. los carbohidratos   c. los productos lácteos

11. Es un hombre de _____ fuerte.
    a. estatura   b. complexión   c. sobrepeso

12. La _____ del señor es de 5'6".
    a. peso   b. edad   c. estatura

13. Después del accidente tenía la vista _____.
    a. nublada   b. grasosa   c. alérgica

14. Tenía la presión muy alta. Por eso el médico me puso _____.
    a. en forma   b. a dieta   c. de peso

9–32 ¡Manténganse en forma! Find the word or expression that is out of place in each group.

1. a. proteína	b. grasas	c. diabetes	d. carbohidratos
2. a. adelgazar	b. engordar	c. dormir	d. estar a dieta
3. a. peso	b. frijoles	c. avena	d. aceite de oliva
4. a. gimnasia	b. levantar pesas	c. aumentar de peso	d. ejercicios aeróbicos
5. a. contribuir	b. guardar la línea	c. estar a dieta	d. mantenerse en forma
6. a. reposo	b. descansar	c. correr	d. llevarla suave
7. a. riesgo	b. cigarrillos	c. colesterol	d. complexión
8. a. grasa	b. carbohidratos	c. manteca	d. mantequilla
9. a. adelgazar	b. bajar de peso	c. obtener	d. perder peso
10. a. vista	b. gafas	c. ojos nublados	d. alimento

9–33 Un examen médico. Read the advertisement and then fill out the questionnaire that appears in it.

CHEQUEO PARA SU SALUD...

Los Hispanos son más propensos a sufrir diabetes...¿por qué correr este riesgo sin necesidad?

En honor a la "Semana de Alerta a la Diabetes", hágase una simple prueba. Este servicio es **gratis** para la comunidad. A continuación unas preguntas, solamente necesita responder SI o NO y debe anotar 10 puntos por cada respuesta afirmativa.

	SÍ	NO
Estoy sintiendo los siguientes síntomas con repetida regularidad:		
Sed excesiva	☐	☐
Orino con frecuencia	☐	☐
Mucho cansancio	☐	☐
Pérdida de peso inexplicable	☐	☐
Vista nublada a veces	☐	☐
Tengo más de 40 años:		
Según las tablas de peso, tengo más peso del debido:	☐	☐
Soy mujer y he tenido niños que han pesado más de 9 lbs. al nacer:	☐	☐
Uno de mis padre es diabético:	☐	☐
Mi gemelo/a tiene diabetes:	☐	☐
Mi hermano/a tiene diabetes:	☐	☐

Si su total es 20 o más de 20 puntos, le recomendamos se haga una prueba de diabetes, absolutamente gratis.

LAS PRUEBAS SE EFECTUARÁN:

Martes, 19 de marzo—8:00 am - 11:00 am
Vestíbulo del Coral Gables Hospital
3100 Douglas Road (SW 37 Avenue)
Coral Gables (se servirá un refrigerio)

Sábado, 23 de marzo—10:00 am - 1:00 pm
Westland Mall
1675 W. 49th treet, Hialeah

Las personas que deseen hacerse esta prueba no deben comer <u>dos horas</u> antes del examen.

Contaremos con una dietista que podrá informarle sobre las comidas y contestar cualquier pregunta que pueda tener.

Para más información o si quiere recibir nuestra revista gratis, llame al **555-6850.**

Coral Gables Hospital
3100 Douglas Road (S.W. 37 Avenue), Coral Gables, FL 33134 • 441-6850

9–34 Lo bueno y lo malo. Using words and expressions from **Vocabulario y expresiones** and other words you know, make a list of **Actividades saludables** and another of **Actividades no saludables.** Each list should have at least four items.

◆ Actividades

9–35 La salud. Copy the items on the list on a separate piece of paper. Then, walk around and find out from your classmates how well they take care of themselves. Write down one answer per item. Give simple answers.

1. guardar cama cuando está resfriado
2. fumar
3. hacer ejercicios todos los días
4. consultar con el médico cuando se siente mal
5. enfermarse mucho
6. hacerse un examen físico anual
7. evitar las comidas grasosas
8. tomar muchas pastillas

9–36 Recomendaciones del doctor. In pairs, take turns reporting a doctor's findings and giving appropriate advice to the patient in each situation. Use the **tú** command form.

MODELO: El doctor me ha dicho que fumo demasiado.
               Fume menos.

PACIENTE	RECOMENDACIÓN DEL DOCTOR
1. …que me encuentra demasiado cansado	a. tomar antibióticos
2. …que trabajo y me preocupo menos	b. levantar pesas
3. …que he engordado mucho	c. mantenerse en forma
4. …que estoy en excelente condición	d. no comer azúcar
5. …que la prueba confirma que soy diabético	e. descansar
6. …que llevo una vida muy sedentaria	f. subir de peso
7. …que soy alérgico a los productos lácteos	g. hacer ejercicios
8. …que tengo el colesterol muy alto	h. llevarla suave
9. …que uso muy poco los músculos	i. ponerse a dieta
10. …que tengo una infección en el oído	j. evitar…
	k. no comer grasas

9–37 Mis sugerencias. What suggestions would you offer the following people? With a classmate, write a short dialog for each situation.

1. One of your close friends wants to lose weight.
2. Your father needs to lower his cholesterol level.
3. Your sister smokes two packs of cigarrettes a day.
4. Your professor wants to keep trim.
5. Someone you know has diabetes.
6. Your boss has a heart condition.

3. The Pluperfect

- The pluperfect is a compound tense. It is formed with the imperfect tense of **haber** + *past participle*. As with the present perfect, **haber** agrees in number with the subject, the past participle is invariable, and no words may be inserted between **haber** and the past participle.

The Pluperfect Tense of *haber* (*to have*)					
		PAST PARTICIPLE			PAST PARTICIPLE
yo	había		*I*	had	
tú	habías		*you*	had	
Ud./él/ella	había	tomado	*you, he, she*	had	*taken*
nosotros(as)	habíamos	comido	*we*	had	*eaten*
vosotros(as)	habías	vivido	*you* (plural)	had	*lived*
Uds./ellos/ellas	habían		*you* (plural), *they*	had	

- The pluperfect is used to refer to an action or event that occurred before another past action or event. Compare the following sentences to the time line.

Mis padres **habían hecho** una cita antes de ➔ ir al consultorio del doctor.
*My parents **had made** an appointment before ➔ going to the doctor's office.*

Ya le **habían puesto** la inyección al niño cuando ➔ el doctor llegó.
*They **had** already **given** the shot to the child when ➔ the doctor arrived.*

9–38 Teófilo and Digna. Teófilo and Digna's parents emigrated to the United States from Peru. Last summer their mother had a coronary by-pass, so she sent the kids to their Peruvian family. Say what Teófilo, Digna, and their family had never done before.

MODELO: Teófilo y Digna viajaron a Lima para sus vacaciones.
            Nunca antes habían viajado a Lima.

1. Digna/volar en avión
2. Digna/estar lejos de sus padres por más de una semana
3. Digna/conocer a sus abuelos
4. la abuela/alegrarse tanto de ver a sus nietos
5. Teófilo/olvidarse de la casa grande y vieja
6. los hermanos/abrazar a tanta gente
7. nadie/los atender tan bien
8. Teófilo y Digna/comer comida tan sabrosa
9. ellos/aprovechar una vacación tanto como ésta
10. Teófilo y Digna/montar a caballo, ¿verdad?
11. Teófilo/interesarse en la pesca
12. Digna/escuchar la lengua de los incas
13. Teófilo/escribirles una carta a sus padres
14. Teófilo y Digna/visitar Cuzco
15. ellos/pasar una vacación tan larga fuera de los Estados Unidos
16. Teófilo y Digna/tener una vacación maravillosa
17. Teófilo y Digna/despedirse de tanta gente en un día
18. el viaje de regreso/parecerles tan largo

9–39 ¿Qué habías hecho antes? You are studying abroad in Spain. A Spanish friend is trying to find out more about your background, your group, and what you did prior to coming to Spain. Enact the situation asking questions and providing answers according to the model.

MODELO: tú/venir a España antes
            —¿Tú habías venido antes a España?
            —No, yo no había venido a España antes. *or*
            —Sí, yo sí había venido a España antes.

1. el grupo/pasear por el Parque del Retiro
2. tú y tu familia/viajar por el sur de España
3. tus compañeros de clase/hacer una visita a Toledo
4. el profesor/visitar el parque de diversiones de Madrid
5. tú/asistir a un concierto de música clásica en los Estados Unidos
6. tu amiga María Elena/comer cochinillo asado
7. tú/pasar un verano fuera de tu casa
8. Uds./ver una película española en los Estados Unidos
9. tu grupo/visitar la Casa Botín
10. tú y to amigo/comer tapas
11. Uds./ir a Segovia
12. tu profesor/asistir al teatro
13. tú/visitar El Corte Inglés
14. tu grupo/ver una corrida de toros
15. tus compañeros/escuchar música española
16. tú/vivir en Madrid de niña

9–40 El accidente de Wilfredo. Wilfredo was the healthiest creature on earth until he had an accident while roller blading. Say what he, his family, and friends had never done before his accident.

MODELO: Wilfredo/siempre/ser/muy sano
           Wilfredo seimpre había sido muy sano.

1. nunca/tener un accidente
2. siempre/hacer mucho ejercicio
3. nunca/romperse un hueso
4. nunca/torcerse un tobillo
5. nunca/ser operado
6. nunca/dolerle la cabeza
7. siempre/salir bien en los exámenes físicos
8. nunca/enfermarse
9. nunca/darle gripe
10. siempre/mantenerse en forma
11. él/siempre/levantar pesas
12. nunca/sacarse/una radiografía
13. nunca/hacerse/una prueba de sangre
14. nunca/guardar cama
15. nosotros/nunca/verlo tan molesto como el día del accidente
16. tú/tener confianza en su complexión tan fuerte
17. sus padres/ nunca/necesitar preocuparse por él
18. su doctor/nunca recetarle nada

◆ Actividades

9–41 La gran comida. In groups of three or four write a skit about a friend who had always led an unhealthy life and suddenly decided to get in shape.

MODELO: Imagínate, nunca había caminado a la universidad, pero ahora…
           ¿Puedes creerlo? Nunca había…

9–42 ¡Nunca había hecho eso! Talk with a classmate about things that you had not done prior to attending the university.

MODELO: vivir en una residencia de estudiantes…
           Nunca había vivido en una residencia de estudiantes.

1. tomar una clase de…
2. vivir con…
3. estudiar…
4. salir con mis amigos(as)…
5. conocer a…
6. ir a…
7. trabajar en…
8. ver…
9. practicar…
10. viajar a…
11. escribir…
12. escuchar…

 Estructuras

5. Possesive Adjectives (Long Forms) and Pronouns

La habitación mía está en el último piso.

- In **Lección 2** you learned the short forms (unstressed) of possessive adjectives. The following chart presents the long forms (stressed).

Possessive Adjectives (Long Forms)		
	SINGULAR	PLURAL
yo	**mío, mía**	**míos, mías**	*my, of mine*
tú	**tuyo, tuya**	**tuyos, tuyas**	*your (fam..), of yours*
usted			*your (form.)*
él	**suyo, suya**	**suyos, suyas**	*his, of his, of its*
ella			*her, of hers, of its*
nosotros	**nuestro, nuestra**	**nuestros, nuestras**	*our, of ours*
vosotros	**vuestro, vuestra**	**vuestros, vuestras**	*your (fam. pl.), of yours*
ustedes			*your (form. pl.), of yours*
ellos	**suyo, suya**	**suyos, suyas**	*their, of theirs*
ellas			*their, of theirs*

- Short forms always precede the noun; long forms of possessive adjectives follow the noun. They also agree with the noun in **gender** and **number**.

El libro **tuyo** está en la mesa.   *Your book is on the table.*
Aquí tienes unas novelas **mías**.   *Here you have some novels **of mine**.*

- As with the short form **su(s),** the long form **suyo(a,os,as)** can be replaced by the construction **de** + *pronoun* in order to clarify the identity of the possessor.

una amiga **suya**	*a friend **of his***
una amiga **de él**	
el profesor **suyo**	***their** professor*
el profesor **de ellas**	

- The long forms of possessive adjectives may be used as pronouns with the definite article. The noun is omitted.

Los libros **nuestros** son interesantes.	***Our** books are interesting.*
Los nuestros son interesantes.	***Ours** are interesting.*
La pluma **mía** no escribe bien.	***My** pen doesn't write well.*
La mía no escribe bien.	***Mine** doesn't write well.*

- If you need to clarify the possessive pronouns in the third person forms **(el suyo, la suya, los suyos, las suyas)** use the *definite article* + *pronoun:* **el(la) de usted, las de ellos,** etc. The definite article must agree in gender and number with the noun it replaces.

La suya (la corbata) es más bonita que la de Paco.	***Yours** (the tie) is prettier than Paco's.*
La de usted es más bonita que la de Paco.	***Yours** is prettier than Paco's.*

◆ Práctica

9–43 En la playa. Complete the narrative with the correct form of the possessive adjectives and pronouns.

El fin de semana pasado el grupo *(our)* _____ pasó dos días en la playa. Como yo no tenía mucho dinero, el cuarto *(mine)* _____ no tenía baño privado. Marcela y Lilia pidieron una habitación doble. La habitación *(theirs)* _____ era grande y cómoda y el baño *(theirs)* _____ también. Jorge y Carlos se quedaron en un hotel enfrente de la playa. *(Theirs)* _____ era más lujoso y más caro que *(ours)* _____ , pero las camareras *(ours)* _____ eran más amables que *(theirs)* _____ . Es verdad que el comedor *(ours)* _____ era pequeño pero los ascensores *(elevators) (theirs)* _____ no funcionaban. El verano próximo volveremos al hotel *(ours)* _____ .

9–44 La casa de verano. A group of guests staying at a health spa for a week has just arrived. Everyone is trying to find out what belongs to whom. Ask and answer the questions following the model.

MODELO: de Ud./la radio
—¿Esta radio es suya?
—No, la mía es ésa.

1. de Ana/vestido de baño
2. de sus amigas/toallas
3. (de ti)/libros
4. de Gabriela/los zapatos de tenis
5. (de mí)/refrescos
6. (de nosotras)/el tocacassetes
7. de Ud./el cesto
8. de Mario/el reloj
9. de Indurain/bicicletas
10. (de nosotros)/sombrillas
11. (de ti)/las pesas
12. de Carla/teléfono celular
13. del equipo brasileño/la pelota
14. de Marielos/el disco compacto

9-45 En el campamento de tenis. Three friends arrive late at a fancy tennis camp. They take everything out of their suitcases and the next morning the room is a mess. Elsa is trying to clean it up and find out what belongs to whom. Ask and answer questions following the model.

MODELO: — ¿Esta maleta es tuya?
— No, no es mía. La mía está allí.

1. la blusa
2. las medias
3. la cámara
4. la raqueta
5. los vestidos
6. la secadora de pelo
7. la pasta de dientes
8. el cepillo de dientes
9. las tijeras
10. el cepillo
11. los aretes
12. la billetera
13. la cadena de oro
14. el desodorante
15. el espejo
16. el pañuelo
17. los pantalones
18. los cinturones
19. las faldas
20. la pulsera

◆ **Actividades**

9–46 ¿De quién es la habitación? With a group of classmates role-play a group of doctor friends attending a medical convention in Madrid. Assign yourselves the room keys in the illustration. Then a group leader will ask questions to determine which room key belongs to whom.

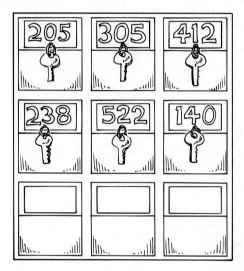

MODELO: —¿De quién es la habitación 205?
           —Es la mía.

           —Roberto, ¿es tuya la habitación 305?
           —No. Es la suya.

9–47 La Clínica Latina de Salud. There's been a fire at Clínica Latina de Salud. Everyone has been evacuated. Later all the patients come back trying to find their things. Write out the questions the patients might ask and the answers they might receive using long forms of possessive adjectives and pronouns. Use the list as a guide.

MODELO: —¿Ésta es tu prueba de sangre?
           —No, no es la prueba de sangre mía. La mía…
           (está aquí/allá/en ese escritorio; no está; la tiene la otra enfermera, etc.)

mis muletas	los antibióticos para la fiebre de mi esposa
tu radiografía del pulmón	su jarabe para la tos
sus inyecciones de vitaminas	los antihistamínicos de mi abuela
mi prueba de sangre	mis instrucciones del doctor
tu receta médica	tus cigarrillos
mis pastillas para el dolor	mis vitaminas y minerales
la penicilina de mi hijo	tu programa de ejercicios
mis radiografías del estómago	…(original)

Estructuras

5. *pero* vs. *sino*

> No queremos el grande sino el pequeño.

- To express the conjunction *but* in Spanish, use **pero.**

  Quiero un trabajo, **pero** un   *I want a job, **but** a good job.*
  trabajo bueno.
  Ser dentista es una buena   *To be a dentist is a good profession, **but***
  profesión, **pero** no me gusta.   *I don't like it.*

- When *but* means *on the contrary* or *rather*, use **sino** instead of **pero.** Always use **sino** in an affirmative statement which contradicts a preceding negative statement.

  No quiero hablar contigo **sino**   *I don't want to talk with you **but***
  con Paco.   *with Paco.*
  No es este libro **sino** aquél.   *It's not this book **but** that one.*

◆ Práctica

9–48 ¡Lo que yo quiero ser! You and your friends have different career goals. Find out what they are by completing the following sentences with either **pero** or **sino.**

1. Quiero ser ingeniero _____ no soy muy bueno en matemáticas.
2. María no desea ser dentista _____ médica.
3. Evelio y Pepe no estudian para maestros _____ para intérpretes.
4. Tú aspiras a ganar mucho dinero _____ no te gusta trabajar.
5. Mirta pretende ser azafata _____ teme volar en avión.
6. No piensan ser psicólogos _____ psiquiatras.
7. María de los Ángeles quiere ser jardinera _____ es alérgica a las flores.
8. Manuelita quiere ser abogada _____ también quiere ser artista.
9. Toño no desea ser piloto_____ astronauta.
10. Isabel no quiere ser una estrella deportiva, _____ una buena entrenadora.
11. Lalo quiere ser campeón de natación, _____ no practica lo suficiente.
12. Julia no desea ser recepcionista del hotel _____ guía turística.
13. Marcelino ya no desea estudiar más, _____ dar clases.
14. Andrina quiere ser doctora, _____ no le gusta cuidar a los enfermos.
15. Conrado no quiere estudiar biología _____ informática.

9–49 Un día ordinario. A group of nurses at Clínica Latina come to work the day after a fire, only to find that a cleaning crew will be working there all day. Since the parking lot was closed, everyone took public transportation. Suddenly they find themselves with a holiday, but without a car. What will they do? Fill in the blanks with **sino** or **pero.**

No era domingo _____ lunes, _____ la clínica de repente había cerrado. No sabíamos qué hacer. No hacía frío como los otros días, _____ bastante calor. Queríamos ir a la playa _____ no teníamos carro. Jorge Manuel le pidió prestado el carro a su hermano _____ él no quiso dárselo. Yo sabía que mamá necesitaba el carro, entonces no la llamé a ella, _____ a papá. _____ desafortunadamente él estaba en una reunión. Patricia llamó a Isolina, nuestra amiga, _____ ella no quería pasear _____ ir de compras. Nosotros no queríamos estar adentro _____ afuera. Entonces fuimos a un concierto de rock en el parque, _____ cuando llegamos no era un concierto de rock _____ de jazz. La música no sólo no era mala, _____ que era muy buena. Entonces decidimos quedarnos, _____ tuvimos que irnos antes del final porque comenzó a llover. No fue un día extraordinario _____ ordinario, _____ por lo menos nos divertimos.

◆ Actividad

9–50 Nadie puede ir. You are a medical resident in a big hospital. It's your day off. You're trying to find a friend to go out with that evening, but for one reason or another, nobody can go. With a classmate, write a dialog about this situation. Use **pero** and **sino.** Use Hispanic names for your characters.

MODELO: ANA CECILIA: Ay, lo siento, pero no puedo. Tengo que estudiar
                         para un examen de química mañana.
                  BETO: Me gustaría, pero ya le dije a Zoila que iba al cine
                         con ella.

Colaboración

Estudiante A

9-51A Las partes del cuerpo humano. Working with a classmate, match parts of the body with their definitions.

LA PARTE DEL CUERPO	EL USO/LA DEFINICIÓN
la boca	los necesitas para abrazar a tu novio(a)
los hombros	la usas para hablar y también para probar la comida
las uñas	con ésta saludas a tus compañeros
la garganta	la necesitas para pensar, y también para ponerte el sombrero
el corazón	los necesitas para tocar el piano y para escribir a máquina
los pulmones	es roja o "azul"
las orejas	con éstos oyes música, y también a tu profesor(a)

9-52A Consejos para mantenerse en forma. Working with a classmate, match the health status with the advice.

EL ESTADO DE SALUD	EL CONSEJO
Cuando uno padece de diabetes…	debes tratar de comer menos grasa.
Si tomas mucho alcohol…	toma productos lácteos.
Si quieres adelgazar…	necesitas más reposo.
Si fumas mucho…	levanta pesas.
Si eres atleta…	visita un centro naturalista.
Si te preocupa el colesterol…	

9-53A ¡No, no lo he hecho! Your brother/sister always blames you for everything that goes wrong. Defend yourself. Then switch roles. Blame him or her.

MODELO: —Enojaste a la abuela, ¿no es cierto? (¿verdad?, ¿no?)
          —¡No, no la he enojado!

ACUSACIONES

perder la tarea de tu clase de español
olvidar tus zapatos de tenis en el gimnasio
prestarle mi nuevo disco compacto a Chepe
romper la copa de vino
tomar mi cepillo del baño
abrir las ventanas y entrar la lluvia

9-54A ¿Ya habías...? You are a store manager exchanging business tips with a colleague. Take turns answering each other's questions.

MODELO: —¿Ya le habías escrito al banco?
          —Sí, pero no me habían contestado.

PREGUNTAS	RESPUESTAS
¿Ya...	
importar cueros de Argentina?	No sólo en China, sino en Korea también.
enviarle el giro monetario al banco?	Unas estaban arregladas, otras no.
abrir una cuenta en quetzales?	Se lo iba a devolver al día siguiente.
arreglarle el reloj al cliente?	No, no había podido abrirla todavía.
pedir los abrigos italianos?	No tenían vestidos, sólo faldas.
pagar todas las cuentas?	No, todavía me quedan algunas.

9-55A ¿De quién es? You are having some friends stay at your beach house. Take turns asking to whom the different items the column on the left belong to. The column on the right provides clues for the answer.

MODELO: —¿De quién es la heladera?
          (Yo les presté la heladera.) —Es mía.
          —¿De quién son las fotos?
          (Rigoberto trajo fotos.) —Son suyas.

¿DE QUIÉN...	PERSONA QUE LO TRAJO
es el perfume francés?	Marcos trajo un balón para jugar al fútbol.
son las raquetas de tenis?	Tú dejaste el cepillo en el carro.
es ese vestido de baño?	Nosotros pusimos las toallas en el baño.
son las cervezas y los refrescos?	Mis hermanas trajeron el tocadiscos.
es la torta de zanahorias?	Los padres vinieron en carro.
es el VCR?	Yo traje sombrillas de playa.

Estudiante B

9-51B Las partes del cuerpo humano. Working with a classmate, match body parts with their definitions.

LA PARTE DEL CUERPO   EL USO/LA DEFINICIÓN

la cabeza   late (*it beats*) locamente cuando estás enamorado(a)
la lengua   sirven para colgar tus gafas
la sangre   cuando está cerrada no puedes decir nada
la mano   en éstos llevas la mochila
los oídos   por ella pasa la comida de la boca al estómago
los dedos de la mano   las necesitas para tocar la guitarra clásica; algunas personas
                               se las pintan
los brazos   son necesarios para respirar

9-52B Consejos para mantenerse en forma. Working with a classmate, match the health status with the advice.

EL ESTADO DE SALUD   EL CONSEJO

Si siempre estás cansado(a)…   es mejor no comer azúcar.
Si comes mucha manteca…   debes comer más proteínas que las personas
                                       menos activas.
Si necesitas más calcio…   trata de beber menos. Si no, te vas a poner
                                       enfermo(a) del hígado *(liver)*.
Si quieres fortalecer *(strengthen)* consulta con tu médico sobre una dieta
  los músculos…   saludable.
Si te gusta la comida orgánica…   deja de comer productos animales.
                                     no puedes hacer ejercicios aeróbicos.

9-53B ¡No, no lo he hecho! You always blame your brother/sister for everything that goes wrong. Listen to his/her defense. Then switch roles and respond to his/her accusations.

MODELO: —Enojaste a la abuela, ¿no es cierto? (¿verdad?, ¿no?)
            —¡No, no la he enojado!

ACUSACIONES

dejar el programa de la tele en casa de la abuela
pelar las papas antes de lavarlas
portarte antipática con la amiga de mamá
perder mi chaqueta de cuero
ponerte mis pantalones nuevos
romper la calculadora

9-54B ¿Ya habías...? You are a store manager exchanging business tips with a colleague. Take turns answering each other's questions.

MODELO: —¿Ya le habías escrito al banco?
             —Sí, pero no me habían contestado.

PREGUNTAS   REPUESTAS

¿Ya...
devolverle el recibo a la señora?   Cueros sí, pero zapatos ya hechos no.
arreglar las vitrinas de la tienda?   Sí, y también pedí unos rusos.
abrir otra tienda en la misma ciudad?   Lo llevé a la relojería.
pedir los vestidos de seda?   Sí, la había abierto desde hacía un mes.
comprar zapatos fabricados en China?   No, todavía me quedan varias por pagar.
vender todas las faldas talla 43?   No, iba a enviárselo al día siguiente.

9-55B ¿De quién es? You are having some friends stay at your beach house. Take turns asking to whom the different items in column on the left belong to. The column on the right provides clues for the answer.

MODELO: —¿De quién es la heladera?
             (Yo les presté la heladera.) —Es mía.
             —¿De quién son las fotos?
             (Rigoberto trajo fotos.) —Son suyas.

¿DE QUIÉN...   PERSONA QUE LO TRAJO

son las toallas en el baño?   Yo puse el vestido de baño en la cocina.
es el cepillo en el carro?   Francisca trajo una torta de zanahorias.
es el balón?   Nosotros trajimos raquetas de tenis.
Son las sombrillas de playa?   Los tíos nos prestaron un VCR.
es el tocadiscos?   Tú pusiste el perfume francés en el cuarto.
es el carro?   Uds. compraron cervezas y refrescos.

Mundo hispánico

España

España está entre el mar Mediterráneo y el Océano Atlántico, y entre dos continentes, Europa y África. Después de Suiza, es el país con más montañas en Europa. Tiene 2.732 kilómetros de playas y es el país favorito de los turistas europeos. Más de 50.000.000 millones de personas de todas partes del mundo van a España todos los años

Datos básicos de España

Nombre oficial: Reino de España
Población: 39.465.000
Área: 504.750 km²
Ciudades principales: Madrid, capital (3.120.000), Barcelona (1.707.000), Valencia (758.000), Sevilla (678.000)
Regiones y lenguas: Castilla y otras regiones (español), Cataluña (catalán), Galicia (gallego), País Vasco (vasco), Valencia (valenciano).

Madrid

- Es una bella ciudad, llena de cultura y arte, con magníficos edificios y amplias avenidas, fuentes y parques,
grandes museos e iglesias antiguas.
- El Palacio Real o Palacio de Oriente, fue inaugurado por el Rey Carlos III y es un ejemplo de arquitectura neoclásica.
- El Museo del Prado es uno de los grandes museos del mundo junto con el Museo del Louvre en París y El Hermitage en Leningrado.
- La Plaza Mayor en el corazón de Madrid fue construida en 1619 por el rey Felipe III. Es uno de los lugares favoritos de los turistas que llegan a tomar aperitivos en sus bares y cafés.

Arte y literatura

- Música y danza: flamenco, regional (sevillanas, jota) y popular; música de zarzuela
- Compositores: Isaac Albéniz, creador de una escuela española de música; Manuel de Falla, *El amor brujo;* Joaquín Rodrigo, *Concierto de Aranjuez.*

- Pintura: Domenico Theotocopulos—'El Greco' (1541–1614), realismo místico, *El entierro del conde Orgaz;* Diego Rodríguez de Silva y Velázquez (1599–1660), pintor extraordinario y gran retratista, *Las meninas;* Francisco de Goya y Lucientes (1746–1828), precursor de la pintura moderna, *Los caprichos;* Pablo Ruiz Picasso (1881–1973), genio versátil, cubista, surrelista y expresionista, *Guernica;* Joan Miró (1893–1983), surrealista, *El carnaval de Arlequín;* Salvador Dalí (1904–1989), impresionista, cubista, dadaísta, surrealista, *La última cena*
- Escritores famosos: Miguel de Cervantes Saavedra (1547–1616), *Don Quijote de la Mancha;* Benito Pérez Galdós (1843–1920), *Fortunata y Jacinta* (novela); Ramón del Valle Inclán (1866–1936), *Divinas palabras* (teatro); Vicente Aleixandre (1898–1984), *Ámbito* (poesía); Antonio Machado (1875–1939), *Soledades* (poesía); Juan Ramón Jiménez (1881–1958), *Platero y yo* (relato); Federico García Lorca (1898–1936), *Bodas de sangre* (teatro), *Romancero gitano* (poesía); Camilo José Cela (1916–); Premio Nóbel (1989), *La colmena* (novela); Antonio Buero Vallejo (1916–). *Historia de una escalera* (teatro); Ana María Matute (1926–), *Los Abel* (novela)
- Cine: Luis Buñuel, *Viridiana;* Carlos Saura, *Ana y los lobos;* Pedro Almodóvar, *Mujeres al borde de un ataque de nervios*

◆ Actividades

9-56 ¿Qué son y dónde están? In pairs, identify and discuss the location of the cities and regions given below. Is each a city or a region? What language is spoken there? Consult the inside cover of your text. What other regions and cities can you identify?

Galicia	Castilla
Palma de Mallorca	el País Vasco
Cataluña	Valencia
Barcelona	Andalucía
Toledo	Sevilla

9-57 ¿Quién es quién?

1. Carlos Saura
2. Benito Pérez Galdós
3. Federico García Lorca
4. Diego Velázquez
5. Luis Buñuel
6. Joaquín Rodrigo
7. Juan Ramón Jiménez
8. El Greco
9. Francisco de Goya
10. Vicente Aleixandre
11. Ana María Matute
12. Ramón del Valle Inclán

a. poeta que escribió *Ámbito*
b. autor de *Divinas palabras*, obra de teatro
c. pintor del siglo XVII que hace retratos excelentes
d. la autora de *Los Abel*
e. director de la película *Ana y los lobos*
f. novelista del siglo XIX
g. pintor místico del siglo XVI y XVII
h. poeta y dramaturgo; escribe *Romancero gitano*
i autor del delicado *Platero y yo*
j. compositor del *Concierto de Aranjuez*
k. precursor de la pintura moderna en el siglo XIX
l. director de *Viridiana* y otras películas surrealistas

Lección 10

Los medios de información y la política

Comunicación

- Expressing Doubt, Denial and Uncertainty
- Expressing Your Point of View
- Persuading Others
- Reacting to Events and Situations

Cultura

- **Periódicos del mundo hispano**
- **Personajes de la política**

Estructuras

Primera parte

- The Subjunctive to Express Doubt or Denial
- The Subjunctive with Impersonal Expressions

Segunda parte

- The Subjunctive in Adjectival Clauses
- The Subjunctive with **ojalá, tal vez** and **quizás**
- The Subjunctive with Adverbial Clauses

PRIMERA PARTE
¡Así es la vida!

Los medios de información

El siguiente editorial apareció en *Novedades*, un periódico mexicano. El autor del editorial ofrece una opinión sobre la situación de los inmigrantes mexicanos en los Estados Unidos. El editorial fue escrito durante una visita del presidente mexicano, Carlos Salinas de Gortari, a Chicago.

El mexicano de fuera

La ciudad de Chicago tiene un gran potencial debido en gran parte al producto del trabajo de miles de mexicanos que emigraron hace muchos años y se establecieron allá. Encontraron condiciones favorables para desarrollar sus actividades y han sido muy útiles. Sin embargo, conservan sentimientos que los identifican como mexicanos y que fueron expresados con entusiasmo en la bienvenida que le dieron al presidente Salinas de Gortari.

Los mexicanos de fuera, como se les conoce porque no han dejado de ser mexicanos, tampoco han sido marginados por México, que los sigue considerando parte integrante de nuestra nacionalidad. Al hablar ante más de 3.000 mexicanos y mexicano-estadounidenses, el presidente Salinas de Gortari expresó que el Gobierno de México va a seguir trabajando intensamente para proteger los derechos y garantizar las libertades de los trabajadores mexicanos migratorios.

Mientras que en el territorio nacional no se puedan ofrecer condiciones de vida que satisfagan las aspiraciones de los que emigran en busca de un mejor nivel de vida, el flujo migratorio continuará. Esto no significa que nuestras autoridades ignoren a los emigrantes. Por el contrario, éste siempre ha sido tema en las negociaciones entre México y Estados Unidos, como ahora que el Presidente de la República de México recorre algunas ciudades del vecino país.

Vocabulario y expresiones

Las secciones del periódico

el artículo	*article*
los avisos clasificados	*classified ads*
la cartelera	*entertainment section*
la columna sentimental	*advice column*
la crónica	*news, story*
el editorial	*editorial page*
la esquela	*obituary*
el horóscopo	*horoscope*
la primera plana	*front page*
el titular	*headline*
la sección deportiva	*sports section*
la sección financiera	*business section*
las tiras cómicas	*comics*

Los medios de comunicación

el acontecimiento	*event, happening*
la cadena	*network*
el canal	*channel*
en directo, en vivo	*live (television)*
la estación de radio	*radio station*
el(la) lector(a)	*reader*
las noticias	*news*
el noticiero	*newscast*
la prensa	*press, news media*
el(la) radioyente	*listener (radio)*
la reseña	*review*
la revista	*magazine*
la telenovela	*soap opera*
el(la) televidente	*television viewer*

Empleados de los medios de comunicación

el(la) anfitrión(ona)	*show host (hostess)*
el(la) comentarista	*newscaster, commentator*
el(la) crítico(a)	*critic*
el(la) locutor(a)	*announcer, D.J.*
el(la) meteorólogo(a)	*weatherperson, meteorologist*
el(la) patrocinador(a)	*sponsor*
el(la) periodista	*journalist*
el(la) reportero(a)	*reporter*

Adjetivos

antiguo(a)	*antique; ancient*
deportivo(a)	*sportive*
dudoso(a)	*doubtful*
extraño(a)	*strange*
importante	*important*
imposible	*impossible*
increíble	*incredible*
influyente	*influential*
posible	*possible*
probable	*probable*
seguro(a)	*sure; safe*
urgente	*urgent*
útil	*useful*

Verbos

continuar	*to continue*
cubrir	*to cover*
desarrollar	*to develop*
distribuir	*to distribute*
dudar	*to doubt*
ejercer	*to exert*
enterarse (de)	*to find out*
establecer(se)	*to establish (oneself)*
fundar	*to found; establish*
informar	*to report*
mencionar	*to mention*
negar(ie)	*to deny*
patrocinar	*to sponsor*
proteger	*to protect*
recorrer	*to travel through, to tour*
satisfacer	*to satisfy*
transmitir	*to transmit*

Otras palabras y expresiones

el certamen	*(beauty) contest or pageant*
el concurso	*game show; competition*
el flujo	*flow*
justo	*just, exactly*
la lástima	*pity*
la mayoría	*the majority*
el negocio	*business*

◆◆◆◆◆◆◆◆◆◆◆◆◆◆◆◆◆◆◆◆◆◆◆◆◆

¡Así lo decimos!

obituary

In English we use the word *obituary* to refer to both the short announcement and the article that sometimes appears in the newspaper when the person who has died is famous or locally well known. Spanish speakers generally make a distinction between the article and the announcement. The article is customarily referred to as **el obituario**, whereas there is more variation in the term used for the announcement.

Argentina, Uruguay	**aviso fúnebre**
Cuba, España	**esquela**
Ecuador	**parte mortuorio**
México	**obituario, esquela**
Venezuela	**invitación**

comics

There is also a great deal of variation in the standard terms used in the Spanish-speaking world to refer to the *comics* in newspapers.

Argentina, Uruguay	**chistes, historietas**
Chile	**monos**
Cuba	**muñequitos**
España	**chistes, viñetas**
México	**muñequitos, monitos, comics, chistes**
Puerto Rico	**comics**
Venezuela	**comiquitas**

Ampliación

- The words **la televisión** and **la radio** refer to television and radio broadcasting in general; **el televisor** and **el radio** refer to the radio and television sets.

- **El editorial** refers to an editorial; **la editorial** is a publishing house.

- **El crítico** refers to a person who reviews films or books; **la crítica** refers to the field of "criticism" in general or to a female critic.

🔊 **¡A escuchar!**

El mexicano de fuera. You will hear a recording of the editorial that appears in **¡Así es la vida!** After listening, indicate whether the statements you hear are **Cierto, Falso** or **No se sabe**.

	Cierto	Falso	No se sabe
1.	_____	_____	_____
2.	_____	_____	_____
3.	_____	_____	_____
4.	_____	_____	_____
5.	_____	_____	_____
6.	_____	_____	_____
7.	_____	_____	_____

◆ Práctica

10–1 Emparejar. Match the words in the columns.

1. los avisos clasificados
2. el horóscopo
3. la primera plana
4. la tira cómica
5. el(la) patrocinador(a)

6. el(la) reportero(a)
7. el(la) comentarista
8. el noticiero

9. la sección financiera
10. el editorial
11. la esquela
12. la cartelera

a. sección donde se da la opinión del periódico
b. sección donde aparecen los espectáculos
c. persona que ofrece su opinión por televisión
d. firma o empresa que paga los anuncios comerciales
e. página del periódico donde aparecen las noticias más importantes
f. persona que reporta las noticias
g. sección donde se leen los anuncios
h. programa que informa los eventos más importantes del día
i. lugar donde se anuncia la muerte de alguien
j. una sección dedicada a la astrología
k. tiene ilustraciones y es muy cómica o divertida
l. la sección para saber cómo está la economía

10–2 Los medios de información. Complete the sentences by choosing the correct word.

1. Tengo tres años como anfitriona de este programa, pero no sé si voy a

   _____.

   a. garantizarlo   b. continuar   c. patrocinarlo

2. Varios reporteros van a _____ el país con los ciclistas.
   a. recorrer   b. proteger   c. ejercer

3. El periódico de la tarde no _____ todo el territorio nacional.
   a. satisface   b. cubre   c. establece

4. Este niño es el que _____ los periódicos en esa ruta.
   a. distribuye   b. niega   c. informa

5. La tienda *Novedades* va a _____ el nuevo programa de la moda.
   a. mencionar   b. dudar   c. patrocinar

6. La columna sentimental dice: "Si la quieres, no debes _____ de ella."
   a. informar   b. dudar   c. enterarte

7. No voy a _____ que me importa mucho lo que dice la crítica sobre mis obras.
   a. enterarme   b. cubrir   c. negar

8. Federico es _____ pero muy interesante, y quizás por eso es tan buen periodista.
   a. reportero   b. deportivo   c. extraño

9. ¿Cuándo fue _____ *La Prensa Libertad*?
   a. ejercida   b. fundada   c. continuada

10. Los medios de comunicación _____ gran influencia sobre la mayoría de la gente.
    a. ejercen   b. protegen   c. informan

11. Al abuelo le gusta _____ todo lo que está pasando en el mundo.
    a. ejercer   b. enterarse de   c. desarollar

12. Por favor, no le _____ a Tita las malas noticias.
    a. cubras   b. menciones   c. satisfagas

13. El anfitrión tiene que _____ a los patrocinadores y a los televidentes.
    a. satisfacer   b. informar   c. garantizar

14. ¡Qué _____ que no den "Como agua para chocolate" en cablecolor!
    a. influyente   b. lástima   c. flujo

15. La comentarista siempre llega _____ a tiempo antes de comenzar el programa.
    a. posible   b. justo   c. útil

10–3 Las comunicaciones. Complete the statements about the media with words and expressions from **Vocabulario y expresiones.**

1. Las noticias sobre el béisbol y el fútbol aparecen siempre en _____ de un periódico.
2. Las personas que miran programas de televisión son los _____.
3. Muchas veces el noticiero se transmite _____.
4. En la televisión existen los canales, mientras que en la radio existen _____.
5. _____ es la persona que habla sobre el clima y el tiempo.
6. Un hombre o una mujer de negocios se interesa mucho en la sección _____ del periódico.
7. Una novela que se presenta en la televisión en varios episodios es una _____.
8. En _____ aparecen anuncios sobre la compra y venta de artículos, propiedades y automóviles.

10–4 Te toca a ti. Answer the questions about your own preferences concerning the media with complete sentences.

1. ¿Cuáles son tus programas favoritos de televisión?
2. ¿Qué programas no te gustan?
3. ¿Te gusta ver las telenovelas? Explica.
4. ¿Cuáles son las secciones del periódico que lees todos los días? ¿Por qué?
5. ¿Qué secciones no lees?
6. ¿Cuál es tu estación de radio favorita?
7. ¿Qué programas de radio te gusta escuchar?
8. ¿Qué opinas sobre los certámenes por televisión?
9. ¿Has participado en algún concurso alguna vez?
10. ¿Te gustaría ser periodista o reportero?
11. ¿Cuál es tu anfitrión favorito de los programas nocturnos después de las once de la noche?
12. Según este anuncio, ¿qué ofrece Radio Mar del Plata? ¿Quién es el comentarista de este canal?

EN EL FIN DE SEMANA
SIEMPRE HAY TIEMPO.

Para compatir y disfrutar la mejor música.
La elegida y presentada por **Néstor Vértiz los sábados
de 13 a 19 y los domingos de 12:30 a 15.**
Y en el momento oportuno, la noticia, el comentario justo,
el hecho importante que usted quiere conocer.
Y también el reportaje.
Con la agenda cultural más completa. Con la calidad
inconfundible de Néstor Vértiz y la complicidad de
Radio Mar del Plata.
Porque para descansar y divertirse,
Siempre Hay Tiempo en Mar del Plata.

SIEMPRE HAY TIEMPO.
Sábados de 13 a 19.
Domingos de 12:30 a 15.

EN EL **670** DEL DIAL
**RADIO
MAR DEL
PLATA**

SIEMPRE MAS RADIO

10–5 Los programas de televisión. Read the television schedule from the Mexican newspaper *Novedades*. Then answer the questions based on information provided in it.

1. ¿Cuál es el canal de la familia mexicana?
2. ¿Cuál es el canal de las estrellas?
3. ¿En qué canal hay un noticiero?
4. ¿Cómo se llama el programa de opinión pública?
5. ¿Qué tema tratarán en ese programa?
6. ¿Ves algunos de los programas que aparecen aquí? ¿Cuáles?
7. ¿Cuáles de los programas te parecen interesantes?
8. ¿Qué películas se pueden ver en algunos de los canales?
9. ¿Qué canal ofrece programas para niños? ¿Cuáles son algunos?
10 ¿Hay algún programa deportivo?
11. ¿Podrían algunos de estos programas ser telenovelas? ¿Cuáles?
12. ¿Hay programas sobre animales y plantas?

10–6 Mi punto de vista. First, indicate whether you agree or disagree with the statements and explain why. Then, create your own statements and have a classmate agree or disagree and give his/her reasons.

MODELO: Estoy de acuerdo
(No estoy de acuerdo)
porque…

1. La prensa en los Estados Unidos es muy sensacionalista.
2. En los Estados Unidos no hay libertad total de prensa.
3. Hay mucha violencia en los programas de televisión.
4. Una persona inteligente no ve las telenovelas.
5. Muchos de los anuncios que pasan por televisión son muy aburridos.
6. La prensa debe ser censurada.

10–7 Tus opiniones. Briefly discuss the following topics with a classmate, giving reasons to support your opinions.

1. el nombre del periódico que más te gusta
2. tu sección favorita del periódico
3. la sección del periódico que menos te gusta
4. tu programa de televisión favorito
5. el programa de noticias que ves todos los días
6. tu reportero(a) o periodista favorito(a) en la televisión
7. si lees el horóscopo o no
8. tu tira cómica favorita
9. ¿A qué se refiere "Anuncios por Palabras" del periódico ABC?

10–8 En el periódico. You and three or four classmates are on the staff of a local newspaper. Prepare a plan for tomorrow's edition, which you may base either on current events or imaginary ones. Use the questions below as a guide, but make your plan as detailed as you can. Be prepared to share it with the class.

1. ¿Cuáles son los titulares de la primera plana?
2. ¿Cuál es el tema del editorial?
3. ¿Cuál es el tema de la sección financiera?
4. ¿Cuál es el tema de la sección deportiva?
5. ¿Cuál es el tema de la columna sentimental?
6. ¿Qué películas, conciertos, obras de teatro se anuncian en la cartelera?
7. ¿Cuántas esquelas hay? ¿Hay esquelas de personas importantes? ¿Quiénes?
8. ¿Cuántos avisos clasificados y de qué tipo hay?
9. ¿Hay horóscopo?
10. ¿Hay tiras cómicas? ¿De qué tratan?

Estructuras

1. The Subjunctive to Express Doubt or Denial

- Use the subjunctive in noun clauses after expressions of doubt, uncertainty or denial. Some verbs that express doubt and denial are: **dudar, negar, no creer, no estar seguro(a) de, no pensar.**

Dudo que Camilo escriba el editorial.	*I doubt that Camilo **will write** the editorial.*
No creo que éste **sea** el canal que queremos.	*I don't believe that this **is** the channel that we want.*
Ana María **no está segura de** que Juan **quiera** ganar el concurso.	*Ana María **isn't sure** that Juan **wants** to win the game show.*
El reportero **niega** que el artículo **sea** demasiado negativo.	*The reporter **denies** that the article **is** too negative.*

- Use the indicative in the noun clause when there is no doubt, uncertainty or disbelief about an action or event and when the subject appears to be certain of the facts.

Estoy segura de que Genaro **va** a la emisora mañana.	*I'm sure that Genaro **is going to** the radio station tomorrow.*
Creemos que **va a escribir** la reseña a tiempo.	*We believe that **he will write the** review on time.*

- **No dudar** and **no negar** express certainty and therefore are followed by the indicative.

No dudo que esa empresa **patrocinará** el evento.	*I don't doubt that this company **will sponsor** the event.*
No niega que Ana **tiene** la revista.	*He doesn't deny that Ana **has** the magazine.*

- **Creer** in a question, implies doubt in the mind of the speaker, so it requires the subjunctive in the dependent clause. If the speaker expresses no opinion, the indicative is preferred. **No creer** in a question implies certainty on the part of the speaker and is thus followed by the indicative.

¿Crees que Claudia me **diga** quién es el crítico?	**Do you believe** that Claudia **will tell** me who the critic is? (Doubt implied)
¿Crees que **sabe** la respuesta?	**Do you believe** that **she knows** the answer? (No opinion)
¿No cree Ud. que Eloy **va** a ver las noticias?	**Don't you think** that Eloy **is going** to watch the news? (Certainty implied)

◆ Práctica

10–9 El(la) desconfiado(a). You have a tendency to doubt everything people at the office tell you. Express your doubts about the following sentences. Follow the model.

MODELO: Jacobo es muy buen periodista.
           Dudo que Jacobo sea muy buen periodista.

1. Ese comentarista sabe mucho.
2. La emisora da muchas noticias.
3. El comentarista dice la verdad.
4. Los artículos de ese periodista tienen temas muy interesantes.
5. Esa editora escribe buenos editoriales.
6. El comentarista deportivo conoce a todos los jugadores.
7. La reportera del canal 3 va a hacer un viaje a Cuba.
8. En ese periódico hay muchos anuncios clasificados.
9. Es la mejor estación de radio del país.
10. Van a transmitir en vivo.

10–10 En la cafetería. You and a group of colleagues from the media are talking shop after work. React to each statement with the indicative or the subjunctive using the cues provided.

MODELO: —Mauricio escribe todas las reseñas de las obras de teatro./Dudo…
           —Dudo que Mauricio escriba todas las reseñas de las obras de teatro.

1. Mañana no transmiten la telenovela *Amor de locura*./Pienso
2. El canal 2 presenta el partido de fútbol entre Brasil y Argentina a las cuatro./Dudo
3. El lunes cambian las telenoticias de las seis a las seis y media de la tarde./No creo
4. Pelé ya no quiere ser el patrocinador del programa./No niego
5. Por ahora no hay patrocinadores para el certamen./Estoy seguro(a)
6. Los radioyentes están furiosos con el locutor./No pienso
7. El canal 11 y Radio Juventud forman parte de la misma cadena./Sé
8. El editorial de la Prensa Matutina hace una crítica muy fuerte del gobierno./Creo
9. En la sección financiera anuncian una nueva devaluación del dólar./Dudo
10. Camilo Fernández prepara las esquelas./No estoy seguro(a)
11. Pepe se va del canal 4./¿Crees…?
12. Emilia va a ser la reportera de la Feria del Libro./No creo

10–11 El consultorio sentimental. You're the editor of the advice column for your local newspaper. A young man writes you the following letter. Offer him advice.

MODELO: Le aconsejo que…(Dudo/Creo/Le recomiendo, etc.)

Estimado(a) Dr. (Dra.) Corazón:

   Soy un chico de veinte años. No soy muy atractivo pero no creo que sea tan feo. Conozco a una chica muy linda y quiero salir con ella, pero dudo que ella quiera salir conmigo. Ella no tiene novio pero tengo miedo que ella me diga que no. ¡No sé qué hacer! ¿Qué me aconseja Ud.?

10–12 El programa de Felipe. Two women friends discuss a sports program in the radio that airs very late at night. Complete their conversation by filling in the blanks with the correct expression. Do not use any expression more than once.

cree	no creo	dudo	niega	sabemos
creo	estoy segura	no dudo	piensa	sabes

— _____ que Felipe venga hoy. Ayer estuvo en la estación hasta las tres de la mañana. Es el locutor de "Comentarios deportivos" en Radio Deportes. ¿Lo sabías, no?

— Sí, cómo no. _____ que es un locutor muy divertido. Soy aficionada a su programa.

— ¿Ah, sí? _____ que Felipe lo sepa. _____ que a las mujeres no nos interesan los deportes.

— Pues no tiene razón. _____ que hay miles y miles de mujeres que escuchan su programa. _____ que los tiempos han cambiado.

— Sí, las chicas de ahora son más activas, pero Felipe lo _____. Casi todas las llamadas que recibe son de muchachos.

— Sí, Hilda, pero _____ que el programa de Felipe lo transmiten muy tarde.

__ Y, ¿cómo es que tú lo escuchas? ¡_____ que tú necesitas dormir tanto como yo!

— Es cierto, pero _____ que soy enfermera. Ahora trabajo de seis de la tarde a una de la mañana. Cuando salgo del hospital voy a comer y escucho el programa de Felipe.

◆ Actividades

10–13 Una entrevista. Get together with a classmate and ask each other the following questions about the status of the media in your country.

1. ¿Estás seguro(a) de que hay libertad de prensa en su país? ¿Por qué?
2. ¿Es cierto que todos los periodistas son objetivos?
3. ¿Crees que el gobierno debe censurar algunos programas de televisión? Explica.
4. ¿Crees que las emisoras y los canales de televisión de tu ciudad son buenos? Explica.
5. ¿Crees que en su país hay una obsesión con las telenovelas?
6. ¿Te parece que hay demasiada violencia en la televisión? ¿demasiado sexo?

10–14 Ante la prensa. With four or five classmates, role-play the following situation using the model as a guide.

A political analyst is interviewed by several journalists. Each journalist asks the analyst two questions. The analyst's replies express a great deal of skepticism.

MODELO: PERIODISTA: ¿Cree que las cosas están bien en el país?
         ANALISTA: No, no creo que las cosas estén bien en el país.

10–15 ¿Qué hacemos? You and your friends are making plans for the weekend. In groups of three or four, take turns suggesting activities. Use the list below as a guide only. React to each suggestion expressing doubt and propose a different plan.

MODELO: ver esta película
      —Veamos esta película.
      —No creo que sea muy buena. Mejor compremos boletos para …

ver…en la televisión	estudiar…	tener una fiesta	leer…
comprar…en…	visitar a…	asistir a…	ir a…
dar un paseo a/en…	trabajar…	hacer ejercicios	escuchar…
jugar un partido de…	escribir….	salir a comer a…	levantarse tarde

10–16 Srta. Dulce Amor. It's your turn to write to the advice column. In pairs write a letter to Srta. Dulce Amor about your sentimental woes.

2. The Subjunctive with Impersonal Expressions

- Use the subjunctive in noun clauses after impersonal expressions that do not convey certainty. If the dependent clause has an expressed subject, use the subjunctive. If it doesn't, use the infinitive. Some common impersonal expressions that require the subjunctive are:

Es bueno	Es importante	Es (una) lástima	Es posible
Es difícil	Es imposible	Es malo	Es preciso
Es dudoso	Es increíble	Es mejor	Es probable
Es extraño	Es indispensable	Es necesario	Es urgente
Es fácil			

Es importante que transmitan en directo.
    *It's **important** that they transmit live.*

Es imposible que la emisora cancele el concurso.
    *It's **impossible** that the radio station will cancel the competition.*

Es difícil enterarse de todo.
    *It's **difficult** to find out about everything.*

Es imposible seguir esa telenovela.
    *It's **impossible** to keep up with that soap opera.*

- Use the **indicative** with impersonal expressions that convey certainty.

> **Es verdad** que Carlota **es** muy   **It's true** that Carlota is very nice.
> simpática.
>
> **Es cierto** que el coche **está** aquí.   **It's true** that the car **is** here.
>
> **Es evidente** que Manuel **es** guapo.   **It's evident** that Manuel **is** handsome.

- However, when expressions of certainty are negated, they require the subjunctive because they then convey uncertainty.

> **No es verdad** que Gloria Estefan   **It's not true** that Gloria Estefan **lives** in
> **viva** en México.   Mexico.
>
> **No es seguro** que Felipe **venga**   **It's not certain** that Felipe will **come** tonight.
> esta noche.

◆ Práctica

10–17 Expresiones de certidumbre e incertidumbre. Read each expression and decide whether it expresses certainty or uncertainty. Then, write a sentence with each one.

Es bueno…	Es urgente…	Es extraño…
Es cierto…	Es verdad…	Es evidente…
Es fácil…	Es importante…	Es probable…
No es seguro…	Es dudoso…	Es malo…
Es posible…	No es evidente…	Es imposible…

10–18 Hablando de papá. Mother and daughter are discussing the father's health and his refusal to see a doctor. Complete the dialog with the infinitive, the present indicative, or the present subjunctive of the verb in parentheses.

MAMÁ: Es importante que Fernando (entender) _____ que no puede seguir así. Estoy segura de que (hacer) _____ más de tres años que no ve al doctor. Es difícil (conversar) _____ con una persona tan terca.

HIJA: De acuerdo, mami, pero no es bueno (insistir) _____ tanto. Es cierto que papá no (ir) _____ nunca al doctor, pero se cuida mucho.

MAMÁ: ¿Mucho? ¡Ja, ja! Ahora, porque se siente mal y tiene miedo, pero es increíble que no (seguir) _____ los consejos del doctor Álvarez. Es preciso que (ponerse) _____ a dieta inmediatamente. Y es todavía más importante que (dejar) _____ de fumar y (hacer) _____ ejercicios.

HIJA: Escúchame, mami. Lo más urgente es que tú (estar) _____ tranquila, porque si no, tú también te vas a enfermar. Papá no puede cambiar en un día. Es mejor que (comenzar) _____ lentamente. Es una lástima que no le (gustar) _____ hacer ejercicios, pero yo le voy a hablar. Es indispensable que por lo menos (caminar) _____ media hora todos los días.

MAMÁ: Sí, mi amor, por favor, háblale. Es necesario que (comprender) _____ que es por cariño, y no por molestarlo, que le decimos estas cosas. Pero es dudoso que te (escuchar) _____. Lo conozco.

HIJA: Sí, es verdad que no (querer) _____ oírnos. Pero es evidente que en esta ocasión (tener) _____ que hacerlo. Ya no te preocupes. Es posible que papá (ver) _____ que tenemos razón. Y ahora, cambiemos de tema, ¿te parece?

10–19 Viaje a México. Your friend is going to Mexico. He or she worries about what to take, what to do, and about getting sick. Advise him/her on what to take, what to eat and drink there, and what to do. Use impersonal expressions.

MODELO: Es evidente que no debes viajar solo porque tienes miedo.

◆ Actividades

10–20 En mi opinión... A friend of yours is going on a trip to a Spanish-speaking country. She doesn't know where to start and turns to you for advice. In pairs, role-play this situation. Use impersonal expressions.

MODELO: Me gustaría hacer un viaje pero no sé por dónde empezar.
             Para empezar es bueno que llames a la agente de viajes.

10–21 Recomendaciones. You work in the personnel department of a multimedia conglomerate. Your boss wants you to recommend people for some positions that are open in your company. In pairs, take turns role-playing the boss and the employee. Base your recommendations on the cues about the candidates. Use impersonal expressions.

MODELO: Para periodista recomiendo a...porque....

CANDIDATOS

- Chalo tiene mucha experiencia con el noticiero.
- Cecilia es la mejor comentarista.
- Claudio es un crítico de cine muy conocido.
- Aurelio es muy tímido para anfitrión de un programa de tele, pero como locutor es bueno.
- Yamilé ganó el premio "Mejor periodista del año." Sabe mucho de economía.
- Silvia Elena se especializa en las artes.
- Marcela ya ha trabajado antes con los avisos clasificados.
- Celina decide qué va en la primera plana.
- Luis Antonio tiene un doctorado en literatura.
- Olman fue entrenador del equipo San Juanense antes de ser reportero de Radio Reloj.
- Margarita estudió ciencias.
- Berta tiene una personalidad extrovertida.
- Lucho ha recorrido todo el país.

TRABAJOS

- reportero(a) deportista
- locutor(a) para un programa de música
- periodista para el editorial de un periódico
- reportero de noticias
- comentarista político
- meteorólogo(a)
- anfitrión(a) de un programa de concursos
- crítico(a) literario
- periodista para la sección financiera de un periódico muy importante
- persona que haga las esquelas, la cartelera y los avisos clasificados.

▼▼▼▼▼▼▼
A propósito...Periódicos del mundo hispano

Por lo general, en cada uno de los países de habla española se publica un periódico principal que se distribuye en toda la nación. Estos periódicos, en su mayoría, se publican en la capital del país y ejercen una gran influencia sobre la política, la industria y el comercio de la nación. A continuación se mencionan algunos de los periódicos más importantes.

El País—Hoy día es el diario de mayor circulación de España. Fue fundado en 1976 en Madrid, justo después de la muerte del dictador Francisco Franco.

El Tiempo—Es el principal diario de Colombia. Publicado en Bogotá, es considerado uno de los periódicos más influyentes de la América Latina.

El Mercurio—Es el diario más importante de Chile y el más antiguo de Latinoamérica. Su circulación cubre todo el territorio chileno y ejerce gran influencia en el campo de la política.

El Nuevo Herald—Publicado en la ciudad de Miami por *The Miami Herald*, es el periódico hispano de mayor circulación en los Estados Unidos. Sus lectores son principalmente los inmigrantes cubanos en la Florida.

La Opinión—Es el diario hispano de mayor importancia en Los Ángeles, California. Sus lectores son en su mayoría los inmigrantes mexicanos. Fundado en 1926, tiene una circulación diaria de más de ciento veinte mil ejemplares.

¡Vamos a comparar!

¿Existe en los Estados Unidos un periódico nacional? ¿Cómo se llama? ¿Cuáles son los periódicos importantes en tu ciudad? ¿Los periódicos tienen gran influencia en la política?

Noticiero por televisión en Managua, Nicaragua.

Primera plana de tres periódicos hispanos.

SEGUNDA PARTE
¡Así es la vida!

El candidato presidencial

Alberto Figueroa es candidato a la presidencia por el partido Alianza con la Naturaleza, un partido "verde". Ahora está pronunciando un discurso.

Patricio Aylwin
ex-presidente deChile.

¡Conciudadanos! Se habla mucho de la inflación, del desempleo, de los impuestos, de la deuda externa y del crimen. Éstos son problemas serios que hay que controlar. Como Uds. saben, la economía es una prioridad del partido Alianza con la Naturaleza. Pero yo me pregunto: ¿Podemos resolver nuestros problemas sin una visión que incluya la protección del medio ambiente? ¿Podemos hablar de desarrollo económico sin tomar en cuenta la infraestructura social? La respuesta es no, y mil veces ¡NO!

Conciudadanos, ha llegado la hora de afrontar los problemas ecológicos que amenazan al país. No podemos seguir ignorando la deforestación, el asalto a los recursos naturales, la destrucción del bosque. ¿Buscan un candidato que represente las aspiraciones ecológicas del pueblo? ¡Ése soy yo! ¿Quieren un líder que elimine la contaminación del medio ambiente? ¡Ése soy yo! ¿Desean un candidato que tenga visión, que piense en prevenir y no sólo en resolver cuando ya sea demasiado tarde? Conciudadanos, ¡Ése soy yo! ¡ÉSE SOY YO!

Para que yo pueda llevar a cabo estos cambios es preciso que voten por mí y por Alianza con la Naturaleza. Sin que todos y cada uno de Uds. nos apoyen, no es posible triunfar. A menos que hagamos sacrificios ahora, no vamos a poder garantizarles a nuestros hijos y a sus hijos un futuro. Conciudadanos, ¡Todos a votar! ¡Vamos a las elecciones a ganar! ¡A votar por Alberto Figueroa y por el partido Alianza con la Naturaleza! Señoras y señores, ¡a votar! ¡a ganar! ¡a triunfar!

Vocabulario y expresiones

Personajes políticos

el(la) alcalde(sa)	*mayor*
el(la) asesor(a)	*consultant, advisor*
el(la) candidato(a)	*candidate*
el(la) ciudadano(a)	*citizen*
el(la) conciudadano(a)	*fellow citizen*
el(la) contrincante	*opponent*
el(la) diputado(a)	*congressperson*
el(la) gobernador(a)	*governor*
el(la) juez(a)	*judge*
el(la) presidente(a)	*president*
el rey/la reina	*king/queen*
el(la) senador(a)	*senator*

La política

el asalto	*assault*
la campaña	*campaign*
el congreso	*congress*
el deber	*duty*
la democracia	*democracy*
el desarrollo	*development*
la dictadura	*dictatorship*
el discurso	*speech*
la elección	*election*
la encuesta	*poll; survey*
el gobierno	*government*
la ley	*law*
el lema	*motto*
la monarquía	*monarchy*
el partido político	*political party*
la prioridad	*priority*
la provincia	*province, state*
el pueblo	*the people, the masses*
el sacrificio	*sacrifice*
el senado	*senate*

Temas de actualidad

el aborto	*abortion*
el bienestar social	*social welfare*
el bosque lluvioso	*rainforest*
la contaminación	*pollution*
el crimen	*crime*
la defensa	*defense*
la deforestación	*deforestation*
el desempleo	*unemployment*
la deuda externa	*foreign debt*

la inflación	*inflation*
los impuestos	*taxes*
el medio ambiente	*environment*
la pena capital	*death penalty*
los recursos naturales	*natural resources*

Verbos

afrontar	*to face*
apoyar	*to support*
combatir	*to fight, to combat*
darse cuenta	*to realize*
destruir	*to destroy*
elegir(i)	*to elect; to choose*
empeorar	*to get worse*
ignorar	*to ignore*
llevar a cabo	*to carry out*
mejorar	*to improve*
prevenir(ie)	*to prevent, to warn*
resolver(ue)	*to resolve*
sacrificar	*to sacrifice*
tomar en cuenta	*to take into account*
triunfar	*to triumph*
votar	*to vote*

Otras palabras

a fin de que	*in order that*
¡a ganar!	*Let's win!*
a menos (de) que	*unless*
¡a triunfar!	*Let's triumph!*
¡a votar!	*Let's vote!*
antes de que	*before*
aunque	*although, even if, even though*
con tal (de) que	*provided (that)*
después (de) que	*after*
en caso de que	*in case*
en cuanto	*as soon as*
hasta que	*until*
luego que	*as soon as*
mientras que	*as long as*
ojalá	*hopefully*
para que	*in order that*
sin que	*without*
tan pronto como	*as soon as*
tal vez	*perhaps, maybe*

◆◆◆◆◆◆◆◆◆◆◆◆◆◆◆◆◆◆◆◆◆◆◆◆◆

¡Así lo decimos!

mugger

In many Spanish-speaking countries, crime is on the rise and is a constant topic of conversation. But just as the levels of crime differ from country to country, so do the words used to refer to the person who assaults you; that is, the person who confronts and robs you. A different word is generally used for the person who robs your house when you are not there.

Argentina, Uruguay	**asaltante, rapiñero, chorro** (*colloquial*)
Chile	**punga**
Cuba	**caco, pillo**
España	**atracador, chorizo**
México	**ratero, asaltante, maleante, malhechor**
Venezuela	**malandro**

El malandro me asaltó en plena luz del día.
The mugger robbed me in total daylight.

unemployment

In this lesson, you learned the typical word **desempleo** for *unemployment*. This term is used everywhere but Spain.

España	**paro**

¡A escuchar!

El candidato presidencial. You will hear the speech in **¡Así es la vida!** After you listen, complete the sentences that follow by choosing the correct word.

1. a. la deforestación   b. la ley   c. el aborto

2. a. la economía   b. el crimen   c. los programas sociales

3. a. la inflación   b. la deuda externa   c. la infraestructura social

4. a. la intervención   b. la prevención   c. la eliminación de los impuestos

5. a. ¡Ése soy yo!   b. ¡A triunfar!   c. ¡A ganar!

6. a. un presidente   b. un pasado   c. un futuro

7. a.   b.   c.

◆ Práctica

10–22 Prudencio Sabelotodo. Complete the paragraph about candidate Sabelotodo with words from **Vocabulario y expresiones.**

Este año voy a _____ por Prudencio Sabelotodo para presidente de la

República. Prudencio es miembro de Acción en Acción, un _____ que

solamente tiene un representante en el congreso. Sin embargo, es un _____

muy fuerte porque tiene buenas ideas y ha hecho una _____ muy limpia. Sabe

conversar como una persona muy educada y por eso sus _____ son

emocionantes. También hay que _____ en cuenta que hace ocho años fue

_____ de la provincia del norte, por tanto (*therefore*), ya tiene experiencia

política. Me parece la mejor persona para _____ los problemas del país. Creo

que el pueblo lo va a _____ y que va a ganar las _____.

10–23 La política. Match the words with their definitions.

1. un sistema de gobierno con elecciones
2. una manera de hablar de los políticos
3. el(la) líder de una monarquía
4. el candidato que se opone a otro candidato
5. el día que la gente vota
6. cada uno tiene un candidato y un programa
7. un sistema con un líder autoritario
8. establece las leyes del país
9. toda la gente de un país
10. lo que un país le debe a otro
11. lo que la gente le tiene que pagar al gobierno
12. es causada por sustancias tóxicas
13. lo que hacen los políticos para ganar las elecciones
14. Yo soy ciudadano y Ud. también. Es mi…

a. el rey o la reina
b. las elecciones
c. el pueblo
d. la contaminación
e. la deuda externa
f. la campaña
g. el discurso
h. el(la) contrincante
i. los partidos políticos
j. la dictadura
k. los impuestos
l. la democracia
m. el gobierno
n. conciudadano

10–24 La discusión política. Three brothers and sisters are discussing politics. Complete their dialog with words from the list using each word once.

apoyar	discurso	medio ambiente	recursos
cuenta	empeorar	mejorar	sacrificios
deuda externa	impuestos	prioridad	triunfar
destrucción	inflación	programas	votar

TOÑO: ¿Por quién vas a _____? Yo voy a _____ al partido Alianza con la Naturaleza. Con Figueroa la ecología va a _____.

ALFREDO: Sí, claro, es su obsesión. Pero y la economía, ¿qué? Probablemente aumente los _____ para financiar su reestructuración ecológica.

ELIZA: El desarrollo económico es su _____, pero, ¡desarrollo "sostenible"!

ALFREDO: Eso es un código que significa más impuestos, más _____ sociales.

TOÑO: ¡Tú no lees los periódicos! Estás repitiendo lo que dice papá. Figueroa va a aumentar el precio de la gasolina de plomo *(lead)*. Así, la gente va a tener que comprar gasolina sin plomo que es mejor para el _____.

ELIZA: Sí, y va a negociar la _____ con el Banco Mundial. Los bancos internacionales toman en _____ que no es suficiente mantener la _____, los intereses y el cambio de moneda bajos. Es preciso no prestar dinero para ningún proyecto sin antes hacer un estudio del impacto del proyecto en el medio ambiente.

ALFREDO: Sí, ya me imagino, van a vender nuestros _____ nacionales.

TOÑO: ¡Qué negativo! Al contrario, en su _____ de ayer dijo que los iba a proteger.

ALFREDO: ¡Eso es retórica! ¿Por qué no habla de los _____ que hay que hacer?

ELIZA: La _____ del bosque lluvioso no es juego. Si destruimos la ecología, la economía va a _____.

ALFREDO: Con esa propaganda no dudo que Figueroa va a _____.

◆ Actividades

10–25 Entrevista. Interview a classmate using the questions below; then switch roles.

1. ¿Crees que votar es un deber? Explica.
2. ¿Votaste en las últimas elecciones? ¿Por quién?
3. ¿Eres miembro de algún partido político? ¿De cuál? ¿Por qué?
4. ¿Te cae bien alguna figura de la política mundial? ¿Quién y por qué?
5. ¿Quieres ser presidente(a) de los Estados Unidos? Explica.
6. ¿Qué consejos puedes darle a tu presidente?

10–26 Temas de actualidad. Look at the following political advertisement. Rank in order of priority the issues you consider most important. Briefly explain your choices to a classmate.

Distrito 105

Alberto
Gutman

Su
Representante Estatal

Siempre Presente con Usted en Mente

ALBERTO GUTMAN TRABAJA...

* para ayudar a las personas mayores
* para combatir el crimen y la drogas
* para controlar lo impuestos
* para mejorar el sistema de salud
* para más y mejores viviendas públicas
* para mejorar el sistema escolar
* para un medio ambiente saludable
* para establecer eficiencia en el gobierno
* para USTED.

Tal vez gane el señor Gutman las próximas elecciones.

10–27 Un informe. Take turns briefly describing to a classmate who each historical/political figure listed below was/is.

1. Isabel la Católica
2. Cristóbal Colón
3. César Chávez
4. Eva Duarte de Perón
5. Fidel Castro
6. la reina Sofía
7. Felipe González
8. Violeta Chamorro

10–28 Tu candidato. In groups of three or four, write a campaign ad for a candidate for your college or university presidency. Use the ad in exercise 10–26 as a model.

Estructuras

3. The Subjunctive in Adjectival Clauses

> Quiero un sombrero que tenga un ala muy grande.

- Use the subjunctive in an adjectival clause—a clause that modifies a noun—when it refers to a person or object that is indefinite or does not exist.

Indefinite antecedent

Buscamos un candidato que **sea** honesto.   *We're looking for a candidate who **is** honest.* (You don't know if he/she exists.)

Quieren un sombrero que **sea** mexicano.   *They want a hat that **is** Mexican.* (They haven't found it yet.)

Nonexistent antecedent

No veo nada que me **guste.**   *I don't see anything I **like**.* (It might not exist.)

No hay nadie aquí que yo **conozca.**   *There's no one here I **know**.* (You don't recognize anyone. A known person does not exist in this situation.)

- Use the indicative in an adjectival clause when it refers to persons or objects whose existence is certain.

Voy a votar por el candidato que **es** honesto.   *I'm going to vote for the honest politician.* (You have someone specific in mind.)

Quieren el sombrero que **es** mexicano.   *They want the hat that **is** Mexican.*

Veo algo que me **gusta** en la vitrina.   *I see something I **like** in the window.* (If you see it, it exists.)

Ahí hay una persona que yo **conozco.**   *There's someone I **know** there.*

- In questions containing adjectival clauses, it is precisely the existence of the person or object that is being asked about. Therefore, those questions take the subjunctive:

> ¿Conoce Ud. a alguien que **trabaje** en el congreso? *Do you know anyone who **works** in Congress?*

> ¿Hay algún asiento que **esté** desocupado? *Is there a seat that **is** free (not in use)?*

◆ Práctica

10–29 La tertulia. Young people in other countries are often very involved in politics. Are you? Imagine that you are at a bar eating *tapas* with your friends. Everyone has questions or comments to make about local politics. Fill in the blanks with the appropriate form of the present indicative or present subjunctive.

1. ¿Conoces al senador que (vivir) _____ en tu estado?
2. Necesitamos votar por unos candidatos que (hablar) _____ español.
3. Necesitamos un represantante que (querer) _____ ayudar al público.
4. No hay ningún político que me (gustar) _____.
5. Buscamos un presidente y un senador que siempre (estar) _____ con la gente.
6. No hay nadie por quien nosotros (poder) _____ votar este año.
7. ¿Buscas al candidato que siempre (hablar) _____ por la radio?
8. ¿Conoces al político que (tener) _____ el lema famoso?
9. Necesito una encuesta que nos (decir) _____ la verdad.
10. No veo nada que (ser) _____ interesante en estas elecciones.
11. Quiero hablar con el reportero que (cubrir) _____ la campaña.
12. Preferimos patrocinar una emisora que (ejercer) _____ más influencia.
13. Busco un periodista que (saber) _____ mucho de historia.
14. ¿Conoces al comentarista que (aparecer) _____ en el canal 4 los sábados?
15. Deseamos un aviso clasificado que (ser) _____ económico y efectivo.
16. Quiero un candidato que (tomar) _____ en cuenta el problema de la inflación.
17. No nos gusta el candidato que (oponerse) _____ al aborto.
18 Apoyamos al senador que (ser) _____ muy fuerte en la defensa del país.

10–30 Una campaña política. You are planning a political campaign in a local election. List at least two skills or characteristics that each person below should have. Use the cues provided.

MODELO: asesor
          Queremos un asesor que tenga mucha experiencia y que sepa mucho de política.

un agente de viajes	directora de campaña	ayudante	abogado
secretario	traductora	chofer	piloto

1. Necesitamos…
2. Estamos interesados en…
3. Queremos…
4. Estamos buscando…
5. Vamos a conseguir…
6. Preferimos…
7. Nos gustaría…
8. Tenemos que encontrar…

10–31 La visita. You are visiting a group of relatives who all seem to have an opinion about political events. Complete their opinions using the indicative or subjunctive of the verbs in parentheses.

1. El candidato necesita un ayudante que (poder) _____ escribir discursos.
2. En el gobierno de ahora hay varios ministros que (ser) _____ muy populares.
3. No conozco a nadie que (trabajar) _____ tanto como el alcalde de la capital.
4. Necesitamos un gobernador que (saber) _____ hablar varios idiomas.
5. Buscan un candidato que (tener) _____ el apoyo del partido.
6. Tienen un lema que sin duda (ir) _____ a ayudarlos a triunfar.
7. No he encontrado un partido político que realmente (combatir) _____ el crimen.
8. ¿Qué candidato nos va a pedir abiertamente que nos (sacrificar) _____?
9. Los pueblos ignorantes necesitan líderes que los (educar) _____.
10. Es un plan de desarrollo que (tomar) _____ en cuenta la infraestructura social.
11. Necesitamos un plan que (poner) _____ fin a la destrucción del bosque lluvioso.
12. Queremos un lema que nos (llevar) _____ a triunfar.
13. Éste es un gobierno que (saber) _____ prevenir los problemas.
14. No queremos un partido que (acabar) _____ con los recursos naturales.
15. Es el senador que (apoyar) _____ la nueva ley contra la deforestación.

10–32 El viaje de Ana. Find out about Ana's trip by matching the phrases in the columns.

1. Tengo un boleto
2. Busco un agente de viajes
3. La verdad es que quiero un viaje
4. Ah, y prefiero un vuelo
5. Tampoco quiero un hotel
6. Sé que hay unas excursiones
7. Necesito una cámara fotográfica
8. Busco un(a) compañero(a) de viaje

a. que ofrezca mucha variedad.
b. que pueda meter en el agua.
c. que no cueste mucho.
d. que no son muy caras.
e. que tenga mucha experiencia.
f. que sepa viajar.
g. que esté muy lejos del centro.
h. que no haga escala en ninguna parte.

10–33 Teleguía. Scan the T.V. schedule. With a classmate, one person says what he/she is looking for, the other finds a program to recommend. Then switch roles.

MODELO: —Quiero ver un programa que tenga un tema religioso.
—Te recomiendo "Tiempo de creer" sobre los musulmanes.

PROGRAMACIÓN TV

martes 18

TVE-1
8.00 **Buenos días**
8.30 **Telediario matinal.**
9.00 **Por la mañana.**
13:00 **Johnny Quest.** *Cautivos de los po-ho.*
13.30 **Tres por cuarto.**
14:30 **Informativos territoriales.**
14.55 **Conexión con la programación nacional.**
15.00 **Telediario 1.**
15.35 **Mount Royal.**
16.30 **Por la tarde.**
17.55 **Avance telediario.**
18.00 **Los mundos de Yupi.** *El fantasma encapuchado.*
18.30 **El misterio de la flor mágica.** *El anillo de la reina egipcia.*
19.00 **Juan el Largo.**
19.30 **Entre líneas.**
20.00 **Casa de locos.** *Madam Butterfat.*
20.30 **Telediario 2.**

21.00 **El tiempo.**
21.15 **Tariro, tariro.**
22.20 **Sesión de noche.** Ciclo Robert Redford. El gran Gatsby.
0.50 **Telediario 3.**
1.10 **Teledeporte.**
1.25 **Testimonio.**
1.30 **La noche.** *Primera plana.*
2:00 **Filmoteca del martes.** *El maquinista de la General.*

TVE-2
13.00 **Programación centros territoriales.**
14.30 **Informativos territoriales.**
15.00 **Telediario 1.**
15.30 **Historia delmimo.**
16.30 **Caballo viejo.**
17.15 **La comedia musical española.** *Róbame esta noche.*
19.00 **El tiempo que vivimos.**
19.55 **Ópera.** *Los maestros contores de Nuremberg, de R. Wagner, desde el Gran Teatro del Liceo de Barcelona.*
1.00 **Tendido cero.**

miércoles 19

TVE-1
8.00 **Buenos días.**
8.30 **Telediario matinal.**
9.00 **Por la mañana.**
13.00 **Los osos Berenstain.**
13.30 **Tres por cuatro.**
14.30 **Informativos territoriales.**
14.55 **Conexión con la programación nacional.**
15.00 **Telediario 1.**
15.35 **El olivar de Atocha.** *La casa abierta.*
16.30 **Por la tarde.**
17.55 **Avance telediario.**
18.00 **Los mundos de Yupi.** *La visita sorpresa.*
18.30 **Historias de aquí y de allá.** *El sombrero roja (Noruega).*
19.00 **El cuenta cuentos.** *La novia verdadera.*
19.30 **Hablando claro.**
20.00 **Throb.**
20.30 **Telediario 2.**
21.00 **El tiempo.**
21.15 **El viaje infinito.** *La gran caza del dinosaurio.*
22.20 **Canción triste de Hill Street.** *El recuerdo.*

23.15 **Historias de music hall.** *Belle époque.*
0.15 **Telediario 3.**
0.35 **Teledeporte.**
0.50 **La noche.** *Sin fronteras.*
2.00 **Reposiciones TVE.** *El hombre del Oeste.*

TVE-2
13.00 **Programación centros territoriales.**
14.30 **Informativos territoriales.**
15.00 **Telediario.**
15.30 **Documental.** *La herrería: los conjuradores del fuego.*
16.00 **Europa en juego.** *Fútbol: semifinales de la Copa de Europa, Galatasaray (Turquía)-teaua (Rumanía).*
18.30 **La conquista del espacio.** *Secretos del cosmos.*
19.00 **Plastic.**
20.00 **Europa en juego.** *Fútbol: Milán-Real Madrid.*
23.00 **A través del espejo.** *El irresistible avance del desierto.*
0.20 **El poeta en su vox.** *María Victoria Atencia.*
0.35 **Tiempo de creer.** *Musulmanes.*

10–34 Discusión. With a classmate, discuss the qualities you look for in political candidates. Use the subjunctive mood.

MODELO: —Prefiero un candidato que sea honesto.
—Necesitamos políticos que cumplan sus promesas.

10–35 La campaña. You and your classmates are on a political campaign staff. In small groups, role-play a meeting in which you discuss the people you want to hire to help with the campaign; the media you want to advertise in; the polls you want to commission; and the slogans that will carry you to victory. Use indefinite and nonexistent antecedents when possible.

10–36 El gran debate. Engage in a debate about the issues below with two classmates. The first student expresses an opinion and the others then express agreement or disagreement. Take turns being the student who kicks off the debate.

MODELO: el crimen en las grandes ciudades
E1: — Dudo que el crimen en las grandes ciudades pueda ser controlado.
E2: — No estoy de acuerdo. Es necesario elegir un gobierno que le dé más poder a la policía.
E3: — Pues yo creo que debemos mejorar la situación económica de la gente.

1. el uso de las drogas entre los jóvenes
2. el suicidio en los adolescentes
3. la separación del estado y la iglesia *(church)*
4. el feminismo y el aborto
5. la asistencia a los pobres
6. cómo mejorar la educación en los Estados Unidos
7. la pena capital *(death penalty)*
8. los programas sensacionalistas en la televisión

4. The Subjunctive with *ojalá, tal vez* and *quizás*

Ojalá que sea una pizza de jamón con champiñones.

- The expression **¡Ojalá!** entered the Spanish language during the Arab occupation of Spain. Its literal translation is "May God (Allah) grant your wish" and its actual meaning is *hopefully*. **¡Ojalá!** may be used with or without **que,** and is followed by the subjunctive.

  ¡Ojalá (que) **tengamos** buen tiempo mañana. ***I hope that we will have*** *good weather tomorrow.*
  ¡Ojalá (que) no **llueva!** ***I hope*** *it doesn't rain.*

- Use the subjunctive with the expressions **tal vez** and **quizá(s)**, *(perhaps* or *maybe)* when the speaker wishes to convey uncertainty or doubt.

  Tal vez vaya al senado.   *Perhaps I'll go to the senate.*
  Quizás vote por tu candidato.   *Maybe I'll vote for your candidate.*

- Use the indicative when **tal vez** or **quizá(s)** follows the verb.

  Voy al senado, **tal vez.**   *Perhaps I'll go to the senate.*
  Voto por tu candidato, **quizás.**   *Maybe I'll vote for your candidate.*

◆ Práctica

10–37 Nuestra presidenta. Amada Nervo has just been elected president of the Republic. List the goals you hope she will accomplish.

MODELO: ¡Ojalá que ella (combatir) _____ el crimen!
          ¡Ojalá que ella combata el crimen!

1. ¡Ojalá que tú (obtener) _____ un puesto en su gobierno!
2. ¡Ojalá que yo (poder) _____ ser su ayudante!
3. ¡Ojalá que nosotros (tener) _____ prosperidad!
4. ¡Ojalá que ella (reducir) _____ la tasa de desempleo!
5. ¡Ojalá que los representantes la (apoyar) _____!
6. ¡Ojalá que ella (aumentar) _____ los programas de ayuda social!
7. ¡Ojalá que ella (establecer) _____ un sistema mejor de educación!
8. ¡Ojalá que su administración (prevenir) _____ el uso de las drogas!
9. ¡Ojalá que los estudiantes (tener) _____ más ayuda del gobierno!
10. ¡Ojalá que no (haber) _____ más guerras!
11. ¡Ojalá que (eligir) _____ buenos ministros.
12. ¡Ojalá que (resolver) _____ el problema de la contaminación.
13. ¡Ojalá que no (ignorar) _____ la deforestación del bosque lluvioso.
14. ¡Ojalá que la deuda externa no (empeorar) _____.
15. ¡Ojalá que sus reformas (triunfar) _____.

10–38 Tal vez. President Nervo has been in power for three years. Soon there will be new elections. You and your friends are talking about them. Change the following statements so that they express uncertainty. Use **quizás** or **tal vez** to change the following statements.

MODELO: La candidata pronuncia un discurso.
          Tal vez la candidata pronuncie un discurso.
          Quizás la candidata pronuncie un discurso.

1. Yo voto por ella otra vez.
2. Nosotros recordamos su lema.
3. Tú ayudas a su contrincante.
4. Apoyamos a su contrincante también.
5. Ambos partidos se unen.
6. Nuestra candidata cumple sus promesas.
7. Los partidos menores van a ganar muchos votos.
8. El presidente controla la inflación justo a tiempo.
9. El congreso le da prioridad y pasa la ley.
10. El senado no apoya la ley nueva.

◆ **Actividades**

10–39 ¡Ojalá que… ! Discuss with a classmate what you wish would happen in the United States or Canada in the next five years.

MODELOS: ¡Ojalá que no suban los impuestos!
          ¡Ojalá los demócratas ganen la presidencia!

10–40 En el año 2000. In small groups, create a dialog about what may happen in the world by the year 2000. Follow the models. Be prepared to share it with the class.

MODELOS: Tal vez no tengamos más guerras.
          Quizás todos los automóviles sean eléctricos.

5. The Subjunctive in Adverbial Clauses

antes (de) que	*before*
a fin de que	*in order that*
a menos (de) que	*unless*
con tal (de) que	*provided (that)*
en caso de que	*in case*
para que	*in order that, so that*
sin que	*without*

¿Te cubre tu póliza los préstamos y el crédito?

- The use of these expressions presupposes that the action described in the dependent clause is uncertain or has not yet taken place, because they express purpose, intent, condition or anticipation. They appear in adverbial clauses and require the subjunctive.

Díselo **para que** sepa la verdad.	*Tell him **so that** he knows the truth.*
No estudiaremos con ellos **a menos que** lleguen a tiempo.	*We won't study with them **unless** they arrive on time.*
No me enojaré **con tal que** él no trate de hablarme.	*I won't get angry **provided that** he doesn't try to talk to me.*
Llevaré el cuaderno **en caso de que** lo necesite.	*I'll bring the notebook **in case** I need it.*
La veré **antes de que** ella regrese del trabajo.	*I'll see her **before** she returns from work.*

- When there is no change in subject, the following expressions are used with the infintive: **a fin de, a menos de, antes de, con tal de, en caso de, para** and **sin.**

Tomamos clases **a fin de aprender.**	*We are taking classes in order to learn.*
No puedes sacar buenas notas **sin estudiar.**	*You cannot get good grades without studying.*
El equipo practica mucho **para ganar** el campeonato.	*The team practices a lot in order to win the championship.*

Expressions with Either Subjunctive or Indicative

aunque	*although, even*	
cuando	*when*	
después (de) que	*after*	
en cuanto	*as soon as*	
hasta que	*until*	
luego que	*as soon as*	
mientras que	*while*	
tan pronto como	*as soon as*	

- Use the subjunctive after expressions that introduce time clauses, because we can't speak with certainty about an action that has not yet taken place. Also, after the conjunction **aunque** when the speaker wishes to convey uncertainty.

Hablaré con él **cuando** entre.	*I will talk to him when he enters.*
Le diremos la verdad **en cuanto** llegue.	*We'll tell her the truth as soon as she arrives.*
No te darán más dinero **hasta que** seas más cortés.	*They will not give you more money until you're more polite.*

- However, use the present or past indicative if the action referred to by the time clause is habitual or has already happened, because we can speak with certainty about things that have already occurred. Also with **aunque** if the speaker wishes to express certainty or refer to a completed event.

Hablaron con la joven **hasta que se fue.**	*They talked with the young lady until she left.*
Cuando veo a mi novia me siento muy bien.	*When I see my girlfriend I feel very good.*
Aunque llueva, iré a verte.	*Even though it may rain, I'll go to see you.*
Aunque es caro, no me gusta.	*Although it's expensive, I don't like it.*
Aunque estabas en la fiesta, no me viste.	*Although you were at the party, you didn't see me.*

◆ **Práctica**

10–41 ¿Indicativo o subjuntivo? Amalia and Rafael love technology. They talk about nothing else. Complete the sentences with the appropriate indicative or subjunctive form of the verbs in parentheses. Verb tenses may vary.

1. Compraré una computadora cuando (tener) _____ dinero.
2. Te voy a enseñar la videograbadora *(videorecorder)* con tal de que (venir) _____ a mi casa.
3. Ayer instalamos la fotocopiadora después de que tú (llegar) _____ del trabajo.
4. Harán la cuenta tan pronto como (conseguir) _____ una calculadora.
5. ¿Me enviará usted un fax antes de que ellos me (llamar) _____ por teléfono?
6. Les voy a comprar una computadora para que ellos (poder) _____ hacer su trabajo.
7. Hablé con Mario cuando él (volver) _____ de su clase de computación.
8. Ellos aprenderán a usar las computadoras luego que tú les (explicar) _____ cómo usarlas.
9. No vimos nada en la pantalla aunque ya la (arreglar) _____ .
10. En caso de que tu teléfono celular no (servir) _____ , yo te presto el mío.
11. Voy a comprar un videoteléfono a fin de que mamá (poder) _____ verme cuando la (llamar) _____ .
12. Quiero un control remoto sofisticado aunque (costarme) _____ mucho dinero.

10–42 Completar. Complete the phrases with personal information, using the indicative or subjunctive as appropriate.

MODELO: Estudiaré español hasta que....
         Estudiaré español hasta que pueda hablarlo tan bien como un mexicano.

1. Seré feliz cuando....
2. Buscaré un trabajo tan pronto como....
3. Mis amigos(as) y yo nos iremos de vacaciones en cuanto....
4. Mi familia celebrará las navidades aunque....
5. No seré millonario(a) hasta que....
6. Esta noche voy a estudiar cuando....
7. Siempre me duermo después que....
8. Por lo general, yo no salgo de casa hasta que....
9. Voy a tener mi título universitario antes de que....
10. Voy a...mientras que....

◆ Actividades

10–43 Mis planes para hoy. Discuss your plans for the day with a classmate. Have your partner say what he/she will do in the same situation. Use the phrases below as a starting point for your conversation.

MODELO: Voy a estudiar tan pronto como....

              —Voy a estudiar tan pronto como llegue a casa.

              —Yo no quiero estudiar. Tan pronto como llegue a casa me voy a acostar.

1. Voy a cenar en cuanto....
2. Voy a ver la televisión cuando....
3. Voy a hacer mi tarea antes de que....
4. Voy a hablar con mis amigos después de que....
5. Voy a salir con mi novio(a) cuando....
6. Voy a dormir hasta que....
7. Voy a limpiar la casa con tal que....
8. No puedo hacer mi tarea sin que....
9. Voy a acostarme temprano a fin de que....
10. Voy a estudiar español en caso de que....

Colaboración

Estudiante A

10-44A Los medios de información: Una encuesta. Interview your classmate about his/her preferences. Write down the answers. Then, switch roles.

MODELO: leer el periódico
—¿Te gusta leer el periódico? ¿Cuál es tu favorito?
—Sí, me gusta mucho. Mi periódico favorito es el....

ACTIVIDAD

leer el periódico	No me gusta nada
ver el noticiero en la televisión	Me gusta poco
escuchar la radio pública	Me da igual
ver telenovelas	Me gusta
leer revistas científicas	Me gusta mucho
ver algún programa deportivo	¡Me encanta!
ver certámenes de belleza	

10-45A Una encuesta política. Interview your classmate about his/her opinions. React to your classmate's opinion by expressing agreement or disagreement. Then switch roles.

MODELO: —¿En este país hay libertad de prensa?
—No creo que haya libertad de prensa.
—Pues, yo estoy seguro(a) de que sí hay libertad de prensa.
or Yo también dudo que haya libertad de prensa.

LA PREGUNTA

¿Pueden los estudiantes expresar sus opiniones políticas?
¿Se prohíben ciertos libros en las bibliotecas de las escuelas públicas de tu estado?
¿Trabajan los políticos para mejorar la situación económica?
¿Dicen siempre la verdad los periodistas?
¿Tienen razón los críticos del gobierno?
¿Controlan los patrocinadores los programas de televisión?
¿Es imparcial el periódico de esta ciudad?
¿Explotan a la mujer los certámenes de belleza?

EXPRESIONES DE DUDA O NEGACIÓN	EXPRESIONES DE CERTIDUMBRE O AFIRMACIÓN
Dudo	No dudo
Niego	No niego
No creo	Creo
No estoy seguro(a)	Estoy seguro(a)
No es cierto	Es cierto
Es dudoso	Es verdad
	Es evidente

10-46A Las opiniones. Comment on the following subjects. Write down your classmate's reaction.
React to your classmate's comments with an impersonal expression. Switch roles.

MODELO: —Muchas más mujeres son candidatas en estas elecciones.
           —Me alegro. Es bueno (malo, importante, etc.) que las mujeres sean candidatas en las elecciones
             porque tienen más experiencia con los problemas de las mujeres y los niños.
           —Estoy/No estoy de acuerdo *(I agree/disagree)* porque….

EL COMENTARIO

   …es (va a ser) candidato a la presidencia.
   El congreso va a aumentar los impuestos.
   Hay mucho desempleo entre los jóvenes.
   Los programas sociales reciben menos apoyo.
   Los políticos son todos ricos.

EXPRESIONES CON EL SUBJUNTIVO	EXPRESIONES CON EL INDICATIVO
es…	es…
bueno (malo)	verdad
posible (imposible)	cierto
probable (improbable)	seguro
difícil (fácil)	evidente
increíble	no hay duda
dudoso	yo sé que
extraño	
importante	
indispensable	
una lástima	
mejor	
necesario	
preciso	
urgente	

10-47A ¿Qué buscas? Ask your classmate what ideal characteristics he/she looks for in the following people,
things, and places. Write down his/her answers. Then tell your classmate what your preference are.

MODELO: un coche
           —¿Qué tipo de coche buscas?
           —Busco un coche que tenga cuatro ruedas y un cinturón de seguridad.

Mi compañero(a) busca…

   un coche   un lugar para las vacaciones
   una clase   un programa de televisión
   un(a) amigo(a)   una novela
   un restaurante

Yo busco… (Posibles descripciones)
   • honesto, trabajador, intelectual, *hablar* español, etc.
   • justo, interesante, activo, divertido, *dar* exámenes fáciles, etc.
   • *pagar* bien, en un lugar interesante, *tener* seguro médico, tener un beneficios de retiro, etc.
   • divertido, tener una banda de rock, *estar* en mi barrio,etc.
   • grande, económico, tener un vista, *estar* en un barrio seguro, etc.
   • *tocar* música de…, pública, etc.
   • *tener* noticias internacionales, tener una sección deportiva, etc.
   • *jugar* en …, activo, bueno, etc.

Estudiante B

10-44B Los medios de información: Una encuesta. Your classmate will interview you about your preferences. Then, switch roles. Write down your classmate's answers.

MODELO: leer el periódico
  —¿Te gusta leer el periódico? ¿Cuál es tu favorito?
  —Sí, me gusta mucho. Mi periódico favorito es el….

ACTIVIDAD

ver la publicidad en la televisión	No me gusta nada
escuchar al(a la) meteorólogo(a)	Me gusta poco
ver los concursos en la televisión	Me da igual
escuchar al(a la) comentarista deportivo(a)	Me gusta
ver la televisión (¿qué canal?)	Me gusta mucho
escuchar la radio (¿qué emisora?)	¡Me encanta!
leer revistas populares (por ejemplo, *People*)	

10-45B Una encuesta política. Your classmate will interview you about your opinions. Answer by expressing doubt or certainty. Then switch roles.

MODELO: —¿En este país hay libertad de prensa?
  —No creo que haya libertad de prensa.
  —Pues, yo estoy seguro(a) de que sí hay libertad de prensa.
  or   Yo también dudo que haya libertad de prensa.

LA PREGUNTA

¿Pueden los estudiantes expresar sus opiniones políticas?
¿Se prohiben ciertos libros en las bibliotecas de las escuelas públicas en su estado?
¿Trabajan los políticos para mejorar la situación económica?
¿Dicen siempre la verdad los periodistas?
¿Tienen razón los críticos del gobierno?
¿Controlan los patrocinadores los programas de televisión?
¿Es objetivo el periódico de esta ciudad?
¿Explotan a la mujer los certámenes de belleza?

EXPRESIONES DE DUDA O NEGACIÓN	EXPRESIONES DE CERTIDUMBRE O AFIRMACIÓN
Dudo	No dudo
Niego	No niego
No creo	Creo
No estoy seguro(a)	Estoy seguro(a)
No es cierto	Es cierto
Es dudoso	Es verdad
	Es evidente

10-46B Las opiniones. React to your classmate's comments with an impersonal expression. Justify your opinion; then switch roles. Comment on the subjects below. Write down your classmate's reaction. React to his/her comments.

MODELO: —Muchas más mujeres son candidatas en estas elecciones.
  —Me alegro. Es bueno (malo, importante, etc.) que las mujeres sean candidatas en las elecciones porque tienen más experiencia con los problemas de las mujeres y los niños.
  —Estoy/No estoy de acuerdo *(I agree/disagree)* porque….

EL COMENTARIO
…es (va a ser) candidato al congreso.
Hay pocas mujeres en el senado de este país.
Pocos políticos se interesan por el medio ambiente.
Los programas de defensa reciben más apoyo que la educación.
Las campañas políticas son cada vez más *(more and more)* negativas.

EXPRESIONES CON EL SUBJUNTIVO	EXPRESIONES CON EL INDICATIVO
es…	es…
bueno (malo)	verdad
posible (imposible)	cierto
probable (improbable)	seguro
difícil (fácil)	evidente
increíble	no hay duda
dudoso	yo sé que
extraño	
importante	
indispensable	
una lástima	
mejor	
necesario	
preciso	
urgente	

10-47B ¿Qué buscas? Your classmate will ask the ideal characteristics you look for in a variety of people, places, and things. Then ask your classmate what he/she looks for. Write down his/her answers.

MODELO: un coche
  —¿Qué tipo de coche buscas?
  —Busco un coche que tenga cuatro ruedas y un cinturón de seguridad.

Yo busco… (posibles descripciones)
• rápido, grande, rojo, económico, de lujo, *tener…*, etc.
• grande, interestante, emocionante, fácil, a las (hora), *tener* un buen profesor, etc.
• inteligente, divertido, intelectual, interesado en los deportes, trabajador, *gustarle…*, etc.
• cosmopolita, internacional, económico, elegante, *servir* comida rápida, etc.
• económico, en el mar, tranquilo, en las montañas, *tener* un paquete turístico, etc.
• larga, corta, de detectives, de suspenso, romántica, en español, escrita por…,

Mi compañero busca…   Su descripción
  un(a) candidato(a) presidencial
  un(a) profesor(a)
  un puesto
  una discoteca
  una apartamento
  una emisora de radio
  un periódico
  un equipo de béisbol

Ampliación gramatical

Estructuras adicionales

- The Future Tense

- The Future Perfect

- The Conditional Tense

- The Conditional Perfect

- The Present Perfect Subjunctive

- The Imperfect Subjunctive

- The Pluperfect Subjunctive

- The Indicative or Subjunctive in **si** Clauses

Estructuras adicionales

1. The Future Tense

● Form the Spanish future tense by adding the present tense endings of the verb **haber** (without the **h**). The **vosotros** form drops the stem **hab-**. There is only one set of endings for the **-ar, -er** and **-ir** verbs. All endings, except for the **nosotros** forms, have a written accent mark.

	TOMAR	COMER	VIVIR
yo	tomaré	comeré	viviré
tú	tomarás	comerás	vivirás
Ud./él/ella	tomará	comerá	vivirá
nosotros(as)	tomaremos	comeremos	viviremos
vosotros(as)	tomaréis	comeréis	viviréis
Uds./ellos/ellas	tomarán	comerán	vivirán

● The English equivalent is **will** + *verb*.

Mañana **comeremos** en casa.	*Tomorrow **we will eat** at home.*
El año próximo **viviré** en España.	*Next year **I will live** in Spain.*
¿**Tomarás** café con leche con tostadas?	**Will you have** coffee and milk with toast?

● There are other ways of expressing future action in Spanish: The present tense, to express the immediate future, and the present tense of **ir a** + *infinitive*.

Regresan ahora mismo.	***They will return** right now.*
Vengo a las cuatro.	***I will come** at four.*
Voy a cenar contigo esta noche.	***I'm going to have dinner** with you tonight.*

● The Spanish future tense does *not* express the idea of **willingness,** as does the English future. Use the present tense instead.

¿**Quieren** ayudarme a hacer las maletas?	***Will you** help me pack the suitcases?*

● To express probability or conjecture in the present in Spanish, use the future tense.

¿**Estará** Ramón en el trabajo?	*I wonder if John is at work.*
¿Qué hora **será? Serán** las dos.	*What time **can it be?** **It's probably** two o'clock.*

- There twelve Spanish verbs that have irregular forms in the future. They form the future by adding the future endings to an irregular stem. The irregular stems can be grouped into three categories.

a. The future stem is different from the stem of the regular verb.

decir	**dir-**	diré, dirás,...
hacer	**har-**	haré, harás,...

b. The **e** of the infinitive is dropped to form the stem of the future.

caber	**cabr-**	cabré, cabrás,...
haber	**habr-**	habré, habrás,...
poder	**podr-**	podré, podrás,...
querer	**querr-**	querré, querrás,...
saber	**sabr-**	sabré, sabrás,...

c. The **e** of the infinitive is replaced by **d** to form the stem of the future.

poner	**pondr-**	pondré, pondrás,...
salir	**saldr-**	saldré, saldrás,...
tener	**tendr-**	tendré, tendrás,...
valer	**valdr-**	valdré, valdrás,...
venir	**vendr-**	vendré, vendrás,...

◆ Práctica

A-1 En busca de empleo. Three friends are looking for part-time jobs. Change the verbs in italics from the construction **ir a** + *infiinitive* to the future tense.

Mañana María Cristina y yo *vamos a pedir* _____ empleo en la Agencia Ruiz. *Vamos a levantarnos* _____ temprano. Luego *vamos a reunirnos* _____ con Pedro y Rosalía en la cafetería Manila que está cerca de la agencia. Yo *voy a tratar* _____ de obtener un trabajo de cocinero en un restaurante. Ana *va a preguntar* _____ si hay trabajo para camarera en el mismo lugar. Como somos novios, para Ana y para mí *va a ser* _____ muy agradable trabajar juntos. Pero Pedro dice que él *va a buscar* _____ un trabajo mejor. En la Agencia Ruiz *va a preguntar* _____ sobre trabajo en los bancos. Después, *va a ir* _____ a ver a un tío suyo que trabaja en el Almacén el Emporio. Ahí el tío lo *va a presentar* _____ a la jefe de personal. El tío cree que le *va a poder* _____ conseguir un buen trabajo a Pedro como vendedor. Pedro *va a llevar* _____ a su tío a almorzar para darle las gracias. Rosalía quiere ser cajera. También *va a averiguar* _____ sobre los bancos. Si no es posible, *va a visitar* _____ varios supermercados. Estoy seguro que, *vamos a tener* _____ un verano muy productivo.

A-2 Los novios. Complete the description of John and Melissa's future plans. Provide the future forms of the verbs in parentheses.

Mi novio y yo (graduarse) _____ en tres años. Cuando seamos *juniors* (pasar) _____ un año en España para aprender bien el español. Después de graduarnos (empezar) _____ nuestros estudios de postgrado. (Estudiar) _____ literatura en español para ser profesores de español. Después de acabar el postgrado yo (enseñar) _____ español en una escuela secundaria. Y él (dar) _____ clases en una universidad. (Ser) _____ unos profesores excelentes y muy motivados. (Viajar) _____ con nuestros estudiantes a países hispanoamericanos. Yo les (mostrar) _____ a mis estudiantes muchas cosas interesantes. Nuestros estudiantes nos (querer) _____ mucho. (Trabajar) _____ varios años para ahorrar dinero. (Casarse) _____ en un bosque cerca de un lago un día de verano. (Vivir) _____ en una ciudad grande y cosmopolita. Más tarde (comprar) _____ una casa pequeña cerca de una ciudad grande. Eventualmente (tener) _____ dos o tres hijos. (Educar) _____ a nuestros hijos tan bien como nuestros padres nos educaron a nosotros.

A-3 Nuestro viaje a España. Two North American students, Stephanie Lippo and Brenda White, will be going to Spain this summer. Find out what their plans are by changing the infinitives to the future verb forms.

MODELO: Este verano (ir) a España.
          Este verano iremos a España.

Primero nosotros (viajar) _____ avión de Johnson City a Nueva York. Allí (reunirse) _____ con el resto del grupo en la terminal de Iberia. En Madrid todos (vivir) _____ en una residencia de estudiantes. Nosotras (tomar) _____ nuestro almuerzo en una cafetería. (Tener) _____ nuestras clases en el colegio mayor. Brenda (visitar) _____ Pamplona para ver los sanfermines. Stephanie (ver) _____ muchos monumentos y palacios interesantes en Madrid. Nosotras (dar) _____ muchos paseos cerca de Madrid. (Salir) _____ al teatro por la noche. Yo (ir) _____ a comer tapas con frecuencia. Brenda (querer) _____ ver una corrida de toros. Nosotras (poder) _____ conocer el Museo del Prado. Yo (bañarse) _____ en la piscina de la universidad todas las tardes. Nosotras (conversar) _____ con los españoles que estudian en la universidad. Nosotras (regresar) _____ a Nueva York el 6 de agosto. Brenda (venir) _____ al club de español a dar una conferencia sobre nuestro viaje.

A-4 ¿Qué hora será? Guess at what time your roommate does the following actions. Follow the model.

MODELO: Está acostándose.
                   Serán las once de la noche.

1. Está lavándose los dientes por la mañana.
2. Está entrando a la clase de español.
3. Está almorzando en la cafetería.
4. Está haciendo ejercicios en una clase de aeróbicos.
5. Está volviendo a la residencia de estudiantes.
6. Está cenando con su amiga Marla.
7. Está estudiando en la biblioteca.
8. Está viendo el programa de David Letterman.
9. Está lavándose los dientes para acostarse.
10. Está durmiendo.

2. The Future Perfect

● Form the future perfect with the future of the auxiliary verb **haber** + *past participle*.

		FUTURE	PAST PARTICIPLE
	yo	**habré**	
	tú	**habrás**	**tomado**
	Ud./él/ella	**habrá**	**comido**
	nosotros(as)	**habremos**	**vivido**
	vosotros(as)	**habréis**	
	Uds./ellos/ellas	**habrán**	

● Use the future perfect to express an action that *will have occurred* by a certain point in time.

| **¿Habrás comido** esta noche para las ocho? | ***Will you have eaten** tonight by eight o'clock?* |
| No, no **habré comido** para las ocho. | *No, I will not have eaten by eight o'clock.* |

● Also, use the future perfect to express probability or conjecture about what may have happened in the past, yet has some relation to the present.

| **¿Habrá venido** el cartero ya? | *I wonder if the mailman **has come** already.* |
| **¿Habremos sacado** una A en el examen? | *I wonder if we got an A on the exam.* |

◆ Práctica

A-5 ¡Qué familia más curiosa! You're visiting some cousins in Ecuador with whom your family has not kept closely in touch over the years. They have many questions about you and your family.

MODELO: ¿Cuándo vas a comprarte un buen estéreo?
El próximo mes ya me habré comprado un buen estéreo.

1. ¿Cuándo vas a terminar el semestre? (en un mes)
2. ¿Cuándo vas a graduarte? (en tres años)
3. ¿Cuándo terminarás de estudiar español (en seis meses)
4. ¿Cuándo te va a comprar tu papá un coche? (el año que viene)
5. ¿Cuándo va a saber tu hermana usar la computadora de tu mamá? (en una semana)
6. ¿Cuándo vas a comprar tu propia computadora? (en tres meses)
7. ¿Cuándo van Uds. a visitar a su familia en México? (en Navidad)
8. ¿Cuándo vas a encontrar un trabajo para el verano? (en mayo)
9. ¿Cuándo irán tus padres a visitar a los abuelos? (para semana santa)
10. ¿Cuándo vas a salir con la chica que conociste en tu clase? (el viernes)
11. ¿Cuándo vas a dejar de usar jeans y empezar a usar trajes? (en el año 2024)
12. ¿Cuándo vas a darles una fiesta de sorpresa a tus padres? (en agosto)
13. ¿Cuándo vas a decidir si haces un postgrado o no? (en unos cinco años)
14. ¿Cuándo te vas a casar? (en diez años)
15. ¿Cuándo comprará tu hermana una casa? (cuando tenga hijos)

A-6 La marcha del tiempo. You are a career counselor at a university or college. You want to make sure the student you are counseling will have everthing done on time. Ask about his/her future plans and activities. Use the cues provided.

MODELO: terminar la tarea antes de las cinco
¿Habrás terminado la tarea antes de las cinco?

1. escribir la composición de inglés para la semana que viene
2. leer la bibliografía antes de comenzar el segundo semestre
3. llevarle el examen de historia al profesor Curtis a eso de las tres de la tarde
4. completar el requisito de español en dos años
5. comprar un diccionario digital para la computadora
6. escuchar la cinta de español en el laboratorio para este fin de semana
7. terminar el requisito de ciencias en tres años
8. hacer el servicio a la comunidad en cuatro años
9. devolver todos los libros a la biblioteca antes del final del semestre
10. tomar una clase de matemáticas para el tercer semestre
11. asistir a por lo menos tres conferencias para el semestre que viene
12. hablar con el profesor de biología para el martes

A-7 Paco. Paco tends to forget his responsibilities and his mother is always worried about him. Write down the questions she is asking herself. Use the clues provided.

MODELO: haber/despertarse/a tiempo
¿Se habrá despertado a tiempo?

1. haber/olvidar/su suéter nuevo
2. haber/arreglar/su cuarto
3. haber/acostar/demasiado tarde
4. haber/desayunar/cereal

5. haber/estudiar/para el examen
6. haber/poner/la mesa
7. haber/dejar/su bicicleta en el jardín
8. haber/cepillarse/los dientes

3. The Conditional Tense

Form the conditional tense in Spanish by adding the imperfect endings for **-er** and **-ir** verbs to the infinitive. The same endings are used for **-ar, -er** and **-ir** verbs.

	TOMAR	COMER	VIVIR
yo	tomaría	comería	viviría
tú	tomarías	comerías	vivirías
Ud./él/ella	tomaría	comería	viviría
nosotros(as)	tomaríamos	comeríamos	viviríamos
vosotros(as)	tomarías	comeríais	viviríamos
Uds./ellos/ellas	tomarían	comerían	vivirían

- Use the conditional to state what you **would** do in some future situation.

¿Qué te **gustaría** comer?	*What would you like to eat?*
Yo **comería** la paella, pero no me gustan los camarones.	*I would eat the paella, but I don't like shrimp.*
¿Me **ayudarías** a prepararla?	***Would you help** me prepare it?*

- The conditional has the same irregular stems as the future.

decir	**dir-**	diría, dirías,…
hacer	**har-**	haría, harías,…
haber	**habr-**	habría, habrías,…
caber	**cabr-**	cabría, cabrías,…
poder	**podr-**	podría, podrías,…
querer	**querr-**	querría, querrías,…
saber	**sabr-**	sabría, sabrías,…
poner	**pondr-**	pondría, pondrías,…
salir	**saldr-**	saldría, saldrías,…
tener	**tendr-**	tendría, tendrías,…
valer	**valdr-**	valdría, valdrías,…
venir	**vendr-**	vendría, vendrías,…

● Also, use the conditional when the speaker is referring to an event that is future in relation to another past event.

Creíamos que **habría** más comida en la fiesta.	*We thought that **there would be** more food at the party.*
Ellos me dijieron que **vendrías** más tarde.	*They told me that **you would come** later.*
Me aseguraron que **estarían** allí.	*They assured me that **they would be** there.*

● The verb **deber,** when used in the conditional tense, is equivalent to *should.*

Deberías buscar empleo.	*You should look for employment.*
Deberíamos hablar con él.	*We should talk with him.*

◆ Práctica

A-7 Sugerencias. You work at a travel agency that has a suggestion box for employees. Offer several suggestions using cues from the list below.

MODELO: darles a los empleados un mes de vacaciones
          Yo les daría a los empleados un mes de vacaciones.

aumentarles el salario a los empleados más responsables
ofrecerles a todos un plan de retiro (*retirement*)
sorprender a los buenos empleados con una promoción
pagarles el seguro médico a los empleados
pedirles tres recomendaciones a los empleados nuevos
poner a los empleados viejos a entrenar a los nuevos
contratar a alguien que hable español y francés
darle cursos de computadoras a todo el personal
comprar más computadoras para la oficina central
enviar al mejor empleado o empleada en un viaje a un lugar muy bonito

A-8 Un empleado responsable. Write sentences explaining what a responsible employee in a restaurant would and wouldn't do.

MODELO: hablar todo el tiempo con los otros empleados
          No hablaría todo el tiempo con los otros empleados.

1. llegar generalmente tarde al restaurante
2. ayudar a los empleados que están ocupados
3. traer el postre antes de la ensalada
4. pasar la cuenta antes de servirles la comida
5. recibir llamadas personales por teléfono
6. atender bien a los clientes
7. ser antipático(a) con los clientes
8. poner bien las mesas
9. poner cubiertos extra
10. leerles el menú del día a los clientes

A-9 Situaciones. Write sentences explaining what you would do in these places.

MODELO: en la playa
          Me bañaría en el mar.

1. en el cine
2. en el restaurante
3. en el centro comercial
4. en la piscina de la universidad
5. en el Museo del Prado
6. en la agencia de trabajo
7. en el gimnasio
8. en la agencia de viajes
9. en la biblioteca
10. en la discoteca
11. en la galería de arte
12. en la librería
13. en el laboratorio de lenguas
14. en la agencia de viajes
15. en la clínica de salud
16. en el estadio

A-10 ¿Qué harías? Now write sentences explaining what you would do in these situations.

1. Has conseguido un trabajo fantástico.
2. Te ha ido muy mal en un examen.
3. Un(a) chico(a) muy guapo(a) te ha invitado a salir.
4. Te has ganado un millón de dólares en la lotería.
5. El jefe tuyo no te ha aumentado el salario.
6. Tu mejor amigo(a) se ha enamorado de tu novio(a).
7. El el último día de clases y mañana sales de vacaciones.
8. Tienes un examen final de español mañana.
9. Tienes un dolor de cabeza y te sientes muy mal.
10. Has sacado una excelente nota en tu examen de informática.
11. Tus padres te han regalado un coche nuevo.
12. En el banco te informan que no tienes dinero en tu cuenta corriente.
13. Tienes mucha hambre, pero no tienes mucho dinero.
14. Quieres hacer un viaje por España pero no quieres ir solo(a).
15. Llegas a un hotel muy caro y no te gusta tu cuarto.

4. The Conditional Perfect

● Form the conditional perfect with the conditional of the auxilliary verb **haber** + *participle*.

	CONDICIONAL	PAST PARTICIPLE
yo	habría	
tú	habrías	
Ud./él/ella	habría	tomado
nosotros(as)	habríamos	comido
vosotros(as)	habríais	vivido
Uds./ellos/ellas	habrían	

● Use the conditional perfect to express an action that would or should have occurred, but did not.

Habría ido al baile, pero me enfermé.

I would have gone to the dance, but I got sick.

Habríamos estudiado más para el examen, pero no pudimos.

We would have studied more for the exam, but we weren't able to.

● Use the conditional perfect to express probability or conjecture in the past perfect.

¿**Habrían hablado** con ella?   *I wonder if they had talked with her.*
¿Me **habría visto?**   *I wonder if he had seen me.*

◆ Práctica

A-11 ¿Qué habría pasado? Óscar is telling Rául all about the problems that his wife María Antonieta had during a job interview today. Complete the dialog using the appropriate form of the conditional perfect of the verbs in parentheses.

RAÚL: ¿Llegó María Antonieta a tiempo a la entrevista?

ÓSCAR: (llegar) _____, pero hubo un accident de tráfico y llegó increíblemente tarde.

RAÚL: ¿Entonces no le hicieron la entrevista?

ÓSCAR: Sí, sí se la hicieron, pero de llegar temprano le (dar) _____ más tiempo, estoy seguro. También ella (ver) _____ al director del departamento.

RAÚL: ¿Cómo, no estuvo presente el director en la entrevista?

ÓSCAR: No. (Estar) _____ pero su mamá se enfermó y tuvo que ir al hospital.

RAÚL: ¡Qué lástima! Si no, ¿crees tú que le (ofrecer) _____ el trabajo?

ÓSCAR: Sí la (escoger) _____ porque estaban muy contentos con ella, pero tiene que volver a otra entrevista con el gerente.

RAÚL: María (estar) _____ muy molesta, me imagino.

ÓSCAR: En otra circumstancia (ponerse) _____ furiosa, pero como prácticamente le dieron el trabajo, está contenta.

RAÚL: Y tú (sentirse) _____ muy nervioso esperando la llamada, ¿no?

ÓSCAR: No lo niego. (sentirse) _____ mejor de saber que ya tenía el trabajo.

RAÚL: Pues sí, todo (ser) _____ más fácil, pero tampoco salió mal, no crees?

A-12 ¿Qué habrías hecho? You were planning a trip to Buenos Aires, but unfortunately, you broke a leg skiing. Write sentences explaining what you would have done if you hadn't had the accident. Use the clues provided.

MODELO: comer churrasco con salsa chimichurri
            Habría comido churrasco con salsa chimichurri.

1. llamar a una agencia de viajes especializada en América Latina
2. comprar un boleto de ida y vuelta pasando por Brasil
3. reservar un asiento de primera clase
4. pedir la sección de no fumar
5. quedarse en un hotel sencillo y barato
6. comer todos los días en un restaurante diferente
7. ir a escuchar tangos
8. comprar discos compactos de Mercedes Sosa y Astor Piazzola
9. ir a un concierto a escuchar a Charlie García y su "nuevo rock"
10. visitar los monumentos principales
11. encontrarse con un amigo muy querido que vive en Buenos Aires
12. enviar muchas tarjetas postales
13. leer sobre Evita Perón
14. oír los testimonios de las madres de la Plaza del 5 de mayo
15. volar en avión a Tucumán para visitar a otra amiga
16. ver muchas películas argentinas para conocer la cultura popular
17. ir de compras a los fabulosos centros comerciales de Buenos Aires
18. ir a la playa a nadar

A-13 Todo habría sido diferente. To express what you might have done under certain conditions, write complete sentences by matching items in the left-hand column with items in the column to the right. Be sure to conjugate the verbs. There are several possible combinations.

1. con un millón de dólares
2. con otro(a) profesor(a) de español
3. conociendo mejor la computadora
4. con más preparación en informática
5. con más ejercicio físico
6. con más tiempo
7. con más conocimiento de los deportes
8. teniendo un(a) novio(a)

a. dormir mejor
b. interesarse más en los partidos de fútbol
c. divertirse más este año
d. conseguir un puesto importante
e. tener con quien salir siempre
f. escribir mis trabajos en la computadora
g. sentirse mejor
h. gustar más la clase
i. salir mejor en los exámenes
j. asistir a esta universidad
k. viajar por el mundo
l. ...(original)

5. The Present Perfect Subjunctive

● Form the present perfect subjunctive with the present subjunctive of the auxiliary verb **haber** + *past participle*.

	PRESENT SUBJUNCTIVE	PAST PARTICIPLE
yo	**haya**	
tú	**hayas**	
Ud./él/ella	**haya**	**tomado**
nosotros(as)	**hayamos**	**comido**
vosotros(as)	**hayáis**	**vivido**
Uds./ellos/ellas	**hayan**	

● Use the present perfect subjunctive when the conditions for using the subjunctive are met and the speaker is referring to a completed event that has some bearing on the present. Generally, the verb in the main clause is in the present tense.

Dudamos que **hayan comprado** una computadora.

*We doubt that **they have bought** a computer.*

No creo que Anita **haya estudiado** para el examen.

*I don't believe that Anita **has studied** for the test.*

Espero que Pepe **se haya comunicado** por fax con Rodrigo.

*I hope that Pepe **has communicated** with Rodrigo by fax.*

◆ Práctica

A-14 El sábado por la noche. You and your roommate have invited some friends to watch a movie on your VCR. You're both wondering whether you've done everything necessary to prepare for the evening. Form sentences eith the present perfect subjunctive, using the cues provided.

1. Pepe/no creer/Luisa/invitar/Mari Carmen
2. nosotros/no pensar/Ramiro/conseguir/película
3. Marcos/no estar seguro de/tú/venir a ver/video
4. Alfonso y Adolfo/esperar/Germán/traer/refrescos
5. Juana y Eloísa/dudar/Pedro/preparar/sándwiches
6. Aida y Marisa/no creer/Pablo/arreglar/videograbadora
7. yo/esperar/Manuel/limpiar/apartamento
8. no es seguro/Rolando/prestarnos/su guitarra
9. tú/desear/Damaris/comprar/los pasteles/¿no?
10. nosotros/dudar/Alejandro/llamar a/Laura
11. es probable/Celina/preparar/una torta
12. todos nosotros/desear/invitados/recibir la invitación

A-15 Reacciones. You are the manager of a small office who has been away for several days. Your assistant reports to you what happened while you were gone. React positively or negatively to the statements, according to the cues.

MODELO: Ayer instalamos todos los programas en la computadora. (Es bueno)
          Es bueno que hayan instalado todos los programas en la computadora.

1. Ayer pagamos todas las cuentas de la oficina. (Es fabuloso)
2. La secretaria no escribió a máquina las cartas. (Es malo)
3. Esta mañana enviamos un fax a los vendedores. (Es bueno)
4. Ayer se rompió la fotocopiadora de la oficina. (Es un desastre)
5. Yo terminé el informe sobre el nuevo proyecto. (Es fantástico)
6. Esta mañana instalamos la base de datos en la computadora. (Es maravilloso)
7. El martes compré unos teléfonos portátiles *(portable)*. (Es bueno)
8. La nueva asistente ya aprendió a usar la computadora. (Es mejor)
9. Me dieron una silla nueva a mí. (Me alegro)
10. Laló no pudo abrir la cuenta en marcos alemanes. (Es un desastre)

A-16 Patricia y Armando. Patricia and Armando won the lottery recently. They bought a house and now they're buying new furniture and appliances. Their family is talking about some of the problems and successes they've had. Complete the sentences with the correct present perfect subjunctive forms.

MODELO: Me alegro que Patricia y Armando (comprar) _____ la casa.
Me alegro de que Patricia y Armando hayan comprado la casa.

1. Dudo que ellos (conseguir) _____ ese modelo de sofá para la sala. Solo quedaba uno.
2. No creo que el escritorio de madera (costar) _____ tanto como el de metal.
3. Lamento que el almacén no (tener) _____ la mecedora de cuero que Patricia quería.
4. Temo que ellos no (poder) _____ comprar el congelador a tiempo para la fiesta de celebración. Usarán has heladeras para poner el hielo y las cervezas.
5. Ojalá que a Patricia le (gustar) _____ el teléfono celular que le dio su papá.
6. El Almacén Sol siente que los empleados no (instalar) _____ el lavaplatos bien. Van a enviar al técnico mañana.
7. Es imposible que el refrigerador no (llegar) _____ esta tarde. Nos dijeron que no llegaría hasta mañana.
8. Es probable que el tocacassettes no (funcionar) _____. No estaba bien conectado.
9. Es una lástima que tú no (ir) _____ a ver la casa. ¡Es preciosa!
10. Niegan que el técnico (saber) _____ explicar bien cómo usar la computadora nueva.
11. Me sorprende que ellos (comprar) _____ un sofá tan moderno para la sala.
12. Es increíble que la lámpara (romperse) _____ al llegar a la casa.
13. Es maravilloso que la televisión (resultar) _____ de tan excelente calidad.
14. Es mejor que ellos (poner) _____ el estéreo en la sala familiar.
15. Es extraordinario que la secadora de ropa (usar) _____ tan poca electricidad.

A-17 Los padres preocupados. Rodrigo and Vinicio are two exuberant twins who love to eat, drink, and celebrate life. Their lifestyle worries their chiropractor father and their acupuncturist mother. Complete the dialog by conjugating the verbs in parentheses with the correct present perfect subjunctive forms.

MAMÁ: Me alegro que Rodrigo (dejar) _____ el cigarrillo, pero me preocupa que no (querer) _____ ponerse a dieta. Es posible que (subir) _____ de peso este semestre. Y ya sabes que si no se pone en forma después no ando muy contenta.

PAPÁ: Y tampoco le gusta hacer ejercicios, excepto nadar en el lago en el verano. No creo que (ir) _____ a levantar pesas ni una sola vez al gimnasio.

MAMÁ: No, no es cierto. Sí, ha estado levantando pesas, pero dudo mucho que (correr) _____ o que (jugar) _____ básquetbol. La verdad es que a Rodrigo le encanta comer pizza, helados, carne, cerdo y otras cosas que no debería comer. ¡Y qué muchacho para divertirse cocinando!

PAPÁ: Sí, cocina delicioso. Vinicio en eso es un poco más disciplinado. Es bueno que (meterse) _____ un programa para adelgazar. Me alegra que (perder) _____ peso y que (practicar) _____ el tenis todos los sábados. Y por supuesto, me parece muy bien que (decidir) _____ caminar a la universidad todos los días.

MAMÁ: De acuerdo, Vinicio sabe guardar la línea, pero en cambio, no me gusta que no (aprender) _____ a beber más moderamente, como Rodrigo.

PAPÁ: El problema es que son demasiados populares y los amigos siempre los están llamando. No está bien que (tener) _____ tantas fiestas durante el semestre. Es bueno que ahora (hacerce) _____ amigos de Mario que es más tranquilo y serio. Espero que sea un buen modelo para ellos.

MAMÁ: Sí, me encanta que Mario los (llevar) _____ al centro naturalista y les (presentar) _____ a esas amigas naturalistas. Quizás aprendan a cuidarse.

PAPÁ: Por supuesto que aprenderán. Mario será muy serio y responsable, pero dudo que (divertirse) _____ tanto como Rodrigo y Vinicio. Tal vez ellos sean un buen balance para Mario, y Mario un buen balance para ellos.

6. The Imperfect Subjunctive

● The Spanish imperfect subjunctive has two conjugations: one form has **-ra** endings and the other **-se** endings. The **-ra** form is more common in daily conversation, while the **-se** form is more formal and used primarily in the written language. The same endings are used for **-ar, -er**, and **-ir** verbs.

● Form the imperfect subjunctive of regular and irregular verbs by dropping the **-ron** ending of the third person plural form of the preterite and adding the endings below.

-ra FORM		**-se** FORM	
-ra	-ramos	-se	-semos
-ras	-rais	-ses	-seis
-ra	-ran	-se	-sen

- A written accent is required on the first person plural of both imperfect subjunctive forms.

arregláramos   arreglásemos
contratáramos   contratásemos
pusiéramos   pusiésemos

- The following chart shows the imperfect subjunctive forms of some common regular and irregular verbs.

INFINITIVE	3RD PERSON PLURAL PRETERITE	1ST PERSON SINGULAR IMPERFECT SUBJUNCTIVE
abrazar	abraza**ron**	abrasa**ra, -se**
beber	bebie**ron**	bebie**ra, -se**
caer	caye**ron**	caye**ra, -se**
conducir	conduje**ron**	conduje**ra, -se**
dar	die**ron**	die**ra, se**
decir	dije**ron**	dije**ra, -se**
escribir	escribie**ron**	escribie**ra, -se**
estar	estuvie**ron**	estuvie**ra, -se**
hacer	hicie**ron**	hicie**ra, -se**
ir	fue**ron**	fue**ra, -se**
poder	pudie**ron**	pudie**ra, -se**
poner	pusie**ron**	pusie**ra, -se**
querer	quisie**ron**	quisie**ra, -se**
saber	supie**ron**	supie**ra, se**
ser	fue**ron**	fue**ra, -se**
tener	tuvie**ron**	tuvie**ra, -se**
traer	traje**ron**	traje**ra, -se**
venir	vinie**ron**	vinie**ra, -se**

- Use the imperfect subjunctive to refer to events that were incomplete and that there was no certainty of completing in the past.

Dudaba que Ángela **fuera** a la reunión. *I doubted that Angela was going to the meeting.*

Ella **quería** que el gobierno **controlara** la contaminación. *She wanted the government to control pollution.*

- Use the imperfect subjunctive to make polite requests or statements. In such instances the forms of the verbs **querer, poder,** and **deber** are used.

Quisiera pedir una sopa de pollo, por favor. *I would like to order some chicken soup, please.*

¿Pudiera prestarme un poco de dinero, Paco? *Could you lend me some money, Paco?*

Debiéramos salir temprano. *We should leave early.*

- With ¡ojalá!, it means *I wish...*

¡Ojalá ganara la lotería! *I wish I could win the lottery.*

◆ Práctica

A-18 ¡A practicar! Practice the Spanish imperfect subjunctive forms of the following verbs.

1. tú/caminar, beber, salir, abrir, gustar, vender, freír
2. usted/contaminar, vivir, dormirse, entender, hervir, alegrarse
3. él/conservar, resolver, estar, pensar, tostar, probar, dormir
4. nosotros/proteger, consumir, sentarse, almorzar, explicar, seguir
5. ellas/aprender, aceptar, vestirse, repetir, atender, pedir, afeitarse, acostarse
6. yo/nadar, escribir, sentirse, volver, recordar, ver, oír

A-19 La conferencia. An environmental expert gave a talk to your class about how to protect the environment better. Summarize his suggestions by changing the infinitives to the imperfect subjunctive.

MODELO: El señor quería que…
         …yo reunirme con Uds. para explicarles sus ideas →
         El señor quería que yo me reuniera con ustedes para explicarles sus ideas.

1. …nosotros consumir menos energía
2. …la clase empezar un programa de reciclaje
3. …todos los estudiantes proteger el medio ambiente
4. …los científicos resolver el problema de la contaminación del aire.
5. …nadie echar basura en el parque
6. …la ciudad empezar un programa de repoblación forestal
7. …el senado de la universidad escribir una carta a nuestro representante
8. …la población ser más consciente de nuestros recursos naturales
9. …el gobierno llevar a cabo un programa de educación en todos los medios de comunicación
10. …los estudiantes elegir candidatos verdes
11. …nosotros fundar una organización para conseguir información
12. …nosotros prevenir la deforestación del bosque

A-20 La mesa redonda. Report what happened at a round table conference on the environment. Complete the statements with the correct form of the verbs in parentheses.

1. José Antonio dudaba que nosotros (poder) _____ buscar otras fuentes de energía.
2. Adela temía que el gobierno (poner) _____ más plantas nucleares.
3. Pilar quería que los represantantes (pasar) _____ leyes más fuertes.
4. Juan y yo no creíamos que el problema de la lluvia ácida (ser) _____ tan serio.
5. Un profesor lamentaba que (haber) _____ tanto tráfico en las ciudades.
6. Ana y Joaquín sentían que sus hijos no (saber) _____ nada sobre la contaminación.
7. Yo esperaba que nosotros (hacer) _____ más para proteger el ambiente.
8. Todos insistieron en que nosotros (comenzar) _____ un programa de reciclaje.
9. Nos pidieron que (votar) _____ por candidatos pro medio ambiente.
10. Una profesora aconsejó que (fundar) _____ una asociación de estudiantes para proteger el medio ambiente.

A-22 Cuando era niño(a). Answer the following questions about your childhood. Use the imperfect subjunctive in your answers.

1. ¿Qué querían tus padres que hicieras en la casa?
2. ¿Qué te prohibían que vieras?
3. ¿Qué te sugerían que hicieras en la escuela?
4. ¿Cómo deseaban tus padres que comieras?
5. ¿Qué profesión esperaban tus padres que estudiaras?
6. ¿Qué te pedían tus maestros que hicieras?
7. ¿Qué deportes querían tus amigos que practicaras?
8. ¿Qué música no les gustaba a tus padres que oyeras?

A-23 Si el mundo fuera perfecto. Express what you and other people would like to happen if we lived in a perfect world. Follow the model.

MODELO: reciclar siempre/ojalá
                  Ojalá siempre reciclara.

1. tener un coche que no gaste mucha gasolina/ojalá que
2. caminar o tomar el autobús siempre/sería bueno que todo el mundo
3. yo buscar un trabajo en una industria que no contamine/mis padres quisieran
4. tú y yo vivir en un lugar que no tuviera mucha contaminación/sería maravilloso
5. hacer todo lo posible para proteger el medio ambiente/nos gustaría que el(la) presidente
6. conservar la energía/ojalá que todos Uds.
7. trabajar por la protección del medio ambiente/sería excelente que todos
8. gastar menos agua cuando se bañan/sería mejor que ellos
9. usar pocos productos químicos/ojalá que la sociedad
10. no ser peligroso asolearse/sería fantástico que
11. haber más casas con energía solar/sería más eficiente que
12. los lagos y mares no estar contaminados/ojalá que
13. poder jugar sin peligro de enfermarsr/como me gustaría que los niños
14. todos los candidatos venir a la conferencia sobre el medio ambiente/me encantaría que
15. la industria, los bancos, el gobierno sentarse con los científicos a resolver los principales problemas del medio ambiente/sería increíble que

7. The Pluperfect Subjunctive

● Form the pluperfect subjunctive with the imperfect subjunctive of the auxiliary verb **haber** + *past participle*.

	IMPERFECT SUBJUNCTIVE	PAST PARTICIPLE
yo	**hubiera**	
tú	**hubieras**	**tomado**
Ud./él/ella	**hubieras**	**comido**
nosotros(as)	**hubiéramos**	**vivido**
vosotros(as)	**hubieraís**	
Uds./ellos/ellas	**hubieran**	

● Use the pluperfect subjunctive in dependent clauses, under the same conditions as the present perfect subjunctive, to refer to events that occurred prior to another past event.

Él **esperaba** que **hubiéramos protegido** más el medio ambiente.

*He **hoped** that **we had protected** the environment more.*

Sentíamos que la niña **se hubiera enfermado.**

We felt sorry** that the girl **had gotten sick.

◆ Práctica

A-24 ¿Por qué tenía que pasar esto? Three friends have a problem getting to their dinner appointment. Find out why. Complete the story with the correct form of the pluperfect subjunctive.

El sábado Lucila, Rafael y yo estábamos invitados a comer a casa de Olguita. Chale, mi hijo, nos prestó su carro y cuando íbamos en camino nos quedamos sin gasolina fuera de la ciudad. Era imposible que Chale (olvidarse) _____ de poner gasolina porque es muy responsable. Era más probable que (tener) _____ algún problema con el tanque de gasolina y no (darse) _____ cuenta.

No había teléfono. Esperábamos que Olguita no (empezar) _____ a cocinar porque era obvio que íbamos a llegar muy tarde. Rafa tuvo que caminar al pueblo más cercano, pero mientras esperábamos, pensábamos que era dudoso que Rafa (poder) _____ conseguir un mecánico. Afortunadamente sí consiguió un mecánico, de lo contrario, no sé que (hacer) _____ nosotros. Sin embargo, no había teléfono.

Además habíamos dicho que íbamos a traer vino. Esperábamos que la licorería no (cerrar) _____ porque todavía no teníamos el vino. Si (saber) _____ que esto iba a pasar, yo lo habría comprado antes. Lucila quería comprar un pan español que es excelente pero que se vende muy rápido. Ahí estábamos viendo al mecánico arreglar el tanque de gasolina y deseando que en la panadería no (vender) _____ todo el pan. Finalmente llegamos a casa de Olguita con el vino, pero sin pan.

Temíamos que Olguita (ponerse) _____ furiosa o que (irse) _____ de la casa. Pero no. Ella está esperándonos y estaba preocupada de que nosotros no (acordarse) _____ de la comida. Ninguno de nosotros jamás se hubiera olvidado, pero yo habría pensado lo mismo. Es de esas cosas que pasan y que todo el mundo quisiera que no (pasar) _____ nunca. Habría sido mejor si nosotros (tener) _____ un teléfono celular.

A-25 ¡No es cierto! Lucía is always reading newspapers at the table when the rest of her large family is talking about different things. She gets everything wrong and then she passes it on to other people. Correct Lucía's misunderstanding of each situation using the pluperfect subjunctive.

MODELO: Carlos y Anita salieron a bailar.
          No **era** cierto que Carlos y Anita **hubieran salido** a bailar.

1. Pedro se fue de vacaciones a Valparaíso.
2. Tía Eda se enfermó muy seriamente.
3. Alejandra y Aida sacaron notas muy malas en español.
4. Tía Evangelina perdió su billetera en el Teatro Nacional
5. Eduardo y Jorge Lenín tuvieron una discusión muy animada.
6. Marisa obtuvo un empleo en una fábrica de zapatos.
7. El estudiante que le gusta a Rosalía vino a visitarla.
8. Mario se ganó trescintos dólares en la lotería.
9. Francisco compró una motocicleta.
10. Mis tíos pusieron una tienda nueva en la avenida 8.
11. El doctor se enojó mucho con la abuela.
12. Marlene conversó mucho con la abuela
13. Sandra oyó un ruido extraño en el garage.
14. Julio y Carlos le dieron flores a mamá.
15. Mi hermanito menor se cayó de la bicicleta.

8. The Indicative or Subjunctive in *si* Clauses

Simple *si* Clauses

● A **si** clause states a condition that must be met in order for something to occur. The verb in a simple **si** clause is usually in the present indicative, while the verb in the result clause is in the present or future tense. A conditional **si** clause does not have a fixed position in the sentence; it may appear at the beginning or end of the sentence.

Si **vas** al parque, **iré** contigo.	*If **you go** to the park, **I'll go** with you.*
Si **trabajas** muy fuerte, **vas a ganar** mucho dinero.	*If **you work** very hard, **you'll earn** a lot of money.*
Veremos la película, si **quieres.**	*We'll see the movie, if you want.*

Contrary-to-fact Conditional Clauses

● When a **si** clause contains implausible or contrary-to-fact information, the imperfect subjunctive is used in the **si** clause and the conditional tense is used in the result clause.

Si **tuviera** mucho dinero me **compraría** un Porsche.	*If **I had** a lot of money **I would buy** myself a Porsche.*
Si **fuéramos** a la piscina, la **veríamos.**	*If **we went** to the pool, **we would see** her.*
Sacaría mejores notas, **si estudiaras** conmigo.	*I would get better grades, if you studied with me.*

- When the **si** clause containing contrary-to-fact information describes a past action, the pluperfect subjunctive is used in the **si** clause, while the conditional perfect isused in the main clause.

> Si **hubiera tenido** dinero, **habría comprado** una corbata.
>
> *If **I had had** money, **I would have bought** a tie.*
>
> Si no **hubiéramos gastado** tanta agua, **habríamos tenido** suficiente para lavar la ropa.
>
> *If **we had not wasted** so much water, **we would have had** enough to wash the clothes.*

◆ Práctica

A-26 Los comentarios de Lupe. Even though Lupe has never been in any of the following situations, she has an opinion about everything. Complete her statements with the correct form of the verbs in parentheses.

MODELO: Si tú (votar) _____ por el partido verde, todo (mejorar) _____.
Si tú votaras por el partido verde, todo mejoraría.

1. Si yo (ver) _____ a una persona echando basura en el parque, yo (llamar) _____ a un policía.
2. Si mi hermana (ser) _____ menos materialista, (dedicarse) _____ a combatir la deforestación.
3. Si mi primo Andrés (usar) _____ mucha electridad en su casa, yo le (sugerir) _____ un cambio de estilo de vida.
4. Si mis padres (tener) _____ otra alternativa, no (trabajar) _____ en una planta nuclear.
5. Si los norteamericanos (querer) _____ proteger el medio ambiente, (usar) _____ menos petróleo.
6. Si a nosotros (preocuparse) _____ nuestro planeta, (proteger) _____ más nuestros recursos naturales.

A-27 Ya es muy tarde. An environmentalist is proposing a series of measures to help control pollution in a particular area, but it's already too late. Say what could have been done if he or she had been consulted earlier.

MODELO: Si el presidente acepta un programa de repoblación forestal, no tendrán el problema de la deforestación. →
Si el presidente hubiera aceptado un programa de repoblación forestal, no habrían tenido el problema de la deforestación.

1. Si ahorran electricidad, conservarán energía.
2. Si usan menos los carros, resolverán el problema de la contaminación.
3. Si el gobierno pasa leyes más fuertes, podrán proteger mejor los recursos naturales.
4. Si el gobierno no establece plantas nucleares, no habrá accidentes catastróficos.
5. Si los habitantes practican medidas higiénicas, no existirá el cólera.
6. Si el presidente desea cambiar la situación, podrá mejorar el medio ambiente.
7. Si venden menos químicos, los lagos estarán más limpios.
8. Si no cortan tantos árboles *(trees)* la deforestación no será tan seria.

A-28 Si yo fuera... Say what you would do in the following situations.

MODELO: Si yo fuera el profesor...
           Si yo fuera el profesor, daría menos exámenes.

1. Si yo me ganara la lotería...
2. Si tuviera un Mercedes Benz...
3. Si mi novio(a) saliera con otra(o)...
4. Si aprendiera bien el español...
5. Si fuera famoso(a)...
6. Si viviera al lado del mar...
7. Si estuviera en España...
8. Si pudiera graduarme este año...
9. Si mi carro se dañara...
10. Si mis padres no me dieran dinero para mis estudios...
11. Si quisiera salir con un(a) chico(a) que no conozco...
12. Si viera a mi mejor amigo(a) usando drogas...
13. Si tuviera mucho tiempo libre...
14. Si me graduara hoy de la universidad...
15. Si tuviera un fax...
16. Si comprara un teléfono celular...
17. Si supiera informática...
18. Si (no) tuviera dos hijos(as)...
19 Si no conociera a los compañeros de clase...
20. Si naciera en México...

A-29 ¿Qué hubieras hecho? Write sentences explaining what you would have done in the following situations.

MODELO: Si hubieras estado en el banco cuando fue asaltado.
           Habría llamado a la policía y una ambulancia.

1. si hubieras estado en el World Trade Center cuando los terroristas pusieron la bomba
2. si hubieras estado en Chernobyl cuando hubo un accidente nuclear
3. si hubieras estado en la Florida cuando llegó el huracán Andrés
4. si hubieras tenido una pierna rota un día antes de participar en un maratón
5. si tu mejor amigo(a) hubiera tratado de suicidarse
6. si tú y tus amigos hubieran tenido un accidente de carro y no hubiera habido teléfono para pedir ayuda
7. si no hubiera podido estudiar porque tenías que ayudar a tus padres en su tienda
8. si hubieras tenido una gran facilidad para tocar la guitarra
9. si tus padres te hubieran enseñado a bailar muy bien de niño(a)
10. si (no) hubieras tenido hermanos

APPENDIX 1
Translations of *¡Así es la vida!*

PRIMERA PARTE

Conversation 1

Hi! What's your name?
Hi! My name is José Delgado.
It's a pleasure to meet you. I'm Elena Sánchez.
The pleasure is mine.

Conversation 2

Hello. What's your name? (formal)
My name is Miranda Pérez.
It's a pleasure to meet you. I'm Professor Hoyos.
Delighted.

Conversation 3
Good morning, Luisa. What's up? How are you?
Fine, Carlos, and you?
So-so.

Conversation 4

Good evening, Mrs. González. How are you doing?
Pretty well, José Manuel. How are you?
Not very well.
Really? I'm sorry, José Manuel.

Conversation 5

See you tomorrow, Pepe.
Good-bye, Pedro.

LECCIÓN 1

PRIMERA PARTE

Who am I?

Hi! My name is Antonio Pacheco. These are my friends.

Her name is Isabel Madrid Davis. She's Argentinian. She is intelligent and very hardworking. She's also very nice. Where are you from?

His name is Leví Gómez Mansur. He's from Madrid, the capital of Spain. He's tall and thin. What are you like?

Where are you from?

PACO: Where are you from, María?
MARÍA: I'm from Miami, but my parents are from Cuba. And you, where are you from?
PACO: I'm from Puerto Rico.
CARLOS: Are you Colombians?
LUPE: No, we are Venezuelan.
CARLOS: Really? I'm also from Venezuela.
LUPE: Is that right? What city do you come from?
CARLOS: From Maracaibo.
LUPE: Gee! So are we!
CARLOS: What a small world!

SEGUNDA PARTE

What do you do?

Andrea Alvarado Salinas
28 years old, Santiago de Chile
I speak Spanish and Italian, and I'm studying medicine at the University of Chile. Today I have to study a lot because I have a biology exam tomorrow.

Marco Aurelio Mora Arce
22 Years old, San José, Costa Rica
I speak Spanish and a little English. I am studying law at the National University and in the evenings I work in a bookstore. Today I have to play soccer with my friends.

Rosalía Bermúdez Fiallo
19 years old, Santo Domingo, República Dominicana
I am studying engineering. Tonight my friends and I are going to go dancing in a discotheque. We don't have classes tomorrow.

LECCIÓN 2

PRIMERA PARTE

What subjects are you going to take?

ALBERTO: Hey, Luis! Do you have your class schedule?

LUIS: Yes. And you? What subjects are you going to take?

ALBERTO: My schedule is fairly tough (rather complicated). I'm going to take five subjects: Algebra, Chemistry, History, and Computer Science.

LUIS: You're crazy! I'm only going to take four subjects this semester...

ALBERTO: Are you going to take Professor Smith's English class?

LUIS: No way, man! He's a very difficult professor.

What time is it?

MELISA: Carmen, what time is it?

CARMEN: It's nine o'clock sharp.

MELISA: Really? It's already nine?

CARMEN: Yes, look at the clock.

MELISA: I'm leaving right now. My biology class is in five minutes!

CARMEN: On Tuesdays I don't have classes in the morning.

Where are you going?

ANA: Hi, Roberto! How are you?

ROBERTO: Very well, Ana! And you? Where are you going?

ANA: I'm going to the Foreign Language department. I have French (class) at quarter after ten.

ROBERTO: But, you're going to take languages?

ANA: Of course, Roberto. In today's world, it's necessary to learn languages.

SEGUNDA PARTE

Where is the bookstore?

It's eleven thirty in the morning. Eda and Dora are chatting in a café near the university while eating a sandwich and drinking a soda.

EDA: What are you going to do after lunch?

DORA: I have to go to the bookstore to buy an English-Spanish dictionary. I need to write a composition for tomorrow.

EDA: And where is the bookstore? I also have to go tomorrow.

DORA: It's behind the library. Why don't we go together now?

EDA: No thanks, Dora. I have to go to the university health center.

DORA: I am going to the Med School that is next door. Let's go together!

EDA: Oh, great! Let's go!

LECCIÓN 3

PRIMERA PARTE

A letter

José Joaquin Jiménez receives a letter from his young, Mexican friend Marilú Fuentes. She studies at the university with him and she's telling him about her family with whom she is spending a few days.

Dear José Joaquin:

Here I am with my family in Guadalajara. It's really fabulous to be able to be with them and to rest.

My family and I are very close. My father is a dentist and my mother works as a teacher at a high school. My oldest sister is named Carmen and she is a lawyer. Ernesto is younger than I am and goes to school. Finally, there is the youngest one, my little sister Lucía, who is very nice and as beautiful as my mother.

My grandparents, on my father's side, live with us and my aunt Julia and Uncle Evelio live close by. They have an only child, my cousin Pedrito, who is as mischievous as my brother Ernesto and is as big a nuisance. They are now playing and are making a lot of noise. Thank God that I am finishing this letter.

I will return to the university next Sunday. When are you coming back? I hope to see you soon.

Love,
Marilú

SEGUNDA PARTE

Among friends

LAURA: Hello?

RAÚL: Yes, I'd like to speak with Laura, please.

LAURA: This is Laura speaking.

RAÚL: Laura, it's Raúl. How are you?

LAURA: Very well. What a surprise!

RAÚL: Well, I'm going to walk around town. Do you want to come along?

LAURA: I'd rather go to a café.

RAÚL: That's OK and afterwards at the Rialto Theater, they are showing one of your favorite movies, "Tears of love."

LAURA: Yeah! Well, let's go. What time is the show?

RAÚL: It's at seven.

LAURA: Alright. We'll go to the movies.

At a party

1. Do you want to dance, my darling?
   No, dear. There's my boyfriend.
2. That guy is very handsome, isn't he?
   Yes, but he doesn't know how to dance very well.
3. You look so beautiful tonight!
   Thank you, you are also very handsome.
4. The truth is that the party is not a lot of fun. Do you want to go to a café or go for a ride?
   Yes, the party is a bit boring.

LECCIÓN 4

PRIMERA PARTE

The weekend

Scene 1

Karen Banks, Ricardo Rubio, Linnette Ortiz and Scott Breslow study at the University of Puerto Rico. It's Saturday morning.

RICARDO: Hey, Karen, why don't we go to the basketball game?

KAREN: I don't know. It's nice out today and I don't want to be inside a gym.

RICARDO: You're right. How about if we go to the international festival?

KAREN: Good idea! But, look, there's Scott and Linnette. Let's go see what they are thinking of doing.

Scene 2

KAREN: Hi, what's new? What are you planning to do today?

LINNETTE: Well, today is a perfect day for going to the beach. It's sunny and very hot. Why don't we go to Luquillo to swim (in the ocean) and afterwards we'll have a picnic?

RICARDO: Great! (Stupendous)

SCOTT: I'll make sandwiches.

LINNETTE: No, it's better if I make them.

SCOTT: Then I'll buy the drinks.

KAREN: And who will bring the umbrella?

RICARDO: I'll bring it.

Scene 3

Upon arriving at the beach

KAREN: Let's go in...

SCOTT: It's (ideal) a great day to swim.

LINNETTE: Listen, Scott, where is the beach bag with our bathing suits? I don't see it in the trunk.

SCOTT: What luck. We're not going to be able to swim.

LINNETTE: But we can play (sing with) the guitar.

SEGUNDA PARTE

Sports

María Silvia Wierna (Argentinian)

I love sports. In the summer when it's hot, I play tennis and cycle and swim. In the winter when it's cold, I like to ski in Bariloche. My favorite sports figure is the tennis player Gabriela Sabatini.

Julio Prenat Anzola (Uruguayan)

I am a soccer coach. I teach my players to be aggressive and disciplined. Because of this, they almost always play well.

Norberto Vázquez Guerra (Dominican)

I play volleyball, basketball and baseball, but the sport I like the most is baseball. I am the left fielder on the university's team. I'm not a star but I usually hit the ball rather well. The Dominican baseball season is from November to January.

Albertina Morales Rulfo (Mexican)

There are sports that I like a lot, and there are others that I don't. I love tennis because it's a very fast sport, but I don't like golf because I find it slow and very boring. I don't like boxing because it's violent and, although I don't understand football, I find it exciting.

LECCIÓN 5

PRIMERA PARTE

Enjoy your meal!

Scene 1

MARTA: I'm dying of hunger, Arturo. ¿Why don't we go and have lunch?

ARTURO: Fine. Let's go to this restaurant. They serve delicious hamburgers with french fries.

MARTA: No I don't like hamburgers. It's better if we go to the restaurant Don Pepe. There they serve local dishes.

Scene 2

ARTURO: Waiter, bring us the menu, please.

WAITER: I'll bring it to you right away. In the meantime, do you want something to drink?

MARTA: Yes. Bring me a glass of wine, please.

ARTURO: And I would like a Coca-Cola, please.

Scene 3

MARTA: Could you tell me what the specialty of the house is?

WAITER: Gladly. The chef's specialty is grilled shrimp.

MARTA: Grilled?

WAITER: Yes, ma'am. They're really exquisite. Do you want to try them?

MARTA: No. I'll have sirloin steak and a salad.

ARTURO: But I will order the shrimp.

Scene 4

MARTA: What are you going to have (ask for) for dessert?

ARTURO: I don't like to eat dessert at lunch, but I want a café con leche.

MARTA: I love desserts. I want the flan and a black coffee.

SEGUNDA PARTE

Chicken and rice

My aunt is a fabulous cook. There isn't a more popular dish in the Caribbean region. I asked her – Aunt Julia – how did you prepare the chicken and rice and here's how she replied.

• First, I cut the chicken into small pieces and then placed it in a container. I added lemon juice and some chopped garlic to it.

• Then I heated up a little olive oil in a casserole pot, added the chicken pieces, and let them fry at medium heat. I added an onion and a green pepper, well-chopped. I let all this simmer for about five minutes.

• Then I added one cup of tomato sauce, one tablespoon of salt, a pinch of pepper and azafrán, half of a cup of white wine, and two cups of chicken broth. I let it simmer for another five minutes.

• Finally, I added two cups of white rice to the casserole pot. I mixed everything well and when it boiled again, I covered the pot and let it cook at low heat for about twenty-five minutes.

The chicken and rice dish was delicious!

LECCIÓN 6

PRIMERA PARTE

Shopping

VILMA: Yesterday, Victoria, Manuel, and I went shopping.

PITI: Oh, really? Where did you go?

VILMA: Well, before leaving, Victoria turned on the television set and saw all the daily sales in the shops and stores of Lima. We then decided to go to the shopping center.

PITI: And did you spend much time there?

VILMA: We walked here and there for more than four hours. Manuel bought a lot of shirts, pants, socks, and a pair of shoes.

PITI: And what did you buy?

VILMA: For myself I could not couldn't find anything, but I bought some interesting leather items for aunt Zoila, a wallet and a belt, for her birthday.

PITI: And did you all go out for the evening?

VILMA: Impossible! We got back home very tired. Victoria slept for three hours before dinner. Mom didn't say anything but asked us to be quiet. I didn't sleep but had to rest. Shopping was very nice but very tiring.

At Wong's Department Store

In the summer, my family always went to Wong's Department Store because they offered many bargains, and we could pay with a credit card or a bank check. If you asked them, they gave good discounts. They had cotton shirts, silk ties, jackets and leather handbags at a discount of 30% or more. Mom bought us many school clothes. They were cheap, but of good quality. And, whenever there was a clearance sale, we left home early, shopped, and went out to eat afterwards. We always saved a lot at Wong's Department Store.

SEGUNDA PARTE

What did you buy?

Andrina is now back home and is chatting about her purchases with her brother Armando, when the phone rings.

ANDRINA: Hello?

VIVIANA: Hello, Andrina. It's Viviana. How are you?

ANDRINA: Fine. What's up, Viviana?

VIVIANA: Listen, I called you at home three times and you weren't there. Nobody answered. Where did you go?

ANDRINA: I went shopping at La Gran Vía. Generally, I go there when I have something special to buy.

VIVIANA: Oh, really? And did you have something special to buy?

ANDRINA: Yes, it's Gustavo's birthday. But, first, I bought those jeans that were in style last summer. Remember? They fit me perfectly. Then, I went to the jewelry store and bought a silver key ring for Gustavo. Finally, I went to the pharmacy and bought a bottle of cologne for dad and a bottle of perfume for mom.

VIVIANA: You spent a lot, right?

ANDRINA: Well, it wasn't cheap, but the good thing is that I didn't have to pay cash. I used my dad's credit card.

VIVIANA: But, Andrina!

ANDRINA: Well, it's not a big deal. Next month I'll pay him back.

ARMANDO: You always say the same thing but you never do it. Poor dad!

LECCIÓN 7

PRIMERA PARTE

Personal routines

Antonio, Beatriz, and Enrique Castillo are three siblings who live in Barquisimeto, Venezuela. Here are their morning routines.

Antonio is an early riser. He always wakes up at six in the morning. After getting up, he brushes his teeth, showers, and dries himself with a towel. Later, he makes breakfast for his mom, which makes her very happy.

Beatriz is also an early riser, but since she didn't sleep well last night, she didn't wake up early today. When she got up this morning, she washed her face, got dressed quickly, and left the house without putting on her make-up. She became very nervous when she arrived at the university because she was late.

Enrique never wakes up when the alarm clock goes off. He likes to sleep during the morning because at night he always goes to bed very late. After getting up, he shaves, puts on shaving lotion, combs his hair, and looks at himself in the mirror. He often arrives late to work and his boss becomes angry with him.

SEGUNDA PARTE

The real estate agent

AGENT: I went by the house of Mr. Dalí. It is fabulous! I think it will interest you.

CLIENT: Oh, really? Tell me, when can I go to see it?

AGENT: Tomorrow, if you like. Go and see it because it is ideal for you. The upstairs has three large bedrooms and two complete bathrooms. The living room is downstairs, below the main bedroom. It is huge and has a porch. Tomorrow, make sure you don't leave before going out to the garden. It is marvelous!

CLIENT: I am interested. Tell me more.

AGENT: Well, the dining room is not too big, but you could place a China cabinet against the large wall and a table for eight to ten people. The kitchen, however, is very large and is next to the garage. The garage is a double garage for two cars. Oh, I forgot, downstairs, between the kitchen and the dining room, there is a half bathroom. There is also a pantry large enough to store food, a vacuum cleaner, and a broom. What it doesn't have is a laundry room, but since the kitchen is big, you could place the washer and drier there.

CLIENT: Well, there is nothing else to talk about. Make an appointment for me for the morning. Does that seem good to you?

The household chores of María Isabel

María Isabel is a hard-working girl. She gets up at six o'clock in the morning. She brushes her teeth, showers, and does her household chores. She makes her bed and straightens up her room. Right away, she does the vacuuming, and irons the clothes she is going to wear. When she's done, she prepares herself a good breakfast. At eight o'clock she leaves the house, gets in her car, and goes to the Castillo and Peralta real estate agency. There, she works as an assistant to the real estate agents from nine o'clock in the morning to five o'clock in the afternoon. She loves the beautiful houses and dreams of some day owning one. At night, if she doesn't go out with friends, she goes back to her house, prepares supper, sets the table, and sits down to eat in front of the television in the dining room. After supper, she dusts the sofa, sweeps the kitchen floor, and takes out the garbage, if there is any to take out. Finally, she lies down to read mystery novels.

LECCIÓN 8

PRIMERA PARTE

A honeymoon trip

Armando Perera and Grisel Esteban are two young Cuban-Americans from Miami who are going to get married soon. They are in the office of Rosario Díaz, a friend of Grisel who works at a travel agency.

ROSARIO: Hello, how are you? What do the soon-to-be newlyweds have to say?

GRISEL: Well, here we are, running from one place to the other.

ROSARIO: Good, and do you already know where you are going on your honeymoon?

ARMANDO: I want to go to Cancún, because that is where we met.

GRISEL: It would be better not to go to Cancún. There are too many tourists there.

ARMANDO: But, Grisel!

ROSARIO: (Showing them a brochure) Just a moment. Don't start fighting now. Look, here they are offering a two-week trip to Costa Rica.

GRISEL: What does the trip include?

ROSARIO: It includes round-trip airfare, lodging, meals, and excursions. All this for only $800 per person!

GRISEL: Marvelous!

ARMANDO: Well, yes, it's O.K. Let's go to Costa Rica!

A month later, Armando and Grisel get married. After the wedding, they leave on their honeymoon for Costa Rica. Now, they find themselves in the LACSA waiting room in Miami's international airport. A bit later, they hear the voice of an agent...

AGENT: Good afternoon, passengers. LACSA announces the departure of flight 621 to San José. Please pass to departure gate number 22. Have a nice trip!

SEGUNDA PARTE

Paulino, a young man from Los Angeles, California, is going to Paraguay as a Peace Corps volunteer. All of his family is at the airport to see him off.

MOM: Son, do you have all of your luggage? And how about your passport and traveler's checks?

PAULINO: Please don't worry, and calm down.

MOM: When you arrive, I want you to let me know right away.

GRANDMA: My boy, how much we are going to miss you! I beg you to write to us.

PAULINO: I promise that to you, Grandma. Now, I suggest that you keep mom company. Please don't leave her alone. Is that O.K.?

GRANDMA: Leave in peace. All of us are going to take good care of her. And, I advise you to be very careful, too!

DAD: Paulino, I want you to open a checking account at the Central Bank of Paraguay in Asunción. You already know the exchange rate, right?

PAULINO: Yes, dad.

PEPITA: Paulino, Please bring me a souvenir from Paraguay.

PAULINO: Yes Pepita, and I in turn ask that you behave yourself and help mom with everything.

DAD: I recommend that you don't sign your travelers checks before using them.

PAULINO: Yes dad, of course. And now I forbid you all from giving me anymore recommendations. Everything is going to be fine.

GRANDMA: You are right, son. Now, let's leave him alone.

LECCIÓN 9

PRIMERA PARTE

How lousy I feel!

Don Evelio is not feeling well. His whole body aches. His wife, Refugio, wants him to go to see the doctor.

Don Evelio: Ooooouch! Refu! How lousy I'm feeling!

Doña Refugio: Evelio, I have already told you to call the doctor. You have been sick for three days.

Don Evelio: No way.

Doña Refugio: Evelio, you are so stubborn! You haven't seen Dr. Estrada Fernández in over a year.

Don Evelio: All right, dear. Don't bother me! Call Dr. Estrada Fernández and ask him to make an appointment, but I've already told you that I don't trust doctors.

At Dr. Estrada's office

Dr. Estrada: Don Evelio, what a pleasure! I haven't seen you for such a long time.

Don Evelio: How are you, doctor? Yes, it's been over a year since I've been here.

Dr. Estrada: And, how are you feeling? What do you have?

Don Evelio: Well, my throat hurts a lot, in addition to my chest and stomach.

Dr. Estrada: Let's see ..., breathe ... cough ... Well, look. What you have is a cold. I am going to prescribe an antibiotic for you... Oh, I almost forgot! You told me that you were allergic to antibiotics, right?

Don Evelio: Well, not allergic. It's just that I don't like to take them because I'm a naturalist, but if I have to take them, it doesn't matter!

Dr. Estrada: O.K., we will avoid the antibiotics. Take these pills and I guarantee you that you will feel better. However, what's most important is that you get a lot of rest. And, I want you to come next week for your annual check up.

Don Evelio: Come again?

Dr. Estrada: Come on Don Evelio, one has to be rational.

SEGUNDA PARTE

Improve your health

A good diet for a healthy heart

We all know how important it is to watch our nutrition in order to stay healthy. It is important to control the consumption of sugar. One also has to control consumption of those foods that contribute to heart disease. According to the American Diabetic Association, a change in diet can significantly lower the risk of heart diseases. The recommendations that the Association makes include the following:

- Limit your cholesterol intake to 300 mg. or less per day. Cholesterol is present in all animal products. Also, try to eat more foods that are rich in protein, such as oatmeal or beans.

- Avoid greasy foods. Use vegetable and olive oils in your kitchen instead of butter or lard.

- Get 50 to 60 percent of your daily calories from carbohydrates (breads, cereals), 12 to 20 percent from protein (meat, fish, milk), and more than 30 percent from fat.

- Don't eat more than is necessary. Excessive eating increases the sugar level in your blood.

Naturally, maintaining an ideal weight, exercising, controlling your sugar level, and avoiding alcohol are important for good health. Talk with your doctor to plan an appropriate diet for you.

LECCIÓN 10

PRIMERA PARTE

The media

The following editorial appeared in Novedades, a Mexican newspaper. The author of the editorial offers an opinion about the situation of Mexican immigrants in the United States. The editorial was written during a visit of the Mexican President, Carlos Salinas de Gortari, to Chicago.

The Outside Mexican

The city of Chicago has a great potential, due mostly to the work of thousands of Mexicans who migrated and settled there many years ago. They found favorable conditions to develop their plans, and have been very useful. However, they still conserve sentiments that identify them as Mexicans, which were enthusiastically expressed in the welcome they gave to President Salinas de Gortari.

The Outside Mexicans, as they are known because they have not ceased being Mexicans, have not been forgotten by Mexico either, which still considers them an integral part of its nationality. Speaking before an audience of more than 3,000 Mexicans and Mexican-Americans, President Salinas de Gortari expressed that the Mexican government will continue working intensely to protect the rights and guarantee the freedoms of Mexican migrant workers.

As long as living conditions in the national territory fail to satisfy the aspirations of those who seek a better life, the migratory flow will continue. That does not mean that our leaders ignore the emigrants. On the contrary, this has always been a topic of the negotiations between Mexico and the United States, as it is now as the president of the Republic of Mexico travels through some cities of the neighboring country.

SEGUNDA PARTE

The Presidential Candidate

Alberto Figueroa is a candidate for the presidency with the Alliance With Nature Party, a "green party". He is now giving a speech.

Fellow citizens! Inflation, unemployment, taxes, external debt, and crime get talked about plenty. These are serious problems that have to be controlled. As you all know, the economy is a priority of the Alliance with Nature Party. But, I ask myself: Can we resolve our problems without a vision which includes protection of the environment? Can we talk about economic development without taking into account the social infrastructure? The answer is no, and a thousand times, NO!

Fellow citizens, the hour has come to affront the ecological problems that threaten the country. We can not continue to ignore deforestation, the assault on natural resources, the destruction of the forest. Are you looking for a candidate who represents the ecological aspirations of the people? That's me! Do you want a leader who eliminates contamination of the environment? That's me! Do you want a candidate who has vision, who thinks about preventing, and not just in resolving when it is already too late? Fellow citizens, that's me! THAT'S ME!

In order for me to be able to bring about these changes, it is of critical importance that you vote for me and for the Alliance with Nature Party. Without each and everyone of you supporting us, it is not possible to win. Unless we make sacrifices now, we will not be able to guarantee a future for our sons and daughters and their sons and daughters. Fellow citizens, let's all vote! Lets go to the polls to win! Let's vote for Alberto Figueroa and for the Alliance with Nature Party! Ladies and gentlemen, let's vote! let's win! let's triumph!

APPENDIX 2

Verb Charts

A. Regular Verbs: Simple Tenses

Infinitive Present Participle Past Partciple	Indicative					Subjunctive		Imperative
	Present	Imperfect	Preterite	Future	Conditional	Present	Imperfect	
hablar hablando hablado	hablo hablas habla hablamos habláis hablan	hablaba hablabas hablaba hablábamos hablabais hablaban	hablé hablaste habló hablamos hablasteis hablaron	hablaré hablararás hablará hablaremos hablaréis hablarán	hablaría hablarías hablaría hablaríamos hablaríais hablarían	hable hables hable hablemos habléis hablen	hablara hablaras hablara habláramos hablarais hablaran	habla tú, no hables hable usted hablemos hablen Uds.
comer comiendo comido	como comes come comemos coméis comen	comía comías comía comíamos comíais comían	comí comiste comió comimos comisteis comieron	comeré comerás comerá comeremos comeréis comerán	comería comerías comería comeríamos comeríais comerían	coma comas coma comamos comáis coman	comiera comieras comiera comiéramos comierais comieran	come tú, no comas coma usted comamos coman Uds.
vivir viviendo vivido	vivo vives vive vivimos vivís viven	vivía vivías vivía vivíais vivíais vivían	viví viviste vivió vivimos vivisteis vivieron	viviré vivirás vivirá viviremos viviréis vivirán	viviría vivirías viviría viviríamos viviríais vivirían	viva vivas viva vivamos viváis vivan	viviera vivieras viviera viviéramos vivierais vivieran	vive tú, no vivas viva usted vivamos vivan Uds.

B. Regular Verbs: Perfect Tenses

	Indicative					Subjunctive	
	Present Perfect	**Past Perfect**	**Preterite Perfect**	**Future Perfect**	**Conditional Perfect**	**Present Perfect**	**Past Perfect**
	he hablado	había hablado	hube hablado	habré hablado	habría hablado	haya hablado	hubiera hablado
	has comido	habías comido	hubiste comido	habrás comido	habrías comido	hayas comido	hubieras comido
	ha vivido	había vivido	hubo vivido	habrá vivido	habría vivido	haya vivido	hubiera vivido
	hemos	habíamos	hubimos	habremos	habríamos	hayamos	hubiéramos
	habéis	habíais	hubisteis	habréis	habríais	hayáis	hubierais
	han	habían	hubieron	habrán	habrían	hayan	hubieran

C. Irregular Verbs

Infinitive Present Participle Past Participle	Indicative					Subjunctive		Imperative
	Present	**Imperfect**	**Preterite**	**Future**	**Conditional**	**Present**	**Imperfect**	
andar andando andado	ando	andaba	anduve	andaré	andaría	ande	anduviera	anda tú,
	andas	andabas	anduviste	andarás	andarías	andes	anduvieras	no andes
	anda	andaba	anduvo	andará	andaría	ande	anduviera	ande usted
	andamos	andábamos	anduvimos	andaremos	andaríamos	andemos	anduviéramos	andemos
	andáis	andabais	anduvistes	andaréis	andaríais	andéis	anduvierais	anden Uds.
	andan	andaban	anduvieron	andarán	andarían	anden	anduvieran	
caer cayendo caído	caigo	caía	caí	caeré	caería	caiga	cayera	cae tú,
	caes	caías	caiste	caerás	caerías	caigas	cayeras	no caigas
	cae	caía	cayó	caerá	caería	caiga	cayera	caiga usted
	caemos	caíamos	caímos	caeremos	caeríamos	caigamos	cayéramos	caigamos
	caéis	caías	caístes	caeréis	caeríais	caigáis	cayerais	caigan Uds.
	caen	caían	cayeron	caerán	caerían	caigan	cayeran	
dar dando dado	doy	daba	di	daré	daría	dé	diera	da tú,
	das	dabas	diste	darás	darías	des	dieras	no des
	da	daba	dio	dará	daría	dé	diera	dé usted
	damos	dábamos	dimos	daremos	daríamos	demos	diéramos	demos
	dais	dabais	disteis	daréis	daríais	deis	dierais	den Uds.
	dan	daban	dieron	darán	darían	den	dieran	

C. Irregular Verbs (continued)

Infinitive / Present Participle / Past Participle	Indicative: Present	Imperfect	Preterite	Future	Conditional	Subjunctive: Present	Imperfect	Imperative
decir / diciendo / dicho	digo	decía	dije	diré	diría	diga	dijera	
	dices	decías	dijiste	dirás	dirías	digas	dijeras	di tú,
	dice	decía	dijo	dirá	diría	diga	dijera	no digas
	decimos	decíamos	dijimos	diremos	diríamos	digamos	dijéramos	diga usted
	decís	decíais	dijisteis	diréis	diríais	digáis	dijerais	digamos
	dicen	decían	dijeron	dirán	dirían	digan	dijeran	digan Uds.
estar / estando / estado	estoy	estaba	estuve	estaré	estaría	esté	estuviera	
	estás	estabas	estuviste	estarás	estarías	estés	estuvieras	está tú,
	está	estaba	estuvo	estará	estaría	esté	estuviéramos	no estés
	estamos	estábamos	estuvimos	estaremos	estaríamos	estemos	estuviera	esté usted
	estáis	estabais	estuvisteis	estaréis	estaríais	estéis	estuvierais	estemos
	están	estaban	estuvieron	estarán	estarían	estén	estuvieran	estén Uds.
haber / habiendo / habido	he	había	hube	habré	habría	haya	hubiera	
	has	habías	hubiste	habras	habrías	hayas	hubieras	
	ha	había	hubo	habrá	habría	haya	hubiera	
	hemos	habíamos	hubimos	habremos	habríamos	hayamos	hubiéramos	
	habéis	habíais	hubistes	habréis	habríais	hayáis	hubierais	
	han	habían	hubieron	habrán	habrían	hayan	hubieran	
hacer / haciendo / hecho	hago	hacía	hice	haré	haría	haga	hiciera	
	haces	hacías	hiciste	harás	harías	hagas	hicieras	haz tú,
	hace	hacía	hizo	hará	haría	haga	hiciera	no hagas
	hacemos	hacíamos	hicimos	haremos	haríamos	hagamos	hiciéramos	haga usted
	hacéis	hacíais	hicistes	haréis	haríais	hagáis	hicierais	hagamos
	hacen	hacían	hicieron	harán	harían	hagan	hicieran	hagan Uds.
ir / yendo / ido	voy	iba	fui	iré	iría	vaya	fuera	
	vas	ibas	fuiste	irás	irías	vayas	fueras	ve tú,
	va	iba	fue	irá	iría	vaya	fuera	no vayas
	vamos	íbamos	fuimos	iremos	iríamos	vayamos	fuéramos	vaya usted
	vais	ibais	fuisteis	iréis	iríais	vayáis	fuerais	vayamos
	van	iban	fueron	irán	irían	vayan	fueran	vayan Uds.

C. Irregular Verbs (continued)

Infinitive Present Participle Past Participle	Indicative					Subjunctive		Imperative
	Present	Imperfect	Preterite	Future	Conditional	Present	Imperfect	
oír oyendo oído	oigo oyes oye oímos oís oyen	oía oías oía oíamos oíais oían	oí oíste oyó oímos oísteis oyeron	oiré oirás oirá oiremos oiréis oirán	oiría oirías oiría oiríamos oiríais oirían	oiga oigas oiga oigamos oigáis oigan	oyera oyeras oyera oyéramos oyerais oyeran	oye tú, no oigas oiga usted oigamos oigan Uds.
poder pudiendo podido	puedo puedes puede podemos podéis pueden	podía podías podía podíamos podíais podían	pude pudiste pudo pudimos pudisteis pudieron	podré podrás podrá podremos podréis podrán	podría podrías podría podríamos podríais podrían	pueda puedas pueda podamos podáis puedan	pudiera pudieras pudiera pudiéramos pudierais pudieran	
poner poniendo puesto	pongo pones pone ponemos ponéis ponen	ponía ponías ponía poníamos poníais ponían	puse pusiste puso pusimos pusisteis pusieron	pondré pondrás pondrá pondremos pondréis pondrán	pondría pondrías pondría pondríamos pondríais pondrían	ponga pongas ponga pongamos pongáis pongan	pusiera pusieras pusiera pusiéramos pusierais pusieran	pon tú, no pongas ponga usted pongamos pongan Uds.
querer queriendo querido	quiero quieres quiere queremos queréis quieren	quería querías quería queríamos queríais querían	quise quisiste quiso quisimos quisisteis quisieron	querré querrás querrá querremos querréis querrán	querría querrías querría querríamos querríais querrían	quiera quieras quiera queramos queráis quieran	quisiera quisieras quisiera quisiéramos quisiérais quisieran	quiere tú, no quieras quiera usted queramos quieran Uds.
saber sabiendo sabido	sé sabes sabe sabemos sabéis saben	sabía sabías sabía sabíamos sabíais sabían	supe supiste supo supimos supisteis supieron	sabré sabrás sabrá sabremos sabréis sabrán	sabría sabrías sabría sabríamos sabríais sabrían	sepa sepas sepa sepamos sepáis sepan	supiera supieras supiera supiéramos supierais supieran	sabe tú, no sepas sepa usted sepamos sepan Uds.
salir saliendo salido	salgo sales sale salimos salís salen	salía salías salía salíamos salíais salían	salí saliste salió salimos salisteis salieron	saldré saldrás saldré saldremos saldréis saldrán	saldría saldrías saldría saldríamos saldríais saldrían	salga salgas salga salgamos salgáis salgan	saliera salieras saliera saliéramos salierais salieran	sal tú, no salgas salga usted salgamos salgan Uds.

C. Irregular Verbs (continued)

Infinitive Present Participle Past Participle	Indicative					Subjunctive		Imperative
	Present	Imperfect	Preterite	Future	Conditional	Present	Imperfect	
ser siendo sido	soy eres es somos sois son	era eras era éramos erais eran	fui fuiste fue fuimos fuisteis fueron	seré serás será seremos seréis serán	sería serías sería seríamos seríais serían	sea seas sea seamos seáis sean	fuera fueras fuera fuéramos fuerais fueran	sé tú, no seas sea usted seamos sean Uds.
tener teniendo tenido	tengo tienes tiene tenemos tenéis tienen	tenía tenías tenía teníamos teníais tenían	tuve tuviste tuvo tuvimos tuvisteis tuvieron	tendré tendrás tendrá tendremos tendréis tendrán	tendría tendrías tendría tendríamos tendríais tendrían	tenga tengas tenga tengamos tengáis tengan	tuviera tuvieras tuviera tuviéramos tuvierais tuvieran	ten tú, no tengas tenga usted tengamos tengan Uds.
traer trayendo traído	traigo traes trae traemos traéis traen	traía traías traía traíamos traíais traían	traje trajiste trajo trajimos trajisteis trajeron	traeré traerás traerá traeremos traeréis traerán	traería traerías traería traeríamos traeríais traerían	traiga traigas traiga traigamos traigáis traigan	trajera trajeras trajera trajéramos trajerais trajeran	trae tú, no traigas traiga usted traigamos traigan Uds.
venir viniendo venido	vengo vienes viene venimos venís vienen	venía venías venía veníamos veníais venían	vine viniste vino vinimos vinisteis vinieron	vendré vendrás vendrá vendremos vendréis vendrán	vendría vendrías vendría vendríamos vendríais vendrían	venga vengas venga vengamos vengáis vengan	viniera vinieras viniera viniéramos viniérais vinieran	ven tú, no vengas venga usted vengamos vengan Uds.
ver viendo visto	veo ves ve vemos véis ven	veía veías veía veíamos veíais veían	vi viste vio vimos visteis vieron	veré verás verá veremos veréis verán	vería verías vería veríamos veríais verían	vea veas vea veamos veáis vean	viera vieras viera viéramos vierais vieran	ve tú, no veas vea usted veamos vean Uds.

D. Stem-changing and Orthographic-changing Verbs

Infinitive / Present Participle / Past Participle	Indicative					Subjunctive		Imperative
	Present	Imperfect	Preterite	Future	Conditional	Present	Imperfect	
incluir (y) incluyendo incluido	incluyo incluyes incluye incluimos incluís incluyen	incluía incluías incluía incluíamos incluíais incluían	incluí incluiste incluyó incluimos incluisteis incluyeron	incluiré incluirás incluirá incluiremos incluiréis incluirán	incluiría incluirías incluiría incluiríamos incluiríais incluirían	incluya incluyas incluya incluyamos incluyáis incluyan	incluyera incluyeras incluyera incluyéramos incluyerais incluyeran	incluye tú, no incluyas incluya usted incluyamos incluyan Uds.
dormir (ue, u) durmiendo dormido	duermo duermes duerme dormimos dormís duermen	dormía dormías dormía dormíamos dormíais dormían	dormí dormiste durmió dormimos dormisteis durmieron	dormiré dormirás dormirá dormiremos dormiréis dormirán	dormiría dormirías dormiría dormiríamos dormiríais dormirían	duerma duermas duerma durmamos durmáis duerman	durmiera durmieras durmiera durmiéramos durmierais durmieran	duerme tú, no duermas duerma usted durmamos duerman Uds.
pedir (i, i) pidiendo pedido	pido pides pide pedimos pedís piden	pedía pedías pedía pedíamos pedíais pedían	pedí pediste pidió pedimos pedisteis pidieron	pediré pedirás pedirá pediremos pediréis pedirán	pediría pedirías pediría pediríamos pediríais pedirían	pida pidas pida pidamos pidáis pidan	pidiera pidieras pidiera pidiéramos pidierais pidieran	pide tú, no pidas pida usted pidamos pidan Uds.
pensar (ie) pensando pensado	pienso piensas piensa pensamos pensáis piensan	pensaba pensabas pensaba pensábamos pensabais pensaban	pensé pensaste pensó pensamos pensasteis pensaron	pensaré pensarás pensará pensaremos pensaréis pensarán	pensaría pensarías pensaría pensaríamos pensaríais pensarían	piense pienses piense pensemos penséis piensen	pensara pensaras pensara pensáramos pensarais pensaran	piensa tú, no pienses piense usted pensemos piensen Uds.

D. Stem-changing and Orthographic–changing Verbs (continued)

Infinitive Present Participle Past Participle	Indicative					Subjunctive		Imperative
	Present	Imperfect	Preterite	Future	Conditional	Present	Imperfect	
producir (zc) produciendo producido	produzco produces produce producimos producís producen	producía producías producía producíamos producíais producían	produje produjiste produjo produjimos produjisteis produjeron	produciré producirás producirá produciremos produciréis producirán	produciría producirías produciría produciríamos produciríais producirían	produzca produzcas produzca produzcamos produzcáis produzcan	produjera produjeras produjera produjéramos produjerais produjeran	produce tú, no produzcas produzca usted produzcamos produzcan Uds.
reír (i, i) riendo reído	río ríes ríe reímos reís ríen	reía reías reía reíamos reíais reían	reí reíste rió reímos reísteis rieron	reiré reirás reirá reiremos reiréis reirán	reiría reirías reiría reiríamos reiríais reirían	ría rías ría riamos riáis rían	riera rieras riera riéramos rierais rieran	ríe tú, no rías ría usted riamos rían Uds.
seguir (i, i) (ga) siguiendo seguido	sigo sigues sigue seguimos seguís siguen	seguía seguías seguía seguíamos seguíais seguían	seguí seguiste siguió seguimos seguisteis siguieron	seguiré seguirás seguirá seguiremos seguiréis seguirán	seguiría seguirías seguiría seguiríamos seguiríais seguirían	siga sigas siga sigamos sigáis sigan	siguiera siguieras siguiera siguiéramos siguierais siguieran	sigue tú, no sigas siga usted sigamos sigan Uds.
sentir (ie, i) sintiendo sentido	siento sientes siente sentimos sentís sienten	sentía sentías sentía sentíamos sentíais sentían	sentí sentiste sintió sentimos sentisteis sintieron	sentiré sentirás sentirá sentiremos sentiréis sentirán	sentiría sentirías sentiría sentiríamos sentiríais sentirían	sienta sientas sienta sintamos sintáis sientan	sintiera sintieras sintiera sintiéramos sintierais sintieran	siente tú, no sientas sienta usted sintamos sientan Uds.
volver (ue) volviendo vuelto	vuelvo vuelves vuelve volvemos volvéis vuelven	volvía volvías volvía volvíamos volvíais volvían	volví volviste volvió volvimos volvisteis volvieron	volveré volverás volverá volveremos volveréis volverán	volvería volverías volvería volveríamos volveríais volverían	vuelva vuelvas vuelva volvamos volváis vuelvan	volviera volvieras volviera volviéramos volvierais volvieran	vuelve tú, no vuelvas vuelva usted volvamos vuelvan Uds.

APPENDIX 3
Spanish-English Vocabulary

A

abajo *adv.* **5** down with; below, downstairs

el/la **abogado(a) 3** lawyer

abordar 8 to board

a **bordo 6** on board

el **aborto 10** abortion

Abran el libro. H Open the book.

abrazar 6 to embrace

el **abrazo 4** hug

el **abrigo 6** coat

abril 2 April

abrir 2 to open

abrocharse 8 to fasten

la **abuela 3** grandmother

el **abuelo 3** grandfather

abundar 4 to be abundant

aburrido(a) 2 bored, boring

acabar de + *inf.* 3 to have just

el **accesorio 8** acccessory

la **acción en ejecución 4** action in progress

el **aceite de oliva 5** olive oil

aceptar 6 to accept

acerca de *prep.* **6** about

el **acero 2** steel

acogedor(a) 5 friendly

acompañar 8 to accompany

aconsejar 8 to advise

el **acontecimiento 10** happening

acordarse (ue) (de) 7 to remember

acostar (ue) 8 to put to bed

acostarse (ue) 7 to go to bed

la **actriz 1** actress

acudir A to turn to

adelgazar 9 to lose weight

además *adv.* **4** besides, moreover

además de *prep.* **4** besides, in addition to

adentro 4 inside

adiós 1 good-bye

el **adjetivo 1** adjective

la **administración de empresas 1** business administration

admirar 2 to admire

¿Adónde?... 2 To where?

adoquinado(a) 4 tiled, paved with cobblestones

la **aduana 8** customs

el/la **aduanero(a) 9** customs agent

el **adverbio 3** adverb

la **aerolínea 3** airline

el **aeropuerto 3** airport

a **eso de 5** at about

el **afecto 4** affection

afeitarse 7 to shave

el/la **aficionado(a) 4** fan

a **fin de que 10** in order that

afrontar 10 to face

afuera 4 outside

la **agencia 7** agency

el/la **agente 6** agent

la **agencia de empleos A** employment agency

la **agencia de viajes 9** travel agency

agosto 2 August

agotador(a) 6 exhausting

agradable *adj.* **5** pleasant

el **agua** *f.* **4** water

el **agua caliente 9** hot water

el **agua de lluvia 5** rain water

el **agua mineral 5** mineral water

ahí 5 there

ahora 6 now

ahora mismo 2 right now

ahorrar 6 to save

el **aire A** air

el **aire acondicionado 9** air conditioning

el **ají verde 5** green pepper

el **ajo 5** garlic

el **ala** *f.* **9** wing

a **la derecha 2** to the right

a **la izquierda 2** to the left

a **la parrilla 5** on the grill

aló 3 hello

el **albergue estudiantil A** student hostel

el **alcalde 10** mayor

el **alcázar 2** palace; fortress

al **comienzo 5** at the beginning

alegrarse (de) 7 to become happy; to be glad (about)

alegre 3 happy

el **alemán 1** German

alergia 9 allergy

alérgico(a) 9 allergic

al **este 2** to the east

la **alfarería 4** pottery

la **alfombra 7** rug

el **álgebra** *f.* **2** algebra

algo 5 something

el **algodón 6** cotton

alguien 5 someone, anyone

alguno(a) 5 any, some

al **lado (de)** *prep.* **2** next to

allá 5 over there

allí H,5 there

al **llegar 8** upon arrival

el **almacén 6** department store

al **mismo tiempo 8** at the same time

la **almohada A** pillow

almorzar (ue) 4 to have lunch

el **almuerzo 5,2** lunch

al **norte 2** to the north

aló 4 hello *(answering the phone)*

al **oeste 2** to the west

el **alojamiento 8** lodging

los **alrededores 4** surrounding areas

al **sur 2** to the south

el **altiplano 10** high plateau

alto(a) 1 tall

la **altura 9** altitude

el **ama** *f.* **de casa 6** housewife

amable 3 kind, friendly, nice

amarillo(a) H yellow
al poco rato 6 a little bit later
el **ambiente A** environment
a menos que *conj.* **10** unless
a menudo *adv.* **8** often
América Central 1 Central America
América del Norte 1 North America
América del Sur 1 South America
el/la **amigo(a) 1** friend
el **amor 4** love
amplio(a) 2 wide
el/la **analista 10** analyst
el/la **analista de sistemas A** systems analyst
anaranjado(a) H orange
el **ancho 7** width
anclado(a) 6 anchored
andar 6 to walk, to go
andar con cuidado 5 to be careful
el/la **anfitrión(a) 10** show host (hostess)
anidado(a) 10 nestled
el **anillo 6** ring
anoche 5 last night
a principios de 5 at the beginning of
anteayer 5 the day before yesterday
el **antepasado A** ancestor
antes *adv.* **8** before, sooner
antes de *prep.* **2** before
antes de Cristo 4 B.C.
antes (de) que *conj.* **10** before
el **antiácido 9** antacid
el **antibiótico 9** antibiotic
antiguo(a) 10 ancient
anitihistamínico 9 antohistamine
antipático(a) 1 unfriendly
el **anuncio 5** announcement
añadir 5,2 to add
año 1 year
el **año pasado 5** last year
apacible *adj.* **4** pleasant, calm
apagado(a) A (turned) off
apagar A to extinguish; to turn off
el **aparador 7** china cabinet
el **aparato** de la cocina **6** kitchen appliance

el **aparato electrónico A** electrical appliance
apellido 1 surname
apenas *adv.* **4** hardly, barely
el **aperitivo 2** apéritif
apoyar 10 to support
aprender (a) 2 to learn
aprovechar 6 to take advantage
el (los) **apunte(s) A** note(s)
apurado(a) 2 in a hurry
apurarse 8 to hurry
aquí H here
el **árbitro 5** referee
archivar A to file
el **arco 2** arch
el **área** *f.* **de estudio 2** field of study
la **arena 4** sand
el **arete 6** earring
argentino(a) 1 Argentine, Argentinian
la **arqueología 4** archaeology
el/la **arquitecto(a) 2** architect
la **arquitectura 2** architecture
arraigado(a) 8 rooted, fixed
arreglar 6 to fix
arreglar la cuenta A to take care of the bill
el **arreglo personal 8** personal care
arriba 5 yea; above; up; high
arriba de *prep.* **7** on top of
arrojar 4 to throw out
el **arroz 5** rice
el **arte** *m./f.* **1** art
el **arte dramático** dramatic art
la **artesanía 4** handicraft
el **artículo 6,9** article, item
el **artículo de tocador 7** personal care product
el **artículo de uso personal 8** personal care item
asalto 10 assault
ascender (ie) A to promote
el **ascensor A** elevator
asegurarse (de) 6 to be sure
el/la **asesor(a) 10** advisor
así 1 thus, that way
así lo decimos 1 this is how we say it

asiento 8 seat
asistir (a) 3 to attend
asolearse 8 to get some sun, to tan
la **aspiradora 7** vacuum cleaner
el/la **aspirante A** applicant
la **aspirina 9** aspirin
el **asunto 3** matter
atar 7 to tie
atender (ie) 6 to wait on someone
atentamente A sincerely
el **aterrizaje 8** landing
a tiempo 8 on time
el **Atlántico 2** Atlantic Ocean
el **atletismo 4** track and field
la **atmósfera A** atmosphere
atracar 5 to hold up, rob
atractivo(a) 3 attractive
atraer 5 to attract
atrasado(a) 7 late, behind schedule
atravesado(a) 10 crossed
a través de 6 through
el **atún 5** tuna
aumentar A to increase
el **aumento A** raise
aunque *conj.* **6,10** although, even if, even though
a veces 4 sometimes
la **avena 9** oatmeal
la **avenida 2** avenue
averiguar 8 to find out
el **avión 1** airplane
avisar 8 to warn
el **aviso clasificado 9** classified ad
ayer 5 yesterday
la **ayuda 6** help
ayudar (a) 5 to help
la **azafata 8** stewardess
el **azafrán 5** saffron
azteca 4 Aztec
el/la **azúcar 5** sugar
azul H blue

B

bailar 1 to dance
bailar en la fiesta 3 to dance at a party

bailar en la discoteca 3 to dance at a discoteque

bajar 6 to descend, go down, get off

bajar de peso 9 to lose weight

bajo(a) 1 short

el **balcón 9** balcony

el **balón 4** ball (soccer, basketball, volleyball)

la **banana 5** banana

bañarse 7 to bathe

el **baño 7** bathroom

el **baño privado A** private bath

barato(a) H cheap, inexpensive

bárbaro(a) 5 awesome

barrer el piso 7 to sweep the floor

el **barrio 6** neighborhood

la **base de datos A** data base

el **básquetbol 4** basketball

bastante *adj.* **2** enough, sufficient

Bastante bien H Pretty well

bastante *adv.* **2** rather

el **basurero 7** garbage can

el **bate 4** bat

batear 4 to bat

el **batido 6** shake

batir 5 to beat

baúl 4 trunk

beber 2 to drink

la **bebida 6** drink

la **bebida alcohólica 9** alcoholic beverage

el **béisbol 1** baseball

bello(a) 1,6 beautiful

el **beneficio A** benefit

el **beso 4** kiss

la **biblioteca 2** library

bicicleta 4 bicycle

bien *adv.* **H** fine; well

bien cocido 5 well done, well cooked

los **bienes raíces 6** the real estate

bienestar social 10 social welfare

bienvenida 7 welcome

el **bigote 1** moustache

el **billete 8** bill (bank note)

la **billetera 6** wallet

los **binoculares 8** binoculars

la **biología 1** biology

el **bistec de solomillo 5** sirloin steak

blanco(a) H white

la **blusa 6** blouse

la **boca 7,9** mouth

la **boletería 3** ticket office

la **boda 3** the wedding

el **boleto 8** (airline) ticket

el **bolígrafo 1** ball-point pen

la **bolsa 6,4** purse

el **bolso 6** purse, handbag

el/la **bombero(a) A** firefighter

la **bonificación anual A** yearly bonus

bonito(a) 1 pretty

el **borrador 1** eraser

borrar A to erase

el **bosque 8** forest

el **bosque lluvioso 10** rain forest

el **bosque pluvial 8** rain forest

la **bota 6** boot

la **botella 6** bottle

el **botones A** bellhop

el **boxeo 4** boxing

el **brazo 9** arm

buen provecho 5 enjoy your meal!

buenas noches H good evening

buenas tardes H good afternoon

bueno(a) 1 good

bueno 4 hello (answering the phone)

buenos días 1 good morning

buscar 6 to look for

la **butaca 8** armchair

el **buzón 8** mailbox

C

el **cabaret 7** nightclub

la **cabeza 9** head

la **cabina 8** cockpit

el **cacique 8** Indian chief

cada 5 each

cada vez más 5 more and more

la **cadena 6,10** chain; network

caer 8 to fall

caer bien 2 to like (*a person*)

caer mal 2 to dislike (*a person*)

el **café 2** coffee; brown (color)

el **café con leche 5** coffee with milk

el **café solo 5** black coffee

la **cafetera 5** coffeepot

la **cafetería 2** cafeteria

la **caja registradora 6** cash register

el/la **cajero(a) 8** teller

el **cajero automático A** automatic teller machine

la **calculadora 2** calculator

caldo 5 broth

calentar 5 to heat up

la **calidad 7** quality

cálido(a) 9 warm

caliente *adj.* **5** hot

la **calificación A** qualification

el **calzado 7** footwear

la **calle 3** street

la **cama 7** bed

la **cámara de representantes A** house of representatives

la **cámara de video 8** cam recorder

la **cámara fotográfica 8** camera

la **camarera A** maid

camarero(a) 5 waiter; waitress

el **camarón 5** shrimp

cambiar 7 to change; to exchange

el **cambio 7,8** exchange; change

caminar 1 to walk

la **camisa 6** shirt

la **campaña 10** campaign

el/la **campeón(a) 4** champion

el **campeonato 4** championship

el/la **campesino(a) A** farmer

el **canal 10** channel

la **cancha 4** court, playing field

el/la **candidato(a) 10** candidate

cansado(a) 2 tired

cansancio 9 fatigue

capaz *adj.* **A** capable

la **capital 1** capital (city)

la **cara 7,9** face

el **carbohidrato 9** carbohydrate

el **cargo A** post; position

el **cariño 4** love

cariñosamente 3 love (in letter closing)

la **carne 6** meat

la **carne de res** 10 beef
la **carnicería** 6 butcher shop
caro(a) H expensive
el/la **carpintero(a) A** carpenter
el **carro** 6 car
la **carta** 8 letter
la **cartelera** 9 entertainment section
  (newspaper)
la **cartera** 6 purse, wallet
el/la **cartero(a)** 9 mailman,
  mailwoman
la **casa** 2 home; house
la **casa de huéspedes A** guest
  house
casado(a) 2 married
casamiento 3 wedding
casi 4 almost
el **casillero A** mailbox
el **caso** 1 case
el **castillo** 2 castle
castizo(a) 8 pure-blooded
la **caza** 5 hunting
la **cazuela** 5 stew pot, casserole dish,
  saucepan
la **cebolla** 5 onion
la **cena** 3,2 dinner
cenar 5 to have dinner
la **ceniza** 7 ash
el **centro** 2 center
el **centro comercial** 6 shopping
  center
el **centro estudiantil** 2 student
  center
el **centro naturalista** 10 health
  store
cepillarse 7 to brush one's—
el **cepillo** 7 brush
el **cepillo de dientes** 7 toothbrush
cerca *adv.* 2 close, near
cerca de *prep.* 4 near, close to
el **cerdo** 10 pig
el **cereal** 5 cereal
cerrar (ie) 6 to close
el **certamen** 10 (beauty) contest,
  pageant
la **cerveza** 5 beer
la **cesta** 4 basket

el **cesto** 4 basket
el **champú** 6 shampoo
la **chaqueta** 6 jacket
el **cheque** 6 (bank) check
el **cheque de viajero** 8 traveler's
  check
el/la **chico(a)** 2 man, kid, boy, girl
  (colloquial)
chileno(a) 2 Chilean
el **chisme** 7 gossip
chismear 7 to gossip
chismoso(a) 5 gossip, fond of gossip
el **chocolate** 6 chocolate
la **chuleta de cerdo** 6 pork chop
el **ciclismo** 4 bicycling
ciencias 2 science
cierren el libro H close the book
cierto(a) 1 true
el **cigarrillo** 9 cigarette
el **cinc** 10 zinc
el **cine** 3 movie
el **cinturón** 6 belt
el **cinturón de seguridad** 8 seat belt
el **cirujano** 9 surgeon
la **cita** 8 appointment, date
la **ciudad** 1 city
el/la **ciudadano(a)** 10 citizen
claro(a) 5 clear
la **clase** 1 class
la **clase turista** 8 coach class
la **clave A** key
el/la **cliente(a)** 5 customer, client
el **clima** 2 climate, weather
cobrar 8 to cash
el **cobre** 10 copper
la **coca-cola** 6 Coca-Cola
el **coche** 1 car
cocido(a) 6 cookcd
la **cocina** 7 kitchen
cocinar 5 to cook
el/la **cocinero(a) A** cook
el **código postal A** ZIP code
la **cola** 9 tail
la **colección** 2 collection
el **colesterol** 9 cholesterol
el **collar** 6 necklace
colombiano(a) 1 Colombian

la **colonia** 6 cologne
el **color** 1 color
el **colorete** 7 rouge, blush
columna sentimental 9 advice
  column
el/la **comandante** 1 major
combatir 10 to fight, to combat
el **comedor** 7 dining room
el/la **comentarista** 10 newscaster,
  commentator
el/la **comentarista deportivo(a) A**
  sportscaster
comenzar (ie)(a) 3 to begin
comer 2 to eat
el **comercio** 7 business
el **comestible** 6 food, foodstuff
la **comida** 7,5 meal
la **comisaría de policía** 1 police
  headquarters
¿**cómo**? 1 how?
¿**Cómo es? H** What is… like?
¿**Cómo estás?** *(familiar)* **H** How are
  you?
¿**Cómo está usted?** *(formal)* **H** How
  are you?
¿**Cómo le va?** *(formal)* **H** How are
  you doing?
¿**Cómo se llama usted?** *(formal)* **H**
  What is your name?
¿**Cómo te llamas?** *(familiar)* **H**
  What is your name?
¿**Cómo te va?** *(familiar)* **H** How are
  you doing?
como 8, 3 as, sincc
la **cómoda** 7 dresser
cómodo(a) 6 comfortable
¿**Como eres?** 1 What are you like?
el **cómpact disc** *(Anglicism)* **A**
  compact disc
compañero de cuarto 2 roommate
el **compartimiento** 6 compartment
la **complexión** 9 body structure
complicado(a) 2 complicated
componerse 9 to get well
comprar 2 to buy
la **computación** 3 computer science
la **computadora** 3 computer

con 1 with
el concierto 5 concert
el/la conciudadano(a) 10 fellow citizen
el concurso 10 game show
el condimento 6 condiment
confiar (en) 9 to trust
con frecuencia 6 frequently
el congelador 5 freezer
el congreso 10 congress
conmigo 5 with me
conocer 3 to know (to be acquainted with a person)
conocido(a) 2 known
con permiso 3 excuse me
¿Con quiénes? 2 With whom… ?
conseguir (i, i) 4 to get, to obtain
el conserje A concierge
conservar A to save
construido(a) 2 constructed
el consultorio 9 doctor's office
el consultorio sentimental A advice column
consumir A to consume, to use
al contado 6 cash
el/la contador(a) A accountant
con tal (de) que 10 provided (that)
la contaminación 10 pollution, contamination
contaminar A to pollute
contar (ue) 4 to tell; to count
contener 2 to contain
contento(a) 2 happy
el contestador automático A answering machine
contestar 1 to answer
Conteste(n) en español H Answer in Spanish
contigo 3 with you (familiar)
el continente 1 continent
continuar 10 to continue
contra 8 against
contratar A to hire
el contrato A contract
contribuir 9 to contribute
el/la contrincante A opponent
controlar 9 to control
conversar 1 to converse, to chat

conversar en un café 3 to chat at a cafe
la coordinador(a) A coordinator
la copa de vino 5 cup of wine
el corazón 9 heart
la corbata 6 tie
cordialmente A cordially
la cordillera 2 mountain chain
el correo 8 mail
el correo aéreo 8 air mail
correr 9 to run; to jog
correr por el parque 3 to run/jog in the park
la corrida de toros 5 bullfighting
cortar 5 to cut
cortar la hierba 7 to mow the lawn
la cortesía 3 courtesy
la corte suprema A Supreme Court
corto(a) 6 short
la cosa 5 thing
la cosecha A harvest
cosechar A to gather the harvest
la costa 4 coast
costar (ue) 4 to cost
costarricense 1 Costa Rican
el crecimiento A growth
creer 2 to believe
la crema de afeitar 7 shaving cream
el crimen 10 crime
la crítica A criticism
el/la crítico(a) 10 critic
la crónica 9 news story
la crónica social A social page (newspaper)
crudo(a) 5 rare; raw
el cuaderno 1 notebook
la cuadra A block (Spanish America)
cuadrado(a) 1 square
el cuadro 8 painting, picture
el cuadro comparativo 7 table
¿cuál? 1 which (one)?
¿cuáles? H which (ones)?
cualquier 5 any
¿cuándo? 2 when?
cuando A when
¿Cuanto cuesta(n)… ? H How much is (are)… ?

¿Cuanto(s)… ? H How much/many?
el cuarto 7 quarter; room; bedroom
cuarto(a) 7 fourth
cubano(a) 2 Cuban
el cubierto 5 place setting
cubierto(a) 2 covered
el cubo 8 bucket, pail
cubrir 9,10 to cover
la cucaracha A roach
la cuchara 5 spoon
la cucharada 6 tablespoon
la cucharadita 6 teaspoon
la cucharita 5 teaspoon
el cucharón 6 large spoon
la cuchilla de afeitar 7 razor blade
el cuchillo 5 knife
el cuello 9 neck
la cuenca 8 river basin
la cuenta 5 bill
la cuenta corriente 8 checking account
la cuenta de ahorros 8 savings account
el cuero 6 leather
el cuerpo 8 body
cuesta(n) H it costs/they cost
cuidadosamente 6 carefully
cuidar 8 to take care of
cuidarse 9 to take care of oneself
el cultivo A crop
la cultura 2 culture
la cumbre 7 peak
cumplir (años) to be someone's birthday
la cuñada 3 sister-in-law
el cuñado 3 brother-in-law
el cupo 9 space, quota, share
curar A to cure
el curso 2 course, class
cuyo(a)/s 4 whose

D

dar 5 to give
dar igual 5 to be all the same
dar la bienvenida 7 to welcome
darle dolor de … 9 to get an ache
darle la gripe 9 to catch the flu

dar guerra 4 to cause trouble
dar un paseo 3 to take a stroll, walk
darse cuenta 10 to realize
datar de 4 to date back to
de 1 of; from
de acuerdo 3 fine with me;OK
de algodón 6 (made of) cotton
debajo (de) 7 below; under
deber 2 to ought to
el **deber 10** duty
de buena/mala calidad 6 good/bad quality
debil 3 weak
decidir 2 to decide
décimo(a) 7 tenth
decir (i) 4 to say, to tell
de cuadros 6 plaid
de cuero 6 made of leather
el **dedo de la mano 9** finger
el **dedo del pie 9** toe
¿De donde... ? 2 From where...?
la **defensa 10** defense
la **deforestación 10** deforestation
dejar 8 to quit
de lana 6 (made of) wool
de la mañana 2 in the morning (A.M.)
de la noche 2 at night (P.M.)
de la tarde 2 in the afternoon (P.M.)
delante de *prep.* **3** in front of
delgado(a) 2 thin
delicioso(a) 5 delicious
el/la **delincuente 4** hoodlum
de lo que 2 than
de manga corta 6 short-sleeved
de manga larga 6 long-sleeved
demasiado(a) 8 too many
demasiado *adv.* **5** too much
la **democracia 10** democracy
demonios 7 darn it!
de nada 1 you're welcome
el/la **dentista A** dentist
dentro de *prep.* **7** inside of
el/la **dependiente(a) 6** clerk
el **deporte 2** sport
el/la **deportista 4** one who participates in a sport, sports fan

deportivo(a) 10 sportive
depositar 8 to deposit
de pronto 1 suddenly
¿De qué? 2 From what?
¿De qué color es? H What color is it?
¿De quienes? 2 Whose... ?
de rayas 6 striped
la **derecha 2** right (side)
derecho *sust.* **1** law; straight
de repente 8 suddenly
desaparecido *p.p.* **1** disappeared
la **desaparición 3** disappearance
desarrollar 10 to develop
desarrollo 10 development
desayunar 5 to have breakfast
el **desayuno 5** breakfast
descansar 3 to rest
descompuesto(a) A broken
el/la **desconocido(a) 3** unknown person
descriptivo(a) 2 descriptive
el **descubrimiento 4** discovery
descubrir 9 to discover
el **descuento 6** discount
desde 8 since; from
desear 5 to wish
de seda 6 made of silk
el **desempleo 10** unemployment
desenfrenado(a) A rampant
los **deshechos A** waste, trash
el **desodorante 6,7** deodorant
la **despedida 1** farewell
despedir (i, i) A to fire
despedirse (i, i) 7 to say good-bye
el **despegue 8** takeoff
la **despensa 7** pantry
el **despertador 7** alarm clock
despertarse (ie) 7 to wake up
la **despoblación forestal A** deforestation
después (de) 10 after; later
el/la **destinatario(a) 8** addressee
destruido(a) 2 destroyed
destruir 10 to destroy
de todas partes 2 from all parts
detrás de *prep.* **2** behind

la **deuda external 10** foreign debt
¿de veras? 1 really?
de vez en cuando 7 from time to time, once in a while
devolver (ue) 6 to return (something)
el **día 2** day
la **diabetes 10** diabetes
el **diccionario 2** dictionary
diciembre 2 December
el/la **dictador(a) A** dictator
la **dictadura 10** dictatorship
el **diente 7** tooth
difícil 2 hard
dígame *(formal)* **2** tell me *(answering telephone)*
el **dinero 6** money
los **dioses 4** gods
el/la **diputado(a) 10** congressperson
el/la **director(a) A** director
el **disco compacto 4** compact disk
el **disco duro A** hard disk
la **discoteca 1** discothèque
el **discurso 10** speech
diseñado(a) 2 designed
diseñar A to design
el **diseño A** design
disfrutar (de) 6 to enjoy
disparar 6 to shoot
disponible A available
distribuír 10 to distribute
divertido(a) 3 fun, enjoyable
divertirse *(ie, i)* **7** to have fun
divorciado(a) 2 divorced
doblar 2 to turn
doblar a la izquierda A to turn left
doblar a la derecha A to turn right
doler (ue) 9 to hurt
dolor 9 ache, pain
el **dolor de cabeza 10** headache
el **dolor de estómago 10** stomachache
el **dolor de garganta 10** sore throat
el **domingo 3** Sunday
dominicano(a) 1 Dominican
¿dónde? 1 where?

dormir (ue, u) 4 to sleep
dormir hasta tarde 8 to sleep late
dormirse (ue, u) 7 to fall asleep
el **dormitorio 7** bedroom
dos veces a— 8 twice a—
la **dosis 9** dose
la **droguería 7** drugstore
ducharse 7 to shower
dudar 10 to doubt
dudoso(a) 10 doubtfull
durante 4 during, for

E

la **economía 2** economics
ecuestre 2 equestrian
echar 5 to add
echar (al correo) A to toss (in the mailbox)
edad 1 age
edificarse 2 to be built
el **edificio 2** building
el **editorial 9** editorial page
la **editorial A** publishing house
el **ejemplo 2** example
ejercer 10 to exert
los **ejercicios aeróbicos 10** aerobics
la **elección 10** election
las **elecciones A** elections
el/la **electricista A** electrician
electrónico(a) A electronic
elegante 3 elegant
elegir (i, i) 10 to elect
elevado(a) 2 elevated
eliminar A to end
el/la **embajador(a) 2** ambassador
la **emisora A** radio station (business entity)
empatar 5 to tie (the score)
empeorar 10 to get worse
empezar (ie) (a) 6 to begin
el **empleo A** employment
emprender A to undertake
enamorarse (de) 7 to fall in love (with)
en busca de 2 in search of
encantado(a) 1 delighted
encantar 2 to enchant; to fascinate
en caso de que 10 in case that

encender (ie) A to turn on
encendido(a) A (turned) on
encima de prep. **8** on top of
encontrar (ue) 4 to find
encontrarse (ue) 4 to meet; to be found
en cuanto 10 as soon as
la **encuesta 10** poll; survey
en directo 10 live (on television)
endosar 8 to countersign, to endorse
en el centro 2 downtown
en efectivo 6 cash
la **energía A** energy
enero 2 January
enfadado(a) 2 angry
enfermarse 7,9 to get or become sick
la **enfermedad 9** sickness, illness
el/la **enfermero(a) 9** nurse
enfermo(a) 2,9 sick
enfrente (de) 2 in front of
engordar 9 to gain weight
enhorabuena A congratulations !
enjuague 7 mouthwash
enojarse (con) **7** to get angry (with)
enorme adj. **6** enormous
la **ensalada 2** salad
el **ensayo A** essay
enseguida 5 right away
enseñar 3 to teach; to show
entender 3 to understand
enterarse (de) 10 to find out (about)
entonces 1 then; therefore
entrar (en) 7 to enter
entre 2 divided by; among; between
el/la **entrenador(a) 4** coach
el **entrenamiento A** training
la **entrevista 3** interview
el **entusiasmo 5** enthusiasm
entusiasta adj. m/f **A** enthusiastic
en vez de 6 rather than
enviar 8 to send
en vivo A live (on television)
la **época 4** time, era
equipado(a) 6 equipped
el **equipaje 8** luggage, baggage

el **equipaje de mano 9** hand luggage
el **equipo 4** team
el **equipo de sonido 7** sound system
es una buena/mala idea 4 it's a good/bad idea
escalar 8 climb (mountains)
escalar montañas 9 to climb mountains
la **escalera 7** stairs
la **escalerilla 6** gangplank
el **escaño A** seat (in Congress); judge's bench
la **escasez A** shortage
la **escoba 7** broom
escojer 8 to choose
Escriba(n) los ejercicios H Write the exercises
escribir 2 to write
escrito(a) p.p. **2** written
escuchar 2 to listen
Escuche(n) H Listen
la **escuela 1** school
la **escuela secundaria 4** high school
esmalte 7 nail polish
España 1 Spain
el **español 1** Spanish
español(a) 1 Spanish
esparcido(a) 8 scattered
el **espárrago 6** asparagus
la **espátula 6** spatula
la **especialidad 6** specialty
la **especialidad de la casa 5** the specialty of the house
la **especialización A** specialization
el **espejo 7** mirror
esperar 8 to wait for; to hope; to expect
espeso(a) 7 dense
espléndido(a) 2 splendid
la **esposa 2** wife
el **esposo 4** husband
la **esquela 9** obituary
el **esquí 5** ski, skiing
el **esquí acuático 5** water ski,
esquiar 4 to ski
la **esquina A** corner

los **esquís 4** skiis
Está bien, vamos 3 O.K. Let's go
establecer 10 to establish; to set
la **estación de radio 10** radio
    station (on the dial)
la **estadía 9** stay
el **estadio 4** stadium
las **estadísticas 2** statistics
el **estado 2** state
Estado Libre Asociado 1
    Commonwealth
Estados Unidos 1 United States
estadounidense adj. **2** of the U. S. A.
esta noche 1 tonight
el **estante 7** shelf
el **estaño 10** tin
estar 2 to be
estar a dieta 9 to be on a diet
estar a tiempo 9 to be on time
estar atrasado(a) 8 to be late
estar contento(a) (de) 10 to be
    happy (that)
estar de moda 6 to be in style
estar demorado(a) 9 to be delayed
estar de vuelta 6 to have returned
estar en manos (de) 4 to be in the
    hands (of)
estar guapo(a) **4** to look
    handsome/pretty
la **estatua 2** statue
la **estatura 9** height
este 1 this
el **estéreo 4** stereo
el **estilo 2** style
el **estómago 9** stomach
Esto es H This is…
estos 2 these
Estoy de acuerdo 4 I agree
estrecho(a) 7 tight
la **estrella 4** star
el/la **estudiante 1** student
estudiar 1 to study
Estudie(n) la lección H Study the
    lesson
la **estufa 6** stove
¡Estupendo! 4 Terrific!
la **ética A** ethics

la **etiqueta 6** price tag
Europa 1 Europe
europeo(a) 2 European
la **evaluación A** evaluation
evitar 9 to avoid
el **examen 2** exam, test
el **examen físico 9** checkup
la **excursión 8** tour, excursion
exigente adj. **2** challenging,
    demanding
el **expediente A** file
la **experiencia práctica A** practical
    experience
explicar 6 to explain
la **expresión 2** expression
la **expresión clave 2** key expression
la expresión de tiempo time
    expression
exquisito(a) 5 exquisite, delicious
extender (ie) A to expand
la **extensión 1** length
el **extranjerismo A** foreign word or
    phrase
el/la **extranjero(a) 2** foreigner
extrañar 8 to miss
extraño(a) 10 strange

F

la **fábrica 10** factory
fabuloso(a) 4 fabulous, great
fácil 2 easy
facturar el equipaje 8 to check in
    luggage
la **Facultad de… 2** the school of
la **Facultad de Arte 3** art school
la **Facultad de Ciencias 3** science
    school
la **Facultad de Derecho 3** law
    school
la **Facultad de Ingeniería 3**
    engineering school
la **Facultad de Medicina 3** medical
    school
la **faja 10** strip
la **falda 6** skirt
falso(a) 1 false

faltar 2 to lack, to miss
famoso(a) 3 famous
el/la **fanático(a) 5** fanatic
el/la **fanfarrón(a) 4** braggart
fantástico(a) 5 fantastic
el/la **farmacéutico(a) 9** pharmacist
la **farmacia 6** pharmacy, drugstore
fascinante 3 fascinating
el **fax** (Anglisism) **A** fax
febrero 2 February
la **fecha 3** date
felicitaciones A congratulations
felicitar 7 to congratulate
feo(a) 1 ugly
la **feria A** fair
fiebre 9 fever
fijo(a) A fixed
el **filete de pescado 5** fish fillet
el **filete de res 5** beef fillet
filosofía y letras 1 humanities/
    liberal arts
finalmente 6 finally
la **finca A** farm, ranch
el **fin de semana 5** weekend
fino(a) 1 fine
firmar 8 to sign
el **flan 5** caramel custard
la **flor 8** flower
flujo 10 flow
el **folleto 8** brochure
formar 1 to form
formado(a) 2 formed
la **foto (fotografía) 2** photo
la **fotocopiadora A** photocopying
    machine
fotocopiar A to photocopy
el **francés 1** French
el **franqueo A** postage
el **frasco 7** bottle
la **frazada A** blanket
frecuente adv. **6** frequent
el **fregadero 5** sink
freír (i, i) 5 to fry
la **frente 9** forehead
frente a 2 in front of
la **fresa 5** strawberry
el **frijol 5** bean

frío(a) 5 cold
la fruta 2 fruit
la frutería 6 fruit store
el fuego 2 fire
el fuego alto 5 high heat
el fuego bajo 5 low heat
el fuego mediano 5 medium heat
la fuente 2 fountain
fuerte adj. 3 strong
fumar 6 to smoke
la función 3 show
funcionar 7 to function, to work
fundar 10 to found, establish
el fútbol 1 soccer
el fútbol americano 4 football

G

las gafas de sol 8 sunglasses
la galería 1 gallery
la ganadería 10 cattle raising
ganar 4 to win
la ganga 6 bargain
el garaje 7 garage
garantizar 9 to guarantee
la garganta 9 throat
la gaseosa 5 soft drink
gastar 6 to spend
el gasto A expense
generalmente 8 generally
la geografía 1 geography
geográfico(a) 2 geographical
el/la gerente 6 manager
la gimnasia 4 gymnastics
el gimnasio 2 gymnasium
giro monetario 8 money order
el/la gobernador(a) 10 governor
el gobierno 10 government
el golf 4 golf
el golfo 4 gulf
gordo(a) 1 fat, heavy, overweight
el/la gorila 5 gorilla
grabar A to record
gracias 1 thanks
Gracias, pero no puedo 3 Thanks, but I can't
gracias a Dios 4 thank God
grande adj. 1 big, large; great
las Grandes Ligas 5 Major Leagues

el grano 6 grain
la grasa 9 fat
grasoso(a) 9 greasy
la gripe 9 flu
gris H gray
gritar 5 to shout
el guante 4,6 glove
guapo(a) 1,3 handsome
guardar 7 to put away
guardar cama 9 to stay in bed
guardar la línea 9 to stay in shape
el/la guía 8 tour guide
la guía turística 8 guide book
gustar 5 to like, to be pleasing to

H

la habichuela 5 green bean
la habitación 2 room
la habitación doble A double room
la habitación sencilla A single room
el/la habitante 1 inhabitant
hablador(a) 5 talkative
hablar 1 to talk
hablar por teléfono 2 to talk on the phone
hace tres días que 2 it has been three days since
hacer 2 to do, to make
hacer a mano A to make by hand
hacer buen (mal) tiempo 4 to be good (bad) weather
hacer calor (frío, fresco, sol, viento) 4 to be hot (cold, cool, sunny, windy)
hacer compras 4 to do the shopping
hacer ejercicios 9 to exercise
hacer falta 8 to miss; to lack
hacer juego 6 to match, to go well with
hacer la cama 4 to make the bed
hacer mandados 4 to run errands
hacer una cita 10 to make an appointment
hacer un picnic 4 to have a picnic
la hacienda 4 ranch

Haga la tarea H Do the homework
la hamaca 4 hammock
la hamburguesa 2 hamburger
la harina de pescado 10 fish meal
hasta 6 until
hasta luego 1, 2 see you later, so long
hasta mañana 1 see you tomorrow
hasta pronto 1 see you soon
hasta que 10 until
hay H,1,2 there is, there are
hay que 2 one has to
he aquí 7,8 here is
la heladera 4 cooler
la heladería 5 ice cream shop
el helado 5 ice cream
la herencia 4 heritage
la hermana 3 sister
la hermanastra 3 stepsister
el hermanastro 3 stepbrother
el hermano 3 brother
hermoso(a) 6 beautiful
el héroe 5 hero
hervir (ie, i) 5 to boil
el hielo 4 ice
el/la hijo(a) único(a) 3 only son/daughter
la hijastra 3 stepdaughter
el hijastro 3 stepson
la hija 3 daughter
el hijo 3 son
el/la hispanohablante 1 Spanish speaker
la historia 1 history
el hockey (Anglicism) 4 hockey
la hoja de vida A résumé
la hoja electrónica A spreadsheet
hola 1 hello, hi
el hombre H man
el hombro 9 shoulder
honrado(a) A honest
la hora 3 hour, time
la hora de llegada 3 arrival time
el horario de clases 2 class schedule
el horario de trabajo A work schedule
hornear 5 to bake
el horno 5 oven
el horóscopo 9 horoscope

horrible 5 horrible
el **hospedaje 9** lodging
el **hostal A** hostel
el **hotel 8** hotel
hoy día 5 nowadays
el **hueso 9** bone
el **huésped A** guest
el **huevo frito 5** fried egg
el **huevo revuelto 6** scrambled egg
humano(a) 10 human
el **humo A** smoke

I

el idioma 2 language
la **iglesia 2** church
ignorar 10 ignore
igualmente 1 likewise
imaginarse 4 to imagine
el **impermeable 6** raincoat
importante 10 important
imposible 10 impossible
impresionante 2 impressive
la **impresora A** printer
imprimir A to print
los **impuestos 10** taxes
inaugurado(a) 2 inaugurated
incomparable 2 incomparable,
    matchless
el/la **inconforme 6** finnicky
    customer
increíble *adj.* **10** incredible
independiente *adj.* **1** independent
indicar 8 to indicate
industrial A industrial
la **infección 9** infection
la **inflación 10** inflation
infuyente 10 influential
la **información 2** information
informar 10 to inform; to report
la **informática 2** computer store
la **ingeniería 1** engineering
el/la **ingeniero(a) A** engineer
el **inglés 1** English
el **ingrediente 6** ingredient
inmediatamente 2 immediately
el **inodoro A** toilet

insistir (en) 2 to insist
inteligente 1 intelligent
intentar 6 to try
interesante 2 interesting
interesar 2 to be interested
el/la **intérprete A** interpreter
invertir (ie, i) A to invest
el **invierno 2** winter
el/la **invitado(a) 6** guest
la **inyección 9** shot, injection
ir 2 to go
ir a la playa 3 to go to the beach
ir a un concieto 4 to go to the
    concert
ir a un partido 4 to go a game
ir al cine 3 to go to the movies
ir de compras 7 to go shopping
ir de excursión 9 to go on an
    outing
irse 7 to go away, to leave
la **isla 1** island
el **italiano 1** Italian
la **izquierda 3** left (side)

J

el **jabón 6,7** soap
jamás 5 never
el **jamón 5** ham
el **jarabe 9** cough syrup
el **jardín 7,8** garden; yard
el/la **jardinero(a) 4** outfielder
los **jeans** *(Anglicism)* **6** jeans
el/la **jefe(a) 1** head, chief; boss
el **jogging** *(Anglicism)* **10** jogging
el/la **joven 1** young
las **joyas 7** jewelry
la **joyería 6** jewelry store
el **juego electrónico A** electronic
    game
el **jueves 3** Thursday
el **juez 10** judge
la **jugada 5** play *(in a game)*
el/la **jugador(a) 4** player
jugar (a) **4** to play
jugar a las cartas 6 to play cards
el **jugo 2** juice

el **jugo de limón 6** lemon juice
el **jugo de naranja 5** orange juice
julio 2 July
la **jungla 4** jungle
junio 2 June
junto(a) 2 together
justo 10 just, exactly
la **juventud 1** youth

K

el **kilo 5** kilogram *(equivalent to 2.2
    pounds)*
el **kilómetro cuadrado 2** square
    kilometer

L

el **labio 7** lip
el **laboratorio 2** laboratory
el **laboratorio de lenguas
    (idiomas) 3** language laboratory
el **lado 5** side
el **lago 6** lake
la **lágrima 3** tear
lamentar 8 to regret
la **lámpara 7** lamp
la **lana 6** wool
la **langosta 5** lobster
el **lápiz 1** pencil
el **lápiz labial 7** lipstick
largo(a) 6 long
el **largo 5** length
la **lástima 10** pity
el **lavabo A** sink
la **lavadora 7** washer
la **lavandería 7** laundry room
el **lavaplatos 5** dishwasher
lavar 8 to wash
lavar la ropa 7 to wash clothes
lavarse 7 to wash (oneself)
Lean la lección H Read the lesson
la **lección 2** lesson
la **leche 2** milk
la **lechuga 5** lettuce
el/la **lector(a) 10** reader
la **lectura 2** reading
leer 2 to read
la **legumbre 1** vegetable

lejos (de) **2** far (from); faraway
el **lema 10** motto
la **lengua 9,2** tongue
lento(a) 6 slow
levantar pesas 9 to lift weights
levantarse 7 to get up
la **ley 10** law
la **leyenda 4** legend
libre 2 free
la **librería 1** bookstore
el **libro 1** book
ligero(a) 6 light
límon 5 lemon
limitar 9 to limit
limpiar 8 to clean
limpiar la casa 7 to clean the house
limpio(a) A clean
lindo(a) 6 pretty
la **lista de espera 8** waiting list
listo 4 ready
la **literatura 2** literature
el **litro 5** liter (equivalent to 1.057 quarts)
la **llamada telefónica 1** telephone call
la **llamada 3** telephone call
llamar 2 to call
llamarse 7 to be called
el **llano 8** plain
la **llave A** key
el **llavero 6** keychain
la **llegada 8** arrival
llegar (a) 2 to arrive
lleno(a) 2 full
llevar 6 to take; to wear
llevar a cabo 10 to accomplish
llevarla suave 9 to take it easy
llover (ue) 4 to rain
lluvioso(a) 10 rainy
lo antes posible 2 as soon as possible
Lo siento, tengo que… 3 I'm sorry, I have to…
el **lobby** (Anglicism) **A** lobby
la **loción 7** shaving lotion
loco(a) 3 crazy
el/la **locutor(a) 10** announcer
lograr 4 to manage; to be successful

lo más pronto posible 2 as soon as possible
lo siento 7 I'm sorry
luego 6 then; later
luego que 10 as soon as
el **lugar 2** place
los **lugares universitarios 3** university places
el **lujo 3** luxury
lujoso(a) 6 luxurious
la **luna de miel 8** honeymoon
el **lunes 3** Monday
la **luz 1** light

M

la **madera 10** wood
la **madrastra 3** stepmother
la **madre 3** mother
madrina 3 godmother
madrugador(a) 7 likes to rise early
madrugar 7 to get up early
el/la **maestro(a) 4** teacher
magnífico(a) 4,6 magnificent; great; wonderful
majadero(a) 3 annoying
mal 1 bad, badly, not well
malcriado(a) 4 spoiled
la **maleta 8** suitcase
el **maletero 5** trunk
malo(a) 2 bad
la **mamá 3** mother
mandar 8 to govern; to command, to order
mandatorio(a) A mandatory
manejar A to manage, to handle
la **mano 7,9** hand
la **mano de obra 8** manual labor
manos arriba 6 hands up!
la **manta A** blanket
la **manteca 9** lard
el **mantel 5** tablecloth
mantenerse en forma 9 to stay in shape
la **mantequilla 5** butter
la **manzana 5** apple; block (Spain)
la **mañana 1** tomorrow
el **mapa 1** map

el **maquillaje 7** makeup
maquillarse 7 to put on makeup
la **máquina de afeitar 7** electric razor
la **máquina de escribir A** typewriter
la **maquinaria agrícola A** agricultural machinery
las **maquinarias 2** machinery
maravilloso(a) 6 marvelous
el **Mar Caribe 1** Caribbean Sea
marcharse A to leave
el **marisco 6** seafood
marrón H brown
el **martes 3** Tuesday
marzo 2 March
más 3 plus
¡Más ánimo! 9 Cheer up!
más de 1,2 more than
más grande 1 larger, largest
más o menos 1 more or less, so-so
las **matemáticas 2** math
la **materia 2** (academic) subject
el **material 7** fabric
maya 4 Mayan
mayo 2 May
la **mayonesa 5** mayonnaise
mayor 3 greater; bigger, biggest; older, oldest
mayoría 10 majority
Me da igual. 4 It's all the same to me.
Me encantaría 3 I would love to
me llamo… H My name is
mecánico(a) A mechanic
mecanografiar A to type
la **mecedora 7** rocking chair
la **medalla 6** medal
mediano(a) 7 medium
mediante A through
las **medias 6** stockings
la **medicina 1,2** medicine
el/la **médico(a) A** physician
la **medida 6** measurement; measure
el **medio ambiente 10** environment
el **Mediterráneo 2** Mediterranean Sea

mejor 2 best; better
mejorar 10 to improve
mencionar 10 to mention
menor 3 smaller, smallest; younger, youngest
menos 3 minus; less
menú 5 menu
mentir (ie, i) 8 to lie
la **merienda** 5 afternoon snack
la **merluza** 5 hake (fish from Bay of Biscay)
la **mermelada** 5 marmalade
el **mes** 2 month
mes pasado 5 last month
la **mesa** 1 table
la **mesa de noche** 7 nightstand
mestizo(a) 5 of mixed blood
la **meta A** goal
el/la **meteorólogo(a)** 10 weatherman, weatherwoman
meter 5 to put in
mexicano(a) 1 Mexican
mezclar 6 to mix
mi 2 my
mi cielo 4 sweetheart, darling (figurative)
la **microcomputadora A** personal computer, microcomputer
el **microondas** 5 microwave
el **microscopio** 2 microscope
la **miel** 5 honey
el **miembro** 4 member
mientras 2 while
mientras tanto 5 in the meantime, meanwhile
mientras que 10 as long as; while

el miércoles 3 Wednesday
los **millones** 1 millions
la **miniprueba** 1 quiz, minitest
mirar 1 to look at, to watch
mirarse 8 to look at oneself
la **mitad** 1 half
mi vida darling (figurative)
la **mochila** 1 backpack
los **modales** 5 manners
el **molde** 6 baking pan
molestar 2 to bother

la **molestia** 10 discomfort
la **monarquía** 10 monarchy
la **moneda** 8 currency; coin
la **montaña** 6 mountain
montañoso(a) 2 mountainous
montar a caballo 8 to ride horses
el **monumento** 8 monument
morado(a) H purple
morir (ue, u) 7 to die
morirse (ue, u) de hambre 7 to be starving; to die of hunger
mostaza 5 mustard
el **mostrador** 6 counter
el **mostrador de la aerolínea** 7 airline counter
mostrar (ue) 4 to show
el **motor** 9 engine
mover (ue) 6 to move
la **muchacha** 1 girl
el **muchacho** 1 boy
muchas gracias H thank you very much
muchas veces 1 often
mucho 1 a lot, plenty, much
mucho gusto H it's a pleasure (to meet you)
los **muebles** 8 furniture
muerto(a) 3 dead
la **mujer H** woman
las **muletas** 9 crutches
la **multa A** fine
multar A to fine
el **mundo** 1 world
el **mundo hispánico** 1 Hispanic world
el **mundo de hoy** 3 today's world
la **muñeca** 9 wrist
la **muralla** 8 wall
el **músculo** 9 muscle
el **museo** 8 museum
la **música** 2 music
muy 1 very
Muy bien H Very well, fine
Muy bien, gracias. ¿Y tú/usted? (fam/formal) **H** Fine, thank you. And you?

N

la **nación** 1 nation
la **nacionalidad** 2 nationality
nada 4 nothing
nadar 1 to swim
nadar en el mar 4 to swim in the ocean
nadie 5 nobody, no one, not anybody
la **naranja** 5 orange
la **naríz** 9 nose
la **natación** 1 swimming
la **naturaleza A** nature
naúsea 9 nausea
la **navaja de afeitar** 8 razor blade
necesario(a) 3 necessary
la **necesidad** 3 necessity
necesitar 6 to need
necesito un/una H I need a…
negar(le) 10 to deny
el **negocio** 10 business
negro(a) H black
neoclásico(a) 2 neoclassical
nevado(a) 10 snow-covered
ni…ni 4 neither…nor
ni modo 9 what the heck (colloquial)
la **nieta** 4 granddaughter
el **nieto** 3 grandson
ninguno(a) 5 none, not any
no muy bien H not very well
no sé 4 I don't know
no tienes razón 4 you're wrong
nocivo(a) 10 hazardous
la **noche** 1 night, evening
no hay lugar 8 there's no room
el **nombre** 2 name
norteamericano(a) 1 American; North American
la **nota** 2 note
notablemente 9 notably
la **noticia** 10 news item
el **noticiero** 10 newscast
notificar 8 to notify
noveno(a) 7 ninth
la **novia** 2 girlfriend
noviembre 2 November

el novio 2 boyfriend
nublado(a) 9 foggy
la **nuera** 3 daughter-in-law

nuevo(a) 5 new
numeroso(a) 2 numerous
nunca 5 never

O

o… o 5 either… or
obligar 6 to force
la **obra 2** work; deed
obtener 9 to obtain
occidental *adj.* **7** western
octavo(a) 7 eighth
octubre 2 October
ocupado(a) 2 busy
ocurrírsele (a uno) A to cross
    one's mind, to occur
la **oferta 6** offer *(in a sale)*
la **oficina 1** office
el **oficio A** occupation
ofrecer 4 to offer
el **oído 9** inner ear
oír 6 to hear
ojalá 10 I hope that
los **ojos 7** eyes
olvidarse (de) 7 to forget
operar 9 to operate
ordenar 8 to order
ordenar el cuarto 7 to pick up
    one's room
la **oreja 9** ear
oriental *adj.* **7** eastern
el **oriente 2** east
originalmente 2 originally
el **oro 6** gold
la **orquesta 3** orchestra
la **orquídea 8** orchid
el **otoño 2** fall
otro(a) 4 other; another
otra vez 8 again
oye listen!

P

el/la **paciente 3,9** patient
el **pacto de paz 5** peace pact
el **padrastro 3** stepfather
el **padre 3** father
los **padres 3** parents
el **padrino 3** godfather

pagar 6 to pay
pagar a plazos 7 to pay in
    installments
pagar al contado 7 to pay cash
pagar en efectivo 7 to pay cash
el **pago 7** payment
el **país 1** country
el **paisaje lunar 7** moonscape
el **pájaro 7** bird
la **palabra 2** word
la **palabra interrogativa 2**
    interrogative word
el **palacio 2** palace
la **palmera 5** palm tree
el **pan 5** bread
la **panadería 6** bakery
panameño(a) 1 Panamanian
el **panecillo 6** roll
la **pantalla A** screen
los **pantalones 6** pants, slacks
las **pantimedias 6** pantyhose
el **pañuelo 6** handkerchief
la **papa 5** potato
el **papá 3** father
las **papas fritas 5** french fries
el **papel 1** paper
la **papelería 7** stationery store
el **papel higiénico A** toilet paper
el **par 6** pair
para 1 for, in order
para chuparse los dedos 6 finger-
    licking good
para nada 5 at all
el **parador A** government inn
para que 10 in order that, so that
parecer 2 to appear, to seem
la **pared 1** wall
parlamentario(a) 2 parliamentary
el **parque 2** park
el **parque nacional 9** national park
la **parte 1** part
el **partido 5** game
el **partido político 10** political
    party
el **pasado 4** past
el **pasaje 8** ticket, fare
el **pasaje de ida y vuelta 8**
    roundtrip fare

el/la **pasajero(a) 8** passenger
pasar 3 go by
pasar 3 to spend
el **pasaporte 9** passport
pasar la aspiradora 7 to vacuum
pasar una película 3 to show a
    movie
el **pasatiempo 4** pastime
el **pase 5** pass (in a game)
pasear por el centro 3 to take a
    walk downtown
el **pasillo 7** hall; aisle
la **pasta de dientes 6** toothpaste
el **pastel 6** pastry
la **pastelería 6** pastry shop
la **pastilla 9** pill; lozenge
patear 4 to kick
patinar 4 to skate
el/la **patrocinador(a) 10** sponsor
patrocinar 10 to sponsor
el **pecho 9** chest
pedir (i, i) 4 to ask for, to request;
    to order
pedir prestado 8 to borrow
peinarse 7 to comb (one's hair)
el **peine 7** comb
la **peinilla 8** comb
pelar 5 to peel
pelearse 7 to have a fight
la **peletería 7** fur store
el **peligro 2** danger
el **pelo 7** hair
la **pelota 4** baseball, tennis ball
el **pelotero 5** baseball player
el/la **peluquero(a) A** hair stylist
la **pena capital 10** death penalty
el **pendiente 6** earring
la **penicilina 9** penicillin
la **Península Ibérica 1** Iberian
    Peninsula
pensar (ie) 3 to think; to intend
pensar en las musarañas 8 to be
    daydreaming
la **pensión A** boarding house
peor 4 worse, worst
pequeño(a) 1 small
la **pera 5** pear
perder (ie) 4 to lose

perdido(a) 2 lost

¡Perdón! 3 Pardon me!

perdurable 4 everlasting

perezoso(a) 1 lazy

el **perfume 6** perfume

la **perfumería 6** perfume store

el **perímetro 2** perimeter

el **periódico A** newspaper

el/la **periodista 10** journalist, newspaper man/woman

la **perla 8** pearl

permitir 9 to permit

pero 1 but

la **persona 1** person

la **persona desaparecida 1** missing person

pertenecer 5 to belong

la **pesadez 1** heaviness

pesado(a) 7 tedious, dull

pesar 9 to weigh

la **pesca 5** fishing

la **pescadería 6** fish market

el **pescado 6** fish

pescar 6 to fish

el **peso 9** weight

el **petróleo 10** oil

picado(a) 6 chopped

picante 5 hot (spices)

picar 5 to chop

el **pie 9** foot

la **pierna 9** leg

el **piloto 8** pilot

la **pimienta 5** pepper

pintarse (las uñas) 7 to polish (one's nails)

pintoresco(a) 4 picturesque

la **pirámide 4** pyramid

la **piscina 4** swimming pool

el **piso 6,7** floor

la **pista 3** trail

la **pistola 6** pistol

la **pizarra 1** blackboard

la **pizca 5** pinch (salt, pepper, etc.)

el **placer 5** pleasure

la **plancha 7** iron

el **plan de retiro A** retirement plan

planchar la ropa 7 to iron

la **planta 7** floor (Spain)

la **planta alta 7** upstairs; upper floor

la **planta baja 7** downstairs, main floor

la **planta nuclear A** nuclear plant

la **plata 6** silver

el **plátano 5** plantain; banana

la **platería 4** items made of silver

el **plato 5** dish

la **playa 2** beach

el/la **plomero(a) A** plumber

la **pluma 1** pen

el **pluriempleo A** moonlighting

la **población 1** population

poblado(a) 10 populated

poder (ue, u) 4 to be able, can

¿Podría (inf)...? 5 Could you...?

el **policía 2** police officer

la **policía 2** police force

político(a) 5 political

el **pollo 5** chicken

pollo asado 5 broiled chicken

poner 5 to put; to place

poner atención 4 to pay attention

poner la radio 4 to turn on the radio

poner la mesa 4 to set the table

poner música 4 to play music

ponerse 7 to put on

ponerse a dieta 9 to go on a diet

ponerse contento 7 to become happy

ponerse en forma 9 to get in shape

ponerse furioso(a) 7 to become angry

ponerse impaciente 7 to become impatient

ponerse nervioso 7 to become nervous

ponerse triste 7 to become sad

por 1 times (multiplication); for

por ahí (allí) 7 around there

por ahora 7 for now

por aquí 7 around here

por cierto 7 by the way

por Dios 7 for God's sake

por donde 2 through which

por ejemplo 7 for example

por eso 4 that's why

por favor 5 please

por fin 7 finally

por la mañana 2 in the morning

por la noche 2 in the evening

por la tarde 1,2 in the afternoon

por lo general 7 in general, generally

por lo menos 8 at least

por lo visto 7 apparently

por poco 7 almost

porque 1 because

¿por qué? 1 why?

¿Por qué no vamos...? 4 Why don't we go?

por supuesto 8 of course

portarse bien/mal 8 to behave well/poorly

portugués(a) 1 Portuguese

la **posada A** lodging; inn, lodge

posible 10 possible

el **postre 6** dessert

la **práctica** practice

practicar 1 to practice

el **precio 6** cost

preciso(a) A essential

preferir (ie, i) 8 to prefer

la **pregunta 1** question

preguntar por 4 to ask about (somebody or something)

prender 5 to light

la **prensa 10** press; news media

preocupado(a) 2 worried

preocuparse 8 to worry

preparar 1 to prepare

preparar la comida 7 to prepare the meal

la **presentación 1** introduction

presentar 5 to present

presentar una película 4 to show a movie

presidente(a) 10 president

la **preción 9** pressure

prestar 8 to lend

presuntamente 6 presumably

el **presupuesto 8** budget

prevenir 10 to prevent, to warn

la **primavera** 2 spring
la **primera clase** 8 first class
la **primera plana** 9 front page
   (newspaper)
primero(a) 7 first
el/la **primo(a)** 3 cousin
la **prioridad** 10 proirity, to resolve
el **prisionero** 2 prisoner
privilegiado(a) 2 privileged
probable 10 probable
el **probador** 6 fitting room
probar (ue) 5 to try (taste); to try on
el **problema** 3 problem
la **procedencia** 3 origin
el **procesador de textos A** word
   processor
el **producto interno bruto** (PIB) **5**
   gross national product (GNP)
los **productos lácteos** 9 milk products
la **profesión A** profession
el/la **profesor(a)** 1 professor
programar A to program
el **programa radial A** radio program
los **programas sociales A** social
   welfare programs
prohibir 10 to prohibit
pronto 8 soon
la **propina** 5 tip
proteger 10 to protect
la **proteína** 9 protein
la **provincia** 10 state
próximo(a) 2 next
la **prueba** 9 test
el/la **psicólogo(a) A** psychologist
el **pueblo** 10 the people, the mass
¿Puedes ir a… ? 3 Can you go to… ?
la **puerta** 1 door
la **puerta de salida** 8 gate; exit door
el **puerto** 6 port
el **puerto libre** 8 duty-free port
puertorriqueño(a) 1 Puerto Rican
pues sí 3 yes, indeed
el **puesto** 6 stand; position; job
el **pulmón** 9 lung
la **pulsera** 6 bracelet
la **punta** 1 tip; point
el **pupitre** 1 student desk

Q

¿qué? 1 what?
que 1 that
¿Qué crees? 4 What do you think?
¡Qué disgracia! 4 How unfortunate!
¿Qué es esto? H What's this?
¿Qué hay? H What's new?
¿Qué hay en? H What's in?
¿Qué piensas? 4 What do you think?
¿Qué tal? H What's up? How goes it?
¿Qué tal si… ? 4 What if… ?
¿Qué te parece? 4 What do you
   think?
¿Qué tiempo hace? 4 What's the
   weather like?
quedar 2 to have left
quedar bien 7 to fit well
quedarse 9 to stay
el **quehacer doméstico** 8 household
   chore
la **queja A** complaint
quejarse A to complain
querer 3 to want, to love
querido(a) 3 dear
¿quién? 1 who
¿Quiere ir a… ? 3 Do you want to
   go to… ?
el **queso** 5 cheese
la **química** 2 chemistry
quinto(a) 7 fifth
quisiera… 5 I would like...
quitar 8 to remove
quitar la mesa 8 to clear the table
quitarse 7 to take off
quizá(s) A perhaps, maybe

R

el **radio** radio set
la **radio** radio (in general)
la **radioactividad A** radioactivity
la **radiografía** 9 x-ray
el **radioyente** 10 (radio) listcncr
rápido(a) 6 fast
raptado(a) 3 kidnapped
la **raqueta** 4 racquet

raro(a) 5 strange
reaccionar 5 to react
real *adj.* 2 royal
realmente 4 really
la **rebaja** 6 sale
rebajar 6 to lower
la **recepción A** front desk
el/la **recepcionista A** front desk clerk
la **receta** 5,9 recipe; prescription
recetar 9 to prescribe
rechazar 4 to reject
recibido(a) 3 received
recibir 2 to receive
el **recibo** 6 receipt
el **reciclaje A** recycling
recientemente 5 recently
el **recipiente** 5 generic pot, bowl,
   dish, etc.
la **reclamación de equipaje** 9
   baggage claim
la **recomendación A** recommendation
recomendar (ie) 8 to recommend
recordar (ue) 6 ro remember
recorrer 10 to travel throughout, to
   tour
recorrer el país 8 to go around
   (across) the country
la **rectoría** 2 administration building
el **recurso natural** 10 natural resource
redondo(a) 1 round
reducir 9 to reduce
reducir de peso 9 to lose weight
la **referencia A** reference
el **refresco** 2,5 refreshment, soda
el **refrigerador** 5 refrigerator
regatear 7 to bargain
el **registro A** guest register
regresar 1 to return
regular 1 so-so
la **reina** 10 queen
el **reinado** 2 reign
el **reino** 2 kingdom
reír (i, i) 4 to laugh
reírse (de) 7 to laugh (at)
el **reloj** 1 clock
el **reloj pulsera** 6 wristwatch
el/la **remitente** 8 sender

renunciar A to resign
reñir (i, i) 5 to quarrel
reparar A to repair
repartir A to deliver; to distribute
repetir (i, i) 4 to repeat; to have a second helping
Repita(n) las frases H Repeat the sentences
la **repoblación forestal A** reforestation
el/la **reportero(a) 10** reporter
reposar 9 to rest
el **reposo 9** rest
el/la **representante A** representative
la **República Dominicana 1** Dominican Republic
el **rescate 3** ransom; rescue operation
la **reseña 10** review
reservar 6 to reserve
reservar una mesa 5 to reserve a table
el **resfriado 9** cold
la **residencia estudiantil 2** student residence, dorm
resolver (ue) 10 to solve; to resolve
la **respiración A** breathing
respirar 9 to breathe
responder (a) 7 to answer
la **responsabilidad A** responsibility
responsable 3 responsible
la **respuesta 1** answer
el **restaurante 2** restaurant
el **retorno 7** return
reunirse 4 to get together
la **revista 10** magazine
el **rey 10** king
rico(a) 3 rich
riesgo 9 risk
el **río 8** river
la **rodilla 9** knee
rogar (ue) 8 to beg
rojo(a) H red
el **rollo de película 8** roll of film (for a camera)
romperse (un hueso) 9 to break (a bone)
la **ropa 6** clothing
rosado(a) H pink

roto(a) A broken
rubio(a) 1 blond(e)
el **ruido 3** noise
la **ruina 2** ruin

S

el **sábado 3** Saturday
la **sábana A** sheet (for a bed)
saber 4 to know (facts, information)
sabroso(a) 5 savory, tasty
sacar la basura 7 to take out the garbage
sacar la lengua 10 to stick out one's tongue
el **saco 7** sportscoat
sacrificar 10 to sacrifice
el **sacrificio 10** sacrifice
sacudir los muebles 7 to dust the furniture
la **sal 6** salt
la **sala 7** living room
la **sala de espera 8** waiting room
el **salario A** salary, wages
la **salida 9** departure
la **salida de emergencia 8** emergency exit
salir 3 to leave, to go out
salir a 5 to go out to do something
salir con 5 to go out with, to date
salir de 5 to leave a place, to leave on a trip
el **salón de conferencias A** convention hall
la **salsa de tomate 5** tomato sauce; ketchup
la **salud 10** health
saludable adj. **9** healthy
saludar 4 to say hello
los **saludos 1** greetings
salvaje adj. **8** wild
la **sandalia 6** sandal
el **sándwich 5** sandwich
la **sangre 9** blood
sano(a) 9 healthy
el **sarape 4** colorful Mexican shawl
el/la **sartén 5** frying pan, skillet

la **sastrería 6** tailor shop
satisfacer 10 to satisfy
la **secadora 7** dryer; hair dryer
secar 8 to dry
secarse 7 to dry oneself
la **sección de no fumar 8** no-smoking section
la **sección deportiva 9** sports section (newspaper)
la **sección de ropa 6** clothing section (newspaper)
la **sección financiera 9** business section (newspaper)
el/la **secretario(a) 1** secretary
secuestrar 6 to kidnap
el **secuestro 7** kidnapping
la **seda 6** silk
la **sede 10** seat (of government)
seguir (i, i) 4 to follow; to continue
según 6,9 according to
segundo(a) 7 second
seguro 10 sure; safe
el **seguro de vida A** life insurance
el **sello 8** stamp
la **selva 7** jungle
la **semana 2** week
la **semana pasada 5** last week
sembrar (ie) A to plant
el **semestre 2** semester
el **senado 10** senate
el/la **senador(a) 10** senator
sentarse (ie) 7 to sit down
sentir (ie, i) 8 to feel; to be sorry for; to regret
sentirse (ie, i) 7 to feel
el **señor (Sr.) 1** Mr
la **señora (Sra.) 1** Mrs
la **señorita (Srta.) 1** Miss
septiembre 2 September
séptimo(a) 7 seventh
ser 1 to be
serio(a) 3 serious
servicial adj. **4** helpful
el **servicio a la habitación A** room service
el **servicio de camarera A** cleaning service

el **servicio de lavandería A** laundry service

la **servilleta 5** napkin

servir (i, i) 4 to serve

sexto(a) 7 sixth

si 1 if

sí 1 yes

¿Sí? 2 Really?

Sí, claro. 3 Yes, of course.

siempre 4 always

la **silla 1** chair

el **sillón 7** armchair, overstuffed chair

simpático(a) 1 nice, friendly

sin A without

sin embargo 9 however

sino A but (on thc contrary, rather)

sin que 10 without

el **síntoma 9** symptom

la **sirvienta 7** maid

el **sirviente 7** servant

situado(a) 1 situated

sobre 1 about; on

el **sobre 8** envelope

el/la **sobrecargo 9** flight attendant

el **sobrepeso 9** overweight

la **sobrina 3** niece

el **sobrino 3** nephew

el **sofá 7** sofa

el **sol 2** sun

solamente 2 only

solicitado(a) 3 requested

la **solicitud** de empleo **A** job application form

sólo *adv.* **1** only

solo(a) *adj.* **3,8** alone

soltero(a) 3 single

la **sombrerería 7** hat store

el **sombrero 6** hat

la **sombrilla 4** sun umbrella

sonar (ue) 7 to ring (bell, alarm, clock)

soñar (ue)(con) 4 to dream (about)

la **sopa 5** soup

la **sopa de vegetales 6** vegetable soup

sorprender 8 to surprise

la **sorpresa 3** surprise

Soy... H I am

subir (a) **6** to climb

subir de peso 9 to gain weight

el **subsuelo 8** subsoil

el **suceso 7** event

sucio(a) 5 dirty

el/la **suegro(a) 3** father/mother-in-law

el **sueldo A** wages, salary

el **suelo 7** soil

el **suéter 6** sweater

la **sugerencia 5** suggestion

sugerir (ie, i) 8 to suggest

el **suite de lujo A** deluxe suite

Suiza 2 Switzerland

la **suma 3** sum

súper 6 very *(slang)*

la **superpoblación A** overpopulation

el/la **supervisor(a) A** supervisor

suponer 5 to suppose

el **sur 1** south

el **sustantivo 10** noun

T

el **tablero 8** information board

talar A to raze

el **talco 6** powder

tal vez 10 perhaps, maybe

la **talla 6** size

el **taller de reparaciones 5** repair shop

el **tamaño 5** size

también 1,5 also; too

tampoco 5 neither, not either

tan... como 4 as... as

tan pronto como 10 as soon as

tanto 3 so much

tanto... como 3 as... as

tapar 5 to cover

la **taquilla 2** ticket booth

tarde *adj.* **2** late

la **tarjeta 8** postcard

la **tarjeta de crédito 6** credit card

la **tarjeta de embarque 8** boarding pass

la **taza 6** cup

el **té 5** tea

el **teclado A** keyboard

tecnológico(a) A technological

el **teléfono inalámbrico A** cordless telephone

el **teléfono portátil A** portable telephone

la **telenovela 10** soap opera

el **televidente 10** television viewer

la **televisión 4** television (in general)

el **televisor A** television set

temer 8 to fear

temperatura 9 temperature

la **temporada 4** season

temprano 4 early

el **tenedor 5** fork

tener 2 to have

tener — años 2 to be (so many) years old

tener calor 2 to be hot

tener confianza en 9 to trust

tener cuidado 2 to be careful

tener dolor 10 to have a pain

tener fiebre 10 to have a fever

tener frío 2 to be cold

tener hambre 2 to be hungry

tener miedo (de) **10** to fear

tener náuseas 10 to be nauseated

tener prisa 2 to be in a hurry

tener que + inf. 1 to have to do (something)

tener razón 5 to be right

tener un resfriado 10 to have a cold

tener sed 2 to be thirsty

tener sueño 2 to be sleepy

el **tenis 1** tennis

el **tenis de mesa 5** table tennis

el/la **tenista 5** tennis player

tercero(a) 7 third

el **tercio 5** third

terco(a) 9 stubborn

el **término deportivo 5** sports term

término medio 5 medium-rare

la **ternera 5** veal

la **terraza 7** terrace

el **territorio 2** territory

el/la **terrorista 4** terrorist

la **tía 3** aunt

el **tiempo** 4 weather/time

la **tienda** 6 store

tienda naturalista 9 health store

tienes razón 4 you're right

la tierra 2 homeland; land; earth

las **tijeras** 7 scissors

tímido(a) 4 timid

el **tío** 3 uncle

el **tipo** 7 type

tirar 8 to throw

las **tiras cómicas** 9 comics

el **titular** 9 headline

el **título** 1 title

la **tiza** 1 chalk

la **toalla** 4 towel

el **tobillo** 9 ankle

el **tocacassettes** 4 cassette player

el **tocadiscos** 8 record player

tocar 4 to play (a musical instrument); to touch

todavía 5 yet, still

todo 4 everything

todos los días 1 every day

tomar 2 to take; to drink

tomar apuntes A to take notes

tomar el sol 3 to sunbathe

tomar en cuenta to take into account

tomarse la presión 10 to take one's blood pressure

tomarse la temperatura 10 to take one's temperature

el **tomate** 5 tomato

tonto 1 dumb

torcerse twist

torcerse el tobillo 10 to twist one's ankle

la **torre de mandos** 9 control tower

la **torta** 5 cake

la **tortilla de papas** 6 egg and potato omelet

tortilla española spanish omelette

toser 9 to cough

la **tostada** 5 toast

la **tostadora** 5 toaster

tostar (ue) 5 to toast

trabajador(a) 1 hardworking

trabajar 1 to work

trabajar a comisión A to work on commission

el **trabajo** 1 work

traer 5 to bring

el **traje** 6 suit

el **traje a la medida** 6 custom-made suit

el **traje de baño** 4 bathing suit

tranquilo(a) 6 calm, quiet

transmitir 10 to transmit

el **tratado** 5 treaty

tratar 9 to try

travieso 3 mischieveus

triste *adj.* 3 sad

triunfar 10 to triumph

trotar 10 to jog

tu 3 your (familiar)

el/la **turista** 2 tourist

turístico(a) 2 tourist

turnarse 10 to take turns

turquesa 4 turquoise

U

la **ubicación** 9 location; situation

último(a) 3 last

una vez a… 8 once a…

único(a) 6 only

unido(a) 3 close

universitario(a) 3 pertaining to the university

la **universidad** a university

un poco 1 a little

la **uña** 7,9 finger/toenail

urgente *adj.* 10 urgent

el **utensilio** 6 utensil

útil 10 useful

la **uva** 5 grape

V

vacío(a) 5 empty

Vamos 3 Let's go

¿Vamos a… ? 1,3 Should we go to… ?

el **vaso** 5 glass

Vayan a la pizarra H Go to the board

el/la **vecino(a)** 4 neighbor

la **vela A** candle

el/la **vendedor(a) A** salesperson

el/la **vendedor(a) ambulante** 7 street vendor

vender 2 to sell

venir 3 to come

venezolano(a) 1 Venezuelan

la **venta-liquidación** 6 clearance sale

la **ventana** 1 window

la **ventanilla** 8 porthole; small window

la **ventanilla de pagos** 8 cashier window

ver 5 to see

el **verano** 2 summer

¿Verdad? H True?

la **verdad** 3 truth

verdadero(a) 7 real

verde H green

la **verdura** 6 vegetable

la **verdurería** 6 vegetable store

el **vestido** 6 dress

vestirse (i, i) 7 to get dressed

el/la **veterinario(a) A** veterinarian

la **vez** 3 time

el/la **viajante A** traveling salesperson

el **viaje** 5 trip

el/la **viajero(a)** 8 traveler

la **videograbadora A** video cassette recorder (VCR)

viejo(a) 1 old

el **viernes** 3 Friday

el **vino tinto** 6 red wine

virar 6 to turn

visita 7 guests

el **visitante** 2 visitor

visitar 3 to visit

la **vista** 8,9 view

la **vitrina** 6 display case or window

viva 5 hurray!

vivir 2 to live

vivo(a) 4 alive; smart, alert

volar (ue) 4 to fly

el **volcán** 8 volcano

el **vólibol 4** volleyball
voltear 5 to turnover
volver (ue) 4 to return, to come back
votar 10 to vote
el **vuelo 3** flight
el **vuelo sin escalas 8** nonstop flight

Y

y 2 and
ya 2 already
el **yate de lujo 6** luxury yacht
el **yerno 3** son-in-law

Z

la **zanahoria 5** carrot
la **zapatería 6** shoe store
el **zapato 6** shoe
los **(zapatos de) tenis 6** tennis
  shoes

APPENDIX 4
English-Spanish Vocabulary

A

a little bit later al poco rato
a lot mucho
abortion el aborto
about sobre; acerca de
above arriba de *prep.*
accept aceptar
accessory el accesorio
accompany *(vb.)* acompañar
accomplish llevar a cabo
according to según
accountant el/la contador(a)
ache, pain dolor
achieve lograr
action in progress la acción en ejecución
actress la actriz
add añadir; echar
addressee el/la destinatario(a)
adjective el adjetivo
administration building la rectoría
admire admirar
adverb el adverbio
advice column el consultorio sentimental
advise aconsejar
advisor el/la asesor(a)
aerobics los ejercicios aeróbicos
affection el afecto
after después (de)
afternoon la tarde
afternoon snack la merienda
again otra vez
against contra
agency la agencia
agent el/la agente
agricultural machinery la maquinaria agrícola
air mail el correo aéreo

air el aire
air conditioning el aire acondicionado
airline la aerolínea
airline ticket el boleto
airline counter el mostrador de la aerolínea
airplane el avión
airport el aeropuerto
aisle el pasillo
alarm clock el despertador
alcoholic beverages las bebidas alcohólicas
alert vivo(a)
algebra el álgebra *f.*
alive vivo(a)
allergic alérgico(a)
allergy alergia
almost casi por poco
already ya
also también
although aunque
altitude la altura
always siempre
ambassador el/la embajador(a)
American, North American norteamericano(a)
among entre
analyst el/la analista
ancestor el antepasado
anchored anclado(a)
ancient antiguo(a)
angry enfadado(a)
ankle el tobillo
announcement el anuncio
announcer el/la locutor(a)
annual anual *adj.*
answer responder (a)
answer la respuesta
answering machine el contestador automático

antacid el antiácido
antibiotic el antibiótico
antihistimine antihistamínico
any cualquier(a); alguno(a)
apéritif el aperitivo
apparently por lo visto
appear parecer
apple la manzana
applicant el/la aspirante
application la solicitud
appointment, date la cita
April abril
arch el arco
archaeology la arqueología
architect el/la arquitecto(a)
architecture la arquitectura
Argentinian argentino(a)
arm el brazo
armchair la butaca; el sillón
around there por ahí (allí)
around here por aquí
arrival time la hora de llegada
arrival la llegada
arrive late llegar tarde
arrive llegar (a)
art el arte, *f.*
art school la facultad de arte
article el artículo
as long as mientras que
as soon as en cuanto, luego que, tan pronto como
as como
as soon as possible lo más pronto posible, lo antes posible
as... as tan... como *adj.*
as... as tanto... como *adj.*
ash la ceniza
ask about (somebody or something) preguntar por
ask for pedir (i, i)

asparagus el espárrago
aspirin la aspirina
assault asalto
at about a eso de
at all para nada
Atlantic Ocean el (Océano)
  Atlántico
at least por lo menos
at the same time al mismo tiempo
atmosphere la atmósfera
attend asistir (a)
attract atraer
attractive atractivo(a)
August agosto
aunt la tía
automatic teller machine el cajero
  automático
available disponible
avenue la avenida
avoid *(vb.)* evitar
awesome bárbaro(a)
Aztec azteca

B

B.C. antes de Cristo (a.C)
backpack la mochila
bad malo(a)
badly mal *adv.*
baggage claim la reclamación de
  equipaje
bake hornear
bakery la panadería
baking pan el molde
balcony el balcón
**ball (soccer, basketball,
  volleyball)** el balón
ball-point pen el bolígrafo
banana la banana, el plátano
bank check el cheque
bargain la ganga
bargain regatear
baseball el béisbol; la pelota
baseball player el pelotero
basket la cesta; el cesto
basketball el básquetbol
bat el bate

bathe bañarse
bathing suit el traje de baño
bathroom el baño
be ser
be __ years old tener __ años
be able poder (ue, u)
be abundant abundar
be afraid tener miedo
be called llamarse
be careful tener cuidado; andar con
  cuidado
be cold tener frío
be daydreaming pensar en las
  musarañas
be delayed estar demorado(a)
be happy estar contento (de)
be hungry tener hambre
be hot tener calor
be in a hurry tener prisa
be in style estar de moda
be in the hands of estar en manos de
be interested in interesar
be late estar atrasado(a)
be nauseated tener náuseas
be on a diet estar a dieta
be on time estar a tiempo
be right tener razón
be sleepy tener sueño
be someone's birthday cumplir
  (años)
be sorry (for) sentir (ie, i)
be starving morirse (ue, u) de hambre
be sure asegurarse (de)
be the same dar igual
be thirsty tener sed
beach la playa
bean el frijol
beat batir
beautiful bello(a), hermoso(a)
because porque
become sad ponerse triste
become angry ponerse furioso
become nervous ponerse nervioso
become impatient ponerse
  impaciente
become happy ponerse contento,
  alegrarse (de)

bed la cama
bedroom el cuarto; el dormitorio
beef la carne de res
beef fillet el filete de res
beer la cerveza
before antes *adv.*; antes de *prep.*;
  antes (de) que *conj.*
beg rogar(ue)
begin comenzar (ie), empezar (ie)
beginning, at the al comienzo, a
  principios de
behave well/poorly portarse
  bien/mal
believe creer
bellhop el botones
belong pertenecer
below debajo (de)
belt el cinturón
benefit el beneficio
besides además (de)
best mejor
better mejor
between entre
bicycling el ciclismo
big grande *adj.*
Big Leagues las Grandes Ligas
bill la cuenta; *(bank note)* el billete
binoculars los binoculares
biology la biología
bird el pájaro
black coffee el café solo
black negro(a)
blackboard la pizarra
blanket la manta, la frazada
block (Spanish America) la cuadra;
  (Spain) la manzana
blond(e) rubio(a)
blood la sangre
blouse la blusa
blue azul
board *(vb.)* a bordo
boarding pass la tarjeta de embarque
boarding house la pensión
body structure la complexión
body el cuerpo
boil hervir (ie, i)
bone el hueso

bonus la bonificación
book el libro
bookstore la librería
boot la bota
bored aburrido(a)
boring aburrido(a)
borrow *(vb.)* pedir prestado
boss el/la jefe(a)
bother molestar
bottle of perfume el frasco de
    perfume
bottle la botella
bottle of cologne el frasco de colonia
boxing el boxeo
boy el muchacho
boyfriend el novio
bracelet la pulsera
braggart el/la fanfarrón(a)
bread el pan
break (a bone) romperse (un hueso)
breakfast el desayuno
breathe respirar
breathing la respiración
bring traer
brochure el folleto
broiled asado(a)
broken descompuesto(a), roto(a)
broom la escoba
brother-in-law el cuñado
brother el hermano
brown marrón
brush cepillarse
brush el cepillo
bucket el cubo
budget el presupuesto
building el edificio
bullfighting la corrida de toros
business el comercio, el negocio
business administration la
    administración de empresas
business section *(newspaper)* la
    sección financiera
busy ocupado(a)
but pero; sino
butcher shop la carnicería
butter la mantequilla
buy comprar
by the way a propósito

C

cafeteria la cafetería
cake la torta
calculator la calculadora
call llamar
calm tranquilo(a)
cam recorder la cámara de video
camera la cámara fotográfica
campaign la campaña
candidate el/la candidato(a)
candle la vela
capable capaz *adj.*
capital (city) la capital
car el coche; el carro
caramel custard el flan
carbohydrate el carbohidrato
carefully cuidadosamente
Caribbean Sea el Mar Caribe
carpenter el/la carpintero(a)
carrot la zanahoria
case el caso
cash cobrar
cash el contado, el efectivo
cash register la caja registradora
cashier window la ventanilla de pagos
casserole dish la cazuela
castle el castillo
catch the flu darle la gripe a
cattle raising la ganadería
cause trouble dar guerra
center el centro
Central America América Central
cereal el cereal
chain la cadena
chair la silla
chalk la tiza
challenging exigente *adj.*
champion el/la campeón(a)
championship el campeonato
change cambiar; el cambio *n.*
channel el canal
chat conversar
cheap barato(a)
check in luggage facturar el
    equipaje
checking account la cuenta
    corriente

checkup el examen físico
Cheer up! ¡Más ánimo!
cheese el queso
chemistry la química
chest el pecho
chicken el pollo
Chilean chileno(a)
china cabinet el aparador
chocolate el chocolate
cholesterol el colesterol
choose *(vb.)* escoger
chopped picado(a)
church la iglesia
cigarette el cigarrillo
citizen el/la ciudadano(a)
city la ciudad
class schedule el horario de clases
class la clase; el curso
classified ads los avisos clasificados
classroom expressions las
    expresiones para la clase
clean limpiar
clean the house *(vb.)* limpiar la casa
clean limpio(a)
cleaning service el servicio de
    camarera
clear the table quitar la mesa
clear claro(a)
clearance sale la venta–liquidación
clerk el/la dependiente(a)
client el/la cliente(a)
climate el clima
climb mountains escalar montañas
climb subir (a)
clock el reloj
close cerca *adv.*; cerca de *prep.*
close unido(a)
close *(vb.)* cerrar (ie)
clothing la ropa
clothing section *(newspaper)* la
    sección de ropa
coach class la clase turista
coach el/la entrenador(a)
coast la costa
coat el abrigo, el saco
Coca-Cola la *coca-cola*
cockpit la cabina
coffee el café

coffee with milk el café con leche
coffeepot la cafetera
coin la moneda
cold frío(a); el resfriado n.
collection la colección
Colombian colombiano(a)
color el color
comb (one's hair) peinarse
comb el peine, la peinilla
combat combatir
comfortable cómodo(a)
comics las tiras cómicas
command mandar
commentator el/la comentarista
Commonwealth Estado Libre
   Asociado
compact disc el cómpact disc
   (Anglicism)
compartment el compartimiento
complain quejarse
complaint la queja
complicated complicado(a)
computer science la computación;
   la informática
computer la computadora
concert el concierto
concierge el conserje
condiment el condimento
congratulate felicitar
congratulations felicitaciones,
   enhorabuena
congress el congreso
congressperson el/la diputado
constructed construido(a)
consume consumir
contest (beauty) el certamen
continent el continente
contract el contrato
contribute (vb.) contribuir
control tower la torre de mandos
control controlar
convention hall el salón de
   conferencias
converse conversar
cook cocinar
cook el/la cocinero(a)
cooked cocido(a)

cooler la heladera
coordinator el/la coordinador(a)
copper el cobre
cordially cordialmente
cordless telephone el teléfono
   inalámbrico
corner la esquina
cost costar (ue)
cost el precio
cotton el algodón
cough syrup el jarabe
cough toser
count contar (ue)
counter el mostrador
countersign endosar
country el país
course el curso
court (sports) la cancha
courtesy la cortesía
cousin el/la primo(a)
cover cubrir
covered cubierto(a)
crazy loco(a)
credit card la tarjeta de crédito
crime el crimen
critic el/la crítico(a) n.
critical crítico(a) adj.
criticism la crítica
crop el cultivo
cross one's mind ocurrírsele (a uno)
crutches muletas
crossed atravesado(a)
Cuban cubano(a)
culture la cultura
cup la taza
cure curar
currency la moneda
customer el/la cliente
custom-made suit el traje a la medida
customs la aduana
customs agent el/la aduanero(a)
cut cortar

D

dance bailar
danger el peligro

darling (figurative) mi cielo, mi vida
darn it! ¡demonios!
data base la base de datos
date la fecha
date salir con
date back to datar de
daughter la hija
daughter-in-law la nuera
day el día
dead muerto(a)
dear querido(a)
death penalty la pena capital
December diciembre
decide decidir
defense la defensa
deforestation la despoblación
   forestal, deforestación
delicious delicioso(a), exquisito(a)
delighted encantado(a)
deliver repartir
deluxe suite el suite de lujo
demanding exigente adj.
democracy la democracia
dense espeso(a)
dentist el/la dentista
deny (vb.) negar (ie)
deodorant el desodorante
department store el almacén
departure la salida
deposit (vb.) depositar
descend, go down, get off (vb.)
   bajar
descriptive descriptivo(a)
design diseñar
design el diseño
designed diseñado(a)
desk (student) el pupitre
dessert el postre
destroy (vb.) destruir
destroyed destruido(a)
develop (vb.) desarrolar
development desarrollo
diabetes la diabetes
dictator el/la dictador(a)
dictatorship la dictadura
dictionary el diccionario
die morir (ue, u)

dining room el comedor
dinner la cena
director el/la director(a)
dirty sucio(a)
disappearance la desaparición
disappeared desaparecido *p.p.*
discomfort la molestia
discothèque la discoteca
discount el descuento
discover descubrir
discovery el descubrimiento
dish el plato
dishwasher el lavaplatos
diskette el disco duro
dislike (a person) caer mal
display case or window la vitrina
distribute repartir, distribuir
divided by *(math)* entre
divorced divorciado(a)
do hacer
doctor's office el consultorio
Dominican Republic la República Dominicana
Dominican dominicano(a)
door la puerta
dorm la residencia estudiantil
dose la dosis
double room la habitación doble
doubt *(vb.)* dudar
doubtful dudoso(a)
down with abajo *exclam.*
downstairs la planta baja; abajo *adv.*
downtown en el centro
dramatic art el arte dramático
dream soñar (ue) (con)
dress vestirse (i, i)
dress el vestido
dresser la cómoda
drink beber
drink la bebida
drugstore la droguería, la farmacia
dry oneself secarse
dry secar
dryer la secadora
dust the furniture sacudir los muebles
duty el deber
duty-free port el puerto libre

E

ear la oreja
earring el arete, el pendiente
earth la tierra
east el oriente
eastern oriental
easy fácil
eat comer
economics la economía
editorial page el editorial
eighth octavo(a)
either...or o...o
elect elegir (i, i)
elections las elecciones
electrical appliance el aparato electrónico
electrician el/la electricista
electronic game el juego electrónico
electronic electrónico(a)
elevated elevado(a)
elevator el ascensor
embrace abrazar
emergency exit la salida de emergencia
employment agency la agencia de empleos
employment el empleo
empty vacío(a)
enchant encantar
end eliminar
endorse endosar
energy la energía
engine el motor
engineer el/la ingeniero(a)
engineering school la facultad de ingeniería
engineering la ingeniería
English el inglés
enjoy your meal! ¡buen provecho!
enjoy disfrutar (de)
enormous enorme adj.
enough bastante adj.
enter entrar (en)
entertainment section *(newspaper)* la cartelera
enthusiasm el entusiasmo
enthusiastic entusiasta

envelope el sobre
environment el ambiente; el medio ambiente
equestrian ecuestre
equipped equipado(a)
erase borrar
eraser el borrador
essay el ensayo
essential preciso(a)
establish establecer
ethics la ética
Europe Europa
European europeo(a)
evaluation la evaluación
even though aunque
event el suceso
everlasting perdurable *adj.*
every day todos los días
exam el examen
example el ejemplo
exchange el cambio
excuse me con permiso
exercise hacer ejercicios
exert *(vb.)* ejercer
exhausting agotador(a)
expand extender (ie)
expense el gasto
expensive caro/a)
explain explicar
expression la expresión
exquisite exquisito(a)
extinguish apagar
eyes los ojos

F

fabric el material
fabulous fabuloso(a)
face afrontar
face la cara
factory la fábrica
fair la feria
fall in love (with) enamorarse (de)
fall asleep dormirse (ue, u)
fall el otoño
fall caer(se)
false falso(a)
famous famoso(a)

fan el/la aficionado(a), el/la fanático(a)
fantastic fantástico(a)
far (from) lejos (de)
farewell la despedida
farm la finca
farmer el/la campesino(a)
fascinate encantar
fast rapido(a)
fasten *(vb.)* abrocharse
fat la grasa
fat gordo(a)
father-in-law el suegro
fatigue el cansancio
father el padre; el papá
fax *(Anglicism)* el fax
fear tener miedo (de), temer
February febrero
feel sentirse (ie, i)
fellow citizen el/la conciudadano(a)
fever fiebre
field of study el área *f.* de estudio
field *(sports)* la cancha
fifth quinto(a)
fight combatir
file el expediente
file archivar
finally por fin, finalmente
find out enterarse, averiguar
find encontrar (ue)
fine multar
fine la multa
fine fino(a); bien *adv.*
finger/toe nails la uñas
finger el dedo de la mano
finger-licking good para chuparse los dedos
finicky person el/la inconforme
fire despedir (i, i)
fire el fuego
firefighter el/la bombero(a)
first primero(a)
first class la primera clase
fish fillet el filete de pescado
fish el pescado
fish market la pescadería
fish pescar
fishing la pesca

fish meal la harina de pescado
fit well quedar bien
fitting room el probador
fix arreglar
fixed fijo(a)
flight attendant el sobrecargo
flight el vuelo
floor la planta *(Spain);* el piso
flow flujo
flower la flor
flu la gripe
fly volar (ue)
foggy nublado(a)
follow seguir (i, i)
food and drink las comidas y bebidas
food el comestible
foot el pie
football el fútbol americano
footwear el calzado
for now por ahora
found, establish *(vb.)* fundar
for God's sake por Dios
for example por ejemplo
for para, por
force obligar
forehead la frente
foreign debt la deuda externa
foreign word or phrase el extranjerismo
foreigner el/la extranjero(a)
forest el bosque
forget olvidarse (de)
fork el tenedor
formed formado(a)
for now por ahora
found, establish *(vb.)* fundar
fountain la fuente
fourth cuarto(a)
freezer el congelador
french fries las papas fritas
French el francés
frequent frecuente *adj.*
frequently con frecuencia
Friday el viernes
fried egg el huevo frito
friend el(la) amigo(a)
friendly acogedor(a), amable

from de
from time to time de vez en cuando
From what? ¿De que?
From where? ¿De donde?
front desk la recepción
front page *(newspaper)* la primera plana
front desk clerk el/la recepcionista
fruit store la frutería
fruit la fruta
fry freír (i, i)
frying pan el/la sartén
full lleno(a)
fun divertido(a)
function funcionar
fur store la peletería
furniture los muebles

G

gain weight engordar, subir de peso
gallery la galería
game show el concurso
game el partido
gangplank la escalerilla
garage el garaje
garbage can el basurero
garden el jardín
garlic el ajo
gate la puerta de salida
gather the harvest cosechar
generally generalmente; por lo general
geographical geográfico(a)
geography la geografía
German el alemán
get conseguir (i, i)
get an ache darle dolor de
get angry enojarse
get dressed vestirse (i, i)
get in shape ponerse en forma
get together reunirse
get sick enfermarse
get some sun asolearse
get conseguir (i, i)
get up levantarse
get up early madrugar
get well *(vb.)* componerse

get worse *(vb.)* empeorar
girl la muchacha
girlfriend la novia
give dar
glass *(for wine)* el vaso; la copa
glove el guante
go ir
go around (across) the country recorrer el país
go away irse
go on a diet ponerse a dieta
go on an outing ir de excursión
go to bed acostarse (ue)
go out to do something salir a
go out with salir con **go shopping** ir de compras
goal la meta
gods los dioses
gold el oro
golf el golf
good evening buenas noches
good-bye adiós
good morning buenos días
good bueno(a) *adj.*
good/bad quality de buena/mala calidad
good afternoon buenas tardes
gorilla el/la gorila
gossip el chisme
gossip chismear
gossipy chismoso(a)
government el gobierno
government inn el parador
governor el/la gobernador(a)
grain el grano
granddaughter la nieta
grandfather el abuelo
grandmother la abuela
grandson el nieto
grape la uva
gray gris
greasy grasoso(a)
great grande *adj.*
greater mayor
green verde
green bean la habichuela
green pepper el ají verde
greeting el saludo

gross national product (GNP) el producto interno bruto (PIB)
growth el crecimiento
guarantee *(vb.)* garantizar
guest house la casa de huéspedes
guest register el registro
guest el/la invitado(a); el/la huésped
guests la visita
guide book la guía turística
gulf el golfo
gymnastics la gimnasia

H

hair el pelo
hair dryer la secadora
hair stylist el/la peluquero(a)
hake *(fish from Bay of Biscay)* la merluza
half la mitad
hall el pasillo
ham el jamón
hamburger la hamburguesa
hammock la hamaca
hand la mano
hand luggage la equipaje de mano
handicraft la artesanía
handkerchief el pañuelo
hands up! manos arriba
handsome guapo(a)
happening el acontecimiento
happy contento(a)
hard difícil *adj.*
hardly apenas
hardworking trabajador(a)
harvest la cosecha
hat el sombrero
hat store la sombrerería
have tener
have breakfast desayunar
have a cold tener un resfriado
have dinner cenar
have a fever tener fiebre
have a fight pelearse
have fun divertirse (ie, i)
have just + *inf.* acabar de + *inf.*
have left quedar
have lunch almorzar (ue)**have a**

picnic hacer un picnic
have a pain tener dolor
have returned estar de vuelta
have to do (something) tener que + *inf.*
hazardous nocivo(a)
head el/la jefe(a); la cabeza
headache el dolor de cabeza
headline el titular
health store el centro naturalista , tienda naturalista
health la salud
healthy saludable, sano(a)
hear oír
heart el corazón
heaviness la pesadez
height la estatura
hello *(answering the phone)* bueno, aló
hello hola
help ayudar (a)
help la ayuda
helpful servicial
here is he aquí
here aquí
heritage la herencia
hero el héroe
high plateau el altiplano
high school la escuela secundaria
high heat el fuego alto
hire contratar
Hispanic world el mundo hispánico
history la historia
hockey *(Anglicism)* el hockey
hold up atracar
home la casa
homeland la tierra
honest honrado(a)
honey la miel
honeymoon la luna de miel
hoodlum el/la delincuente
hope esperar
horoscope el horóscopo
horrible horrible
hostel el hostal
hot caliente *adj.*
hot water el agua caliente
hotel el hotel
house la casa

house of representatives la cámara de representantes
household chore el quehacer doméstico
housewife el ama *f.* de casa
how cómo *interrogative*
How unfortunate! ¡Que desgracia!
however sin embargo
hug el abrazo
human humano(a)
humanities filosofía y letras
hunting la caza
hurray! viva
hurried apurado(a)
hurry apurarse
hurt doler (ue)
husband el esposo

I

I would like... quisiera...
I hope that ojalá
Iberian Peninsula la Península Ibérica
ice el hielo
ice cream shop la heladería
ice cream el helado
if si
ignore *(vb.)* ignorar
imagine imaginarse
immediately inmediatamente
important importante
impossible imposible
impressive impresionante
improve mejorar
in search of en busca de
in order para *prep.*
in order that a fin de que, para que
in front of frente a
in addition (to) además (de)
in case that en caso de que
include *(vb.)* incluir
inaugurated inaugurado(a)
incomparable incomparable *adj.*
increase aumentar
incredible increíble *adj.*
independent independiente *adj.*

Indian chief el cacique
indicate indicar
industrial industrial
infection la infección
inflation la inflación
influential influyente
inform informar
information board el tablero
information la información
ingredient el ingrediente
inhabitant el/la habitante
inn la posada
inner ear el oído
inside of dentro de *prep.*
insist insistir (en)
intelligent inteligente
interesting interesante
interpreter el/la intérprete
interrogative word la palabra interrogativa
interview la entrevista
introduction la presentación
invest invertir (ie, i)
iron la plancha
iron *(vb.)* planchar la ropa
island la isla
Italian italiano(a)
item el artículo

J

jacket la chaqueta
January enero
jeans *(Anglicism)* los jeans
jewelry las joyas
jewelry store la joyería
job application form la solicitud de empleo
jog correr; trotar
jogging *(Anglicism)* el jogging
journalist el/la periodista
judge el juez
juice el jugo
July julio
June junio
jungle la jungla; la selva
just, exactly justo

K

ketchup la salsa de tomate
key la llave; la clave
key chain el llavero
key expression la expresión clave
keyboard el teclado
kick patear
kidnap secuestrar
kidnapped raptado(a)
kidnapping el secuestro
kilogram *(equivalent to 2.2 pounds)* el kilo
king el rey
kingdom el reino
kiosk el estanco
kiss el beso
kitchen la cocina
kitchen appliance el aparato de la cocina
knee la rodilla
knife el cuchillo
know *(facts, information)* saber
know *(to be acquainted with a person)* conocer
known conocido(a)

L

lack faltar
lake el lago
lamp la lámpara
land la tierra
landing el aterrizaje
language el idioma; la lengua
language laboratory el laboratorio de lenguas
lard la manteca
large spoon el cucharón
large grande *adj.*
last último(a)
late tarde *adv.*
late, behind schedule atrasado(a)
later luego *adv.*
laugh reír (i, i); reírse (de)
laundry service el servicio de lavandería

laundry room lavandería
law la ley
law school la facultad de derecho
law el derecho
lawyer el/la abogado(a)
lazy perezoso(a)
learn aprender (a)
leather el cuero
leave salir; salir de; marcharse
leg la pierna
legend la leyenda
lemon juice el jugo de limón
lend prestar
length la extensión; el largo
less menos *adv.*
lesson la lección
letter la carta
lettuce la lechuga
library la biblioteca
lie mentir (ie, i)
life insurance el seguro de vida
lift weights levantar pesas
light ligero(a)
light la luz
like gustar
like *(a person)* caer bien
likewise igualmente
limit *(vb.)* limitar
lip el labio
lipstick el lápiz labial
listen escuchar
listener *(radio)* el radioyente
liter *(equivalent to 1.057 quarts)* el litro
literature la literatura
live vivir
live *(on television)* en vivo, en directo
living room la sala
lobby *(Anglicism)* el lobby
lobster la langosta
location la ubicación
lodging el hospedaje; el alojamiento
long largo(a)
long-sleeved de manga larga
look (at) mirar; mirarse
look for *(vb.)* buscar
lose weight bajar de peso, adelgazar, reducir de peso

lose perder (ie)
lost perdido(a)
love el cariño, el amor
love *(in letter closing)* cariñosamente
low heat el fuego bajo
lower rebajar
luckily por suerte
luggage el equipaje
lunch el almuerzo
lung el pulmón
luxurious lujoso(a)
luxury el lujo

M

machinery las maquinarias
(made of) leather de cuero
(made of) silk de seda
(made of) wool de lana
magazine la revista
magnificent magnífico(a)
maid la sirvienta; la camarera
mail el correo
mailbox el casillero, el buzón
mailman *(mailwoman)* el/la cartero(a)
main floor la planta baja
major el/la comandante
majority la mayoría
make the bed hacer la cama
make by hand hacer a mano
make an appointment hacer una cita
make hacer
makeup el maquillaje
man el hombre; *(colloquial)* el/la chico(a)
manage lograr; manejar
manager el/la gerente
mandatory mandatorio(a)
manners los modales
manual labor la mano de obra
map el mapa
March marzo
marmalade la mermelada
married casado(a)
marvelous maravilloso(a)
match hacer juego

math las matemáticas
matter el asunto
May mayo
Mayan maya
maybe quizá(s), tal vez
mayor el/la alcalde
meal la comida
meantime mientras tanto
measurement la medida
meat la carne
mechanic el/la mecánico(a)
medal la medalla
medical school la facultad de medicina
medicine la medicina
Mediterranean el Mediterráneo
medium heat el fuego mediano
medium mediano(a)
meet encontrarse
member el miembro
mention mencionar
Mexican mexicano(a)
microscope el microscopio
microwave el microondas
milk la leche
milk products los productos lácteos
millions millones
mineral water el agua mineral
minitest la miniprueba
minus *(math)* menos
mirror el espejo
miss, to lack faltar; extrañar, hacer falta
Miss la señorita (Srta.)
missing person la persona desaparecida
mix mezclar
mixed blood mestizo(a)
monarchy la monarquía
Monday el lunes
money dinero
money order giro monetario
monument el monumento
moonlighting el pluriempleo
moonscape el paisaje lunar
more or less más o menos
more than más de
more and more cada vez más

morning la mañana
mother la mamá, la madre
mother-in-law la suegra
motto el lema
mountain la montaña
mountain chain la cordillera
mountainous montañoso(a)
moustache el bigote
mouth la boca
mouthwash enjuage dental
move mover (ue)
movie el cine
mow the lawn cortar la hierba
Mr. el señor (Sr.)
Mrs. la señora (Sra.)
much mucho
muscle el músculo
museum el museo
music la música

N

nail polish esmalte
name el nombre
napkin la servilleta
nation la nación
national park el parque nacional
nationality la nacionalidad
natural sciences las ciencias naturales
natural resource el recurso natural
nature la naturaleza
nausea naúsea
near cerca *adv.;* cerca de *prep.*
necessary necesario(a)
necessity la necesidad
neck el cuello
necklace el collar
need *(vb.)* necesitar
neighbor el/la vecino(a)
neighborhood el barrio
neither...nor ni...ni
neither tampoco
neoclassical neoclásico(a)
nephew el sobrino
nestled anidado(a)
network la cadena

never nunca; jamás
new nuevo(a)
news story la crónica
news item la noticia
newscast el noticiero
newscaster el/la comentarista
newspaper el periódico
next próximo(a)
nice simpático(a)
niece la sobrina
night la noche
nightclub el cabaret
nightstand la mesa de noche
ninth noveno(a)
no-smoking section la sección de no fumar
nobody nadie
noise el ruido
none ninguno(a)
nonstop flight el vuelo sin escalas
North America América del Norte
nose la nariz
notably notablemente
note la nota
notebook el cuaderno
notes los apuntes
nothing nada
notify *(vb.)* notificar
noun el sustantivo
November noviembre
now ahora
nowadays hoy día
nuclear plant la planta nuclear
numerous numeroso(a)
nurse el/la enfermero(a)

O

O.K. de acuerdo
oatmeal la avena
obituary la esquela
obtain obtener
occupation el oficio
October octubre
of de
of course por supuesto
off apagado(a)

offer *(in a sale)* la oferta
offer ofrecer
office la oficina
often muchas veces; a menudo
oil el petróleo
old viejo(a)
older mayor *adj.*
olive oil el aceite de oliva
on time a tiempo
on top of arriba de, encima de
on encendido(a)
on board a bordo
on the grill a la parrilla
onion la cebolla
only sólo *adv.;* solamente, único(a)
only daughter/son el/la hija(o) única(o)
open abrir
operate operar
opponent el/la contrincante
orange juice el jugo de naranja
orange anaranjado(a) *adj.;* la naranja *n.*
orchestra la orquesta
orchid la orquídea
order pedir (i, i); mandar, ordenar
origin la procedencia
originally originalmente
other otro(a)
ought to deber
out of order no funcionar
outfielder el/la jardinero(a)
oven el horno
overpopulation la superpoblación
overweight el sobrepeso

P

pail el cubo
painting el cuadro
pair el par
palace el palacio, el alcázar
palm tree la palmera
Panamanian panameño(a)
pantry despensa
pants los pantalones
pantyhose las pantimedias
paper el papel

pardon perdonar
parents los padres
park el parque
parliamentary parlamentario(a)
part la parte
pass *(in a game)* el pase
passenger el/la pasajero(a)
passport el pasaporte
past el pasado
pastime el pasatiempo
pastry shop la pastelería
pastry el pastel
patient el/la paciente
pay *(vb.)* pagar
pay in installments pagar a plazos
pay cash pagar en efectivo, pagar al contado
payment el pago
peace pact el pacto de paz
peak la cumbre
pear la pera
pearl la perla
peel pelar
pen la pluma
pencil el lápiz
penicillin la penicilina
people, masses el pueblo
perfume store la perfumería
perhaps quizá(s), tal vez
perimeter el perímetro
permit permitir
person la persona
personal care product el artículo de tocador
personal care item el artículo de uso personal
personal care el arreglo personal
personal computer la micro-computadora
pharmacist el/la farmacéutico(a)
pharmacy la farmacia
photo la foto
photocopy fotocopiar
photocopying machine la fotocopiadora
physician el/la médico(a)
pick up one's room ordenar el cuarto

picturesque pintoresco(a)
pig el cerdo
pill la pastilla
pillow la almohada
pilot el piloto
pinch *(of salt, pepper, etc.)* la pizca
pink rosado(a)
pistol la pistola
pity la lástima
place setting el cubierto
place el lugar
plaid de cuadros
plain el llano
plant sembrar (ie)
plantain el plátano
play tocar; jugar (a)
play *(in a game)* la jugada
player el/la jugador(a)
pleasant apacible; agradable
please por favor
pleasure el placer
plumber el/la plomero(a)
plus *(math)* más
police headquarters la comisaría de policía
police force la policía
police officer el policía
polish *(one's nails)* pintarse *(las uñas)*
political político(a)
political party el partido político
pollute contaminar
pollution la contaminación
populated poblado(a)
population la población
pork chop la chuleta de cerdo
port el puerto
portable telephone el teléfono portátil
porthole la ventanilla
Portuguese portugués(a)
position el cargo; el puesto
possible posible
postage el franqueo
postcard la tarjeta
pot el recipiente
potato la papa
pottery la alfarería
powder el talco

practical experience la experiencia práctica
practice la práctica
practice practicar
prefer preferir (ie, i)
prepare preparar
prepare the meal prepar la comida
prescribe recetar
prescription la receta
present presentar
president el/la presidente(a)
press la prensa
presumably presuntamente
pretty well bastante bien
pretty bonito(a); lindo(a)
prevent prevenir
price tag la etiqueta
print imprimir
printer la impresora
prisoner el prisionero
private bath el baño privado
privileged privilegiado(a)
probable probable
problem el problema
profession la profesión
professor el/la profesor(a)
program programar
prohibit prohibir
promote ascender (ie)
protect proteger
protein la proteína
provided (that) con tal (de) que
province, state la provincia
psychologist el/la psicólogo(a)
publishing house la editorial
Puerto Rican puertorriqueño(a)
pure-blooded castizo(a)
purple morado(a)
purse la bolsa, el bolso
put on ponerse
put on makeup maquillarse
put to bed acostar (ue)
put poner
put away *(vb.)* guardar
pyramid la pirámide

Q

qualification la calificación
quality la calidad
quarrel reñir (i, i)
quarter el cuarto
queen la reina
question la pregunta
quiet tranquilo(a)
quit dejar

R

racquet la raqueta
radio la radio
radio set el radio
radio program el programa radial
radio station (business entity) la emisora; (on the dial) la estación de radio
radioactivity la radioactividad
rain water el agua de lluvia
rain forest el bosque pluvial
rain llover (ue)
raincoat el impermeable
rainy lluvioso(a)
raise el aumento
rampant desenfrenado(a)
ranch la hacienda; la finca
ransom el rescate
rare crudo(a)
rather bastante *adv.*
rather than en vez de
raze talar
razor blade la cuchilla de afeitar, la navaja de afeitar
react reaccionar
read leer
reader el/la lector(a)
reading la lectura
real verdadero(a)
real estate los bienes raíces
realize darse cuenta
really de veras; realmente; ¿Sí?
receipt el recibo
receive recibir
received recibido(a)

recently recientemente
recipe la receta
recommend recomendar (ie)
recommendation la recomendación
record grabar
record player el tocadiscos
recycling el reciclaje
red wine el vino tinto
reduce (vb.) reducir
red rojo(a)
referee el árbitro
reference la referencia
reforestation la repoblación forestal
refreshment el refresco
refrigerator el refrigerador
regret lamentar
reign el reinado
reject rechazar
remember acordarse (ue) (de)
remove quitar
repair shop taller de reparaciones
repair reparar
repeat repetir (i, i)
reporter el/la reportero(a)
representative el/la representante
request pedir (i, i)
requested solicitado(a)
reserve reservar
resign renunciar
resolve (vb.) prioridad
responsibility la responsabilidad
rest el reposo
rest descansar, reposar
restaurant el restaurante
résumé el curriculum vitae
retirement plan el plan de retiro
return el retorno
return (something) devolver (ue)
return regresar, volver (ue)
review la reseña
rice el arroz
rich rico(a)
ride horses montar a caballo
right now ahora mismo
right derecho(a)
right away enseguida
right now ahora mismo

ring (bell, alarm, clock) sonar (ue)
ring el anillo
river el río
river basin la cuenca
roach la cucaracha
rocking chair la mecedora
roll of film (for a camera) el rollo de película
roll el panecillo
room service el servicio a la habitación
roommate compañero de cuarto
room la habitación, el cuarto
rooted arraigado(a)
rouge el colorete
round redondo(a)
roundtrip de ida y vuelta
royal real
rug la alfombra
ruin la ruina
run correr

S

sacrifice el sacrificio, sacrificar
sad triste
saffron el azafrán
salad la ensalada
salary el salario
sale la rebaja
salesperson el/la vendedor(a)
salt la sal
sand la arena
sandal la sandalia
satisfy (vb.) satisfacer
Saturday el sábado
save ahorrar; conservar
savings account la cuenta de ahorros
savory sabroso(a)
say decir (i)
say goodbye (vb.) despedirse (i, i)
scattered esparcido(a)
school la escuela
science school la facultad de ciencias
scissors las tijeras
scrambled egg el huevo revuelto

screen la pantalla
seafood el marisco
season la temporada
seat el asiento
seat belt el cinturón de seguridad
seat *(of government)* la sede; *(in Congress)* el escaño
second segundo(a)
secretary el/la secretario(a)
see ver
seem parecer
sell vender
semester el semestre
senate el senado
senator el/la senador(a)
send enviar
sender el/la remitente
September septiembre
serious serio(a)
servant el/la sirviente(a)
serve servir (i, i)
set the table poner la mesa
seventh séptimo(a)
shake el batido
shampoo el champú
shave afeitarse
shaver la máquina de afeitar
shaving cream la crema de afeitar
shaving lotion la loción
sheet la sábana
shelf el estante
shirt la camisa
shoe store la zapatería
shoe el zapato
shoot disparar
shopping center el centro comercial
short bajo(a), corto(a)
short-sleeved de manga corta
shortage la escasez
shot la inyección
shoulder el hombro
shout gritar
show la función
show host (hostess) el/la anfitrión(a)
show enseñar; mostrar (ue)
show a movie pasar o presentar una película
shower ducharse

shrimp el camarón
sick enfermo(a)
sickness la enfermedad
side el lado
sign firmar
silk la seda
silver la plata
since desde, como
sincerely atentamente
single room la habitación sencilla
single soltero(a)
sink el fregadero; el lavabo
sirloin steak el bistec de solomillo
sister-in-law la cuñada
sister la hermana
sit (down) sentarse (ie)
situated situado(a)
sixth sexto(a)
size la talla, el tamaño
skate patinar
ski esquiar
skiing el esquí
skirt la falda
sleep dormir (ue, u)
sleep late dormir (ue, u) hasta tarde
slow lento
small pequeño(a)
smaller menor
smile sonreír
smoke el humo
smoke fumar
snow covered nevado(a)
so much tanto *adj.*
so-so regular; más o menos
so long hasta luego
soap opera la telenovela
soap el jabón
soccer el fútbol
social page *(newspaper)* la crónica social
social welfare el bienestar social
social welfare program el programa social
sofa el sofá
soft drink la gaseosa
soil el suelo
solve resolver (ue)
some alguno(a)

someone alguien
something algo
sometimes a veces
son el hijo
son-in-law el yerno
soon pronto
sore throat el dolor de garganta
sound system equipo de sonido
soup la sopa
south el sur
South America América del Sur
Spain España
Spanish el español; español(a) *adj.*
Spanish egg omelette tortilla española
Spanish speaker el/la hispanohablante
spatula la espátula
specialization la especialización
specialty la especialidad
speech el discurso
spend gastar
spend *(vb.)* pasar
splendid espléndido(a)
spoiled malcriado(a)
sponsor patrocinar
sponsor el/la patrocinador(a)
spoon la cuchara
sport el deporte
sportive deportivo(a)
sports section *(newspaper)* la sección deportiva
sports-related term el término deportivo
sportscaster el/la comentarista deportivo(a)
spreadsheet la hoja electrónica
spring la primavera
square kilometer el kilómetro cuadrado
square cuadrado(a)
stairs la escalera
stamp el sello
stand el puesto
star la estrella
state el estado
stationery store la papelería
statistics las estadísticas

statue la estatua
stay in bed guardar cama
stay in shape mantenerse en forma
stay trim guardar la línea
stay quedarse
stay la estadía
steel el acero
stepbrother el hermanastro
stepdaughter la hijastra
stepfather el padrastro
stepmother la madrastra
stepsister la hermanastra
stepson el hijastro
stewardess la azafata
stick out (one's tongue) sacar (la
  lengua)
still todavía *adv.*
stockings las medias
stomach el estómago
stomachache el dolor de estómago
store la tienda
stove la estufa
straight ahead derecho *adv.*
strange raro(a); extraño(a)
strawberry la fresa
street la calle
street vendor el/la vendedor(a)
  ambulante
strip la faja
striped de rayas
strong fuerte *adj.*
stubborn terco
student hostel el albergue
  estudiantil
student center el centro estudiantil
student residence la residencia
  estudiantil
student el/la estudiante
study estudiar
style el estilo
subject *(academic)* la materia
subsoil el subsuelo
suddenly de pronto, de repente
sufficient bastante *adj.*
sugar el/la azúcar
suggest sugerir (ie, i)
suggestion la sugerencia
suit el traje

suitcase la maleta
sum la suma
summer el verano
sun el sol
sun umbrella la sombrilla
sunbathe tomar el sol
Sunday el domingo
sunglasses las gafas de sol
supervisor el/la supervisor(a)
support apoyar
suppose suponer
supreme court la corte suprema
sure, safe seguro(a)
surgeon el cirujano
surprise sorprender
surprise la sorpresa
surrounding areas los alrededores
survey, poll la encuesta
sweater el suéter
sweep the floor barrer el piso
sweetheart *(figurative)* mi cielo, mi
  vida
swim nadar
swimming la natación
Switzerland Suiza
symptom el síntoma
systems analyst el/la analista de
  sistemas

T

table la mesa; el cuadro comparativo
table tennis el tenis de mesa
tablecloth el mantel
tablespoon la cucharada
tail la cola
tailor shop la sastrería
take turns turnarse
take out the garbage sacar la basura
take one's temperature tomarse la
  temperatura
take notes tomar apuntes
take off quitarse
take one's blood pressure tomarse
  la presión
take tomar; llevar
take care of the bill arreglar la cuenta
take into account tomar en cuente

take care of cuidar; cuidarse
take a stroll dar un paseo, pasear
take advantage of aprovechar
takeoff el despegue
talk hablar
talkative hablador(a)
tall alto(a)
tasty sabroso(a)
tax el impuesto
tea el té
teach enseñar
teacher el/la maestro(a)
team el equipo
tear la lágrima
teaspoon la cucharadita
technological tecnológico(a)
tedious pesado(a)
telephone call la llamada *(telefónica)*
television set el televisor
television viewer el televidente
television la televisión
tell contar (ue)
teller el/la cajero(a)
temperature temperatura
tennis player el/la tenista
tennis shoes los (zapatos de) tenis
tennis el tenis
tenth décimo(a)
terrace la terraza
terrific estupendo
territory el territorio
terrorist el/la terrorista
test prueba
than de lo que; que
thank God gracias a Dios
thanks gracias
that que
that's why por eso ,
then entonces *adv.;* luego *adv.*
there allí
there is (there are) hay
there is no room no hay lugar
these esto(a)s
thin delgado(a)
thing la cosa
think pensar (ie)
third tercero(a); el tercio n.
this este(a)

throat la garganta
through a través de; mediante
through which por donde
throw tirar
throw out arrojar
Thursday el jueves
thus así
ticket el pasaje
ticket office la boletería
tie atar
tie *(the score)* empatar
tie la corbata
tight estrecho(a)
tiled adoquinado(a)
time la vez; la época
times *(multiplication)* por
timid tímido(a)
tin el estaño
tip la propina
tip la punta
tired cansado(a)
title el título
to take it easy llevarla suave
to the east al este
to the north al norte
to the south al sur
to the west al oeste
To where? ¿Adónde?
toast la tostada
toast tostar (ue)
toaster la tostadora
today's world el mundo de hoy
toe el dedo del pie
together junto(a)
toilet el inodoro
toilet paper el papel higiénico
tomato el tomate
tomato sauce la salsa de tomate
tomorrow mañana
tongue la lengua
tonight esta noche
too también
too many demasiado(a)
too much demasiado *adv.*
tooth el diente
toothbrush el cepillo de dientes
toothpaste la pasta de dientes

toss echar
tour la excursión
tour guide el/la guía
tourist el/la turista
touristic turístico(a)
towel la toalla
track and field el atletismo
trail la pista
training el entrenamiento
transmit transmitir
travel agency la agencia de viajes
travel through recorrer
traveler el/la viajero(a)
traveler's check el cheque de viajero
traveling salesperson el/la viajante
treaty el tratado
trip el viaje
triumph *(vb.)* triunfar
true cierto(a)
trunk el maletero
trust *(vb.)* confiar (en)
truth la verdad
try intentar
try food probar (ue), tratar
try on (clothes) probar (ue)
Tuesday el martes
tuna el atún
turn off apagar
turn right doblar a la derecha
turn on encender (ie)
turn to acudir
turn left doblar a la izquierda
turn doblar; virar
turquoise turquesa
twist torcerse
twist one's ankle torcerse el tobillo
type el tipo
type pasar o escribir a máquina, mecanografiar
typewriter la máquina de escribir

U

U.S.A., of the estadounidense *adj.*
ugly feo(a)
uncle el tío
under de bajo (de)

undertake emprender
unemployment el desempleo
unfriendly antipático(a)
United States Estados Unidos
university building el edificio universitario
unknown person el/la desconocido(a)
unless a menos que
until hasta; hasta que *conj.*
up arriba *adv.*
upon arrival al llegar
upstairs la planta alta
urgent urgente *adj.*
U.S.A., of the estadounidense *adj.*
useful útil
utensil el utensilio

V

vacuum pasar la aspiradora
vacuum cleaner la aspiradora
veal ternera
vegetable la legumbre; la verdura
vegetable soup la sopa de vegetales
vegetable store la verdurería
Venezuelan venezolano(a)
¿Verdad? True?
very muy, súper (slang)
veterinarian el/la veterinario(a)
video cassette recorder (VCR) la videograbadora
view la vista
visit visitar
visitor el/la visitante
volcano el volcán
volleyball el vólibol
vote votar

W

wages el sueldo, el salario
wait for esperar
wait on someone atender (ie)
waiting list la lista de espera
waiting room la sala de espera
wake up despertarse (ie)
walk caminar, andar

wall la pared; la muralla
wallet la billetera
warm cálido(a)
wash clothes lavar ropa
wash lavar; lavarse
washer la lavadora
waste los deshechos
water el agua f.
water ski el esquí acuático
wear llevar
weather el clima; el tiempo
weatherman (weatherwoman) el/la meteorólogo(a)
Wednesday el miércoles
weekend el fin de semana
weigh pesar
weight el peso
welcome la bienvenida
welcome dar la bienvenida
well bien adv.
western occidental
What are you like? ¿Como eres?
What the heck? ni modo
when cuándo interrogative; cuando
which cuál(es) interrogative
while mientras; mientras que
white blanco(a)
whose cuyo(a)/s, ¿De quiénes?
wide amplio(a)
width el ancho
wife la esposa
wild salvaje adj.
win ganar
window la ventana
wing el ala f.
winter el invierno
wish desear
with me conmigo
With whom... ? ¿Con quiénes?
with you contigo
with con
without sin, sin que
woman la mujer
wood la madera
wool la lana
word la palabra

word processor el procesador de textos
work on commission trabajar a comisión
work trabajar; funcionar
work schedule el horario de trabajo
work el trabajo; la obra
world el mundo
worried preocupado(a)
worry preocuparse
worse (worst) peor
wrist muñeca
wristwatch el reloj pulsera
write escribir
written escrito(a) p.p.

X

x-ray la radiografía

Y

yacht el yate
yard el jardín
yea! arriba
yellow amarillo(a)
yes sí
yet todavía
you're welcome de nada
young el/la joven
younger menor adj.
your (familiar) tu
youth la juventud

Z

zinc el cinc
ZIP code el código postal

Index

For a listing of chapter themes, cultural information, and vocabulary groupings, please consult the Table of Contents.

Credits

Photos

1 (both) Robert Frerck/ Odyssey Productions; 27 (top left, middle, right) Peter Menzel, (bottom) Chris Brown/Stock Boston, Inc.; 30 Robert Frerck/Odyssey Productions; 37 Focus on Sports; 44 (all) Robert Frerck/Odyssey Productions; 58 (top) Robert Frerck/Odyssey Productions, (bottom) Peter Menzel; 59 Eric A. Wessman/Stock Boston, Inc., 61 (left) Peter Menzel, (right) Robert Frerck/Odyssey Productions; 81 Peter Menzel; 82 Robert Frerck/Odyssey Productions; 98 (left) Robert Frerck/Odyssey Productions, (right) Comstock; 99 Philip Jon Bailey/Stock Boston, Inc.; 101 Gary Conner/Photoedit;

102; 116 (left) Mike Mazzaschi/Stock Boston, Inc., (right); 127 (both) Robert Frerck/Odyssey Productions; 132 (top) Robert Frerck/Odyssey Productions, (bottom) Peter Menzel; 133 (left) Robert Frerck/Odyssey Productions, (right) Peter Menzel; 135 (both) Robert Frerck/Odyssey Productions; 148 AP/Wide World Photos; 149 (all) Robert Frerck/Odyssey Productions; 169 Peter Menzel; 170 (both) Robert Frerck/Odyssey Productions; 171 Owen Franken/Stock Boston, Inc.; 172 Grant Leduc/Stock Boston, Inc.; 177 Robert Frerck/Odyssey Productions; 192 Barbara Alper/Stock Boston, Inc.; 193 Arlene Collins/Monkmeyer Press; 209 (both) Robert Frerck/Odyssey Productions; 229 (both) Robert Frerck/Odyssey Productions; 263 (both) Robert Frerck/Odyssey Productions; 264 Peter Menzel; 293 Robert Frerck/Odyssey Productions; 377 Robert Frerck/Odyssey Productions; 391 Peter Menzel; 392 C. Goldin/Latin Stock, D. Donne/Bryant Stock Photography;